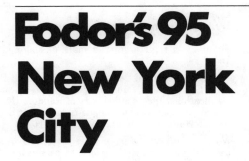

Fodor's 95 New York City

W9-BJP-185

Fodor's Travel Publications, Inc.
New York • Toronto • London • Sydney • Auckland

Copyright © 1994
by Fodor's Travel Publications, Inc.

Fodor's is a registered trademark of Fodor's Travel Publications, Inc.

All rights reserved under International and Pan-American Copyright Conventions. Published in the United States by Fodor's Travel Publications, Inc., a subsidiary of Random House, Inc., New York, and simultaneously in Canada by Random House of Canada Limited, Toronto. Distributed by Random House, Inc., New York.

No maps, illustrations, or other portions of this book may be reproduced in any form without written permission from the publisher.

ISBN 0–679–02742–4

"The New York Babel," by V. S. Pritchett, was originally printed in *New York Proclaimed.* Copyright © 1965 by V.S. Pritchett. Reprinted by permission of Sterling Lord Literistic, Inc.

"What Makes New Yorkers Tick," by Calvin Trillin. Copyright © 1990 by Calvin Trillin. Originally appeared in *Time.* Reprinted by permission of Lescher & Lescher, Ltd.

Fodor's New York City

Editor: Christopher Billy
Contributors: Steven K. Amsterdam, Robert Blake, Andrew Collins, Karen Cure, Theodore Fischer, Janet Foley, Echo Garrett, Holly Hughes, Dick Kagan, Ann LaForge, David Low, Bevin McLaughlin, Denise Lewis Patrick, Paula Rackow, Mary Ellen Schultz, Kate Sekules, Terry Trucco, Nancy van Itallie, Jay Walman, Susan Spano Wells
Creative Director: Fabrizio La Rocca
Cartographer: David Lindroth
Illustrator: Karl Tanner
Cover Photograph: Francesco Ruggeri

Design: Vignelli Associates

Special Sales

Fodor's Travel Publications are available at special discounts for bulk purchases for sales promotions or premiums. Special editions, including personalized covers, excerpts of existing guides, and corporate imprints, can be created in large quantities for special needs. For more information, contact your local bookseller or write to Special Markets, Fodor's Travel Publications, 201 East 50th Street, New York, NY 10022. Inquiries from Canada should be directed to your local Canadian bookseller or sent to Random House of Canada, Ltd., Marketing Department, 1265 Aerowood Drive, Mississauga, Ontario L4W 1B9. Inquiries from the United Kingdom should be sent to Fodor's Travel Publications, 20 Vauxhall Bridge Road, London, England SW1V 2SA.

MANUFACTURED IN THE UNITED STATES OF AMERICA
10 9 8 7 6 5 4 3 2 1

Contents

3 Exploring Manhattan 42

4 Exploring the Other Boroughs 134

5 Exploring New York City with Children 158

6 Sightseeing Checklists 169

7 Sports, Fitness, Beaches 177

8 Shopping 187

Maps and Charts

Foreword

While every care has been taken to ensure the accuracy of the information in this guide, the passage of time will always bring change, and consequently, the publisher cannot accept responsibility for errors that may occur.

All prices and opening times quoted here are based on information supplied to us at press time. Hours and admission fees may change, however, and the prudent traveler will avoid inconvenience by calling ahead.

Fodor's wants to hear about your travel experiences, both pleasant and unpleasant. When a hotel or restaurant fails to live up to its billing, let us know and we will investigate the complaint and revise our entries where the facts warrant it.

Send your letters to the editors of Fodor's Travel Publications, 201 E. 50th Street, New York, NY 10022.

Highlights'95 and Fodor's Choice

Highlights '95

Neighborhoods At press time, various New York City neighborhoods were in the process of sprucing themselves up. Recently rejuvenated Bryant Park and Herald Square were joined by Union Square and the 50-odd blocks surrounding Grand Central Terminal, the area roughly between 38th and 48th streets and 3rd and 5th avenues. This latter beautification project—still in progress—will encompass renovation of sidewalks, street signs, and crosswalks. Union Square, meanwhile, has become an even more popular spot to hang out: the expanded Greenmarket now operates four days a week, new stores and restaurants have opened up south and east of the square, and an open-air café run by the purveyors of the ever-trendy Coffee Shop now sits in the middle of it all.

Dining New restaurants are opening (and closing) with the usual dizzying speed, and chefs revolving more than most doors with that appellation. **Gramercy Tavern,** the combined effort of Danny Meyer (who also owns the Union Square Café) and his chef and co-owner Tom Colicchio (formerly of Mondrian), stole the show as the most talked-about opening of 1994. Chef John Deleo (formerly of Zoë) held court for a while at the beautifully designed **Iridium** (owned by Ellen Hart of Ellen's Stardust Diner) after Rick Laakkonen left for the River Café; he has since been replaced by John Loughlin, who was chef de cuisine at River Café before Laakkonen took over. Pino Luongo of Coco Pazzo and Le Madri opened two important restaurants: **Amarcord,** which emphasizes the style of Italy circa World War II, and **Mad. 61,** a serious Italian restaurant in Barneys Uptown. There's no visible end to the bistro/trattoria mania: The latest entrant is Jean Denoyer's baby, **La Gouloue** (Mr. Denoyer has also recently opened **Le Colonial,** a stylish Vietnamese lounge and restaurant on East 57th Street). Spanish is in, and although **Bolo** (presided over by Bobby Flay and Laurence Kretchmer of Mesa Grill) may not remind you of Madrid, its state-of-the-art kitchen, tasty tapas, and swinging crowd are sure to please. Jerome Kretchmer, Laurence's father (he also owns Gotham Bar & Grill), has his own new superstar restaurant: **Judson Grill.** Chef Terrance Brennan, of the late Prix Fixe presides over the range at **Picholine.** Samuel de Marco, of the ill-fated Luxe, has a hot hit at **First,** a funky East Village restaurant. And Philip Suarez of Vong and Jo Jo's has a new Latin success, **Patria,** with chef Doug Rodriguez, who scored in Miami with Yuca. **Shaan,** glorious to behold with its 3,000 square feet of Italian and Portuguese marble, serves many regional dishes never before seen in New York. Also new and noteworthy, **Gauguin,** in the Plaza Hotel. See Chapter 9 for more on these and other restaurants, and when you make one of these trendy scenes, wear black and kiss anyone who offers a spare cheek.

Lodging On the hotel scene, nothing so exciting as the major opening of the **Four Seasons** in 1993 has happened lately, though a few major renovations have been completed. The **Ritz-Carlton** on Central Park South lavished about $22 million on its rethink, which involved expanding the park-view fitness center; adding several new suites; upgrading the telephone, heat, and air-conditioning networks; and remodeling all the guest rooms and public areas. Two 2-line phones and fax are now standard guest room issue, and there's an excellent new northern Italian restaurant, **Fantino,** in the former Jockey Club premises.

Downtown, the **New York Vista,** which was damaged in the World Trade Center bombing of February 1993, has been completely rejuvenated, with brand-new smart decor, freshly renovated guest rooms with improved fixtures and amenities, and a spectacular health club complete with pool and jogging track (the club now ranks among the city's best). In the heart of Greenwich Village, the much smaller **Washington Square Hotel** (103 Waverly Pl.) has spent $10 million on a major refurbishment. They succeeded in replacing all the furnishings, air-conditioning, and bathrooms without affecting the hotel's reasonable rates or European ambience. It still looks like a Parisian hotel, and swanky extras like bellhops and room service are still missing, which makes it possible for the owners to offer a single room here for under $60 a night. At press time, it was looking like one other downtown landmark hotel is going to stay under scaffolding for yet another year: the **Mercer** overlooking the SoHo branch of the Guggenheim Museum is still dogged by planning blight and the projected opening for 1995 is looking doubtful.

Tours An enterprising operation run by New Yorker Kristin Muma Bell began offering its **Downtown Tours** (tel. 212/932–2744) in spring 1994. Aimed at capturing the "elusive other downtown scene," these rambles below Union Square seek to reveal how a city's culture evolves, where the ethnic communities have carved their niche, and where the artists and bohemians are creating tomorrow's masterpieces. Running west from Chelsea to Greenwich Village, and east from SoHo to the Lower East Side, these downtown investigations introduce the cultural explorer to the best of Off-Off Broadway theater at the likes of La Mama, PS 122, the Public, and the Performance Garage; to the art scene of SoHo and beyond; to the film world of TriBeCa, the literary landmarks of Greenwich Village, the ethnic diversity of Chinatown and Little Italy; as well as the food, nightlife, and music throughout the entire territory.

Anniversaries One of the most festive of a multiplicity of 1995 anniversaries is being planned for the **New York Public Library Centennial.** This 82-branch cultural monument, visited by over 7 million people every year, is planning many events to mark its 100th year, starting in May 1994 and continuing until the following April. Events include special exhibitions, educational programs, and galas, plus a library-wide birthday party, and, late in the year, the opening of the brand-new **Science, Industry, and Business**

Library, which uses the latest information technology to bring its vast resources to the public.

Another much-loved institution celebrating its centenary is the **Bronx Zoo and Wildlife Conservation Park.** "Wildlife Weeks," featuring treasure hunts, a 5-K race, and a centennial sweepstakes are due to mark the occasion, with many conservation-related events at the society's outposts in the planning. A not-unrelated silver anniversary is also being celebrated, on April 23, when New York, wearing its "Earth Day International City of the Year" hat, hosts the **Parade for the Planet** to mark the 25th International Earth Day. Approximately 1½ million people are expected to line the parade route (which has yet to be announced) to cheer on artists, musicians, and performers from all over the world.

Not one, but two of Manhattan's major museums are 125 years old in 1995, and both are celebrating in style. The **American Museum of Natural History** is following last year's unveiling of the Hall of Human Biology and Evolution with the opening of two new Dinosaur Halls in June, with an Orientation Center and a Hall of Primitive Vertebrates due to follow in 1996. Besides this, various events and exhibitions are planned for the anniversary year. The other 125-year-old is America's largest art museum, the **Metropolitan Museum of Art.** Needless to say, the event is being marked by a series of important exhibitions, starting in September 1994, with *The Origins of Impressionism*—a guaranteed sellout featuring early works of the French faves, Monet, Manet, and Renoir. Following that, at the end of the year through March 1995, is *Greek Gold, Jewelry of the Classical World*, with an *R. B. Kitaj Retrospective* running from February to May.

Just one more institution celebrates a big anniversary in 1995— the one responsible for popularizing the sobriquet "The Big Apple" back in a 1971 promotion: Throughout the year the **New York Convention and Visitors Bureau** will be working extra hard to market the city that never sleeps. Watch out for special offers.

Fodor's Choice

No two people will agree on what makes a perfect vacation, but it's fun and helpful to know what others think. We hope you'll have a chance to experience some of Fodor's Choices yourself while visiting New York City. For detailed information about each entry, refer to the appropriate chapters within this guidebook.

Views

The lower Manhattan skyline, seen from the Brooklyn Heights Promenade

The vista of skyscrapers ringing Central Park, best viewed from the reservoir's northwest corner

A moonlit look at the harbor from the Staten Island Ferry

The sun setting over New Jersey and the lights of Manhattan snapping on one by one, from the World Trade Center's observation deck, 107 stories up

Architecture

The Woolworth Building, the Flatiron Building, the Empire State Building, and the World Trade Center's twin towers—each, in its time, the world's tallest building

The Chrysler Building, with its Art Deco chrome spire

The Dakota, grande dame of apartment buildings

The unbroken front of cast-iron beauties along Greene Street in SoHo

The graceful town houses along St. Luke's Place in the West Village

The Cathedral of St. John the Divine, an immense Gothic cathedral still abuilding

Museums

The Pierpont Morgan Library, and Morgan's personal library within

The newly restored dinosaur dioramas at the American Museum of Natural History

The American Wing's garden courtyard, among other delights at the Metropolitan Museum of Art

The restored and expanded Guggenheim Museum

The medieval Cloisters, especially its unicorn tapestries

Holidays and Seasonal Events

The lighting of the Christmas tree in Rockefeller Plaza

Cherry blossoms at the Brooklyn Botanical Garden

Late August when the Mets play at Shea and nearby the U. S. Open is held at Flushing Meadows

The Halloween parade in Greenwich Village

The giant balloons for Macy's Thanksgiving Day Parade being inflated the night before on West 77th and West 81st streets

Entertainment

The first preview of any new play—before the critics' verdict

Jazz into the wee hours at the Blue Note

Standing-room tickets for the Metropolitan Opera

Cabaret at the Algonquin, the Carlyle, or Rainbow & Stars

Viewing any movie at the Film Forum, the Angelika, the Walter Reade, or MoMA

Standing in line at the TKTS booth

Restaurants

Chanterelle, *$$$$*

Lespinasse, *$$$$*

San Domenico, *$$$$*

La Caravelle, *$$$*

Le Périgord, *$$$*

Patria, *$$$*

Duane Park Café, *$$*

Tatou, *$$*

Carmine's, *$–$$*

Pisces, *$*

Takahachi, *$*

Triple Eight Palace, *$*

Shopping

Ralph Lauren's Polo store on the East Side

Zabar's, an outstanding food store and cultural institution

Barneys New York for men's and women's clothing

F.A.O. Schwarz, the ultimate toy store

Annex Antiques Fair and Flea Market, for everything from earrings to end tables

Hunting for used books at the Argosy or Strand

Hotels

The Carlyle, *$$$$*

Essex House, *$$$$*

The Mayfair Baglioni, *$$$$*

The Ritz-Carlton, *$$$$*

Embassy Suites, *$$$*

U.N. Plaza–Park Hyatt, *$$$*

The Fitzpatrick, *$$*

Manhattan Suites East, *$$*

Morgans, *$$*

Gramercy Park, *$*

Hotel Edison, *$*

Paramount, *$*

Street Life

Crowds surging through Grand Central Terminal at rush hours, viewed from a balcony above the fray

The steps of the New York Public Library, weekdays at lunchtime

Lincoln Center's central plaza, just before an 8 PM concert.

Central Park's Mall, Bethesda Terrace, and Conservatory Water on weekend afternoons

Walking east to west on Bleecker Street on a weekend

Quintessentially New York

Browsing among the melon-squeezers on a Saturday morning at the Union Square Greenmarket.

Watching the frenzy on the floor of the New York Stock Exchange

Going to a deli restaurant for a pastrami-on-rye, garlic pickles, and an egg cream

Spotting celebrities—anywhere and everywhere

Buying the Sunday *New York Times* on Saturday night

Walking out of Shubert Alley onto 44th or 45th Street to gaze at the marquees

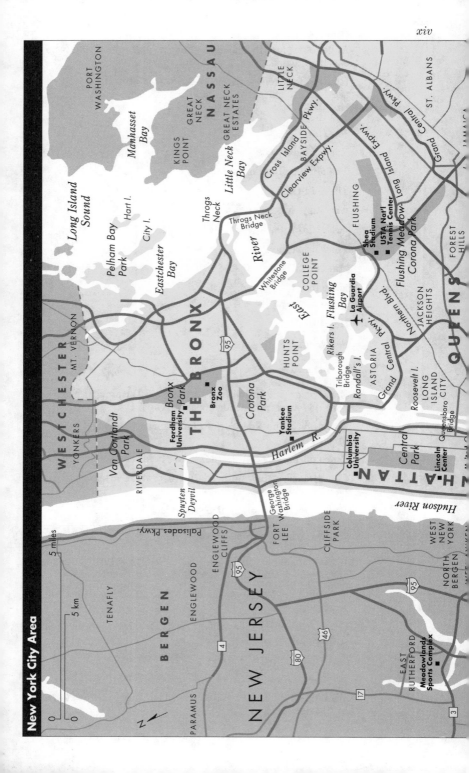

New York City Area

World Time Zones

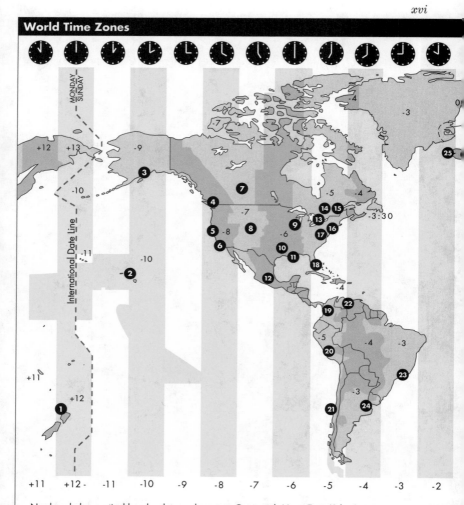

Numbers below vertical bands relate each zone to Greenwich Mean Time (0 hrs.).
Local times frequently differ from these general indications,
as indicated by light-face numbers on map.

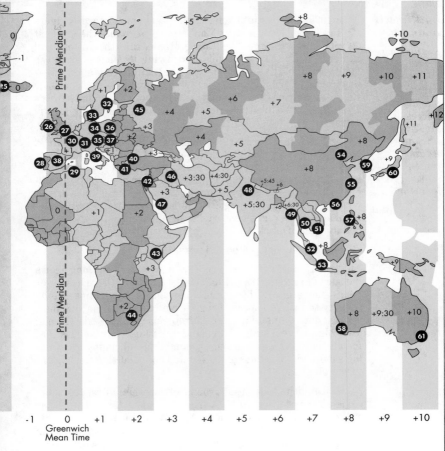

Introduction

By Michael Adams

Senior writer for the business travel magazine Successful Meetings, Michael Adams finally moved to his hometown, New York City, 12 years ago.

In 1925, the youthful songwriting team of Richard Rodgers and Larry Hart wrote "Manhattan," arguably the loveliest city anthem ever. "We'll have Manhattan, the Bronx, and Staten Island, too," it promises, drawing its images from the merry scramble that was the city more than 60 years ago: "sweet pushcarts," "baloney on a roll," a subway that "charms," Brighton Beach, Coney Island, and the popular comedy *Abie's Irish Rose.* "We'll turn Manhattan into an isle of joy," coos the refrain.

Several decades later, in 1989, an album called simply *New York*, by aging enfant terrible rocker Lou Reed, views the same city with glasses fogged by despair and cynicism: Drugs, crime, racism, and promiscuity reign in what Reed considers to be a sinkhole of "crudity, cruelty of thought and sound." His voice brittle with weary irony, he sings, "This is no time for celebration." Manhattan's "sweet pushcarts" now apparently overflow with deadly vials of crack.

So, whom to believe—Lou or Larry?

The truth of the matter is slippery, for New York has long been a mosaic of grand contradictions, a city for which there has never been—nor ever will be—a clear consensus. Hart himself took the city to task in another song, "Give It Back to the Indians," whose lyrics count off a litany of problems that still exist: crime, dirt, high prices, traffic jams, and all-around urban chaos. Yet for all that, millions live here, grumbling but happy, and millions more visit, curious as cats to find out what the magnificent fuss is all about.

I was in eighth grade in suburban Detroit when I first really became aware of New York. A friend's Manhattan-born mother still subscribed to the Sunday *New York Times,* and at their house I'd pore over the "Arts and Leisure" section, as rapt as an archaeologist with a cave painting. The details of what I read there have blurred, but I remember vividly the sensation I felt while reading: a combined anticipation and nostalgia so keen it bordered on pain. Although I had never been there, I was homesick for New York.

It's my home now, yet I can still understand and appreciate the impulse that draws visitors here. In a city so ripe with possibilities, we are all more or less visitors.

I think of this on an uncharacteristically warm day in late March, as I and fellow New Yorkers escape from the hives of offices and homes to celebrate spring's first preview. We unbutton our jackets, leave buses a stop or two before our usual destinations, quicken our resolve to visit that new exhibit at the Met or jog around the Central Park Reservoir. A jubilant sense of renewal infects us all, and I overhear one happy fellow saying to a friend, "I felt just like a tourist yesterday."

Whenever I get the New York blues, the best tonic for me is to glimpse the city through the eyes of a visitor. One day, after subway construction had rerouted me well out of my usual path, I found myself in the grimy Times Square station—hardly the place for a spiritual conversion. As usual I had that armor of body language that we New Yorkers reflexively assume to protect ourselves from strangers bent on (1) ripping us off, (2) doing us bodily harm, (3) converting us, (4) making sexual advances, or (5) being general pains-in-the-butt just for the hell of it. But that day, tucked away in a corner, was a group of musicians—not an uncommon sight in New York—playing the guitar, organ, and accordion with gusto and good spirits behind a homemade sign that dubbed them the "Argentinian Tango Company." Like many street musicians in Manhattan, they were *good*, but I was only half listening, too intent on cursing the city. Just as I passed the band, however, I noticed four teenagers drawn to the music—visitors surely, they were far too open and trusting to be anything else. Grinning as widely as the Argentinians, they began to perform a spontaneous imitation of flamenco dancing—clapping hands above their heads, raising their heels, laughing at themselves, and only slightly self-conscious. Passersby, myself included, broke into smiles. As I made my way to the subway platform, buoyed by the impromptu show, I once again forgave New York. This minor piece of magic was apology enough.

I wonder whether that was the moment one of those teenagers happened to fall in love with the city. It *can* happen in a single moment, to a visitor or to a longtime resident. Perhaps it hits during a stroll through Riverside Park after a blanketing snowfall, when trees have turned to crystal and the city feels a hush it knows at no other time; or when you turn a corner and spy, beyond a phalanx of RVs and a tangle of cables and high-beam lights, the filming of a new movie.

That moment could also come when the house lights begin to dim at the Metropolitan Opera, and the gaudily sparkling chandeliers make their magisterial ascent to the ceiling; or when you first glimpse the magnificently bright Prometheus statue in Rockefeller Center, gleaming like a giant present under the annual Christmas tree as dozens of skaters cut swirls of seasonal colors on the ice below. You may even be smitten in that instant when, walking along the streets in the haze of a summer afternoon, you look up above the sea of anonymous faces to see—and be astonished by—the lofty rows of skyscrapers, splendid in their arrogance and power. At times like these it is perfectly permissible to stop for a moment, take a breath, and think, "Wow! *This is New York!*" We who live here do it every so often ourselves.

For some, of course, that special moment comes with a happy shock of recognition when they spot a street or building made familiar by movies or television, anything from *I Love Lucy* to *On the Waterfront*. At the Empire State Building, who can help but remember King Kong's pathetically courageous swing from its pinnacle? Or at the brooding Dakota, the chilling destiny created for Rosemary's baby within those fortresslike walls? In the mind's eye, Audrey Hepburn is eternally pairing diamonds and a doughnut as she wends her swank way down Fifth Avenue to have breakfast at Tiffany's. And the miniature park on Sutton Place will always be where Woody Allen and Diane Keaton began their angst-ridden *Manhattan* love affair, with the 59th Street bridge gleaming beyond and Gershwin music swelling in the background.

There's a moment of sudden magic when a New York stereotype, seen so often on screen that it seems a joke, suddenly comes to life: when a gum-cracking waitress calls you "hon," or a stogie-sucking cabbie asks, "How 'bout them Yankees, Mac?" There's also the thrill of discovering one of New York's cities-within-the-city: Mulberry Street in Little Italy; Mott Street in Chinatown; Park Avenue's enclave of wealth and privilege; SoHo and TriBeCa, with their artistic types dressed in black from head to toe; or Sheridan Square, the nexus of the city's prominent lesbian and gay communities. The first glimpse of a landmark could begin the visitor's infatuation, too: frenetic Grand Central Station, abustle with suburban commuters; the concrete caverns of Wall Street, throbbing with power and ambition; or the Statue of Liberty, which neither cliché nor cheap souvenir can render common.

As you ready yourself to take on New York's contradictions, prepare to wonder and to exult. Here, on a single day, you might catch a glimpse of John Kennedy, Jr. or Rollerena, the gloriously tacky drag-queen-cum-fairy-godmother on roller skates, who waves her magic wand to bestow blessings on select public events. Here you can eat sumptuously at a hot dog stand or at a world-celebrated gourmet shrine.

Excess and deprivation mingle here: As a limousine crawls lazily to take its pampered passengers to their luxe destination, it rolls past a threadbare beggar seeking the warmth that steams from the city's belly through an iron grate. It's a ludicrously bright cartoon and a sobering documentary, New York—almost too much for one city to be. It's maddening and it's thrilling; monstrous, yet beautiful beyond parallel.

And I envy anyone their first taste of it.

1 Essential Information

Before You Go

Visitor Information

The **New York Convention and Visitors Bureau** (2 Columbus Circle, New York, NY 10019, tel. 212/397–8222 or 212/484–1200, fax 212/484–1280) provides brochures, subway and bus maps, an up-to-date calendar of events, listings of hotels and weekend hotel packages, and discount coupons for Broadway shows. **The New York Division of Tourism** (1 Commerce Plaza, Albany, NY 12245, tel. 518/474–4116 or 800/225–5697) offers a free series of "I Love New York" booklets listing New York City attractions and tour packages.

Tours and Packages

Should you buy your travel arrangements to New York packaged or do it yourself? There are advantages either way. Buying packaged arrangements saves you money, particularly if you can find a program that includes exactly the features you want. You also get a pretty good idea of what your trip will cost from the outset. You have two options: fully escorted tours and independent packages. Escorted tours mean having limited free time and traveling with strangers. Escorted tours are most often via motorcoach, with a tour director in charge. Your baggage is handled, your time rigorously scheduled, and most meals planned. Escorted tours are therefore the most hassle-free way to see New York, as well as generally the least expensive. Independent packages allow plenty of flexibility. They generally include airline travel and hotels, with certain options available, such as sightseeing, car rental, and excursions. Independent packages are usually more expensive than escorted tours, but your time is your own.

Travel agents are your best source of recommendations for both tours and packages. They will have the largest selection, and the cost to you is the same as buying direct. Whatever program you ultimately choose, be sure to find out exactly what is included: taxes, tips, transfers, meals, baggage handling, ground transportation, entertainment, excursions, sports or recreation (and rental equipment if necessary). Ask about the level of hotel used, its location, the size of its rooms, the kind of beds, and its amenities, such as pool, room service, or programs for children, if they're important to you. Find out the operator's cancellation penalties. Nearly everyone charges them, and the only way to avoid them is to buy trip-cancellation insurance. Also ask about the single supplement, a surcharge assessed to solo travelers. Some operators do not make you pay it if you agree to be matched up with a roommate of the same sex, even if one is not found by departure time.

Fully Escorted Tours Escorted tours are usually sold in three categories: deluxe, first-class, and tourist or budget class. The most important differences are the price and the level of accommodations. Some operators specialize in one category, while others offer a range. **Bixler Tours** (Box 37, Hiram, OH 44234, tel. 216/569–3222 or 800/325–5087) has fournight programs that include accommodations at the Waldorf-Astoria and Broadway show tickets. **CIT Tours** (342 Madison Ave., Suite 207, New York, NY 10173, tel. 212/697–2100 or 800/248–8687; western U.S., tel. 310/670–4269 or 800/248–7245) and **Domenico Tours** (751 Broadway, Bayonne, NJ 07002, tel. 201/823–8687 or 800/554–8687) have a variety of packages. **Gadabout Tours** (700 E. Tahquitz Canyon Way, Palm Springs, CA 92262, tel. 619/325–5556 or 800/952–5068) has seasonal specials to the Big Apple. **Go America Tours** (733 3rd Ave., 7th Floor, New York, NY 10017, tel. 212/370–5080) offers escorted tours to Gotham. **Mayflower Tours** (1225 Warren Ave., Downers Grove, IL 60515, tel. 708/960–3430 or 800/323–7604) has two New York City packages. **Maupintour** (Box 807, Lawrence, KS 66044, tel. 913/843–1211 or 800/255–4266) has one program, offered at Thanksgiving, to view the Macy's Thanksgiving Day parade.

Most itineraries are jam-packed with sightseeing, so you see a lot in a short amount of time. To judge just how fast-paced the tour is, review the itinerary carefully. If you are in a different hotel each night, you will be getting up early each day to head out, travel to your next destination, do some sightseeing, have dinner, and go to bed, then you'll start all over again. If you want some free time, make sure it's mentioned in the tour brochure; if you want to be escorted to every meal, confirm that any tour you consider does that. Also, when comparing programs, be sure to find out if the motorcoach is air-conditioned and has a rest room on board. Make your selection based on price and stops on the itinerary.

Independent Packages Independent packages are offered by airlines, tour operators who may also do escorted programs, and any number of other companies from large, established firms to small, new entrepreneurs. **Bixler Tours** and **CIT TOURS** (*see above*), **City Tours** (26A Oak St., East Rutherford, NJ 07073, tel. 201/939–4154), and **Go America** (*see above*) also do independent programs. Among the other operators are **Amtrak** (tel. 800/872–7245) and **SuperCities** (tel. 800/333–1234). Among the major airlines offering packages to New York are **American Airlines Fly AAway Vacations** (tel. 800/321–2121), **Continental's Grand Destinations** (tel. 800/634–5555), **Delta Dream Vacations** (tel. 800/872–7786), **TWA Getaway Vacations** (tel. 800/438–2929), and **United Airlines' Vacation Planning Center** (tel. 800/328–6877).

Independent programs come in a wide range of prices based on levels of luxury and options—in addition to hotel and airfare, sightseeing, car rental, transfers, admission to local attractions, theater tickets, and other extras. Note that when pricing different packages, it sometimes pays to purchase the same arrangements separately, as when a rock-bottom promotional airfare is being offered, for example.

Special-Interest Travel Special-interest programs may be fully escorted or independent. Some require a certain amount of expertise, but most are for the average traveler with an interest and are usually hosted by experts in the subject matter. When the program is escorted, it enjoys the advantages and disadvantages of all escorted programs; because your fellow travelers are apt to be passionate about the subject, they can prove as enjoyable a part of your travel experience as the destination itself. The price range is wide, but the cost is usually higher—sometimes a lot higher—than for ordinary escorted tours and packages, because of the expert guiding and special activities. For special-interest tours around the city, *see* Guided Tours, *below.*

Music **Dailey-Thorp Travel** (330 W. 58th St., New York, NY 10019, tel. 212/307–1555; book through travel agents), a performing arts specialist, has lively New York City programs.

Special Events **Gadabout Tours** (*see above*) does packages at Christmas, with tickets to the Radio City holiday spectacular; at Thanksgiving, with a stay at a hotel with a good vantage point on the parade; and at Easter, with a special dinner.

Tennis **Steve Furgal's International Tennis Tours** (11828 Rancho Bernardo Rd., San Diego, CA 92128, tel. 619/487–7777 or 800/258–3664) has a package for aficionados combining the excitement of the U.S. Open with Broadway theater tickets.

Theater **Broadway Theatours, Inc.** (71 Broadway, New York, NY 10006, tel. 212/425–6410 or 800/843–7469) does Broadway, as does **Sutherland "Hit Show" Tours** (370 Lexington Ave., New York, NY 10017, tel. 212/532–7732 or 800/221–2442). **Keith Prowse & Co.** (234 W. 44th St., New York, NY 10036, tel. 212/398–1430 or 800/669–8687) has "New Yorkers" packages for most of the performing arts in the city.

Tips for British Travelers

Passports and Visas British citizens need a valid 10-year passport. A visa is not necessary unless 1) you are planning to stay more than 90 days; 2) your trip is for purposes other than vacation; 3) you have at some time been refused a visa or refused admission to the United States, or have been required to leave by the U.S. Immigration and Naturalization Service; or 4) you do not have a return or onward ticket. You will need to fill out the Visa Waiver Form, 1–94W supplied by the airline. To apply for a visa or for more information, call the U.S. Embassy's Visa Information Line (tel. 0891/200–290; calls cost 48p per minute or 36p per minute cheap rate).

Customs British visitors age 21 or over may import the following into the United States: 200 cigarettes or 50 cigars or 2 kilograms of tobacco; one U.S. liter of alcohol; gifts to the value of $100. Restricted items include meat products, seeds, plants, and fruits. Never carry illegal drugs.

Returning to the United Kingdom, you may import duty-free 200 cigarettes, 100 cigarillos, 50 cigars or 250 grams of tobacco; 1 liter of spirits or 2 liters of fortified or sparkling wine; 2 liters of still table wine; 60 milliliters of perfume; 250 milliliters of toilet water; plus £36 worth of other goods, including gifts and souvenirs.

Insurance Most tour operators, travel agents, and insurance agents sell specialized policies covering accidents, medical expenses, personal liability, trip cancellation, and loss or theft of personal property. Some policies include coverage for delayed departure and legal expenses, winter-sports accidents, or motoring abroad. You can also purchase an annual travel-insurance policy valid for every trip you make during the year in which it's purchased (usually only trips of less than 90 days). Before you leave, make sure you will be covered if you have a preexisting medical condition or are pregnant; your insurers may not pay for routine or continuing treatment, or may require a note from your doctor certifying your fitness to travel.

The **Association of British Insurers,** a trade association representing 450 insurance companies, advises extra medical coverage for visitors to the United States.

For advice by phone or a free booklet, "Holiday Insurance," which sets out what to expect from a holiday-insurance policy and gives price guidelines, contact the Association of British Insurers (51 Gresham St., London EC2V 7HQ, tel. 071/600–3333; 30 Gordon St., Glasgow G1 3PU, tel. 041/226–3905; Scottish Provincial Bldg., Donegall Sq. W, Belfast BT1 6JE, tel. 0232/249176; call for other locations).

Tour Operators Tour operators offering packages to New York City include **Americana Vacations Ltd.** (Morley House, 320 Regent St., London W1R

5AD, tel. 071/637–7853), **Jetsave** (Sussex House, London Rd., East Grinstead, Sussex RH19 1LD, tel. 0342/312033), **Key to America** (15 Feltham Rd., Ashford, Middx., TW15 1DQ, tel. 0784/248777), **Trailfinders** (42–50 Earls Court Rd., London W8 7RG, tel. 071/937–5400; 58 Deansgate, Manchester M3 2FF, tel. 061/839–3636), and **Transamerica Holidays** (3a Gatwick Metro Centre, Balcombe Rd., Horley RH6 9GA, tel. 0293/774441).

Airfares Fares vary enormously. Fares from consolidators are usually the cheapest, followed by promotional fares such as APEX (advance purchase excursion). A few phone calls should reveal the current picture. When comparing fares, don't forget to figure airport taxes and weekend supplements. Once you know which airline is going your way at the right time for the least money, book immediately, since seats at the lowest prices often sell out quickly. Travel agents will generally hold a reservation for up to 5 days, especially if you give a credit card number.

Seven airlines fly direct from Heathrow to La Guardia, JFK, or Newark: **British Airways** (tel. 081/897–4000), **American Airlines** (tel. 0800/010151), **Virgin Atlantic** (tel. 0293/747747), **United Airlines** (tel. 0426/915500), **Air India** (081/759-1818), **Kuwait Airways** (081/745–7772), and **El Al** (081/759–9771); BA and Virgin also serve Gatwick, as does **Continental Airlines** (tel. 0293/567977), and Virgin and AA both fly direct to Manchester, too. Flight time is approximately seven hours on all routes.

Some travel agencies that offer cheap fares to New York City include **Trailfinders** (*see above*), specialists in Round-The-World fares and independent travel: **Travel Cuts** (295a Regent St., London W1R 7YA, tel, 071/637–3161), the Canadian Students' travel service; **Flightfile** (49 Tottenham Court Rd., London W1P 9RE, tel. 071/700–2722), a flight-only agency.

When to Go

At one time, it seemed New York's cultural life was limited to the months between October and May, when new Broadway shows opened, museums mounted major exhibitions, and formal seasons for opera, ballet, and concerts held sway. Today, however, there are Broadway openings even in mid-July, and a number of touring orchestras and opera and ballet companies visit the city in summer. In late-spring and summer, the streets and parks are filled with ethnic parades, impromptu sidewalk concerts, and free performances under the stars. Except for regular closing days and a few holidays (such as Christmas, New Year's Day, and Thanksgiving), the city's museums are open year-round. The parks are always free, so in winter you can cross-country ski, in summer you can swim or sunbathe, and in summer and fall you can watch migrating birds make their semiannual New York visits.

Climate Although there's an occasional bone-chilling winter day, with winds blasting in off the Hudson, snow hardly ever accumulates in the city (the winter of 1993/94 aside). Summer is the only unpleasant time of year, especially the humid, hot days of August, when many Manhattanites vacate the island for summer homes. Most hotels are air-conditioned, but if you're traveling in the summer and choosing budget accommodations, it's a good idea to ask whether your room has an air conditioner. Air-conditioned stores, restaurants, theaters, and museums provide respite from the heat; so do the many green expanses of parks. Subways and buses are usually air-conditioned, but subway stations can be as hot as saunas (and considerably dirtier).

Because the metropolitan area's water needs are so enormous, occasional summer droughts may entail strict conservation, with the result that air-conditioning is cut back, grass goes unwatered, fountains stand dry, and restaurants serve water only upon request.

The following table shows each month's average temperatures for New York City—the daily highs and lows, expressed in both Fahrenheit and centigrade:

Jan.	41F	5C	**May**	70F	21C	**Sept.**	76F	24C
	29	- 2		54	12		61	16
Feb.	43F	6C	**June**	81F	27C	**Oct.**	67F	19C
	29	- 2		63	17		52	11
Mar.	47F	8C	**July**	85F	29C	**Nov.**	56F	13C
	34	1		70	21		43	6
Apr.	61F	16C	**Aug.**	83F	28C	**Dec.**	43F	6C
	45	7		68	20		31	- 1

Information For current weather conditions and forecasts for cities in the United
Sources States and abroad, plus the local time and helpful travel tips, call the **Weather Channel Connection** (tel. 900/932–8437; 95¢ per minute) from a touch-tone phone.

Festivals and Seasonal Events

When it comes to special events, New York is indeed, as one classic song puts it, "the city that doesn't sleep." Here is a list of some of the more important or unusual events projected to take place throughout the year; for more up-to-date information, pick up a copy of *New York* magazine, the *Village Voice*, or the Friday edition of the *New York Times* upon your arrival in the city; contact the New York Convention and Visitors Bureau (*see* Visitor Information, *above*); or contact the event sponsor noted at the end of some listings.

Dec. 31–Jan. 1: New Year's Eve is marked by the famous countdown in Times Square; expect throngs of somewhat unruly revelers waiting for the ball to drop. Fireworks and a midnight run are held in Central Park.
Jan.: Ice Capades makes its regular winter appearance at Madison Square Garden. Tel. 212/465–6000.
Jan. 6–15: The National Boat Show, at the Jacob K. Javits Convention Center, gives the public a look at all sorts of seaworthy vessels and related equipment. Tel. 212/922–1212.
Jan.: The Winter Antiques Show, an exhibition of 17th- and 18th-century furniture, paintings, and statues, is held at the Seventh Regiment Armory, Park Avenue at 67th Street. Tel. 212/439–0300.
Feb.: The Chinese New Year crackles with fireworks and energy as the Chinatown community prepares for and celebrates the lunar New Year.
Feb.: The Westminster Kennel Club Dog Show showcases top-of-the-line pooches at Madison Square Garden. Tel. 212/465–6000.
Feb.: The Millrose Games, an international track-and-field competition, is held at Madison Square Garden. Tel. 212/465–6000.
Early Mar.: The International Cat Show, at Madison Square Garden, displays favorite breeds along with varieties you've never heard of. Tel. 212/465–6000.
Mar.: Big East Basketball Championships, at Madison Square Garden, provide some exciting basketball action. Tel. 212/465–6000.
Mar. 9–13: Artexpo NY displays artworks in all media to the public at the Jacob K. Javits Convention Center. Tel. 800/331–5706.
Mar. 17: St. Patrick's Day Parade, a classic parade down 5th Avenue,

reflects the vitality of the Irish and Irish-American sector of the city's population.

Mid-Mar.–Apr.: Ringling Bros. Barnum & Bailey Circus brings its three-ring act to Madison Square Garden. Tel. 212/465–6000.

Mar.–Apr.: Radio City Easter Extravaganza fills last couple of weeks before Easter with dancers, spectacle, and other nonreligious pageantry. Tel. 212/247–4777.

Apr.–June: The New York City Ballet (tel. 212/870–5570) and **American Ballet Theatre** (tel. 212/362–6000) launch the spring season with performances at Lincoln Center.

Apr.–Oct.: The major-league baseball season sees the Yankees play their home games at Yankee Stadium in the Bronx (tel. 718/293–6000), while the Mets hold court at Shea Stadium, Queens (tel. 718/507–8499).

Apr. 16: Easter Parade, takes place along 5th Avenue from 49th to 59th streets.

Late Apr.: The Cherry Blossom Festival is in full bloom at the Brooklyn Botanic Garden. Tel. 718/622–4433.

May: Ukrainian Festival, held on 7th Street between 2nd and 3rd avenues, is a refreshingly homespun event with what is probably the best food of any of the street fairs. Tel. 212/228–6840.

May: Martin Luther King, Jr., Parade marches down 5th Avenue in memory of the civil rights leader.

Mid-May: The 9th Avenue International Food Festival features food and merchandise from 32 countries. Tel. 212/581–7217.

Late May–early June: Washington Square Art Show (also held in early Sept.) displays artists' current work around the Greenwich Village central square for two weekends, starting Memorial Day weekend. Tel. 212/982–6255.

June–July: Metropolitan Opera performs free on weekday evenings in parks throughout the five boroughs. Tel. 212/769–7000.

June 1–13: Feast of St. Anthony spills over from SoHo to Little Italy. Tel. 212/777–2755.

June 11: Welcome Back to Brooklyn Day is a gala celebration from noon to 5 along Eastern Parkway from Grand Army Plaza to Washington Avenue. Tel. 718/855–7882.

June 27: Lesbian and Gay Pride Day Parade runs down 5th Avenue to Washington Square. Tel. 212/463–9030.

Late June: JVC Jazz Festival features vintage stars and newcomers at venues all around town. Tel. 212/787–2020.

July 4: Independence Day is celebrated with fireworks and street fairs at various locations.

July–Aug.: Shakespeare in the Park presents free productions at the Delacorte Theater in Central Park. Tel. 212/598–7100.

July–Aug.: The New York Philharmonic chips in with free concerts in various city parks. Tel. 212/360–1333.

Mid-July–Aug.: Mostly Mozart Festival presents a distinguished series of classical concerts at Avery Fisher Hall in Lincoln Center. Tel. 212/875–5030.

July–Nov.: New York City Opera performs at the New York State Theater in Lincoln Center. Tel. 212/870–5570.

Aug. 7–21: Harlem Week presents a series of workshops, street fairs, gospel festivals, and cultural events. Tel. 212/427–7200.

Late Aug.–Sept.: Lincoln Center Out-of-Doors hosts a variety of cultural events on the complex's plazas. Tel. 212/875–5400.

Late Aug.–early Sept.: U.S. Open Tennis Championships bring world-class excitement to the National Tennis Center in Flushing Meadows, Queens. Tel. 718/271–5100.

Late Aug.–Dec.: New York Giants and **New York Jets** play NFL football at Giants Stadium in East Rutherford, New Jersey. Tel. 201/ 935–3900.

Mid-Sept.: New York Is Book Country transforms 5th Avenue into a reader's paradise.

Mid-Sept.: Feast of San Gennaro, a popular, somewhat overcrowded 10-day extravaganza in Little Italy, features games, vendors, and fabulous food. Tel. 212/226–9546.

Sept.–June: New York Philharmonic plays at Lincoln Center's Avery Fisher Hall. Tel. 212/875–5030.

Late Sept.–early Oct.: New York Film Festival features an eclectic mix of new and notable international films at Lincoln Center's Alice Tully Hall. Tel. 212/875–5050.

Oct. 1: Feast of St. Francis at the Cathedral of St. John the Divine draws a crowd of thousands to watch the Blessing of the Animals, which includes everything from pet hamsters to circus elephants. Tel. 212/316–7400.

Oct. 9: Columbus Day Parade gives New York's Italian-Americans a chance to strut their stuff.

Oct.: The International Antique Dealers Show, a vetted exhibition of antique furniture, porcelain, and other decorative objets d'art, is held at the Seventh Regiment Armory, Park Avenue at 67th Street. Tel. 212/439–0300.

Oct.–Apr.: Metropolitan Opera commands center stage at Lincoln Center. Tel. 212/362–6000.

Oct.–Apr.: New York Knicks Basketball and **New York Rangers Hockey** get underway at Madison Square Garden. Tel. 212/465–6000.

Oct. 31: Halloween Parade, New York's most outrageous parade, is held in Greenwich Village.

Early Nov.: New York City Marathon starts at the Verrazano-Narrows Bridge in Staten Island and proceeds through all five boroughs. Tel. 212/860–4455.

Mid-Nov.: Virginia Slims Tennis Tournament brings top women pros to Madison Square Garden. Tel. 212/465–6000.

Nov. 23: Macy's Thanksgiving Day Parade sends giant balloons and a sleigh-borne Santa from Central Park West at 77th Street to Broadway and 34th Street.

Mid-Nov.–Jan.: Christmas Spectacular, a musical performance featuring the high-kicking Rockettes, hits the Radio City Music Hall stage. Tel. 212/247–4777.

Late Nov.–early Jan.: Lord & Taylor and **Saks Fifth Avenue** present animated window displays.

Dec.–early Jan.: The New York City Ballet's *Nutcracker* performances are a seasonal fixture at Lincoln Center. Tel. 212/870–5570.

What to Pack

Clothing Jackets and ties are required for men in a number of restaurants. For sightseeing and casual dining, jeans and sneakers are acceptable just about anywhere in the city. Sneakers or other flat-heeled walking shoes are highly recommended for pounding the New York pavements; you may even see businesspeople in button-down office attire lacing them on for the sprint from one appointment to another.

Miscellaneous Pack light, because porters and luggage trolleys can be hard to find at New York airports. You may need a fistful of quarters to rent a trolley, if no personnel are on duty by the coin-operated trolley racks.

Bring an extra pair of eyeglasses or contact lenses in your carry-on luggage. If you have a health problem that requires a prescription drug, pack enough to last the duration of the trip. Don't pack them in luggage that you plan to check in case your bags go astray. Pack a list of the offices that supply refunds for lost or stolen traveler's checks.

Luggage Free airline baggage allowances depend on the airline, the route,
Regulations and the class of your ticket; ask in advance. In general, on domestic flights you are entitled to check two bags—neither exceeding 62 inches, or 158 centimeters (length + width + height), or weighing more than 70 pounds (32 kilograms). A third piece may be brought aboard; its total dimensions are generally limited to less than 45 inches (114 centimeters), so it will fit easily under the seat in front of you or in the overhead compartment. In the United States the Federal Aviation Administration gives airlines broad latitude to limit carry-on allowances and tailor them to different aircraft and operational conditions. Charges for excess, oversize, or overweight pieces vary.

Safeguarding Before leaving home, itemize your bags' contents and their worth in
Your Luggage case they go astray. To minimize that risk, tag them inside and out with your name, address, and phone number. (If you use your home address, cover it so that potential thieves can't see it.) Put a copy of your itinerary inside each bag, so that you can easily be tracked. At check-in, make sure that the tag attached by baggage handlers bears the correct three-letter code for your destination. If your bags do not arrive with you, or if you detect damage, immediately file a written report with the airline before you leave the airport.

Insurance In the event of loss, damage, or theft on domestic flights, airlines' liability is $1,250 per passenger, excluding the valuable items such as jewelry, cameras, and more that are listed in the fine print on your ticket. Excess-valuation insurance can be bought directly from the airline at check-in. Your homeowner's policy may fill the gap; or firms such as **The Travelers Companies** (1 Tower Sq., Hartford, CT 06183, tel. 203/277–0111 or 800/243–3174) and **Wallach and Company** (107 W. Federal St., Box 480, Middleburg, VA 22117, tel. 703/687–3166 or 800/237–6615) sell baggage insurance.

What It Will Cost

There's no doubt that New York is an expensive city to visit. Hotel rooms with views of Central Park can easily run as high as $250 a night; dinner for two at a moderate restaurant, plus orchestra seats at a Broadway show, can set you back $150–$200 (*see* Chapters 8, 9, and 10). If you're on a budget, don't despair. New Yorkers themselves know how to find bargains; they comb discount clothing outlets, grab food at corner delis, walk just about everywhere, and attend free concerts and plays in the parks. You, too, can moderate the cost of your visit if you do as they do (*see* Manhattan for Free in Chapter 3 and Discount Tickets in Chapter 10).

Hotel taxes add up to 21¼% once you get past the $100-a-night rate level (which covers most New York hotels!). The customary tipping rate is 15%–20% for taxi drivers and waiters (see Chapter 8 for further tipping advice), and bellhops are usually given $2 in luxury hotels, $1 elsewhere. Hotel maids should be tipped around $1 per day of your stay.

Getting Money from Home

Cash Machines Many automated-teller machines (ATMs) are tied to international networks such as **Cirrus** and **Plus.** You can use your bank card at ATMs to withdraw money from an account and get cash advances on a credit-card account if your card has been programmed with a personal identification number, or PIN. Check in advance on limits on withdrawals and cash advances within specified periods. On cash advances you are charged interest from the day you receive the money from ATMs as well as from tellers. Transaction fees for ATM withdrawals outside your home turf may be higher than for withdrawals at home.

For specific Cirrus locations in the United States and Canada, call 800/424–7787. For U.S. Plus locations, call 800/843–7587 and press the area code and first three digits of the number you're calling from (or of the calling area where you want to find an ATM).

Wiring Money You don't have to be a cardholder to send or receive a **MoneyGram** from **American Express** for up to $10,000. Go to a MoneyGram agent in retail and convenience stores and American Express travel offices, pay up to $1,000 with a credit card and anything over that in cash. You are allowed a free long-distance call to give the transaction code to your intended recipient, who needs only present identification and the reference number to the nearest MoneyGram agent to pick up the cash. MoneyGram agents are in more than 70 countries (call 800/926–9400 for locations). Fees range from 3% to 10%, depending on the amount and how you pay.

You can also use **Western Union.** To wire money, take either cash or a cashier's check to the nearest office or call and use Mastercard or Visa. Money sent from the United States or Canada will be available for pickup at agent locations in 78 countries within minutes. Once the money is in the system it can be picked up at *any* one of 22,000 locations (call 800/325–6000 for the one nearest you.

Traveling with Cameras, Camcorders, and Laptops

About Film and Cameras If your camera is new or if you haven't used it for a while, shoot and develop a few test rolls of film before you leave. Store film in a cool, dry place—never in the car's glove compartment or on the shelf under the rear window.

Airport security X-rays generally aren't harmful to film with ISO below 400. To protect your film, carry it with you in a clear plastic bag and ask for a hand inspection. Such requests are honored at U.S. airports. Don't depend on a lead-lined bag to protect film in checked luggage.

About Camcorders Before your trip, put camcorders through their paces, invest in a skylight filter to protect the lens, and check all the batteries.

About Videotape Videotape is not damaged by X-rays, but it may be harmed by the magnetic field of a walk-through metal detector, so ask for a hand-check. Airport security personnel may ask you to turn on the camcorder to prove that it's what it appears to be, so make sure the battery is charged.

About Laptops Security X-rays do not harm hard-disk or floppy-disk storage, but you may request a hand check, at which point you may be asked to turn on the computer to prove that it is what it appears to be. (Check your battery before departure.) Most airlines allow you to use your laptop aloft except during takeoff and landing (so as not to interfere with navigation equipment).

Traveling with Children

See Chapter 5 for the many free and exciting activities for children in the Big Apple.

Publications *Family Travel Times*, published 10 times a year by Travel With
Newsletter Your Children (TWYCH, 45 W. 18th St., 7th Floor Tower, New York, NY 10011, tel. 212/206–0688; annual subscription $55), covers destinations, types of vacations, and modes of travel. TWYCH also publishes *Cruising with Children* and *Skiing with Children*.

Books *Great Vacations with Your Kids*, by Dorothy Jordan and Marjorie Cohen ($13; Penguin USA, 120 Woodbine St., Bergenfield, NJ 07621, tel. 800/253–6476), and *Traveling with Children—And Enjoying It*, by Arlene K. Butler ($11.95 plus $3 shipping per book; Globe Pequot Press, Box 833, 6 Business Park Rd., Old Saybrook, CT 06475, tel. 800/243–0495, or 800/962–0973 in CT), help plan your trip with children, from toddlers to teens. From the same publisher are *Recommended Family Resorts in the United States, Canada, and the Caribbean*, by Jane Wilford with Janet Tice ($12.95), and *Recommended Family Inns of America* ($12.95).

Tour **Grandtravel** (6900 Wisconsin Ave., Suite 706, Chevy Chase, MD
Operators 20815, tel. 301/986–0790 or 800/247–7651) offers tours for people traveling with their grandchildren. The catalogue, as charmingly written and illustrated as a children's book, positively invites armchair traveling with lap-sitters aboard.

Getting There On domestic flights, children under 2 not occupying a seat travel
Air Fares free, and older children currently travel on the "lowest applicable" adult fare.

Baggage The adult baggage allowance applies for children paying half or more of the adult fare.

Safety Seats The FAA recommends the use of safety seats aloft and details approved models in the free leaflet "Child/Infant Safety Seats Recommended for Use in Aircraft" (available from the Federal Aviation Administration, APA–200, 800 Independence Ave. SW, Washington, DC 20591, tel. 202/267–3479); Information Hot Line, tel. 800/322–7873). Airline policy varies. U.S. carriers allow FAA-approved models bearing a sticker declaring their FAA approval. Because these seats are strapped into regular passenger seats, airlines may require that a ticket be bought for an infant who would otherwise ride free.

Facilities Aloft Some airlines provide other services for children, such as children's meals and freestanding bassinets (only to those with seats at the bulkhead, where there's enough legroom). Make your request when reserving. The annual February/March issue of *Family Travel Times* details children's services on dozens of airlines ($10; *see above*). "Kids and Teens in Flight," free from the U.S. Department of Transportation's Office of Consumer Affairs (R-25, Washington, DC 20590, tel. 202/366–2220), offers tips for children flying alone.

Baby-Sitting You can usually make child-care arrangements through your hotel's
Services concierge. For New York City agencies, *see* Chapter 5.

Around Town Children under age 6 travel free on subways and buses; children over age 6 must pay full fare. Clean rest rooms are often difficult to find; your best bet is to use the washrooms at museums, department stores, hotels, and restaurants while you are there.

If you find you need a stroller once you get here, ask your hotel concierge to find one for you, or contact **AAA-U-Rent** (861 Eagle Ave., Bronx, NY 10456, tel. 718/665–6633).

Hints for Travelers with Disabilities

Many buildings in New York City are now wheelchair-accessible. The subway is still hard to navigate, however; people in wheelchairs do better on public buses, most of which "kneel" to facilitate getting on and off. For brochures and further information, contact the **Mayor's Office for People with Disabilities** (52 Chambers St., Office 206, New York, NY 10007, tel. 212/788–2830). Blind or visually impaired visitors may appreciate a visit to the **Andrew Heiskell Library for the Blind and Physically Handicapped** (40 W. 20th St., tel. 212/206–5400), a public library branch with a large collection of Braille, large-print, and recorded books, housed in a layout specially designed for easy access by the visually impaired.

Organizations Several organizations provide travel information for people with disabilities, usually for a membership fee, and some publish newsletters and bulletins. Among them are the **Information Center for Individuals with Disabilities** (Fort Point Pl., 27–43 Wormwood St., Boston, MA 02210, tel. 617/727–5540; in MA, 800/462–5015 between 11 and 4, or leave message; TTY 617/345–9743); **Mobility International USA** (Box 10767, Eugene, OR 97440, tel. and TTY 503/343–1284, fax 503/343–6812), the U.S. branch of an international organization based in Britain (*see below*) that has affiliates in 30 countries; **MossRehab Hospital Travel Information Service** (tel. 215/456–9603, TTY 215/456–9602); the **Travel Industry and Disabled Exchange** (TIDE, 5435 Donna Ave., Tarzana, CA 91356, tel. 818/344–3640, fax 818/344–0078); and **Travelin' Talk** (Box 3534, Clarksville, TN 37043, tel. 615/552–6670, fax 615/552–1182).

In the United Important information sources include the **Royal Association for**
Kingdom **Disability and Rehabilitation** (RADAR: 12 City Forum, 250 City Rd., London EC1V 8AF, tel. 071/250–3222), which publishes travel information for people with disabilities in Britain, and **Mobility International** (228 Borough High St., London SE1 1JX, tel. 071/403–5688), an international clearinghouse of travel information for people with disabilities.

Travel **Flying Wheels Travel** (143 W. Bridge St., Box 382, Owatonna, MN
Agencies 55060, tel. 507/451–5005 or 800/535–6790) is a travel agency specia-
and Tour lizing in domestic and worldwide cruises, tours, and independent
Operators travel itineraries for people with mobility problems. Adventurers should contact **Wilderness Inquiry** (1313 5th St. SE, Minneapolis, MN 55414, tel. and TTY 612/379–3838), which orchestrates action-packed trips like white-water rafting, sea kayaking, and dog sledding for people with disabilities. Tours are designed to bring together people who have disabilities with those who don't.

Publications The New York Division of Tourism (1 Commerce Plaza, Albany, NY
Local 12245, tel. 518/474–4116 or 800/225–5697) offers the *I Love New*
Resources *York Travel and Adventure Guide*, which includes ratings of various facilities' accessibility. The New York State Parks Department (Empire State Plaza, Albany, NY 12238, tel. 518/474–0456) provides information on handicapped facilities in the *Guide to New York State Parks, Historic Sites and Programs*.

General Several free publications are available from the U.S. Consumer In-
Information formation Center (Pueblo, CO 81009): "New Horizons for the Air
Traveler with a Disability" (include Dept. 608Y in the address), a
U.S. Department of Transportation booklet describing changes resulting from the 1986 Air Carrier Access Act and from the 1990
Americans with Disabilities Act, and the Airport Operators Council's *Access Travel: Airports* (Dept. 5804), which describes facilities
and services for people with disabilities at more than 500 airports
worldwide.

Travelin' Talk Directory (see Travelin' Talk, *above)* was published in
1993. This 500-page resource book ($35 check or money order with a
money-back guarantee) is packed with information for travelers
with disabilities. Twin Peaks Press (Box 129, Vancouver, WA 98666,
tel. 206/694–2462 or 800/637–2256) publishes the *Directory of Travel Agencies for the Disabled* ($19.95), listing more than 370 agencies
worldwide; and *Wheelchair Vagabond* ($14.95), a collection of per-
sonal travel tips. Add $2 per book for shipping. Fodor's publishes
Great American Vacations for Travelers with Disabilities detailing
services and accessible attractions, restaurants, and hotels in New
York City and other U.S. destinations (available in bookstores, or
call 800/533–6478).

Hints for Older Travelers

Organizations The **American Association of Retired Persons** (AARP, 601 E St. NW,
Washington, DC 20049, tel. 202/434–2277) provides independent
travelers who are members of the AARP (open to those age 50 or
older; $8 per person or couple annually) with the Purchase Privilege
Program, which offers discounts on lodging, car rentals, and sightseeing, and the AARP Motoring Plan, which furnishes domestic
trip-routing information and emergency road-service aid for an annual fee of $39.95 per person or couple ($59.95 for a premium version). AARP also arranges group tours, cruises, and apartment
living through AARP Travel Experience from American Express
(400 Pinnacle Way, Suite 450, Norcross, GA 30071, tel. 800/927–
0111) or 800/745–4567).

Two other organizations offer discounts on lodgings, car rentals,
and other travel products, along with such nontravel perks as magazines and newsletters: the **National Council of Senior Citizens** (1331
F St. NW, Washington, DC 20004, tel. 202/347–8800; membership
$12 annually) and **Mature Outlook** (6001 N. Clark St., Chicago, IL
60660, tel. 800/336–6330; $9.95 annually).

Note: Mention your senior-citizen identification card when booking
hotel reservations for reduced rates, not when checking out. At restaurants, show your card before you're seated; discounts may be limited to certain menus, days, or hours. If you are renting a car, ask
about promotional rates that might improve on your senior-citizen
discount.

Educational The nonprofit **Elderhostel** (75 Federal St., 3rd Floor, Boston, MA
Travel 02110, tel. 617/426–7788) has offered inexpensive study programs
for people 60 and older since 1975. Held at more than 1,800 educational institutions, courses cover everything from marine science to
Greek myths and cowboy poetry. Participants usually attend lectures in the morning and spend the afternoon sightseeing or on field
trips; they live in dorms on the host campuses. Fees for programs in
the United States and Canada, which usually last one week, run
about $300, not including transportation.

Tour Operators The following tour operators specialize in older travelers: If you want to take your grandchildren, look into **Grandtravel** (*see* Traveling with Children, *above*). **Saga International Holidays** (222 Berkeley St., Boston, MA 02116, tel. 800/343–0273) caters to those over age 60 who like to travel in groups. **SeniorTours** (508 Irvington Rd., Drexel Hill, PA 19026, tel. 215/626–1977 or 800/227–1100) arranges motorcoach tours throughout the United States and Nova Scotia, as well as Caribbean cruises.

Hints for Gay and Lesbian Travelers

Organizations The **International Gay Travel Association** (Box 4974, Key West, FL 33041, tel. 305/292–0217, 800/999–7925, or 800/448–8550), which has 700 members, will provide you with names of travel agents and tour operators who specialize in gay travel. The **Gay & Lesbian Visitors Center of New York Inc.** (135 W. 20th St., 3rd Floor, New York, NY 10011, tel. 212/463–9030 or 800/395–2315; $100 annually) mails a monthly newsletter, valuable coupons, and more to its members.

Travel Agencies and Tour Operators The dominant travel agency in the market is **Above and Beyond** (3568 Sacramento St., San Francisco, CA 94118, tel. 415/922–2683 or 800/ 397–2681). Tour operator **Olympus Vacations** (8424 Santa Monica Blvd. #721, West Hollywood, CA 90069; tel. 310/657–2220 or 800/ 965–9678) offers all-gay and lesbian resort holidays. **Skylink Women's Travel** (746 Ashland Ave., Santa Monica, CA 90405, tel. 310/452–0506 or 800/225–5759) handles individual travel for lesbians all over the world and conducts two international and five domestic group trips annually.

Publications The premiere international travel magazine for gays and lesbians is *Our World* (1104 North Nova Road, Suite 251, Daytona Beach, FL 32117, tel. 904/441–5367; $35 for 10 issues). "Out & About" (tel. 203/ 789–8518 or 800/929–2268; $49 for 10 issues, full refund if you aren't satisfied) is a 16-page monthly newsletter with extensive information on resorts, hotels, and airlines that are gay-friendly.

Further Reading

Many a famous writer has set down his or her impressions of this fascinating city. Some of the best full-length accounts are *Christopher Morley's New York*, a mid-1920s essay; *A Walker in the City*, by Alfred Kazin; and *Apple of My Eye*, a 1978 account of writing a New York guidebook, by Helene Hanff. *New York Style*, by Suzanne Slesin, Stafford Cliff, and Daniel Rozensztroch, has several sections devoted to the city. Dan Wakefield recalls his early literary days in *New York in the 50s*. Perhaps the best of all is E. B. White's 1949 essay "Here Is New York."

The early history of New York is wittily told in the classic *Knickerbocker's History of New York*, by Washington Irving. For a fine historical introduction to the city, find the heavily illustrated *Columbia Historical Portrait of New York*, by John Kouwenhoven. *New York, New York*, by Oliver E. Allen, is a well-rounded, up-to-date history of the city. *You Must Remember This*, by Jeff Kisseloff, is an oral history of ordinary New Yorkers early in this century. *The Park and its People*, by Roy Rosenzweig and Elizabeth Blackmar, tells how Central Park evolved.

Fiorello H. La Guardia and the Making of Modern New York, by Thomas Kessner, is a biography of the charismatic Depression-era mayor. *The Power Broker* by Robert Caro is a fascinating biography of Robert Moses, one of the city's most influential parks commissioners. Robert Daley's *Prince of the City* is a true-life drama of New York police corruption. Highly critical accounts of the city's recent politics can be found in *The Streets Were Paved with Gold*, by Ken Auletta; *The Rise and Fall of New York City*, by Roger Starr; *Imperial City*, by Geoffrey Moorhouse; and *City for Sale*, by Jack Newfield and Wayne Barrett. *A License to Steal*, by Benjamin J. Stein, concerns Wall Street's notorious Michael Milken, as does *Den of Thieves*, by James B. Stewart.

Theater lovers may want to read *Act One*, the autobiography of playwright Moss Hart; for more up-to-date essays on the city's theater scene, try David Mamet's *The Cabin*. *The Kingdom and the Power*, by Gay Talese, offers a behind-the-scenes look at the *New York Times;* life at one of the city's most venerable magazines is recounted in *Here at The New Yorker*, by Brendan Gill. Speaking of that august publication, *Up in the Old Hotel* brings together Joseph Mitchell's *New Yorker* stories, which deal with colorful New York characters. *From Manet to Manhattan*, by Peter Watson, explores the city's art world. *Literary New York*, by Susan Edmiston and Linda D. Cirino, traces the haunts of famous writers, neighborhood by neighborhood. *The Heart of the World*, by Nik Cohn, is a block-by-block history of Manhattan's most famous street, Broadway.

AIA Guide to New York City, by Elliot Willensky and Norval White, is the definitive guide to the city's many building styles; Paul Goldberger's *The City Observed* describes Manhattan building by building. *The WPA Guide to New York City (The Federal Writers' Project Guide to 1930s New York)* was written in 1939, and many still consider it an unbeatable guide to the city's history and geography. John Kieran's *A Natural History of New York* explores the wildlife of the city's parks, while Eugene Kinkead concentrates on the most famous park in *Central Park: The Birth, Decline, and Renewal of a National Treasure*.

Perhaps because so many writers have lived in New York City, there is a wealth of fiction set here. Jack Finney's *Time and Again* is a delightful time-travel story illustrated with 19th-century photos; *Winter's Tale*, by Mark Helprin, uses surreal fantasy to create a portrait of New York's past. Novels set in 19th-century New York include Henry James's *Washington Square*, Edith Wharton's *The Age of Innocence*, and Stephen Crane's *Maggie, A Girl of the Streets*. O. Henry's short stories depict the early years of this century, while Damon Runyon's are set in the raffish underworld of the 1930s and 1940s. F. Scott Fitzgerald (*The Beautiful and Damned*, 1922), John Dos Passos (*Manhattan Transfer*, 1925), John O'Hara (*Butterfield 8*, 1935), and Mary McCarthy (*The Group*, 1938) also wrote about this city. J. D. Salinger's *The Catcher in the Rye* (1951) partly takes place here, as does Thomas Pynchon's *V* (1965). Truman Capote's 1958 novella *Breakfast at Tiffany's* is a special favorite of many New Yorkers.

More current New York novels include *The Bonfire of the Vanities*, by Tom Wolfe; *The Mambo Kings Play Songs of Love*, by Oscar Hijuelos; *The New York Trilogy*, by Paul Auster; and *People Like Us*, by Dominick Dunne. For portraits of gay life, try Larry Kramer's *Faggots*, David Leavitt's *The Lost Language of Cranes*, Sarah Schulman's *After Delores* and *People in Trouble*, and John Weir's *The Irreversible Decline of Eddy Socket*. The downtown scene is depicted in Tama Janowitz's *Slaves of New York* and Jay McInerney's *Bright Lights, Big City*.

The black experience in Harlem has been chronicled in Ralph Ellison's *Invisible Man*, James Baldwin's *Go Tell It on the Mountain*, and Claude Brown's *Manchild in the Promised Land*. For a portrait of Harlem during the 1920s, there's *When Harlem Was in Vogue*, by David Levering Lewis. The history of New York's Jewish population can be traced through such books as *World of Our Fathers*, by Irving Howe; *Call It Sleep*, by Henry Roth; *The Promise*, by Chaim Potok; *Enemies, A Love Story*, by Isaac Bashevis Singer; and *Our Crowd*, by Stephen Birmingham.

Greenwich Village and How It Got That Way is a fascinating study of that fascinating neighborhood by Terry Miller. Francine Prose's *Household Saints* is a fictional portrait of life in Little Italy. *The New Chinatown*, by Peter Kwong, is a recent study of the community across Canal Street. Kate Simon's *Bronx Primitive*, Laura Cunningham's autobiographical *Sleeping Arrangements*, and E. L. Doctorow's novel *World's Fair* are set in the Bronx. Brooklyn's history is beautifully illustrated in *Brooklyn: People and Places, Past and Present*, by Grace Glueck and Paul Gardner.

Mysteries set in New York City range from Dashiell Hammett's urbane 1933 novel *The Thin Man*, to Rex Stout's series of Nero Wolfe mysteries (continued by Robert Goldsborough) to more recent picks: *While My Pretty One Sleeps*, by Mary Higgins Clark; *Greenwich Killing Time*, by Kinky Friedman; *Dead Air*, by Mike Lupica; and *Unorthodox Practices*, by Marissa Piesman.

Arriving and Departing

By Plane

Flights are either nonstop, direct, or connecting. A **nonstop** flight requires no change of plane and makes no stops. A **direct** flight stops at least once and can involve a change of plane, although the flight number remains the same; if the first leg is late, the second waits. This is not the case with a **connecting** flight, which involves a different plane and a different flight number.

Airports and Airlines Virtually every major U.S. and foreign airline serves one or more of New York's three airports: **La Guardia Airport** (tel. 718/533–3400) and **JFK International Airport** (tel. 718/244–4444), both in the borough of Queens, and **Newark International Airport** (tel. 201/961–6000) in New Jersey.

U.S. carriers serving the New York area include **America West** (tel. 800/247–5692); **American** (tel. 800/433–7300); **Continental** (tel. 800/525–0280); **Delta** (tel. 800/221–1212); **Northwest** (tel. 800/225–2525); **TWA** (tel. 800/221–2000); **United** (tel. 800/241–6522); and **USAir** (tel. 800/428–4322).

Cutting Costs The Sunday travel section of most newspapers is a good source of deals. When booking, particularly through an unfamiliar company, call the Better Business Bureau and your local or state Consumer Protection Bureau to find out whether any complaints have been registered against the company, pay with a credit card if you can, and consider trip-cancellation and default insurance.

Promotional Airfares Less expensive fares, called promotional or discount fares, are round-trip and involve restrictions, which vary according to the route and season. You must usually buy the ticket—commonly called an APEX (advance purchase excursion) when it's for international travel—in advance (seven, 14, or 21 days are usual), although some of the major airlines have added no-frills, cheap flights to compete with new bargain airlines on certain routes. These new low-cost carriers include: **Kiwi** (tel. 800/538–5494), based in Newark, New Jersey, and serving Chicago, Atlanta, Tampa, Orlando, West Palm Beach, and San Juan; and **Private Jet** (tel. 800/949–9400), based in Atlanta and serving Miami, Dallas, St. Thomas, St. Croix, Las Vegas, New York's JFK, Los Angeles, Chicago, and San Francisco.

With the major airlines, the cheaper fares generally require minimum- and maximum-stays (for instance, over a Saturday night or at least seven and no more than 30 days). Airlines generally allow some return date changes for a $25 to $50 fee, but most low-fare tickets are nonrefundable. Only a death in the family would prompt the airline to return any of your money if you cancel a nonrefundable ticket. However, you can apply an unused nonrefundable ticket toward a new ticket, again with a small fee. The lowest fare is subject to availability, and only a small percentage of the plane's total seats will be sold at that price. Contact the U.S. Department of Transportation's Office of Consumer Affairs (I–25, Washington, DC 20590, tel. 202/366–2220) for a copy of "Fly-Rights: A Guide to Air Travel in the U.S." *The Official Frequent Flyer Guidebook* by Randy Petersen (4715-C Town Center Dr., Colorado Springs, CO 80916, tel. 719/597–8899, 800/487–8893 or 800/485–8893; $14.99, plus $3 shipping and handling) yields valuable hints on getting the most for your air-travel dollars.

Consolidators Consolidators or bulk-fare operators—"bucket shops"—buy blocks of seats on scheduled flights that airlines anticipate they won't be able to sell. They pay wholesale prices, add a markup, and resell the seats to travel agents or directly to the public at prices that still undercut the airline's promotional or discount fares (higher than a charter ticket but lower than an APEX ticket, and usually without the advance-purchase restriction). Moreover, some consolidators sometimes give you your money back. Carefully read the fine print detailing penalties for changes and cancellations. If you doubt the reliability of a company, call the airline once you've made your booking and confirm that you do, indeed, have a reservation on the flight.

Discount Travel clubs offer members unsold space on airplanes, cruise ships, *Travel Clubs* and package tours at as much as 50% below regular prices. Membership may include a regular bulletin or access to a toll-free hot line giving details of available trips departing from three or four days to several months in the future. Most also offer 50% discounts off hotel rack rates, but double check with the hotel to make sure it isn't offering a better promotional rate independent of the club. Clubs include **Discount Travel International** (114 Forrest Ave., Suite 203, Narberth, PA 19072, tel. 215/668–7184; $45 annually, single or family), **Entertainment Travel Editions** (Box 1014, Trumbull, CT 06611, tel. 800/445–4137; price ranges $28–$48), **Great American Traveler** (Box 27965, Salt Lake City, UT 84127, tel. 800/548–2812; $29.95 annually), **Moment's Notice Discount Travel Club** (425 Madison Ave., New York, NY 10017, tel. 212/486–0503; $45 annually, single or family), **Privilege Card** (3391 Peachtree Rd. NE, Suite 110, Atlanta, GA 30326, tel. 404/262–0222 or 800/236–9732; domestic annual membership $49.95, international $74.95), **Travelers Advantage** (CUC Travel Service, 49 Music Sq. W, Nashville, TN 37203, tel. 800/548–1116; $49 annually, single or family), and **Worldwide Discount Travel Club** (1674 Meridian Ave., Miami Beach, FL 33139, tel. 305/534–2082; $50 annually for family, $40 single).

Publications The newsletter "Travel Smart" (40 Beechdale Rd., Dobbs Ferry, NY 10522, tel. 800/327–3633; $44 a year) has a wealth of travel deals in each monthly issue.

Smoking Since February 1990, smoking has been banned on all domestic flights of less than six hours' duration; the ban also applies to domestic segments of international flights aboard U.S. and foreign carriers.

Between the **Taxis** cost $18–$23 plus tolls (which may be as high as $4) and take
Airports and 20–40 minutes. Group taxi rides to Manhattan are available at taxi
Manhattan dispatch lines just outside the baggage-claim areas during most
La Guardia travel hours (except on Saturday and holidays). Group fares run
Airport $8–$9 per person (plus a share of tolls).

Carey Airport Express buses (tel. 718/632–0500, 800/456–1012, or 800/284–0909) depart for Manhattan every 20 minutes from 6 AM to midnight, from all terminals. It's a 20- to 30-minute ride to 42nd Street and Park Avenue, directly opposite Grand Central Terminal. The bus continues from there to the Port Authority Bus Terminal, the New York Hilton, Sheraton Manhattan, Holiday Inn Crowne Plaza, and Marriott Marquis hotels. Other midtown hotels are a short cab ride away. The bus fare is $8.50 ($10 to the hotels); pay the driver. **The Gray Line Air Shuttle Minibus** (tel. 212/315–3006 or 800/622–3427) serves major Manhattan hotels directly to and from the airport. The fare is $12 per person; make arrangements at the airport's ground transportation center or use the courtesy phone.

The most economical way to reach Manhattan is to ride the Q-33 bus (there are no luggage facilities on this bus) to either the Roosevelt Avenue–Jackson Heights station, where you can catch the E or F subway, or the 74th Street–Broadway station (it's the same station), where you can catch the No. 7 subway. Allow 90 minutes for the entire trip to midtown; the total cost is two tokens ($2.50 at press time). You can use exact change for your bus fare but will have to purchase a token to enter the subway.

JFK **Taxis** cost $25–$30 plus tolls (which may be as much as $4) and take
International 35–60 minutes.
Airport

Carey Airport Express buses (tel. 718/632–0500, 800/456–1012, or 800/284–0909) depart for Manhattan every 30 minutes from 6 AM to midnight, from all JFK terminals. The ride to 42nd Street and Park Avenue (Grand Central Terminal) takes about one hour. The bus continues from there to the Port Authority Bus Terminal, the New York Hilton, Sheraton Manhattan, Holiday Inn Crowne Plaza, and Marriott Marquis hotels; it's a short cab ride to other midtown hotels. The bus fare is $11 ($12.50 to the hotels); pay the driver.

The Gray Line Air Shuttle Minibus (tel. 212/315–3006 or 800/622–3427) serves major Manhattan hotels directly from the airport; the cost is $15 per person. Make arrangements at the airport's ground transportation counter or use the courtesy phone.

New York Helicopter (tel. 800/645–3494) offers daily flights between the airport and the heliport at East 34th Street and the East River. Planes leave from International Terminal 3 beginning at 8:50 AM, running roughly every 45 minutes in the morning and every half hour from 2:30 to 7:15 PM. Many passengers who use helicopter transport do so because it has been included in their long-distance airfare (check with your airline, especially if you are traveling first or business class); for other passengers the one-way fare is $65 plus tax. Reservations are recommended.

The cheapest but slowest means of getting to Manhattan is to take the Port Authority's free shuttle bus, which stops at all terminals, to the Howard Beach subway station, where you can catch the A train into Manhattan. Alternatively, you can take the Q-10 bus (there are no luggage facilities on this bus) to the Union Turnpike–Kew Gardens station, where you can catch the E or F subway, or to the Lefferts Boulevard station, where you can catch the A subway. Allow at least two hours for the trip; the total cost is one token ($1.25 at press time) if you use the shuttle or two tokens ($2.50) if you use the Q-10. You can use exact change for your fare on the Q-10, but you will need to purchase a token to enter the subway.

Newark **Taxis** cost $28–$30 plus tolls ($4) and take 20–45 minutes. "Share
Airport and Save" group rates are available for up to four passengers between 8 AM and midnight; make arrangements with the airport's taxi dispatcher.

NJ Transit Airport Express buses (tel. 201/762–5100) depart every 15–30 minutes for the Port Authority Bus Terminal, at 8th Avenue and 42nd Street. From there it's a short cab ride to midtown hotels. The ride takes 30–45 minutes. The fare is $7; buy your ticket inside the airport terminal.

Olympia Airport Express buses (tel. 212/964–6233) leave for Grand Central Terminal, Penn Station, and 1 World Trade Center (next to the Vista hotel) about every 30 minutes from around 6 AM to midnight. The trip takes 35–45 minutes to Grand Central and Penn Station, 20 minutes to WTC. The fare is $7.

The Gray Line Air Shuttle Minibus (tel. 212/757–6840 or 800/622–3427) serves major Manhattan hotels directly to and from the airport. You pay $17 per passenger; make arrangements at the airport's ground transportation center or use the courtesy phone.

Passengers arriving in Newark can also take New Jersey Transit's **Airlink buses** (tel. 201/762–5100), leaving every 20 minutes from 6:15 AM to 2 AM, to Penn Station in Newark. The ride takes about 20 minutes; the fare is $4. From there they can catch **PATH Trains** (tel. 800/234–7284), which run to Manhattan 24 hours a day. The trains run every 10 minutes on weekdays, every 15–30 minutes on weeknights, every 20–30 minutes on weekends, and stop at the World Trade Center and at five stops along 6th Avenue—Christopher Street, 9th Street, 14th Street, 23rd Street, and 33rd Street. The fare is $1.

Car Services Car services are a great deal, because the driver will often meet you on the concourse or in the baggage-claim area and help you with your luggage. You ride in late-model American-made cars that are comfortable, if usually a bit worn. New York City Taxi and Limousine Commission rules required that all be licensed and pick up riders only by prior arrangement. Call 24 hours in advance for reservations, or at least a half-day before your flight's departure. Try **All State Car and Limo** (tel. 212/741–7440), **Carey Limousines** (tel. 212/599–1122), **Carmel Car and Limousine Service** (tel. 212/662–2222), **Eastside Limo Service** (tel. 212/744–9700), **Fugazy Continental** (tel. 212/645–4242), **La Limousine** (tel. 212/736–0484), **London Towncars** (tel. 212/988–9700), **Manhattan Limo** (tel. 718/729–4200), **Sherwood Silver Bay Limousine Service** (tel. 718/472–0183), **Skyline** (tel. 212/741–3711), and **Wheels of New York** (tel. 212/465–1630).

Airline Ticket Many airlines have ticket offices in convenient midtown and lower-
Offices Manhattan locations. American, Continental, Delta, Northwest, and Virgin Atlantic, for example, all have offices at the **Airlines Building** (100 E. 42nd St.), and United, USAir, and TWA have of-

fices in the other **Airlines Building** next door at 101 Park Avenue. Offices are generally open weekdays 8–7, weekends 9–5, but hours vary among carriers.

Ticket offices are also clustered in three other Manhattan locations: the New York Hilton Hotel at 1335 6th Avenue (American, Continental, and Delta); the Sherry Netherland Hotel at 1 East 59th Street (American, Continental, Delta, TWA, United, and USAir); and 1 World Trade Center (American, British Airways, Continental, Delta, Lufthansa, Northwest, TWA, United, and USAir). Many foreign carriers have ticket offices along 5th Avenue north of 50th Street.

By Car

If you plan to drive into Manhattan, try to time your arrival in late morning or early afternoon. That way you'll avoid the morning and evening rush hours (a problem at the crossings into Manhattan) and lunch hour.

The **Lincoln Tunnel** (I–495), **Holland Tunnel**, and **George Washington Bridge** (I–95) connect Manhattan with the New Jersey Turnpike system and points west. The Lincoln Tunnel comes into midtown Manhattan; the Holland Tunnel into lower Manhattan; and the George Washington Bridge into northern Manhattan. Each of the three arteries requires a toll ($4 for cars) eastbound into New York, but no toll westbound.

The **Bayonne Bridge** connects Route 440 in Staten Island with Route 440 in New Jersey; a $4 toll for cars is collected southbound into New York. The **Outerbridge Crossing** and **Goethals Bridge** connect Staten Island with the New Jersey Turnpike and points west. The Outerbridge Crossing, which also feeds into the Garden State Parkway, comes into southern Staten Island, the Goethals Bridge into the northern part of the borough. Both bridges are linked through Route 278 to the Verrazano-Narrows Bridge into southern Brooklyn. The Goethals and Outerbridge require a toll ($4 for cars) eastbound into New York, but no toll westbound. The Verrazano requires a toll of $5 for cars westbound only.

From Long Island, the **Midtown Tunnel** (I–495) and **Triborough Bridge** (I–278) are the most direct links to Manhattan. Both require tolls ($2.50 for cars) in both directions.

From upstate New York, the city is accessible via the **New York (Dewey) Thruway** (I–87) (toll) to the **Major Deegan Expressway** (I–87) through the Bronx and across the **Triborough Bridge** ($2.50 toll), or via the **Taconic State Parkway** to the **Saw Mill River Parkway** ($1.25 toll bridge) into upper Manhattan.

From New England, the **Connecticut Turnpike** (I–95) connects with the **New England Thruway** (I–95) (toll) and then the **Bruckner Expressway** (I–278). Take the Bruckner to the **Triborough Bridge** ($2.50 toll) or to the **Cross Bronx Expressway**, which enters upper Manhattan on the west side ($1.25 toll bridge).

Manhattan has two major north–south arteries that run the length of the island. The **West Side Highway** skirts the Hudson River from Battery Park (where it's known as West Street) through midtown (it then becomes the Henry Hudson Parkway north of 72nd Street) and past the George Washington Bridge. Both the Holland and Lincoln tunnels enter Manhattan just a few blocks east of this route; the Cross Bronx Expressway connects with the Henry Hudson Parkway in northern Manhattan at the George Washington Bridge. **Franklin D. Roosevelt Drive** (FDR Drive) runs along the East River from Battery Park into upper Manhattan, where it becomes Harlem River Drive north of 125th Street. Both the Queens Midtown Tunnel (East 36th Street) and the Queensboro Bridge (East 59th Street) can be entered a few blocks west of FDR Drive, which connects with the Triborough Bridge at East 125th Street.

Be forewarned: The deterioration of the bridges linking Manhattan, especially those spanning the East River, is a serious problem, and repairs will be ongoing for the next few years. Don't be surprised if a bridge is entirely or partially closed.

Driving within Manhattan can be a nightmare of gridlocked streets and predatory motorists. Free parking is difficult to find in midtown, and violators may be towed away literally within minutes. All over town, parking lots charge exorbitant rates—as much as $15 for two hours in some neighborhoods. If you do drive, don't plan to use your car much for traveling within Manhattan.

Car Rentals

If you find you absolutely need a car—perhaps for a weekend escape or because Manhattan is part of a longer trip—you'll have to sort out Manhattan's confusing array of car-rental possibilities. Although rates were once cheaper out of Newark airport, that is no longer the case; prices charged by national firms are the same at Newark, JFK, and La Guardia, as well as at Manhattan rental locations. Companies with multiple Manhattan and airport locations include **Avis** (tel. 800/331–1212, 800/879–2847 in Canada); **Budget** (tel. 800/527–0700); **Dollar** (tel. 800/800–4000); **Hertz** (tel. 800/654–3131, 800/263–0600 in Canada); and **National** (tel. 800/227–7368). Some regional budget companies, such as **Rent-A-Wreck** (tel. 212/721–0080), offer lower rates. If you are flying into La Guardia or JFK, you might look into some local Queens agencies with lower rates, such as **Universal** (tel. 718/786–0786). **Sunshine Rent-A-Car** (tel. 212/989–7260) is good for budget rentals in Greenwich Village. Unlimited-mileage rates range from $64 per day for an economy car to $82 for a large car; weekly unlimited-mileage rates range from $226 to $330. This does not include tax, which in New York State is 12¼% on car rentals.

Extra Charges Picking up the car in one city and leaving it in another may entail substantial drop-off charges or one-way service fees. Some rental agencies will charge you extra if you return the car *before* the time specified on your contract. Ask before making unscheduled drop-offs. Fill the tank when you turn in the vehicle to avoid being charged for refueling at what you'll swear is the most expensive pump in town.

Cutting Costs Major international companies have programs that discount their standard rates by 15% to 30% if you make the reservation before departure (anywhere from 24 hours to 14 days), rent for a minimum number of days (typically three or four), and prepay the rental. More economical rentals may come as part of fly/drive or other packages, even bare-bones deals that only combine the rental and an airline ticket (*see* Tours and Packages, *above*).

Insurance and Collision Damage Waiver Before you rent a car, find out exactly what coverage, if any, is provided by your personal auto insurer and by the rental company. Don't assume that you are covered. If you do want insurance from the rental company, secondary coverage may be the only type offered. You may already have secondary coverage if you charge the rental to a credit card. Only Diner's Club (tel. 800/234–6377) provides primary coverage in the United States and worldwide.

In general if you have an accident, you are responsible for the automobile. Car rental companies may offer a collision damage waiver (CDW), which ranges in cost from $4 to $14 a day. You should decline the CDW only if you are certain you are covered through your personal insurer or credit card company. California, New York, and Illinois have outlawed the sale of CDW altogether.

By Train

Amtrak (tel. 800/872–7245) offers frequent service within the Northeast Corridor, between Boston and Washington, DC. Trains arrive at and depart from **Pennsylvania Station** (31st–33rd Sts., between 7th and 8th Aves.). Amtrak trains serve Penn Station from upstate New York, Montréal, the Southeast, Midwest, and Far West. Penn Station also handles **Long Island Railroad** trains (tel. 718/217–5477), with service to and from all over Long Island, and **New Jersey Transit** trains (tel. 201/762–5100), with frequent service from the northern and central regions of New Jersey.

Metro-North Commuter Railroad (tel. 212/340–3000) serves the northern suburbs and Connecticut as far east as New Haven from Grand Central Terminal. The other Metro-North Manhattan stop is at 125th Street and Park Avenue in East Harlem—not a good place to get off the train unless you are visiting this neighborhood.

PATH Trains (tel. 201/963–2557, 212/466–7649, or 800/234–7284) run 24 hours a day to New York City from terminals in Hoboken, Jersey City, Harrison, and Newark, New Jersey; they connect with seven major New Jersey Transit commuter lines at Hoboken Station, Broad Street Station (Newark), and Penn Station (Newark). PATH trains stop in Manhattan at the World Trade Center and along 6th Avenue at Christopher Street, 9th Street, 14th Street, 23rd Street, and 33rd Street. They run every 10 minutes on weekdays, every 15–30 minutes on weeknights, and every 20–30 minutes on weekends. The fare is $1.

By Bus

All long-haul and commuter bus lines feed into the **Port Authority Terminal** (tel. 212/564–8484), a mammoth multilevel structure that occupies a nearly 2-square-block area between 40th and 42nd streets and 8th and 9th avenues. Though it was recently modernized and is fairly clean, large numbers of vagrants make the terminal an uncomfortable place to spend much time. Especially with night arrivals, plan to move through the terminal swiftly. Beware of hustlers trying to help you hail a cab on 8th Avenue—they will demand a tip for performing this unnecessary service and can be hostile and aggressive if crossed.

For information on any service into or out of the Port Authority Terminal, call 212/564–8484. Some of the individual bus lines serving New York include **Greyhound** (tel. 800/231–2222); **Adirondack Pine Hill Trailways** from upstate New York (tel. 800/225–6815); **Bonanza Bus Lines** from New England (tel. 800/556–3815); **Martz Trailways** from northeastern Pennsylvania (tel. 800/233–8604); **New Jersey Transit** from around New Jersey (tel. 201/762–5100); **Peter Pan Bus Lines** from New England (tel. 413/781–2900); and **Vermont Transit** from New England (tel. 802/862–9671).

The **George Washington Bridge Bus Station** (tel. 212/564–1114) is located at Fort Washington Avenue and Broadway between 178th and 179th streets in the Washington Heights section of Manhattan. Six bus lines, serving northern New Jersey and Rockland County, New York, make daily stops there from 5 AM to 1 AM. The terminal connects with the 175th Street Station on the A subway, making it slightly more convenient for travelers going to and from the West Side.

Staying in New York

Important Addresses and Numbers

Tourist Information New York Convention and Visitors Bureau. The main office is at 2 Columbus Circle (tel. 212/397–8222) and is open weekdays 9–6, weekends 10–6.

Emergencies Dial 911 for **police, fire,** or **ambulance** in an emergency.

Deaf Emergency Teletypewriter (tel. 800/342–4357), for medical, fire, and ambulance emergencies.

Doctor **Doctors On Call, 24-hour house-call service** (tel. 212/737–2333). Near midtown, 24-hour emergency rooms are open at **St. Luke's-Roosevelt Hospital** (58th St. at 9th Ave., tel. 212/523–6800) and **St. Vincent's Hospital** (7th Ave. and 11th St., tel. 212/790–7997).

Dentist The **Dental Emergency Service** (tel. 212/679–3966; after 8 PM, tel. 212/679–4172) will make a referral.

24-Hour Pharmacy **Kaufman's Pharmacy** (Lexington Ave. and 50th St., tel. 212/755–2266) is convenient but its prices are exorbitant; **Genovese** (2nd Ave. at 67th St., tel. 212/772–0104) is less expensive. Before 10 or 11 PM, look for a pharmacy in a neighborhood that keeps late hours, such as Greenwich Village or the Upper West Side for better deals.

Hot Lines The New York Telephone Company lists important emergency and community services numbers in the front of its white-pages directory. Here are some numbers that may come in handy:

Better Business Bureau of Metropolitan New York (tel. 212/533–6200).

Crime Victims' Hotline (tel. 212/577–7777).

Mental Health (tel. 212/566–4766).

NYC On Stage (tel. 212/768–1818) provides up-to-the-minute information on tickets for theater, music, and dance performances.

Sex Crimes Report Line (tel. 212/267–7273).

Telephones

There are more than 58,000 public telephones in New York City, nearly 25,000 of which are in Manhattan. A visitor should never have to hunt more than three or four blocks before finding a coin-operated phone. If you're making a brief call—and don't mind the cacophonous sound of traffic or subways rumbling in the background—street phones are probably your best bet. If you want to consult a directory or make a more leisurely call, pay phones in the lobbies of office buildings or hotels (some of which take credit cards) are a better choice.

The area code for Manhattan is 212; for Brooklyn, Queens, the Bronx, and Staten Island, it's 718. Pay telephones cost 25¢ for the first three minutes of a local call (this includes calls between 212 and 718 area codes); an extra deposit is required for each additional minute.

Rest Rooms

Public rest rooms in New York run the gamut when it comes to cleanliness. Facilities in Penn Station, Grand Central Terminal, and the Port Authority bus terminal are often quite dirty and are inhabited by homeless people. Rest rooms in subway stations are even more filthy and are often downright unsafe.

As a rule, the cleanest bathrooms are in midtown department stores such as Macy's, Lord & Taylor, and Bloomingdale's, in museums, or in the lobbies of large hotels. Public atriums, such as the Citicorp Center and Trump Tower, also provide good public facilities. Restaurants, too, have rest rooms, but usually just for patrons. If you're dressed well and look as if you belong, you can often just sail right on in. Be aware that cinemas, Broadway theaters, and concert halls have limited amenities, and there are often long lines before performances, as well as during intermissions.

Precautions

Despite New York's bad reputation in the area of crime, most people live here for years without being robbed or assaulted. Nevertheless, as in any large city, travelers make particularly easy marks for pickpockets and hustlers, so caution is advised.

Ignore the panhandlers on the streets (some agressive, many homeless); people who offer to hail you a cab (they often appear at Penn Station, Port Authority, and Grand Central Terminal); and limousine and gypsy cab drivers who offer you a ride. Someone who appears to have had an accident at the exit door of a bus may flee with your wallet or purse if you attempt to give aid; the individual who approaches you with a complicated story is probably playing a confidence game and hopes to get something from you. Beware of strangers jostling you in crowds, or someone tapping your shoulder from behind.

Keep jewelry and valuables out of sight on the street; better yet, leave them at home. Don't wear gold chains, or gaudy jewelry, even if it's fake. Women should never hang their purse on a chair in a restaurant or on a hook in a rest-room stall. Men are advised to carry wallets in their front pants pockets rather than in their hip pockets.

Avoid deserted blocks in out-of-the-way neighborhoods. If you end up in an empty area or a side street that feels unsafe, it probably is. Go to the nearest avenue and hail a cab. A brisk, purposeful pace helps deter trouble wherever you go.

The subway is usually most safe to ride during the day and early evening; after the theater or a concert, travel by bus or taxi. You can also ride the subway in relative safety; just ride in the center car of the subway train, with the conductor, and wait among the crowds on the center of the platform. Watch out for unsavory characters lurking around the inside or outside of stations, particularly at night. When you're waiting for a train, stand away from the edge of the subway platform, especially when trains are entering or leaving the station, so you can avoid being pushed on to the tracks, either accidentally or intentionally. Once the train pulls into the station, avoid empty cars. When disembarking from a train, stick with the crowd until you reach the comparative safety of the street.

Though they're slower, buses are often more pleasant than subways, particularly when you sit next to a window and can view the passing street life. Buses are usually safer than the subways because they carry fewer passengers than the average subway car, and each bus has a driver who can stop the vehicle at a moment's notice.

Opening and Closing Times

New York is very much a 24-hour city. Its subways and buses run around the clock, and plenty of services are available at all hours and on all days of the week. To compensate for being open at odd times, however, many businesses close during what one would expect to be their normal workweek, so it's always a good idea to check ahead.

Banks are open weekdays 9–3 or 9–3:30, although a few branches in certain neighborhoods may stay open late on Friday or open on Saturday morning.

Post offices are generally open weekdays 10–5 or 10–6. The main post office on 8th Avenue between 31st and 33rd streets is open daily 24 hours.

Museum hours vary greatly, but most of the major ones are open Tuesday–Sunday and keep later hours on Tuesday or Thursday evenings.

Stores are normally open Monday–Saturday 10–5 or 10–6. Major department stores usually have late hours at least one evening a week. In business districts, stores may open earlier, while in neighborhoods such as the Village and SoHo, they open later and close later. Many stores in residential neighborhoods are open on Sunday.

Changing Money

Foreign travelers visiting New York can exchange foreign currency and traveler's checks at a number of offices around Manhattan. Large banks—Bank Leumi, Chase Manhattan, Chemical, and Citibank, for example—accommodate travelers during weekday business hours. Other companies provide exchange services up to seven days a week and often quote rates over the phone. They include:

American Express Travel Service, with nine Manhattan locations including: 822 Lexington Avenue, tel. 212/758–6510; Bloomingdale's, 59th Street and Lexington Avenue, tel. 212/705–3171; 150 East 42nd Street, tel. 212/687–3700; 374 Park Avenue, tel. 212/421–8240; American Express Tower, 200 Vesey Street, tel. 212/640–5130; and Macy's Herald Square, 151 West 34th Street, tel. 212/695–8075. Hours vary among locations.

Chequepoint USA, 551 Madison Avenue at 55th Street, tel. 212/980–6443. Open weekdays 8–7, weekends 10–6.

Freeport Exchange, 708 7th Avenue (at 47th Street), tel. 212/765–7900. Open weekdays 8:30–7, weekends 9:30–5. At 49 West 57th Street, tel. 212/223–1200. Open weekdays 8:30–7, weekends 9:30–6.

Harold Reuter & Co., Metropolitan Life Building, 200 Park Avenue, Room 332 East, 3rd Floor, tel. 212/661–0826. Open weekdays 8–5. At Abraham & Straus, 32nd Street and 6th Avenue, 6th Floor, tel. 212/268–8517, open Mon.–Sat., 10–6, Sun. 11–6, and at Grand Central Terminal, 42nd Street, between Vanderbilt and Lexington avenues, open weekdays 7–7, Saturday 8–3.

New York Foreign Exchange, 61 Broadway, Suite 805, tel. 212/248–4700. Open weekdays 9–5.

People's Foreign Exchange, 500 5th Avenue (at 42nd Street), Suite 200, tel. 212/391–5270. Open daily 9–6.

Thomas Cook Currency Service has branches at 630 5th Avenue in Rockefeller Center (tel. 212/757–6915); 41 East 42nd Street (tel. 212/883–0400); and 29 Broadway (tel. 212/363–6208). Open weekdays 9–5, Saturdays 10–3.

Getting Around

On Foot The cheapest, sometimes the fastest, and usually the most interesting way to explore this city is by walking. Because New Yorkers by and large live in apartments rather than in houses, and travel by cab, bus, or subway rather than by private car, they end up walking quite a lot. As a result, street life is a vital part of the local culture. On crowded sidewalks, people gossip, snack, sunbathe, browse, buy drugs, cement business deals, make romantic rendezvous, encounter long-lost friends, and fly into irrational quarrels with strangers. It's a wonderfully democratic hubbub. Also sharing the streets, however, are increasing numbers of panhandlers, some aggressive, others more or less insane.

The typical New Yorker, if there is such an animal, walks quickly, dodging around cars, buses, bicycle messengers, construction sites, and other pedestrians. Although the natives seem hurried and rude, they will often cheerfully come to the aid of a lost pedestrian, so don't hesitate to ask a passerby for directions.

Before you start out, keep a few simple rules in mind: Above 14th Street, the city is planned along a grid, with 5th Avenue marking the dividing line between east and west. The streets, numbered from 1 to 220, are straight lines running east to west. The avenues—from 1st to 12th—run north to south. Below 14th Street, however, chaos reigns (*see* Orientation in Chapter 3).

By Subway The 230-mile subway system operates 24 hours a day and, especially within Manhattan, serves most of the places you'll want to visit. It's cheaper than a cab and, during the workweek, often faster than either cabs or buses. The trains have finally been rid of their graffiti (some New Yorkers, of course, perversely miss the colorful old trains), and sleek new air-conditioned cars predominate on many lines. The New York subway deserves much of its negative image, however. Many trains are crowded, dirty, and noisy, and even occasionally unsafe. Although trains are scheduled to run frequently, especially during rush hours, you never know when some incident somewhere on the line may stall traffic indefinitely. Unsavory characters lurk around certain stations, and panhandlers frequently work their way through the cars. Don't write off the subway—some 3.5 million passengers ride it every day without incident—but stay alert at all times (*see* Precautions, *above*).

The subway fare at press time was $1.25, but transit authority officials were already predicting that it would be raised to $1.50, which may have occurred by the time you visit New York. Reduced fares are available for handicapped people and senior citizens during nonrush hours. If you're just taking a few trips, you should pay with tokens; they are sold at token booths that are *usually* open at each station. It is advisable to buy several tokens at one time to prevent waiting in line later. For four or more subway trips, you might find it easier to use the MTA's new MetroCard, a thin, plastic card with a magnetic strip that you swipe through a reader. The cards were in-

Manhattan Subways

Subway Lines

— BMT

— IND

— IRT

troduced in early 1994, and subway stations are gradually upgrading to be able to accept them. By 1995, most major subway stations will accept the cards. They are sold at all subway stations where they are accepted; at some Metro-North and Long Island Rail Road commuter rail stations; and at some stores—look for an "Authorized Sales Agent" sign. You can buy a card for a minimum of $5 (4 trips) and a maximum of $80, in $5 increments. You can add more money to a card, and more than one person can use the same card: Swipe it through once for each rider. Both tokens and MetroCards permit unlimited transfers within the system.

This book's subway map covers the most-visited parts of Manhattan. Maps of the full subway system are posted on many trains and at some stations, but don't rely on finding one when you need it. You may be able to pick up free maps at token booths, too, but they are often out of stock. Make sure the map you refer to is up-to-date— lengthy repair programs can cause reroutings that last long enough for new "temporary" maps to be printed.

For route information, ask the token clerk or a transit policeman. Call 718/330–1234 (a local call, 25¢ from pay phones) for information from 6 AM to 9 PM daily. And don't hesitate to ask a fellow rider for directions: Once New Yorkers realize you're harmless, most bend over backward to be helpful.

By Bus Most buses follow easy-to-understand routes along the Manhattan grid. Routes go up or down the north–south avenues, or east and west on the major two-way crosstown streets. Most bus routes operate 24 hours, but service is infrequent late at night. Buses are great for sightseeing, but traffic jams—a potential threat at any time or place in Manhattan—can make rides maddeningly slow. Certain bus routes now offer "Limited-Stop Service"; buses on these routes stop only at major cross streets and transfer points and can save traveling time. The "Limited-Stop" buses usually run on weekdays and during rush hours. For information about routes, bus stops, and hours of operation, call 718/330–1234 daily 6–9.

Bus fare is the same as subway fare: $1.25 at press time, in coins (no pennies; no change is given) or a subway token or MetroCard (some buses will start accepting the card in 1995, and all will accept them by the end of 1996, according to the MTA). When you get on the bus you can ask the driver for a free transfer coupon, good for one change to an intersecting route. Legal transfer points are listed on the back of the slip. Transfers have time limits of at least two hours, often longer. You cannot use the transfer to enter the subway system.

Guide-A-Rides, which consist of route maps and schedules, are posted at many bus stops in Manhattan and at major stops throughout the other boroughs. Each of the five boroughs of New York has a separate bus map, and they are scarcer than hens' teeth. They are occasionally available in subway token booths, but never on buses. The best places to obtain them are the Convention and Visitors Bureau at Columbus Circle or the information kiosks in Grand Central Terminal and Penn Station.

By Taxi Taxis are usually easy to hail on the street or from a taxi rank in front of major hotels. You can tell if a cab is available by checking its rooftop light; if the center panel is lit, the driver is ready to take passengers. Taxis cost $1.50 for the first ⅕ mile, 25¢ for each ⅕ mile thereafter, and 25¢ for each 75 seconds not in motion. A 50¢ surcharge is added to rides begun between 8 PM and 6 AM. There is no charge for extra passengers, but you must pay any bridge or tunnel tolls incurred during your trip (sometimes a driver will personally pay a toll to keep moving quickly, but that amount will be added to the fare when the ride is over). Taxi drivers also expect a 15% tip. Barring performance above and beyond the call of duty, don't feel obliged to give them more.

To avoid unhappy taxi experiences, try to have a general idea of where you want to go. A few cab drivers are dishonest; some are ignorant; some can barely understand English. If you have no idea of the proper route, you may be taken for a long and costly ride.

By Trolley The **Manhattan Neighborhood Trolley** (180 Eldridge St., New York, NY 10002, tel. 212/677–7268), a 1900 vintage red-and-green car seating 30 passengers, runs weekends and holidays, noon–6 PM, April through October, making stops every hour at South Street Seaport, Battery Park, the World Trade Center, the World Financial Center, City Hall Park, Chatham Square in Chinatown, Grand Street in Little Italy, and Orchard Street on the Lower East Side. Tickets, which are valid for boarding and reboarding all day, cost $4 for adults, $3 for senior citizens and children under age 12, and may be purchased from a tour guide on board, who provides a running narration.

By Limousine If you want to ride around Manhattan in style, you can rent a chauffeur-driven car from one of many limousine services. Companies usually charge by the hour or offer a flat fee for sightseeing excursions. The Manhattan yellow pages provides a full listing of limousine operators, but here are several recommended companies: **All State Car and Limo** (tel. 212/741–7440); **Bermuda Limousine International** (tel. 212/249–8400); **Carey Limousines** (tel. 212/599–1122); **Carmel Car and Limousine Service** (tel. 212/662–2222); **Chris Limousines** (tel. 718/356–3232); **Concord Luxury Limousine** (tel. 212/230–1600); **Eastside Limo Service** (tel. 212/744–9700); **Gordon's Limousine Service** (tel. 212/921–0081); **La Limousine** (tel. 212/736–0484); **London Towncars** (tel. 212/988–9700); **Sherwood Silver Bay Limousine Service** (tel. 718/472–0183).

Guided Tours

Orientation Tours
Boat Tours The most pleasant way to get a crash orientation to Manhattan is aboard a **Circle Line Cruise.** Once you've finished the three-hour, 35-mile circumnavigation of Manhattan, you'll have a good idea of where things are and what you want to see next. Narrations are as interesting and individualized as the guides who deliver them. *Pier 83, west end of 42nd St., tel. 212/563–3200. Fare: $16 adults, $8 children under 12. Operates early Mar.–Dec., daily.*

For a shorter excursion, the **TNT Express,** a hydroliner, will show you the island of Manhattan in 75 minutes. *Pier 11, 2 blocks south of South St. Seaport, tel. 800/342–5868. Fare: $15 adults, $13 senior citizens, $8 children under 12, children under 5 free. Boats depart Apr.–Sept., weekdays and Sat. at noon and 2 PM.*

World Yacht Cruises (Pier 81, W. 42nd St. at Hudson River, tel. 212/630–8100) serve lunch ($27.50) and Sunday brunch ($39.95) on two-hour cruises, and dinner (Sun.–Thurs. $62; Fri.–Sat. $69.50; drinks extra) on three-hour cruises. The Continental cuisine is restaurant quality, and there's even music and dancing on board. The cruises run daily year-round, weather permitting.

The Spirit of New York (Pier 9, three blocks south of South Street Seaport on East River, tel. 212/742–7278) sails on lunch ($22.95), brunch ($29.95), dinner ($42.95–$48.95), and moonlight cocktail ($18) cruises.

At South Street Seaport's Pier 16 you can take two- or three-hour voyages to New York's past aboard the iron cargo schooner *Pioneer* (tel. 212/669–9400) or 90-minute tours of New York Harbor aboard the sidewheeler *Andrew Fletcher* or the *DeWitt Clinton,* a re-created steamboat (tel. 212/269–3200).

Bus Tours **Gray Line** (254 W. 54th St., tel. 212/397–2620) offers a taste of yesteryear with their "NY Trolley Tour" on coaches replicating New York trolleys of the '30s, in addition to a number of standard city bus tours, plus cruises and day trips to Brooklyn and Atlantic City. **Central Park Trolley Tours** tempts visitors to explore parts of the park that even native New Yorkers may have never seen. Or climb to the top of an authentic London double-deck bus operated by **New York Doubledecker Tours** (tel. 212/967–6008); hop on and off to visit attractions as often as you like.

Helicopter **Island Helicopter** (heliport at E. 34th St. and East River, tel. 212/
Tours 683–4575) offers four fly-over options, from $47 (for 7 miles) to $119 (for 35 miles). From the West Side, **Liberty Helicopter Tours** (heliport at W. 30th St. and Hudson River, tel. 212/465–8905) has three tours ranging from $55 to $119.

Special-Interest **Backstage on Broadway** (tel. 212/575–8065) is a talk about the
Tours Broadway theater held in an actual theater, given by a theater professional. Reservations are mandatory; groups of 25 or more only. **Radio City Music Hall Productions** (tel. 212/632–4041) schedules behind-the-scenes tours of the theater. Call **The Metropolitan Opera House Backstage** (tel. 212/769–7020) for a tour of the scene and costume shops, stage area, and rehearsal facilities. **Madison Square Garden** (tel. 212/465–6080) also has tours of the sports mecca's inner workings. If TV is your thing, call **NBC Studio Tour** (212/664–7174) for a guided tour of the television studios. **Stardom Tours** (tel. 800/ STARDOM) offers a tour around the city emphasizing celebrity homes and memorable movie locations. **Gracie Mansion Conservancy Tour** (tel. 212/570–4751) will show you the 1799 house, official residence of New York City mayors since 1942. **Art Tours of Manhattan** (tel. 609/921–2647) custom-designs tours of museum and gallery exhibits as well as artists' studios and lofts. **Gallery Passports** (tel. 212/ 288–3578) takes you to galleries and museums in Manhattan. **Arts & Events** (tel. 212/921–0924) tours include visits to museums, theaters, and artists' studios and private collections. **Literary Tours of Greenwich Village** (tel. 212/924–0239) walks in the footsteps of famous American writers. **Doorway to Design** (tel. 212/221–1111) tours fashion and interior design showrooms as well as artists' private studios. **South Street Seaport Tours** (tel. 212/233–4800 or 800/ 552–2626) explores historic ships and takes evening music cruises. **Harlem Your Way!** (tel. 212/690–1687), **Harlem Spirituals, Inc.** (tel. 212/757–0425), and **Penny Sightseeing Co., Inc.** (tel. 212/410–0080) offer bus and walking tours and Sunday gospel trips to Harlem. **The Lower East Side Tenement Museum** (tel. 212/431–0233) offers Sunday tours through former immigrant communities. **River to River Downtown Tours** (tel. 212/321–2823) specializes in lower Manhattan for two-hour walking tours. **Fulton Fish Market** tours give an insider's view of the early morning seafood market (tour guide Richard Lord, tel. 201/798–3901). **Louis Singer** (tel. 718/875–9084), an encyclopedia of New York trivia, provides tours of Brooklyn and Manhattan.

Walking Tours **New York City Cultural Walking Tours** (tel. 212/979–2388) focuses on the city's architecture, landmarks, memorials, outdoor art, and historic sites. **Sidewalks of New York** (tel. 212/517–0201 or 212/662–6300) hits the streets from various thematic angles—"Ye Old Tavern" tours, "Celebrity Home" tours, "Famous Murder Sites," "Chelsea Saints and Sinners," and so forth. These walks are offered on weekends year-round; weekday tours are available by appointment. **Adventure on a Shoestring** (tel. 212/265–2663) is an organization dating from 1963 that explores New York neighborhoods. Tours are scheduled periodically for $5 per person. **Big Onion Walking Tours** (tel. 212/439–1090) has theme tours: try "From Naples to Bialystock to Beijing: A Multi-Ethnic Eating Tour." **Walks of the Town** (tel. 212/222–5343) strolls through neighborhoods of historic and architectural interest, usually on weekends. **Citywalks** (tel. 212/989–2456) offers two-hour walking tours exploring various neighborhoods in depth, weekends at 1 PM for $12. **Urban Explorations** (tel. 718/721–5254) runs Thursday, Friday, and weekend tours with an emphasis on architecture and urban planning; Chinatown is a specialty. The **Municipal Art Society** (tel. 212/935–3960) operates a series of bus and walking tours. The **Museum of the City of New York** (tel. 212/534–1672) sponsors Sunday afternoon walking tours. **SoHo Art Tours** (tel. 212/431–8005) gives an inside look at the SoHo art community with visits to galleries, artists' studios, and the area's unusual cast-iron buildings. The **Urban Park Rangers** (tel. 212/427–4040) offer weekend walks and workshops, most of them free, in city parks. The **92nd Street Y** (tel. 212/996–1100) often has something special to offer on weekends and some weekdays. Other knowledgeable walking-tour guides include **Arthur Gelfand** (tel. 212/222–5343), **Joyce Gold** (tel. 212/242–5762), and **Arthur Marks** (tel. 212/673–0477).

The most comprehensive listing of tours offered during a particular week is published in the "Other Events" section of *New York* magazine's "Cue" listings.

Self-Guided Walking Tours The **New York Convention and Visitors Bureau's** "I Love New York Visitors Guide and Map" is available at the bureau's information center (2 Columbus Circle, tel. 212/397–8222). Walkers in Brooklyn can pick up two maps—"Brooklyn on Tour" and "Downtown Brooklyn Walking Tours"—as well as a handy "Brooklyn Neighborhood Book," all free of charge, at the public affairs desk of the **Brooklyn Borough President'**s office (209 Joralemon St., 3rd Floor).

The **Municipal Art Society of New York** has prepared a comprehensive "Juror's Guide to Lower Manhattan: Five Walking Tours" for the benefit of jurors who are often required to kill time while serving in downtown courthouses. Along with an explanation of the New York jury system, the pamphlet includes tours of lower Manhattan and Wall Street, the City Hall district, Chinatown and Little Italy, South Street Seaport, and TriBeCa. Nonjurors can purchase copies for $5 at **Urban Center Books** (457 Madison Ave. at 51st St., inside the courtyard of the New York Palace hotel, tel. 212/935–3592).

A free "Walking Tour of Rockefeller Center" pamphlet is available from the information desk in the lobby of the GE building (30 Rockefeller Plaza).

Another option is to pop one of the **Guides-on-Tape** (21 E. 90th St., Suite 7B, New York, NY 10128, tel. 212/289–8805, $9.95 per tape) into your Walkman and start strolling to an in-your-ear anecdotal history of midtown, downtown, or Greenwich Village.

Credit Cards

The following credit-card abbreviations are used throughout this guide: AE, American Express; D, Discover; DC, Diners Club; MC, MasterCard; V, Visa. It's always a good idea to call ahead and confirm an establishment's credit-card policy.

2 Portraits of New York City

The New York Babel

By V. S.
Pritchett

One of the
great living
masters of
English
prose,
V. S.
Pritchett
expounds
delightfully
on his
impressions
of the city in
New York
Proclaimed.
Here are
some choice
passages
from the
book.

If Paris suggests Intelligence, if London suggests Experience, then the word for New York is Activity. York itself is an almost intolerably famous name, but adding New to it was one of the lucky prophetic insights of nomenclature, for newness, from day to day, was to be the moral essence of the place. There is no place where newness is so continuously pursued.

What is not naturally active in New York soon has to turn to and become so. There is not an inactive man, woman, or child in the place. It might be thought that a contemplative, passive New Yorker, one who is inhabited by his feelings and his imaginings, who lives in an inner world, or was born torpid, must be immune to the active spirit. This is not so in New York, where states like passivity, contemplation, vegetativeness, and often sleep itself are active by prescription. Pragmatism sees to that. The prime example is the bum or derelict. There he lies asleep or drunk on the doorstep or props himself against a wall in the Bowery, an exposed, accepted, but above all an established figure of a 51st state. In a city where all activity is specialized, he has his specialty: he must act in protest against activity, which leads him from time to time on a chase for alcohol, a smoke, or a coin as persistent as a salesman's, but in solitude. Virginia Woolf used to ask where Society was; the notion was metaphysical to her. But Skid Row exists as a recognized place. You go there when the thing comes over you. You graduate in dereliction. You put in a 20-hour day of internal fantasy-making in your studied rejection of the New York norm. The Spanish mendicant has his rights and takes his charity with condescension; the bum grabs with resentment. He is busy. You have upset his dream. The supremely passive man in theory, he will stop in the middle of the street as he crosses the Bowery, holding up his dirty hand at the traffic, and scream in the manner of madness at the oncoming driver. Screaming like that—and New York is dotted with screamers on a scale I have seen in no other city in the world, though Naples has its share—reveals the incessant pressure of the active spirit.

For ourselves who are trying to settle first what we see before our eyes, this active, practical spirit has curious manifestations. New York City is large, but Manhattan is small in extent, so small that a large part of its population has to be pumped out of it every night by bridges and tunnels. Despite the groans about the congestion of its traffic, it is easy to dash from one end to the other of the island and to drive fast all around it. And most people do dash. The only real difficulty is in the downtown tangle of named streets in old New York; the grid has settled the rest. The grid is an unlovely system. It is not originally American: Stuttgart and Berlin hit upon this method of automatically extending cities in the 17th century. By the 18th century Europe had discovered that cities must be designed before they are extended: mere pragmatism and planning will not do. It absolutely will not do if left to engineers, soldiers, or what are called developers. The makers of the New York grid confused the idea that parallel lines can be projected into infinity without meeting, with the idea of design. The boredom this has inflicted upon the horizontal life of Manhattan has turned out to be endurable to the primarily active man who is impatient of the whole idea of having neighbors. The striping, unheeding avenues of the grid have given one superb benefit. They cut through long distances, they provide long vistas that excite the eye, and these are fine where the buildings are high, if they are featureless where the buildings are low. No other city I can think of has anything like the undulating miles that fly down Park Avenue from 96th Street to Grand Central, blocked now though it is by the brutal mass of the Metropolitan Life Building—a British affront to the city and spoken of as a revenge for Suez—or the longer streak of Madison. These two avenues impress most as a whole, other avenues in part, by their assurance as they cleave their way through the cliffs.

Of course, being a stranger, you have been living it up, for if you want a night city, this is preeminently the one. There is a large fluorescent population of pale faces—who is that old man sitting alone in the Automat at this late hour? Where are all those taxis streaking to endlessly through the night? You have been listening to the jazz in Birdland perhaps, listening to the long drumming that says "Encroach, encroach, encroach, encroach, overcome, come!" or to that woman with the skirling voice which is shoving, pushing, and struggling cheerfully to get all her energy out of her body and into her mouth as she sings what is really the theme song of the city: "And it's good. It's all good, good, good." She was wired in to some dynamo.

Those words never fade from the mind. In sleep you still hear them. You are a receiving station for every message Babel sends out day and night. The sirens of the police cars, the ambulances and fire engines, mark the hours, carrying the mind out to fantasies of disaster. I say "fantasies," for surely all these speeding crews are studiously keeping alive the ideal of some ultimate dementia while the rest of us sleep. New York demands more than anything else that one should never fail to maintain one's sense of its drama; even its social manners, at their most ceremonious, have this quality. Where the crowds of other cities are consolidating all day long, filling up the safes and cellars of the mind, the New York crowd is set on the pure function of self-dispersal. A couple of cops idling through the night in a police car will issue their noise as if it were part of the uniform and to keep up their belief in their own reality and in the sacred notion of the Great Slaying or the Great Burglarization. Then there is light traffic on the highways, with its high, whipping, cat-gut whine. On 104th Street on the West Side I used to have the sensation of being flayed alive all night by knives whipping down Riverside Drive; it was not disagreeable. City life is for masochists. On many other avenues the trucks bulldozed the brain. There were bursts of noctambulist shouting off Madison and 60th at 3 or 4; followed by the crowning row of the city, the clamor of the garbage disposers, successors to Dickens's gentlemanly swine, that fling the New York garbage cans across the pavement and grind the stuff to bits on the spot. Often I have sat at my window to watch these night brutes chew up the refuse. The men have to rush to keep up with its appetite. As a single producer of shindy this municipal creature is a triumph.

The only way of pinning some sort of identity onto the people is to think of them as once being strangers like yourself and trace them to their districts. The man who used to bring my breakfast, saying, every morning, "Lousy day," was a 115th Street Puerto Rican, of five years' standing. You learn to distinguish. You know where the Ukrainians, the Sephardic Jews, early and late Italians, degrees of Irish, live. You build up a map of the black and Puerto Rican pockets. You note the Germans are at 86th Street and yet the Irish are there, too; that, at the bottom, on East End Avenue, the neighborhood has become suddenly fashionable. The Greenwich Village Italians are pretty fixed; the several Harlems have established their character, for they have stuck to their district for 60 years, which must be a record for New York. You know the Greeks are on 9th Avenue. The Lower East Side, now largely transformed, is Jewish and Puerto Rican. But large groups break away; poor give place to poorer. Sometimes poor give place to rich. In Sutton Place they cleared the poor away from that pleasant little cliff on the East River. But one must not understand these quarters as being the old parishes or the ancient swallowed-up villages of European cities, though they were sometimes the sites of farms. Topographically they are snippings of certain avenues and cross streets. For the avenues stripe the city and the groups live on a block or two along or across the stripe. One would have to analyze New York street by street, from year to year, to know the nuances of racial contact.

Statistics deceive, but it is clear that the oldest American stock of Dutch, British, and German, though dominant in wealth and traditional influence, is a small minority in New York. The question no one can answer is how far the contents of the melting pot have really melted and whether a new race has yet been created. For a long time the minorities resist, huddle into corners. Some foreign groups of New Yorkers melt slowly or not at all. O. Henry in his time called Lower Manhattan "Bagdad-on-the-Subway," thinking then of the unchanging Syrians and Armenians around Rector Street, but they have almost vanished. The Ukrainians still have their shops and churches near Avenue A. The Russian Orthodox priest walks down the street. The Poles shout from their windows or sit on the cagelike fire escapes east of Greenwich Village. Slowly these people, no doubt, merge; but the tendency for social classes to be determined by race is marked. Many groups of Orthodox Jews remain untouched. Over in Williamsburg you see a sect wearing beards, the men in black hats and long black coats, their hair often long, with curls at the ears, walking with a long loping shuffle as if they traveled with knees bent. They look like a priesthood, and the boys, curled in the same way, might be their acolytes. You will meet them with their black cases of treasure between their feet, standing on the pavement outside the diamond markets of 47th Street.

The foreign are tenacious of their religions—there must be more Greek Orthodox and Russian Orthodox churches than in any other city outside of Europe—and of their racial pride. The old Romanian who cleans your suit has never seen Romania, but he speaks with his old accent; as one looks at his settled, impersonal, American face, one sees the ghost person of another nation within its outlines, a face lost, often sad and puzzled. The Italian cop stands operatically in the full sun at the corner of Union Square; the nimble Greek with his four pairs of hands in the grocer's has the avidity of Athens under that slick, standard air of city prosperity. It occasionally happens that you go to restaurants in New York kept by the brother-in-law or uncle, say, of the man who has the founding place in London, Naples, or Paris; you fall into family gossip, especially with Italians, who are possibly more recent but who are still entangled in the power politics of the European family system. I once talked to an Irish waiter who rushed away into the bar crying, "D'ye see that bloody Englishman? He knows me father." I didn't, but I did know that his father was a notorious leader of one of those "columns" of the I.R.A. in the Irish Civil War.

In this quality of being lost and found there is the mixture of the guilt, the sadness, the fading mind of exile with the excited wonder at life which is an essential New York note. New York tolerance allows the latitude to civilization. People are left alone and are less brutally standardized than in other cities. "Clearly"—these foreigners tell you with resignation—"this is not Europe. But"—they suddenly brighten, tense up, and get that look of celebration in their eyes—"it is New York." That is to say, the miracle. Although New Yorkers of all kinds curse the city for its expense and its pressures, and though all foreigners think it is the other foreigners who make it impossible, they are mad about the place. There is no place like it in the world. And although a Londoner or a Parisian will think the same about their cities, here the feeling has a special quality: that of a triumphant personal discovery of some new thing that is getting bigger, richer, higher, more various as every minute of the day goes by. They have come to a ball. And this is felt not only by the New Yorker with the foreign strain, but also by the men and women who come in from the other states, drawn by its wealth but even more by the chances, the freedom, and the privacy that a metropolis offers to human beings. Its very loneliness and ruthlessness are exciting. It is a preemptive if not a literal capital. Scott Fitzgerald speaks of his wife Zelda coming up because she wanted "luxury and largeness beyond anything her world provided," and that precisely describes the general feeling of many a newcomer.

What Makes New Yorkers Tick

By Calvin
Trillin

Calvin
Trillin, who
considers
himself a
"resident
out-of-towner"
in
Manhattan
for 34 years,
writes
regularly for
The New
Yorker and
The Nation.
His most
recent book
is Deadline
Poet.

In the first place, we have more weird-looking people in New York City than can be found in any other American city. Also, more rich people. We have so many rich people that I once came to the conclusion that other cities were sending us the rich people they wanted to get rid of ("Listen, if Frank down at the bank doesn't quit talking about how much his Jaguar cost, we're just going to have to put him in the next shipment to New York"). Some of the weird-looking people and some of the rich people are the same people. Why would a rich person want to look weird? As we New Yorkers like to say: Go know.

When I moved to New York, back in 1961, I remember saying that 90% of the people walking along the street in Manhattan would be interviewed in any other town, and the other 10% would be arrested. It's got a lot weirder since then.

Of course, it's got weirder everywhere since then. But someone in a silly getup in Houston or Cleveland or Denver has to be aware that everyone is looking at him. If a 300-lb. man costumed as Eleanor of Aquitaine walks onto a crosstown bus in New York carrying both an attaché case and a rib roast, the other passengers might glance up for a second, but then they'd go back to their tabloids. If you asked the driver why he didn't seem to be registering such a sight, he'd say, "Hey whadaya—kidding? I seen a million guys like that. You think I'm some kinda farmer or something?"

So if you're making a list of how New Yorkers differ from other Americans—even other city dwellers—write "funny looking" near the top. Also write "jaded" or maybe "blasé": New Yorkers have seen a million guys like that no matter what the guy is like. We've seen everything. We've seen everybody. We are not impressed. The common response of New Yorkers to the presence of the President in their city is not excitement but irritation: His motorcade is going to tie up traffic. He may think he's in town to address the United Nations or raise money at one of those fat-cat banquets at the Waldorf, but as far as New Yorkers are concerned, he is there to cause them aggravation. And why, as a matter of fact, is the United Nations in New York? Also to cause aggravation, this time by taking up a lot of curb space with diplomatic-plate-only parking zones. In the minds of true New Yorkers, an awful lot that happens in the world happens to cause them aggravation. In fact, "aggravation," in that particular usage, is basically a New York word. I know there are people who think it's a Yiddish word—nobody thinks it's an English word—but a Yiddish word and a New York word are the same thing. It's true that you can detect an Italian bounce to some New York phrases, and it's true that white students at expensive Manhattan private schools are as likely as Harlem teenagers to shout "Yo!" when they come across a friend, but I think the basic structure and inflection of the language New Yorkers speak owe their greatest debt to Yiddish. The only purely New York word I can think of—cockamamie—sounds Yiddish, even though it isn't. It means ridiculous or harebrained and is commonly used in such phrases as "another one of the mayor's cockamamie schemes."

A scheme thus classified was launched some years ago by the then mayor, Edward Koch, who had come back from China smitten with the idea of bicycle transportation. He had protective strips of concrete installed to create a bicycle lane up 6th Avenue. As someone who schlepps around (as we say here) on an old Raleigh three-speed, I was pathetically grateful for the bike lane myself: I suppose that shows that no matter how long I live in New York, I am, at heart, an out-of-towner. The cabdrivers, of course, hated it ("He likes China so much, he shoulda stood in China"). Some storekeepers hated it. But who complained most bitterly about the bike lanes? The bicyclers. The true New York bicyclers complained that the bike lane was full of pedestrians and garment-center pushcarts and people who schlepped around on Raleigh three-speeds. And slush. "It's October," I said to the bicycler who made that complaint: "there's no slush in October." "When there's slush," he said, "the bike lane will have slush."

The bike-lane episode reminds me that you'd better put "contentious" near the top of that list, right under "funny looking." (Not just "funny looking" come to think of it, but also "funny": New York is the only city I've ever been in where almost everyone you meet on the street considers himself a comedian—a fact brought home to me a couple of years ago when a panhandler near my subway stop said to me, "Can you spare some change? I'd like to buy a few junk bonds.") In the matter of contentiousness, I once tried to indicate the difference between New York and the Midwest, where I grew up, by saying that in the Midwest if you approach someone who is operating a retail business and ask him if he has change for a quarter, he is not likely to call you a fascist. He is certainly not going to say, "G'wan—get lost." He would never say, "Ya jerky bastard, ya."

New Yorkers are not polite. If you asked a New York cabdriver why he wasn't more polite, he might say something like "Polite! Where do you think you are—Iowa or Indiana or one of them?" New York cabdrivers do not usually bother to distinguish among states that begin with *I*.

Earlier this year, some booster organization in New York got the idea of launching a campaign to make New Yorkers more polite. Talk about cockamamie ideas! What are they—crazy? Do they think this is Illinois or Idaho or someplace? In the first place, the whole idea of a booster organization is as foreign to New York as Girl Scout cookies. (Yes, I know that thousands of Girl Scout cookies are sold every year in places like Queens and Staten Island. You think I'm a farmer or something?) I have never heard of a New York Chamber of Commerce. If it exists, I suspect it spends most of its time putting out press releases about aggravations. Also, telling New Yorkers not to be rude is the equivalent of telling Neapolitans not to talk with their hands: it could render us speechless.

I don't think there's anything particularly surprising about the level of rudeness in New York. A lot of it is just show. New York has been portrayed in so many books and movies and stand-up acts that the stock characters know how to behave badly. They've all read their press clippings. The Jewish deli waiter knows what to say to an out-of-towner who asks if he could get a pastrami sandwich ("When I'm ready, I'll get" or "Listen, the pastrami here I wouldn't wish on Arafat"). The Irish cop knows how to act like an Irish cop who does not go overboard in showing respect to the citizenry. Some of the newer stock characters, like the Korean greengrocer and the Indian news dealer, aren't certain how to act yet—there haven't been enough movies about them—but when they do get it all hardened into a New York shtick, I rather doubt that they're going to sound like the flight attendant of the month.

Also, I believe rudeness tends to vary in direct proportion to the size of the city, so it's only natural that the largest city is the rudest. It isn't just that the little daily irritations tend to build up in a large city faster than they do in a small town; it's the anonymity. In a small town, what you shout at someone who makes a sudden turn in front of you without a signal is limited in nastiness by the realization that you might find yourself sitting beside that person the next day at the Kiwanis lunch or the PTA meeting. If the town is small enough, the chance that you'll never see the offending party again is nonexistent. That puts a sort of governor on your behavior. In New York, the odds are almost the opposite; you are almost certainly not going to see that person again. The governor is removed. Knowing that, you might do a lot worse than "Ya jerky bastard, ya."

Not you? Yes, you. Right at the top of the list you should write down that there's nothing genetic about any of this. New Yorkers weren't born that way. A lot of New Yorkers weren't even born in New York. Some of them were born on farms. I was born in Kansas City. If you moved to New York, you'd be a New Yorker, and you'd act like a New Yorker. You'd only glance for a moment at the guy costumed as Eleanor of Aquitaine. You'd scheme to get the last seat on the subway car. You'd become a comedian. You might even use harsh language with taxi drivers. You wouldn't behave that way? Well, how about Mother Teresa?

Mother Teresa! Right. In Calcutta, Mother Teresa is probably an absolute pussycat, but if she moved to New York, she'd be a New Yorker. A couple of years ago, I started to use a true story about Mother Teresa to illustrate how all New Yorkers, living in what I believe could be considered a rather challenging environment, find themselves trying to get a little edge. Around 1987, Mayor Koch was briefly hospitalized with a slight stroke, and a few days later he got a surprise visit from Mother Teresa, who happened to be in town to establish a hospice. She told him he had been in her prayers, and he took the occasion to say that New York was grateful for her presence and that she should let him know if there was any way he could be of assistance. She said that as a matter of fact, there was one thing he might do. It would be helpful at the hospice to have a reserved parking spot. So envision this scene: here is Mother Teresa, perhaps a saint, making a sick call on a man who has just had a stroke—and she's trying to hustle him for a parking spot. You've got to say it's a tough town.

3 Exploring Manhattan

Manhattan is, above all, a walker's city. Along its busy streets there's something else to look at every few yards. Attractions, many of them world-famous, are crowded close together on this narrow island, and because it has to grow up, not out, new layers are simply piled on top of the old. The city's character changes every few blocks, with quaint town houses shouldering sleek glass towers, gleaming gourmet supermarkets sitting around the corner from dusty thrift shops, and soot-smudged warehouses inhabited at street level by trendy neon-lit bistros. Many a visitor has been beguiled into walking a little farther, then a little farther still—"Let's just see what that copper dome and steeple belongs to . . ."—and ending up with a severe case of blisters. So be warned: Wear your most comfortable shoes, preferably sneakers, and take time along the way to stop and rest.

Our walking tours cover a great deal of ground, yet they only scratch the surface. If you plod dutifully from point to point, nose buried in this book, you'll miss half the fun. Look up at the tops of skyscrapers and you'll see a riot of mosaics, carvings, and ornaments. Go inside an intriguing office building and study its lobby decor; read the directory to find out what sorts of firms have their offices there. Peep around corners, even in crowded midtown, and you may find fountains, greenery, and sudden bursts of flowers. Find a bench or ledge to perch on, and take time just to watch the street life. New York has so many faces that every visitor can discover a different one.

Orientation

The map of Manhattan bears a Jekyll-and-Hyde aspect. The rational, Dr. Jekyll part prevails above 14th Street, where the streets form a regular grid pattern, imposed in 1811. Consecutively numbered streets run east and west (crosstown), while broad avenues, most of them also numbered, run north (uptown) or south (downtown). The chief exceptions are Broadway (which runs on a diagonal from East 14th to West 79th streets) and the thoroughfares that hug the shores of the Hudson and East rivers.

Fifth Avenue is the east–west dividing line for street addresses: in both directions, they increase in regular increments from there. For example, on 55th Street, the addresses 1–99 East 55th Street run from 5th, past Madison, to Park (the equivalent of 4th) avenues, 100–199 East 55th would be between Park and 3rd avenues, and so on; the addresses 1–99 West 55th Street are between 5th and 6th avenues, 100–199 West 55th would be between 6th and 7th avenues, and so forth. Above 59th Street, where Central Park interrupts the grid, West Side addresses start numbering at Central Park West, an extension of 8th Avenue. Avenue addresses are much less regular, for the numbers begin wherever each avenue begins and increase at different increments. An address at 552 3rd Avenue, for example, will not necessarily be anywhere near 552 2nd Avenue. New Yorkers themselves cannot master the complexities of this system, so in their daily dealings they usually include cross-street references along with avenue addresses (as far as possible, we follow that custom in this book). New Yorkers also rely on the handy Manhattan Address Locator found in the front of the local phone book.

Below 14th Street—the area that was already settled before the 1811 grid was decreed—Manhattan streets reflect the disordered personality of Mr. Hyde. They may be aligned with the shoreline or they may twist along the route of an ancient cow path. Below 14th Street you'll find West 4th Street intersecting West 11th Street,

Manhattan Neighborhoods

Greenwich Street running roughly parallel to Greenwich Avenue, Leroy Street turning into St. Luke's Place for one block and then becoming Leroy again. There's an East Broadway and a West Broadway, both of which run north–south and neither of which is an extension of plain old Broadway. Logic won't help you below 14th Street; only a good street map and good directions will.

You may also be confused by the way New Yorkers use "uptown" and "downtown." These terms refer both to locations and to directions. Uptown means north of wherever you are at the moment; downtown means to the south. But Uptown and Downtown are also specific parts of the city (and, some would add, two very distinct states of mind). Unfortunately, there is no consensus about where these are—as are: Downtown may mean anyplace from the tip of Lower Manhattan through Chelsea; it depends on the orientation of the speaker.

A similar situation exists with "East Side" and "West Side." Someone may refer to a location as "on the east side," meaning somewhere east of 5th Avenue. A hotel described as being "on the west side" may be on West 42nd Street. But when New Yorkers speak of the East Side or the West Side, they usually mean the respective areas above 59th Street, on either side of Central Park. Be prepared for misunderstandings.

Exploring

Highlights for First-Time Visitors

Rockefeller Center, Tour 1
Times Square, Tour 3
The United Nations, Tour 3
The Metropolitan Museum of Art, Tour 5
Central Park, Tour 7
The American Museum of Natural History, Tour 8
The Statue of Liberty, Tour 17
The World Trade Center, Tour 17
South Street Seaport, Tour 18
The Brooklyn Bridge, Tour 18

Tour 1: Rockefeller Center and Midtown Skyscrapers

Numbers in the margin correspond to points of interest on the Tours 1–3: Midtown map.

When movies and TV shows are set in Manhattan, they often start with a panning shot of Rockefeller Center, for no other city scene— except perhaps the downtown skyline—so clearly says "New York." Begun during the Great Depression of the 1930s by John D. Rockefeller, this 19-building complex occupies nearly 22 acres of prime real estate between 5th and 7th avenues and 47th and 52nd streets. Its central cluster of buildings are smooth shafts of warm-hued limestone, streamlined with glistening aluminum, but the real genius of the complex's design was its intelligent use of public space: plazas, concourses, and street-level shops that create a sense of community for the nearly quarter of a million human beings who use it daily. Restaurants, shoe-repair shops, doctors' offices, barbershops, banks, a post office, bookstores, clothing shops, variety stores—all are accommodated within the center, and all parts of the complex are linked by underground passageways.

Rockefeller Center helped turn midtown into New York City's second "downtown" area, which now rivals the Wall Street area in the number of its prestigious tenants. The center itself is a capital of the communications industry, containing the headquarters of a TV network (NBC), several major publishing companies (Time-Warner, McGraw-Hill, and Simon & Schuster), and the world's largest newsgathering organization, the Associated Press.

Let's begin the tour with a proud symbol of the center's might: the huge statue of Atlas supporting the world that stands sentry before the **International Building** (5th Ave., between 50th and 51st Sts.). The building, with a lobby inspired by ancient Greece and fitted with Grecian marble, houses many foreign consulates, international airlines, and a U.S. passport office.

One block south on 5th Avenue, between 49th and 50th streets, you'll come to the head of the **Channel Gardens,** a promenade with six pools surrounded by flowerbeds filled with seasonal plantings, conceived by artists, floral designers, and sculptors—10 shows a season. They are called the Channel Gardens because they separate the British building to the north from the French building to the south (above each building's entrance is a coat of arms bearing that country's national symbols). The French building contains among other shops the **Librairie de France,** which sells French-language books, periodicals, and records; its surprisingly large basement contains a Spanish bookstore and a foreign-dictionary store.

At the foot of the Channel Gardens is perhaps the most famous sight in Rockefeller Center (if not all of New York): the great gold-leaf statue of the fire-stealing Greek hero **Prometheus,** sprawled on his ledge above the **Lower Plaza.** A quotation from Aeschylus is carved into the red granite wall behind, and 50 jets of water spray around the statue. The plaza's trademark ice-skating rink is open from October through April; the rest of the year, it becomes an open-air café. In December the plaza is decorated with an enormous live Christmas tree. On the Esplanade above the Lower Plaza, flags of the United Nations' members alternate with flags of the states.

The backdrop to the Lower Plaza is the center's tallest tower, the 70-story **GE Building** (formerly the RCA Building until GE acquired RCA in 1986), occupying the block bounded by Rockefeller Plaza, Avenue of the Americas (which New Yorkers call 6th Avenue), and 49th and 50th streets. The block-long street called Rockefeller Plaza, officially a private street (to maintain that status, it closes to all traffic on one day a year), is often choked with celebrities' black limousines, for this is the headquarters of the NBC television network. From this building emanated some of the first TV programs ever; the *Today* show has been broadcast from here since 1952, and a shot of this building is included in the opening credit sequence of *Saturday Night Live.*

One way to see what goes on inside is to spend $7.75 to take a tour of the NBC studios: One leaves from the street level of the GE Building every 15 minutes, 9:30–4:30, Monday–Saturday, and on Sunday during the summer. You can also buy a T-shirt, Frisbee, and other items with the logos of your favorite NBC programs at a boutique in the black granite lobby.

As you enter the GE Building from Rockefeller Plaza, look up at the striking sculpture of Zeus above the entrance doors, executed in limestone cast in glass by Lee Lawrie, the same artist who sculpted the big Atlas on 5th Avenue. Inside, crane your neck to see the dramatic ceiling mural by Jose Maria Sert: Wherever you stand, the figure seems to be facing you. From the lobby information desk, go down the escalator in the right-hand corner and turn right to find a detailed exhibit on the history of the center (admission free; open weekdays 9–5). Then wander around the marble catacombs that connect the various components of Rockefeller Center. There's a lot to see: restaurants in all price ranges, from the chic American Festival Café to McDonald's; a post office and clean public rest rooms (scarce in midtown); and just about every kind of store. To find your way around, consult the strategically placed directories or obtain the free "Shops and Services Guide" at the GE Building information desk.

Returning to the GE Building lobby, you can take an elevator to the 65th floor to enjoy the spectacular view with drinks or a meal at the **Rainbow Room** (*see* Chapter 8). Exit the GE Building on 6th Avenue to see the allegorical mosaics above that entrance.

❹ Across 50th Street from the GE Building is America's largest indoor theater, the 6,000-seat **Radio City Music Hall.** Home of the fabled Rockettes chorus line (which actually started out in St. Louis in 1925), Radio City was built as a movie theater with a stage suitable for live shows as well. Its days as a first-run movie house are long over, but after an announced closing in 1978 Radio City has had an amazing comeback, producing concerts, awards presentations, and special events, along with its own Christmas and Easter extravaganzas. On most days you can take a one-hour tour of the premises. *Tel. 212/247–4777; tour information, 212/632–4041. Tour admission: $9 adults, $5 children under 6. Tours usually leave from main lobby every 30 min, Mon.–Sat. 10–4:45, Sun. 11:15–4:45.*

Later additions to Rockefeller Center include 6th Avenue's skyscraper triplets—the first between 47th and 48th streets, the second (the **McGraw-Hill Building**) between 48th and 49th streets, and the third between 49th and 50th streets—and their cousin immediately to the north, the **Time & Life Building,** between 50th and 51st streets. All have street-level plazas, but the most interesting is McGraw-Hill's, where a 50-foot steel sun triangle points to the seasonal positions of the sun at noon and a pool demonstrates the relative size of the planets.

Time Out For supercasual eating when the weather is good, the **6th Avenue food vendors** near Rockefeller Center offer the best selection in the city. These "à la carte" diners offer far more than trite hot dogs—there's a truly international menu of tacos, falafel, souvlaki, tempura, Indian curry, Afghani kofta kebabs, and Caribbean beef jerky.

NBC isn't the only network headquartered in Manhattan. The **CBS Building** is a black monolith popularly called Black Rock, on 6th Avenue between 52nd and 53rd streets. (ABC, once a close neighbor, has now moved its main office to 66th Street on the West Side.) From here, you can choose among a cluster of museums: the Museum of Television and Radio, the American Craft Museum, or the major collection at the Museum of Modern Art. Go east on 52nd Street to the **❺ Museum of Television and Radio,** housed in a new limestone building by Philip Johnson and John Burgee that reminds everyone of a 1930s-vintage radio. Three galleries exhibit photographs and artifacts relating to the history of broadcasting, but most visitors to this museum come to sit at a console and sample its stupendous collection of more than 32,000 TV shows, 13,000 commercials, and 16,000 radio programs. *25 W. 52nd St., tel. 212/621–6800 for daily events or 212/621–6600 for other information. Suggested contribution: $5 adults,*

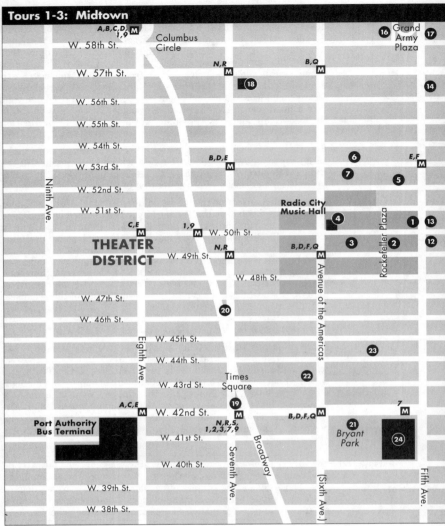

Tours 1-3: Midtown

Algonquin Hotel, **23**

American Craft Museum, **7**

Bryant Park, **21**

Carnegie Hall, **18**

Chrysler Building, **26**

Citicorp Center, **10**

Duffy Square, **20**

Ford Foundation Building, **27**

GE Building, **3**

General Motors Building, **17**

Grand Central Terminal, **25**

IBM Building, **15**

International Building, **1**

ICP Mid-Town, **22**

Lever House, **8**

Lower Plaza, **2**

Museum of Modern Art, **6**

Museum of Television and Radio, **5**

New York Public Library, **24**

The Plaza, **16**

Radio City Music Hall, **4**

St. Bartholomew's Church, **11**

St. Patrick's Cathedral, **13**

Saks Fifth Avenue, **12**

Seagram Building, **9**

Times Square, **19**

Trump Tower, **14**

United Nations Headquarters, **28**

KEY

AE American Express Office

0   880 yards

0   800 meters

E. 58th St.

E. 57th St.

E. 56th St.

E. 55th St.

E. 54th St.

E. 53rd St.

TURTLE BAY

E. 52nd St.

E. 51st St.

E. 50th St.

E. 49th St.

E. 48th St.

E. 47th St.

E. 46th St.

E. 45th St.

E. 44th St.

E. 43rd St.

E. 42nd St.

E. 41st St.

E. 40th St.

E. 39th St.

E. 38th St.

4,5,6

E,F

6

4,5,6,7,S

Madison Ave.

Park Ave.

Vanderbilt Ave.

Lexington Ave.

Third Ave.

Second Ave.

First Ave.

Sutton Pl.

FDR Drive

Tudor City Pl.

Park Ave.

Grand Central Terminal

Queens-Midtown Tunnel

East River

$4 students, $3 senior citizens and under 13. Open Tues.–Wed. and Fri.–Sun. noon–6, Thurs. noon–8.

Just east of the Museum of Television and Radio, you'll pass the famous restaurant **The "21" Club,** with its trademark row of jockey statuettes parading along the wrought-iron balcony. Now wonderfully restored after an extensive renovation, it still has a burnished men's-club atmosphere and a great downstairs bar. In the movie *The Sweet Smell of Success,* Burt Lancaster as a powerful Broadway columnist held court at his regular table here, besieged by Tony Curtis as a pushy young publicist.

To reach the other museums, on 53rd Street, walk toward 5th Avenue and turn left to cut through the shopping arcade of 666 5th Avenue. On the north side of 53rd is the **Museum of Modern Art** (MOMA), in a bright and airy six-story structure built around a secluded sculpture garden. In the second- and third-floor galleries of painting and sculpture, some of the world's most famous modern paintings are displayed: Van Gogh's *Starry Night,* Picasso's *Les Demoiselles d'Avignon,* Matisse's *Dance.* The collection also includes photography, architecture, decorative arts, drawings, prints, illustrated books, and films. Afternoon and evening film shows, mostly foreign films and classics, are free with the price of admission; tickets are distributed in the lobby on the day of the performance, and often they go fast. Programs change daily; call 212/708–9480 for a schedule. There's a good bookstore just off the lobby, and the even more interesting MOMA Design Store across the street. And leave time to sit outside in that wonderful Sculpture Garden. *11 W. 53rd St., tel. 212/708–9500. Admission: $7.50 adults, $4.50 students and senior citizens; children under 16 free. Pay what you wish Thurs. and Fri. 5–8:30. Open Sat.–Tues. 11–6, Thurs. and Fri. 11–8:30.*

On the south side of 53rd, the **American Craft Museum** spotlights the work of contemporary American and international craftspersons working in clay, glass, fabric, wood, metal, paper, or even chocolate. Distinctions between "craft" and "high art" become irrelevant here, for much of this work is provocative and fun to look at. *40 W. 53rd St., tel. 212/956–3535. Admission: $4.50 adults, $2 students and senior citizens. Open Tues. 10–8, Wed.–Sun. 10–5.*

For a look at some of the city's landmark skyscrapers, head east on 53rd Street across 5th Avenue. At Madison Avenue, you may want to detour left (north) to 55th Street to see the **American Telephone & Telegraph Co. Building,** designed by architect Philip Johnson. Unlike the sterile ice-cube-tray buildings of 6th Avenue, AT&T's rose granite columns, its regilded statue of the winged *Golden Boy* in the lobby, and its peculiar "Chippendale" roof have made it an instant landmark for New Yorkers, who consider it the first postmodern skyscraper. There's also a pleasant open-air atrium on the street level where you can sit.

East of Madison Avenue, the next street is broad Park Avenue, with its planted median. On the west side of Park Avenue between 53rd and 54th streets is **Lever House,** a 1952 creation by Gordon Bunshaft, of Skidmore, Owings & Merrill. It's basically a sheer, slim glass box, resting on one end of a one-story-thick shelf that seems to float above the street, balanced on square chrome columns. Because the tower occupies only half of the space above the lower floors, a great deal of air space is left open, and the tower's side wall displays a reflection of its neighbors.

On the other side of Park Avenue, one block south between 52nd and 53rd streets, the **Seagram Building** is the only New York building by German architect Mies van der Rohe, a leading interpreter of the International style. This, too, is a simple boxlike tower, although the black metal and bronze glass exterior looks more severe than Lever House's cool blue-green. Built in 1958, it created a sense of spaciousness with its ground-level plaza, an innovation at the time that has since become a common element in urban skyscraper design. Inside is one of New York's most venerated restaurants, **The Four Seasons** (*see* Chapter 9).

Go one block east to Lexington Avenue, between 53rd and 54th streets, to see the soaring, luminescent white shaft of the **Citicorp Center** (1977), designed by Hugh Stubbins & Associates. Its most striking feature is the angled top, originally intended to carry an immense solar-energy collector that was never installed. At street level, the Citicorp Center has a pleasant mall of restaurants and shops. Attached to the Center, on the corner of 54th Street and Lexington Avenue, is **St. Peter's Church** (tel. 212/935–2200), which offers jazz vespers on late Sunday afternoon; below the church is a theater where various acting troupes perform.

For a pleasing contrast, return to Park Avenue and walk down to 51st Street, where you'll see **St. Bartholomew's Church** nestled amid the skyscrapers. Built in 1919, it has rounded arches, while its intricate tiled dome is Byzantine. Church fathers have been eager to sell the air space over St. Bart's, to take advantage of the stratospheric property values in this part of town, but landmark preservation forces have so far prevented any such move.

Tour 2: 5th Avenue and 57th Street

The stretch of 5th Avenue upward from Rockefeller Center glitters with elegant shops, but the rents are even higher along East 57th Street, a parade of very exclusive smaller shops and upmarket art galleries. This is one of the world's great shopping districts, and every year more and more international fashion firms try to muscle in on this turf. The list of designer boutiques reads like a roll call of haute couture—Dior, Gucci, Vuitton, Ferragamo, Fendi, Chanel—and we have space here to point out only a few major stores. If your goal here is to spend a lot of money, *see* Chapter 8 for more details.

The string of stores begins right across the street from Rockefeller Center's Channel Gardens (*see* Tour 1, *above*), with **Saks Fifth Avenue** (5th Ave. and 50th St.), the flagship of the national department store chain. On the next block is Gothic-style **St. Patrick's**, the Roman Catholic Cathedral of New York. Dedicated to the patron saint of the Irish—then and now one of New York's principal ethnic groups—the white marble and stone structure was begun in 1858, consecrated in 1879, and completed in 1906. Among the statues in the alcoves around the nave is a striking modern interpretation of the first American-born saint, Mother Elizabeth Seton. From outside, catch one of the city's most photographed views: the ornate white spires of St. Pat's against the black glass curtain of **Olympic Tower,** a multiuse building of shops, offices, and luxury apartments.

Cartier, Inc., displays its wares in a jewel box of a turn-of-the-century mansion on the southeast corner of 52nd Street and 5th Avenue; similar houses used to line this street, and many of their occupants were parishioners of **St. Thomas Church** (5th Ave. at 53rd St.), an Episcopal institution that has occupied the site since 1911. The impressive huge stone reredos behind the altar holds the statues of more than 50 apostles, saints, martyrs, missionaries, and church figures. The Christmas Eve services here have become one of the season's highlights.

On the northwest corner of 5th Avenue and 54th Street, you'll see the imposing bulk of the **University Club,** a granite palace built by New York's leading turn-of-the-century architects, McKim, Mead & White, for this exclusive midtown men's club, one of several that only recently have begun accepting women members. Pick out the crests of various prestigious universities above its windows. Across the street is **Takashimaya New York** (683 5th Ave.), a branch of Japan's largest department-store chain. The elegant store features a garden atrium, a two-floor gallery, and three floors of men's and women's clothing and household items that combine Eastern and Western styles.

Fifth Avenue Presbyterian Church, a grand brownstone church (1875), sits on the northwest corner of 5th Avenue and 55th Street. On the same block is **Henri Bendel** (712–716 5th Ave.), a fashion store organized like a little tower of intimate boutiques; the facade's René Lalique art-glass windows from 1912 can be viewed at close range from balconies ringing the four-story atrium. Next door is **Harry Winston** (718 5th Ave.), with a spectacular selection of fine jewelry.

⑭ Trump Tower, on 5th Avenue between 56th and 57th streets, is an exclusive 68-story apartment and office building named for its developer, Donald Trump. The grand 5th Avenue entrance leads into a glitzy six-story shopping atrium paneled in pinkish-orange marble and trimmed with lustrous brass. A fountain cascades against one wall, drowning out the clamor of the city.

Just north of Trump Tower, the intersection of 5th Avenue and 57th Street is ground zero for high-class shopping. And what more fitting resident for this spot than **Tiffany & Co.** (727 5th Ave. at 57th St.), the renowned jewelers, with its Fort Knox–like Art Deco entrance. One quintessential New York movie, *Breakfast at Tiffany's,* opens with Audrey Hepburn, dressed in an evening gown, emerging from a yellow cab at dawn to stand here window-shopping with a coffee and Danish.

Around the corner on East 57th Street, anchoring the north side of Trump Tower, is the new French contender for most glamorous New York department store, **Galeries Lafayette,** a branch of the Paris fashion emporium. Its stylish salons occupy the six-story space that was formerly Bonwit Teller. Both English and French are spoken here, and you can convert your French francs to American dollars on premises.

⑮ At Madison Avenue and 57th Street, look up at the **IBM Building, a five-sided sheath of dark gray-green granite and glass by Edward Larrabee Barnes. On the ground level there's the entrance to the subterranean **IBM Gallery of Science and Art,** which presents a variety of temporary art shows and the permanent science exhibition *Think,* including lasers, magnets, and superconductors. *Tel. 212/ 745–6100. Admission free. Open Tues.–Sat. 11–6.*

Time Out At the 56th Street corner, step into IBM's high, cool atrium, one of the most inviting public spaces in town. Small marble-topped tables and wrought-iron chairs are provided, live music plays at noontime most weekdays, and a small café serves lunch. The atrium closes at 10 PM.

Cross 57th Street and head back toward 5th Avenue on the north side of the street, with its stellar lineup of boutiques: the French shop **Hermès** (11 E. 57th St.), the English shop **Burberrys Ltd.** (9 E. 57th St.), the German shop **Escada** (7 E. 57th St.), and the French classic **Chanel** (appropriately located at 5 E. 57th St.). Back at 5th Avenue (at 754, to be exact), you can visit **Bergdorf Goodman:** The women's boutiques are on the west side of the avenue and the men's store on the east side, both between 57th and 58th streets. **Van Cleef & Arpels** jewelers is located within Bergdorf's 57th Street corner.

Cross 58th Street to **Grand Army Plaza,** the open space along 5th Avenue between 58th and 60th streets. The southern block features the Pulitzer Fountain, donated by publisher Joseph Pulitzer of Pulitzer Prize fame. Appropriately enough for this ritzy area, the fountain is crowned by a female figure representing Abundance. The block to the north holds a gilded (some say *too* gilded) equestrian statue of Civil War general William Tecumseh Sherman; beyond it is a grand entrance to Central Park (*see* Tour 7, *below*).

16 Appropriately named **The Plaza,** the famous hotel (*see* Chapter 9) at the western edge of this square is a registered historical landmark built in 1907. Its architect, Henry Hardenbergh, was the same man who designed the rather dour Dakota apartment building (*see* Tour 8, *below*), but here he achieved a sprightly birthday-cake effect with white-glazed brick busily decorated and topped off with a copper-and-slate mansard roof. The hotel has been featured in many movies, from Alfred Hitchcock's *North by Northwest* to more recent films such as *Arthur, Crocodile Dundee, Home Alone 2,* and of course, *Plaza Suite.* Among the many upper-crust parties that have taken place in the Plaza's ballroom was Truman Capote's Black and White Ball of 1966, attended by everyone who was anyone—all dressed, naturally, in black and white.

17 Adjacent to Grand Army Plaza stands the **General Motors Building,** a 50-story tower of Georgia marble. One section of the main floor is the flagship of the legendary **F.A.O. Schwarz** toy store, with its fantastic mechanical clock right inside the front doors. Bigger than it looks from outside, the toy-o-rama offers a vast, wondrously fun selection, although it definitely tends toward expensive imports. Browsing here should bring out the child in everyone, as it did in the movie *Big,* when Tom Hanks and his boss got caught up in tap-dancing on a giant keyboard.

Now return to 57th Street and head west, where the glamour eases off a bit (but not much). You'll pass the excellent **Rizzoli** bookstore at 31 West 57th (Robert DeNiro and Meryl Streep trysted here in their bomb movie *Falling In Love*), and beyond that is arguably the handsomest McDonald's in the land, with an elegant blue-neon decorating scheme that's definitely not standard-issue for the burger chain. Across 6th Avenue (remember, New Yorkers *don't* call it Avenue of the Americas, despite the street signs), you'll know you're in classical-music territory when you peer through the showroom windows at **Steinway** (109 W. 57th St.). But before you get to Carnegie Hall, you may want to cross the street to grab a bite (or at least steal a peek) at **Planet Hollywood** (140 W. 57th St., tel. 212/333–7827), where, behind the pink-and-green striped awnings and plastic palm trees, you'll find a trendy restaurant stuffed with movie memorabilia—everything from Humphrey Bogart's Maltese Falcon to *Star Wars'* R2D2 and C3PO robots. To assemble such a cache, you'd need good Tinseltown connections, but since the restaurant's owners include actors Arnold Schwarzenegger, Bruce Willis, and Sylvester Stallone, as well as producer-director John Hughes, apparently it was a cinch. A few doors down from Planet Hollywood is the more staid, but no less celebrity-studded, **Russian Tea Room** restaurant (150 W. 57th St., tel. 212/265–0947) in its bright turquoise town house.

An old joke says it all: A tourist asks an old guy with a violin case, "How do you get to Carnegie Hall?" His reply: "Practice, practice, practice." Presiding over the southeast corner of 7th Avenue and 57th Street, **Carnegie Hall** has been hosting musical headliners since 1891, when its first concert was conducted by no less than Tchaikovsky. Outside it's a stout, square brown building with a few Moorish-style arches added, almost as an afterthought, to the facade. Inside, however, is a simply decorated, 2,804-seat auditorium that is considered one of the finest in the world. It was extensively restored before its gala 1990–1991 centennial season, although critics still debate whether the main auditorium's acoustics will ever be as perfect as they were before. The lobby is bigger now, though, and a museum has been added just east of the main auditorium, displaying memorabilia from the hall's illustrious history. Hour-long guided tours of Carnegie Hall are also available. *Carnegie Hall Museum: 881 7th Ave., tel. 212/903–9629. Admission free. Open daily 11–4:30. Guided tours (tel. 212/247–7800) offered Mon., Tues., and Thurs. 11:30, 2, and 3 (performance schedule permitting); admission: $6 adults, $5 students and seniors, $3 children.*

Devotees of classical music may want to head from here up to nearby Lincoln Center (*see* Tour 8, *below*). If rock-and-roll music is more to your liking, head west one more block to the **Hard Rock Café** (221 W. 57th St., tel. 212/459–9320), New York City's outpost of the restaurant chain. Since the opening of Planet Hollywood, which was inspired by the Hard Rock's success, the sidewalk lines behind the velvet rope here are a little shorter, but it's still a popular scene. If you don't want to eat, you can always drop into the adjacent shop to buy one of those ubiquitous T-shirts.

A few blocks south and west is the old **Ed Sullivan Theater** (1697 Broadway, between 53rd and 54th Sts.), now home to the "David Letterman Show." Many of the shopkeepers and restaurateurs on this block have become minor late-night celebrities as a result of the talk-show host's periodic forays onto the street to get acquainted with (and cajole and harrass) his neighbors.

Tour 3: Across 42nd Street

As midtown Manhattan's central axis, 42nd Street ties together several major points of interest, from the United Nations on the East River, past the Grand Central Terminal, to Times Square. While it's never less than a busy commercial thoroughfare, a few blocks of 42nd Street are downright disreputable, living up to the often-held image of New York as a den of pickpockets, porno houses, prostitutes, and destitutes. An ambitious plan to redevelop Times Square is currently under way, but in the meantime try to imagine West 42nd Street as a scene out of the movie *Taxi Driver*, lyrical in its squalor.

While it may not exactly be the Crossroads of the World, as it is often called, **Times Square** is one of New York's principal energy centers. It's one of many New York City "squares" that are actually triangles formed by the angle of Broadway slashing across a major avenue—in this case, crossing 7th Avenue at 42nd Street. The square itself is occupied by the former Times Tower, now resheathed in white marble and called **One Times Square Plaza.** When the *New York Times* moved into its new headquarters on December 31, 1904, it publicized the event with a fireworks show at midnight, thus starting a New Year's Eve tradition. Each December 31, workmen on this roof lower a 200-pound ball down the flagpole by hand, just as they have since 1908. The huge intersection below is mobbed with revelers, and when the ball hits bottom on the stroke of midnight, pandemonium ensues.

The present headquarters of the *New York Times* (229 W. 43rd St.) occupies much of the block between 7th and 8th avenues; look for the blue delivery vans lined up along 43rd Street. From 44th to 51st streets, the cross streets west of Broadway are lined with some 30 major theaters (*see* Chapter 11). This has been the city's main theater district since the turn of the century; movie theaters joined the fray beginning in the 1920s. As the theaters drew crowds of people in the evenings, advertisers began to mount huge electric signs here, which gave the intersection its distinctive nighttime glitter. Even the developers who want to change this area intend to preserve the signs, making them bigger and brighter with new technology. One of the newest features a 42-foot-tall bottle of Coca-Cola hanging over Broadway and 47th Street, and a steaming Eight O'Clock Bean Coffee cup now warms up 46th Street.

②⓪ The northern triangle of the intersection, which reaches up to 47th Street, is named **Duffy Square** after World War I hero Father Francis P. Duffy, the "Fighting Chaplain," who later was pastor of a theater district church on West 42nd Street. Besides the suitably military statue of Father Duffy, there's also one of George M. Cohan, the indomitable trouper who wrote "Yankee Doodle Dandy." Today Duffy Square is an important place to visit for the **TKTS discount ticket booth,** which sells half-price and 25%-off tickets to Broadway and some Off-Broadway shows (*see* Chapter 11). Some days it seems that almost every show in town is up for grabs; at other times there may be nothing available but a few long-running hits and some sleepers. The lines may look long, but they move surprisingly fast.

The main live theater on 42nd Street is provided by a group of thriving Off-Broadway playhouses, called **Theatre Row** (*see* Chapter 11), between 9th and 10th avenues. As you walk east, peek into No. 330, between 8th and 9th avenues, behind the Port Authority Bus Terminal. Originally the McGraw-Hill Building, it was designed in 1931 by Raymond Hood, who later worked on Rockefeller Center. The lobby is an Art Deco wonder of opaque glass and stainless steel. The rehabilitation of the block between 7th and 8th avenues that was once the heart of the theater district, but which has for many years been nothing but a sleazy strip of X-rated bookstores, peep shows, and movie theaters has at last begun. The most prominent vestige of the old 42nd Street is the **New Amsterdam** (214 W. 42nd St.), a designated landmark that opened in 1903, showcasing the likes of Eddie Cantor, Will Rogers, Fanny Brice, and the Ziegfeld Girls. It's now dark, though the Walt Disney Company has been showing interest in presenting productions there. Next door to the New Victory, the **Times Square Theater** was due to reopen late 1994 with a state-of-the-art tourist information center and multimedia extravaganza providing an introduction to New York. For two decades after its 1920 opening, the Times Square staged top hits as *Gentlemen Prefer Blondes, The Front Page,* and *Strike Up the Band;* Noël Coward's *Private Lives* opened here with Gertrude Lawrence, Laurence Olivier, and the author himself.

Heading east on 42nd Street, you'll pass **Hotaling's News** (142 W. 42nd St., tel. 212/840–1868), a bustling little shop that carries more than 220 daily newspapers from throughout the United States, most issues only a day or two old. The rear section stocks current newspapers, magazines, and foreign-language books from more than 40 countries.

At the intersection of 42nd Street and 6th Avenue, look north to see, on the side of a low 43rd Street building, the **National Debt Clock,** an electronic display established by real-estate developer Seymour Durst to remind passersby of how much deeper in debt the United States gets every second. Across 6th Avenue you'll see steps rising into the shrubbery and trees of the handsomely renovated **Bryant Park,** named for the poet and editor William Cullen Bryant (1794–1878). This was the site of America's first World's Fair, the Crystal Palace Exhibition of 1853–54; today it's the backyard of the New York Public Library's central research branch. One reason to enter the park is to visit the **Bryant Park Dance and Music Tickets Booth,** which, in a setup similar to that of TKTS, sells tickets for music and dance performances throughout the city (*see* Chapter 11).

On the northwest corner of 6th Avenue and 43rd Street, you can visit a branch of the International Center of Photography (*see* Tour 5, *below*), **ICP Mid-Town,** which presents several photography shows a year in an ultracontemporary, multilevel space. *Tel. 212/768–4680. Admission: $4 adults, $2.50 students and senior citizens, $1 children under 12. Open Tues. 11–8, Wed.–Sun. 11–6.*

A block north, you'll see the **Algonquin Hotel** (59 W. 44th St.; *see* Chapter 10), which is surprisingly unpretentious considering its history as a haunt of well-known writers and actors. Its most famous association is with a witty group of literary Manhattanites who gathered in its lobby and dining rooms in the 1920s—a clique that included short-story writer Dorothy Parker, humorist Robert Benchley, playwright George S. Kaufman, and actress Tallulah Bankhead. One reason they met here was the hotel's proximity to the former offices of the *New Yorker* magazine at 28 West 44th (it finally moved in 1991, to 20 West 43rd Street).

Next door to the Algonquin is the more humble (and cheaper) **Iroquois Hotel** (49 W. 44th St.; *see* Chapter 10), where struggling actor James Dean lived in the early 1950s. Across the street is the **Royalton Hotel** (44 W. 44th St.; *see* Chapter 10), chicly redone by French designer Philippe Starck. You might want to step into its lobby for a peek, but unless your clothes are suitably trendy, you may be hustled along by the staff. The hotel restaurant, 44, has become a popular meeting place for the publishing industry. Next door, at 42 West 44th Street, is the **Association of the Bar of the City of New York,** with a neoclassical facade resembling the courthouses where its members spend so much of their time.

Back on the north side of the street, at 37 West 44th Street is the **New York Yacht Club,** former longtime home of the America's Cup trophy. Notice its swelling windowfronts, looking just like the sterns of ships, complete with stone-carved water splashing over the sill. The redbrick **Harvard Club** (27 W. 44th St.) echoes the Harvard campus with its modest Georgian-style architecture. Even if you're not a Harvard graduate who belongs to the Club, you may stay here if recommended by a member. At 20 West 44th, the **Mechanics' and Tradesmen's Institute Building,** in a turn-of-the-century prep school building, has a wonderful library in a three-story-high hall; here you'll also find the intriguing **Mossman Collection of Locks,** open free to the public (tel. 212/840–1840; open weekdays 10–3, except the first Wed. of every month).

At the corner of 5th Avenue, look left to notice the large clock on a pedestal set in the 5th Avenue sidewalk, a relic of an era when only rich people could afford watches. Then turn right and walk south. Between 40th and 42nd streets on 5th Avenue, you'll find the central research building of the **New York Public Library.** This 1911 masterpiece of Beaux Arts design was financed largely by John Jacob Astor, whose previous library building downtown has since been turned into the Public Theater (*see* Tour 13, *below*). Its grand front steps are guarded by two crouching marble lions—dubbed "Patience" and "Fortitude" by Mayor Fiorello La Guardia, who said he visited the facility to "read between the lions." After admiring the white marble neoclassical facade (crammed with statues, as is typical of Beaux Arts buildings), walk through the bronze front doors into the grand marble lobby with its sweeping double staircase. Turn left and peek into the Periodicals Room, decorated with trompe l'oeil paintings by Richard Haas commemorating New York's importance as a publishing center. Then take a (quiet) look upstairs at the huge, high-ceilinged main reading room, a haven of scholarly calm, or visit the current exhibition in the art gallery. Among the treasures you might see are Gilbert Stuart's portrait of George Washington, Charles Dickens's desk, and Thomas Jefferson's own handwritten copy of the Declaration of Independence. Free one-hour tours, each as individual as the library volunteer who leads it, are given Tuesday–Saturday at 11 AM and 2 PM. *Tel. 212/ 930–0800. Open Tues.–Wed. 11–7:30, Thurs.–Sat. 10–6.*

Continue east on 42nd Street to **Grand Central Terminal** (not a "station," as many people call it, since all runs begin or end here). Constructed between 1903 and 1913, this Manhattan landmark was originally designed by a Minnesota architectural firm and later gussied up with Beaux Arts ornamentation. Stop on the south side of 42nd Street to admire the three huge windows separated by columns, and the Beaux Arts clock and sculpture crowning the facade above the elevated roadway (Park Avenue is routed around Grand Central's upper story). Go in the side doors on Vanderbilt Avenue to enter the cavernous main concourse, with its 12-story-high ceiling displaying the constellations of the zodiac. If you can handle it, the best time to visit is at rush hour, when this immense room crackles with the frenzy of scurrying commuters, dashing every which way. (You may remember the scene in Terry Gilliam's *The Fisher King,* when the crowds stopped running for trains, turned to each other, and waltzed instead.) *Free tours Wed. at 12:30 PM (meet in front of Chemical Bank inside terminal on main level), tel. 212/935–3960.*

On the southwest corner of Park Avenue and 42nd Street, directly opposite Grand Central, the **Whitney Museum of American Art at Philip Morris** (120 Park Ave.) occupies the ground floor of the Philip Morris Building. Each year this free branch of the Whitney Museum (*see* Tour 5, *below*) presents five successive exhibitions of 20th-century painting and sculpture. An espresso bar and seating areas make it a much more agreeable place to rest than anywhere in Grand Central. *Tel. 212/878–2550. Admission free. Sculpture court open Mon.–Sat. 7:30 AM–9:30 PM, Sun. 11–7; gallery open Mon.–Wed. 11–6, Thurs. 11–7:30, Fri.–Sat. 11–6. Lectures on Wed. at 1 PM.*

The southeast corner of 42nd and Park is a major departure point for buses to the three New York area airports, and upstairs at 100 East 42nd Street you'll find ticket counters for most major U.S. airlines. Next door is the **Home Bank for Savings,** better known as **Bowery Savings Bank** (110 E. 42nd St.), whose massive arches and 70-foot-high marble columns give it a commanding presence. At the end of the block is the **Chanin Building** (122 E. 42nd St.), notable for the geometric Art Deco patterns that adorn its facade. Across the street you'll see the **Grand Hyatt** (Park Ave. at Grand Central Terminal), which was created by wrapping a new black glass exterior around the former Commodore Hotel.

Ask New Yorkers to name their favorite skyscraper and most will choose the Art Deco **Chrysler Building** at 42nd Street and Lexington Avenue. Although the Chrysler Corporation itself moved out a long time ago, this graceful shaft culminating in a stainless-steel spire still captivates the eye and the imagination. The building has no observation deck, but you can go inside its elegant dark lobby, which is faced with African marble and covered with a ceiling mural that salutes transportation and human endeavor.

Although its future seemed in question when publisher Mortimer Zuckerman bought it, laying off many staff members, the *Daily News* is still being produced in the **Daily News Building** (220 E. 42nd St.), an Art Deco tower designed with brown-brick spandrels and windows to make it seem loftier than its 37 stories. Step into the lobby for a look at its revolving illuminated globe, 12 feet in diameter; the floor is laid out as a gigantic compass, with bronze lines indicating air mileage from principal world cities to New York. A small gallery displays *News* photos.

The **Ford Foundation Building** (320 E. 43rd St., with an entrance on 42nd St.) encloses a 12-story, ⅓-acre greenhouse. With a terraced garden, a still pool, and a couple of dozen full-grown trees, the Ford atrium is open to the public—for tranquil strolling, not for picnics—weekdays from 9 to 5.

Climb the steps along 42nd Street between 1st and 2nd avenues to enter **Tudor City,** a self-contained complex of a dozen buildings featuring half-timbering and lots of stained glass. Constructed between 1925 and 1928, two of the apartment buildings of this residential enclave originally had no east-side windows, lest the tenants be forced to gaze at the slaughterhouses, breweries, and glue factories then located along the East River. Today, however, they're missing a wonderful view of the United Nations Headquarters; you'll have to walk to the terrace at the end of 43rd Street to overlook the UN. This will place you at the head of the **Sharansky Steps** (named for Natan—formerly Anatoly—Sharansky, the Soviet dissident), which run along the **Isaiah Wall** (inscribed "They Shall Beat Their Swords Into Plowshares"); you'll also look down into **Ralph J. Bunche Park** (named for the African-American UN undersecretary) and **Raoul Wallenberg Walk** (named for the Swedish diplomat and World War II hero who saved many Hungarian Jews from the Nazis).

The **United Nations Headquarters** complex occupies a lushly landscaped 18-acre riverside tract just east of 1st Avenue between 42nd and 48th streets. Its rose garden is especially pleasant to stroll in, although picnicking is strictly forbidden. A line of flagpoles with banners representing the current roster of 159 member nations stands before the striking 550-foot-high slab of the Secretariat Building, with the domed General Assembly Building nestled at its side. The headquarters were designed in 1947–53 by an international team of architects led by Wallace Harrison. You can enter the General Assembly Building at the 46th Street door; the interior corridors overflow with imaginatively diverse artwork donated by member nations. Free tickets to most sessions are available on a first-come, first-served basis 15 minutes before sessions begin; pick them up in the General Assembly lobby. (The full General Assembly is in session from the third Tuesday in September to the end of December.) Visitors can take early luncheon in the Delegates Dining Room (jacket required for men) or eat from 9:30 to 4:30 in the public coffee shop. *Tel. 212/963–7713. Tours offered Mon.–Fri. 10–4:15. 1-hr tours leave the General Assembly lobby every 30 min. Tour admission: $6.50 adults, $4.50 students and senior citizens, $3.50 students in 8th grade and under. Children under 5 not permitted.*

Tour 4: Murray Hill to Gramercy Park

Numbers in the margin correspond to points of interest on the Tour 4: Murray Hill to Gramercy Park map.

As the city grew progressively north throughout the 19th century, one neighborhood after another had its fashionable heyday, only to fade from glory. But three neighborhoods, east of 5th Avenue roughly between 20th and 40th streets, have preserved much of their historic charm, in Murray Hill's brownstone mansions and town houses, Madison Square's classic turn-of-the-century skyscrapers, and Gramercy Park's London-like leafy square. The only "must-see" along this route is the Empire State Building, but the walk as a whole is worth taking for the many moments en route when you may feel as if you've stepped back in time.

Begin on East 36th Street, between Madison and Park avenues, at the **Pierpont Morgan Library.** The core of this small, patrician museum is the famous banker's own study and library, completed in 1906 by McKim, Mead & White. If you walk east past the museum's main entrance on 36th Street, you'll see the original library's neoclassical facade, with what is believed to be McKim's face on the sphinx in the right-hand sculptured panel. Around the corner, at 37th Street and Madison Avenue, is the latest addition to the library, an 1852 Italianate brownstone that was once the home of Morgan's son, J. P. Morgan, Jr. The elder Morgan's own house stood at 36th Street and Madison Avenue; it was torn down after his death and replaced with the simple neoclassical annex that today holds the library's main exhibition space. On your left as you enter are handsome benches, but don't be fooled into thinking that you can sit and rest on them; the guards will shoo you off them. But you can go inside and visit the galleries for rotating exhibitions; go straight to see items from the permanent collection, principally drawings, prints, manuscripts, and rare books, and to pass through the new glass-roofed garden court to the fine bookstore. Turn right just past the entrance and go down a long cloister corridor for the library's most impressive rooms: the elder Morgan's personal study, its red-damask-lined walls hung with first-rate paintings, and his majestic personal library with its dizzying tiers of handsomely bound rare books, letters, and illuminated manuscripts. *29 E. 36th St., tel. 212/685–0008. Suggested contribution: $5 adults, $3 students and senior citizens. Open Tues.–Sat. 10:30–5, Sun. 1–5.*

As you proceed south on Madison Avenue, at 35th Street you'll pass the **Church of the Incarnation,** a broodingly dark brownstone version of a Gothic chapel. Inside, however, there's enough jewellike stained glass to counteract the dour effect. Look especially for the north aisle's 23rd Psalm Window, by the Tiffany Glass works, or the south aisle's two Angel windows dedicated to infants, which are by the 19th-century English writer-designer William Morris.

At 35th Street and Madison Avenue, veteran globe-trotters will enjoy a stop at **The Complete Traveller Bookstore** (199 Madison Ave.,

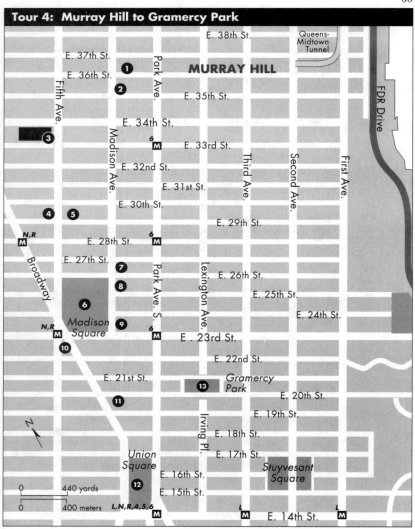

Tour 4: Murray Hill to Gramercy Park

Appellate Division of the State Supreme Court, **8**

Church of the Incarnation, **2**

Church of the Transfiguration, **5**

Empire State Building, **3**

Flatiron Building, **10**

Gramercy Park, **13**

Madison Square, **6**

Marble Collegiate Church, **4**

Metropolitan Life Insurance Tower, **9**

New York Life Insurance Building, **7**

Pierpont Morgan Library, **1**

Theodore Roosevelt Birthplace, **11**

Union Square, **12**

tel. 212/679–4339), a comprehensive shop for travel literature and a charming old-world bookstore in its own right.

Occupying the block between 35th and 34th streets from Madison to 5th avenues is a landmark building that from 1906 to 1989 was the home of **B. Altman,** one of New York's grand old department stores, which was speedily driven into bankruptcy by its last owner, the Australian conglomerate the Hooker Corporation.

❸ At 5th Avenue and 34th Street, you can't miss the **Empire State Building.** It may no longer be the world's tallest building, but it is certainly one of the world's best-loved skyscrapers. The Art Deco playground for King Kong opened in 1931 after only about a year of construction. The crowning spire was originally designed as a mooring mast for dirigibles, but none ever docked here; in 1951, a TV transmittal tower was added to the top, raising the total height to 1,472 feet. Today more than 16,000 people work in the building, and more than 2½ million people a year visit the 86th- and 102nd-floor observatories. At night the top 30 stories are illuminated with colors appropriate to the season (red and green around Christmas; orange and brown for Halloween). In 1956, revolving beacons named the Freedom Lights were installed. These lights are illuminated from dusk to midnight.

Pass beneath the stainless-steel canopy on 34th Street to enter the three-story-high marbled lobby, where illuminated panels depicting the Seven Wonders of the World brazenly add the Empire State as the Eighth Wonder. Go to the concourse level to buy a ticket for the observation decks. The 102nd-floor spot is glassed in; the 86th floor is open to the air. In the movie *An Affair to Remember,* Cary Grant waited here impatiently for his rendezvous with Deborah Kerr, an event around which Nora Ephron built the entire screenplay of the 1993 hit, *Sleepless in Seattle. 5th Ave. and 34th St., tel. 212/736–3100. Admission: $3.75 adults, $1.75 children 5–11. Open daily 9:30 AM–midnight; the last elevator up leaves at 11:30 PM.*

Also on the concourse level of the Empire State Building, you'll find the **Guinness World of Records Exhibition,** where clever displays tell the story of various unusual record-holders. *Tel. 212/947–2335. Admission: $7 adults, $3.25 children under 12. Open Mon.–Thurs. 9–9, Fri.–Sun. 9 AM–9:30 PM.*

❹ Continue south on 5th Avenue to 29th Street and the **Marble Collegiate Church** (1854), a marble-fronted structure built for the Reformed Protestant Dutch Congregation first organized in 1628 by Peter Minuit, the canny Dutchman who bought Manhattan from the native Indians for $24. Its pulpit was once occupied by Dr. Norman Vincent Peale *(The Power of Positive Thinking),* Marble Collegiate's pastor from 1932 to 1984.

❺ Go east on 29th Street to the **Church of the Transfiguration** (1 E. 29th St.), which is better known as the Little Church Around the Corner. Set back in a shrub-filled New York version of an old English churchyard, it won its memorable appellation in 1870 when other area churches refused to bury actor George Holland, a colleague of well-known thespian Joseph Jefferson. Jefferson was directed to the "little church around the corner," which did that sort of thing, and the Episcopal institution has welcomed literary and show-biz types ever since. Go inside to see the south transept's stained-glass window, by John LaFarge, depicting 19th-century superstar actor Edwin Booth in his most famous role, Hamlet.

Bordered by 5th Avenue, Broadway, Madison Avenue, 23rd and 26th streets, **Madison Square** was the site (circa 1845) of New York's first baseball games. On the north end, an imposing 1881 statue by Augustus Saint-Gaudens memorializes Civil War naval hero Admiral Farragut.

The block at 26th Street and Madison Avenue is occupied by the ornate **New York Life Insurance Building,** designed in 1928 by Cass Gilbert, who also did the Woolworth Building (*see* Tour 17, *below*). Its birthday-cake top is capped by a gilded pyramid that is stunning when lit at night. Go inside to admire the soaring lobby's coffered ceilings and ornate bronze doors. This was formerly the site of the second (1890–1925) Madison Square Garden, designed by architect and playboy Stanford White, who was shot in the Garden's roof garden by Harry K. Thaw, the jealous husband of actress Evelyn Nesbit—a lurid episode more or less accurately depicted in the movie *Ragtime.*

Coincidentally, other scenes in *Ragtime* were filmed in front of the **Appellate Division of the State Supreme Court,** which is at Madison Avenue and 25th Street. The roof balustrade of this imposing white marble Corinthian structure depicts great lawmakers of the past: Moses, Justinian, Confucius, and others, although a statue of Muhammed had to be removed because it offended the Islamic religion.

The **Metropolitan Life Insurance Tower** (Madison Ave., between 23rd and 24th Sts.) made this building the world's tallest when it was added in 1909. The 700-foot tower re-creates the campanile of St. Mark's in Venice. The four dials of its clock are each three stories high; wait for the quarter hour to hear it chime. Met Life's North Building, between 24th and 25th streets, is connected by a skywalk. Its Art Deco loggias have attracted many film crews—it appeared in such films as *After Hours, Radio Days,* and *The Fisher King.* Step into the lobby of the South Building during weekday business hours to see a fine set of Wyeth murals; the guard may stop you, but if you explain what you want to see, you should be issued a pass.

The Renaissance-style **Flatiron Building,** by architect Daniel Burnham, occupies the triangular lot formed by Broadway, 5th Avenue, and 23rd Street. This, too, was the tallest building in the world when it opened (1902). Its rounded front point is only 6 feet wide, but gentle waves built into the molded limestone-and-terra-cotta side walls soften the wedge effect. Winds invariably swooped down its 20-story, 286-foot height, billowing up the skirts of women pedestrians on 23rd Street, and local traffic cops had to shoo away male gawkers—coining the phrase "23 Skiddoo." Originally named the Fuller Building, it was instantly rechristened by the public because of its resemblance to a flatiron, and eventually the nickname became official.

The Flatiron Building has lent its name to the once seedy, now trendy Flatiron District that lies to the south between 5th Avenue and Park Avenue South. The neighborhood's massive buildings, the last of the preskyscraper era, have had their ornate Romanesque facades gleamingly restored; hip boutiques and restaurants occupy their street levels, while advertising agencies, publishing houses, architects' offices, graphic design firms, and residential lofts fill the upper stories.

Time Out A good stop for hearty soups, salads, or wonderful sandwiches on thick, crusty bread is **La Boulangère** (49 E. 21st St., tel. 212/475-8582). You can either sit at one of the tiny tables or order take-out (enjoy a picnic on a bench in either Madison Square or Union Square to the south).

Continue south on Broadway and turn east on 20th Street to the **⑪ Theodore Roosevelt Birthplace,** a reconstruction of the Victorian brownstone where Teddy lived until he was 15 years old. Before becoming president, Roosevelt was New York City's police commissioner and the governor of New York State. The house contains Victorian period rooms and Roosevelt memorabilia; a selection of videos about the namesake of the teddy bear can be seen on request. Saturday-afternoon chamber-music concerts are offered each fall, winter, and spring. *28 E. 20th St., tel. 212/260–1616. Admission: $2 adults, free to senior citizens and children under 17. Open Wed.– Sun. 9–5; guided tours 9–3:30.*

If you pass by **890 Broadway** (between 19th and 20th Sts.), you may see actors and actresses leaving and entering the building. At this address is the Lawrence A. Wein Center for Dance and Theater, a honeycomb of rehearsal halls for upcoming plays and musicals. The space was founded by the late Broadway director-choreographer Michael Bennett, and it was here that he developed the award-winning musical *Dreamgirls.*

⑫ Union Square lies between Park Avenue South and Broadway and 14th and 17th streets. Its name, originally signifying the fact that two main roads merged here, proved doubly apt in the early 20th century when the square became a rallying spot for labor protests and mass demonstrations; many unions, as well as fringe political parties, moved their headquarters nearby. Over the years the area deteriorated into a habitat of drug dealers and kindred undesirables, until a massive renewal program in the 1980s transformed it. If possible, visit on Greenmarket day (Monday, Wednesday, Friday, and Saturday), when farmers from all over the Northeast, including some Pennsylvania Dutch and latter-day hippies, bring their goods to the big town: fresh produce, homemade bakery goods, cheeses, cider, New York State wines, even fish and meat. The trendy, Warhol-founded *Interview* has its offices here, while the most recent developments have included renovation of the 1932 **Pavilion,** now flanked by playgrounds and an open-air café run by the Coffee Shop, and much new retail activity at the south (14th Street) end, and along the east side.

Just east of Union Square on rather disreputable 14th Street is the **Palladium** (126 E. 14th St.), a former movie palace turned into a cavernous, innovative disco—now well past its brief "in" moment—by Ian Schrager and the late Steve Rubell, of Studio 54 fame, and designed by Arata Isozaki. The Palladium is now owned by Peter Gatien, who also controls three other New York nightclubs: Limelight, the Tunnel, and Club USA. The Palladium stands at the foot of Irving Place, named after the writer Washington Irving (1783–1859), author of *The Legend of Sleepy Hollow.* Walk north to 40 Irving Place, where you'll see a huge bust of the writer outside **Washington Irving High School,** alma mater of Claudette Colbert and Whoopi Goldberg. A plaque on the redbrick house at 17th Street and Irving Place proclaims it as the home of Washington Irving, but it was his nephew's house, though the famous writer did visit there often.

More than a century later another famous chronicler of New York life, O. Henry, whose real name was William Sidney Porter, lived at 55 Irving Place, in a building long ago demolished. But his legend lives on at **Pete's Tavern** (18th St. and Irving Pl., tel. 212/473–7676), which claims that O. Henry wrote "The Gift of the Magi" while sitting in the second booth to the right. Pete's Tavern also claims to be the oldest saloon in New York (1864); both facts are disputed, but stop here anyway for a casual drink and absorb the atmosphere of the Gaslight Era. Across the street is **Fresh Art** (71 Irving Pl., tel. 212/955–5044), an attractive plant store, and **Friend of a Farmer** (77 Irving Pl., tel. 212/477–2188), a popular country-style café.

At the top of Irving Place, between 20th and 21st streets, lies **⑬ Gramercy Park,** a picture-perfect city park complete with flower beds, bird feeders, sundials, and cozy benches. It stays nice largely because it's surrounded by a locked cast-iron fence, and, alas, only residents of the property around the park can obtain keys. Laid out in 1831 according to a design inspired by London's residential squares, Gramercy Park is surrounded by interesting buildings.

On the south side of the square, peek inside the park and you'll see a statue of actor Edwin Booth playing Hamlet. Booth lived at No. 16, which he remodeled in the early 1880s to serve as an actors' club, **The Players Club.** Stanford White, the architect for the renovation, was a member of the club, as were many other nonactors. Members over the years have included Mark Twain, Booth Tarkington, John and Lionel Barrymore, Irving Berlin, Winston Churchill, Lord Laurence Olivier, Frank Sinatra, Walter Cronkite, Jack Lemmon, and Richard Gere.

The **National Arts Club** (15 Gramercy Park S) was once the home of Samuel Tilden, a governor of New York and the Democratic presidential candidate who, in 1876, received more popular votes than Rutherford B. Hayes, who won more electoral college votes—and the election. Calvert Vaux, codesigner of Central Park, remodeled this building in 1874, conjoining two houses. Among its Victorian Gothic decorations are medallions portraying Goethe, Dante, Milton, and Benjamin Franklin. The Club now houses the Poetry Society of America, which sponsors poetry readings (*see* Readings and Lectures in Chapter 11).

On the west end of the square, note the row of redbrick Greek Revival town houses, with their fanciful cast-iron verandas looking like something out of New Orleans's French Quarter. Mayor James Harper (elected in 1888) lived at No. 4, behind the pair of street lanterns. The actor John Garfield died in 1952 while staying at No. 3.

At the northeast corner, the white terra-cotta apartment building at **36 Gramercy Park East** is guarded by concrete knights in silver-paint armor. The turreted redbrick building at **34 Gramercy Park East** was one of the city's first cooperative apartment houses; its tenants have included actors James Cagney, John Carradine, and Margaret Hamilton, who played the Wicked Witch in *The Wizard of Oz*. The austere gray-brown Friends Meeting House at 28 Gramercy Park South became **The Brotherhood Synagogue** in 1974, and a narrow plaza just east of the synagogue contains a Holocaust memorial. **19 Gramercy Park South** was the home in the 1880s of society doyenne Mrs. Stuyvesant Fish, a fearless iconoclast who shocked Mrs. Astor and Mrs. Vanderbilt when she reduced the time of formal dinner parties from several hours to 50 minutes, thus ushering in the modern social era.

If you're still energetic, wander over to Lexington Avenue in the high 20s, a neighborhood affectionately known as Little India, where Indian restaurants, spice shops, imported-video stores, and clothing stores abound. The area also plays host to Middle Eastern, Indonesian, and Vietnamese restaurants. In this multicultural part of town, better seen during the day, don't be surprised to find a Spanish-language playhouse across the street from an Islamic bookstore.

Tour 5: Museum Mile

Numbers in the margin correspond to points of interest on the Tours 5 and 6: Museum Mile, Upper East Side map.

Once known as Millionaire's Row, the stretch of 5th Avenue between 79th and 104th streets has been fittingly renamed Museum Mile, for it now contains an impressive cluster of cultural institutions. The connection is more than coincidental: Many museums are housed in what used to be the great mansions of merchant princes and wealthy industrialists. In 1979 a group of 10 5th Avenue institutions formed a consortium that, among other activities, sponsors a Museum Mile Festival each June. The Frick Collection and the Whitney Museum of American Art are not officially part of the Museum Mile Consortium, but they're located close enough to be added to this tour.

It would be impossible to do justice to all these collections in one outing; the Metropolitan Museum alone contains too much to see in a day. You may want to select one or two museums to linger in and simply walk past the others, appreciating their exteriors (this in itself constitutes a minicourse in modern architecture). Save the rest for another day—or for your next trip to New York.

Be sure to pick the right day of the week for this tour: Most of these museums are closed on Monday, but some have free admission during extended hours on Tuesday evening.

❶ Begin at 5th Avenue and 70th Street with **The Frick Collection,** housed in an ornate, imposing Beaux Arts mansion built in 1914 for coke-and-steel baron Henry Clay Frick, who wanted the superb art collection he was amassing to be kept far from the soot and smoke of Pittsburgh, where he'd made his fortune. The mansion was designed by architects Carrère and Hastings (also responsible for the Public Library on 5th Avenue at 40th Street); opened as a public museum in 1935 and expanded in 1977, it still resembles a gracious private home, albeit one with a bona fide masterpiece in almost every room. Strolling through the mansion, one can imagine how it felt to live with Vermeers by the front stairs, Gainsborough and Reynolds portraits in the dining room, canvases by Constable and Turner in the library, and Titians, Holbeins, a Giovanni Bellini, and an El Greco in the living room. Some of the collection's best pieces include Rembrandt's *The Polish Rider* and Jean-Honoré Fragonard's series *The Progress of Love.* You can rest in the tranquil indoor court with a fountain and glass ceiling. *1 E. 70th St., tel. 212/288–0700. Admission: $3 adults, $1.50 students and senior citizens. Children under 10 not admitted. Open Tues.–Sat. 10–6, Sun. 1–6, closed holidays.*

Walk one block east to Madison Avenue and head up to 75th Street to **❷** **The Whitney Museum of American Art.** This museum grew out of a gallery in the studio of the sculptor and collector Gertrude Vanderbilt Whitney, whose talent and taste were fortuitously accompanied by the wealth of two prominent families. The current building, opened in 1966, is a minimalist gray granite vault, separated from Madison Avenue by a dry moat; it was designed by Marcel Breuer, a member of the Bauhaus school, which prized functionality in architecture. The monolithic exterior is much more forbidding than the interior, where changing exhibitions offer an intelligent survey of 20th-century American works; the second floor offers, among other

Americas
Society, **15**

Asia Society, **16**

Bloomingdale's, **12**

Carl Schurz
Park, **19**

Conservatory
Garden, **11**

Cooper-Hewitt
Museum, **6**

El Museo del
Barrio, **10**

Frick
Collection, **1**

Gracie
Mansion, **20**

Guggenheim
Museum, **4**

Henderson Place
Historic
District, **18**

International
Center of
Photography, **8**

Jewish
Museum, **7**

Metropolitan
Museum of
Art, **3**

Museum of the
City of New
York, **9**

National
Academy of
Design, **5**

Ralph
Lauren, **17**

Seventh
Regiment
Armory, **14**

Temple Emanu-
El, **13**

Whitney
Museum of
American Art, **2**

Tours 5 and 6: Museum Mile, Upper East Side

KEY

AE American Express Office

E. 106th St.

E. 104th St.

E. 102nd St.

E. 101st St.

E. 100th St.

E. 99th St.

E. 98th St.

E. 97th St.

E. 96th St.

E. 95th St.

E. 94th St.

E. 93rd St.

E. 92nd St.

E. 91st St.

E. 90th St.

E. 89th St.

E. 88th St.

E. 87th St.

E. 86th St.

E. 85th St.

E. 84th St.

E. 83rd St.

E. 82nd St.

E. 81st St.

E. 80th St.

E. 79th St.

E. 78th St.

E. 77th St.

E. 76th St.

E. 75th St.

E. 74th St.

E. 73rd St.

E. 72nd St.

E. 71st St.

E. 70th St.

E. 69th St.

E. 68th St.

E. 67th St.

E. 66th St.

E. 65th St.

E. 64th St.

E. 63rd St.

E. 62nd St.

E. 61st St.

E. 60th St.

E. 59th St.

E. 58th St.

FDR Dr.

Fifth Ave.

Madison Ave.

Park Ave.

Lexington Ave.

Third Ave.

First Ave.

Second Ave.

York Ave.

East End Ave.

East River

FDR Dr.

CENTRAL PARK

N

Queensboro
Bridge

B, Q

AE

N, R

N, R
4, 5, 6

4, 5, 6

0 440 yards

0 400 meters

exhibits, daring new work from American video artists and film-makers, and the third-floor gallery features a sample of the perma-nent collection, including Edward Hopper's haunting *Early Sunday Morning* (1930), Georgia O'Keeffe's *White Calico Flower* (1931), and Jasper Johns's *Three Flags* (1958). Alexander Calder's *Circus*, a playful construction he tinkered with throughout his life (1898–1976), stands near the front entrance. The Whitney also has a branch across from Grand Central Terminal (*see* Tour 3). *945 Madison Ave. at 75th St., tel. 212/570–3676. Admission: $6 adults, $5 students and senior citizens. Open Wed. and Fri.–Sun. 11–6, Thurs. 1–8.*

Cut back to 5th Avenue and walk north to **The American Irish Historical Society,** in a town house once owned by U.S. Steel president William Ellis Corey, who scandalized his social class by marrying musical comedy star Mabelle Gilman. With its ornamentation and mansard roof, this is another fine example of the French-influenced Beaux Arts style that was so popular at the turn of the century. The society's library holdings chronicle people of Irish descent who became successful in the United States. *991 5th Ave. at 81st St., tel. 212/288–2263. Admission free by appointment. Open Tues.–Sat. 11–4:30.*

❸ **The Metropolitan Museum of Art** offers valid evidence for billing it-self as "New York's number one tourist attraction"; certainly the quality and range of its holdings make it one of the world's greatest museums. It's the largest art museum in the Western Hemisphere (1.6 million square feet), and its permanent collection of more than 3 million works of art from all over the world includes objects from prehistoric to modern times. The museum, founded in 1870, moved to this location in 1880, but the original redbrick building by Calvert Vaux has since been encased in other architecture. The majestic 5th Avenue facade, designed by Richard Morris Hunt, was built in 1902 of gray Indiana limestone; later additions eventually surrounded the original building on the sides and back. (On a side wall of the new ground-floor European Sculpture Court, you can glimpse the muse-um's original redbrick facade.)

The 5th Avenue entrance leads into the Great Hall, a soaring neo-classical chamber that has been designated a landmark. Past the ad-mission booths, a vast marble staircase leads up to the European painting galleries, whose highlights include Botticelli's *The Last Communion of St. Jerome,* Pieter Brueghel's *The Harvesters,* El Greco's *View of Toledo,* Johannes Vermeer's *Young Woman with a Water Jug,* and Rembrandt's *Aristotle with a Bust of Homer.* At press time, the galleries housing the Met's fine Impressionist collec-tion were being remodeled into graceful neoclassical rooms, with the focal point of an oval gallery displaying 15 large Manets. During the remodeling, all of the important pictures of this era were on view in the European painting galleries, but if all goes according to sched-ule, the refurbished rooms for the Impressionist paintings should be open by early 1994. The arcaded European Sculpture Court includes Auguste Rodin's massive bronze *The Burghers of Calais.*

American art has its own wing, back in the northwest corner; the best approach is on the first floor, where you enter through a re-freshingly light and airy garden court graced with Tiffany stained-glass windows, cast-iron staircases by Louis Sullivan, and a marble Federal-style facade taken from the Wall Street branch of the United States Bank. Take the elevator to the third floor and begin working your way down through the rooms decorated in period fur-niture—everything from a Shaker retiring room to a Federal-era ballroom to the living room of a Frank Lloyd Wright house—and excellent galleries of American painting.

In the realm of 20th-century art, the Met was a latecomer, allowing the Museum of Modern Art and the Whitney to build their collections with little competition until the Metropolitan's contemporary art department was finally established in 1967. The big museum has been trying to make up for lost time, however, and in 1987 it opened the three-story Lila Acheson Wallace Wing, in the southwest corner. Pablo Picasso's 1906 portrait of Gertrude Stein is the centerpiece of this collection.

There is much more to the Met than paintings, however. Visitors with a taste for classical art should go immediately to the left of the Great Hall on the first floor to see the Greek and Roman statuary, not to mention a large collection of rare Roman wall paintings excavated from the lava of Mount Vesuvius. Directly above these galleries, on the second floor, you'll find room after room of Grecian urns and other classical vases. The Met's awesome Egyptian collection, spanning some 3,000 years, lies on the first floor directly to the right of the Great Hall. Its centerpiece is the Temple of Dendur, an entire Roman-period temple (circa 15 BC) donated by the Egyptian government in thanks for U.S. help in saving ancient monuments. Placed in a specially built gallery with views of Central Park to refresh the eye, the temple faces east, as it did in its original location, and a pool of water has been installed at the same distance from it as the river Nile once stood. Another spot suitable for contemplation is directly above the Egyptian treasures, in the Asian galleries: The Astor Court Chinese garden reproduces a Ming Dynasty (1368–1644) scholar's courtyard, complete with water splashing over artfully positioned rocks.

There's also a fine arms and armor exhibit on the first floor (go through the medieval tapestries, just behind the main staircase, and turn right). The Met's medieval collection here is lovely, but to see the real medieval treasures, don't miss a trip to **The Cloisters,** the Met's annex in Washington Heights (*see* Chapter 6). Keep going straight from the medieval galleries until you enter the cool skylit white space of the Lehman Pavilion, where the small but exquisite personal collection of the late donor, investment banker Robert Lehman, is displayed in rooms resembling those of his West 54th Street town house. This is one of the lesser-known wings of the Met (perhaps because it's tucked away behind so many other galleries), so it's a good place to go when the other galleries begin to feel crowded.

Although it exhibits only a portion of its vast holdings, the Met offers more than can reasonably be seen in one visit. Be aware also that cuts in cultural funding have forced the museum to close certain galleries either mornings or afternoons Tuesday–Thursday; in the course of a day, you can still see anything you want, but ask at the desk for an alternating-gallery schedule to avoid frustration. Choose what you want to see, find a map, and plan your tour accordingly. Walking tours and lectures are free with your admission contribution. Tours covering various sections of the museum begin about every 15 minutes on weekdays, less frequently on weekends; they depart from the Tour Board in the Great Hall. Self-guided audio tours can also be rented at a desk in the Great Hall. Lectures, often related to temporary exhibitions, are given frequently. *5th Ave. at 82nd St., tel. 212/535–7710. Suggested contribution: $6 adults, $3 students and senior citizens. Open Tues.–Thurs. and Sun. 9:30–5:15, Fri. and Sat. 9:30–8:45.*

Time Out While the Metropolitan has a good museum café, only a block away is a friendly, sparkling-clean coffee shop: **Nectar of 82nd** (1090 Madison Ave. at 82nd St., tel. 212/772–0916). Omelets, salads, soups, burgers—the portions are generous and the prices quite reasonable.

Across from the Met, between 82nd and 83rd streets on 5th Avenue, one Beaux Arts town house stands its ground amid newer apartment blocks. It now belongs to the Federal Republic of Germany, which has installed a branch of the Goethe Institute here. **Goethe House** (tel. 212/439–8700; closed Sun.–Mon.) offers a changing series of art exhibitions as well as lectures, films, and chamber-music concerts; its extensive library (closed in the summer) includes current issues of German newspapers and periodicals. Up at 86th and 5th, a brightly embellished limestone-and-redbrick mansion, designed by Carrère and Hastings to echo the buildings on the Place des Vosges in Paris, was once the home of Mrs. Cornelius Vanderbilt III. It now houses the **Yivo Institute for Jewish Research** (tel. 212/535–6700; open Mon. 9:30–8:30, Tues. and Thurs.–Fri. 9:30–5:30), with occasional exhibitions focusing on Eastern European and American Jewish history.

❹ Frank Lloyd Wright's **Guggenheim Museum** (opened in 1959) is a controversial work of architecture—even many of those who like its assertive six-story spiral rotunda will admit that it does not result in the best space in which to view art. Inside, under a 92-foot-high glass dome, a quarter-mile-long ramp spirals down past changing exhibitions of modern art. The museum has especially strong holdings in Wassily Kandinsky, Paul Klee, and Pablo Picasso; the oldest pieces are by the French Impressionists. A new annex called the Tower Galleries opened in June 1992, creating additional gallery space to display the newly acquired Panza Collection of Minimalist art, among other works. The 10-story annex designed by Gwathmey Siegel and based on Wright's original designs offers four spacious galleries that can accommodate the extraordinarily large art pieces that the Guggenheim owns but previously had no room to display. *1071 5th Ave. at 88th St., tel. 212/423–3500. Admission: $7 adults, $4 students and senior citizens, children under 12 free. Joint admission to both branches of the Guggenheim, $10 adults, $6 students and senior citizens. Open Sun.–Wed. 10–6, Fri. and Sat. 10–8.*

❺ A block north is **The National Academy of Design,** housed in a stately 19th-century mansion and a pair of town houses on 89th Street. The academy itself, which was founded in 1825, required each elected member to donate a representative work of art, which has resulted in a strong collection of 19th- and 20th-century American art. (Members have included Samuel F. B. Morse, Winslow Homer, John Singer Sargent, Frank Lloyd Wright, and Robert Rauschenberg.) *1083 5th Ave. at 89th St., tel. 212/369–4880. Admission: $3.50 adults, $2 senior citizens and children under 16; free Tues. 5–8. Open Tues. noon–8, Wed.–Sun. noon–5.*

At 91st Street you'll find the former residence of industrialist Andrew Carnegie, now the home of the **Cooper-Hewitt Museum** (officially the Smithsonian Institution's National Museum of Design). Carnegie sought comfort more than show when he built this 64-room house on what were the outskirts of town in 1901; he administered his extensive philanthropic projects from the first-floor study. (Note the low doorways—Carnegie was only 5 feet 2 inches tall.) The core of the museum's collection was begun in 1897 by the three Hewitt sisters, granddaughters of inventor and industrialist Peter Cooper; major holdings include drawings, prints, textiles, furniture, metalwork, ceramics, glass, woodwork, and wall coverings. The Smithsonian rescued their museum from financial ruin in 1963, and the Carnegie Corporation donated the mansion in 1972. The changing exhibitions, which focus on various aspects of contemporary or historical design, are invariably well researched, enlightening, and often amusing. *2 E. 91st St., tel. 212/860–6868. Admission: $3 adults, $1.50 students and senior citizens, children under 12 free; free Tues. 5–9. Open Tues. 10–9, Wed.–Sat. 10–5, Sun. noon–5.*

Across 91st Street from the Cooper-Hewitt, the **Convent of the Sacred Heart** is in a huge Italianate mansion originally built in 1918 for financier Otto Kahn, a noted patron of the arts.

Time Out **Jackson Hole** (Madison Ave. and 91st St., tel. 212/427–2820) is a cheerful spot that serves the great American hamburger plus other sandwiches, omelets, chicken, and salads. Ski posters evoke the mood of the eponymous Wyoming resort.

❼ **The Jewish Museum** opened its expanded and renovated facilities in June 1993. The expansion preserved the gray stone Gothic-style 1908 mansion occupied by the museum since 1947 and enlarged the 1963 addition. At the same time, the mansion facade was extended, giving the museum the appearance of a late–French Gothic château. The permanent two-floor exhibition, presented alongside temporary shows, traces the development of Jewish culture and identity over 4,000 years. The exhibition draws on the museum's enormous collection of art works, ceremonial objects, and electronic media. *1109 5th Ave. at 92nd St., tel. 212/423–3200. Admission: $6 adults, $4 students and senior citizens, children under 12 free (pay-as you-wish Tues. after 5). Open Sun., Mon., Wed., Thurs. 11–5:45; Tues. 11–8. Closed national and Jewish holidays.*

The handsome, well-proportioned Georgian-style mansion on the corner of 5th Avenue and 94th Street was built in 1914 for Willard Straight, founder of the *New Republic* magazine. Today it is the **❽** home of **The International Center of Photography** (ICP), a relatively young institution—founded in 1974—building a strong collection of 20th-century photography. Its changing exhibitions often focus on the work of a single prominent photographer or one photographic genre (portraits, architecture, etc.). The bookstore carries an impressive array of photography-oriented books, prints, and postcards. *1130 5th Ave. at 94th St., tel. 212/860–1777. Admission: $4.50 adults, $2.50 students and senior citizens, $1 children under 12. Open Tues. 11–8, Wed.–Sun. 11–6.*

As you proceed north on 5th Avenue, you may want to walk a few paces east on 97th Street to see the onion-domed tower of the **Russian Orthodox Cathedral of St. Nicholas,** built in 1902. Between 98th and 101st streets, 5th Avenue is dominated by the various buildings of **Mount Sinai Hospital,** which was founded in 1852 by a group of wealthy Jewish citizens and moved here in 1904. The 1976 addition, the Annenberg Building, is a looming tower of Cor-Ten steel, which has deliberately been allowed to develop a patina of rust.

❾ **The Museum of the City of New York** traces the course of Big Apple history, from the Dutch settlers of Nieuw Amsterdam to the present day, with period rooms, dioramas, slide shows, and clever displays of memorabilia. An exhibit on the Port of New York illuminates the role of the harbor in New York's rise to greatness; the noteworthy Toy Gallery has several meticulously detailed dollhouses. Weekend programs appeal especially to children. *5th Ave. at 103rd St., tel. 212/534–1672. Suggested contribution: $5 adults; $3 students, sen-*

ior citizens, and children; $8 family. Open Wed.–Sat. 10–5, Sun. and holidays 1–5; closed Mon., Tues. (tour groups only).

⑩ **El Museo del Barrio,** founded in 1969, concentrates on Latin culture in general, with a particular emphasis on Puerto Rican art. ("El Barrio" means "the neighborhood," and the museum is positioned on the edge of Spanish Harlem.) The permanent collection includes numerous pre-Columbian artifacts. *1230 5th Ave. at 104th St., tel. 212/831–7272. Suggested contribution: $2. Open Wed.–Sun. 11–5.*

⑪ Having completed this long walk, you may want to reward yourself by crossing the street to Central Park's **Conservatory Garden.** The entrance, at 105th Street, is through elaborate wrought-iron gates that once graced the mansion of Cornelius Vanderbilt II. In contrast to the deliberately rustic effect of the rest of the park, this is a symmetrical, formal garden. The central lawn is bordered by yew hedges and flowering crab apple trees, leading to a reflecting pool flanked by a large wisteria arbor. To the south is a high-hedged flower garden named after Frances Hodgson Burnett, author of the children's classic *The Secret Garden.* To the north is the Untermeyer Fountain, with its three spirited girls dancing at the heart of a huge circular bed where 20,000 tulips bloom in the spring, and 5,000 chrysanthemums in the fall.

Tour 6: The Upper East Side

The Upper East Side epitomizes the high-style, high-society way of life most people associate with the Big Apple. Between 5th and Lexington avenues, up to about 86th Street, is an elegant enclave of wealth. Luxury co-ops and condominiums, exquisite town houses, private schools, posh galleries, and international shops line streets where even the sidewalks seem more sparkling clean than any others in Manhattan. You may find the people who live and work in this neighborhood a bit snobbish compared with other New Yorkers, but take it in stride—they treat everybody that way.

⑫ A fitting place to begin your exploration of the moneyed Upper East Side is that infamous shrine to conspicuous consumption, **Bloomingdale's** (59th St. between Lexington and 3rd Aves., tel. 212/705–2000). This block-long behemoth is noisy, trendy, and crowded; you'll find everything from designer clothes to high-tech teakettles in slick, sophisticated displays. Not one to shrink from the spotlight, Bloomie's has appeared in more than a few Manhattan movies. Diane Keaton and Michael Murphy shared a perfume-counter encounter here in Woody Allen's *Manhattan*; Robin Williams, playing a Russian musician, defected to the West in *Moscow on the Hudson*; and mermaid Darryl Hannah, in *Splash*, took a crash course in human culture in front of a bank of TVs in the electronics department.

Time Out On Bloomingdale's sixth floor, frazzled shoppers can take a break at **Le Train Bleu** restaurant (tel. 212/705–2100), decorated like a snappy railroad car and overlooking the 59th Street Bridge. Besides à la carte snacks, it offers one of the best bargains in town for afternoon tea (3–4:30 PM).

Leaving Bloomingdale's, head west on 60th Street toward 5th Avenue. As you cross Park Avenue, stop for a moment on the wide, neatly planted median strip. Look south toward midtown and you'll see the Met Life Building, which New Yorkers will probably always refer to as the Pan Am Building, since the letters were only changed when that venerable airline went under in 1992. Then turn to look uptown, and you'll see a thoroughfare lined with massive buildings that are more like mansions stacked atop one another than apartment complexes. As you proceed into the Upper East Side, observe the trappings of wealth: well-kept buildings, children in private school uniforms, nannies wheeling grand baby carriages, dog-walkers, limousines, doormen in braided livery. This is the territory where Sherman McCoy, protagonist of Tom Wolfe's *The Bonfire of the Vanities*, lived in pride before his fall, and where the heroine of Woody Allen's movie *Alice* felt suffocated amidst the trappings of wealth.

On the northwest corner of 60th Street and Park Avenue is **Christ Church United Methodist Church** (520 Park Ave., tel. 212/838–3036), built during the Depression but designed to look centuries old, with its random pattern of limestone blocks. Inside, the Byzantine-style sanctuary (open Sundays and holidays) glitters with golden handmade mosaics.

Continue west on 60th Street to pass a grouping of very different kinds of clubs. Ornate grillwork curls over the doorway of the scholarly **Grolier Club** (47 E. 60th St., tel. 212/838–6690), founded in 1884 and named after the 16th-century French bibliophile Jean Grolier. Its members are devoted to the bookmaking crafts; one of them, Bertram Grosvenor Goodhue, designed this neatly proportioned redbrick building in 1917. The club presents public exhibitions and has a specialized reference library open by appointment only. On the next block over, at 10 East 60th Street, a red canopy shelters the entrance to the **Copacabana** (tel. 212/755–6010), the once swanky nightclub; in a memorable scene in the movie *Goodfellas*, mobster Henry Hill wows a new girlfriend by nonchalantly slipping in from the back door to swing a front-row table here. From the time it opened in 1940 until well into the 1950s, the Copa was one of Manhattan's most glamorous night spots, featuring such performers as Ella Fitzgerald, Sid Caesar, Frank Sinatra, Tony Bennett, Sammy Davis, Jr., Nat King Cole, Jimmy Durante, and Lena Horne. The club closed in 1973, although it has since had various comebacks, currently keeping a low profile as a disco and group-function space. Right next door is the **Harmonie Club** (4 E. 60th St.), one of several private men's clubs (many of which now admit women) in this area. Built in 1905 by McKim, Mead & White, this pseudo-Renaissance palace, awkwardly stretched to high-rise proportions, is closely guarded by a doorman, so it's best to admire it from afar. Across the street is the **Metropolitan Club** (1 E. 60th St.), an even more lordly neoclassical edifice built in 1893, also by McKim, Mead & White. J. P. Morgan established this club when a friend of his was refused membership in the Union League Club; its members today include rulers of foreign countries and presidents of major corporations.

Take a right at 5th Avenue. On the next block you'll pass **The Pierre** (*see* Chapter 10), a hotel that opened in 1930; notice its lovely mansard roof and tower. As you cross 62nd Street, take a look at the brick-and-limestone mansion at 2 East 62nd, the home of the **Knickerbocker Club,** a private social club founded in 1871. Across the street is the **Fifth Avenue Synagogue** (5 E. 62nd St., tel. 212/838–2122), a limestone temple built in 1959. Its pointed oval windows are filled with stained glass in striking abstract designs. You may want to detour down this elegant block of town houses; take special note of No. 11, which has elaborate Corinthian pilasters and an impressive wrought-iron entryway.

13 Continue up 5th Avenue to 65th Street, where you'll see **Temple Emanu-El,** the world's largest Reform Jewish synagogue (it has seats for 2,500 worshipers). Built in 1929 of limestone, it is covered with mosaics and designed in the Romanesque style with Byzantine influences; the building features Moorish and Art Deco ornamentation. *Tel. 212/744–1400. Services Fri. 5 PM, Sat. 10:30 AM. Weekday services Sun.–Thurs. 5:30 PM held around corner at community house, 1 E. 65th St. Guided group tours of synagogue by appointment.*

Head east on 66th Street, past the site of the house (3 E. 66th St.) where Ulysses S. Grant spent his final months, before moving permanently up to Grant's Tomb (*see* Tour 9). (If you are interested in presidential homes, you may want to detour over to 65th Street between Madison and Park avenues to Nos. 45 and 47 East 65th Street, a pair of town houses built in 1910 for Sara Delano Roosevelt and her son, Franklin; FDR once lay recovering from polio at No. 47.) Next door, at 5 East 66th Street, is the **Lotos Club,** a private club founded in 1870. Its current home is a handsomely ornate French Renaissance mansion originally designed as a private residence by Richard Howland Hunt.

Continue east to Park Avenue. Railroad tracks once ran down the middle of Park Avenue; they were covered with a roadway just after World War I, and the grand sweeping street that resulted became a distinguished residential address. The red Victorian castle-fortress at 66th Street and Park Avenue is the **Seventh Regiment Armory** (643 Park Ave.). This huge structure is no longer used as a military headquarters, but it has plenty of meeting and social space, which is used for a tennis arena, a restaurant, a shelter for homeless people, and an exhibit hall that hosts, among other events, two posh annual antiques shows. Both Louis Comfort Tiffany and Stanford White helped design its surprisingly residential interior; go up the front stairs into the wood-paneled lobby and take a look around. Tours are available by appointment (tel. 212/744–2968).

On the west side of Park Avenue, a pair of grand mansions face each other across 68th Street. Though houses have generally been replaced by apartment buildings along Park Avenue, these survivors give you an idea of how the neighborhood once looked. The grandly simple silvery limestone palace on the southwest corner, built in 1920, now houses the prestigious **Council on Foreign Relations** (58 E. 68th St.). The dark-red brick town house on the northwest corner was built in 1909–1911 by McKim, Mead & White for Percy Pyne, the grandson of noted financier Moses Taylor. From 1948 to 1963, this mansion was the Soviet Mission to the United Nations; when the Russians moved out, developers wanted to raze the town house, but in 1965 the marquesa de Cuevas acquired the property and presented it to the Center for Inter-American Relations. Now called the **Americas Society,** it has an art gallery that's open to the public. *680 Park Ave., tel. 212/249–8950. Suggested contribution: $3. Open Tues.–Sun. noon–6.*

Note how the three houses to the north—built during the following decade, and designed by three different architects—carried on the Pyne mansion's Georgian design to create a unified block. Today these buildings hold the **Spanish Institute** (684 Park Ave.), the **Instituto Italiano di Cultura** (Italian Cultural Institute, 686 Park Ave.), and the **Italian Consulate** (690 Park Ave.).

Two blocks north, on the east side of Park Avenue, is the **Asia Society,** a museum and educational center in an eight-story red granite building in striking contrast to the older, more traditional architecture of the street. While this is the headquarters of a nonprofit educational society, not technically a museum, it does offer public exhibitions of Asian art, including South Asian stone and bronze sculptures; art from India, Nepal, Pakistan, and Afghanistan; bronze vessels, ceramics, sculpture, and paintings from China; Korean ceramics; and paintings, wood sculptures, and ceramics from Japan. *725 Park Ave. at 70th St., tel. 212/288-6400. Admission: $2 adults, $1 students and senior citizens; free Fri. 6–8. Open Tues.– Thurs. and Sat. 11–6, Fri. 11–8, Sun. noon–5.*

At this point, shoppers may want to double back to Madison Avenue and get down to shopping business (*see* Chapter 8). The catchphrase "Madison Avenue" no longer refers to the midtown advertising district (most major agencies have moved away from there anyway) but instead to Uptown's fashion district: Madison Mile, between 59th and 79th streets, an exclusive area of haute couture designer boutiques, patrician art galleries, and unique specialty stores. For the most part, these shops are small, intimate, expensive—and almost invariably closed on Sunday. Even if you're just window-shopping, it's fun to step inside the tony digs of **Ralph Lauren** (867 Madison Ave. at 72nd St., tel. 212/606–2100), which hardly seems like a store at all. In fact, it's in the landmark Rhinelander Mansion and has preserved the grand house's walnut fittings, oriental carpets, and family portraits as an aristocratic setting in which to display high-style preppy clothing (it's draped about casually, as though waiting to be put away). Be sure to visit the fourth-floor home-furnishings section, where merchandise is arrayed in to-the-manor-born dream suites.

At Madison Avenue and 76th Street is the **Carlyle Hotel,** one of the city's most elite and discreet properties (*see* Chapter 10). In the early 1960s President John F. Kennedy frequently stayed here; rumor has it that he entertained Marilyn Monroe in his rooms when Mrs. Kennedy was not around. The hotel's current roster of rich-and-famous guests includes Elizabeth Taylor, George C. Scott, Steve Martin, Paul Newman, and Warren Beatty and Annette Bening.

West of Madison is the so-called **Gucci Town House** (16 E. 76th St.), the former Gucci family mansion, which in 1988 sold for $7 million, at the time the most ever paid for a New York town house.

The final leg of this tour is several blocks away, so walk up Lexington or 3rd avenues, where there are plenty of shops and restaurants at street level to entertain you. This is the part of the East Side where more ordinary mortals can manage to live.

Time Out Among the many restaurants clustered along 3rd Avenue in the 70s and 80s, one of the least pretentious is **Luke's Bar and Grill** (1394 3rd Ave., between 79th and 80th Sts., tel. 212/249–7070), with its friendly staff, cozy wood paneling, and red-checkered tablecloths. Reasonably priced burgers, salads, sandwiches, and pasta fill the lunch menu.

As you get closer to 86th Street, the neighborhood becomes more modest and ethnic. Until the 1830s, when the New York & Harlem Railroad and a stagecoach line began racing through the area, this neighborhood was the quiet, remote hamlet of **Yorkville,** a predominantly German community. Over the years it has also welcomed waves of immigrants from Austria, Hungary, and Czechoslovakia, and local shops and restaurants still bear reminders of this European heritage.

 On 86th at East End Avenue, the **Henderson Place Historic District** includes 24 small-scale town houses built in the 1880s in the Queen

Anne style, which was developed in England by Richard Norman Shaw. Designed to be comfortable yet romantic dwellings, they combine elements of the Elizabethan manor house with classic Flemish details. Note, especially, the lovely bay windows, the turrets marking the corner of each block, and the symmetrical roof gables, pediments, parapets, chimneys, and dormer windows.

⑲ When you reach East End Avenue, you'll be facing **Carl Schurz Park,** overlooking the East River. Stand by the railings and look out at the Triborough and Hell's Gate bridges, Ward's and Randall's islands, and, on the other side of the river, Astoria, Queens. During the American Revolution, a house on this promontory was used as a fortification by the Continental army, then was taken over as a British outpost. In more peaceful times, the land became known as East End Park. It was renamed in 1911 to honor Carl Schurz (1829–1906), a famous 19th-century German immigrant who eventually served the United States as a minister to Spain, a major general in the Union Army, and a senator of Missouri. During the Hayes administration, Schurz was Secretary of the Interior; he later moved back to Yorkville and worked as editor of the *New York Evening Post* and *Harper's Weekly.*

⑳ Stroll up Carl Schurz Park to reach one of the city's most famous residences, **Gracie Mansion,** the official home of the mayor of New York. Surrounded by a small lawn and flowerbeds, this Federal-style yellow frame house still feels like a country manor house, which is what it was built as in 1779 by wealthy merchant Archibald Gracie. The Gracie family entertained many notable guests at the mansion, including Louis Philippe (later king of France), President John Quincy Adams, the marquis de Lafayette, Alexander Hamilton, James Fenimore Cooper, Washington Irving, and John Jacob Astor. The city purchased Gracie Mansion in 1887, and, after a period of use as the Museum of the City of New York (now at 5th Ave. and 103rd St.—*see* Tour 5, *above*), Mayor Fiorello H. La Guardia made it the official mayor's residence. *Admission: $3 adults, $2 senior citizens. Guided tours mid-Mar.–mid-Nov., Wed. at 10, 11, 1, and 2, by reservation only. Tel. 212/570–4751.*

Tour 7: Central Park

Numbers in the margin correspond to points of interest on the Tour 7: Central Park map.

It's amazing that 843 acres of the world's most valuable real estate should be set aside as a park, yet the city's 1856 decision to do so has proved to be marvelous wisdom, for Central Park contributes mightily toward helping New Yorkers maintain their sanity. It provides space large enough to get lost in (the entire principality of Monaco would fit within its borders), space where you can escape from the rumble of traffic to hear a bird sing or watch an earthworm tumble through the soil.

Although it appears to be simply a swath of rolling countryside exempted from urban development, Central Park is in fact one of the most cunningly planned artificial landscapes ever built. When they began in 1858, designers Frederick Law Olmsted and Calvert Vaux were presented with a swampy neighborhood of a few farms, houses, and a church. It took them 16 years, $14 million, and 5 million cubic yards of moved earth to create this playground of lush lawns, thick forests, and quiet ponds. Hills and tunnels artfully conceal transverse roads (65th, 79th, 86th, and 97th streets) so crosstown traffic will not disturb park goers, and a meandering circular drive carries vehicular traffic in the park (the drive is closed to auto traffic on weekends year-round).

Today Central Park hosts just about any activity that a city dweller might engage in outdoors: jogging, cycling, horseback riding, softball, ice skating, roller skating, croquet, tennis, bird-watching, boating, chess, checkers, theater, concerts, skateboarding, and folk dancing. If you're traveling with children, you'll especially appreciate how much there is to do and see. Try to come on a weekend, when local residents gratefully flock here to play—free entertainment is on tap, and the entire social microcosm is on parade.

Weekend crowds also make it safe to go into virtually any area of the park, although even on weekdays you should be safe anywhere along this tour. Despite its bad reputation, Central Park has the lowest crime rate of any precinct in the city—though the spectacularly ugly and frightening attack on a jogger in 1989 has reminded New Yorkers that the wisest course is to stay out of it at night (unless you are attending a free concert along with thousands of others).

Our route covers a lot of territory, but Olmsted and Vaux scattered their attractions so generously that there's something to see or do at almost every turn. One caveat, however: Although there are cafés connected with several attractions, as well as food stands near many entrances, the range of food is limited and predictable. Do as most New Yorkers do and stop beforehand at a deli or gourmet food shop for a picnic to carry in with you. *Tel. 212/794–6565 for general information, 212/794–6564 for a recorded message on city park events, 212/427–4040 for information on weekend walks and talks led by Urban Park Rangers.*

At Grand Army Plaza, or most intersections of Central Park South (59th Street's name between 5th and 8th avenues), you can hire a ride in a horse-drawn carriage through the park. Carriages operate all year, except in extremely hot or cold weather, and blankets are provided when it's cool. The official rates are $34 for the first 30 minutes and $10 for each additional 15 minutes, although drivers may try to get more, so agree on a price in advance. By the way: You can charge the ride to an American Express card.

To explore the park on foot, begin at Grand Army Plaza. Enter the park along the main road (East Drive), turning down the first path ❶ to your left to the **Pond.** Walk along the shore to the Gapstow Bridge (each of the park's 30 bridges has its own name and individual design), where you can look back at the often-photographed view of midtown skyscrapers reflected in the pond. From left to right, you'll see the peak-roofed brown Sherry-Netherland hotel, the black-and-white General Motors building, the rose-colored "Chippendale" top of the AT&T building, the black glass shaft of Trump Tower, and in front the green gables of the white Plaza Hotel.

❷ Return to the main path and continue north to **Wollman Memorial Rink,** a skating rink that was once a symbol of municipal inefficiency to New Yorkers. Fruitless and costly attempts by the city to repair the deteriorated facility had kept it closed for years, until real-estate mogul Donald Trump adopted the project and quickly completed it. Even if you don't want to join in, you can stand on the terrace here to watch the skaters—ice-skating throughout the winter, roller-blading and playing miniature golf April through October. The blaring loudspeaker system in this otherwise quiet park makes the rink hard to ignore. *Tel. 212/517–4800. Admission: $6.15 adults, $3.25 children under 13. Skate rental: $3.25. Open daily 10–9:30.*

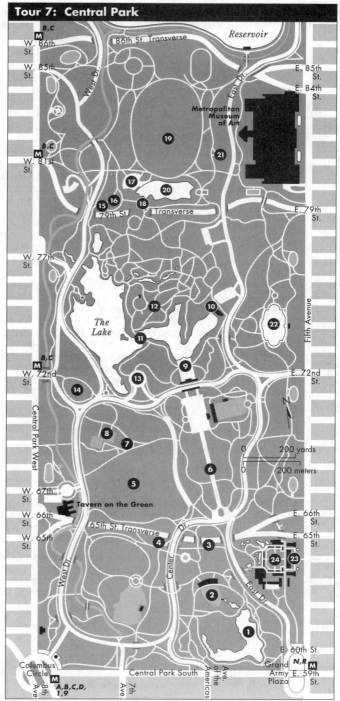

Tour 7: Central Park

From April through October part of the rink becomes the **Gotham Miniature Golf** course, where putters maneuver around scale models of various city landmarks. *Tel. 212/517–4800. Admission: $6.50 adults, $3.50 children under 13. Open Mon. 10–5, Tues.–Thurs. 10–9:30, Fri. and Sat. 10 AM–11 PM, Sun. 10–9:30.*

Turn your back to the rink and you'll see the painted, pointed eaves, steeple, and high-pitched slate roof of the **Dairy**, originally an actual dairy built in the 19th century when cows grazed here. Today it's the park's visitor center, offering maps, souvenirs, videos, children's programs, and some very interesting hands-on exhibits. *Tel. 212/794–6565. Open Tues.–Sun. 11–4, Fri. 1–4.*

As you leave the Dairy, follow the path to your right (west) and under the Playmates Arch—aptly named, because it leads to a large area of ballfields and playgrounds. Coming through the arch, you'll hear the jaunty music of the **Carousel**. Although this isn't the park's original one, it was built in 1908 and later moved here from Coney Island. Its 58 ornately hand-carved steeds are three-quarters the size of real horses, and the organ plays a variety of tunes, new and old. *Tel. 212/879–0244. Admission: 90¢. Open summer, weekdays 10:30–5:30, weekends 10:30–6:30; winter, weekends only 10:30–4:30, weather permitting.*

Climb the slope to the left of the Playmates Arch and walk beside the Center Drive. From here you can choose between two parallel routes: Turn left onto the paved path that runs alongside the chain-link fence of the **Sheep Meadow**, or go all the way to the circular garden at the foot of the **Mall**. The broad formal walkway of the Mall called **"The Literary Walk"** is a peaceful spot, lined with the largest group of American elms in the Northeast and statues of famous men, including Shakespeare, Robert Burns, and Sir Walter Scott. The other path, however, buzzes on weekends with human activity: volleyball games, roller-skating, impromptu music fests. Watch out for speeding in-line skaters. By contrast, the 15 grassy acres of the Sheep Meadow make an ideal spot for picnicking or sunbathing. It's an officially designated quiet zone, where the most vigorous sports allowed are kite-flying and Frisbee-tossing. This lawn was actually used for grazing sheep until 1934; the nearby sheepfold was turned into the Tavern on the Green restaurant (*see* Tour 8, *below*).

The gravel path that borders the Sheep Meadow on the north is heady with the scent of lilacs in spring; it leads to the **Mineral Springs Pavilion**, where there's a snack bar. Behind it are the beautifully manicured **Croquet Grounds** and **Lawn Bowling Greens**. During the season (May–November), you can peer through gaps in the high hedges to watch the players, usually dressed in crisp white. To play, you must have a season permit (tel. 212/360–8133).

The 72nd Street transverse—the only crosstown street that connects with the East, Center, and West drives—cuts across the park just north of here, but you can cross it or pass beneath it through a lovely tiled arcade to reach **Bethesda Fountain**, set on an elaborately patterned paved terrace on the edge of the **Lake** and featured in the film *Home Alone 2*. This ornate, three-tiered fountain is named after the biblical Bethesda pool in Jerusalem, which was supposedly given healing powers by an angel (hence the angel rising from the center). Perch on the low terrace wall or the edge of the fountain and watch the rowboaters stroke past on the lake. If you want to get out on the water yourself, take the path east from the terrace to **Loeb Boathouse**, where in season you can rent a rowboat. The boathouse also operates a bike-rental facility and a better-than-average restaurant, where the characters in the movie *Three Men and a Little Lady* dined. *Boat rental $10 per hr, $20 deposit; tel. 212/517–4723. Bicycle rental $6 per hr, tandems $12 per hr; tel. 212/861–4137. Open May–Oct., daily 11–6.*

11 The path to the west of the terrace leads to **Bow Bridge,** a splendid cast-iron bridge arching over a neck of the lake. The view from either side is postcard-perfect, with the water reflecting a quintessentially New York image of vintage apartment buildings peeping above the treetops. If you continue across the bridge, you'll enter
12 the **Ramble,** a heavily wooded 37-acre area laced with twisting, climbing paths. This is prime bird-watching territory; a rest stop along a major migratory route, it shelters many of the 269 species of birds that have been sighted in the park. Because it is so dense and isolated, however, it may not be a good place to wander alone.

If you don't venture into the Ramble, recross Bow Bridge and con-
13 tinue west on the lakeside path to **Cherry Hill,** where a circular plaza sets off a wrought-iron-and-gilt fountain that is smaller, but no less lovely, than Bethesda Fountain. This area was originally a carriage turnaround and watering area for horses. The path ahead leads back to the 72nd Street transverse; on the rocky outcrop directly across the road, you'll see a statue of a falconer gracefully lofting his bird. Turn to the right and you'll see a more prosaic statue, a pompous bronze figure of Daniel Webster with his hand thrust into his coat. Cross the drive behind Webster, being careful to watch for bikes hurtling around the curve.

14 You've now come to **Strawberry Fields,** the "international peace garden" memorializing John Lennon. Climbing up a hill, its curving paths, shrubs, trees, and flower beds create a deliberately informal pastoral landscape, reminiscent of the English parks Lennon may have been thinking of when he wrote the Beatles song "Strawberry Fields Forever" in 1967. A black-and-white mosaic set into one of the sidewalks contains simply the word "Imagine," another Lennon song title. Just beyond the trees, at 72nd Street and Central Park West, is the Dakota (*see* Tour 8, *below*), where Lennon and his wife, Yoko Ono, lived at the time of his death in 1980.

Cross the road at the top of Strawberry Fields' hill, turn right through a rustic wood arbor thickly hung with wisteria vines, then head back on the path down the hill and follow the West Drive north (cross the drive as soon as possible so you can walk along the lake). Shortly past the lake, you'll see on your right a dark-wood chalet that looks like something straight out of Germany's Black Forest.
15 This is the **Swedish Cottage,** where marionette shows are staged. *Tel. 212/988–9093. Shows Sat. noon and 3, call for reservations.*

16 Turn right and walk past the cottage to the **Shakespeare Garden,** one of the park's few formal flower plantings, tucked onto terraces on the side of a relatively steep hill. In the garden, you'll find plants that William Shakespeare mentioned in his writings. The open-air
17 **Delacorte Theater,** where the Joseph Papp Shakespeare Theater Company performs each summer (*see* Chapter 11), is just around the corner. But for the best view of the Delacorte, head for the top of the hill, aptly called **Vista Rock.**

18 Vista Rock is dominated by **Belvedere Castle,** built in 1872 of the same gray Manhattan schist that thrusts out of the soil in dramatic outcrops throughout the park. If you step through the pavilion out onto the lip of the rock, you can examine some of this schist, polished and striated by Ice Age glaciers. From here you can look down di-
19 rectly upon the stage of the Delacorte; you can also see the **Great**

Lawn stretching beyond, a series of softball fields that hum with action on weekends and most summer evenings. In summer, should you see a few hundred people picnicking in a row around the oval edge of the lawn, you'll know they're waiting to pick up free tickets to a Shakespeare performance at the Delacorte.

The castle itself, a typically 19th-century mishmash of styles—Norman, Gothic, Moorish—was deliberately kept small so that when it was viewed from across the lake, the lake would seem bigger. (The Ramble's forest now obscures the lake's castle view.) Since 1919 it has been a measurement station of the U.S. Weather Bureau; look up to see the twirling meteorological instruments atop the tower. Climb out onto its balconies for a dramatic view, or get a minilesson in geology from the exhibits within. If you've got children with you, visit the ground-floor learning center. *Tel. 212/772–0210. Admission free. Open mid-Feb.–mid-Oct., Tues.–Thurs. and weekends 11–5, Fri. 1–5; winter hours (mid-Oct.–mid-Feb.), closes at 4 PM.*

20 From the castle's plaza, follow the downhill path east along **Turtle Pond,** populated by fish, ducks, and dragonflies, as well as turtles. At the east end of the pond you'll pass a statue of King Jagiello of Poland; groups gather here for folk-dancing on weekends. Follow
21 the path north to nearby **Cleopatra's Needle,** a pollution-worn obelisk covered with hieroglyphics; it was a gift to the city in 1881 from the khedive of Egypt. The copper crabs supporting the huge stone at each corner almost seem squashed by its weight. If you look just past the trees, you can see the glass-enclosed wing of the Metropolitan Museum (*see* Tour 5, *above*) that holds the Egyptian Temple of Dendur.

Vigorous walkers may want to continue north to the **Reservoir,** popular with New Yorkers for the running track that surrounds it, and, in springtime, for its fragrant flowering trees. The city's main reservoirs are upstate; this one is more or less a holding tank.

Others can return south from Cleopatra's Needle, following the path to the left under Greywacke Arch, which leads around the back corner of the Metropolitan Museum. This side of the park, perhaps in keeping with its proximity to the East Side, has a tamer landscape than the west side, and here you'll see more uniformed nannies and fussy little dogs on leashes. A few minutes' walk will take you to one of the park's most formal areas: the symmetrical stone basin of the
22 **Conservatory Water,** where you can watch some very sophisticated model boats being raced each Saturday morning at 10. (Unfortunately, model boats are not for rent here.) At the north end of the pond is one of the park's most beloved statues, José de Creeft's 1960 bronze sculpture of **Alice in Wonderland,** sitting on a giant mushroom with the Mad Hatter, White Rabbit, and leering Cheshire Cat in attendance. Children are encouraged to clamber all over it. On the west side of the pond, a bronze statue of **Hans Christian Andersen,** the Ugly Duckling at his feet, is the site of storytelling hours on summer weekends.

Climb the hill at the far end of the Conservatory Water, cross the 72nd Street transverse, and follow the path south to the Children's Zoo, oft-threatened by city budget cuts and currently closed pending reconstruction. Pass under the Denesmouth Arch to the **Delacorte Clock,** a delightful glockenspiel set above a redbrick arch. Every hour its six-animal band circles around and plays a tune while monkeys on the top hammer their bells. A path to the left will take
23 you around to the front entrance of the **Arsenal,** the Parks Department's headquarters, occupying what was a pre–Civil War arsenal.

Since the city acquired it in 1857, it has served as, among other things, the first home of the American Museum of Natural History, now on Central Park West at 79th Street (*see* Tour 8, *below*). The downstairs lobby has some WPA-era great murals; an upstairs gallery features changing exhibitions, often of great interest to kids. *Tel. 212/360–8163. Open weekdays 9:30–4:30.*

㉔ Just past the clock is the **Central Park Zoo,** recently renamed the **Central Park Wildlife Conservation Center,** a small but delightful menagerie. Clustered around the central Sea Lion Pool are separate exhibits for each of the earth's major environments; the Polar Circle features a huge penguin tank and polar-bear floe; the open-air Temperate Territory is highlighted by a pit of chattering monkeys; and the Tropic Zone contains the flora and fauna of a miniature rain forest. This is a good zoo for children and adults who like to take time to watch the animals; even a leisurely visit will take only about an hour, for there are only about 100 species on display. Go to the Bronx Zoo (*see* Chapter 4) if you need tigers, giraffes, and elephants—the biggest specimens here are the polar bears. *Tel. 212/439–6500. Admission: $2.50 adults, $1.25 senior citizens, 50¢ children 3–12. No children under 16 allowed in without adult. Open Apr.–Oct., Mon. and Wed.–Fri. 10–4:30, Tues. 10–7, weekends and holidays 10–5; Nov.–Mar., daily 10–4.*

Tour 8: The Upper West Side

Numbers in the margin correspond to points of interest on the Tours 8 and 9: Upper West Side, Columbia map.

The Upper West Side has never been as fashionable as the East Side, despite the fact that it has a similar mix of real estate—large apartment buildings along Central Park West, West End Avenue, and Riverside Drive, and town houses on the shady, quiet cross streets. Once a haven for the Jewish intelligentsia, by the 1960s the West Side had become a rather grungy multiethnic community. In the 1970s gentrification began slowly, with actors, writers, and gays as the earliest settlers. Today, however, this area is quite desirable, with lots of restored brownstones and high-priced co-op apartments. Young families have gravitated to its large apartments, young professionals to its smaller ones. On weekends, the sidewalks are crowded with couples pushing babies around in their imported strollers, giving way in the evenings to something resembling a singles scene, as ever more restaurants and bars open. Columbus Avenue is one such boutique-and-restaurant strip; Amsterdam Avenue is slowly following suit, its shopfronts a mix of bodegas and boutiques. Along upper Broadway, new luxury apartment towers are slowly blocking in the horizon. Many longtime West Siders decry the "yuppification" of their neighborhoods, but the good news is that small businesses now thrive on blocks that a few years ago were not safe to walk on.

❶ The West Side story begins at **Columbus Circle,** where a statue of Christopher himself crowns a stately pillar at the intersection of Broadway, 8th Avenue, Central Park West, and Central Park South. Columbus Circle is a good place to begin any tour of New York, for it is the headquarters of the **New York Convention and Visitors Bureau,** located in a weird pseudo-Byzantine structure, ostensibly modeled after the Doge's Palace in Venice but locally nicknamed the Lollipop Building. Count on the bureau for brochures; bus and subway maps; hotel, restaurant, and shopping guides; a seasonal calendar of events; free TV-show tickets (sometimes) and discounts

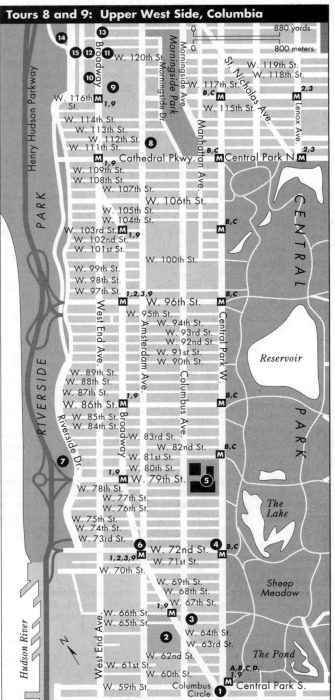

American
Museum of
Natural History
and Hayden
Planetarium, **5**

Barnard
College, **10**

Cathedral of St.
John the
Divine, **8**

Columbia
University, **9**

Columbus
Circle, **1**

The Dakota, **4**

Grant's
Tomb, **14**

Jewish
Theological
Seminary, **13**

Lincoln
Center, **2**

Museum of
American Folk
Art, **3**

Riverside
Church, **15**

Riverside
Park, **7**

Teachers
College, **11**

Union
Theological
Seminary, **12**

Verdi Square, **6**

on Broadway theater; and sound advice. *2 Columbus Circle, tel. 212/ 397–8222. Open weekdays 9–6, weekends 10–6.*

On the southwest quadrant of the circle, the **New York Coliseum,** a blank functional-looking white brick building, was the city's chief convention and trade-show venue before the opening of the Jacob Javits Center. A soaring multiuse complex proposed for the site was bitterly opposed by New Yorkers determined not to let its huge shadow be cast across Central Park; the site continues to be embroiled in suits and countersuits. On the northeast corner of the circle, an entrance to Central Park is presided over by the Maine Monument, with its florid bronze figures atop a stocky limestone pedestal. The pie-shape wedge of land between Central Park West and Broadway holds the **Paramount Communications Building,** headquarters of a media empire. The box office of the subterranean Paramount movie theater juts above the ground on the Broadway side of the plaza.

At the world headquarters of the **American Bible Society** (1865 Broadway at 61st St., tel. 212/408–1200), ascend red-carpeted stairs to a little-known second-floor library (open weekdays 9–4:30), which displays, among other things, Helen Keller's massive 10-volume braille Bible, a replica of the original Gutenberg press, and a Torah (Jewish scriptures) from China.

When you pass **The Ballet Shop** (1887 Broadway, between 61st and 62nd Sts.), a mecca for balletomanes searching for books, prints, and recordings, you'll know you're getting close to New York's major site for the performing arts: **Lincoln Center,** covering an eight-block area west of Broadway between 62nd and 66th streets. This unified complex of pale travertine marble was built during the 1960s to supplant an urban ghetto (*West Side Story* was filmed on the slum's gritty, deserted streets just before the demolition crews moved in). Lincoln Center can seat nearly 18,000 spectators at one time in its various halls (*see* Chapter 11).

Stand on Broadway, facing the central court with its huge fountain. The three concert halls on this plaza clearly relate to one another architecturally, with their symmetrical bilevel facades, yet each has slightly different lines and different details. To your left, huge honeycomb lights hang on the portico of the **New York State Theater,** home to the New York City Ballet and the New York City Opera. Straight ahead, at the rear of the plaza, is the **Metropolitan Opera House,** its brilliant-colored Chagall tapestries visible through the arched lobby windows; the Metropolitan Opera and American Ballet Theatre perform here. To your right, abstract bronze sculptures distinguish **Avery Fisher Hall,** host to the New York Philharmonic Orchestra.

Wander through the plaza, then angle to your left between the New York State Theater and the Metropolitan Opera House into **Damrosch Park,** where summer open-air festivals are often accompanied by free concerts at the **Guggenheim Bandshell.** Angle to your right from the plaza, between the Metropolitan and Avery Fisher, and you'll come to the North Plaza, with a massive Henry Moore sculpture reclining in a reflecting pool. To the rear is the **Library and Museum of the Performing Arts,** a branch of the New York Public Library with an extensive collection of books, records, and scores on music, theater, and dance; visitors can listen to any of 50,000 records and tapes, or check out its four galleries. Next to the library is the wide glass-walled lobby of the **Vivian Beaumont Theater,** officially considered a Broadway house although it is far removed from the theater district. Below it is the smaller **Mitzi E. Newhouse Theater,** where many award-winning plays have originated.

An overpass leads from this plaza across 65th Street to the world-renowned **Juilliard School** (for music and theater). Check here to see if there's a concert or a play going on; actors Kevin Kline and Patti LuPone once performed here. Turn right for an elevator down to street level and **Alice Tully Hall,** home of the Chamber Music Society of Lincoln Center and the New York Film Festival. Or turn left from the overpass and follow the walkway west to Lincoln Center's newest arts venue, the **Walter Reade Theater,** opened in the fall of 1991, showing several unusual American and foreign films a day, seven days a week (*see* Chapter 11).

Visitors can wander freely through the lobbies of all these buildings. A one-hour guided "Introduction to Lincoln Center" tour covers the center's history and wealth of artworks and usually visits the three principal theaters, performance schedules permitting. *Tel. 212/875–5350 for schedule and reservations. Admission: $7.75 adults, $6.75 students and senior citizens, $4.50 children 6–12.*

Conveniently close to Lincoln Center, at the northwest corner of Broadway and 66th Street, is **Tower Records,** the uptown branch of that vast emporium of tapes and CDs—and, less than a block north, **Tower Video,** a haven of videotapes and laser discs.

❸ Across the busy intersection, the **Museum of American Folk Art** has found a new home at Columbus Avenue and 66th Street. Its collection includes naïve paintings, quilts, carvings, dolls, trade signs, painted wood carousel horses, and a giant Indian-chief copper weathervane. *2 Lincoln Sq., tel. 212/977–7298. Suggested contribution: $2. Open Tues.–Sun. 11:30–7:30.*

Around the corner on 66th Street is the headquarters of the ABC television network; ABC owns several buildings along Columbus Avenue as well, including some studios where news shows and soap operas are filmed, so keep an eye out for your favorite daytime doctors, tycoons, and temptresses.

Turn onto West 67th Street and head toward Central Park along one of the city's most handsome blocks. Many of the apartment buildings here were designed as "studio buildings," with immense windows that make them ideal for artists; look up at the facades and imagine the high-ceilinged spaces within. Also notice the Gothic motifs, carved in white stone or wrought in iron, that decorate several of these buildings at street level. Perhaps the finest apartment building on the block is the **Hotel des Artistes** (1 W. 67th St.), built in 1918, with its elaborate mock-Elizabethan lobby. Its tenants have included Isadora Duncan, Rudolph Valentino, Norman Rockwell, Noël Coward, Fannie Hurst, and contemporary actors Joel Grey and Richard Thomas and artist Leroy Neiman; another tenant, Howard Chandler Christy, designed the lush, soft-toned murals in the excellent ground-floor restaurant, **Café des Artistes** (*see* Chapter 9), where Louis Malle's *My Dinner with André* was filmed.

Another dining landmark is just inside Central Park at 66th Street, **Tavern on the Green** (*see* Chapter 9). Originally built as a sheepfold, in the days when sheep grazed on the meadows of the park, it was converted into a restaurant in the 1930s. True, the high tone is not what it once was, but many of its dining rooms have fine park views; at night white lights strung through the surrounding trees create a magical effect.

Movie buffs may want to detour down to 65th Street, where you'll find the Art Deco building that was supposedly "Spook Central" in the movie *Ghostbusters* (55 Central Park West).

Continue up Central Park West to 72nd Street, where the stately ● **Dakota** presides over the northwest corner. Its tenants have included Boris Karloff, Judy Holliday, José Ferrer and Rosemary Clooney, Lauren Bacall, Rex Reed, and Gilda Radner. Resembling a buff-colored castle, with copper turrets, its slightly spooky appearance was played up in the movie *Rosemary's Baby*, which was filmed here. Stop by the gate on 72nd Street; this is the spot where, in December 1980, a deranged fan shot John Lennon as he came home from a recording session. Lennon is memorialized in Central Park's Strawberry Fields, across the street (*see* Tour 7, *above*).

Proceed up Central Park West and you'll see several other famous apartment buildings, including **The Langham** (135 Central Park West), where Mia Farrow's apartment was featured in Woody Allen's film *Hannah and Her Sisters;* the twin-towered **San Remo** (145–146 Central Park West), over the years home to Rita Hayworth, Dustin Hoffman, Raquel Welch, Paul Simon, Tony Randall, and Diane Keaton—but not to Madonna, whose application was rejected because of her flamboyant lifestyle; and **The Kenilworth** (151 Central Park), with its immense pair of ornate front columns, once home to Basil Rathbone, film's quintessential Sherlock Holmes.

● The **American Museum of Natural History,** the attached **Hayden Planetarium,** and their surrounding grounds occupy a four-block tract bounded by Central Park West, Columbus Avenue, and 77th and 81st streets. As you approach at 77th Street, you can see the original architecture in the pink granite corner towers, with their beehive crowns. A more classical facade was added along Central Park West, with its centerpiece an enormous equestrian statue of President Theodore Roosevelt, naturalist and explorer.

With a collection of more than 30 million artifacts, the museum displays something for every taste, from a 94-foot blue whale to the 563-carat Star of India sapphire. Among the most enduringly popular exhibits are the wondrously detailed dioramas of animal habitat groups, on the first and second floors just behind the rotunda, and the fourth-floor halls full of dinosaur skeletons. A five-story-tall cast of *Barosaurus* rears on its hind legs in the Roosevelt Rotunda, protecting its fossilized baby from a fossil allosaur. The Hall of Human Biology and Evolution, which opened in April 1993, investigates the workings of the human body and features a computerized archaeological dig and an electronic newspaper about human evolution. The Naturemax Theater projects films on a giant screen; the Hayden Planetarium (on 81st Street) has two stories of exhibits, plus several different Sky Shows projected on 22 wraparound screens; its rock-music laser shows draw crowds of teenagers on Friday and Saturday nights. *Museum: tel. 212/769–5100. Suggested contribution: $5 adults, $2.50 children. Open Sun.–Thurs. 10–5:45; Fri.–Sat. 10– 8:45. Planetarium: tel. 212/769–5920. Admission: $5 adults, $3.75 senior citizens and students; $2.50 children 2–12; $7 for laser show. Open weekdays 12:30–4:45, Sat. 10–5:45, Sun. noon–5:45. Naturemax Theater film admission: $5 adults, $3.75 senior citizens and students, $2.50 children. Call 212/769–5650 for show times.*

Directly behind the museum is Columbus Avenue, where shoppers may want to forsake this tour for boutique-shopping. If you do, work your way up one side of the street and back down the other, going north to 86th Street and south to 67th Street (*see* Chapter 8).

Time Out For a delicious lunch of pizza or pasta, stop by **Presto's** (434 Amsterdam Ave. at 81st St., tel. 212/721–9141), a casual neighborhood restaurant where kids are welcome. Or try the homey, brick-walled **Phoebe's** (380 Columbus Ave. near 78th St., tel. 212/724–5145), which serves unpretentious American fare, such as chicken pot pie, in a country-style ambience.

Return to Broadway to join New Yorkers in a pilgrimage to some of the city's greatest food shrines, all on the west side of the street. **Zabar's** (between 80th and 81st Sts.) offers exquisite delicatessen items, prepared foods, gourmet groceries, coffee, and cheeses; a mezzanine level features cookware, dishes, and small appliances. Be prepared to muscle a lot of pushy strangers for elbow room, for Zabar's prides itself on carrying a vast range of hard-to-get foods, and at prices that are reasonable. **H & H Bagels** (at 80th St., southwest corner) sells several varieties of huge, chewy bagels hot from the oven, along with juices, cream cheese, and lox (but they will not dress your bagel in any way). **Citarella's** fish store (at 75th St., southwest corner) features intricate, often absurd arrangements of seafood on shaved ice in the front window. The fresh produce in the bountiful but unpretentious **Fairway Market** (2127 Broadway at 74th St.) practically bursts onto the street. Have a look at the handmade signs describing the produce and cheeses; they can be as fresh as the merchandise itself.

At 73rd Street and Broadway, look up at the white facade and fairy-castle turrets of the **Ansonia Hotel,** a turn-of-the-century luxury building whose thick, soundproof walls made it attractive to musicians; once home to Enrico Caruso, Igor Stravinsky, Arturo Toscanini, Florenz Ziegfeld, Theodore Dreiser, and Babe Ruth, today it consists of condominiums. The Ansonia served as the facade for the building in which Jennifer Jason Leigh terrorized Bridget Fonda in the film *Single White Female.* Here, where Broadway cuts across
❻ Amsterdam Avenue, the triangle north of 72nd is **Verdi Square** (for Italian opera composer Giuseppe Verdi). In the '70s, however, Verdi Square was better known as Needle Park because of the drug addicts who hung out there. The neighborhood has vastly improved, and elderly West Siders schmooze on the wood benches, but there are those who fear the area is returning to its inglorious past. The triangle south of 72nd Street is **Sherman Square** (named for Union Civil War general William Tecumseh Sherman); the **subway kiosk** here is an official city landmark, a structure with rounded neo-Dutch moldings that was the first express station north of 42nd Street.

Having bought your picnic lunch, you may now want to head west to
❼ **Riverside Park,** a long, slender green space along the Hudson River landscaped by Central Park architects Olmsted and Vaux. Beginning at about 80th Street is the **Promenade,** a broad formal walkway with a stone parapet looking out over the river. Descend the steps here and go through the underpass beneath Riverside Drive, to reach the **79th Street Boat Basin,** a rare spot in Manhattan where you can walk right along the river's edge, smell the salt air, and watch a flotilla of houseboats bob in the water.

If you walk to the end of the Promenade, you'll see a patch of its median strip exploding with flowers tended by nearby residents. Look up to your right, where the Civil War **Soldiers' and Sailors' Monu-**

ment, a tight circle of white marble columns, crests a hill along Riverside Drive. (The monument appeared in the PBS TV mini-series *The Civil War*.) Climb to the monument for a refreshing view of Riverside Park, the Hudson River, and the New Jersey waterfront.

Tour 9: Columbia University and Environs

On the high ridge just north and west of Central Park, a cultural outpost grew up at the end of the 19th century, spearheaded by a triad of institutions: Columbia University, which developed the mind; St. Luke's Hospital, which cared for the body; and the Cathedral of St. John the Divine, which tended the soul. Idealistically conceived of as an American Acropolis, the cluster of academic and religious institutions that developed here managed to keep these blocks stable during years when neighborhoods on all sides were collapsing into decay. In the past decade, West Side gentrification has reclaimed the area to the south, while the Harlem areas north and east of here haven't changed as much. Yet within the gates of the Columbia or Barnard campus, or inside the hush of the cathedral or Riverside Church, the pace of life seems slower, more contemplative. Being a student neighborhood, the area has a casual atmosphere that is hip, friendly, and fun.

⑧ Our first stop will be at the **Cathedral of St. John the Divine,** New York's major Episcopal church. When it is completed, it will be the largest cathedral in the world (St. Peter's of Rome is larger, but it's technically a basilica). Here you can have a rare, fascinating look at a Gothic cathedral in progress. Before you go in the main entrance on Amsterdam Avenue at 112th Street, peer into the side lot just to the north—the cathedral's **stone-cutting yard,** one of the few such operations in the United States. This immense limestone-and-granite church has been built in spurts. Its first cornerstone was laid in 1892 and a second in 1925, but with the U.S. entry into World War II, construction came to a "temporary" halt that lasted until 1982. St. John's follows traditional Gothic engineering—it is supported by stonemasonry rather than by a steel skeleton—so new stonecutters, many of them youngsters from nearby Harlem neighborhoods, had to be trained before the current work could proceed on the two front towers, the transept, and, finally, the great central tower. The proposed south transept is a radical conception: a "bioshelter" with branching columns, a glass roof, and an upper-level arboretum where sunlight will filter down through lush greenery, echoing the effect of stained glass. A model in the superb gift shop inside shows what the cathedral might look like when completed, probably quite a few years into the future. The shop (open daily 9–5) is known for its fine selection of international crafts, jewelry, religious artifacts, and ecological literature.

On the wide steps climbing to the Amsterdam Avenue entrance, you'll see five portals arching over the entrance doors; the central one shows St. John having his vision of the Lord in glory. Statuary is still being slowly added to the portals. Before you go inside, take a closer look at the facade's huge blocks of limestone: Each one carries a pattern of rough chisel marks called "boasting," the individual mason's distinctive signature.

Inside is a vast nave, the length of two football fields, which can seat 5,000 worshipers. The small chapels that border the nave have a surprisingly contemporary outlook. The second chapel to your left is the only **Poet's Corner** in the United States; the right-hand aisle's chapels movingly mourn tragedies such as the Holocaust and the spread of AIDS.

Beneath the 155-foot-high central dome, which could comfortably contain the Statue of Liberty, you can see another quirk of the cathedral: Its original Romanesque-Byzantine design was scrapped in 1907, when architect Ralph Adams Cram took over and instated a Gothic style. Here, where the transept will someday cross the nave, note the rough granite walls of the original scheme (they will eventually be covered with limestone); note also that the side nearer the entrance has a pointed Gothic arch, while the arch near the altar is still rounded Romanesque. The altar area itself expresses the cathedral's interfaith tradition with menorahs, Shinto vases, and golden chests presented by the king of Siam; the church's international mission is represented in the ring of chapels behind the altar, dedicated to various ethnic groups. The **Baptistry,** to the left of the altar, is an exquisite octagonal chapel with a 15-foot-high marble font and a polychrome sculpted frieze commemorating New York's Dutch heritage.

To the south of the cathedral itself is the **cathedral close,** a peaceful precinct of Gothic-style châteaus that includes the Bishop's House, the Deanery, and the Cathedral School. A circular plaza just off Amsterdam at 111th Street features the Peace Fountain, which is not for all tastes.

Along with Sunday services (8, 9, 9:30 [in Spanish], 10 and 11 AM, and 7 PM), the cathedral operates a score of community outreach programs and presents a full calendar of nonreligious (classical, folk, winter solstice) concerts. *Amsterdam Ave. and 112th St., tel. 212/316–7540, box office tel. 212/662–2133. Suggested contribution: $2. Tours Mon.–Sat. 11, Sun. 12:45. Open daily 7–5.*

Time Out	On the other side of Amsterdam Avenue, between 110th and 111th streets, you'll find two casual restaurants: **V & T Restaurant** (1024 Amsterdam, tel. 212/663–1708) for spicy pizza and Italian cooking; and the **Hungarian Pastry Shop** (1030 Amsterdam Ave., tel. 212/866–4230) for luscious desserts and coffees.

From here you have two options: go north on Amsterdam to Columbia University, or take a swing east on 113th Street to secluded **Morningside Drive.** On 113th Street you can still see the baroque 1896 core of **St. Luke's Hospital,** which has grown rather awkwardly into a jumble of newer buildings. On Morningside Drive at 114th Street you'll find **Eglise de Notre Dame,** a Roman Catholic church that features, behind the altar, a replica of the French grotto of Lourdes; stop in, if possible, during one of the frequent daily services. At 116th Street you may want to pause on the overlook on the right to gaze into **Morningside Park,** tumbling steeply into a wooded gorge. Designed by Central Park's Olmsted and Vaux, it's a lovely landscape, but bordered as it is by some rough blocks of Harlem, it may not be a safe place to take a stroll.

At 116th Street and Amsterdam, you can pass through the campus gates of **Columbia University,** a wealthy, private, coed institution that is New York City's only Ivy League school. The gilded crowns on the black wrought-iron gates serve as a reminder that this was originally King's College when it was founded in 1754, before American independence. Walk along the herringbone-patterned brick paths of College Walk into the refreshingly green main quadrangle, dominated by massive neoclassical **Butler Library** to your left (south) and the rotunda-topped **Low Memorial Library** to your right (north). Butler, built in 1934, holds the bulk of the university's 5 million books; Low, built in 1895–97 by McKim, Mead & White (who laid out the general campus plan when the college moved here in 1897), is now mostly offices, but on weekdays you can go inside to see its domed, templelike former Reading Room. The steps of Low Library, presided over by Daniel Chester French's statue Alma Mater, have been a focal point for campus life, not least during the student riots of 1968. Here Dan Aykroyd and Bill Murray, playing recently fired Columbia research scientists, hit upon the idea of going into business as Ghostbusters.

Before Columbia moved here, this land was occupied by the Bloomingdale Insane Asylum; the sole survivor of those days is **Buell Hall**, the gabled orange-red brick house just east of Low Library. Just north is **St. Paul's Chapel** (1907), an exquisite little Byzantine-style domed church laid out in the shape of a cross. Step inside to admire the tiled vaulting. *Tel. 212/854–6625. Open Sept.–May, weekdays 11–8; Sat. 11–2; Sun. for services, 7:30–1 and 5–9. Greatly reduced hours June–Aug., so call ahead for Sun. schedule. Free organ recitals Thurs. noon.*

A student-run art gallery has been opened downstairs in the chapel's Postcrypt. *Tel. 212/854–1953. Admission free. Open Tues.–Fri. 2–6 and Sat. 9 PM–1 AM as a coffee house, offering poetry readings and folk music.*

The university's renowned Journalism School, founded by Joseph Pulitzer (and the reason why Columbia bestows those Pulitzer Prizes each spring), holds classes in the building just south of the campus's west gates. Go through the gates and onto Broadway to find the official college bookstore at 115th Street and Broadway.

⑩ Across Broadway from Columbia is its sister institution, **Barnard College,** established in 1889. One of the former Seven Sisters of women's colleges, Barnard has steadfastly remained a single-sex institution and has maintained its independence from Columbia, although its students can take classes there (and vice versa). Note the bear (the college's mascot) on the shield above the main gates at 117th Street. Through the gates is **Barnard Hall,** its brick-and-limestone design echoing Columbia's buildings. Turn right to follow the path north through the narrow but neatly landscaped campus; turn left from the main gate to peek into a quiet residential quadrangle.

Follow Broadway north to 120th Street, where on your right you'll see the redbrick Victorian buildings of Columbia University's **⑪** **Teachers College,** founded in 1887 and today still the world's largest graduate school in the field of education. Notice the band of stone along the Broadway facade, inscribed with the names of famous teachers throughout history. On your left is the interdenomination-**⑫** al **Union Theological Seminary** in its rough gray collegiate Gothic quadrangle. Founded in 1836, the seminary moved here in 1910; it has one of the world's finest theological libraries. Step inside the main entrance, on Broadway at 121st Street, and ask to look around the pleasant central quadrangle. At the corner of 122nd Street and Broadway, behind a large blank-walled redbrick tower that fronts **⑬** the intersection at an angle, is the **Jewish Theological Seminary,** founded in 1887 as a training ground for rabbis, cantors, and scholars of Conservative Judaism. This complex was built in 1930, although the tower, which housed part of the seminary's excellent library, was extensively renovated after a fire in 1966. Walk west on 122nd Street; at Claremont Avenue, you'll see the prestigious **Manhattan School of Music** on your right, with musical instruments carved into the stone beneath its upper-story windows. Between Claremont and Riverside Drive, you may want to sit for a moment in **Sakura Park,** a quiet formal garden.

⓮ Across Riverside Drive, in Riverside Park, stands **Grant's Tomb,** where Civil War general and two-term president Ulysses S. Grant rests beside his wife, Julia Dent Grant. The white granite mausoleum, with its imposing columns and classical pediment, is modeled after Les Invalides in Paris, where Napoleon is buried. Under a small white dome, the Grants' twin black marble sarcophagi are sunk into a deep circular chamber, which you view from above; minigalleries to the sides display photographs and Grant memorabilia. In contrast to this austere monument, the surrounding plaza features fanciful 1960s-era mosaic benches, designed by local schoolchildren. *Riverside Dr. and 122nd St., tel. 212/666–1640. Admission free. Open Wed.–Sun. 9–4:30.*

Just south of Grant's Tomb, on Riverside Drive at 120th Street, **⓯** **Riverside Church** is a modern (1930) Gothic-style edifice whose smooth, pale limestone walls seem the antithesis of St. John the Divine's rough gray hulk; in fact, it feels more akin to Rockefeller Center, not least because John D. Rockefeller was a major benefactor of the church. While most of the building is refined and restrained, the main entrance, on Riverside Drive, explodes with elaborate stone carving (modeled after the French cathedral of Chartres, as are many other decorative details here). Inside, look at the handsomely ornamented main sanctuary, which seats only half as many people as St. John the Divine does; take the elevator to the top of the 22-story, 356-foot tower (admission: $1), with its 74-bell carillon, the largest in the world. Although affiliated with the Baptist church and the United Church of Christ, Riverside is basically nondenominational, interracial, international, extremely political, and socially conscious. Its calendar includes political and community events, dance and theater programs, and concerts, along with regular Sunday services at 10:45 AM. *Tel. 212/222–5900. Open Mon.–Sat. 9–5, Sun. noon–4; service each Sun. 10:45.*

Time Out Returning to Broadway, eat with the Columbia and Barnard students at **Ollie's Noodle Shop** (2957 Broadway at 116th St., tel. 212/ 932–3300). The eclectic menu includes everything from eggplant parmesan to Mexican chili to grilled shrimp kebabs, but the main attraction is the savory Cantonese and Mandarin Chinese food. The dumplings and the noodle dishes are divine.

Tour 10: Harlem

Numbers in the margin correspond to points of interest on the Tour 10: Harlem map.

Harlem has been the mecca for African-American culture and life for nearly a century. Originally called Nieuw Haarlem and settled by Dutch farmers, Harlem was a well-to-do suburb in the 19th century; black New Yorkers began settling here in large numbers in about 1900, moving into a surplus of fine apartment buildings and town houses built by real-estate developers for a middle-class white market that never materialized. By the 1920s, Harlem (with one "a") had become the most famous black community in the United States, perhaps in the world. In an astonishing confluence of talent known as the Harlem Renaissance, black novelists, playwrights, musicians, and artists gathered here. Black performers starred in chic

Harlem jazz clubs—which, ironically, only whites could attend. Throughout the Roaring '20s, while whites flocked here for the infamous parties and nightlife, blacks settled in for the opportunity this self-sustaining community represented. But the Depression hit Harlem hard. By the late 1930s, it was no longer a popular social spot for downtown New Yorkers, and many successful African-American families began moving out to homes in the suburbs of Queens and New Jersey.

By the 1960s, Harlem's population had dropped dramatically, and many of those who remained were disillusioned enough to join in civil rights riots. A vicious cycle of crowded housing, poverty, and crime was choking the neighborhood, turning it into a simmering ghetto. Today, however, Harlem is well on its way to restoring itself. Mixed in with some of the seedy remains of the past are old jewels such as the refurbished Apollo Theatre and such new attractions as the Studio Museum. A great number of Harlem's classic brownstone and limestone homes are being restored and lived in by young families, bringing new life to the community.

Deserted buildings, burned-out shopfronts, and yards of rubble still scar certain parts; although a few whites have begun to move in here, some white visitors may feel conspicuous in what is still a largely black neighborhood. But Harlemites are accustomed to seeing tourists on their streets; only common traveler's caution is necessary during daytime excursions to any of the places highlighted, although for nighttime outings it's smart to take a taxi. Bus tours may be a good alternative way to see Harlem, because they cover more areas than the central Harlem walk outlined below (*see* Special-Interest Tours in Chapter 1).

Sunday is a good time to tour Harlem, because that's when you can listen to gospel music at one of the area's many churches. Soulful, moving, often joyous, gospel music blends elements from African songs and chants, American spirituals, and rhythm and blues. Gospel fans and visitors are welcome at the **Canaan Baptist Church of Christ,** where Wyatt Tee Walker is pastor. *132 W. 116th St., tel. 212/ 866–0301; Sun. services 10:45 AM.*

As you head east from the church, notice on the southwest corner of 116th Street and Lenox Avenue the aluminum onion dome of the **Malcolm Shabazz Mosque** (102 W. 116th St.), a former casino that was converted in the mid-1960s to a black Muslim temple (Malcolm X once preached here). Several Muslim stores are located nearby.

On weekdays you may want to begin your tour at the next stop, ❷ **Marcus Garvey Park,** which interrupts 5th Avenue between 120th and 124th streets. Renamed after Marcus Garvey (1887–1940), who led the back-to-Africa movement, this rocky plot of land is interesting less for itself than for the handsome buildings of the surrounding Mount Morris Historic District (Mount Morris Square was the park's original name). Walk up the west side of the park to admire the fine town houses facing the park or on the side streets.

Time Out At the other end of Marcus Garvey Park is **La Famille** (2017 5th Ave. between 124th and 125th Sts., tel. 212/722–9806), a bar and restaurant that serves great food upstairs and a changing nighttime menu of jazz downstairs (Wed.–Sun.). La Famille offers standard soul-food fare plus a more Continental menu.

Harlem's main street is **125th Street,** the chief artery of its cultural, retail, and economic life. Real-estate values here have never come

Abyssinian
Baptist
Church, **7**
Apollo
Theater, **4**
Black Fashion
Museum, **5**
Canaan Baptist
Church of
Christ, **1**
Marcus Garvey
Park, **2**
Schomburg
Center for
Research in
Black Culture, **6**
Striver's Row, **8**
The Studio
Museum in
Harlem, **3**

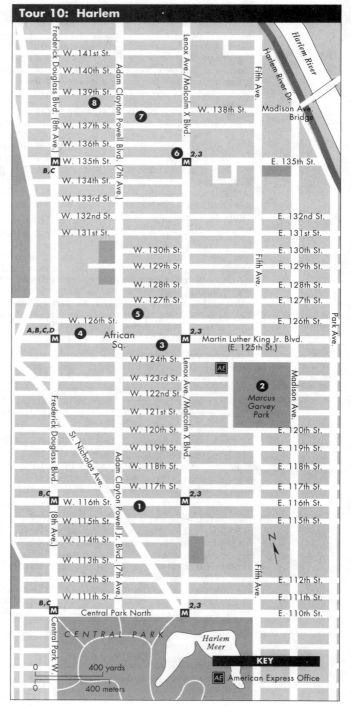

Tour 10: Harlem

close to those downtown along 5th Avenue or even Broadway, and many of the commercial buildings rise only a few stories. New businesses have moved in of late, however, bringing smart new shopfronts along a retail row that used to see many "For Rent" signs. Above the street-level stores is the home of the **National Black Theater** (2033 5th Ave., between 125th and 126th Sts., tel. 212/722–3800), which produces new works by contemporary African-American writers. As you walk west on 125th Street, notice a peculiarity of Harlem addresses: The city's numbered north–south avenues acquire different names up here, commemorating heroes of black history. 6th Avenue becomes Lenox Avenue or Malcolm X Boulevard, 7th Avenue is Adam Clayton Powell Boulevard, and 8th Avenue is Frederick Douglass Boulevard. Even 125th Street has an alias: Martin Luther King Jr. Boulevard. However, just about everybody still uses the streets' former names.

On Lenox Avenue between 126th and 127th streets is **Sylvia's Soul Food Restaurant** (*see* Chapter 9), owned by Sylvia Woods, the self-proclaimed "Queen of Soul Food" in New York who remains most nights until 10 chatting with her customers.

❸ **The Studio Museum in Harlem,** one of the community's showplaces, is a small art museum that houses a large collection of paintings, sculpture, and photographs (including historic photographs of Harlem by James Van DerZee, popular in the 1930s). The museum often offers special lectures and programs, and its gift shop is full of black American and African-inspired books, posters, and jewelry. *144 W. 125th St., tel. 212/864–4500. Admission: $5 adults, $3 students and senior citizens, $1 children under 12. Open Wed.–Fri. 10–5, weekends 1–6.*

❹ A fantastic restoration brought the **Apollo Theatre,** one of Harlem's greatest landmarks, back to life in 1986. When it opened in 1913 it was a burlesque hall for white audiences only, but after 1934, music greats such as Billie Holiday, Ella Fitzgerald, Duke Ellington, Count Basie, and Aretha Franklin performed here. The theater fell on hard times and closed for a while in the early 1970s. The current Apollo's roster of stars isn't as consistent as it was in the past, but its regular Wednesday-night amateur performances at 7:30 PM are as wild and raucous as they were in the theater's heyday. *253 W. 125th St., tel. 212/749–5838. Call for performance schedules.*

Return to 7th Avenue and head north to 126th Street, where the
❺ **Black Fashion Museum** is housed in a brownstone. Costumes from black theater and films are displayed, and the work of black fashion designers of the past century is highlighted. *155 W. 126th St., tel. 212/666–1320. Suggested contribution: $1.50 adults, $1 students and senior citizens, 50¢ children under 12. Open weekdays 12:30–7:30 by appointment.*

As you head up 7th Avenue, between 131st and 132nd streets you'll pass what is today the Williams Institutional (Christian Methodist Episcopal) Church. Once this was the **Lafayette Theater,** which presented black revues in the 1920s and housed the WPA's Federal Negro Theater in the 1930s. A tree outside the theater was considered a lucky charm for black actors; having fallen victim to exhaust fumes, it has been replaced by the abstract metal "tree" on the traffic island in the center of 7th Avenue.

At 135th Street, cross back to Lenox Avenue, where you'll find the
❻ **Schomburg Center for Research in Black Culture.** In 1926 the New York Public Library's Division of Negro History acquired the vast collection of Arthur Schomburg, a scholar of black and Puerto Rican

descent. In 1940, after Schomburg died, this collection, which includes more than 100,000 books, documents, and photographs recording black history, was named after him. In 1972, the ever-growing collection was designated a research library, and in 1980 it moved into this modern redbrick building from the handsome Victorian one next door (designed by McKim, Mead & White), which is now a branch library. The expansion and renovation of the original Schomburg building was completed in 1991 and includes the new **American Negro Theater,** with seating for 380, and increased gallery space. The center's resources include rare manuscripts, art and artifacts, motion pictures, records, and videotapes. Regular exhibits, performing-arts programs, and lectures continue to contribute to Harlem culture. *515 Lenox Ave. at 135th St., tel. 212/491–2200. Admission free. Open Mon.–Wed. noon–8, Thurs.–Sat. 10–6. Open Sun. noon–5 to view exhibits only.*

7 Founded downtown in 1808, the **Abyssinian Baptist Church** was one of the first black institutions to settle in Harlem when it moved here in the 1920s. The Gothic-style bluestone church was further distinguished by its famous family of ministers—Adam Clayton Powell, Sr., and his son, Adam Clayton Powell, Jr., the first black U.S. congressman. Stop in on Sunday to hear the gospel choir and the fiery sermon of its present minister, Rev. Calvin Butts. *132 W. 138th St., tel. 212/862–7474. Sun. services 9 and 11 AM.*

8 Across 7th Avenue from the church is a handsome set of town houses known as **Striver's Row** (W. 138th and W. 139th Sts. between 7th and 8th Aves.). Since 1919, African-American doctors, lawyers, and other middle-class professionals have owned these elegant homes, designed by famous period architects such as Stanford White (his contributions are on the north side of 139th Street). Musicians W. C. Handy ("The St. Louis Blues") and Eubie Blake ("I'm Just Wild About Harry") were among the residents here. The area became known as Striver's Row because less affluent Harlemites felt its residents were "striving" to become well-to-do. These quiet, tree-lined streets are a remarkable reminder of the Harlem that used to be.

Tour 11: Chelsea

Numbers in the margin correspond to points of interest on the Tour 11: Chelsea map.

Like the London district of the same name, New York's Chelsea has preserved its villagelike personality. Both have their quiet nooks where the 19th century seems to live on; both have been havens for artists, writers, and bohemians. Although London's Chelsea is a much more upscale chunk of real estate, New York's Chelsea is catching up, with town-house renovations reclaiming block after block of the side streets. 7th, 8th, and 9th avenues may never be the shopping mecca that King's Road in London's Chelsea has been, but they have plenty of hip, one-of-a-kind boutiques sprinkled among the grubby grocery stores and other remnants of the neighborhood's immigrant tenement past.

Precisely speaking, the New York neighborhood was named not after Chelsea itself but after London's Chelsea Royal Hospital, an old soldiers' home. Running from 14th to 24th streets, from 8th Avenue west, it was one family's country estate until the 1830s, when Clement Clarke Moore saw the city moving north and decided to divide his land into lots. With an instinctive gift for urban planning, he dictated a pattern of development that ensured street after street of graceful row houses. A clergyman and classics professor, Moore is probably best known for his 1822 poem "A Visit from St. Nicholas," which he composed while bringing a sleigh full of Christmas treats from lower Manhattan to his Chelsea home.

❶ Begin your tour of Chelsea at the corner of 7th Avenue and 17th Street, in front of **Barneys New York** (tel. 212/929–9000), a fashionable department store that grew out of an outstanding menswear store. If nothing else, stroll past its store windows, where fashion is displayed with a quirky wit. Across 7th Avenue are branches of **Williams-Sonoma** (gourmet cookware) and **Pottery Barn** (trendy home furnishings); a block uptown, at 18th Street, you'll find one of the city's best children's bookstores, **Books of Wonder** (132 7th Ave., tel. 212/989–3270).

It's appropriate to begin the Chelsea tour with a spate of shopping, because nearby 6th Avenue was once known as Ladies Mile for its concentration of major department stores. After the stores moved uptown in the early 1900s, the neighborhood declined and the grand old store buildings stood empty and dilapidated. The 1990s, however, brought the renaissance of the Flatiron District to the east (*see* Tour 4, *above*), and now renovations are in progress all along 6th Avenue. Stand at 6th Avenue and 18th Street and imagine it in the latter part of the 19th century, when the elevated tracks of the 6th Avenue El train still cast their shadow along this street. From the west side of the avenue, you can look across at the elaborately embellished, glazed terra-cotta building just north of 18th Street. **❷** Originally the **Siegel-Cooper Dry Goods Store**, built in 1895, it contains 15½ acres of space, yet it was built in only five months. In its retail heyday, the store's main floor featured an immense fountain—a circular marble terrace with an enormous white-marble-and-brass replica of "The Republic," the statue Daniel Chester French displayed at the 1883 Chicago World's Fair—which became a favorite rendezvous point for New Yorkers. During World War II, the building was a military hospital. Today its main tenant is **Bed, Bath & Beyond** (tel. 212/255–3550), an impressive emporium with 11 sections of household items at discounted prices. Look up at the building's splendid ornamentation: round wreathed windows, Corinthian and Doric pilasters, Romanesque rounded arches, lion heads, and more.

Now cross 6th Avenue and take a look at the building on the west **❸** side: the original **B. Altman Dry Goods Store,** built in 1876 with additions in 1887 and 1910. Look closely at the exposed columns at the base of the building—it's constructed of cast iron. B. Altman moved out of this giant in 1906 to set up shop in imposing quarters at 5th Avenue and 34th Street. The latter store closed in 1990.

Time Out About a half-block east on 18th Street you can take a restful lunch, tea, or coffee break at the **Book Friends Cafe** (16 W. 18th St., tel. 212/255–7407), a literary hangout and bookstore in this newly artsy neighborhood. On the same block, bibliophiles will also enjoy perusing the shelves of **Academy Bookstore** (10 W. 18th St., tel. 212/242–4848), **Skyline Books and Records** (13 W. 18th St., tel. 212/759–5463), and **Barnes and Noble Sale Annex** (18th St. and 5th Ave., tel. 212/633–3500), with its main store across the street (105 5th Ave., tel. 212/807–0099).

On the east side of 6th Avenue at 20th Street is the Gothic-style **❹** **Church of the Holy Communion,** an Episcopal house of worship built in 1846 and designed by architect Richard Upjohn. To the horror of

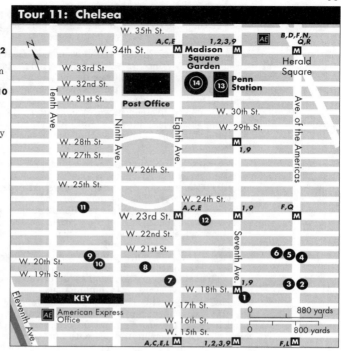

Tour 11: Chelsea

some preservationists, it was converted a few years ago into **Limelight,** a nightclub with state-of-the-art sound and video systems.

On the west side of 6th Avenue between 20th and 21st streets stands another former retail palace, the **Hugh O'Neill Dry Goods Store.** Constructed in 1875, this cast-iron building features Corinthian columns and pilasters; its corner towers were once topped off with huge bulbous domes. The recently renovated structure now houses the Elsevier Science Publishing Company. Look up at the pediment and you'll see the name of the original tenant proudly displayed.

Turn left on 21st Street for a look at **The Third Cemetery of the Spanish & Portuguese Synagogue, Shearith Israel,** a private green oasis with a hardy old ailanthus tree. In use from 1829 to 1851, it is one of three graveyards created in Manhattan by this congregation (*see* Tours 12 and 16, *below*).

Continue west on 21st Street to 8th Avenue, where the **Chelsea Historic District** officially begins. Between 20th and 23rd streets, from 8th to 10th avenues, you'll find examples of all of Chelsea's architectural periods: Greek and Gothic Revival, Italianate, and 1890s apartment buildings. But before you start prowling around there, you may want to head down to 19th Street and 8th Avenue to see the Art Deco **Joyce Theater** (175 8th Ave., tel. 212/242–0800). The former Elgin movie house was gutted and transformed in 1982 into this sleek modern theater; if you have any interest in modern dance (*see* Chapter 11), it's well worth checking out who is performing at the Joyce during your stay. Its presence, which helped revitalize the area, has attracted several good, moderately priced restaurants along 8th Avenue.

Time Out A pair of restaurants on 8th Avenue between 20th and 21st streets are busily competing to see which can offer the best deal for a stylish nouvelle lunch. Take your pick—**Intermezzo** (202 8th Ave., tel. 212/929–3433) or **Chelsea Foods** (198 8th Ave., tel. 212/691–3948)—you can hardly go wrong.

---

❽ At 344 West 20th Street, between 8th and 9th avenues, you'll find **St. Peter's Church,** built between 1836 and 1838. The Greek Revival–style **rectory** (1832), to the right of the main church, originally served as the sanctuary. Four years after it was built, the congregation had already laid foundations for a bigger church when, it is said, a vestryman returned from England bursting with excitement over the Gothic Revival that had just taken hold there. The fieldstone **church** that resulted ranks as one of New York's earliest examples of Gothic Revival architecture. To the left of the church, the brick **parish hall** is an example of the so-called Victorian Gothic style; its churchlike front was added in 1871. The wrought-iron fence framing the three buildings once enclosed St. Paul's Chapel downtown *(see Tour 17, below).*

❾ When Clement Clarke Moore divided up his estate, he began by deeding a large section to the **General Theological Seminary,** where he taught Hebrew and Greek. At 9th Avenue and 20th Street, the Episcopal seminary still occupies a block-long stretch. The stoutly fenced campus is accessible through the modern building on 9th Avenue; during off hours you can view the grounds from West 20th Street. The **West Building** (1836) is another early example of Gothic Revival architecture in the city. Most of the rest of the complex was completed in 1883–1902, when Eugene Augustus Hoffman, the school's third dean, hired architect Charles Coolidge Haight to design a campus that would rival those of most other American colleges of the day, in the style known as English Collegiate Gothic, which Haight had pioneered. The general campus plan is in an "E" shape, with the spine facing 21st Street. In the center is the **Chapel of the Good Shepherd,** with its 161-foot-high bell tower. **Sherred Hall,** a three-story classroom building flanked by dormitories, expresses beautifully the simple quality and uniform look Haight strove for. **Hoffman Hall,** the refectory-gymnasium, has an enormous dining hall that resembles a medieval knight's council chamber. A 1960s-era building facing 9th Avenue houses administrative offices, a bookstore, and the 210,000-volume **St. Mark's Library,** generally considered the nation's greatest ecclesiastical library; it has the world's largest collection of Latin Bibles. *Tel. 212/243–5150. Open weekdays noon–3, Sat. 11–4, Sun. 2–4 (no admission after 1 hour before closing), and by appointment.*

Across the street from the seminary, at **404 West 20th Street,** is the oldest house in the historic district. Built between 1829 and 1830 in the Federal style, it still has one clapboard side wall, although over the years it acquired a Greek Revival doorway and Italianate windows on the parlor floor, and the roof was raised one story. The **❿** houses next door, from 406 to 418 West 20th, are **Cushman Row,** some of the country's most perfect examples of Greek Revival town houses. Built by dry-goods merchant Don Alonzo Cushman, a friend of Clement Clarke Moore who became a millionaire by developing Chelsea, the houses retain such details as the tiny wreath-encircled attic windows, deeply recessed doorways with brownstone frames, and handsome iron balustrades, newels, and fences. Notice the pineapples, a traditional symbol of welcome, atop the newels in front of Nos. 416 and 418.

Farther down West 20th Street, at **Nos. 446 to 450,** you'll find some exceptional examples of Italianate houses. The arched windows and doorways are hallmarks of this style, which prized circular forms—not least because, being expensive to build, they showed off the owner's wealth.

When you reach 10th Avenue, turn right and walk north (uptown). Movie buffs might make a quick detour right onto 21st Street to take a peek at **467 West 21st Street,** where, in the 1960s and '70s, Anthony Perkins of *Psycho* was the live-in landlord.

West 22nd Street also has a string of handsome old row houses just east of 10th Avenue. **No. 435** was the longtime residence of actors Geraldine Page and Rip Torn; they nicknamed this Chelsea town house the Torn Page. In 1987, a year after winning an Oscar for *The Trip to Bountiful*, Page suffered a fatal heart attack here.

⑪ On the block spanning 23rd and 24th streets, between 9th and 10th avenues on the north side of the block, you can't miss the **London Terrace Apartments,** a huge complex containing 1,670 apartments. When it first opened in 1930, the doormen dressed as London bobbies. It's actually made up of two rows of interconnected apartment buildings, which enclose a block-long private garden. As you walk along 23rd Street, notice the lions on the arched entryways: From the side they look as though they're snarling, but from the front they display wide grins.

The site of the Clarke family manor (where Clement Clarke Moore was born in 1779) was just across 23rd Street here, on what was then a high bluff overlooking the Hudson.

During the 1880s and Gay '90s, 23rd Street was the heart of the entertainment district, lined with theaters, music halls, and beer gardens. Today it is an undistinguished, even run-down, commercial thoroughfare, but there is one relic of its once-proud past: the **⑫** **Chelsea Hotel** (tel. 212/243–3700) at 222 West 23rd Street, between 7th and 8th avenues. Built of red brick with lacy wrought-iron balconies and a mansard roof, it opened in 1884 as a cooperative apartment house and became a hotel in 1905, although it has always catered to long-term tenants, with a tradition of broad-mindedness that has attracted many creative types. Its literary roll call of former tenants includes Mark Twain, Eugene O'Neill, O. Henry, Thomas Wolfe, Tennessee Williams, Vladimir Nabokov, Mary McCarthy, Brendan Behan, Arthur Miller, Dylan Thomas, William S. Burroughs, and Arthur C. Clarke (who wrote the script for *2001: A Space Odyssey* while living here). In 1966, Andy Warhol filmed artist Brigid Polk in her Chelsea hotel room, which eventually became *The Chelsea Girls*, considered by many to be Warhol's best film. More recently, the hotel was seen on screen in *Sid and Nancy* (1986), a dramatization of a true-life Chelsea Hotel murder, when drugged punk rocker Sid Vicious accidentally stabbed to death his girlfriend Nancy Spungeon. The shabby, seedy aura of the Chelsea Hotel is part of its allure. Read the commemorative plaques outside and then step into the lobby to look at the unusual artwork, some of it donated in lieu of rent by residents down on their luck.

Go back to 7th Avenue and walk uptown a few blocks—you'll be leaving Chelsea and entering the garment district, where wheeled racks of clothing add to the traffic volume, and you may well stumble upon your dream designer sale (accept all flyers). Officially, the clothing quarter begins at 28th Street, but the bulk of the ateliers are farther **⑬** up in the 30s, past **Penn Station.** Manhattan's other Amtrak/LIRR station lies beneath the two-square-block Penn Plaza. Much to the dismay of architects and preservationists, the great 1910 McKim, Mead & White iron-and-glass train shed and vast Roman Revival waiting room were demolished in 1962 to make way for the station and the concrete-clad cylinder that is the 20,000-seat **Madison Square Garden,** home of the New York Knicks and Rangers (*see* Chapter 7), other sporting events, and major concerts. Behind-the-scenes tours, from locker rooms to stage, are now available. *Tel. 212/465–6080. Tours Mon.–Sat. 10, 11, noon, 1; Sun. 11, noon, 1. Admission $7.50 adults, $6.50 senior citizens, students and children.*

Tour 12: Greenwich Village

Numbers in the margin correspond to points of interest on the Tours 12 and 13: Greenwich Village and the East Village map.

Greenwich Village, which New Yorkers almost invariably speak of simply as "the Village," enjoyed a raffish reputation for years. Originally a rural outpost of the city—a haven for New Yorkers during early 19th-century smallpox and yellow fever epidemics—many of its blocks still look somewhat pastoral, with brick town houses and low-rises, tiny green parks and hidden courtyards, and a crazy-quilt pattern of narrow, tree-lined streets. In the mid-19th century, however, as the city spread north of 14th Street, the Village became the province of immigrants, bohemians, and students (New York University, today the nation's largest private university, was planted next to Washington Square in 1831). Its politics were radical and its attitudes tolerant, which is one reason it is now home to such a large gay community.

Today Village apartments and town houses go for high rents, and several posh restaurants have put down roots. Except for the isolated western fringe, where a string of tough gay bars along West Street attracts some drug traffic and prostitution, the Village is about as safe and clean as the Upper East Side. Nevertheless, something about the tangled street plan and the small buildings encourages anarchy. Shabby shopfronts, hole-in-the-wall restaurants, and nonmainstream arts groups persist and thrive here. There's still a large student population, and several longtime residents remain, paying cheap rents thanks to rent-control laws. The Village is no longer dangerous, but it still feels bohemian.

Several generations of writers and artists have lived and worked here: in the 19th century, Henry James, Edgar Allan Poe, Mark Twain, Walt Whitman, and Stephen Crane; at the turn of the century, O. Henry, Edith Wharton, Theodore Dreiser, and Hart Crane; and during the 1920s and '30s, John Dos Passos, Norman Rockwell, Sinclair Lewis, John Reed, Eugene O'Neill, Edward Hopper, and Edna St. Vincent Millay. In the late 1940s and early 1950s, the Abstract Expressionist painters Franz Kline, Jackson Pollock, Mark Rothko, and Willem de Kooning congregated here, as did the Beat writers Jack Kerouac, Allen Ginsberg, and Lawrence Ferlinghetti. The 1960s brought folk musicians and poets, notably Bob Dylan and Peter, Paul, and Mary.

Begin a tour of Greenwich Village at Washington Arch in **Washington Square** at the foot of 5th Avenue. Designed by Stanford White, a wood version of Washington Arch was built in 1889 to commemorate the 100th anniversary of George Washington's presidential inauguration and was originally placed about half a block north of its present location. The arch was reproduced in stone in 1892, and the statues—*Washington at War* on the left, *Washington at Peace* on

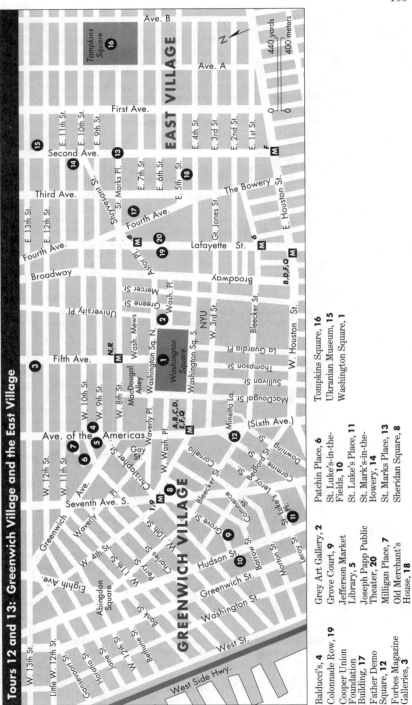

Tours 12 and 13: Greenwich Village and the East Village

Ave. B

Tompkins Square **16**

EAST VILLAGE

Ave. A

First Ave.

15

Second Ave.

13

14

Stuyvesant St.

St. Marks Pl.

Third Ave.

17

Fourth Ave.

6

20

19

Lafayette St.

Fourth Ave.

Broadway

Mercer St.

Greene St.

University Pl.

Wash. Mews

Wash. Pl.

2

NYU

W. 3rd St.

Fifth Ave.

3

1

Washington Square

Washington Sq. N.

Washington Sq. S.

Broadway

Bleecker St.

W. Houston St.

La Guardia Pl.

Thompson St.

Sullivan St.

MacDougal St.

Minetta La.

E. 13th St.

E. 12th St.

E. 11th St.

E. 10th St.

E. 9th St.

E. 7th St.

E. 6th St.

E. 5th St.

The Bowery

Gt. Jones St.

E. Houston St.

E. 4th St.

E. 3rd St.

E. 2nd St.

E. 1st St.

18

MacDougal Alley

Washington Sq. N.

W. 8th St.

W. 9th St.

4

W. 10th St.

5

Waverly Pl.

Ave. of the Americas

7

6

W. 12th St.

W. 11th St.

Gay St.

Christopher St.

W. Wash. Pl.

(Sixth Ave.)

12

Downing St.

Carmine St.

Bedford St.

Cornelia St.

Seventh Ave. S.

GREENWICH VILLAGE

8

Grove St.

Bleecker St.

Commerce St.

9

11

St. Luke's Pl.

Leroy St.

Morton St.

Barrow St.

Waverly

Greenwich Ave.

W. 4th St.

Charles St.

Perry St.

W. 10th St.

W. 11th St.

Bank St.

Abingdon Square

Hudson St.

10

Greenwich St.

Washington St.

West St.

West Side Hwy.

Eighth Ave.

Bethune St.

Jane St.

Horatio St.

Gansevoort St.

Little W. 12th St.

W. 12th St.

W. 13th St.

N,R

A,B,C,D,E,F,Q

1,9

6

B,D,F,Q

F

440 yards

400 meters

0

0

Balducci's, **4**
Colonnade Row, **19**
Cooper Union Foundation Building, **17**
Father Demo Square, **12**
Forbes Magazine Galleries, **3**

Grey Art Gallery, **2**
Grove Court, **9**
Jefferson Market Library, **5**
Joseph Papp Public Theater, **20**
Milligan Place, **7**
Old Merchant's House, **18**

Patchin Place, **6**
St. Luke's-in-the-Fields, **10**
St. Luke's Place, **11**
St. Mark's-in-the-Bowery, **14**
St. Marks Place, **13**
Sheridan Square, **8**

Tompkins Square, **16**
Ukranian Museum, **15**
Washington Square, **1**

the right—were added in 1913. Bodybuilder Charles Atlas modeled for *Peace*.

Washington Square started out as a cemetery, principally for yellow-fever victims, and an estimated 10,000–22,000 bodies lie below. In the early 1800s it was a parade ground and the site of public executions; bodies dangled from a conspicuous Hanging Elm that still stands at the northwest corner of the square. Later Washington Square became the focus of a fashionable residential neighborhood and a center of outdoor activity.

By the early 1980s, Washington Square had deteriorated into a tawdry place only a drug dealer could love. Then community activism motivated a police crackdown that sent the drug traffic elsewhere and made Washington Square comfortable again for Frisbee players, street musicians, skateboarders, jugglers, stand-up comics, sitters, strollers, and a huge outdoor art fair each spring and fall.

Most of the buildings bordering Washington Square belong to New York University. **The Row,** a series of Federal-style town houses along Washington Square North between 5th Avenue and University Place, now serves as university offices and faculty housing. At 7–12 Washington Square North, in fact, only the fronts were preserved, with a 5th Avenue apartment building taking over the space behind. Developers were not so tactful when they demolished 18 Washington Square, once the home of Henry James's grandmother, which he later used as the setting for his novel *Washington Square* (Henry himself was born just off the square, in a long-gone house on Washington Place). The house at 20 Washington Square North is the oldest building (1820) on the block. Notice its Flemish bond brickwork—alternate bricks inserted with the smaller surface (headers) facing out—which before 1830 was considered the best way to build stable walls.

On the east side of the square, NYU's main building contains the **❷** **Grey Art Gallery,** whose changing exhibitions usually focus on contemporary art. *33 Washington Pl., tel. 212/998–6780. Suggested contribution: $2.50. Open Sept.–July, Tues., Thurs. and Fri. 11–6:30, Wed. 11–8:30, Sat. 11–5.*

On the south side of the square, a trio of red sandstone hulks represents an abortive 1960s attempt to create a unified campus look for NYU, as envisioned by architects Philip Johnson and Richard Foster. At one time, plans called for all of the Washington Square buildings to be refaced in this red stone; fortunately, the cost proved prohibitive. On La Guardia Place, the undistinguished modern **Loeb Student Center** stands on the site of a famous boardinghouse, nicknamed the House of Genius for the talented writers who had lived there over the years: Theodore Dreiser, Stephen Crane, Willa Cather, O. Henry, and Eugene O'Neill, among others. A block west of the Student Center, at the corner of Washington Square South and Thompson Street, is the square-towered **Judson Memorial Church** (the tower is now an NYU dormitory), designed by McKim, Mead & White.

Go up 5th Avenue half a block to **Washington Mews,** a cobblestoned private street lined on one side with the former stables of the houses on the Row. Writer Walter Lippmann and artist-patron Gertrude Vanderbilt Whitney (founder of the Whitney Museum) once had homes in the mews; today it's mostly owned by NYU. A similar Village mews, **MacDougal Alley,** can be found between 8th Street and the square just off MacDougal Street, one block west.

Walk up 5th Avenue, past the **Church of the Ascension** (5th Ave. and W. 10th St.), a Gothic-style brownstone designed by Richard Upjohn. Inside, you can admire a mural depicting the Ascension of Jesus and stained-glass windows by John LaFarge and a marble altar sculpture by Louis Saint-Gaudens. In 1844, President John Tyler married Julia Gardiner here. Just past 12th Street, you can stop in ❸ the **Forbes Magazine Galleries,** where the late publisher Malcolm Forbes's idiosyncratic personal collection is on display. Exhibits change in the large gallery while permanent highlights include U.S. presidential papers, more than 500 intricate model boats, jeweled Fabergé eggs, and some 12,000 toy soldiers. *62 5th Ave. at 12th St., tel. 212/206–5548. Admission free. Open Tues.–Wed. and Fri.–Sat. 10–4.*

Time Out If you walk a block east of the Forbes galleries to University Place, you'll find several dining spots located between 8th and 12th streets. At the corner of University Place and 12th Street, **Japonica** (tel. 212/243–7752) serves reasonably priced Japanese lunches, including fresh sushi and excellent sukiyaki. The owners change the restaurant decorations to coincide with the changing seasons and Japanese holidays.

Backtrack on 5th Avenue to **West 11th Street** and turn right to see one of the best examples of a Village town-house block. One exception to the general 19th-century redbrick look is the modern, angled front window of 18 West 11th Street, usually occupied by a stuffed bear whose outfit changes from day to day. This house was built after the original was destroyed in a 1970 explosion; members of the radical Weathermen faction had started a bomb factory in the basement. At the time, actor Dustin Hoffman lived next door at No. 16; he was seen on TV news trying to rescue his personal possessions. Hoffman's costar in *The Graduate,* Anne Bancroft, later lived down at 52 West 11th Street with her husband, director Mel Brooks. At the end of the block, behind a low gray stone wall on the south side of the street, is the **Second Shearith Israel graveyard,** used by the country's oldest Jewish congregation after the cemetery in Chinatown (*see* Tour 16, *below*) and before the one in Chelsea (*see* Tour 11, *above*).

On Avenue of the Americas (6th Avenue), turn left to sample the ❹ wares at **Balducci's** (6th Ave. and 9th St., tel. 212/673–2600), a full-service gourmet food store that sprouted from the vegetable stand of the late Louis Balducci, Sr. Along with more than 80 Italian cheeses and 50 kinds of bread, this family-owned enterprise features imported Italian specialties and a prodigious selection of fresh seafood.

Directly opposite, the triangle formed by West 10th Street, 6th Avenue, and Greenwich Avenue originally held a greenmarket, a jail, ❺ and the magnificent towered courthouse that is now the **Jefferson Market Library** (tel. 212/243–4334). Critics variously termed the courthouse's hodgepodge of styles Venetian, Victorian, or Italian; Villagers, noting the alternating wide bands of red brick and narrow strips of granite, dubbed it the Lean Bacon Style. Over the years, the structure has housed a number of government agencies (public works, civil defense, census bureau, police academy); it was on the verge of demolition when public-spirited citizens saved it and turned it into a public library in 1967. Note the fountain at the corner of West 10th Street and 6th Avenue, and the seal of the City of New York on the east front; inside, look at the handsome interior doorways and climb the graceful circular stairway. If the gate is open, visit the flower garden behind the library, a project run by local green thumbs.

Just west of 6th Avenue on 10th Street is the wrought-iron gateway
6 to a tiny courtyard called **Patchin Place**; around the corner, on 6th
7 Avenue just north of 10th Street, is a similar cul-de-sac, **Milligan Place,** which few New Yorkers even know is there. Both were built around 1850 for the waiters (mostly Basques) who worked at the high-society Brevoort Hotel, long ago demolished, on 5th Avenue. Patchin Place later became home to several writers, including Theodore Dreiser, e.e. cummings, Eugene O'Neill, and Djuna Barnes.

Take Christopher Street, which veers off from the southern end of the library triangle, a few steps to **Gay Street.** A curved lane lined with small row houses circa 1810, Gay Street was originally a black neighborhood and later a strip of speakeasies. Ruth McKinney lived and wrote *My Sister Eileen* in the basement of No. 14, and Howdy Doody was designed in the basement of No. 12. At the end of Gay Street go west on Waverly Place to Christopher Street.

If you continue west on Christopher Street, you'll pass steps leading down to the **Lion's Head** (59 Christopher St.), a longtime hangout for literary types, which, at press time, was still going strong, despite financial troubles. Before she found stardom, Jessica Lange was a waitress here, and book covers by semi-resident authors line the walls. The restaurant faces a green triangle that's technically called **Christopher Park,** but it contains a statue of Civil War general Philip Sheridan; this confuses New Yorkers, because there's another triangle to the south (between Washington Place, Barrow Street, and 7th
8 Avenue) called **Sheridan Square,** which was recently landscaped following an extensive dig by urban archaeologists, who unearthed artifacts dating back to the Dutch and Native American eras.

Sheridan Square was the site of a nasty 1863 riot in which a group of freed slaves was nearly lynched; in 1969, gays and police clashed nearby during a protest march that galvanized the gay-rights movement. Across the busy intersection of 7th Avenue, **Christopher Street** comes into its own as the symbolic heart of New York's gay community. Many bars and stores along here cater to that clientele, although the street is by no means off-limits to other people. Two shops worth a visit are **McNulty's Tea and Coffee Co.** (109 Christopher St., tel. 212/242–5351), with a large variety of tea and coffee blends, and **Li-Lac Chocolate Shop** (120 Christopher St., tel. 212/242–7374), a longtime favorite in the area for its homemade chocolate and buttercrunch.

West of 7th Avenue, the Village turns into a picture-book town of twisting, tree-lined streets, quaint houses, and tiny restaurants. Follow Grove Street from Sheridan Square past the house where Thomas Paine died (59 Grove St.) and the boyhood home of poet Hart Crane (45 Grove St.).

Time Out **The Pink Tea Cup** (42 Grove St., tel. 212/807–6755) is a typical Village restaurant only insofar as it is quirky and one-of-a-kind. Stop here if you have a hankering for down-home hamhocks, chitterlings, or fried pork chops; more standard fare is featured on the menu as well.

At this point, you'll be close to the intersection of Grove and Bleecker streets. You may now choose to take a leisurely stroll along the portion of Bleecker Street that extends west of 7th Avenue from Grove to Bank Street, heading in the direction of Abingdon Square.

This section of Bleecker Street is full of crafts and antiques shops, coffeehouses, and small restaurants. Some shopping highlights along the way include **An American Craftsman** (317 Bleecker St., tel. 212/727–0841) for handcrafted gifts; **Pierre Deux** (367–369 Bleecker St., tel. 212/243–7740) and **Susan Parrish** (tel. 212/645–5020) for antiques; **Simon Pearce** (385 Bleecker St., tel. 212/924–1142) for fine glass and pottery; **Biography Bookstore** (400 Bleecker St., tel. 212/807–8655); and **Bird Jungle** (401 Bleecker St., tel. 212/242–1757), with unusual, often colorful species of birds on display in the windows.

If you choose to forego Bleecker Street, continue your walk west on Grove Street. The secluded intersection of Grove and Bedford streets seems to have fallen through a time warp into the 19th century. On the northeast corner stands one of the few remaining clapboard structures in the city (17 Grove St.); wood construction was banned as a fire hazard in 1822, the year it was built. The house has since served many functions; it housed a brothel during the Civil War. Behind it, at 102 Bedford Street, is **Twin Peaks,** an 1835 house that was rather whimsically altered in the 1920s, with stucco, half-timbers, and a pair of steep roof peaks added on.

9 Grove Street curves in front of the iron gate of **Grove Court,** an enclave of brick-fronted town houses from the mid-1800s. Built originally as apartments for employees at neighborhood hotels, Grove Court used to be called Mixed Ale Alley because of the residents' propensity to pool beverages brought from work. It now houses a more affluent crowd: A town house there recently sold for $3 million.

Walk down Bedford Street a couple of blocks to 77 Bedford Street, the oldest house in the Village (1799). The place next door, 75½ Bedford Street, has an even greater claim to fame: Not only was it the residence (at different times) of both Edna St. Vincent Millay and John Barrymore, it is also, at 9½ feet wide, New York's narrowest house. The lot was an alley until rising real-estate prices inspired construction in 1873.

Heading west on Commerce Street, you soon reach the **Cherry Lane Theater** (tel. 212/989–2020), one of the original Off-Broadway houses and the site of American premieres of works by O'Neill, Beckett, Ionesco, and Albee. Across the street stand two nearly identical brick houses separated by a garden. Popularly known as the **Twin Sisters,** the houses were said to have been built by a sea captain for two daughters who loathed each other. Historical record insists that they were built by a milkman who needed the two houses and an open courtyard for his work.

Follow Barrow Street to Hudson Street, so named because this was originally the bank of the Hudson River. The block to the northwest **10** is owned by **St. Luke's-in-the-Fields,** built in 1822 as a country chapel for downtown's Trinity Church; its first warden was Clement ("'Twas the Night Before Christmas") Clarke Moore, who figured so largely in Chelsea's history (*see* Tour 11, *above*). An unadorned structure of soft-colored brick, St. Luke's was nearly destroyed by fire in 1981, but a flood of donations, many quite small, from residents of the West Village financed restoration of the square central tower. Bret Harte once lived at 487 Hudson Street, at the end of the row.

Time Out At the corner of Hudson Street and St. Luke's Place, the **Anglers and Writers Cafe** (420 Hudson St., tel. 212/675–0810) lives up to its name with bookshelves, fishing tackle, and pictures of Door County,

Wisconsin, hung on the walls. A meal here can be pretty pricey, but weary wanderers may linger over a pot of tea and a slice of cake for an hour or so, absorbing the place's restful charm.

---

⑪ East of Hudson Street, for the length of a block, Leroy Street becomes **St. Luke's Place,** a row of classic 1860s town houses shaded by graceful gingko trees. Novelist Theodore Dreiser wrote *An American Tragedy* at No. 16; poet Marianne Moore lived at No. 14, playwright Sherwood Anderson at No. 12. Mayor Jimmy Walker (first elected in 1926) lived at No. 6; the lampposts in front are "mayor's lamps," which were sometimes placed in front of the residences of New York mayors. This block is often used as a film location, too: No. 12 was shown as the Huxtables' home on *The Cosby Show* (although the family supposedly lived in Brooklyn), and No. 4 was the setting of the Audrey Hepburn movie *Wait Until Dark.* Before 1890 the playground on the south side of the street was a graveyard where, according to legend, the dauphin of France—the lost son of Louis XVI and Marie Antoinette—is buried.

Across 7th Avenue, St. Luke's Place becomes Leroy Street again, which terminates in an old Italian neighborhood at Bleecker Street. Amazingly unchanged amid all the Village gentrification, Bleecker between 6th and 7th avenues seems more vital these days than Little Italy does. Right at the corner of Leroy and Bleecker, **Grandpa's** restaurant (252 Bleecker St., tel. 212/627–9119) isn't particularly atmospheric, but it has celebrity value: It's owned by actor Al Lewis, best known as the vampire Grandpa on the old TV show *The Munsters,* and he is often there greeting patrons. For more authentic Italian ambience, stop into one of the fragrant Italian bakeries (**A. Zito & Sons,** 259 Bleecker St., and **Rocco's,** 243 Bleecker St.), or look inside the old-style butcher shops (**Ottomanelli & Sons,** 285 Bleecker St., and **Faicco's,** 260 Bleecker St.). **John's Pizzeria** (278 Bleecker St., tel. 212/243–1680) is one of those places that locals swear by. Be forewarned, however: no slices; whole pies only. You may also be tempted to stop in at the **Lafayette Bakery** (298 Bleecker St.); it's French rather than Italian, but the treats are luscious all ⑫ the same. The activity here focuses on **Father Demo Square** (Bleecker St. and 6th Ave.). Across Bleecker Street you'll see the **Church of Our Lady of Pompeii,** where Mother Cabrini, a naturalized Italian immigrant who became the first American saint, often prayed.

Head up 6th Avenue to 3rd Street and check out the playground caged there within a chain-link fence. NBA stars of tomorrow learn their moves on this patch of asphalt, where city-style basketball is played all afternoon and evening in all but the very coldest weather.

Return along Washington Square South to MacDougal Street and turn right. The **Provincetown Playhouse** (133 MacDougal St., tel. 212/477–5048) premiered many of Eugene O'Neill's plays. Louisa May Alcott wrote *Little Women* while living at 130–132 MacDougal Street. The two houses at 127 and 129 MacDougal Street were built for Aaron Burr in 1829; notice the pineapple newel posts, a symbol of hospitality.

Time Out The neighborhood's oldest coffeehouse is **Caffe Reggio** (119 MacDougal St., tel. 212/475–9557), where an antique machine steams forth espresso and cappuccino. The tiny tables are close together, but the crowd usually makes for interesting eavesdropping.

At **Minetta Tavern** (113 MacDougal St., tel. 212/475–3850), a venerable Village watering hole, turn right onto **Minetta Lane,** which leads to narrow **Minetta Street,** another former speakeasy alley. Both streets follow the course of Minetta Brook, which once flowed through this neighborhood and still bubbles deep beneath the pavement.

The foot of Minetta Street returns you to the corner of 6th Avenue and Bleecker Street, where you reach the stomping grounds of 1960s-era folksingers (many of them performed at the now-defunct Folk City one block north on West 3rd Street). This area still attracts a young crowd—partly because of the proximity of NYU—to its cafés, bars, jazz clubs, coffeehouses, theaters, and cabarets (*see* Chapter 12), not to mention its long row of unpretentious ethnic restaurants.

Tour 13: The East Village

The gritty tenements of the East Village—an area bounded by 14th Street on the north, 4th Avenue or the Bowery on the west, Houston Street on the south, and the East River—provided inexpensive living places for artists, writers, and actors after real estate prices in SoHo (*see* Tour 14, *below*) zoomed sky-high. New residents brought in their wake new restaurants, shops, and somewhat cleaner streets, while the old East Villagers maintained the trappings of the counterculture. Longtime bastions of the arts, such as the theaters CSC and LaMaMa, St. Mark's-in-the-Bowery Church, and the repertory movie house Theater 80 St. Marks, were joined by newer institutions such as P.S. 122, and several "hot" art galleries opened in narrow East Village storefronts. But the East Village scene lasted only a couple of years—just long enough to drive up rents substantially on some blocks, but not long enough to drive out all of the neighborhood's original residents. Today, an interesting mix has survived: artistic types in black leather, some homeless people and drug addicts (more so as you head deeper east into the slums of so-called Alphabet City along Avenues A, B, C, and D), and longtime members of various immigrant enclaves, principally Polish, Ukrainian, and Slovene.

To explore the East Village, begin at the intersection of East 8th Street, 4th Avenue, and Astor Place. Sculpture adorns two traffic islands here: One island contains *Alamo*, a massive black cube sculpted by Bernard Rosenthal; another bears an ornate cast-iron replica of a Beaux Arts subway entrance, providing access to the uptown No. 6 line. Go down into the station to see the authentically reproduced wall tiles.

🚩 Go straight east to **St. Marks Place** (the name given to 8th Street in the East Village), the longtime hub of the "hip" East Village. During the 1950s, beatniks such as Allen Ginsberg and Jack Kerouac lived and wrote in the area; the 1960s brought Bill Graham's Fillmore East concerts, the Electric Circus, and hallucinogenic drugs. The black-clad, pink-haired or shaven-headed punks followed, and some of them remain today. St. Marks Place between 2nd and 3rd avenues is lined with vegetarian restaurants, jewelry stalls, leather shops, and stores selling books, posters, and weird clothing, although the recent arrival of a branch of The Gap seems to signal that this street has lost its countercultural relevance. Late in the evening, this stretch of St. Marks Place sometimes attracts unpleasant characters you may wish to avoid.

Time Out Restaurants along St. Marks Place may come and go, but **DoJo** (24 St. Marks Pl., tel. 212/674–9821) lives on. The menu is heavy on brown rice, tofu, vegetables, and legumes, all tastily cooked. The atmosphere is casual, and prices are so low even impoverished students are happy.

Second Avenue, which St. Marks crosses after one block, was known in the early part of this century as the Yiddish Rialto. Between Houston and 14th streets, eight theaters presented Yiddish-language productions of musicals, revues, and heart-wrenching melodramas. Today the theaters are gone; all that remains are Hollywood-style stars that have been embedded in the sidewalk in front of the **Second Avenue Deli** (2nd Ave. and 10th St., tel. 212/677–0606) to commemorate Yiddish stage luminaries.

Catercorner to the Second Avenue Deli is another East Village landmark, **St. Mark's-in-the-Bowery Church,** a 1799 fieldstone country church to which a Greek Revival steeple and a cast-iron front porch have been added. This, the city's oldest continually used church building (the old Dutch governor Peter Stuyvesant and Commodore Perry are buried here), had to be completely restored after a disastrous fire in 1978. Over the years, St. Mark's has hosted much countercultural activity. In the 1920s a forward-thinking pastor injected the Episcopalian ritual with Native American chants, Greek folk dancing, and Eastern mantras. During the hippie era, St. Mark's welcomed avant-garde poets and playwrights. Today dancers, poets, and performance artists cavort in the main sanctuary, where pews have been removed to accommodate them.

From in front of the church, you can investigate **Stuyvesant Street,** which angles southwest back to Astor Place. This area was once Governor Stuyvesant's "bouwerie," or farm; among the handsome redbrick row houses is one at 21 Stuyvesant Street that was built in 1804 as a wedding gift for a great-great-granddaughter of the governor.

Continue up 2nd Avenue to the **Ukrainian Museum,** a small upstairs gallery celebrating the cultural heritage of the Ukraine. Now that this country has become independent again, there's something especially poignant about this collection, nurtured in exile throughout the years of Soviet domination: ceramics, jewelry, hundreds of brilliantly colored Easter eggs, and an extensive collection of Ukrainian costumes and textiles. *203 2nd Ave., between 12th and 13th Sts., tel. 212/228–0110. Admission: $1 adults, 50¢ students and senior citizens. Open Wed.–Sun. 1–5.*

Time Out For some of the best Italian pastries in the city, try **De Robertis Pasticceria** (176 1st Ave., tel. 212/674–7137) or the more famous **Veniero Pasticerria** (342 E. 11th St. near 1st Ave., tel. 212/674–7264), both with rows and rows of incredibly fresh cannolis, fruit tarts, cheesecakes, and other desserts on display.

As you continue down 1st Avenue, you'll pass at 9th Street **P.S. 122** (150 1st Ave., tel. 212/477–5288), a former public school building transformed into a complex of spaces for avant-garde entertainment (*see* Chapter 11), and, just west of the avenue on St. Marks Place, **Theater 80 St. Marks** (80 St. Marks Pl., tel. 212/254–7400), one of New York's few remaining revival movie houses. Check out the posters in front to see what today's vintage double bill may be. Also, be sure to look down at the sidewalk, where you'll find the handprints, footprints, and autographs of such past screen luminaries as Joan Crawford, Ruby Keeler, Alexis Smith, and Gloria Swanson.

Turn left on St. Marks Place and head east, to where the avenues are labeled with letters, not numbers. Until relatively recently, this area's nickname, Alphabet City, meant a burned-out territory of slums and drug haunts, but some blocks and buildings were gentrified during the height of the East Village art scene a few years ago. The old and new East Villagers several times clashed around **Tompkins Square,** the leafy park bordered by Avenues A and B and 7th and 10th streets. The square's well-established tent city of homeless people provided the spark in the summers of 1988 and 1989, as police moved to rid the park of vagrants, and neighborhood residents vociferously took up sides. Riots broke out, and tempers ran high. The homeless people have since moved on, and the park has received a much-needed renovation, making it a pleasant place to sit on a bench on a sunny afternoon.

To head back west, follow 7th Street away from the southwest corner of Tompkins Square, studying the mix of small stores and restaurants to get a reading on the neighborhood's culture-in-flux. After crossing 1st and 2nd avenues, note **McSorley's Old Ale House** (15 E. 7th St., tel. 212/473–9138), one of several claimants to the distinction of being New York's oldest bar, often crammed with collegiate types enticed by McSorley's own brands of ale. McSorley's opened in 1854 but didn't admit women until 1970. Just past McSorley's is **Surma, The Ukrainian Shop** (11 E. 7th St., tel. 212/477–0729), with its exotic stock of Ukrainian books, magazines, cassettes, and greeting cards, as well as musical instruments, painted eggs, and an exhaustive collection of peasant blouses. Across the street is **St. George's Ukrainian Catholic Church** with its mosaic dome.

Across 3rd Avenue, the massive brownstone **Cooper Union Foundation Building** dominates **Cooper Square,** the large open space created where 3rd and 4th avenues merge into the Bowery. A statue of industrialist Peter Cooper, by Augustus Saint-Gaudens, presides over the square. Cooper founded this college in 1859 to provide a forum for public opinion and free technical education for the working class; it still offers tuition-free education in architecture, art, and engineering. Cooper Union was the first structure to be supported by steel railroad rails—rolled in Cooper's own plant. Three galleries present changing exhibitions during the academic year (admission free; open weekdays noon–7, Sat. noon–5).

Musicians may want to stop in at the **Carl Fischer Music Store** (62 Cooper Sq., tel. 212/677–1148) to select from the infinitude of sheet music, confer with the knowledgeable staff, and hang out with the musicians here.

If you're here on a Sunday, go down to the foot of Cooper Square and head a half-block east on 4th Street to the **Old Merchant's House.** Built in 1830, this Federal-style house was home to the Tredwell family from 1835 to 1933, when the last of the elderly Tredwell sisters died. The original furnishings and architectural features remain intact, offering a rare glimpse of family life in the mid-19th century. *29 E. 4th St., tel. 212/777–1089. Admission: $3 adults, $2 students and senior citizens. Open Sun. 1–4; other times by appointment ($60 charge for private tour).*

One block west of Cooper Square, turn right up Lafayette Street. The long block between East 4th Street and Astor Place contains on the west side **Colonnade Row** (1833), a grand sweep of four houses (originally nine) fronted by marble Corinthian columns. Although sadly run-down today, in their time these houses were home to millionaires John Jacob Astor and Cornelius Vanderbilt; writers Washington Irving, William Makepeace Thackeray, and Charles Dickens all stayed here at one time or another.

In 1854 Astor opened the city's first free library in the imposing Italian Renaissance–style structure directly across the street, which was renovated in 1967 to serve as the New York Shakespeare Festival's **Joseph Papp Public Theater** (425 Lafayette St., tel. 212/598–7150). Under the leadership of the late Joseph Papp, the Public's five playhouses and one cinema built a fine reputation for bold and innovative performances (*see* Chapter 11); the long-running hit *A Chorus Line* had its first performances here, but so have many less commercial plays.

West of Astor Place, turn left on Broadway to hit a trendy downtown shopping strip, especially strong in funky secondhand and surplus clothing stores. Above street level, the old warehouses here have mostly been converted into residential lofts. Walk south to 4th Street, where you'll see **Tower Records** (692 Broadway, tel. 212/505–1500), a very big and very good tape-and-CD store that also serves as a mingling place for young hipsters (or would-be hipsters).

Time Out   For splendid soups, juicy burgers, large salads, omelets, and great french fries, sample **NoHo Star** (333 Lafayette St. at Bleecker St., tel. 212/925–0070), a sleek, friendly place that attracts an artsy crowd. After 6, dishes with an Asian accent are added to the menu.

Tour 14: SoHo and TriBeCa

Numbers in the margin correspond to points of interest on the Tours 14–16: SoHo, TriBeCa, Little Italy, Chinatown map.

Today the names of these two downtown neighborhoods are virtually synonymous with a certain postmodern chic—an amalgam of black-clad artists, hip young Wall Streeters, track-lit loft apartments, hip art galleries, and restaurants with a minimalist approach to both food and decor. It's all very urban, very cool, very now. But 25 years ago, they were virtual wastelands. SoHo (so named because it is the district *S*outh of *H*ouston Street, bounded by Broadway, Canal Street, and 6th Avenue) was described in a 1962 City Club of New York study as "commercial slum number one." It was saved by two factors: (1) preservationists discovered here the world's greatest concentration of cast-iron architecture and fought to prevent demolition, and (2) artists discovered the large, cheap, well-lit spaces that cast-iron buildings provide. At first it was technically illegal for artists to live in their loft studios, but so many did that eventually the zoning laws were changed to permit residence.

By 1980, the tide of loft dwellers, galleries, and trendy shops and cafés had made SoHo so desirable a residential area, despite the still-gritty look of the neighborhood, that none but the most successful artists could afford it anymore. Seeking similar space, artists moved downtown to another half-abandoned commercial district, for which a new SoHo-like name was invented: TriBeCa (the *Tri*angle *Be*low *Ca*nal Street, although in effect it goes no farther south than Murray Street and no farther east than West Broadway). The same scenario played itself out again, and TriBeCa's rising rents are already beyond the means of most artists, who have moved instead to Long Island City (*see* Queens in Chapter 4) or areas of Brooklyn or

New Jersey. But just because the artists have left doesn't mean that SoHo and TriBeCa aren't still a vital scene.

Perhaps the best introduction to these areas is a walk up Greene Street, where the block between Canal and Grand streets contains the longest continuous row of cast-iron buildings anywhere (Nos. 8–34 Greene St.). The architectural rage between 1860 and 1890, cast-iron buildings were popular because they did not require massive walls to bear the weight of the upper stories. With no need for load-bearing walls, they were able to have more interior space and larger windows. They were also versatile, with various architectural elements produced from standardized molds to mimic any style—Italianate, Victorian Gothic, neo-Grecian, to name but a few visible in SoHo. Look, for example, at 28–30 Greene Street, an 1873 building

❶ nicknamed the **Queen of Greene Street.** Besides its pale paint job, notice how many decorative features have been applied: dormers, columns, window arches, and projecting central bays. Handsome as they are, these buildings were always commercial, containing stores and light manufacturing, principally textiles. Along this street notice the iron loading docks and the sidewalk vault covers studded with glass disks to let light into basement storage areas. In front of 62–64 Greene Street there's one of the few remaining turn-of-the-century bishop's-crook lampposts, with various cast-iron curlicues from the base to the curved top.

❷ At 72–76 Greene Street is the so-called **King of Greene Street,** a five-story Renaissance-style building with a magnificent projecting porch of Corinthian columns. Today the King (now painted yellow) houses the **M-13** art gallery (tel. 212/925–3007) and **The Second Coming,** which sells vintage clothing, furniture, and other curiosities.

Time Out The desirable deli **Dean & Deluca** operates a spacious, skylit café (121 Prince St., tel. 212/254–8776) where you can join the well-heeled gallery-hoppers and shoppers in capuccino and wicked cakes, or a lunchtime brie baguette, roasted vegetables and lemon chicken, or pasta salad. Opposite, **Olive's** (120 Prince St., tel. 212/941–0111) outdoes even D&D in the spectacular sandwich stakes, but it's take-out only.

Take Prince Street west to Wooster Street, which, like a few other SoHo streets, still has its 19th-century pavement of Belgian blocks, a smoother successor to traditional cobblestones. Before embarking

❸ on a gallery-hop, check out the well-established **Street Market** on the southwest corner of Prince and Wooster. With the feeling of a flea market (though it isn't because nothing is secondhand), this cluster of stalls sells trendy clothing, jewelry, socks, hats, and ethnic accessories, many of which bear remarkable similarities to the wares in surrounding shops, but at a tenth of the price. Now on to the art.

❹ Start at the **Paula Cooper Gallery** (149–155 Wooster St., tel. 674–0766), one of SoHo's oldest galleries. At 141 Wooster Street, one of

❺ several outposts of the DIA Art Foundation, you can visit the **New York Earth Room,** Walter de Maria's avant-garde 1977 artwork that consists of 140 tons of gently sculpted soil filling a second-floor gallery. *Tel. 212/473–8072. Admission free. Open Wed.–Sat. noon–6. Closed Memorial Day–Labor Day.*

At 131 Wooster Street, a store named **Home Town** (tel. 212/674–5770) has the serendipitous quality of an upscale flea market, an eclectic stock of "found objects" and country-style antiques for making trendy lofts feel homey. Across the street is the **Gagosian Gallery** (136 Wooster St., tel. 212/228–2828), operated by prominent uptown dealer Larry Gagosian. The gallery's silver-and-glass front resembles a very wide garage door.

West Broadway (which, somewhat confusingly, runs parallel to and four blocks west of regular Broadway) is SoHo's main drag, and on Saturday it can be crowded with smartly dressed uptowners and suburbanites who've come down for a little store- and gallery-hopping (*see* Chapter 8). In the block between Prince and Spring streets alone there are three major art stops: **420 West Broadway,** with six separate galleries including two of the biggest SoHo names, Leo Castelli (tel. 212/431–5160) and the Sonnabend Gallery (tel. 212/966–6160); the **Mary Boone Gallery** (417 W. Broadway tel. 212/431–1818); and another excellent cluster of galleries at **415 West Broadway,** including the Witkin Gallery (tel. 212/925–5510) for photography. One block south, at **383 West Broadway,** OK Harris (tel. 212/431–3600) has its digs.

Time Out The crowded, lively **Cupping Room Cafe** (359 W. Broadway, tel. 212/925–2898) specializes in comforting soups, muffins, cakes, and brunch, with excellent Bloody Marys.

Go east to Broome Street and Broadway, where, on the northeast corner, you'll see the sadly unrestored classic of the cast-iron genre, the **Haughwout Building** (488 Broadway), nicknamed the Parthenon of Cast Iron. Built in 1857 to house Eder Haughwout's china and glassware business, the exterior was inspired by a Venetian palazzo. Inside, it contained the world's first commercial passenger elevator, a steam-powered device invented by Elisha Graves Otis.

Head north up Broadway, which temporarily loses its SoHo ambience in the midst of discount clothing stores. Just below Prince Street, the 1907 **Singer Building** (561 Broadway) shows the final flower of the cast-iron style, with wrought-iron balconies, terracotta panels, and broad expanses of windows. Across the street is one of New York's gourmet shrines, the gleaming **Dean & DeLuca** food market (560 Broadway, tel. 212/431–1691), whose bread and produce arrangements often are worthy of still-life paintings. The smartly restored **560 Broadway** building also houses a respected multigallery exhibit space; another such space is just up the street at **568 Broadway.** On the ground floor at 568 Broadway is the **Armani Exchange** store (tel. 212/431–6000), featuring a new line by the famous Italian designer—casual, basic clothes several notches up from The Gap, just right for post-recession chic.

On the west side of Broadway, the Guggenheim Museum opened a SoHo branch in 1992: the **Guggenheim Museum SoHo,** which displays a revolving series of exhibitions, both contemporary work and pieces from the Guggenheim's permanent collection. The museum occupies space in a landmark 19th-century redbrick structure with its original cast-iron storefronts and detailed cornice. Arata Isozaki designed the two floors of stark, loftlike galleries as well as the museum store facing West Broadway. Scheduled exhibitions for 1995 include a Claes Oldenburg "Anthology," which goes up in April, following Ross Bleckner and Felix Gonzalez-Torres shows. *575 Broadway, tel. 212/423–3500. Admission: $5 adults, $3 senior citizens and students. Open Sun., Mon., Wed. 11–6; Thurs.–Sat. 11–10. Admission higher for special exhibitions.*

A few doors up the street, the **New Museum of Contemporary Art** shows experimental, often radically innovative work by unrecognized artists, none of it more than 10 years old. *583 Broadway, tel. 212/219–1222. Admission: $3.50 adults, $2.50 students, senior citi-*

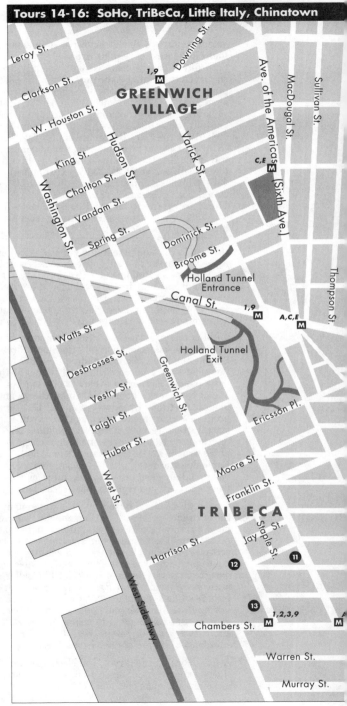

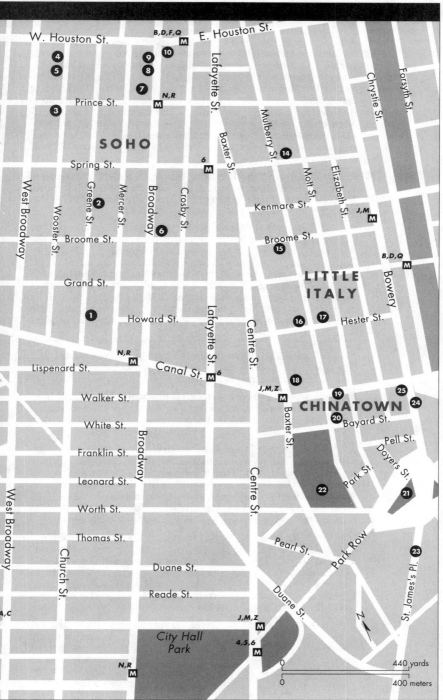

zens, and artists. Open Wed., Thurs., Fri., and Sun. noon–6; Sat. noon–8.

A few doors up the street (north) from the New Museum is the **Museum for African Art,** dedicated to contemporary and traditional African art. This fascinating addition to the SoHo scene is housed in a handsome, two-story space designed by Maya Lin, who also designed Washington, DC's Vietnam Veterans Memorial. Exhibits may include contemporary sculpture, ceremonial masks, architectural details, costumes, and textiles. The museum store features African crafts, clothing, and jewelry. *593 Broadway, tel. 212/966–1313. Admission: $3 adults; $1.50 students, senior citizens, and children under 12. Open Tues.–Fri. 10:30–5:30; Sat. noon–8; Sun. noon–6.*

Across Broadway, the **Alternative Museum,** a gallery that exhibits art with a political or sociopolitical twist, has moved up to SoHo from its former TriBeCa home. *594 Broadway, tel. 212/966–4444. Suggested contribution: $3. Open Tues.–Sat. 11–6.*

Go one block west to Mercer Street, where the sidewalks may be cluttered with cartons of cloth or leather remnants discarded by the sweatshops upstairs (artists find a lot of good collage material here).

Time Out | Amid all the artful minimalism of SoHo restaurants, **Fanelli's Cafe** (corner of Mercer and Prince Sts., tel. 212/226–9412) is a breath of fresh air. It's been in operation since 1872 and it looks it, with its etched-glass front door, carved mahogany bar, and pressed-tin walls. Order some standard bar food—burgers, omelets, or pizza with a thin, crisp crust.

Next to Fanelli's is **A Photographer's Place** (133 Mercer St., tel. 212/966–2356), which features photography books, calendars, postcards, and antique cameras and pictures.

Between Broome and Spring streets is **Enchanted Forest** (85 Mercer St., tel. 212/925–6677), with a fanciful selection of stuffed animals, books, and handmade toys that almost deserves to be considered an art gallery. Both kids and adults have a great time here.

At the foot of Mercer Street, bustling Canal Street leads east to Chinatown (*see* Tour 16, *below*); across the street, TriBeCa officially begins. To avoid Canal Street's commercial chaos, cross as soon as you can and then turn south down West Broadway. A life-size iron Statue of Liberty crown rises above the blue-tiled entrance to **El Teddy's** (219 W. Broadway, tel. 212/941–7070), a gourmet Mexican restaurant. Stop in for a drink, if only to see the kitschy decor.

 In the mid-19th century, Worth Street was the equivalent of 7th Avenue today, the center of the garment trade; the area to the west, near the Hudson River docks, became the heart of the wholesale food business. Turn right onto Duane Street to reach **Duane Park,** preserved since 1800 as a calm, shady triangle; it is still surrounded by cheese, butter, and egg warehouses (note the Land O'Lakes sign facing the south tip of the park).

One block north on Hudson Street, on your right, you'll see the Art Deco **Western Union Building** (60 Hudson St.), where 19 subtly shaded colors of brick are laid in undulating patterns. Turn up quiet Jay Street and pause at narrow Staple Street, little more than an alley, where a green pedestrian walkway overhead links two warehouses. The street is named for the staple products unloaded here by ships in transit that didn't want to pay duty on any extra cargo.

Framed at the end of the alley is the redbrick **New York Mercantile Exchange,** its square corner tower topped by a bulbous roof. On the ground floor is an acclaimed restaurant, **Chanterelle** (*see* Chapter 9).

If you continue west on Jay Street, you'll pass the loading docks of a very active food wholesaler, **Bazzini's Nuts and Confections.** Tucked into a corner of its extensive warehouse is its upscale retail shop (corner of Jay and Greenwich Sts., tel. 212/334–1280), where you can buy nuts, coffee beans, candies, cookies, and various other delicacies.

On Greenwich Street near Harrison Street, the **TriBeCa Grill** (*see* Chapter 9) is located on the first floor of the old Martinson Coffee Building, which now houses actor Robert De Niro's **Tribeca Film Center,** a movie production complex. Movie fans may want to continue north to Moore Street, where a right turn will take you two blocks to 14 Moore Street, the firehouse (still in use) that was filmed as the **Ghostbusters' headquarters** in the movies *Ghostbusters* and *Ghostbusters II*.

As you walk back down Greenwich Street, notice on your right a surprising row of early 19th-century town houses nestled in the side of a huge high-rise apartment complex. These three-story redbrick houses were moved here to Harrison Street from various sites in the neighborhood when, in the early 1970s, the food-wholesalers' central market nearby was razed and moved to the Bronx. Walk around the houses to peer into the green yard they enclose.

🄬 The high-rise towers belong to **Independence Plaza,** a pleasant, if somewhat utilitarian, project of the mid-1970s that was supposed to be part of a wave of demolition and construction—until the preservationists stepped in. For several years Independence Plaza remained a middle-class island stranded downtown, far from stores, schools, and neighbors; with TriBeCa's growing chic, however, plus the development of Battery Park City to the south, it has become a much more desirable address.

Continuing south on Greenwich Street, you'll soon come to the 2½-acre **Washington Market Park,** a much-needed recreation space for 🄭 this neighborhood. Named after the great food market that once sprawled over this area, it is a green, landscaped oasis with tennis courts, a playground, and even a gazebo. Just across Chambers Street, P.S. 234, a public elementary school, has opened to serve TriBeCa's younger generation. At the corner, a stout little red tower resembles a lighthouse, and iron ship figures are worked into the playground fence—reminders of the neighborhood's long-gone dockside past.

Tour 15: Little Italy

Mulberry Street is the heart of Little Italy; in fact, at this point it's virtually the entire body. In 1932 an estimated 98% of the inhabitants of this area were of Italian birth or heritage, but since then the growth and expansion of neighboring Chinatown have encroached on the Italian neighborhood to such an extent that merchants and community leaders of the Little Italy Restoration Association (LIRA) negotiated a truce in which the Chinese agreed to let at least Mulberry remain an all-Italian street. If you want the flavor of a whole Italian neighborhood, you'd do better visiting Carroll Gardens in Brooklyn or Arthur Avenue in the Bronx (*see* Chapter 4); or rent a video of the Martin Scorsese movie *Mean Streets*, which was filmed in Little Italy back in the very early 1970s.

Start at the intersection of Spring and Mulberry streets, which still
⑭ has a residential feel to it. The **D & G Bakery** (45 Spring St., tel. 212/
226–6688) is one of the last coal-oven bakeries in the United States.
Buy a loaf of savory prosciutto bread, a meal in itself, with the Italian ham baked right into the bread.

Walk down Mulberry Street to Broome Street, where the classic
Little Italy really begins, crowded with restaurants, cafés, bakeries, imported-food shops, and souvenir stores. Especially on weekends, when suburbanites flock here, this is a street for strolling,
gawking, and inhaling the aroma of garlic and olive oil. Some restaurants and cafés display high-tech Eurodesign; others seem dedicated to staying exactly as their old customers remember them. At
the southwest corner of Broome and Mulberry streets, stairs lead
down through a glass entrance to what seems to be a blue-tiled
⑮ cave—and, appropriately enough, it is the **Grotta Azzurra** (Blue
Grotto) restaurant (387 Broome St., tel. 212/925–8775), a longtime
favorite for both the hearty food and the very Italian ambience.
Across Mulberry Street is **Caffe Roma** (385 Broome St., 212/226–
8413), a traditional pastry shop where you can eat cannoli at post-
age-stamp-size wrought-iron tables.

At the corner of Mulberry and Grand streets, stop to get the lay of
the land. Facing north (uptown), on your right you'll see a series of
wide, four-story houses from the early 19th century, built long before the great flood of immigration hit this neighborhood between
1890 and 1924. Turn and look south along the east side of Mulberry
Street to see Little Italy's predominant architecture today: tenement buildings with fire escapes projecting over the sidewalks.
Most of these are of the late-19th-century New York style known as
railroad flats: six-story buildings on 25-by-90-foot lots, with all the
rooms in each apartment placed in a straight line like railroad cars.
This style was common in the densely populated immigrant neighborhoods of lower Manhattan until 1901, when the city passed an or-
dinance requiring air shafts in the interior of buildings. On the
southeast corner, **E. Rossi & Co.** (191 Grand St., tel. 212/966–6640;
established in 1902) is an antiquated little shop that sells housewares, espresso makers, embroidered religious postcards, and jocu-
lar Italian T-shirts. Down Grand Street is **Ferrara's** (195 Grand St.,
tel. 212/226–6150), a 100-year-old pastry shop that ships its creations—cannoli, peasant pie, Italian rum cake—all over the world.
Another survivor of the pretenement era is at 149 Mulberry Street,
formerly the Van Rensselaer House (built in 1816); notice its dormer
windows. Today it houses **Paolucci's Restaurant** (tel. 212/226–9653).

⑯ **Umberto's Clam House** (129 Mulberry St., tel. 212/431–7545) is perhaps best known as the place where mobster Joey Gallo was munch-
ing scungili in 1973 when he was fatally surprised by a task force of
mob hit men. Quite peaceful now, Umberto's specializes in fresh
shellfish in a spicy tomato sauce. Turn onto Hester Street to visit yet
⑰ another Little Italy institution, **Puglia** (189 Hester St., tel. 212/966–
6006), a restaurant where guests sit at long communal tables, sing
along with house entertainers, and enjoy moderately priced southern Italian specialties with quantities of homemade wine. (For other
Little Italy restaurants, *see* Chapter 9.)

One street west, on Baxter Street toward Canal Street, stands the
⑱ **San Gennaro Church** (officially, Most Precious Blood Church, National Shrine of San Gennaro), which each year around September
19 sponsors Little Italy's keynote event, the annual Feast of San
Gennaro. (The community's other big festival celebrates St. Anthony of Padua, in June; that church is at Houston and Sullivan streets,

in what is now SoHo.) During the feasts, Little Italy's streets are closed to traffic, arches of tinsel span the thoroughfares, the sidewalks are lined with booths offering games and food, and the whole scene is one noisy, crowded, kitschy, delightful party.

Tour 16: Chinatown

Visibly exotic, Chinatown is a popular tourist attraction, but it is also a real, vital community, where about half of the city's population of 300,000 Chinese still live. Its main businesses are restaurants and garment factories; some 55% of its residents speak little or no English. Theoretically, Chinatown is divided from Little Italy by Canal Street, the bustling artery that links the Holland Tunnel (to New Jersey) and the Manhattan Bridge (to Brooklyn). However, in recent years, an influx of immigrants from the People's Republic of China, Taiwan, and especially Hong Kong has swelled Manhattan's Chinese population, and Hong Kong residents, anticipating the return of the British colony in 1997 to PRC domination, have been investing their capital in Chinatown real estate. Consequently, Chinatown now spills over its traditional borders into Little Italy to the north and the formerly Jewish Lower East Side to the east.

Originally Canal Street was a tree-lined road with a canal running its length. Today the Chinatown stretch of Canal Street is almost overwhelmed with sidewalk markets bursting with stacks of fresh seafood and strange-shaped vegetables in extraterrestrial shades of green. Food shops proudly display their wares: If America's motto is "a chicken in every pot," then Chinatown's must be "a roast duck in every window."

⓳ The slightly less frantic **Kam Man** (200 Canal St., tel. 212/571–0330), a duplex supermarket, sells an amazing assortment of fresh and canned imported groceries, herbs, and the sort of dinnerware and furniture familiar to patrons of Chinese restaurants. Choose from dozens of varieties of noodles or such delicacies as dried starch and fresh chicken feet.

⓴ The **Chinatown History Museum,** at the corner of Bayard and Mulberry streets, shows interactive photographic exhibitions on Asian-American labor history. It also has a resource library and bookstore and offers a walking tour of Chinatown from April to November. *70 Mulberry St., 2nd Floor, tel. 212/619–4785. Admission: $1. Open weekdays and Sun. noon–5.*

Mott Street, the principal business street of the neighborhood, looks the way you might expect Chinatown to look: narrow and twisting, crammed with souvenir shops and restaurants in funky pagoda-style buildings, crowded with pedestrians at all hours of the day or night. Within the few dense blocks of Chinatown, hundreds of restaurants serve every imaginable type of Chinese cuisine, from fast-food noodles or dumplings to sumptuous Hunan, Szechuan, Cantonese, Mandarin, and Shanghai feasts (*see* Chapter 9). Every New Yorker thinks he or she knows the absolute, flat-out best, but whichever one you try, at 8 PM on Saturday, don't be surprised if you have to wait in line to get in.

As you proceed down Mott Street, take a peek down Pell Street, a narrow lane of wall-to-wall restaurants whose neon signs stretch halfway across the thoroughfare. At 35 Pell Street is **May May Chinese Gourmet Bakery** (tel. 212/267–6733), a good place to stop for Chinese pastries, rice dumplings, and vegetarian specialties, such as yam cakes and vegetarian spring rolls.

Time Out A few steps down Pell Street, turn onto Doyers Street to find the **Viet-Nam Restaurant** (11 Doyers St., tel. 212/693–0725), an informal, inexpensive little basement Vietnamese restaurant, then turn right off Mott onto Bayard Street for dessert at the **Chinatown Ice Cream Factory** (65 Bayard, tel. 212/608–4170) for green tea, red bean, or coconut ice cream.

At the corner of Mott and Mosco streets stands the **Church of the Transfiguration.** Built in 1801 as the Zion Episcopal Church, this imposing Georgian structure with Gothic windows is now a Chinese Catholic church where mass is said in Cantonese, Mandarin, and English. Directly across the street from the church is **Quong Yuen Shing & Co.** (32 Mott St., tel. 212/962–6280), one of Chinatown's oldest curio shops, with porcelain bowls, teapots, and cups for sale.

㉑ At the end of Mott Street is **Chatham Square,** which is really more of a labyrinth than a square: 10 streets converge here, creating pandemonium for cars and a nightmare for pedestrians. A Chinese arch honoring Chinese casualties in American wars stands on an island in the eye of the storm. On the far end of the square, at the corner of Catherine Street and East Broadway, you'll see a branch of the Manhattan Savings Bank, built to resemble a pagoda (in this neighborhood, even some public phone booths have been styled as pagodas).

Skirting Chatham Square, head back to the right to go down Worth Street. The corner of Worth, Baxter, and Park streets was once known as Five Points, the central intersection of a tough 19th-century slum of Irish and German immigrants. Today it has been replaced **㉒** by **Columbus Park,** a shady, paved urban space where children play and elderly Chinese gather to reminisce about their homelands.

Return to Chatham Square, cross Park Row (on your right) and take a sharp right turn on St. James Place to find two remnants of this **㉓** neighborhood's pre-Chinatown past. On St. James Place is the **First Shearith Israel graveyard** (predecessor of the cemeteries in Greenwich Village and Chelsea; *see* Tours 11 and 12, *above*). The first Jewish cemetery in the United States, this site was consecrated in 1656, when it was considered to be well outside of town. Walk a half block farther, turn left on James Street, and you'll see **St. James Church,** a stately 1837 Greek Revival edifice where Al Smith, who rose from this poor Irish neighborhood to become New York's governor and a 1928 Democratic presidential candidate, once served as altar boy.

㉔ Go back past Chatham Square and up the Bowery to **Confucius Plaza,** the open area monitored by a statue of Confucius and the sweeping curve of a redbrick high-rise apartment complex named for him. At 18 Bowery, at the corner of Pell Street, stands one of Manhattan's oldest homes, a Federal and Georgian structure built in 1785 by meat wholesaler Edward Mooney. A younger side of Chinatown is **㉕** shown at the **Asian American Arts Centre,** which displays current work by Asian American artists. *26 Bowery, tel. 212/233–2154. Admission free. Open weekdays 10–6.*

For some exotic shopping, duck into the **Canal Arcade,** a passage linking the Bowery and Elizabeth Street. A few doors down, at 50 Bowery, you'll see the **Silver Palace** restaurant (*see* Chapter 9), worth a peek inside for its Chinese rococo interior, complete with dragons whose eyes are blinking lights.

At the intersection of the Bowery and Canal Street, a grand arch and colonnade mark the entrance to the Manhattan Bridge, which leads to Brooklyn. This corner was once the center of New York's diamond district. Many jewelry dealers have moved uptown to 47th Street between 5th and 6th avenues (*see* Off the Beaten Track, *below*), but a substantial number still occupy shops on the Bowery and the north side of Canal. The selection is pretty good, but don't pay the first price quoted.

Tour 17: Wall Street and the Battery

Numbers in the margin correspond to points of interest on the Tours 17 and 18: Lower Manhattan map.

Lower Manhattan doesn't cover many acres, but it is packed with attractions, for it has always been central to the city's networks of power and wealth. It was here that the New Amsterdam colony was established by the Dutch in 1625; in 1789, the first capital building of the United States was located here. The city did not really expand beyond these precincts until the middle of the 19th century. Today Lower Manhattan is in many ways dominated by Wall Street, which is both an actual street and a shorthand name for the vast, powerful financial community that clusters around the New York and American stock exchanges. Visit on a weekday to catch the district's true vitality—but expect to be jostled on the crowded sidewalks if you stand too long, peering at the great buildings that surge skyward on every corner. A different but equally awe-inspiring sight can be found on the tip of the island, as you look out across the great silvery harbor and see enduring symbols of America: the Statue of Liberty and Ellis Island, port of entry for countless immigrants to a new land.

Our tour begins at the southernmost point of Manhattan, at the **Staten Island Ferry Terminal** (for subway riders, that's just outside the
❶ South Ferry station on the No. 1 line). The **Staten Island Ferry** is still the best deal in town: The 20- to 30-minute ride across New York Harbor provides great views of the Manhattan skyline, the Statue of Liberty, the Verrazano-Narrows Bridge, and the New Jersey coast—and it costs only 50¢ round-trip (you must use quarters in the turnstiles). Boats embark on various schedules: every 15 minutes during rush hours, every 20–30 minutes most other times, and every hour after 11 PM and on weekend mornings. A word of advice, however: While commuters love the ferry service's swift, new low-slung craft, the boats ride low in the water and have no outside deck space. Wait for one of the higher, more open old-timers. Once you're on Staten Island, you can, of course, stay as long as you like.

❷ To the west of South Ferry lies **Battery Park,** a verdant landfill, loaded with monuments and sculpture, at Manhattan's green toe. The park's name refers to a line of cannons once mounted here to defend the shoreline (which ran along what is currently State Street). Head north along the water's edge to the **East Coast Memorial,** a statue of a fierce eagle that presides over eight granite slabs inscribed with the names of U.S. servicemen who died in the Western Atlantic during World War II. Climb the steps of the East Coast Memorial for a fine view of the main features of **New York Harbor;** from left to right: **Governors Island,** a Coast Guard installation; hilly **Staten Island** in the distance; the **Statue of Liberty** on Liberty Island; **Ellis Island,** gateway to the New World for generations of immigrants; and the old railway terminal in **Liberty State Park,** on the mainland in Jersey City, New Jersey.

Continue north past a romantic **statue of Giovanni da Verrazano,** the Florentine merchant who piloted the ship that first sighted New York and its harbor in 1524. The Verrazano-Narrows Bridge be-

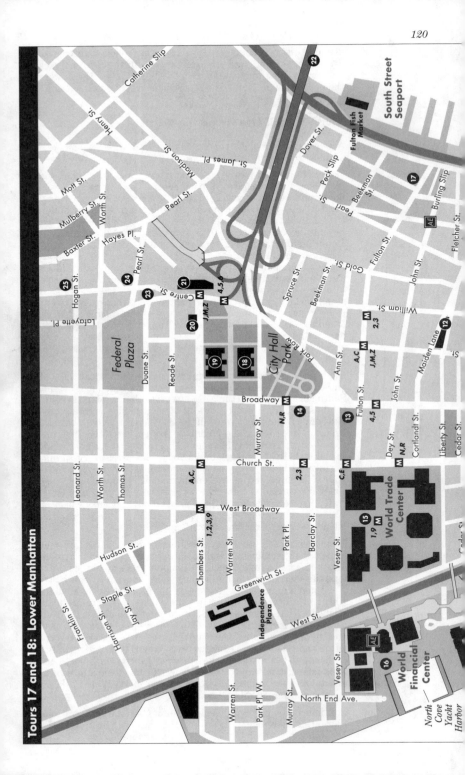

Tours 17 and 18: Lower Manhattan

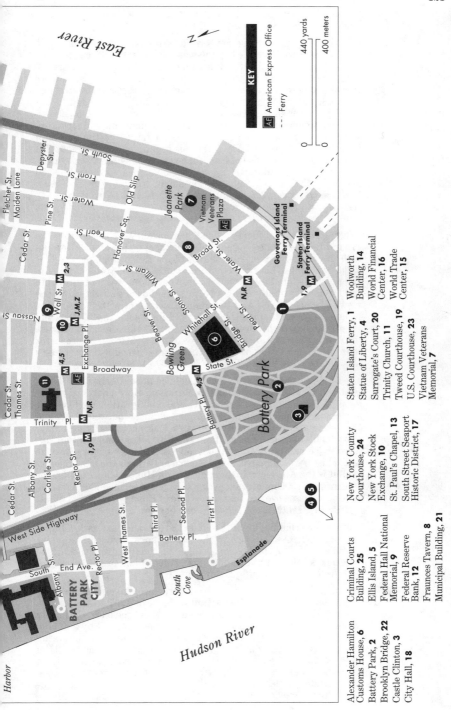

Harbor

Hudson River

East River

KEY

AE American Express Office

--- Ferry

N

0   440 yards

0   400 meters

BATTERY PARK CITY

Battery Park

South Cove

Esplanade

Alexander Hamilton
Customs House, 6
Battery Park, 2
Brooklyn Bridge, 22
Castle Clinton, 3
City Hall, 18

Criminal Courts
Building, 25
Ellis Island, 5
Federal Hall National
Memorial, 9
Federal Reserve
Bank, 12
Fraunces Tavern, 8
Municipal Building, 21

New York County
Courthouse, 24
New York Stock
Exchange, 10
St. Paul's Chapel, 13
South Street Seaport
Historic District, 17

Staten Island Ferry, 1
Statue of Liberty, 4
Surrogate's Court, 20
Trinity Church, 11
Tweed Courthouse, 19
U.S. Courthouse, 23
Vietnam Veterans
Memorial, 7

Woolworth
Building, 14
World Financial
Center, 16
World Trade
Center, 15

tween Brooklyn and Staten Island—the world's longest suspension bridge—is visible from here, just beyond Governors Island.

❸ Built in 1811 as a defense for New York Harbor, the circular brick fortress now called **Castle Clinton** was, when first built, on an island 200 feet from shore. In 1824 it became Castle Garden, an entertainment and concert facility that reached its zenith in 1850 when more than 6,000 people (the capacity of Radio City Music Hall) attended the U.S. debut of the "Swedish Nightingale," Jenny Lind. After landfill connected it to the city, Castle Clinton became, in succession, an immigrant processing center, an aquarium, and now a restored fort, museum, and ticket office for ferries to the **Statue of Liberty** and **Ellis Island.** The ferry ride is one loop; you can get off at Liberty Island, visit the statue, then reboard any ferry and continue on to Ellis Island, boarding another boat once you have finished exploring the historic immigration facility there. *Ferry information: tel. 212/269–5755. Round-trip fare: $6 adults, $5 senior citizens, $3 children 3–17. Daily departures every 45 min 9:30–3:30; more frequent departures and extended hours in summer.*

❹ After arriving on Liberty Island, you have two choices from the ground-floor entrance to the **Statue of Liberty** monument: you can take an elevator 10 stories to the top of the 89-foot-high pedestal, or if you're strong of heart and limb, you can climb 354 steps (the equivalent of a 22-story building) to the crown. (Visitors cannot go up into the torch.) It usually takes two to three hours to walk up to the crown because of the wait beforehand. Erected in 1886 and refurbished for its centennial, the Statue of Liberty weighs 225 tons and stands 151 feet from her feet to her torch. Exhibits inside illustrate the statue's history, including videos of the view from the crown for those who don't make the climb. There is also a model of the statue's face for the blind to feel. *Tel. 212/363–3200. Admission free.*

❺ The ferry's other stop, **Ellis Island,** opened in September 1990 to record crowds after a $140 million restoration. Now a national monument, Ellis Island was once a federal immigration facility that processed 17 million men, women, and children between 1892 and 1954—the ancestors of more than 40% of Americans living today. The island's main building contains the **Ellis Island Immigration Museum,** with exhibits detailing not only the island's history but the whole history of immigration to America. Perhaps the most moving exhibit is the American Immigrant Wall of Honor, where the names of nearly 400,000 immigrant Americans are inscribed along an outdoor promenade overlooking the Statue of Liberty and the Manhattan skyline. *Tel. 212/363–3200. Admission free.*

A broad mall that begins at the landward entrance to Castle Clinton leads back across the park to the **Netherlands Memorial,** a quaint flagpole depicting the bead exchange that bought from the Native Americans the land to establish Fort Amsterdam in 1626. Inscriptions describe the event in English and Dutch.

❻ As you leave the park, across State Street you'll see the imposing **Alexander Hamilton Customs House,** built in 1907 in the ornate Beaux Arts style fashionable at the time. Above the base, the facade features massive columns rising to a pediment topped by a double row of statuary. Daniel Chester French, better known for the statue of Lincoln in the Lincoln Memorial in Washington, DC, sculpted the lower statues, which symbolize various continents (left to right: Asia, the Americas, Europe, Africa); the upper row represents the major trading cities of the world. The Customs House facade appeared in the movie *Ghostbusters II* as the fictional New York Museum of Art. Federal bankruptcy courts are currently housed in the Customs House; in fall 1994, the National Museum of the American Indian (*see* Chapter 6) was scheduled to move here and be renamed the George Gustav Heye Center.

The Customs House faces onto **Bowling Green,** an oval greensward at the foot of Broadway that became New York's first public park in 1733. On July 9, 1776, a few hours after citizens learned about the signing of the Declaration of Independence, rioters toppled a statue of British King George III that had occupied the spot for 11 years; much of the statue's lead was melted down into bullets. In 1783, when the occupying British forces fled the city, they defiantly hoisted a Union Jack on a greased, uncleated flagpole so it couldn't be lowered; patriot John Van Arsdale drove his own cleats into the pole to replace the flag with the Stars and Stripes.

From Bowling Green, head south on State Street. A stunning semicircular office tower in reflective glass hugs the bend of the street at 17 State Street. Next door is the **Shrine of St. Elizabeth Ann Seton** (7–8 State St.). What is now the rectory of the shrine is a redbrick Federal-style town house with a distinctive wood portico shaped to fit the curving street. This house was built in 1793 as the home of the wealthy Watson family; Mother Seton and her family lived here from 1801 to 1803. She joined the Catholic Church in 1805, after the death of her husband, and went on to found the Sisters of Charity, the first American order of nuns. In 1975 she became the first American-born saint. Masses are held here daily.

Continue around onto Water Street, passing on your right **New York Plaza,** a complex of high-tech office towers linked by an underground concourse. Just beyond it is the **Vietnam Veterans Memorial,** where letters from servicemen and servicewomen have been etched into a wall of greenish glass.

Return to Broad Street and go one block inland to **Fraunces Tavern,** a complex of five largely 19th-century buildings housing a museum, restaurant, and bar (*see* Chapter 9). The main building is a Colonial home (brick exterior, cream-colored marble portico and balcony) built in 1719 and converted to a tavern in 1762. This was the site where, in 1783, George Washington delivered a farewell address to his officers celebrating the British evacuation of New York; later, the building housed some offices of the fledgling U.S. government. Today Fraunces Tavern contains two fully furnished period rooms and other displays of 18th- and 19th-century American history. *Broad and Pearl Sts., tel. 212/425–1778. Admission: $2.50 adults, $1 students, senior citizens, and children under 12. Museum open weekdays 10–4:45, Sat. 12–4.*

Walk through the lobby of the office building at **85 Broad Street,** which, paying due homage to urban archaeology, traces the course of the old Dutch Stone Street with a line of brown paving stones. At the side of the building, on Pearl Street, peer through the transparent panel in the sidewalk to see the excavated foundations of the 17th-century Stadt Huis, the old Dutch City Hall.

Time Out   The brick plaza behind 85 Broad Street is flanked by a variety of small restaurants. Order a take-out meal or snack and eat it out here on the benches, where you can watch busy office workers milling past and enjoy not being one of them.

Head up Pearl Street to **Hanover Square,** a quiet tree-lined plaza that stood on the waterfront when the East River reached Pearl

Street. This was the city's original printing-house square; on the site of 81 Pearl Street, William Bradford established the first printing press in the colonies. The pirate Captain Kidd lived in the neighborhood, and the brownstone **India House** (1837) used to house the New York Cotton Exchange. Today it holds Harry's at Hanover Square, a vintage Wall Street bar.

Walk inland up Hanover Square to the rounded corner of South William and Beaver streets, where a graceful columned porch marks the entrance to **Delmonico's** restaurant, opened in 1888 on the site of an earlier Delmonico's founded in 1827. A pioneer in serving Continental cuisine, it was *the* place to go at the turn of the century; under different ownership, it is still a restaurant today.

Two blocks farther north, William Street crosses **Wall Street,** so called because it traces the course of a wood wall built across the island in 1653 to defend the Dutch colony against the native Indians. Arguably the most famous thoroughfare in the world, though only a third of a mile long, Wall Street began its financial career with stock traders conducting business along the sidewalks or at tables beneath a sheltering buttonwood tree. Today it's a dizzyingly narrow canyon—look to the right and you'll glimpse a sliver of East River waterfront; look to the left and you'll see the spire of Trinity Church, tightly framed by skyscrapers at the head of the street.

To learn the difference between Ionic and Corinthian columns, look at the **Citibank Building** to your right (55 Wall St.). The lower stories were part of an earlier U.S. Customs House, built in 1863, and it was literally a bullish day on Wall Street when oxen hauled its 16 granite Ionic columns up to the site. When the National City Bank took over the building in 1907, the architects McKim, Mead & White added a second tier of columns but made them Corinthian.

One block west on Wall Street, where Broad Street becomes Nassau Street, you'll find on your right a regal statue of George Washington on the steps of the **Federal Hall National Memorial.** This 1883 statue by noted sculptor and presidential relative John Quincy Adams Ward marks the spot where Washington was sworn in as the first U.S. president in 1789. After the capital moved to Philadelphia in 1790, the original Federal Hall became New York's City Hall, then was demolished in 1812 when the present City Hall (*see* Tour 18, *below*) was completed. The clean and simple lines of the current structure, built as (yet another) U.S. Customs House in 1842, were modeled after the Parthenon, a potent symbol for a young nation striving to emulate classical Greek democracy. It's now a museum featuring exhibits on New York and Wall Street. *26 Wall St., tel. 212/264–8711. Admission free. Open weekdays 9–5.*

In building a two-story investment bank at the corner of Wall and Broad streets, J. P. Morgan was in effect declaring himself above the pressures of Wall Street real-estate values. Now **Morgan Guaranty Trust,** the building bears pockmarks near the fourth window on the Wall Street side, created when a bomb that had been placed in a pushcart exploded in 1920.

Perhaps the heart of Wall Street is the **New York Stock Exchange,** which has its august Corinthian main entrance around the corner at 20 Broad Street. Compared with the Federal Hall memorial, this neoclassical building is much more elaborately decorated, as befitted the more grandiose national image of 1901, when it was designed. Inside, after what may be a lengthy wait, you can take an elevator to the third-floor visitor center. A self-guided tour, informative slide shows, video displays, and guides may help you interpret the seeming chaos you'll see from the visitors' gallery overlooking the immense (50-foot-high) trading hall. *Tickets available at 20 Broad St., tel. 212/656–5165. Free tickets are distributed beginning at 9:05; come before 1 PM to assure getting in. Open weekdays 9:15–3:35.*

⑪ Trinity Church (Broadway and Wall St.) was established as an Anglican parish in 1697. The present structure (1846), by Richard Upjohn, ranked as the city's tallest building for most of the second half of the 19th century. Its three huge bronze doors were designed by Richard Morris Hunt to recall Ghiberti's doors for the Baptistry in Florence, Italy. After the exterior sandstone was restored in 1991, New Yorkers were amazed to discover that a church they had always thought of as black was actually a rosy pink. The church's Gothic Revival interior is surprisingly light and elegant, although you may see derelicts napping in the pews. On the church's south side is a 2½-acre graveyard: Alexander Hamilton is buried beneath a white stone pyramid; and a monument commemorates Robert Fulton, the inventor of the steamboat (he's actually buried in the Livingstone family vault, with his wife).

Just north of the church is tiny Thames Street, where a pair of skyscrapers playfully called the **Thames Twins**—the Trinity and U.S. Realty buildings—display early 20th-century attempts to apply Gothic decoration to skyscrapers. Across the street at 120 Broadway, the 1915 **Equitable Building** rises 30 stories straight from its base with no setback; its overpowering shadow on the street convinced the city government to pass the nation's first zoning law. Large public plazas around the bases of skyscrapers have helped to alleviate this problem, and a good example is between Cedar and Liberty streets, where the black-glass **Marine Midland Bank** (1971) features in its street-level plaza a red-and-silver Noguchi sculpture, *Cube*. Two blocks east at William and Pine streets, the plaza surrounding the 65-story **Chase Manhattan Bank Building** holds a striking black-and-white sculpture, *Group of Four Trees*, by Jean Dubuffet.

Liberty Street converges with William Street and Maiden Lane at triangular **Louise Nevelson Plaza,** which contains four black welded-steel abstract Nevelson sculptures, three middle-size pieces and one ⑫ huge 70-footer. Sit in the plaza and contemplate the **Federal Reserve Bank** directly across the street, which looks the way a bank ought to look: gray, solid, imposing, absolutely impregnable—and it had better be, for its vaults reputedly contain a third of the world's gold reserves. *33 Liberty St., tel. 212/720–6130. Admission free. 1-hr tour by advance (at least one month) reservation, weekdays at 10, 11, 1, and 2.*

Proceed one block north to John Street, where you'll see the **John Street Methodist Church** (44 John St.), on the site of the first Methodist Church in America. Then return to Broadway and head north ⑬ to **St. Paul's Chapel** (Broadway and Fulton St.), the oldest (1766) surviving church in Manhattan and the site of the prayer service following George Washington's inauguration as president. Built of rough Manhattan stone, it was modeled after London's St. Martin-in-the-Fields. It's open until 4 (Sunday until 3) for prayer and meditation; look in the north aisle for Washington's pew.

Two blocks up Broadway is the so-called Cathedral of Commerce, ⑭ the ornate white terra-cotta **Woolworth Building** (Park Pl. and Broadway). When it opened in 1913 it was, at 792 feet, the world's tallest building; it still houses the Woolworth corporate offices. Among its extravagant Gothic-style details are sculptures set into arches in the lobby ceiling; one of them represents an elderly F. W. Woolworth pinching his pennies, while another depicts the architect, Cass Gilbert, cradling in his arms a model of his creation.

⑮ Go west on Park Place and turn down Church Street to the **World Trade Center,** a 16-acre, 12-million-square-foot complex that contains New York's two tallest buildings (1,350 feet high). To reach the observation deck on the 107th floor of 2 World Trade Center, elevators glide a quarter of a mile into the sky—in only 58 seconds. The view potentially extends 55 miles, although signs at the ticket window disclose how far you can see that day and whether the outdoor deck is open. In late February 1993, the Center was the site of a bombing, attributed to terrorists, that killed six people and caused extensive damage to the area. However, the Center has, for the most part, returned to normal operations, though security has been tightened considerably within the complex. *Tel. 212/435–7397. Admission: $4 adults, $2.25 senior citizens, $2 children. Open June–Sept., daily 9:30 AM–11:30 PM; Oct.–May, daily 9:30 AM–9:30 PM.*

From early 1995, you will once again be able to get the same view with a meal at **Windows on the World** atop 1 World Trade Center—a New York favorite that has been sorely missed during its long closure (jacket required).

Some 50,000 people work in this seven-building complex, and at street level and underground it contains more than 60 stores, services, and restaurants, as well as the adjacent New York Vista hotel (*see* Chapter 11). There's a TKTS booth selling discount tickets to Broadway and Off-Broadway shows (*see* Chapter 11) in the mezzanine of 2 World Trade Center (open weekdays 11–5:30, Sat. 11–1), and on the ninth floor of 4 World Trade Center, a visitors' gallery overlooks the trading floor of the Commodities Exchange (tel. 212/938–2025; open weekdays 9:30–3).

More than a million cubic yards of rock and soil were excavated for the World Trade Center—and then moved across West Street to help beget the 100-acre Battery Park City development, a complete neighborhood built from scratch. Take the pedestrian overpass north of 1 World Trade Center to Battery Park City's centerpiece, **⑯** the **World Financial Center,** a four-tower complex designed by Cesar Pelli, with some heavy-duty corporate tenants, including Merrill Lynch, American Express, and Dow Jones. You'll come out into the soaring **Winter Garden Atrium,** its mauve marble cascade of steps spilling down into a vaulted plaza with 16 giant palm trees, framed by a vast arched window overlooking the Hudson. This stunning space has become a popular venue for free performances by top-flight musicians and dancers (tel. 212/945–0505). Surrounding the atrium are several upscale shops—Godiva chocolatiers, Rizzoli bookshop, Ann Taylor for women's clothing, Mark Cross for leather goods—plus a skylit food court.

Time Out While the courtyard also offers several full-service restaurants, for a quick bite head for **Minters** (tel. 212/945–4455)—and be sure to leave room for great ice-cream cones.

Of the few spots in Manhattan that directly overlook the rivers, **Battery Park City** just may be the best. The outdoor plaza right behind the atrium curls around a tidy little yacht basin; take in the view of the Statue of Liberty and read the stirring quotations worked into the iron railings. Just north of the basin is the terminal for ferry service to Hoboken, New Jersey (tel. 908/463–3779; fare: $2), on the other side of the Hudson River. It's an eight-minute ride to Frank Sinatra's hometown, with a spectacular view of lower Manhattan.

To the south, a longer riverside promenade that eventually will extend to Battery Park accompanies the residential part of Battery Park City, a mix of high rises, town houses, shops, and green squares that does a surprisingly good job of duplicating the rhythms of the rest of the city. Especially noteworthy among the art works populating the esplanade are Ned Smyth's columned plaza with chessboards; and the South Cove, a collaborative effort, a romantic curved stage set of wood piers and a steel-frame lookout. Slated to open in early 1996 behind South Cove is the **Living Memorial to the Holocaust–Museum of Jewish Heritage** (Battery Pl. between 1st and 2nd Pl., tel. 212/687–9141).

Tour 18: The Seaport and the Courts

New York's role as a great seaport is easiest to understand downtown, with both the Hudson River and East River waterfronts within walking distance. While the deeper Hudson River came into its own in the steamship era, the more sheltered waters of the East River saw most of the action in the 19th century, during the age of clipper ships. This era is preserved in the South Street Seaport restoration, centered on Fulton Street between Water Street and the East River. Only a few blocks away, you can visit another seat of New York history: the City Hall neighborhood, which includes Manhattan's magisterial collection of court buildings.

Walk down Fulton Street, named after the ferry to Brooklyn that once docked at its foot (the ferry itself was named after its inventor, Robert Fulton), to Water Street, which was once the shoreline. On ❶⁊ the 19th-century landfill across the street is the 11-block **South Street Seaport Historic District,** which was created in 1967 to save this area from being overtaken by skyscrapers. The Rouse Corporation, which had already created slick so-called "festival marketplaces" in Boston (Quincy Market) and Baltimore (Harborplace), was later hired to restore and adapt the existing historic buildings.

The little white lighthouse at Water and Fulton streets is the **Titanic Memorial,** commemorating the sinking of the RMS *Titanic* in 1912. Beyond it, Fulton Street, cobbled in blocks of Belgian granite, is a pedestrian mall that swarms with visitors, especially on fine-weather weekends. Immediately to your left is the **Cannon's Walk Block,** which contains 15 restored buildings.

At 211 Water Street is **Bowne & Co.,** a reconstructed working 19th-century print shop. Around the corner, a narrow court called Cannon's Walk, lined with shops, opens onto Fulton Street; follow it around to Front Street. Directly across Front Street is the **Fulton Market Building,** a modern building, full of shops and restaurants, that re-creates the bustling commercial atmosphere of the old victual markets that were on this site from 1822 on. On the south side of Fulton Street is the seaport's architectural centerpiece, **Schermerhorn Row,** a redbrick terrace of Georgian- and Federal-style warehouses and countinghouses built in 1811–12. Today the ground floors are occupied by upscale shops, bars, and restaurants, and the **South Street Seaport Museum.** *Tel. 212/669–9400. Admission to ships, galleries, walking tours, Maritime Crafts Center, films, and other seaport events: $6 adults, $5 senior citizens and students, $3 children. Open fall–spring, daily 10–5; summer, daily 10–6.*

Cross South Street under an elevated stretch of the FDR Drive to **Pier 16,** where the historic ships are docked, including the *Peking*, the second-largest sailing ship in existence; the full-rigged *Wavertree;* and the lightship *Ambrose.* A restored **Pilothouse** is the pierside information center. Pier 16 is also the departure point for the 90-minute **Seaport Line Harbor Cruise.** *Tel. 212/233–4800. Fare: $12 adults, $11 senior citizens, $10 students, $6 children. Runs May–Sept. Combination fares—for the cruise and the other attractions—run $15.25, $13.50, $12, and $7.50.*

To the north is **Pier 17,** a multilevel dockside shopping mall. Its weathered-wood rear decks make a splendid spot from which to sit and contemplate the river; look north to see the Brooklyn, Manhattan, and Williamsburg bridges, and look across to see Brooklyn Heights.

Time Out   If you're hungry, head for the fast-food stalls on Pier 17's third-floor **Promenade Food Court.** The cuisine is nonchain eclectic: Seaport Fries, Pizza on the Pier, Wok & Roll, the Yorkville Packing House, and the Salad Bowl. What's really spectacular is the view from the tables in a glass-walled atrium.

As your nose may already have surmised, the blocks along South Street north of the museum complex still house a working fish market, which has been in operation since the 1770s. Although the city has tried to relocate the hundreds of fishmongers of the **Fulton Fish Market** to the South Bronx, the area remains a beehive of activity. Get up early (or stay up late) if you want to see it: The action begins around midnight and ends by 8 AM. To arrange an early morning, behind-the-scenes tour of the market, call tour guide Richard Lord (tel. 201/798–3801) as far in advance as possible.

Return to Fulton Street and walk away from the river to Broadway, where St. Paul's Chapel is (*see* Tour 17, *above*). As you turn right, forking off to your right is **Park Row,** which was known as Newspaper Row from the mid-19th to early 20th century, when most of the city's 20 or so daily newspapers had offices there. In tribute to that past, however, a statue of Benjamin Franklin (who was, after all, a printer) stands in front of Pace University farther up on Park Row.

To the left of Park Row is triangular **City Hall Park,** originally the town common. A bronze statue of patriot Nathan Hale, who was hanged as a spy by the British troops occupying New York City, stands on the Broadway side of the park. In its day this green spot has hosted hangings, riots, and demonstrations; it is also the finish line for ticker-tape parades up lower Broadway (though ticker-tape is nowadays replaced with perforated margin strips torn off from tractor-feed computer paper).

⓲ **City Hall,** built between 1803 and 1812, is unexpectedly sedate, small-scale, and charming. Its exterior columns reflect the classical influence of Greece and Rome, and the handsome cast-iron cupola is crowned with a statue of Lady Justice. Originally its front and sides were clad in white marble while the back was faced in cheap brownstone, because the city fathers assumed New York would never grow farther north than this. (Limestone now covers all four sides.) The major interior feature is a domed rotunda from which a sweeping marble double staircase leads to the second-floor public rooms. The wood-paneled City Council Chamber in the east wing is small and clubby; the Board of Estimate chamber to the west has colonial paintings and church-pew-style seating; and the Governor's Room at the head of the stairs, used for ceremonial events, is filled with historic portraits and furniture. The mayor's office is on the ground floor.

⑲ Looming directly behind City Hall is the **Tweed Courthouse,** named after notorious politician "Boss" William Marcy Tweed, under whose corrupt management this building took some $12 million and nine years to build (it was finally finished in 1872, but the ensuing public outrage drove Tweed from office). Although it is imposing, with its columned classical pediment outside and seven-story rotunda inside, almost none of the boatloads of marble that Tweed had shipped from Europe made their way into this building. Today it houses municipal offices; it has also served as a location for several films, most notably *The Verdict.*

⑳ Across Chambers Street the **Surrogate's Court,** also called the **Hall of Records** (31 Chambers St.), is the most ornate of this City Hall trio. In true Beaux Arts fashion, sculpture and ornament seem to have been added wherever possible to the basic neoclassical structure, yet the overall effect is graceful rather than cluttered. A courtroom here was the venue for *Johnson* v. *Johnson,* where the heirs to the Johnson & Johnson fortune waged their bitter battle.

㉑ On the east side of Centre Street is the city government's first skyscraper, the **Municipal Building,** built in 1914 by McKim, Mead & White. The "roof" section alone is 10 stories high, bristling with towers and peaks and topped by a gilt statue of Civic Fame. This is where New Yorkers come to pay parking fines and get marriage licenses. An immense arch straddles Chambers Street (traffic used to flow through here); the vaulted plaza in front was the site of a scene in the movie *Crocodile Dundee,* in which the Aussie hunter coolly scares off would-be muggers with his bowie knife.

㉒ Just south of the Municipal Building, a ramp curves up into the pedestrian walkway over the **Brooklyn Bridge.** The Great Bridge promenade takes a half-hour to walk and is a New York experience on a par with the Statue of Liberty trip or the Empire State Building ascent. Before this bridge was built, Brooklynites had to rely on the Fulton Street ferry to get to Brooklyn—a charming way to travel, surely, but unreliable in the fog and ice of winter. After some 50 years of talk about a bridge, John Augustus Roebling, a respected engineer, was handed a bridge construction assignment in 1867. As the project to build the first steel suspension bridge slowly took shape over the next 15 years, it captured the imagination of the city; on its completion in 1883, it was called the Eighth Wonder of the World. Its twin Gothic-arched towers rise 268 feet from the river below. The roadway is supported by a web of steel cables, hung from the towers and attached to block-long anchorages on either shore. It is hardly the longest suspension bridge in the world anymore, but it remains a symbol of what man can accomplish. As you look south from the walkway, the pinnacles of downtown Manhattan loom on your right, Brooklyn Heights stands sentinel on your left, and before you yawns the harbor, with Lady Liberty showing herself in profile. Turn about for a fine view up the East River, spanned within sight by the Manhattan and Williamsburg bridges. You don't need binoculars to enjoy the vistas, but you'd do well to bring a hat or scarf, because the wind whips through the cables like a dervish.

㉓ Head north up Centre Street to **Foley Square,** a name that has become synonymous with the New York court system; the district attorneys on the TV series *Law and Order* frequently hold their on-screen colloquies in this vicinity. The **U.S. Courthouse** at 40 Centre Street, designed by Cass Gilbert, has marble steps climbing to a massive columned portico; above this rises a 32-story tower topped by a gilded pyramid, not unlike that with which Gilbert crowned the New York Life building uptown. This courthouse has been the site of such famous cases as the tax evasion trial of hotel queen Leona Helmsley.

With its stately columns, pediments, and 100-foot-wide flight of marble steps, the **New York County Courthouse,** built in 1926, set the precedent here for neoclassical grandeur. It's actually more eccentric than it looks, having been built in a hexagonal shape to fit an irregular plot of land. That quintessential courtroom drama *Twelve Angry Men* was filmed here, as was the more recent *Legal Eagles*.

Turn to look across Foley Square at **Federal Plaza,** which sprawls in front of the gridlike skyscraper of the **Javits Federal Building.** The black glass box to the left houses the **U.S. Court of International Trade.**

Continue up Centre Street past neoclassical civic office buildings to 100 Centre Street, the **Criminal Courts Building,** a rather grim Art Deco tower connected by a skywalk to the detention center known as The Tombs. In *The Bonfire of the Vanities*, Tom Wolfe wrote a chilling description of this court's menacing atmosphere.

In contrast, the **Civil and Municipal Courthouse** across the way at 111 Centre Street is an uninspired modern cube, although it, too, has held sensational trials, including that of subway vigilante Bernhard Goetz. On the west side of this small square is the slick blank granite **Family Court** (60 Lafayette St.), with its off-putting angular facade.

As you walk up Leonard Street, which runs just south of the Family Court, take a look at the ornate Victorian building that runs the length of the block on your left. This is the old New York Life Insurance Company headquarters (346 Broadway), an 1870 building that was remodeled and enlarged in 1896 by McKim, Mead & White. The ornate clocktower facing Broadway is now occupied by the avant-garde **Clocktower Gallery,** an outpost of P.S. 1 in Long Island City, Queens (*see* Tour 21 in Chapter 4). The gallery showcases the work of contemporary sculptors, photographers, painters, and other artists. After looking at the art on the 13th floor, the adventurous will want to climb a narrow spiral stairway inside the clocktower to see the huge clock's mechanism or step outside on the balcony for a dramatic view of New York City. *108 Leonard St., tel. 212/233–1096. Admission free. Open Wed.–Sat. noon–6.*

Manhattan for Free

One of the best, and least expensive, places to be in New York is out on the streets, soaking up the city. That's where you're likely to stumble upon the many free performances—both scheduled and impromptu—given by professionals and amateurs year-round. Music, dance, mime, acting, magic tricks, and more are offered for free or at pass-the-hat prices in parks and plazas all around town (*see* Chapter 11).

Parks and Public Places Another free-but-fascinating New York pastime is people-watching, and one of the best places to go for that is **Central Park** (*see* Tour 7, *above*), where the Mall and the areas around Bethesda Fountain and the Conservatory Water buzz with activity on weekends and holidays from about noon to dusk. Stroll over to Wollman Rink and watch the skaters, or head up to the Great Lawn to find groups of folk dancers. In the summer, take a picnic, a blanket, and a Frisbee to the Great Lawn in the early afternoon (before noon on weekends) to stake out a spot in line for free tickets to that evening's performance (usually a Shakespeare play) at the Delacorte Theater. While you're waiting, settle back to watch the strollers, joggers, softball teams, soccer players, and even snake charmers who congregate in this area. It makes for a long day—tickets aren't handed out until around 6:15 ᴘᴍ, and the plays begin at 8—but the experience is unforgettable.

Another lovely way to spend a day in Central Park is on a walking tour given by **Urban Park Rangers** (tel. 212/427–4040), who are knowledgeable about the history, design, geology, wildlife, and botany of the park. Call the park's **Events Hotline** (tel. 212/794–6565) for an up-to-date list of events.

Rockefeller Center (*see* Tour 1, *above*) is another good place to enjoy New York for free. In summer, there are various outdoor entertainment programs; in winter, you can watch ice skaters swirl about beneath the giant Christmas tree (should you care to ice-skate here, that's another costly story). **Lincoln Center** (*see* Tour 8, *above*) hosts crafts fairs and outdoor performances frequently throughout the summer. The **World Financial Center** (*see* Tour 17, *above*) often has free concerts at lunchtime and on weekends in its Winter Garden Atrium. **South Street Seaport** (*see* Tour 18, *above*) offers an assortment of fun free activities year-round: concerts on the pier during summer, a jazz festival in winter, and daily street entertainment.

Free Tours Volunteers lead free guided tours daily of the **New York Public Library's Central Research Branch.** For a free guided tour of **Grand Central Terminal,** meet in front of the terminal's Chemical Bank branch at 12:30 PM on Wednesday (*see* Tour 3, *above*). Admission to official meetings of the General Assembly at the **United Nations** is free (pick up tickets at the information desk in the General Assembly lobby, at 46th St. and 1st Ave.). The mayor's residence, **Gracie Mansion,** in the Upper East Side's Carl Schurz Park, can be toured for free on Wednesday by advance appointment (*see* Tour 6, *above*).

The **New York Stock Exchange** on Wall Street offers free tours that include a multimedia presentation and a stop in the visitors' gallery overlooking the trading floor. You can also arrange in advance for a free tour of the **Federal Reserve Bank** (33 Liberty St., tel. 212/720–6130).

Museums On Tuesday evening, the **National Academy of Design** (1083 5th Ave. at 89th St.) and the **Cooper-Hewitt Museum** (2 E. 91st St.) charge no admission.

The **Metropolitan Museum of Art** (5th Ave. at 82nd St.), the **Museum of the City of New York** (1220 5th Ave. at 103rd St.), **El Museo Del Barrio** (1230 5th Ave. at 104th St.), the **Cloisters** (Fort Tryon Park, at the northern tip of Manhattan), the **American Museum of Natural History** (Central Park West at 79th St.), the **Museum of American Folk Art** (Columbus Ave. and 66th St.), the **Grey Art Gallery** (33 Washington Pl.), the **Pierpont Morgan Library** (29 E. 36th St.), and the **Museum of Television and Radio** (1 E. 53rd St.) all have pay-what-you-wish or suggested-donation policies. If all you can spare is a penny, they may not look too happy, but they'll still let you in. You can also pay what you wish to get into the **Jewish Museum** (5th Ave. at 92nd St.) on Tuesday evening and the **Museum of Modern Art** (11 W. 53rd St.) on Thursday evening.

Off the Beaten Track

Public Spaces   Under the city's zoning laws, new office buildings can receive a variance—to add extra stories, for example—by designing and maintaining a portion of interior or exterior space for public use. Such spaces are a boon for city dwellers and visitors: They provide clean, safe, attractive areas where you can sit, relax, read a newspaper, and people-watch (although you may see some people you'd rather avoid). Most are planted with greenery, from potted plants to towering trees, or have some form of falling water to muffle the sounds of the city. Many have snack bars, working telephones, and—what can be very difficult to find elsewhere in Manhattan—clean public rest rooms. The following public spaces are listed from lower Manhattan up.

In the modernistic atrium of the **Continental Insurance Building** (180 Maiden La. at Front St.) just two blocks south of the South Street Seaport Museum, benches surround copious foliage amid an ultramodern structure that looks as if it's made out of Tinker Toys. *Near Tours 17 and 18.*

ChemCourt (272 Park Ave., between 47th and 48th Sts.) in the Chemical Bank Building provides benches around plantings of exotic shrubs, all informatively labeled in English and Latin. A glass roof lets the sunshine into the ground floor of the 50-story silver-gray tower. *Near Tour 1.*

On the mezzanine and basement floors of **875 Third Avenue** (between 52nd and 53rd Sts.), tables and chairs are set in a lobby surrounded by an array of fast-food establishments selling pizza, bagels, muffins, Chinese food, sandwiches, and salads. The basement also connects with the 53rd Street subway station (E, F lines). *Near Tour 2.*

A boon to midtown's weary, **Paley Park** (3 E. 53rd St.), named for the former CBS executive William Paley, was the first of New York's "pocket parks" to be inserted among the high-rise behemoths, placed on the site of the former society night spot the Stork Club. A waterfall blocks out traffic noise, and feathery honey locust trees provide shade. There's a snack bar that opens when weather permits. *Near Tour 1.*

Another pocket park, **McGraw-Hill Park** (6th Ave., between 48th and 49th Sts.), behind the McGraw-Hill Building, has a stunning walk-through wall of water during most fair-weather days. *Near Tour 1.*

Nice Places to Live   Many of the loveliest residential areas of the city remain so precisely because they *are* off the beaten track, and hence out of the commercial flow. Here, from south to north, is an utterly subjective sampling, uptown and down.

The city's longest stretch of redbrick town houses preserved from the 1820s and 1830s runs along the north side of **Charlton Street** (west of 6th Ave.), with high stoops, paneled front doors, leaded-glass windows, and narrow dormer windows all intact. While you're here, stroll along parallel King and Vandam streets for more fine Federal houses. This quiet enclave was once an estate called Richmond Hill, whose various residents included George Washington, John and Abigail Adams, and Aaron Burr. *Near Tours 12 and 14.*

Sniffen Court (off 36th St. between Lexington and 3rd Aves.) is an easily overlooked cul-de-sac of 19th-century brick stables converted into town houses, with an atmosphere that's equal parts old London and New Orleans. Sniffen Court was for many years the home of sculptor Malvina Hoffman. *Near Tour 4.*

In the exclusive East Side neighborhood known as Turtle Bay, the secluded two-block-long **Beekman Place** (east of 1st Ave. between 49th and 51st Sts.) has an aura of unperturbably elegant calm. Residents of its refined town houses have included the Rockefellers, Alfred Lunt and Lynn Fontanne, Ethel Barrymore, Irving Berlin, and of course, Auntie Mame, a character in the well-known Patrick Dennis play of the same name. Go down the steps at 51st Street to reach a walkway along the East River. *Near Tour 2.*

Roosevelt Island (East River, 48th to 85th Sts.) is a 2½-mile-long East River island that was taken over by a residential complex in the 1970s, although only half of the high-rise buildings originally planned have been built. Some fragments remain of the asylums and hospitals once clustered here, when it was known as Welfare Island. Walkways along the edge of the island provide fine river views, and it's surprisingly quiet, compared with the city so near. The real treat, however, is the 3½-minute ride over on an aerial tram. The one-way fare is $1.40. *Near Tour 6.*

Built at the turn of the century, the white Beaux Arts town houses lining **West 105th Street** (between West End Ave. and Riverside Dr.) are like a vision of Paris. The apartment building at the northeast corner of Riverside Drive now belongs to the American Buddhist Academy; go around the corner to see its immense bronze Buddha. Marion Davies, mistress of William Randolph Hearst, once lived in the house at 331 Riverside Drive. *Near Tours 8 and 9.*

Commercial Districts The tendency in New York is for merchants in similar trades to cluster together in certain neighborhoods, where their customers can hop from one office to another. As you walk about the streets, you'll come upon sudden thickets of fur dealers, hat makers, button sellers, or flower suppliers, to name just a few. These three districts are particularly large and vibrant:

Gansevoort Market (around Gansevoort and Greenwich Sts.) features otherwise undistinguished warehouse buildings that each morning become the meat market for the city's retailers and restaurants. Racks of carcasses make a fascinating if not very pretty sight. Action peaks on weekdays from 5 to 9 AM. *Near Tours 11 and 12.*

The **Garment District** (7th Ave., between 31st and 41st Sts., also called Fashion Avenue) teems with warehouses, workshops, and showrooms that manufacture and finish mostly women's and children's clothing. On weekdays the streets are crowded with trucks and the sidewalks swarm with daredevil deliverymen wheeling garment racks between factories and specialized subcontractors. *Near Tour 3.*

The relatively unglitzy jewelry shops at street level in the **Diamond District** (47th St., between 5th and 6th Aves.) are just the tip of the iceberg; upstairs, millions of dollars' worth of gems are traded, and skilled craftsmen cut precious stones. Wheeling and dealing goes on at fever pitch, all rendered strangely exotic by the presence of a host of Hasidic Jews in severe black dress, beards, and curled sidelocks. If you're in a hurry, avoid this street during the day, when it becomes one of the slowest streets to navigate by foot in Manhattan. *Near Tour 1.*

4 Exploring the Other Boroughs

Many visitors to Manhattan notice the four outer boroughs—Brooklyn, Queens, the Bronx, and Staten Island—only from a Circle Line cruise, leaving those areas to remain ciphers, part of the city yet not. *Don't fall asleep on the subway,* the unschooled tourist tells himself, *or you may end up in the Bronx!*

Manhattanites themselves, many driven over the river by astronomical rents, discovered the outer boroughs some years back. They found sky, trees, and living space among the 19th-century brownstones, and converted industrial lofts, Art Deco apartment palaces, and tidy bungalows. They also found fascinating ethnic enclaves and a host of museums and parks.

The reality is that Manhattan is only a small part of New York City. Its population of 1.5 million is smaller than that of either Brooklyn (2.3 million) or Queens (1.9 million), and only slightly larger than that of the Bronx (1.2 million). Staten Island may be less populous (378,000), but it's 2½ times the size of Manhattan.

There are things to see and do in the outer boroughs that you simply won't find in Manhattan, and most are just a subway ride away from midtown. Manhattanites may try to put you off such a journey, but don't be daunted. After a couple of beers, those same people may rave about their favorite place for cheesecake (Junior's on Flatbush Avenue in Brooklyn), or a great outdoor barbecue they had at their sister-in-law's mock Tudor brick house (in Forest Hills Gardens, Queens); you may even have to listen to a story about their life's peak experience—found in the bleachers of Yankee Stadium in . . . the Bronx!

Brooklyn

Tour 19: Brooklyn Heights, Cobble Hill, and Carroll Gardens

Numbers in the margin correspond to points of interest on the Tour 19: Brooklyn Heights, Cobble Hill, and Carroll Gardens map.

"All the advantages of the country, with most of the conveniences of the city." So ran the ads for a real-estate development that sprang up in the 1820s just across the East River from downtown Manhattan. Brooklyn Heights—named for its enviable hilltop position—was New York's first suburb, linked to the city first by ferry and later by the Brooklyn Bridge. Feverish construction quickly transformed the airy heights into a fashionable upper-middle-class community. Happily, some 600 buildings more than 100 years old remain intact today, making Brooklyn Heights a kind of picture book of 19th-century American architecture.

Take the No. 2 or 3 subway from Manhattan to Clark Street. Exit the subway station and turn left on Henry Street toward Pineapple Street. (Street names in the Heights are an eccentric collection, reportedly created by a certain Miss Middagh, who despised the practice of naming streets for the town fathers and preferred instead various fruits.) Above the rooftops, look up to see the blue towers of the Manhattan Bridge linking Brooklyn to Manhattan; you'll have a view of the Brooklyn Bridge itself in a few minutes. Turn left onto Orange Street. On the north side of the block between Henry and

❶ Hicks streets is a formidable institution: the **Plymouth Church of the Pilgrims,** which was the vortex of abolitionist sentiment in the years before the Civil War, thanks to the stirring oratory of Brooklyn's

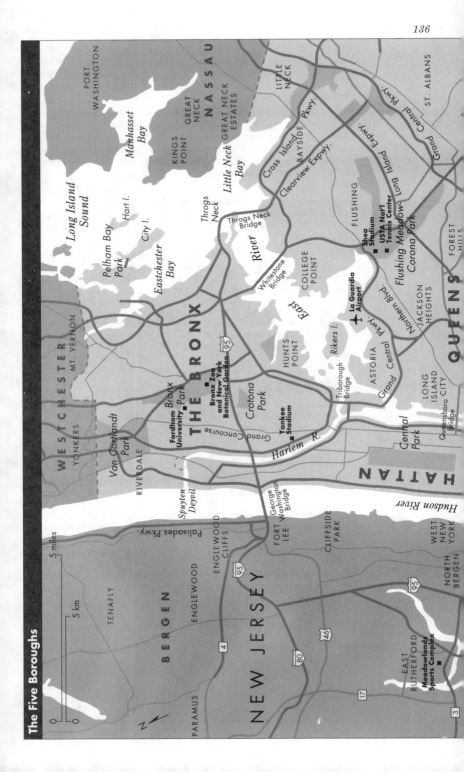

The Five Boroughs

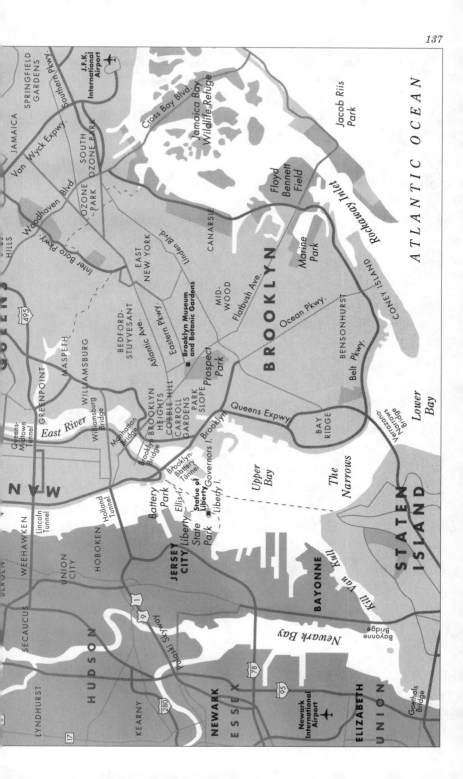

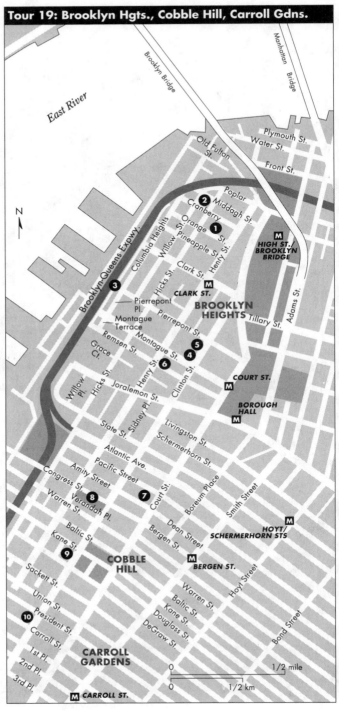

most eminent theologian, Henry Ward Beecher. In the Underground Railroad that smuggled slaves to freedom, Plymouth Church was more or less "Grand Central Station." Beside the church is a courtyard (locked, alas) with a statue of Beecher. Walk on to Willow Street and turn right to see Beecher's house, a prim Greek Revival brownstone, at **22 Willow Street.** At the corner of Willow and

 Middagh (pronounced *mid*-awe) streets, **24 Middagh Street** is the oldest home in the neighborhood—an 1824 Federal-style wood residence with a mansard roof. Peer through a door in the wall on the Willow Street side for a glimpse of the cottage garden and carriage house in the rear. Now turn around and catch a glimpse between the buildings of the **Brooklyn Bridge,** the historic steel suspension bridge designed by John Augustus Roebling and completed in 1883 (*see* Tour 18 in Chapter 3). In the foreground you can also spot the world headquarters of the **Jehovah's Witnesses,** located in the Heights since 1909. Venture a few steps west on Middagh to watch neighborhood children and their parents playing at the **Harry Chapin Playground,** a pleasant neighborhood park named after the late singer-songwriter.

Backtrack on **Willow Street,** which between Clark and Pierrepont streets is one of the prettiest and most architecturally varied blocks in the Heights. Note Nos. 108–112, built in the blend of terra-cotta reliefs, bay windows, and towers known as the Shingle or Queen Anne style. Farther down the block, on the other side, stand three distinguished brick Federal row houses allegedly part of the Underground Railroad.

As you turn right onto Pierrepont Street, heading toward the river, glance down Columbia Heights to your right, where Nos. 210–220 comprise a brownstone grouping often cited as the most graceful in New York. Norman Mailer lives on this street—lucky Mr. Mailer—and from a rear window in No. 111, John Roebling's son Washington (who in 1869 succeeded his father as chief engineer for the Brooklyn Bridge) directed the building of the bridge from his sickbed.

❸ Pierrepont Street ends at the **Brooklyn Heights Promenade,** a sliver of park one-third of a mile long, hanging over the ferry district like one of Babylon's fabled gardens. Cantilevered over two lanes of the Brooklyn–Queens Expressway and a service road, this quiet esplanade area has benches offering views of the Manhattan skyline. Circling gulls squawk, tugboats honk, and the city seems like a vision from another planet.

As you leave the Promenade (via Montague Street), look left to see Nos. 2 and 3 **Pierrepont Place,** two brownstone palaces built in the 1850s by a China trader and philanthropist, and used as a location for John Huston's film *Prizzi's Honor* (the frightful Mafia chieftain Don Corrado lived here). On your right lies **Montague Terrace,** where Thomas Wolfe lived when he finished *You Can't Go Home Again.* In the 1940s and 1950s, the neighborhood was said to be home to the city's largest number of writers outside Greenwich Village, among them Carson McCullers, W. H. Auden, Arthur Miller, and Truman Capote.

As you head east, Montague Street turns into a commercial district often disparaged for its homogeneous yuppie character. Still, restaurants here feature everything from Greek to Mexican to Japanese food, and window shopping can be fun. The **Church of St. Ann and the Holy Trinity** lies at the northwest corner of Montague and Clinton streets. Its historic stained-glass windows—the first made in the United States—are currently being restored. In recent years, the church has become a performing arts center frequented by downtown Manhattan types. *157 Montague St., tel. 718/858-2424. Box office open Tues.-Sat. noon-6.*

Beyond Clinton on the north side of Montague Street, note an interesting row of banks: **Chemical** (No. 177), a copy of the Palazzo della Gran Guardia in Verona, Italy; a **Citibank** (No. 183) that looks like a latter-day Roman temple; and the Art Deco **Municipal Credit Union** (No. 185).

A block north of Montague, at the corner of Clinton and Pierrepont, **5** is the **Brooklyn Historical Society,** with its 1989 Shellens Gallery. The collection includes Brooklyn Dodgers' bats and balls, trick mirrors from Coney Island, and a 300-pound cast-zinc eagle saved from the offices of the *Brooklyn Eagle.* The society's library on the second floor—with its rich carved-wood bookcases and lustrous stained-glass windows—is a showcase for late-19th-century interior design; it also holds 12,000 rare photographs and 110,000 books. *128 Pierrepont St., tel. 718/624-0890. Library research fee: $5. Open Tues.-Sat. noon-4:45. Shellens Gallery admission: $2.50 adults, $1 children under 12; Wed. free. Open Wed.-Sat. noon-5.*

Return south along Clinton Street, then turn right onto Remsen Street. At the corner of Remsen and Henry streets, stop to take in **6** the Romanesque Revival **Our Lady of Lebanon Maronite Cathedral** (113 Remsen St.), designed by prolific architect Richard Upjohn. It features the Shrine of St. Sharbel Makhlouf and doors salvaged from the 1943 wreck of the ocean liner *Normandie.*

If you want to see more of Brooklyn Heights, turn left onto Hicks Street to visit another Upjohn creation, the Gothic Revival **Grace Church** (254 Hicks St.). Across Hicks Street is **Grace Court Alley,** a traditional mews with a score of restored carriage houses, where the stables used to be. Then stroll west on Joralemon Street, where a row of **Greek Revival brownstones** (nos. 29-75) delicately sidestep their way down the hill toward the river and the piers. Follow **Willow Place** south along the peaceful block between Joralemon and State streets; in late afternoon, the houses take on the colors of a faded quilt.

To reach Cobble Hill and Carroll Gardens, return to Clinton Street and go south across Atlantic Avenue, a busy thoroughfare crowded with Middle Eastern restaurants and downscale antiques shops.

Time Out Between Court and Clinton streets on Atlantic Avenue are a half dozen Middle-Eastern gourmet markets and eateries, where you can sample everything from olives imported by the bucket from Lebanon, Greece, and Italy, to the Turkish Delight (a chewy, nutty candy) that's made in the back room. Other specialties include dried fruits, halvah, and very cheap spices. Try **Sahadi Importing** (187–189 Atlantic Ave., tel. 718/624-4550) for the basic delicacies, **Damascus Bread & Pastry** (195 Atlantic Ave., tel. 718/625-7070) for spinach pie and baklava, and the **Yemeni Cafe** (176 Atlantic Ave., tel. 718/834-9533) for anything made with lamb.

Atlantic Avenue is the official dividing line between the neighborhoods of Brooklyn Heights and **Cobble Hill,** the latter a peaceful residential area of leafy streets lined with notable town houses of varying architectural styles. The neighborhood is popular with young families, and on most days you can see an assortment of people pushing strollers, walking dogs, or returning home with grocery-laden bags. Go south down Clinton Street to Amity, two blocks

➐ south of Atlantic. Turn left and make your way to **197 Amity,** where Jennie Jerome, the mother of Winston Churchill, was born in 1854. (Perversely, a plaque at 426 Henry Street, southwest of here, identifies *that* building as the famous woman's birthplace. The Henry Street address is actually where Jennie's parents lived before she was born.)

➑ Return to Clinton and go one more block south, where on the west side of the street you'll find **Cobble Hill Park,** a small oasis of green encircled by pavement, with a playground at one end. Rest on one of the benches here and drink in the sounds of children playing and neighbors chatting. Bordering the park's south side between Clinton and Henry streets is **Verandah Place,** a charming row of converted stable buildings where Thomas Wolfe once lived.

➒ Proceed south down Clinton Street to observe the block after block of distinguished row houses, ranging from Romanesque Revival to neoclassical to Italianate brownstone. Three blocks south of the park, at the southwest corner of Kane and Clinton streets, is the Episcopal **Christ Church** (320 Clinton St.), a sandstone structure that is yet another creation of Richard Upjohn, who lived near here at 296 Clinton Street. Interior furnishings in the church, including the pulpit, lecturn, and altar, were designed by Louis Comfort Tiffany. The church's setting, on a tree-embowered patch of green enclosed by a wrought-iron fence, has the tranquil air of an English churchyard.

As you approach President Street, Cobble Hill gives way to the largely Italian neighborhood of **Carroll Gardens,** an area distinguished by unusually deep blocks that allow for large—by New York standards—front yards. Wander down President, Carroll, 1st, and 2nd places to see the lovingly tended gardens; notice the abundance of religious statuary that attests to the largely Catholic makeup of the neighborhood.

➓ On the northwest corner of Carroll and Clinton streets is the **Guido Funeral Home** (440 Clinton St.), once the John Rankin Residence. Built in 1840, this freestanding redbrick building may be the finest example of a Greek Revival town house in the city.

Go east on Carroll Street to reach Court Street, the main commercial thoroughfare of the neighborhood, where you can gather a few edible mementos of your visit here. Fresh pasta, cheeses, sausages, olives, and prepared Italian dishes are available at a number of shops, including **Pastosa Ravioli** (347 Court St.), where the gnocchi is particularly good, and **Caputo's Dairy** (460 Court St.), with a wide selection of homemade pasta sauces. Bakeries also abound here, but movie buffs will want to cut over to Henry Street to the **Cammareri Brothers Bakery** (502 Henry St.), where Nicholas Cage worked in the 1987 film, *Moonstruck.* Buy a loaf of the pepperoni-studded lard bread here and remind yourself that not all cholesterol is bad.

Time Out **Mola Pizzeria** (404 Court St., tel. 718/852–0240) and **Leonardo's Brick Oven Pizza** (383 Court St., tel. 718/624–9620), across the street from each other, both serve delectable pizza baked in brick ovens.

To return to the city, catch the F train at the corner of 2nd Place and Smith Street, two blocks northwest of Leornardo's. Note also that although cruising cabs are rare in Brooklyn, a number of them do travel north on Clinton Street en route to Manhattan; you may be able to catch one there.

Tour 20: Park Slope

Numbers in the margin correspond to points of interest on the Tour 20: Park Slope map.

This neighborhood, which grew up in the late 1800s on the west side of Prospect Park, is today one of Brooklyn's most sought-after sections. Many families have moved in to renovate the handsome brownstones that line its blocks—beware the heavy traffic in baby strollers!

Begin on **7th Avenue,** the area's main commercial street, accessible by the D, F, Q, 2, or 3 subway trains. Here, among other interesting shops, you'll find a wine store of real distinction, **Leon Paley Ltd.** (88 7th Ave.), the neighborhood's current favorite Thai restaurant, the **Lemongrass Grill** (61 A 7th Ave., tel. 718/399–7100), as well as two diet-defying bakeries: **Cousin John's** (70 7th Ave.); and the **New Prospect At Home** (52 7th Ave.). The corner of 7th Avenue and Sterling Place was the site of a horrendous plane crash in 1960, which leveled several buildings around the intersection.

Turn east on Lincoln Place to find the Slope's most venerable edifice, the **Montauk Club** (25 8th Ave.), an 1891 mansion modeled on Venice's Ca' d'Oro. Notice the friezes of Montauk Indians and the private side entrance, built especially for members' wives in the 19th century.

Make your way south along 8th Avenue, sampling the brownstones on various streets along the way (President and Carroll streets are especially handsome), until you reach **Montgomery Place,** a block-long street between 8th Avenue and Prospect Park West. This is considered by many to be the neighborhood's finest block, lined by a picturesque variety of town houses designed by the Romanesque Revival genius C.P.H. Gilbert.

Return along Prospect Park West to **Grand Army Plaza,** a geographic star from which radiate Prospect Park West, Eastern Parkway, and Flatbush and Vanderbilt avenues. At its center stands the **Soldiers' and Sailors' Memorial Arch,** honoring Civil War veterans and patterned on the Arc de Triomphe in Paris. Three heroic sculptural groupings adorn the arch: atop, a four-horsed chariot by Frederick MacMonnies, so dynamic that it almost seems on the verge of catapulting off the arch; to the sides, the victorious Union Army and Navy of the Civil War. Inside are bas-reliefs of Presidents Abraham Lincoln and Ulysses S. Grant, sculpted by Thomas Eakins and William O'Donovan, respectively. To the northwest, Neptune and a passel of debauched tritons leer over the edges of the **Bailey Fountain,** where tulle-drenched brides and grooms in technicolor tuxes come to pose after exchanging vows.

To the southeast of the plaza is the main entrance to **Prospect Park,** a 536-acre urban playground designed in 1866 by Frederick Law Olmsted and Calvert Vaux, who considered it superior to their earlier creation, Central Park, because no streets divided it and no bordering skyscrapers would break its rural illusion. Woods, water, and meadows remain the park's three basic thematic elements. Inside the entrance is the 90-acre **Long Meadow,** full of picnickers and kite-fliers on weekends, and the site of free New York Philharmonic and Metropolitan Opera performances in the summer. Follow the circular drive to the right, and at the entrance at Prospect Park West and 3rd Street you'll see the **Litchfield Villa,** an Italianate mansion built

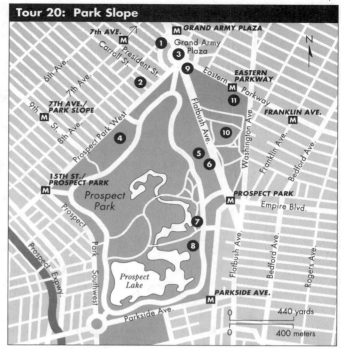

Tour 20: Park Slope

in 1857 for a wealthy lawyer. It now holds the park's administrative offices, but visitors are welcome to step inside and view the interior. Across the main drive is the **Picnic House** (tel. 718/965–6516), stage for a year-round schedule of drama, dance, music, and puppetry, as well as yoga and t'ai chi.

If you follow the drive to the left of the main entrance, you'll come to the **zoo,** recently renamed the **Prospect Park Wildlife Conservation Center.** Reopened in 1993, the Center offers a state-of-the art children's zoo, with such exhibits as "World of Animals" and "Animal Lifestyles." *Tel. 718/399–7339. Admission: $2.50 adults, 50¢ children 3–12. Open daily 10–4:30 in winter; weekdays 10–5, weekends 10–5:30 in summer.* Just beyond the zoo is a restored 1912 **carousel** (50¢ a ride; closed winter months) and the **Lefferts Homestead,** a gambrel-roofed Dutch colonial farmhouse (1783) that was moved here in 1918 and now holds a museum of period home furnishings and changing exhibitions. *Tel. 718/965–6505. Admission free. Open mid-Apr.–mid-Dec., weekends noon–4.*

The middle of the park is a forested ravine, cut by a stream and dotted with bridges. Follow the circular drive. A smaller central drive that branches off to your right leads to the **Quaker Cemetery,** not open to the public (the Urban Park Rangers lead periodic tours through here, tel. 718/287–3400). Montgomery Clift is among the people buried in this quiet cemetery. If you stay on the circular drive, you'll soon pass the terra-cotta **Boathouse** (tel. 718/287–3474; closed winter months), styled after the Library of St. Marks in Venice; today the 1905 structure houses a visitor center, art exhibitions, and a café. Farther down the path is the giant, gnarled **Camperdown Elm,** which Marianne Moore immortalized in a poem in the 1960s.

8 Moore became one of the park's chief advocates, a labor she termed "my only mortal entanglement." South of here is **Concert Grove,** site of outdoor summer performances, near the shore of 60-acre **Prospect Lake** inhabited by ducks and swans.

9 If you return to Grand Army Plaza, to the east of the park's main entrance, you will find the main branch of the **Brooklyn Public Library.** Built in 1941, it applies Art Deco streamlining to the grand neoclassical look of Beaux Arts public buildings. Notice the bas-relief carvings and the inscription picked out in gold above the entrance. Step inside to admire the murals in the lobby. *Tel. 718/780–7700. Open Tues.–Thurs. 9–8, Fri. and Sat. 10–6, Sun. 1–5.*

Eastern Parkway, which runs from Grand Army Plaza past the library, mimics the grand sweep of the boulevards of Paris and Vienna. Every Labor Day weekend the parkway hosts the biggest and liveliest carnival outside the Caribbean—a cacophony of calypso, steel band, and reggae music, with plenty of conch curry, spice bread, and meat patties to go around.

10 A couple of hundred yards along the parkway is an entrance to the **Brooklyn Botanic Garden,** which occupies 52 acres across Flatbush Avenue from Prospect Park. The garden exudes a beguiling Oriental atmosphere, due to the presence of a **Japanese Garden,** complete with a blazing red torii gate and a pond laid out in the shape of the Chinese character for "heart." The Japanese cherry arbor turns into a heart-stopping cloud of pink every May. Wander through the **Cranford Rose Garden** (5,000 bushes, 1,200 varieties); the **Fragrance Garden,** designed especially for the blind; the **Shakespeare Garden,** featuring 80 plants immortalized by the bard (including roses of many names); and **Celebrity Path,** Brooklyn's answer to Hollywood's famous sidewalk, with the names of homegrown stars—including Mel Brooks, Woody Allen, Zero Mostel, Barbara Stanwyck, and Mae West—inscribed on stepping-stones. A complex of handsome greenhouses called the **Steinhardt Conservatory** holds thriving desert, tropical, temperate, and aquatic vegetation, as well as a display charting the evolution of plants over the past 140 million years. The **C.V. Starr Bonsai Museum** in the Conservatory grows about 75 miniature Japanese plants. The Botanic Garden Shop is a fine place to stop, particularly if you're a gardener yourself. *1000 Washington Ave. near Empire Blvd., tel. 718/622–4433. Admission to garden free. Admission to Steinhardt Conservatory Nov.–Mar. free; Apr.–Oct., $2 adults, $1 senior citizens and children 3–12. Garden open Tues.–Fri. 8–4:30, weekends and holidays 10–4:30. Closed Thanksgiving, Dec. 25, and Jan. 1. Conservatory open Apr.–Sept., Tues.–Sun. 10–5; Oct.–Mar., Tues.–Sun. 10–4.*

11 **The Brooklyn Museum,** designed by the McKim, Mead & White team in 1897, sports huge Daniel Chester French statues of Brooklyn and Manhattan (as classical ladies) on its Eastern Parkway front. With more than 2 million objects, the Brooklyn collection is the seventh largest in the country. The museum's renovation and expansion project by Japanese architect Arata Isozaki and New York firm James Stewart Polshek includes a new auditorium with a wave-like ceiling, and new galleries in the oldest part of the building, adding 30,000 square feet of exhibition space. Look especially for its **Egyptian Art** collection (third floor), considered the best of its kind anywhere outside London or Cairo, or the **African and Pre-Columbian Art** (first floor), another collection recognized worldwide. In the gallery of **American painting and sculpture** (fifth floor) you'll find *Brooklyn Bridge* by Georgia O'Keeffe, as well as striking works by Winslow Homer, John Singer Sargent, and Gilbert Stuart. The **Peri-**

od Rooms (fourth floor) include the complete interior of the Jan Martense Schenck House, built in the Brooklyn Flatlands section in 1675, as well as a suite of rooms decorated in Moorish style from the 54th Street mansion of John D. Rockefeller. Outdoors, the **Frieda Schiff Warburg Memorial Sculpture Garden** features relics from "lost New York," such as a lion's head from Coney Island's Steeplechase Park. The museum also offers excellent special exhibitions, a treasure chest of a gift shop, and dramatic views of Manhattan from its Eastern Parkway–Washington Avenue corner. *200 Eastern Pkwy., tel. 718/638–5000. Suggested contribution: $4 adults, $1.50 senior citizens, $2 students with valid ID. Open Wed.–Sun. 10–5.*

Queens

Tour 21: Long Island City

Numbers in the margin correspond to points of interest on the Tours 21 and 22: Long Island City and Astoria map.

In the 1800s, along the East River in Queens, a string of neighborhoods thrived due to their ferry links with Manhattan. One of the busiest ferries connected a finger of land called Hunters Point with East 34th Street, Manhattan. Here, a business district known as Long Island City burgeoned. (Queens is, after all, on the western end of Long Island, as is Brooklyn.) Factories, boardinghouses, municipal buildings, and restaurants clustered around the intersection of Vernon Boulevard and Jackson Avenue, while north along Vernon Boulevard tycoons built summer homes, with boathouses and lawns that reached gracefully to the banks of the river. Today the community has found new life as a mecca for artists, who've migrated with their paint pots and welding tools to airy, low-rent studios.

A 10-minute ride on the No. 7 subway from Times Square or Grand Central Terminal will take you to the 45th Road Court House Square station. This noisy intersection is a fine introduction to this part of Queens, where the dark, clanking hulk of the El keeps the sunlight from penetrating to the street.

Long Island City's streets puzzle cartographers and visitors alike; you'll find numbered streets running north and south, and numbered avenues, roads, and drives going east–west. Consider 45th Avenue: To its south lies 45th Road, and to its north is 44th Road, 44th Avenue, and 44th Drive. But bear with this confusion and turn

❶ east onto 45th Avenue, where you'll find the **Hunters Point Historic District**, full of immaculate row houses, dating from 1870, with their original stoops and cornices. Their fine condition is due partly to their having been faced in resilient Westchester stone. At 21st Street, a small park offers benches (for pigeons and people) and a setting for a large metal sculpture called *Bigger Bird* by Daniel Sinclair. The warehouses surrounding the park are a warren of artists' studios; above their low roofs there's an unobstructed view of Manhattan.

❷ On 21st Street, between 46th Road and 46th Avenue, is **P.S.1 Museum,** a contemporary art museum housed in what was originally a public elementary school. The founders of P.S.1 were the first of the art-conscious to see the possibilities in the area; back in 1976 they turned the old school into lecture rooms, studio space for artists, and galleries. On display are special exhibitions and a number of permanent works, including James Turrell's sky piece *Meeting* and Alan Saret's *Fifth Colar Chthonic Wall Temple. 46–01 21st St., tel. 718/*

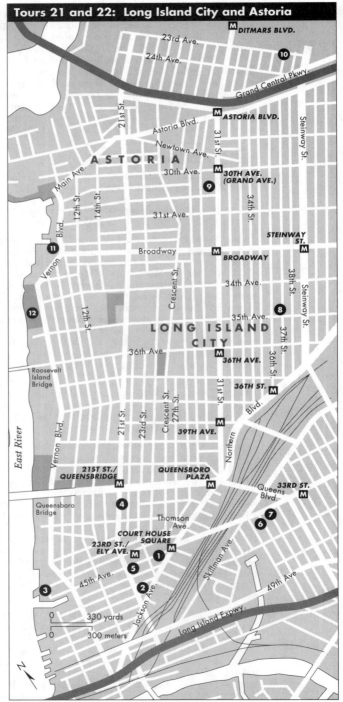

Tours 21 and 22: Long Island City and Astoria

784–2084. Suggested contribution: $2. Open Wed.–Sun. noon–6 when a show is on display.

The intersection of **Jackson Avenue** and **Vernon Boulevard** is still the commercial center of the neighborhood, as it was when the ferry operated from the foot of Borden Avenue. Modest shingled homes, butcher shops, diners, and the Vernon–Jackson subway stop crowd together beneath the huge, four-barreled stacks of the old Pennsylvania Railroad generating plant. (Schwartz Chemicals, as the structure is identified on its eastern face, was a later occupant; today the behemoth contains an assortment of smaller manufacturing firms and some indoor tennis courts.) At 49th Avenue and Vernon Boulevard, the steeple of **St. Mary's Roman Catholic Church** rises more spiritually into the sky than the stacks of old Schwartz.

Vernon Boulevard, originally called the Williamsburg Turnpike Road, was Queens's first true highway, leading to the mansions along the river, all now demolished. The area to the west of Vernon is slated to change dramatically, when the Hunters Point Development plan turns 90 acres of riverfront and landfill between the Midtown Tunnel and Queensboro Bridge into an apartment complex.

Time Out   Only locals know about **Café Vernon** (46–18 Vernon Blvd., tel. 718/472–9694), a tiny, unassuming Italian restaurant at Vernon Boulevard and 46th Road. Don't let its modesty fool you, though, because it offers splendid, filling repasts of Italian sandwiches, soups, and pastas. Prices are moderate; the atmosphere is homey.

A white concrete block of a building rises at the foot of 44th Drive. **③** Another warehouse? Hardly. This is the **Water's Edge Restaurant** (44th Dr. and East River, tel. 718/482–0033), a Queens dining spot where in summertime umbrellas sprout up on the dock, and boaters check in for quick drinks. Inside is an elegant restaurant that charges Manhattan prices, bringing in its sophisticated clientele via a complimentary ferry service from the city's 34th Street Marina Tuesday–Saturday in summer, weekends in winter. From the pier outside you can survey the **Queensboro Bridge,** which extends 7,000 feet, from Manhattan's East 60th Street to Crescent Street, Queens. Finished in 1909, its construction claimed the lives of 50 workers. A detour north on Vernon Boulevard will take you to the bridge's base at Queens Plaza, where there's a riverfront park and a lonely remnant of the past century, the old **New York Architectural Terra Cotta Company,** complete with Tudor Revival adornments and chimney pots.

It's ironically appropriate that the sometimes tatty western section of Queens should have become an outpost for America's glitziest industry, the motion pictures. In Long Island City, filmmakers began to gather in 1983 to make movies and commercials at a three-block-long complex, converted from a bakery into 14 soundstages. **④** **Silvercup Studios** (42–25 21st St., tel. 718/784–3390) can be reached by walking east from Vernon to the intersection of 21st Street and 43rd Avenue. Such movies as *Godfather III, Sea of Love,* and *When Harry Met Sally* were shot within the walls of old Silvercup.

Now hike back down 21st Street to 45th Avenue, which will bring **⑤** you back to **Court House Square.** Notice first—you probably couldn't fail to—the towering green **Citicorp Building.** When it was built, Manhattan office space ran at $40–$95 per square foot, while in Queens you could rent at a cool $17–$27. I. M. Pei is responsible for the building's basic design, which carries over some general themes from Manhattan's Citicorp Building.

Much more modest is the **New York State Supreme Courthouse** (25–10 Court House Sq.) across from Citicorp. Built in 1909 in a jumbled Beaux Arts architectural style, the courthouse is being restored through the 1990s, but depending on where the work is being done, you may be able to step inside the four-story-high lobby to see the mosaic tile floors, elaborate iron banisters, and stained-glass ceiling. The courthouse's orginal construction entailed so much graft and corruption that the Queens borough president, Joseph Bermel, resigned and the architect, Peter M. Coco, was tried for grand larceny in one of the very courtrooms he had designed. Today it's frequently used as a location by neighborhood movie studios.

Thomson Avenue will lead you—perilously, due to roaring traffic alongside—over the mind-boggling mesh of the Long Island Railroad tracks. Just past here, Thomson Avenue merges into **Queens Boulevard,** one of the borough's chief transverses.

To your right lie the shells of several once-thriving industries: the **Sunshine Biscuit Company** (Skillman between 29th St. and 30th St.), **American Eveready Building** (29–10 Thomson Ave.), **Adams Chewing Gum Factory** (30–30 Thomson Ave.), and **White Motor Company Factory** (31–10 Thomson Ave.), all built between 1914 and 1920 in a delightful mix of the practical and the ornamental. The **❻ International Design Center** (tel. 718/937–7474), completed in 1985, now occupies the former three structures. This vast marketplace (1 million square feet) for the products of interior designers was built at a cost of more than $125 million. Peek inside to see the ballooning central atrium, surrounded by showrooms ad infinitum. Gigantic elevators for unloading train cars occupied those central spaces back in the days when these buildings still turned out crackers, bubble gum, and auto parts.

❼ Next door, in the old White Motor Company factory, is **La Guardia Community College,** whose **Archives** (31–10 Thomson Ave., Room E-238; open Mon.–Fri. 9–5, but call 718/482–5065 for appointment to view documents) contain the papers of the city's most colorful mayor, Fiorello H. La Guardia. New York's "Little Flower," as La Guardia came to be called, presided over the metropolis during the Depression.

Tour 22: Astoria

One of New York's most vital ethnic neighborhoods, Astoria was originally German, then Italian, but today you're likely to hear more Greek spoken. It has been said that Astoria is home to more Greeks than any place in the world except Athens; whether that was ever true is disputable, but now that the tide of Greek immigration has ebbed somewhat and many second-generation Greek-Americans have moved to the suburbs, a safe guess would put Astoria's Greek population at around 35,000. There are also lots of Asians, Eastern Europeans, Irish, and Hispanic immigrants in Astoria, not to mention a healthy contingent of young people born in the United States who can't afford Manhattan rents and appreciate Astoria's proximity to the city and safe, friendly atmosphere. Our tour emphasizes the Greek population of Astoria only because it is so established—and because their food is so good.

From Manhattan, take the N train to the Broadway stop in Queens. Here, at the intersection of Broadway and 31st Street, you'll be at the epicenter of the Greek community, where Greek *xaxaroplasteion* (pastry shops) and *kaffenion* (coffeehouses) shoot heady smells onto the avenue. On the northeast corner is one of the neighborhood's few architectural landmarks, a four-story building from the early 1860s that now houses Interbank. During the 1920s, it contained a bar owned by the same family that runs the **Oyster Bay Restaurant and Crystal Palace** caterers at 31–01 and 31–11 Broadway; the Crystal Palace part was originally a movie theater. Late into the night the **Grecian Cave** nightclub next door resounds with Greek crooners and bouzouki music. The **Omonia Cafe,** one block east at 32–20 Broadway, is another temptation; if you don't want to sit at a table, you can still stop by the bakery counter to buy such pastries as cream-filled *ekmek* or flaky layered *pontikaki.*

Time Out Two blocks east, the **Roumeli Taverna** (33–04 Broadway, tel. 718/278–7533) is a standout among the many Greek restaurants here; try the house specialty, *mezedakia,* or Greek hors d'oeuvres.

Farther east on Broadway, the **K & T Deli** (37–11 Broadway, tel. 718/545–2890) sends 500 whole lambs to city kitchens every week.

Go south on 36th Street for one of the neighborhood's main attractions, though it has nothing to do with the Greeks. In the 1920s, such stars as Gloria Swanson, Rudolph Valentino, and the Marx Brothers came to this neighborhood to work at "the Big House," Paramount's movie-making center in the east. Today the 13-acre **Kaufman Astoria Studios** (34–12 36th St., tel. 718/392–5600), with its monumentally columned entrance, remains a principal player in the movie biz. Since 1977, scores of pictures have been produced here, including *The Cotton Club, The Verdict, Arthur, The Wiz,* and *Scent of a Woman.*

❽ A visit to the **American Museum of the Moving Image** next door should satisfy almost any film fan's cravings. Opened in September 1988, the museum houses a 195-seat theater and a 60-seat screening room where fascinating film series flicker by—among them tributes to Hollywood directors, cinematographers, writers, and stars. Galleries feature exhibitions such as "Behind the Screen: Producing, Promoting Motion Pictures and Television" and hands-on displays that allow visitors to try their skills at film editing. Commissioned artworks are on display, such as the Red Grooms and Lysiane Luong theater; *Tut's Fever Movie Palace,* a metaphorical recapitulation of Egyptian-style picture palaces of the 1930s (you'll find lifelike figures of Theda Bara at the ticket booth and Mae West serving up popcorn); and Korean Nam June Paik's video installation, "The Getaway Car," a commentary on movies. The museum's collection of movie memorabilia includes 83,000 items; in the costume display you might find outfits worn by Rudolph Valentino or Bette Davis. *35th Ave. at 36th St., tel. 718/784–0077. Admission: $5 adults, $4 senior citizens, $2.50 students and children. Open Tues.–Fri. noon–4, weekends noon–6.*

Return to Broadway and 31st Street to explore the Greek community in more depth. Two blocks up 31st Street, you'll see Astoria's ❾ heart, the Greek Orthodox **St. Demetrios Cathedral** (30–11 30th Dr., tel. 718/728–1718), a brick building with a red-tile roof and the largest Orthodox congregation outside Greece.

Continue up 31st Street to 31st Avenue, where you may want to turn right three blocks to visit **Zenon Taverna Meze House** (34–10 31st Ave., tel. 718/956–0133), a restaurant run by immigrants not from Greece but from Greek Cyprus, a group that keeps growing as Greek and Turkish forces continue to dispute ownership of the island. The **Pan Cypriot Community Center** is eight blocks north on 31st Street, above **Taverna Vraka** (23–15 31st St.). Continue north on 31st Street to reach 23rd Avenue, where Greek-owned businesses bustle. Among the popular spots here is, one block north of 23rd Avenue, **Elias Corner** (24–01 31st St., tel. 718/932–1510). It isn't open for lunch, but if you love seafood, you should think seriously about hanging around for an early dinner here. There are no menus, so just go to the fish case and point.

⑩ Five blocks east of 31st Steet on 23rd Avenue is **St. Irene Chrysovalantou Cathedral,** an independent Greek church where worshipers can pray to an icon that reportedly wept real tears at the outbreak of the Persian Gulf war in 1991. There was an outcry when the icon was stolen several months later; it was mysteriously returned through the regular mail, wrapped in brown paper, minus its jewel-encrusted frame. While the congregation rejoiced, the mainstream Greek Orthodox priests down at St. Demetrios took the opportunity to denounce the apostates once again and to deny that the icon ever wept at all.

The ancient Greeks excelled in the art of sculpture, so it is appropriate that Astoria should contain two sculpture parks. If you're up for a hike, return to Broadway and head eight blocks west until you
⑪ reach the East River, at Vernon Boulevard. Before you is **Socrates Sculpture Park** (Vernon Blvd. at Broadway, tel. 718/956–1819), 4.2 acres of large, abstract artworks that first appear almost as an urban hallucination. You can get a fine view of Manhattan across the
⑫ water here. Three blocks south is **The Isamu Noguchi Garden Museum,** where Japanese sculptor Isamu Noguchi took studio space in a photo-engraver's factory some 30 years ago. Part of it now holds 12 galleries that offer Noguchi devotees a concentration of the sculptor's evocative work in stone, and garden and stage-set design, along with videos documenting his long career. A small sculpture garden adjoins the museum. *32–37 Vernon Blvd., tel. 718/204–7088. Suggested contribution: $2. Museum open Apr.–Nov., Wed. and Sat. 11–6. Saturday bus service to Noguchi Museum leaves every hour on the half-hour, 11:30–3:30, from the Asia Society, Park Ave. and 70th St. in Manhattan. Fare: $5.*

The Bronx

Tour 23: Fordham and the Bronx Zoo

Numbers in the margin correspond to points of interest on the Tour 23: Fordham and the Bronx Zoo map.

The only borough attached to the North American mainland, the Bronx was first settled by Dutch, French, English, and Swedish country squires, who established manorial holdings there while fighting off Indians. The Village of Fordham was founded by John Archer in the mid-1600s, although little now remains from the Colonial era. But the area does dramatically illustrate another aspect of Bronx history—the influx of immigrant groups from the 1840s onward: first the Irish, then Germans, Italians, and Jews. Later waves included African-Americans and Hispanics, and today there are new infusions of Albanian and Cambodian immigrants.

To reach the old Village of Fordham, ride the D subway to the Kingsbridge Road station (or take a Metro North train to the Fordham stop and pick up the tour just past bullet number 3 below). From the Kingsbridge Road subway station, you'll alight alongside a fine stretch of that Bronx Champs-Elysées, the **Grand Concourse.** Here you get a sense of the roadway as engineer Louis Riis envisioned it—a 4-mile-long "speedway," facilitating excursions into the country—as well as a view to the west of the **Kingsbridge Armory,** built in 1912, one of the largest such structures in the world.

Poe Park, at East Kingsbridge Road and the Grand Concourse, is so named because it contains the **Edgar Allan Poe Cottage,** with its quaint white wood siding and green shutters. Here Poe and his sickly wife, Virginia, sought refuge from Manhattan and from the vicissitudes of the writerly life between 1846 and 1849. He wandered the countryside on foot and listened to the sound of the church bells at nearby St. John's College Church (now Fordham University). Among the works he completed during this period are the poems "Ulalume," "The Bells," "Eureka," and "Annabel Lee." *Tel. 718/ 881–8900. Admission: $2. Open Sat. 10–4, Sun. 1–5.*

A couple of blocks south is the intersection of Fordham Road and the Grand Concourse, the Times Square of the Bronx. Venture south on the Grand Concourse to **Loew's Paradise Theatre** (2413 Grand Concourse, tel. 718/367–1288), which many claim is the best remaining 1930s-style movie house. The exterior ornamentation looks like a claymation fantasy; inside, a sloping, tiled entryway leads to a gorgeously garish Baroque-style lobby. Tell the ticket-taker that you're an architecture student and you may be able to get in without paying for the latest kung fu movie. John Eberson, the dean of bijou-builders, designed this gem in 1929; it was converted to a quadplex in 1981.

Don't stroll farther south on the Grand Concourse from the Paradise—the neighborhood swiftly declines. Instead, turn west on East 188th Street to peek at the **Creston Avenue Baptist Church** (114 E. 188th St.), built in 1905 and looking like it belongs not among the commercial chaos of Fordham Road, but in Merry Old England.

The Bx 12 bus will take you east along Fordham Road to Arthur Avenue; if you prefer the hike, you'll pass myriad coffee shops and discount stores, the Metro North train's Fordham stop, 1 Fordham Plaza (a modern green-and-white birthday-cake-like construction), and the looming Theodore Roosevelt High School.

Belmont, the neighborhood surrounding the intersection of Arthur Avenue and East 187th Street, has come to be called the Bronx's Little Italy—although actually it's a bigger Little Italy than the one in Manhattan. It really lights up after the sun sets, but it's also a daytime place, where some 14,500 families socialize, shop, work, and eat fabulously. Along Arthur Avenue you'll pass **Ciccarone Playground,** sporting a huge painted Italian flag. Indeed, as you study the surrounding two-story frame homes and tenements, the neighborhood begins to seem tinted exclusively in shades of white, red, and green: Italy's colors. A left turn onto East 187th Street takes you into an Italian commercial panoply; on one stellar block between Hughes and Belmont avenues you'll find **Egidio's Pastry Shop** (622 E. 187th St.), **Danny's Pork Store** (626 E. 187th St.), **Catholic Goods** (630 E. 187th St.), which sells Italian greeting cards, **Borgatti's Ravioli & Egg Noodles** (632 E. 187th St.), and the **Roma Luncheonette** (636 E. 187th St.). Across the street, residents' spiritual lives are tended to at **Our Lady of Mt. Carmel Roman Catholic Church** (627 E. 187th St.). The church, built in 1907, is an imposing brick structure with columned arches and four jutting flagpoles; inside, amid the marble columns and the intricate stained-glass windows, there is an indescribable scent of old religion.

A block south is the **Enrico Fermi Cultural Center/Belmont Branch New York Public Library** (610 E. 186th St., tel. 718/933–6410),

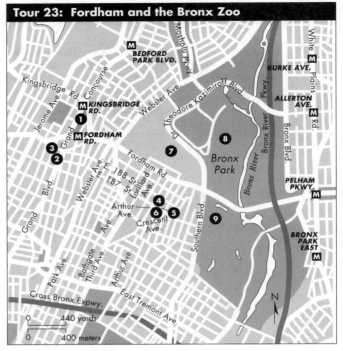

Tour 23: Fordham and the Bronx Zoo

where the Heritage Collection contains several volumes outlining the contributions of Italians and Italian-Americans. Nearby the **Arthur Avenue Retail Market** (2344 Arthur Ave.), a skylit shopping mart, offers 70 stalls, where Italian sausages and cheeses hang from on high.

Time Out   **Dominick's** (2335 Arthur Ave., tel. 718/733–2807) enjoys a reputation as Belmont's best restaurant. Here there are no menus, no wine lists—just hearty Italian food, savored at congested common tables, and cooked by members of a family that's been at Dominick's for 30 years. Finish off your meal with an espresso laced with sambuco.

---

7   Return to Fordham Road to explore the 85-acre campus of **Fordham University,** built around the site of the old Rose Hill Manor House (1838). Begun in 1841 as a Jesuit college, Fordham now has an undergraduate enrollment of 7,500, and an auxiliary campus near Lincoln Center.

Enter the grounds via Bathgate Avenue and you'll find yourself in an enclave of Collegiate Gothic architecture, shady trees, and green turf. Maps are posted around the campus or are available in the admissions office at Dealy Hall; use them to locate such highlights as the **Old Rose Hill Manor Dig;** the **University Church,** with its stained glass donated by King Louis Philippe of France (1773–1850); the pleasant **Edward's Parade;** and **Keating Hall,** sitting like a Gothic fortress in the center of things. After meandering through Fordham, make your way to the university's main entrance, fronting on Bronx (or, properly, New York Zoological) Park.

8 One of the best reasons to make a trip to the Bronx is the **New York Botanical Garden.** The Fordham entrance leads into this serene but extraordinarily varied treasury, the dream of a husband-and-wife botanical team, Dr. Nathaniel Lord and Elizabeth Britton. After visiting England's Kew Gardens in 1889, they returned full of fervor to create a similar haven in New York. In 1991, the New York Botanical Garden celebrated its centennial.

The garden stretches for 250 acres around the dramatic gorge of the Bronx River. It holds the historic **Lorillard Snuff Mill,** built by two French Huguenot manufacturers in 1840 to power the grinding of tobacco for snuff. Nearby, the Lorillards grew roses to supply fragrance for their blend. The snuff mill now houses a café, open daily 10–5. A walk along the Bronx River from the mill leads the visitor to the botanical garden's 40-acre **Forest,** the only uncut woodland in New York City. Outdoor plant collections include the **Erpf Compass Garden,** where cobblestones denoting the points of a compass are surrounded by flowers. Inside the luminous **Enid A. Haupt Conservatory** are displays of ferns, tropical flora, and Old and New World deserts. At the **Museum Building,** there's a gardening shop, a library, and a world-renowned herbarium holding 5.5 million dried plant specimens. *Bronx Park, tel. 718/220–8700. Conservatory admission: $3 adults, $2 senior citizens and students; free Sat. 10–noon. Last admission 1 hr before closing. Open Nov.–Mar., Tues.–Sun. and Mon. holidays 10–4; Apr.–Oct., Tues.–Sun. and Mon. holidays 10–6. Parking: $4.*

9 Also in Bronx Park is the **Bronx Zoo,** the nation's largest urban zoo and recently renamed the **International Wildlife Conservation Park.** It deserves nearly an entire day's visit on its own; if you want to return on another day, you can take the Liberty Lines BxM11 bus that runs up Madison Avenue (Tel. 718/652–8400. Fare: $3.50).

At the zoo you'll see two different historical methods of keeping wild animals. The turn-of-the-century zoological garden houses monkeys, sea lions, and elephants (among many others) in fancy Beaux Arts–style edifices at **Astor Court.** It's being gradually replaced by the animal-in-habitat approach used in the **World of Birds,** with its capacious walk-through indoor natural habitats; in **Jungleworld,** an indoor tropical rain forest complete with five waterfalls, millipedes, flowering orchids, and pythons; and in the new **Baboon Reserve.** The **Children's Zoo** ($1.50 admission; open Apr.–Oct.) features many hands-on learning activities, as well as a large petting zoo. At the **Zoo Center,** visitors will find a rare Sumatran rhino. The zoo as a whole has more than 4,000 animals representing 667 species. *Bronx Zoo, tel. 718/367–1010. Admission: Thurs.–Tues. $5.75 adults, $2 senior citizens and children 2–12 (Nov.–Feb. $2.50 adults, $1 senior citizens and children); Wed. voluntary contribution. Open Feb.–Oct., weekdays 10–5, weekends and holidays 10–5:30; Nov.–Jan., daily 10–4:30.*

Staten Island

Tour 24: Snug Harbor and Richmondtown

Numbers in the margin correspond to points of interest on the Tour 24: Staten Island map.

Even though Staten Island is officially a borough of New York City, many Staten Islanders (as do the rest of the bridge and tunnel crowd) refer to Manhattan as "the City." Perhaps that's because farms and vast woodlands have distinguished it from the more crowded and developed Manhattan since 1661, when Staten Island was permanently settled as a farming community by the Dutch (after several fatal battles with the Native American tribes who already inhabited the area). When oystering became a thriving industry in the early 1800s, farmers brought free blacks up from Maryland to help plant new oyster beds. The black community on the south shore became known as Sandy Ground; descendants of the first black oystermen still live there. Factories came later, as did shipbuilding. Today Staten Island still feels more residential than the other boroughs. (A recent election revealed that an overwhelming majority of the S. I. natives support secession as a way to rid themselves of the many responsibilities of being part of "the city.") Getting around can be somewhat difficult for visitors because the various attractions are so spread out, but bus service is convenient.

The greatest way to introduce yourself to Staten Island is by taking the 20-minute ride across New York Harbor on the **Staten Island Ferry,** which leaves regularly from the southern tip of Manhattan (*see* Tour 17 in Chapter 3). On the boats with outer decks, passengers can get a better look at the spectacular views of lower Manhattan's skyscrapers and the splendidly restored Ellis Island and Statue of Liberty.

From the ferry terminal, a seven-minute ride on the S40 bus or on a special trolley will take you to the **Snug Harbor Cultural Center,** which on a warm summer afternoon might be hosting a New York Philharmonic concert, an art show, or an old-fashioned flea market. Once part of a sprawling farm, then a home for "aged and decrepit sailors," the 80-acre center is based around a row of five columned Greek Revival temples, built between 1831 and 1880, facing onto the Kill Van Kull, a wide stream that flows into Upper New York Bay. The former chapel is now the 210-seat **Veterans Memorial Hall,** site of many indoor concerts and gatherings. *1000 Richmond Terr., tel. 718/448–2500. Admission free; various charges for special events. Open 8 AM–dusk. Free guided tours Sat.–Sun. 2 PM.*

On the Snug Harbor grounds, the **Newhouse Center for Contemporary Art** features changing exhibitions. *Suggested contribution: $1. Open Wed.–Sun. noon–5.*

The **Staten Island Botanical Gardens,** also on the Snug Harbor grounds, feature a perennial garden, a greenhouse, 10 acres of natural marsh habitat, a fragrance garden for the blind, and a bonsai collection. *Tel. 718/273–8200. Admission free. Open 9 AM–dusk.*

The **Staten Island Children's Museum,** also in Snug Harbor, offers four revolving hands-on exhibitions to introduce children to such diverse topics as news and media, storytelling, and insects. *1000 Richmond Terr., tel. 718/273–2060. Admission: $3. Open Tues.–Sun. noon–5.*

Return to the ferry terminal and catch the S52–Bay Street bus for the 2-mile ride to Hylan Boulevard and the **Alice Austen House.** Photographer Alice Austen (1866–1952) defied tradition when, as a girl of 10, she received her first camera as a gift from an uncle and promptly began taking pictures of everything around her. Austen went on to make photography her lifetime avocation, recording on film a vivid social history of Staten Island in the early part of the century; one of the local ferries is actually named for her. The cozy, ivy-covered Dutch-style cottage known as Clear Comfort, where she lived almost all her life, has been restored, and many of her pho-

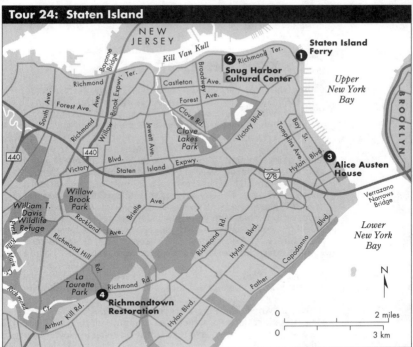

Tour 24: Staten Island

NEW JERSEY

Staten Island Ferry

Kill Van Kull

Bayonne Bridge

Richmond Ter.

Broadway

Snug Harbor Cultural Center

Richmond Ter.

Richmond

Willow Brook Expwy.

Castleton Ave.

Forest Ave.

Upper New York Bay

BROOKLYN

South Ave.

Forest Ave.

Clove Rd.

Clove Lakes Park

Victory Blvd.

Bay St.

Tompkins Ave.

Hylan Blvd.

440

Richmond Ave.

Jewett Ave.

440

Blvd.

Victory

Staten Island Expwy.

278

Alice Austen House

Willow Brook Park

Brielle Ave.

Verrazano Narrows Bridge

William T. Davis Wildlife Refuge

Rockland Ave.

Richmond Rd.

Hylan Blvd.

Capodanno Blvd.

Lower New York Bay

Richmond Hill Rd.

La Tourette Park

Richmond Rd.

Father

N

Arthur Kill Rd.

Richmond Rd.

Richmondtown Restoration

Hylan Blvd.

0   2 miles

0   3 km

tographs are on exhibit. *2 Hylan Blvd., tel. 718/816–4506. Suggested contribution: $2 adults. Open Thurs.–Sun. noon–5.*

Take the S74–Richmond Road bus from the ferry terminal to the **Richmondtown Restoration,** a unique museum village on the site of Staten Island's first permanent settlement, founded in 1685. The 26 historic buildings on this 96-acre complex have been restored inside and out; some were here originally, while others were relocated from other spots on the island. Many of the buildings, such as the Greek Revival courthouse that serves as the **visitor center,** date from the 19th century; other architectural styles on site range from Dutch Colonial to Victorian Gothic Revival. The **Voorlezer's House,** built in 1695, is the oldest elementary schoolhouse in the United States; it looks like the mold from which all little red schoolhouses were cast.

During the warmer months, costumed interpreters demonstrate Early American crafts and trades such as printing, tinsmithing, and baking. The **Staten Island Historical Society Museum,** built in 1848 as the second county clerk's and surrogate's office, now has in its archives American china, furniture, toys, and tools, plus a collection of Staten Island photographs.

During a summer visit, you might want to make reservations for the 19th-century dinner, cooked outdoors and served with utensils of the period. The Autumn Celebration shows off craftspeople demonstrating their skills; the annual Encampment in June is a reenactment of a Civil War battle; December brings a month-long Christmas celebration. Richmondtown regularly hosts other fairs, flea markets, and tours of the historic buildings. There is a tavern where folk music is played. *Tel. 718/351–1611. Admission: $4 adults, $2.50 senior citizens and children 6–18. Open Jan.–Mar., Wed.–Fri. 1–5; Apr.–Dec., Wed.–Sun. 1–5.*

Off the Beaten Track

Brooklyn **Coney Island.** At the last stop on the B, D, F, and N train is the home of the hot dog, "the king of roller coasters" (the "Cyclone"), the "Wonder Wheel," suntan lotion, crowds, fried clams, girls and boys necking under the boardwalk, and old men staring vacantly out to sea. While it may have declined from its glory days early in this century—when visitors lunched at an ocean-side hotel built in the shape of an elephant, glided across the nation's biggest dance floor at Dreamland, or toured a replica of old Baghdad called Luna Park—Coney Island still has a boardwalk, a 2.7-mile-long beach, and a huge amusement park. The **Aquarium for Wildlife Conservation** (tel. 718/265–3474) keeps watery beasts—sharks, black-footed penguins, octopuses, piranhas, and Beluga whales —on view nearby. A lively sideshow, complete with a fire-eater, a sword-swallower, and a contortionist, can be seen along with historic Coney Island memorabilia at the nearby **Sideshows By the Seashore** museum (W. 12th St. and Boardwalk, tel. 718/372–5159; admission: 99¢; open Memorial Day–Labor Day, Wed.–Sun.; rest of year, weekends only). On the first Saturday after summer solstice, the cast of the sideshow and an amazing array of local legends take part in the Boardwalk's increasingly renowned Mermaid Parade. Two blocks away is **Brighton Beach Avenue,** the main street of a community of some 30,000 Soviet émigrés, where inexpensive restaurants serving up Soviet Georgian cuisine abound.

Green-Wood Cemetery (25th St. and 5th Ave.). Built in the 1840s, the cemetery features a stately Gothic Revival gatehouse, designed by Richard Upjohn, that still moves visitors to a sublime pitch of melancholy. The 478 acres contain five lakes, 22 miles of lanes, and 209 paths named for bushes, flowers, and trees. Among the illustrious—or infamous—citizens interred there are Samuel F.B. Morse, Boss Tweed, and Peter Cooper. It's open daily 8–4; call the superintendent (tel. 718/768–7300) for permission to tour. The closest subway stop is 25th Street and 4th Avenue (R train).

Queens **Flushing.** This Queens neighborhood, which played a role in the fight for religious freedom in America, is surrounded by a multiethnic community that is increasingly dominated by people of Asian descent; it's a bubbling melting pot rarely visited by New Yorkers themselves. Take the No. 7 subway to its final stop, the Main Street–Flushing station. Main Street and its two parallel neighbors, Prince and Union streets, serve up a banquet for Korean, Chinese, and Indian gourmands. Go north on Main Street to Northern Boulevard, where the wood-shingled, tiny-windowed **Friends Meeting House** (137–16 Northern Blvd.) is New York City's oldest place of worship. Built in 1694, it's still used for the Quakers' 11 AM Sunday services. Turn right on Bowne Street to see **Bowne House** (37–01 Bowne St., tel. 718/359–0528; admission: $2 adults, $1 senior citizens and children under 12; open Tues. and weekends 2:30–4:30), occupied from 1661 to 1945 by the same family, descendants of John Bowne, a Quaker leader who led a historic fight for religious tolerance. The Bowne House displays household furnishings used by nine generations of the family and is the oldest house in Queens. Across Bowne Street you can see the **Fox Oaks Rock,** marking the site of an impassioned sermon delivered in 1672 by George Fox, founder of the

Quaker sect. North of Bowne House, inside the **Kingsland Homestead** (143–35 37th Ave., tel. 718/939–0647; admission: $2 adults, $1 students, senior citizens, and children; open Tues., Sat., and Sun. 2:30–4:30), a gambrel-roofed wood farmhouse built circa 1785, the Queens Historical Society mounts exhibits about local history. In the park beside the Kingsland Homestead is the **Weeping Beech,** a huge beech tree with trailing branches, planted from a cutting brought by Samuel Parsons from Belgium in 1847.

Bronx **Riverdale.** This is perhaps the Bronx's plushest neighborhood; wide-open territory for outer-borough explorers, it's best visited by car, taking the Kappock Street exit from the Henry Hudson Parkway. If you don't have a car, take the Metro North train to the Riverdale stop. Manhattan millionaires built summer homes here, with stirring views of the New Jersey Palisades across the Hudson River, in the early part of this century. A drive along Palisade Avenue, picturesque Sycamore Avenue above West 252nd Street, and Independence Avenue between West 248th and 254th streets will take you past some of Riverdale's handsomest mansions. Only **Wave Hill** (675 W. 252nd St., tel. 718/549–2055) is open to the public, but a visit to this 28-acre estate will conjure up the image of Riverdale's wealthy past. Built in 1844, then lavishly added onto by J. P. Morgan's partner George Perkins, the estate offers two mansions and splendid views of the Hudson. *Admission: weekends, $4 adults, $2 senior citizens and students; weekdays, free. Open mid-May–mid-Oct., Sun.–Tues. and Thurs.–Fri., 10–5:30, Sat. and Wed. 10–7; mid-Oct.–mid-May, Tues.–Sun. 9:30–4:30.*

City Island. At the extreme west end of the Bronx is a bona fide island measuring 230 acres wide. Back in 1761, a group of the area's residents planned a port to rival New York's, but when that scheme hit the shoals, they returned to perennial maritime pursuits such as fishing and boatbuilding. City Island–produced yachts have included a number of America's Cup contenders. Connected to Pelham Bay Park by bridge, City Island offers visitors a maritime atmosphere and good seafood restaurants. To reach City Island, take the No. 6 subway to Pelham Bay Parkway and then catch the No. 29 bus. While you're there, be sure to stop by the **North Wind Undersea Museum,** with its displays devoted to marine mammal rescue and deep-sea diving. *610 City Island Ave., Bronx, tel. 718/885–0701. Admission: $3 adults, $2 children under 12. Open weekdays 10–5, weekends noon–5.*

Staten Island **Staten Island Train.** There's no subway on Staten Island, but there is one above-ground train line, and it accepts New York City subway tokens. For a leisurely look at Staten Island's topography, ride the train its full route, from the Staten Island ferry terminal to Tottenville, about a 40-minute trip. You'll get a stunning view of the Verrazano-Narrows Bridge and then ramble through residential neighborhoods, woods, and wetlands.

5 Exploring New York City with Children

By Kate
Sekules

New York is as magical a place for children as it is for adults. Although hotels and restaurants tend to be geared firmly to the grown-ups, when provision has been made for children, it is usually accomplished in a grand way. The world's best and largest toy shop, the biggest dinosaur skeletons, the biggest and best park, the nicest city seaport, the best burgers, and of course, some of the world's tallest buildings are here. Besides such sights, there are rare ambient treats to stumble upon—from brightly colored pictograms in Chinatown to exotic-looking Hasidim in the Diamond District, from Central Park squirrels to Greenwich Village street musicians good enough to appear on television (and sometimes they do).

For calendars of children's events, consult *New York* magazine and the weekly *Village Voice* newspaper, available at newsstands. The Friday *New York Times* "Weekend" section and the Friday edition of *New York Newsday* also provide a good listing of children's activities.

Two other good sources of information on happenings for kids are the monthly magazines **New York Family** (141 Halstead Ave., Mamaroneck, NY 10543, tel. 914/381–7474), and the **Big Apple Parents' Paper** (36 E. 12th St., New York, NY 10003, tel. 212/533–2277), which is available free at toy stores, children's museums and clothing stores, and other places around town where parents and children are found.

To get children psyched up for a New York trip, give them *Eloise*, by Kay Thompson, *Harriet the Spy*, by Louise Fitzhugh, or *Stuart Little*, by E.B. White.

Sightseeing

As far as outdoors sights are concerned, there is plenty to please; surprising pockets of street sculpture, graffiti art, strange building facades, and quirky shop windows may be found on almost every block. In no other city are you more likely to entertain offspring simply by wandering. Children get a kick from the sheer size of the buildings, and from riding cabs, or even buses and subways (especially the first or last car, with a view of the track and tunnels). For more exotic transportation, try the **horse-drawn carriages** around Central Park (at Grand Army Plaza or intersections of Central Park S between 5th and 7th Aves.; $34 for the first 30 minutes); summer sailboats, named *The Pioneer* (South St. Seaport, tel. 212/669–9417; $15 adults, $5 children under 12, for 2 hours) or *The Petrel* (Battery Park, tel. 212/825–1976; $14–$25 adults, $10 children under 13, for 45 mins.–2 hours); or an **Island Helicopter** tour (34th St. and East River, tel. 212/683–4575; $41–$94).

For little more than the price of a subway token, the **Roosevelt Island Aerial Tramway** across the East River is a sure hit. Trams board at 2nd Avenue and 60th Street and run every 15 minutes during regular hours, and every 7½ minutes during rush hours, which you might wish to avoid.

Don't miss the **Statue of Liberty, Ellis Island,** (*see* Tour 17 in Chapter 3) or the **South Street Seaport** (*see* Tour 18 in Chapter 3), all appreciated by children. Ferry rides are always fun; try the bargain 50¢ ride on the **Staten Island Ferry** (terminal in Battery Park), or a cruise on the beautiful sidewheeler and steamboat of the **Seaport Line** (*see* Tour 18 in Chapter 3).

While in lower Manhattan, visit **Fraunces Tavern,** whose museum holds kids' workshops; the fairy-tale palacelike lobby of the **Woolworth Building** (*see* Tour 17 in Chapter 3); the indoor jungle at Battery Park City's **Winter Garden Atrium;** and the great sweep of **Brooklyn Bridge** (*see* Tour 18 in Chapter 3). Of course, the **World Trade Center's** 107th-floor panorama is another popular downtown sight (*see* Tour 17 in Chapter 3). The favorite midtown high-level view is from the **Empire State Building,** (*see* Tour 4 in Chapter 3). Hop uptown to **Grand Central Terminal** (*see* Tour 3 in Chapter 3) for the whispering gallery, star-bedecked ceiling, and amazing bustle.

Museums

Although just about every major museum in New York City has something to interest children, certain ones hold special appeal. At the top of the list is the **American Museum of Natural History** (Central Park at 79th St., tel. 212/769–5100), with its lifelike dioramas and giant dinosaurs (partially off-limits until 1995, when restoration of the entire collection will be completed). Also intriguing are the Discovery Room, with hands-on exhibits for children, and the Naturemax Theater, which shows awesome nature films on a gigantic screen. The adjacent **Hayden Planetarium** offers astronomical exhibits and sky shows; there is also a preschool show (reservations required; tel. 212/769–5920) (*see* Tour 8 in Chapter 3).

The **Children's Museum of Manhattan,** is a kind of indoor playground for kids 2–12, with interactive exhibits organized around common childhood experiences. Children can paint, make collages, and try on costumes. *212 W. 83rd St., tel. 212/721–1234. Admission: $4 adults and children, $2 senior citizens. Open Mon., Wed., and Thurs. 1:30–5:30; Fri.–Sun. 10–5.*

The **Children's Museum of the Arts,** in a loftlike space in Soho, allows children ages 18 months to 10 to become actively involved in visual and performing arts. Highlights include the Monet Ball Pond, where children can play with brightly colored balls near a water-lily mural; the Lines and Shapes alcove, where kids have access to computer drawing; and the Creative Play area, which provides a large playpen, a reading corner, art activities, and cushions and futons for relaxation. Weekend workshops are included in the admission price. *72–78 Spring St., tel. 212/941–9198. Admission: $4 adults under 65 and children over 18 months. Admission free, Thurs. 4–7. Open Tues.–Sun. 11–5; Thurs. 11–7.*

Another favorite with the younger generation is the *Intrepid* Sea-Air-Space Museum, an immense World War II aircraft carrier. On deck is a startling array of aircraft; inside there are aviation and military exhibits, as well as skinny hallways, winding staircases, and dozens of knobs, buttons, and wheels to manipulate. *Pier 86 at 12th Ave. and W. 46th St., tel. 212/245–0072. Admission: $7 adults, $6 senior citizens and veterans, $4 children 6–12. Open Wed.–Sun. 10–5.*

Kids tend to like the **Forbes Magazine Galleries** (62 5th Ave. at 12th St., tel. 212/206–5548) for the collections of toy soldiers and boats, and rooms with the bejeweled Fabergé eggs (*see* Tour 12 in Chapter 3). Another good bet is the **New York City Fire Museum** (278 Spring St., tel. 212/691–1303), with displays of fire-fighting equipment and tours given by real firefighters (*see* Chapter 6).

Other museums offer special programs for kids or families. Among these are the **Museum of Modern Art,** the Junior Museum at the **Met-**

ropolitan Museum of Art, the Jewish Museum, the Museum of the City of New York, with wonderful collections of dollhouses and antique toys, the El Museo del Barrio (*see* Tour 5 in Chapter 3), and the Lower East Side Tenement Museum (*see* Chapter 6). At the Whitney Museum of American Art (*see* Tour 5 in Chapter 3), children like the Calder circus.

The Brooklyn Museum (*see* Tour 20 in Chapter 4) has special programs for kids and families. For children who like hands-on involvement, the place to go is the Brooklyn Children's Museum, considered one of the best in the world, and full of tunnels, bubbles, animals, and neon lights. Exhibits cover the environment, nature, science, and more. *145 Brooklyn Ave., tel. 718/735–4432. Suggested contribution: $3. Open June–Aug., Wed.–Sun. noon–5; Sept.–May, Wed.–Fri. 2–5; weekends and holidays noon–5.*

In Queens, the New York Hall of Science in Flushing Meadows–Corona Park allows budding researchers access to 150 exhibits (many of them touchable) on such topics as color and illusion, the atom, self-sensory machines, and microorganisms. *111th St. at 40th Ave., tel. 718/699–0005. Admission: $3.50 adults, $2.50 senior citizens and children; free Wed. and Thurs. 2–5. Open Wed.–Sun. 10–5.*

Astoria, Queens has the American Museum of the Moving Image (*see* Tour 22 in Chapter 4), the only museum in the United States devoted to both film and television.

The Staten Island Institute of Arts and Sciences offers kids' programs and wonderful exhibits covering natural history and the arts from nearly all angles. *75 Stuyvesant Pl., tel. 718/727–1135. Suggested contribution: $2.50 adults, $1.50 senior citizens and children. Open Mon.–Sat. 9–5, Sun. 1–5.*

Also on Staten Island are the hands-on exhibits of the Staten Island Children's Museum (*see* Tour 24 in Chapter 4). Children may also enjoy Richmondtown Restoration's Staten Island Historical Society (*see* Tour 24 in Chapter 4), which has a Museum of Childhood with displays of antique dolls, toys, and children's furniture.

The Liberty Science Center, the largest science museum in the New York metropolitan area, opened in 1993 in Liberty State Park, New Jersey. This impressive four-floor center is guaranteed to keep kids busy for hours with more than 250 interactive exhibits that concentrate on three themes—environment, health, and invention. Highlights include laser light and sound displays, an insect zoo, a 100-foot touch tunnel, an amazing 700-pound geodesic globe, and the Kodak OMNI Theater, for viewing OMNIMAX movies on a gigantic screen. *Liberty State Park, 251 Philip St., Jersey City, NJ, tel. 201/200–1000. Admission: $8 adults, $7 students and senior citizens, $5 children 5–12. OMNI Theater admission: $7 adults, $6 students and senior citizens, $5 children 5–12. Combined admission to exhibits and OMNI Theater: $12 adults, $10 students and senior citizens, $8 children 5–12. Admission "pay-as-you-wish" on first Wed. of every month 1 PM–closing. Open Tues.–Thurs. 9:30–5:30, Fri.–Sun. and holidays 9:30–6:30.*

The center is reached from Manhattan by car by taking the Holland Tunnel to Exit 14B on the New Jersey Turnpike (about a 10-minute drive without heavy traffic).

To reach the center by train from Manhattan, take the PATH train (tel. 800/234–7284) in the direction of Jersey City to Exchange Place, Journal Square, or Grove Street stops and then take a Central Avenue bus to the center. Visitors can also take a Port Imperial ferry (tel. 800/53–

FERRY) from the World Financial Center in downtown Manhattan to Liberty State Park.

Parks and Playgrounds

New York's great outdoors sounds like a contradiction in terms, especially when you add children to the equation. But, in addition to the wide open spaces of Central Park, pockets of green all over town provide relief from concrete.

In Central Park, children can ride bicycles, play tennis, row boats, go horseback riding, ice-skate, roller-skate, rollerblade, skateboard, fly kites, feed ducks, throw Frisbees, and much more (*see* Tour 7 in Chapter 3; *see also* Chapter 7). Favorite destinations include the **Zoo** (*see below*) and the **Conservatory Water,** which attracts owners of large, remote-controlled model boats and is located near the statues of Alice in Wonderland and Hans Christian Andersen. Younger children enjoy the hands-on activities at the **Dairy** and **Belvedere Castle** (tel. 212/772–0210), as well as an antique **Carousel** (midpark at 65th St., tel. 212/879–0244), complete with painted horses that prance to jaunty organ music; it costs only 90¢ a ride. The **Wollman Rink** (tel. 212/517–4800) has rollerblading and roller-skating classes and sessions—ice-skating in winter—and a **Miniature Golf** course, with obstacles of city buildings (*see* Chapter 7).

At Brooklyn's 536-acre **Prospect Park,** enjoy kite flying and picnicking on the 90-acre Long Meadow (*see* Tour 20 in Chapter 4). Near the park, bring the family for a stroll at the **Brooklyn Botanic Garden** (*see* Tour 20 in Chapter 4).

In the Bronx, adjacent to the Bronx Zoo, the **New York Botanical Garden** (*see* Tour 23 in Chapter 4) is one of the world's largest botanical gardens, with a large conservatory, 12 outdoor gardens, walking trails, and 40 acres of forest.

Off the beaten track, there are short marked nature trails suitable for young hikers at the **Alley Pond Environmental Center** (228–06 Northern Blvd., Douglastown, tel. 718/229–4000) and **Jamaica Bay Wildlife Refuge** (tel. 718/474–0613) in Queens, and at **Van Cortlandt Park** (tel. 212/430–1890) in the Bronx. (For more park listings, *see* Chapter 6.)

Manhattan has wonderful state-of-the-art playgrounds. **Central Park's** adventure playgrounds are full of slides, bridges, bars, swings, towers and tunnels; they're carpeted with sand or soft rubber matting and often cooled in summer by sprinklers, fountains, or running water. Good ones can be found along 5th Avenue at 67th Street near the Zoo, at 71st and 77th streets, and at 85th Street near the Metropolitan Museum. Along Central Park West, the best ones are at 68th, 85th, 93rd (with a Wild West theme), and 96th streets. The large **Hecksher Playground,** midpark at 62nd Street, for toddlers, has good water features.

Also top-rated by Manhattan kids are the playgrounds at **Battery Park City** (West St. south of Vesey St.), **Washington Square Park** (at foot of 5th Ave., between Waverly Pl. and W. 4th St.), **Abingdon Square Park** (at the triangular junction of Bleecker, Bank, and Hudson Sts. in the West Village), **Carl Schurz Park** (84th St. near East End Ave.), **John Jay Park** (off York Ave. near 77th St., within sight of the East River), and the **Pearl Street Playground** (Fulton, Water, and Pearl Sts.). In **Riverside Park,** west of Riverside Drive, the best playgrounds are at 77th and 91st streets; the one at 77th Street has a circle of spouting elephant fountains. The new **Asser Levy Play-**

ground (23rd St., one block from the East River) is the first in Manhattan that caters fully to disabled children, with giant, multicolored mazelike structures, helter-skelter slides with wheelchair stations, and textured pavement for the blind; **All Children** (Flushing Meadows–Corona Park, Corona Ave. and 111th St., Queens, tel. 718/699–8283) is its Queens predecessor. Three more— in Coney and Staten islands and the Bronx—are on the way.

Zoos

Central Park Zoo, recently renamed the **Central Park Wildlife Conservation Center,** is of a very manageable size, even for toddlers (*see* Tour 7 in Chapter 3). With only 100 or so mostly small species on display, it may disappoint older children, but everyone loves the penguins on display.

On the more impressive side is the largest zoo of any city in the United States: the **Bronx Zoo,** recently renamed the **International Wildlife Conservation Park** (*see* Tour 23 in Chapter 4). Most of the animals here live in replicas of their natural habitats. Don't miss the Children's Zoo area (open Apr.–Oct.), with fishes, reptiles, and small animals behind glass, as well as a petting farm.

Brooklyn's **Prospect Park Zoo,** recently renamed the **Prospect Park Wildlife Conservation Center** reopened in 1993 after extensive renovations (*see* Tour 20 in Chapter 4).

The **Queens Zoo,** recently renamed the **Queens Wildlife Conservation Center,** shows North American animals in approximations of their natural habitat. The inhabitants include black bears, mountain lions, sea lions, bobcats, coyotes, bison, and elk. *53–51 111th St., Flushing Meadows Park, tel. 718/271–7761. Admission: $2.50 adults, $1.25 seniors, 50¢ children 3–12. Open Apr.–Oct., Mon.– Fri. 10–5, weekends and holidays 10–5:30; Nov.–Mar., daily 10– 4:30.*

The **Staten Island Zoo** is small but of high quality and features one of the world's finest collections of reptiles, as well as a separate Children's Zoo. *Barrett Park, 614 Broadway, Staten Island, tel. 718/442–3100. Admission: $3 adults, $2 children 3–11. Pay-as-you-wish Wed. 2–4:45. Open daily 10–4:45.*

Nearly 300 different varieties of fish are on display in Brooklyn at the **Aquarium for Wildlife Conservation.** You'll marvel at the dolphins, sea lions, and electric eels; be sure to catch the penguin and shark feedings. *Surf Ave. at W. 8th St., Coney Island, tel. 718/265– 3474. Admission: $5.75 adults, $2 senior citizens and children 2–12. Open June–Aug., weekdays 10–5:45, weekends and holidays 10–8; Sept.–May., daily 10–5:45.*

Shopping

Adults and children alike find shopping nirvana in New York. One of the world's best toy stores, **F.A.O. Schwarz** (where Tom Hanks danced on the giant piano in the movie *Big*), is probably highlight number one (*see* Toys in Chapter 8), but even shopping for clothes, often resented by children, can be fun here.

In addition to the stores listed under Children's Clothing in Chapter 8, try, on the Upper West Side, **Morris Brothers** (2322 Broadway, between 84th and 85th Sts., tel. 212/724–9000) and **Monkeys & Bears** (506 Amsterdam Ave., tel. 212/873–2673) for hip, all-age clothes;

and **Shoofly** (465 Amsterdam Ave., tel. 212/580–4390) for designer footwear. The Upper East Side's boutiques of choice are **Magic Windows** (infant–sixth grade, 1046 Lexington at 75th St., tel. 212/517–7271; infant–preteen, 1186 Madison Ave. at 87th St., tel. 212/289–0028), and **Chocolate Soup** (946 Madison Ave., between 74th and 75th Sts., tel. 212/861–2210) for handsewn and imported clothes for kids. Downtown boys like **Boy Oh Boy!** (18 E. 17th St., tel. 212/463–8250) for sizes 2–20. SoHo's **Too Cute** (113 Prince St., between Greene and Wooster Sts., tel. 212/777–5974), stocks casual clothes embroidered with cartoon characters.

Also visit the clothing and toy departments at **Macy's** for the thrill of size and **A&S** for the cool atrium plaza. Go to Macy's during the holiday season between Thanksgiving and Christmas, and enjoy the enchanting Christmas window displays for free. Don't miss the animated windows at **Lord & Taylor,** either; the elegant ones at **Bergdorf Goodman, Bloomingdale's, Saks Fifth Avenue** and, especially, at **Barneys New York** tend to be aimed squarely at adults, but kids usually enjoy them, too (*see* Department Stores in Chapter 8).

For stores featuring toys, games, magic, and general gizmos, *see* Fun and Games in Chapter 8. **Think Big!** (390 W. Broadway, tel. 212/925–7300) and **Dollhouse Antics** (1343 Madison Ave. at 94th St., tel. 212/876–2288), at opposite ends of town, make intriguing partners—one stocks giant replicas of common objects while the other features miniature furnishings at 1″ scale. Children should also enjoy the **Big City Kite Co.** (1201 Lexington Ave., between 81st and 82nd Sts., tel. 212/472–2623), which has one of the best kite selections anywhere. For older kids, there's **Forbidden Planet** (821 Broadway at 12th St., tel. 212/473–1576), stocking everything relating to science fiction and fantasy, such as comic books, fiction, and monster masks; **Sabado Bazaar** (54 Greene St., between Broome and Grand Sts., tel. 212/941–6152) for its colorful carnival of Mexican toys and ceramics; and **Pull Cart** (31 W. 21st St., 7th Floor, tel. 212/727–7089), a ceramics studio where you paint your own tablewares. For small consumer monsters, **Toys "Я" Us** (1293 Broadway in Herald Center, tel. 212/594–8697) may be of interest.

The most pleasant sources for children's reading materials are **Bank Street Bookstore, Books of Wonder,** and **Eeyore's Books for Children** (*see* Children's Books in Chapter 8), but you can also find kids' books at a discount at **Barnes and Noble** and **Tower Books** (*see* Books in Chapter 8).

For comics, besides **Forbidden Planet** (*see above*), try **Village Comics** (163 Bleecker St., 2nd Floor, tel. 212/777–2770) and **Funny Business Comics** (656 Amsterdam Ave., tel. 212/799–9477), which both carry a delightful stock of old and new issues.

Babies have their own shopping needs, though they don't know it. Their parents may be interested in, on the Upper West Side, the comprehensively stocked **Albee's** (715 Amsterdam Ave. at 95th St., tel. 212/662–5740) and the very upscale **Bellini** (473 Columbus Ave. at 83rd St., tel. 212/362–3700), which also has a branch for East Siders (1305 2nd Ave. at 68th St., tel. 212/517–9233). **Hush-A-Bye** (1459 1st Ave. at 76th St., tel. 212/988–3540) also caters to Upper East Siders, and **Schneider's** (20 Ave. A at 2nd St., tel. 212/228–3540) is a very well-stocked store for downtown infants and discount hunters.

Dining

The following is a diverse selection of places, both for everyday refueling and for special family-dining occasions.

In lower Manhattan, the younger ones should enjoy **Minter's Fun Food and Drink** (4 World Financial Ctr., tel. 212/945–4455) for chocolate beverages, and **Minter's Ice Cream Kitchen** (Pier 17, 3rd Floor, South St. Seaport, tel. 212/608–2037). At South Street Seaport, Pier 17's **Promenade Food Court** has a variety of quick foods. The surprising charms of the only **McDonald's** branch with doorman, pianist, and table service (160 Broadway, between Maiden La. and Liberty St., tel. 212/385–2063) are obvious. In TriBeCa, **Bubby's** (120 Hudson St. at N. Moore, tel. 212/219–0666) has casual dining and great baked goods; and the **Royal Canadian Pancake House** (145 Hudson St., tel. 212/219–3038) offers more than 50 flavors, with real maple syrup, and long lines on weekends. In Chinatown, don't miss the green-tea and red-bean ice cream at the **Chinatown Ice Cream Factory** (65 Bayard St., tel. 212/608–4170). Chinatown is also a good place to take the whole family for lunch or dinner at reasonable prices, whether it be for noodles and dumplings at **Noodle Town** or **Wong Kee** or for dim sum at **Mandarin Court** (*see* Chapter 9).

In SoHo, **5&10 No Exaggeration** (77 Greene St., between Spring and Broome Sts., tel. 212/925–7414) is fun for the piles of antique knick-knacks, all for sale, and vintage movies; **Fanelli's Café** (corner of Mercer and Prince Sts., tel. 212/226–9412) serves good burgers, fries, and pizza; **Tennessee Mountain** (143 Spring St. at Wooster St., tel. 212/431–3993) serves BBQ; and the **Cupping Room Café** (359 W. Broadway, near Broome St., tel. 212/925–2898) provides waffles and other light meals throughout the day. In the West Village, try **Arturo's** (106 W. Houston St. at Thompson St., tel. 212/475–9828) and its pizza; **Aggie's** (146 W. Houston St. at MacDougal St., tel. 212/673–8994), a funky coffee shop with sprightly soups and sandwiches; **Elephant and Castle** (68 Greenwich Ave. near 11th St., tel. 212/243–1400) for burgers and great french fries; and **Benny's Burritos** (113 Greenwich Ave. at Jane St., tel. 212/727–0584) for huge Cal-Tex servings at low prices. Also take time out for **Tea and Sympathy** (108 Greenwich Ave., tel. 212/807–8329), offering an authentic British afternoon tea, and the **Cowgirl Hall of Fame** (519 Hudson St. at W. 10th St., tel. 212/633–1133) for Cajun cooking and cowgirl memorabilia.

As you head uptown, just off Union Square, **America** (9 E. 18th St., tel. 212/505–2110) has huge everything—menu, portions, spaces—except checks. Chelsea offers the hip, all-rounder **Empire Diner** (210 10th Ave. at 22nd St., tel. 212/243–2736) and the fun, bustling, neon-decorated **Lox Around the Clock** (676 6th Ave. at 21st St., tel. 212/691–3535). Higher up, near the Flatiron Building, teens go for the scene at **Live Bait** (14 E. 23rd St., tel. 212/243–7969), which bears some resemblance to the **Coffee Shop** (129 Union Sq. W, tel. 212/243–7969), at least in the model-photographer-trendy-pretty clientele. Near Gramercy Park, **Friend of a Farmer** (77 Irving Pl., tel. 212/477–2188), with its chintzy, stripped-pine decor and homey cooking, is perfect for Laura Ashley-clad daughters.

Midtown, the **American Festival Café** (Rockefeller Center, 20 W. 50th St., tel. 212/246–6699) is the essential N.Y.C. family dining experience. Other midtown choices include the casual **Hamburger Harry's** (145 W. 45th St., tel. 212/840–2756), **Stage Delicatessen** (834 7th Ave. at 54th St., tel. 212/245–7850), and **Au Café** (7th Ave. at

53rd St., tel. 212/757–2233). On the East Side, **The Brasserie** (100 E. 53rd St., tel. 212/751–4840) is always open, and the French bistro food's popular all 'round. The other branch of the **Royal Canadian Pancake House** (1004 2nd Ave. at 53rd St., tel. 212/980–4131) is also liked by all.

As you go farther north, **Serendipity 3** (225 E. 60th St., tel. 212/838–3531), "the ice cream parlor to the stars," is perfect for a light meal or dessert. **Jackson Hole** (232 E. 64th St., tel. 212/371–7187) is a reliable, pleasant burger joint with branches around town, and the **7th Regiment Mess** (643 Park Ave., between 66th and 67th Sts., tel. 212/ 744–4107) serves wonderful American fare for families. Central Park's **Boathouse Café** (near 72nd St., tel. 212/517–2233) is somewhat overpriced for the average food, but it's pretty on a spring day.

As you move west, the three highlights are the inevitable **Hard Rock Café** (326 W. 57th St., tel. 212/459–9320), **Planet Hollywood** (140 W. 57th St., tel. 212/333–7827), and the newest theme-burger restaurant, the **Harley Davidson Café** (1370 6th Ave. at 56th St., tel. 212/ 245–6000). **Mickey Mantle's** (42 Central Park S near 6th Ave., tel. 212/688–7777) excites ball-crazy kids, while the upscale ice cream parlor **Rumpelmayer's** (50 Central Park S near 5th Ave., tel. 212/ 755–5800) is always popular.

Good bets near Lincoln Center are **The Saloon** (1920 Broadway at 64th St., tel. 212/874–1500), with a long menu and an occasional skating waiter; **Fiorello's Roman Café** (1900 Broadway near 63rd St., tel. 212/595–5330) for individual pizzas and outside seating; and **Vince & Eddie's** (70 W. 68th St., tel. 212/721–0068). Farther north, try **Sidewalkers** (12 W. 72nd St., tel. 212/799–6070) for buckets of spiced blue crabs; **EJ's Luncheonette** (433 Amsterdam Ave. near 80th St., tel. 212/873–3444); **Amsterdam's** (428 Amsterdam Ave., between 80th and 81st Sts., tel. 212/874–1377), a good-value rotisserie joint; **Presto's** (434 Amsterdam at 81st St., tel. 212/721–9141) for pasta and pizza; **Phoebe's** (380 Columbus Ave. near 78th St., tel. 212/ 724–5145) for its homey atmosphere; **Lucy's** (503 Columbus Ave. at 84th St., tel. 212/787–3009); and the brasserie-style **Boulevard** (2398 Broadway at 88th St., tel. 212/874–7400), where kids can draw on the tablecloths.

And don't forget the **Steve's Ice Cream** (286 Columbus Ave. at 74th St., tel. 212/496–1325), where Oreo cookies, sprinkles, and other tidbits can be blended into your favorite flavor.

Lodging

Since the vast majority of hotels are in midtown Manhattan, your choice of which neighborhood to pick for a family stay is limited. If anything, it may be best to avoid the environs of seedy Times Square, just in case your offspring escapes alone or gets lost. That said, **Embassy Suites** (*see* Chapter 10), a few blocks from Times Square, is among the best places for families because it has "child-proof" suites available and a complete day-care center. Generally speaking, as in any other big city, most Manhattan hotels will provide an extra bed, baby-sitting, and stroller rental—all the common requirements of families traveling with young children—but calling ahead before you make reservations is a good idea to ascertain how child-friendly your chosen base will turn out to be.

If you prefer to make your own baby-sitting arrangements, rather than leave it to the hotel concierge or housekeeper, the **Babysitters' Guild** (60 E. 42nd St., Suite 912, tel. 212/682–0227), in business for more than 40 years, has a multilingual staff that can take your children on sightseeing tours. Rates start at $10 an hour for one or two children over age two; $12.50 an hour for an infant, plus a $4.50 transportation charge ($7 after midnight); minimum booking is for four hours. Two other reliable agencies, though they cater more to long-term child care than to baby-sitting, are the **Gilbert Child Care Agency** (25 W. 39th St., Suite 700, tel. 212/921–4848) and the **Avalon Registry** (250 W. 57th St., Suite 723, tel. 212/245–0250). If you need a stroller, ask your hotel concierge to find one for you, or contact **AAA-U-Rent** (861 Eagle Ave., Bronx, tel. 718/665–6633).

Good bets for families include, at the top end of the scale, the aforementioned **Embassy Suites** and—largely for their child-pleasing swimming pools, which are rare in Manhattan—the **Holiday Inn Crowne Plaza,** the **Sheraton Manhattan,** the **Vista** and the **UN Plaza– Park Hyatt.** Less costly, any of the **Manhattan Suites East** properties would make an excellent choice, since they resemble tiny apartments. **The San Carlos**'s larger suites likewise have kitchen facilities that enable families to save on restaurant bills, and the hotel is secure; also, **The Wyndham's** large rooms are suitable for families. On the far Upper West Side, near Columbia University, **International House,** formerly for students only, has four family-sized apartments for under $100 per night, while the **Vanderbilt Y** in midtown has some family rooms with two bunk beds apiece for a rock-bottom $88 per night. (*See* Chapter 10 for detailed information about all the hotels mentioned above.)

Or plan ahead for a **bed-and-breakfast** stay (*see* Chapter 10) or a **home exchange** (*see* Traveling with Children in Chapter 1).

The Arts and Entertainment

In New York, theater groups exist just for children, art museums organize special programs, and kids can choose among art classes, summer courses, the circus, music concerts, storytelling, parades, and puppet shows.

Madison Square Garden (7th Ave. between 31st and 33rd Sts., tel. 212/465–6000) offers, besides sports events (*see* Chapter 7), some Disney and *Sesame Street* extravaganzas that appeal especially to children. There are major ice shows in winter, and each spring brings the **Ringling Bros. Barnum & Bailey Circus** (check local newspapers for dates, times, and ticket information). Meanwhile, the **Big Apple Circus** (35 W. 35th St., tel. 212/268–0055) charms the toughest New Yorkers in locations all over the five boroughs during spring and summer and in residence at Lincoln Center from October through January.

Music

The **Little Orchestra Society** (220 W. 42nd St., tel. 212/704–2100) organizes concert series that introduce classical music to children ages 3–5 at Florence Gould Hall (55 E. 59th St.) and ages 6–12 at Lincoln Center; the **Metropolitan Opera** offers its **Growing Up with Opera** program (tel. 212/769–7022). Lincoln Center (tel. 212/875–5400) also sponsors an **Out-of-Doors** summer arts program, with plenty in it for children. The **92nd Street Y** (1395 Lexington Ave., tel. 212/415–5440) and **Brooklyn Academy of Music** (30 Lafayette Ave., tel. 718/636–4100) both organize musical entertainment for young people.

Theater

Hartley House Theater (413 W. 46th St. tel. 212/666–1716) stages classic fairy tales; Henry Street Settlement (466 Grand St., between Pitt and Willett Sts., tel. 212/598–0400) has an Arts for Family weekend program; Little People's Theater (The Courtyard Playhouse, 39 Grove St., between W. 4th St. and 7th Ave., tel. 212/765–9540) brings fairy tales and nursery rhymes to life on Sunday afternoons; New York Children's Theater (Lincoln Sq. Theater, 250 W. 65th St., tel. 212/496–8009) is determinedly realistic in style and explores topics such as literacy and aging; The Open Eye: New Stagings for Youth (270 W. 89th St., tel. 212/769–4143) presents both classic and new plays; Paper Bag Players (tel. 212/362–0431) performs amusing productions for children ages four through nine, with a winter season at Symphony Space (Broadway at 95th St., tel. 212/864–6400); Tada! (120 W. 28th St., tel. 212/627–1732) is a popular children's group with a multiethnic perspective; Theaterworks/USA (Promenade Theater, Broadway at 76th St., tel. 212/677–5959) mounts classic stories and original productions about historical figures; 13th Street Theater (50 W. 13th St., tel. 212/675–6677) presents its children's offerings on weekends; Vineyard Theater (108 E. 15th St. and 309 E. 26th St., tel. 212/353–3366) offers kids' events in December.

Puppet Shows

The International Festival of Puppet Theater, sponsored by the Jim Henson Foundation, takes place in September at the Joseph Papp Public Theater (425 Lafayette St., tel. 212/598–7107); Marionette Theater (Swedish Cottage, Central Park at 81st St., tel. 212/988–9093) features Saturday programs; Puppet Playhouse (Asphalt Green, 555 E. 90th St., tel. 212/369–8890) offers weekend shows with puppets and marionettes; Puppetworks (338 6th Ave., Park Slope, Brooklyn, tel. 718/965–3391) presents marionettes performing classic children's stories on weekends.

Storytelling

Eeyore's Books for Children (2212 Broadway at 79th St., tel. 212/362–0634; 25 E. 83rd St., tel. 212/988–3404) has storytelling hours on weekends, except July–August. Storyland (1369 3rd Ave. at 78th St., tel. 212/517–6952) offers weekly story hours on Wednesday, Saturday, and Sunday; call ahead for locations.

Film

Several museums sponsor special film programs aimed at families and children, including the Museum of Modern Art, the Museum of Television and Radio (*see* Tour 1 in Chapter 3), and the American Museum of the Moving Image (*see* Tour 22 in Chapter 4). Kids thrill at the amazing nature films shown on the huge screen at the Naturemax Theater (tel. 212/769–5650) at the American Museum of Natural History (*see* Tour 8 in Chapter 3). The immaculate Walter Reade Theater (70 Lincoln Center Plaza, Broadway at W. 65th St., tel. 212/875–5600) shows films for children on Saturday and sponsors children's film festivals.

6 Sightseeing Checklists

The following checklists organize New York City's attractions by category, so you can supplement sights from the walking tours with related places of interest throughout the five boroughs. They may also help you choose walking tours by showing you which routes include sights that may be related to your own special interests. Attractions that have already been covered in Chapters 3 or 4 include nothing more than a reference to the walking tour in which they appear. Attractions that appear here only are followed by a brief description and useful information.

Museums and Galleries

Abigail Adams Smith Museum. Once the converted carriage house of the home of President John Adams's daughter Abigail and her husband, Colonel William Stephen Smith, this 18th-century treasure is now owned by the Colonial Dames of America. Nine rooms display furniture and articles of the Federal and Empire periods, and an adjoining garden is designed in 18th-century style. *421 E. 61st St., tel. 212/838-6878. Admission: $3 adults, $2 senior citizens and students. Open Mon.-Fri. noon-4, Sun. 1-5. Closed Aug.*

Afro Arts Cultural Centre. Artifacts from East, West, North, and Central Africa are on exhibit. *2191 Adam Clayton Powell, Jr., Blvd. (7th Ave.), tel. 212/996-3333. Suggested contribution: $3.75 adults, $2.75 children. Open daily 9-5.*

American Craft Museum. *See* Tour 1 in Chapter 3.

American Museum of the Moving Image. *See* Tour 22 in Chapter 4.

American Museum of Natural History. *See* Tour 8 in Chapter 3.

American Numismatic Society. The society, founded in 1858, displays its vast collection of coins and medals, including many that date back to ancient civilizations, in one of several museums in the Audubon Terrace complex. *Broadway at 155th St., tel. 212/234-3130. Admission free. Open Tues.-Sat. 9-4:30, Sun. 1-4.*

Americas Society. *See* Tour 6 in Chapter 3.

Asia Society. *See* Tour 6 in Chapter 3.

Asian American Arts Center. *See* Tour 16 in Chapter 3.

Black Fashion Museum. *See* Tour 10 in Chapter 3.

Brooklyn Children's Museum. *See* Museums in Chapter 5.

Brooklyn Historical Society. *See* Tour 19 in Chapter 4.

Brooklyn Museum. *See* Tour 20 in Chapter 4.

Children's Museum of Manhattan. *See* Museums in Chapter 5.

China House Gallery (China Institute). A pair of fierce, fat stone lions guards the doorway of this pleasant redbrick town house, where changing public exhibitions of Chinese art are held. *125 E. 65th St., tel. 212/744-8181. Admission: $3. Open Mon.-Sat. 10-5.*

Clocktower Gallery (Institute for Contemporary Art). *See* Tour 18 in Chapter 3.

The Cloisters. Perched atop a wooded hilltop near Manhattan's northernmost tip, the Cloisters houses the Metropolitan Museum of Art's medieval collection in the style of a medieval monastery. Colonnaded walks connect authentic French and Spanish monastic cloisters, a French Romanesque chapel, a 12th-century chapter house, and a Romanesque apse. An entire room is devoted to a superb set of 15th- and 16th-century tapestries depicting a unicorn hunt. The view of the Hudson River and the New Jersey Palisades (an undeveloped Rockefeller family preserve) enhances the experience. The M-4 "Cloisters–Fort Tryon Park" bus provides a lengthy but scenic ride; catch it along Madison Avenue below 110th Street, or Broadway above; or take the A subway to 190th Street. *Fort Tryon Park, tel. 212/923-3700. Suggested contribution: $6 adults,*

$3 senior citizens and students. Open Tues.–Sun. 9:30–5:15. Closes at 4:45 Nov.–Feb.

Cooper-Hewitt Museum (Smithsonian Institution's National Museum of Design). *See* Tour 5 in Chapter 3.

Federal Hall National Memorial. *See* Tour 17 in Chapter 3.

Forbes Magazine Galleries. *See* Tour 12 in Chapter 3.

Fraunces Tavern Museum. *See* Tour 17 in Chapter 3.

Frick Collection. *See* Tour 5 in Chapter 3.

Garibaldi-Meucci Museum. Housed in an altered Federal farmhouse, this museum offers letters and photographs from the life of fiery Italian patriot Giuseppe Garibaldi; it also documents Antonio Meucci's indisputable claim to having invented the telephone before Alexander Graham Bell did. *420 Tompkins Ave., Staten Island, tel. 718/442–1608. Admission free. Open Tues.–Fri. 10–5, weekends 1–5.*

George Gustav Heye Center (Smithsonian Institution). This new museum—inaugurated in October 1994—houses the collection of the former National Museum of the American Indian, with artifacts from the entire Western Hemisphere spanning more than 10,000 years. This is the world's second largest grouping of Native American materials. *Alexander Hamilton Customs House, 1 Bowling Green, tel. 212/238–2420. Admission free. Open daily 10–5.*

Grolier Club. *See* Tour 6 in Chapter 3.

Guggenheim Museum. *See* Tour 5 in Chapter 3.

Guggenheim Museum SoHo. *See* Tour 14 in Chapter 3.

Guinness World of Records Exhibition. *See* Tour 4 in Chapter 3.

Harbor Defense Museum of New York City. Located at the Brooklyn end of the Verrazano-Narrows Bridge in Fort Hamilton, an active military base, this museum features small arms, uniforms, artillery equipment dating to the 18th century, and an array of military miniatures. *Bldg. 230, Fort Hamilton, Brooklyn, tel. 718/630–4349. Admission free. Open Mon.–Fri. 1–4.*

Hayden Planetarium. *See* Tour 8 in Chapter 3.

Hispanic Society of America. A collection of ancient and modern Hispanic paintings, sculpture, and decorative arts is housed in a richly appointed building. *Broadway at 155th St., tel. 212/926–2234. Admission free. Open Tues.–Sat. 10–4:30, Sun. 1–4. Closed holidays.*

IBM Gallery of Science and Art. *See* Tour 2 in Chapter 3.

ICP Mid-Town. *See* Tour 3 in Chapter 3.

International Center of Photography. *See* Tour 5 in Chapter 3.

Intrepid Sea-Air-Space Museum. *See* Museums in Chapter 5.

Isamu Noguchi Garden Museum. *See* Tour 22 in Chapter 4.

Japan Society Gallery. This wonderfully serene setting holds exhibitions from well-known Japanese and American museums, as well as private collections. Also offered are movies, lectures, classes, concerts, and dramatic performances. *333 E. 47th St., tel. 212/832–1155. Suggested contribution: $2.50. Open Tues.–Sun. 11–5, but only when shows are installed.*

Jewish Museum. *See* Tour 5 in Chapter 3.

Library and Museum of the Performing Arts (New York Public Library at Lincoln Center). *See* Tour 8 in Chapter 3.

Lower East Side Tenement Museum. America's first urban "living-history" museum preserves and interprets the life of immigrants and migrants in New York's Lower East Side. Models of Hester Street, Little Italy, and Chinatown are featured. Gallery exhibits, walking tours, and dramatic performances are offered. *97 Orchard St., tel. 212/431–0233. Suggested contribution: $3 adults, $1 senior citizens, students, and children. Tours: Sun. at 2 PM, $12 adults, $10 senior citizens, students, and children. Open Tues.–Fri. 11–5, Sun. 10–5.*

Marchais Center of Tibetan Art. One of the largest private, nonprofit collections of Tibetan sculpture, scrolls, and paintings outside of Tibet is displayed in a museum resembling a Tibetan temple. Try to visit on a day when the monks bless the temple—and you. *338 Lighthouse Ave., Staten Island, tel. 718/987–3478. Admission: $3 adults, $2.50 senior citizens, $1 children; occasionally, an additional $2 charge for special Sun. programs. Open Apr.–Nov., Wed.–Sun. 1–5; Dec.–Mar., by appointment.*

Metropolitan Museum of Art. *See* Tour 5 in Chapter 3.

Municipal Art Society. A revolving series of exhibitions at this midtown gallery illuminates the art and architecture of the city. *457 Madison Ave. at 50th St., tel. 212/935–3960. Admission free. Open Mon.–Wed., Fri.–Sat. 11–5.*

Museo del Barrio. *See* Tour 5 in Chapter 3.

Museum for African Art. *See* Tour 14 in Chapter 3.

Museum of American Financial History. On the site of Alexander Hamilton's law office (today the Standard Oil Building), this one-room museum displays artifacts of the financial markets' history, including a vintage ticker-tape machine. *24 Broadway, tel. 212/908–4519. Admission free. Open weekdays 11:30–2:30 or by appointment.*

Museum of American Folk Art. *See* Tour 8 in Chapter 3.

Museum of Colored Glass and Light. *See* Tour 14 in Chapter 3.

Museum of Television and Radio. *See* Tour 1 in Chapter 3.

Museum of the City of New York. *See* Tour 5 in Chapter 3.

Museum of Modern Art. *See* Tour 1 in Chapter 3.

National Academy of Design. *See* Tour 5 in Chapter 3.

New Museum of Contemporary Art. *See* Tour 14 in Chapter 3.

New York City Fire Museum. Hand-pulled and horse-drawn apparatus, engines, sliding poles, uniforms, and fireboat equipment are featured in this comprehensive collection of authentic fire-fighting tools from the 18th, 19th, and 20th centuries. *278 Spring St., tel. 212/691–1303. Suggested contribution: $3 adults, 50¢ children. Open Tues.–Sat. 10–4. Closed Sun., Mon., and holidays.*

New York City Transit Museum. A converted 1930s subway station displays 18 restored classic subway cars and has an operating signal tower. *Boerum Pl. at Schermerhorn St., Brooklyn Heights, tel. 718/330–3060. Admission: $3 adults, $1.50 senior citizens and children. Open Tues.–Fri. 10–4, Sat.–Sun. 11–4.*

New York Hall of Science. *See* Museums in Chapter 5.

Nicholas Roerich Museum. Housed in an Upper West Side town house (built in 1898), this small, eccentric museum displays the work of the Russian artist who, among many other things, designed sets for Diaghilev ballets. Vast paintings of the Himalayas are a focal point of the collection. *319 W. 107th St., tel. 212/864–7752. Admission free. Open Tues.–Sun. 2–5.*

North Wind Undersea Museum. *See* Off the Beaten Track in Chapter 4.

Pierpont Morgan Library. *See* Tour 4 in Chapter 3.

Police Academy Museum. The second floor of the city's police academy is full of law-enforcement memorabilia—uniforms, firearms, batons, badges, even counterfeit money—dating back to the time of the Dutch. *235 E. 20th St., tel. 212/477–9753. Admission free. Open weekdays 9–3, large groups by appointment.*

P.S. 1 Museum. *See* Tour 21 in Chapter 4.

Queens Historical Society (Kingsland Homestead). *See* Off the Beaten Track in Chapter 4.

Queens Museum. In Flushing Meadows–Corona Park, at the end of the World's Fair mall, this museum is housed in what was the New York City Pavilion for the 1939 fair. Its most notable exhibit is the recently restored Panorama, a 9,355-square-foot architectural model of New York City's five boroughs. *Tel. 718/592–2405. Suggested contribution: $3 adults, $1.50 senior citizens, students, and children over 5. Open Tues.–Fri. 10–5, weekends noon–5.*

Schomburg Center for Research in Black Culture (New York Public Library). *See* Tour 10 in Chapter 3.

Snug Harbor Cultural Center. *See* Tour 24 in Chapter 4.

Society of Illustrators Museum of American Illustration. A 1,000-piece collection features contemporary and historical works. Solo, group, and themed shows are exhibited. *128 E. 63rd St., tel. 212/838–2560. Admission free. Open weekdays 10–5, Tues. 10–8.*

South Street Seaport Museum. *See* Tour 18 in Chapter 3.

Staten Island Children's Museum. *See* Tour 24 in Chapter 4.

Staten Island Historical Society Museum. *See* Tour 24 in Chapter 4.

Studio Museum in Harlem. *See* Tour 10 in Chapter 3.

Ukrainian Museum. *See* Tour 13 in Chapter 3.

Urban Center. Exhibits on architecture, urban design, and historic preservation are housed in the north wing of the Villard Houses, at the foot of the New York Palace Hotel. *457 Madison Ave., between 50th and 51st Sts., tel. 212/935–3960. Admission free. Open Mon.–Wed., Fri. and Sat. 11–5.*

Whitney Museum of American Art. *See* Tour 5 in Chapter 3.

Whitney Museum of American Art at Philip Morris. *See* Tour 3 in Chapter 3.

Architectural Landmarks

Alexander Hamilton Customs House (1907, Cass Gilbert). *See* Tour 17 in Chapter 3.

American Telephone & Telegraph Building (1983, Philip Johnson and John Burgee). Now occupied by the Sony Corporation, this rose granite postmodern skyscraper is distinguished on the skyline by its pediment roofline, shaped like a Chippendale cabinet top. *Madison Ave. at 55th St.*

Bayard Building (1898, Louis Sullivan). Built in 1898, this is the only structure in New York City designed by Louis Sullivan, one of the Chicago School's leading architects. Its simplicity and emphatic vertical lines made it radically different from the then-prevailing Beaux Arts style. *65–69 Bleecker St. near Lafayette St.*

Carnegie Hall (1891, William B. Tuthill). *See* Tour 2 in Chapter 3.

Chrysler Building (1929, William Van Alen). *See* Tour 3 in Chapter 3.

Citicorp Center (1977, H. Stubbins & E. Roth). *See* Tour 1 in Chapter 3.

City Hall (1812, Mangin, McComb). *See* Tour 18 in Chapter 3.

Dakota Apartments (1884, Henry J. Hardenbergh). *See* Tour 8 in Chapter 3.

Empire State Building (1931, Shreve, Lamb, Harmon). *See* Tour 4 in Chapter 3.

Flatiron Building (1902, Daniel H. Burnham). *See* Tour 4 in Chapter 3.

GE Building, formerly the **RCA Building** (1933, Raymond Hood). *See* Tour 1 in Chapter 3.

Grand Central Terminal (1913, Warren & Wetmore, Reed & Stem). *See* Tour 3 in Chapter 3.

Guggenheim Museum (1959, Frank Lloyd Wright). *See* Tour 5 in Chapter 3.

Haughwout Building (1857, John P. Gaynor). *See* Tour 14 in Chapter 3.

Jacob K. Javits Convention Center (1986, I. M. Pei). The largest of its kind in the Western Hemisphere, the center contains 1.8 million gross square feet set on a 22-acre, five-block site. The glassed-in entry lets in lots of sky, earning it the nickname the Crystal Palace. *11th Ave. at 35th St.*

Lever House (1952, Skidmore, Owings & Merrill). *See* Tour 1 in Chapter 3.

Metropolitan Life Building (1963, Emery Roth & Sons, Pietro Belluschi, and Walter Gropius). What began as the notorious Pan Am Building—detested not only for its faceted walls of precast concrete but also for the fact it shuts off the light from much of Park Avenue—is now considered a stately-looking 59-story monolith. *200 Park Ave. at 45th St.*

New York Public Library (1911, Carrere & Hastings). *See* Tour 3 in Chapter 3.

Plaza Hotel (1907, Henry J. Hardenbergh). *See* Tour 2 in Chapter 3.

Seagram Building (1958, Mies van der Rohe with Philip Johnson). *See* Tour 1 in Chapter 3.

United Nations (1953, Wallace K. Harrison and international committee). *See* Tour 3 in Chapter 3.

Villard Houses (1886, McKim, Mead & White). Now part of the New York Palace hotel, these three brownstone mansions, conceived by newspaper publisher Henry Villard, form an early Italian Renaissance–style courtyard set off by elaborate ironwork. *Madison Ave. at 50th St.*

Woolworth Building (1913, Cass Gilbert). *See* Tour 17 in Chapter 3.

World Financial Center (1989, Cesar Pelli). *See* Tour 17 in Chapter 3.

World Trade Center (1977, Yamasaki & Roth). *See* Tour 17 in Chapter 3.

Worldwide Plaza (1989, Skidmore, Owings & Merrill and Frank Williams). This massive, rose-colored multiuse complex sits on the border between Hell's Kitchen and midtown, on the former site of the second Madison Square Garden. An impressive office tower on 8th Avenue is followed by a pleasing midblock plaza with a fountain; lower-scaled residential units and movie theaters fill the block through to 9th Avenue. *50th–51st Sts., between 8th and 9th Aves.*

Historical Sites

Bartow-Pell Mansion. This Federal-style building with a Greek Revival interior restoration—and sunken gardens, period furnishings, paintings, and a 200-volume library—was built in 1842. *895 Shore Rd. N, Pelham Bay Park, Bronx, tel. 718/885–1461. Admission: $2 adults, $1 senior citizens. Open Wed. and weekends noon–4.*

Bowne House. *See* Off the Beaten Track in Chapter 4.

Castle Clinton. *See* Tour 17 in Chapter 3.

Edgar Allan Poe Cottage. *See* Tour 23 in Chapter 4.

Ellis Island. *See* Tour 17 in Chapter 3.

Fraunces Tavern. *See* Tour 17 in Chapter 3.

Gracie Mansion. *See* Tour 6 in Chapter 3.

Kingsland Homestead. See Off the Beaten Track in Chapter 4.

Morris-Jumel Mansion. In 1776 George Washington spent six weeks at this hilltop house, built in 1765. His office can still be seen in what is Manhattan's oldest residence. *1765 Jumel Terr., 160th St. west of Edgecombe Ave., tel. 212/923–8008. Admission: $3 adults, $2 senior citizens and students. Open Tues.–Sun. 10–4.*

New York Stock Exchange. *See* Tour 17 in Chapter 3.

Old Merchant's House. *See* Tour 13 in Chapter 3.

Radio City Music Hall. *See* Tour 1 in Chapter 3.

Richmondtown Restoration. *See* Tour 24 in Chapter 4.

South Street Seaport. *See* Tour 18 in Chapter 3.
Theodore Roosevelt Birthplace. *See* Tour 4 in Chapter 3.
Van Cortlandt Museum. This 1748 house is full of furnishings and household goods that reflect both its Dutch and British owners. It's now run by the National Society of Colonial Dames. *Broadway at 246th St., Bronx, tel. 718/543-3344. Admission: $2 adults, $1.50 senior citizens and students. Open Tues.–Fri. 10–3, Sat.–Sun. 11–4.*
Wave Hill. *See* Off the Beaten Track in Chapter 4.

Churches and Temples

Abyssinian Baptist Church (Baptist). *See* Tour 10 in Chapter 3.
Brotherhood Synagogue (Conservative Jewish). *See* Tour 4 in Chapter 3.
Cathedral of St. John the Divine (Episcopal). *See* Tour 9 in Chapter 3.
Central Synagogue (Reform Jewish). Built in 1872, this Moorish-style temple is the oldest continually used synagogue building in the city. Note its onion-domed exterior and colorfully stenciled interior. *652 Lexington Ave. at 55th St.*
Church of Our Lady of Pompeii (Roman Catholic). *See* Tour 12 in Chapter 3.
Fifth Avenue Synagogue (Orthodox Jewish). *See* Tour 6 in Chapter 3.
Friends Meeting House (Quaker). *See* Off the Beaten Track in Chapter 4.
Grace Church (Episcopal). This fine mid-19th-century example of an English Gothic Revival church, the site of many society weddings (including that of the P.T. Barnum show member Tom Thumb), is set in a small green yard in Greenwich Village. Topped by a finely ornamented octagonal marble spire, this design by James Renwick, Jr., has some excellent pre-Raphaelite stained-glass windows inside. *802 Broadway at E. 10th St.*
Islamic Cultural Center of New York (Islamic). This stunning gray granite mosque looks sleek and contemporary under its vast copper dome, a slender minaret rising to the side. *1711 3rd Ave. at 97th St.*
John Street Methodist (United Methodist). *See* Tour 17 in Chapter 3.
Little Church Around the Corner (Church of the Transfiguration) (Episcopal). *See* Tour 4 in Chapter 3.
Marble Collegiate (Reformed). *See* Tour 4 in Chapter 3.
Riverside Church (Interdenominational). *See* Tour 9 in Chapter 3.
Spanish & Portuguese Synagogue, Shearith Israel (Orthodox Jewish). Built in 1897, this is the fifth home of the oldest Jewish congregation in the United States, founded in 1654. The adjoining "Little Synagogue" is a replica of Shearith Israel's Georgian-style first synagogue. *8 W. 70th St.*
St. Bartholomew's (Episcopal). *See* Tour 1 in Chapter 3.
St. Luke's-in-the-Fields (Episcopal). *See* Tour 12 in Chapter 3.
St. Mark's-in-the-Bowery (Episcopal). *See* Tour 13 in Chapter 3.
St. Patrick's Cathedral (Roman Catholic). *See* Tour 2 in Chapter 3.
St. Paul's Chapel (Episcopal). *See* Tour 17 in Chapter 3.
St. Paul's Chapel at Columbia University (Nondenominational). *See* Tour 9 in Chapter 3.
Temple Emanu-El (Reform Jewish). *See* Tour 6 in Chapter 3.
Trinity Church (Episcopal). *See* Tour 17 in Chapter 3.

Parks and Gardens

Battery Park. *See* Tour 17 in Chapter 3.
Brooklyn Botanic Garden. *See* Tour 20 in Chapter 4.
Carl Schurz Park. *See* Tour 6 in Chapter 3.
Central Park. *See* Tour 7 in Chapter 3.
Flushing Meadows–Corona Park. Running from Flushing Bay to the Grand Central Parkway, this large Queens park offers a marina, boats, a carousel, bicycling paths, an indoor ice-skating rink, picnic grounds, a swimming pool, a zoo, and theaters and museums, not to mention **Shea Stadium,** home of the New York Mets, and the U. S. **Tennis Association National Tennis Center** (*see* Chapter 7). The park was the site of both the 1939 and 1964 World's Fair, and several structures from those expositions remain, including the **Unisphere,** a 380-ton steel globe, and the 1939 New York Pavilion (now home to the **Queens Museum**).
Fort Tryon Park. At the northern tip of Manhattan, high over the Hudson, this park offers stunning views of the Palisades, plus an attractive though somewhat wild garden. It also contains the Cloisters (*see* Museums and Galleries, *above*).
Jamaica Bay Wildlife Refuge. A series of parks sprawling across Brooklyn and Staten Island, this large refuge offers temporary accommodations for migrating birds, plus nature trails around ponds, marshes, and wooded uplands. Stop in the visitor center (Crossbay Blvd., Broad Channel, Queens, tel. 718/474–0613; open daily 8–5) for a free permit to explore the refuge.
Kissena Park. Located in southwest Flushing, Queens, this park protects precious acres of original Long Island forests and marshland. Visitors can enjoy the new walking trails. *Tel. 718/353–1047.*
New York Botanical Garden. *See* Tour 23 in Chapter 4.
Pelham Bay Park. With more than 2,000 acres, this Bronx park is the largest in the city. Purchased by Thomas Pell from the Indians in 1654, its facilities include a mile-long beach, nature paths, a canoe launch, bridle path, fishing, picnic grounds, and tennis courts.
Prospect Park. *See* Tour 20 in Chapter 4.
Riverside Park. *See* Tours 8 and 9 in Chapter 3.
Staten Island Botanical Gardens. *See* Tour 24 in Chapter 4.
United Nations Rose Garden. *See* Tour 3 in Chapter 3.
Van Cortlandt Park. Located on 2 square miles of the north-central Bronx, this park includes facilities for tennis, swimming, running, baseball, soccer, cricket, and rugby. The nation's oldest municipal golf course is here, as is Van Cortlandt Museum (*see* Historical Sites, *above*).
Washington Market Park. *See* Tour 14 in Chapter 3.

Zoos

Aquarium for Wildlife Conservation. *See* Zoos in Chapter 5.
Bronx Zoo (International Wildlife Conservation Park) & Children's Zoo. *See* Tour 23 in Chapter 4.
Central Park Zoo (Central Park Wildlife Conservation Center) & Children's Zoo. *See* Tour 7 in Chapter 3.
Prospect Park Zoo (Prospect Park Wildlife Conservation Center). *See* Tour 20 in Chapter 4.
Queens Zoo (Queens Wildlife Conservation Center). *See* Zoos in Chapter 5.
Staten Island Zoo. *See* Zoos in Chapter 5.

7 Sports, Fitness, Beaches

By Karen Cure

Updated by Kate Sekules

New Yorkers think the outdoors is a wonderful place, and they are stopped by nothing in their passion for their sports: You can see them jogging in the park when it's sleeting, or heading for a tennis bubble on the most blustery of Sunday winter afternoons. From boccie to croquet, no matter how esoteric the sport, there's a place to pursue it in New York. You'll find oases of greenery you'd never imagine here (13% of the city, in fact, is parkland). And if you strike up a conversation while waiting to rent a boat or a bike at the Loeb Boathouse, or while stretching before a jog around the Reservoir in Central Park, you'll discover a friendly, relaxed side of New Yorkers that you might not otherwise get the chance to see.

Just one word before you set out: Weekends are very busy. If you need to rent equipment or secure specific space—for instance, a tennis court—go very early or be prepared to wait.

Spectator Sports

Many events described below take place at **Madison Square Garden** (7th Ave. between 31st and 33rd Sts.); tickets can be ordered by phone through the box office (tel. 212/465–6000) or Ticketmaster (tel. 212/307–7171). The area's other major sports venue is across the Hudson River at the **Meadowlands** (Rte. 3, East Rutherford, NJ; for box office and information, tel. 201/935–3900). When events are sold out, you can sometimes pick up a ticket on the day of the game outside the venue from a fellow sports fan whose guests couldn't make it at the last minute. Ticket agencies, listed in the Manhattan yellow-pages phone directory and the sports pages of the *Daily News* and *New York Newsday*, can be helpful—for a price.

Baseball

The **New York Mets** play at Shea Stadium (tel. 718/507–8499, or call Ticketmaster at 212/307–6387), at the penultimate stop on the No. 7 subway in Flushing, Queens. Yankee Stadium (tel. 718/293–6000), accessible by the No. 4, D, or C subway to the 161st Street station in the Bronx, is the home of the **New York Yankees.** Baseball season runs from April through October.

Basketball

Only recently have the **New York Knickerbockers** (the "Knicks") aroused any hometown passion, but the team turnaround has made tickets for home games at Madison Square Garden hard to come by. For up-to-date game roundups, phone the New York Knickerbockers Hot Line (tel. 212/465–5867). Another NBA team, the **New Jersey Nets,** plays at the Meadowlands in the Brendan Byrne Arena. Basketball season is late-October–April.

Boxing and Wrestling

The *Daily News*'s annual Golden Gloves **boxing** bout and other major competitions are staged in Madison Square Garden. **Wrestling,** a more frequent Garden presence since the days of "Gorgeous" George and "Haystack" Calhoun in the late '50s, is stagy and outrageous, drawing a rowdy but enthusiastic crowd.

Football

The **New York Giants** and the **New York Jets** play September–December at Giants Stadium in East Rutherford, New Jersey (tel. 201/935–8111 for the Giants; 516/538–6600 for the Jets). All seats for Giants games and most for Jets games are sold on a season-ticket basis, and there's a waiting list for those; remaining Jets tickets for scattered singles are snapped up almost as soon as they go on sale in August. The **Columbia Lions** (tel. 212/854–1754) of Columbia University may be college football's traditionally least successful team (losing streaks have been known to hit 40-plus games), but a fan can still revel in the charms of Ivy League tradition some Saturday afternoons at Columbia's Wein Stadium each September through November.

Hockey

The **New York Rangers** play at Madison Square Garden (tel. 212/465–6741); the **New York Islanders** at Nassau Veterans Memorial Coliseum in Uniondale, Long Island (for tickets call 516/888–9000); and the **New Jersey Devils** at the Brendan Byrne Arena at the Meadowlands (tel. 201/935–3900). Tickets for the Islanders and Devils are usually available at game time; Rangers tickets are more difficult to find. The hockey season runs from October through April.

Horse Racing

Thoroughbreds Modern **Aqueduct Racetrack** (110th St. and Rockaway Blvd., Ozone Park, Queens), with its spate of new lawns and gardens, holds races late-October–early May. The action moves in May to **Belmont Park** (Hempstead Turnpike, Elmont, Long Island), home of the third jewel in horse racing's triple crown, the Belmont Stakes. Horses run here May–July; then after a few weeks upstate at Saratoga, they return to Belmont from late-August through October. Races are held Wednesday–Monday. For information on the New York tracks, call 718/641–4700.

The **Meadowlands** (East Rutherford, NJ, tel. 201/935–8500), generally a trotting venue, also has a flat track season from Labor Day through December.

Standardbreds **Yonkers Raceway** (Central Ave., Yonkers, NY, tel. 718/562–9500) features harness racing daily year-round.

The **Meadowlands** (East Rutherford, NJ, tel. 201/935–8500) runs both trotters and pacers January–mid-August.

Running

The **New York City Marathon** has taken place annually on a Sunday in early November since 1970, and New Yorkers love to cheer on the pack of 25,000 (some 16,000 of them finish). Racewalkers, "jogglers," oldsters, youngsters, and disabled competitors help to make this what former Olympic Organizing Committee president Peter V. Ueberroth called "the best sporting event in the country." Spectators line rooftops and sidewalks, promenades, and terraces all along the route—but don't go near the finishing line in Central Park around 2 PM unless you relish mob scenes.

Tennis

The annual **U.S. Open,** held from late-August through early September at the U.S.T.A. National Tennis Center, is one of the high points of the tennis buff's year, and tickets to watch the late rounds are some of the hottest in town. Early-round matches are entertaining, too, and with a stadium court ticket you can also view matches in outlying courts—where the bleachers are so close you can almost count the sweat beads on the players' foreheads—and in the grandstand, where bleacher seating is first-come, first-served. During early rounds, ushers may help you move down to better seats in the stadium court or the grandstand (you may wish to consider giving a gratuity of $5 or $10). Wherever you sit, the eclectic mix of casual visitors, tennis groupies, and celebrities makes for terrific people-watching. The U.S. Tennis Center box office (tel. 914/696–7284) sells tickets beginning in May; Visa card only, or try ticket agency, Telecharge (tel. 800/524–8440).

The tennis year winds up in Madison Square Garden with the **Virginia Slims Tournament,** a major women's pro event in mid-November (tel. 212/465–6500), with tickets on sale beginning in September.

Participant Sports

Bicycling

Although space comes at a premium in Manhattan apartments, many locals keep a bicycle around for a few of the glorious rides that this city has to offer. A sleek pack of dedicated racers zooms around Central Park at dawn and at dusk daily, and on weekends, parks swarm with recreational cyclists. **Central Park**'s 7.2-mile circular drive is closed to traffic in summer from 10 AM to 3 PM and 7 to 10 PM on weekdays, and from 7 PM Friday to 6 AM Monday. On holidays, it's closed from 8 PM the night before until 6 AM the day after. In **Riverside Park,** the promenade between 72nd and 110th streets, with its Hudson River view, gets a more easygoing crowd. Other good bets: the **Wall Street** area, deserted on weekends; the Hudson-view **Battery Park Esplanade;** or the winding roads in Brooklyn's **Prospect Park,** also closed to cars.

Bike Rentals Expect to leave a deposit or a credit card at the following: **AAA Bikes in Central Park** (Loeb Boathouse, mid-park near E.74th St., tel. 212/861–4137); **85th Street Bicycles** (204 E. 85th St., tel. 212/722–2201); **Gene's Bicycles** (242 E. 79th St., tel. 212/249–9218); **Metro Bicycles** (1311 Lexington Ave. at 88th St., tel. 212/427–4450); or **Pedal Pusher** (1306 2nd Ave., between 68th and 69th Sts., tel. 212/288–5592). Some rent only 3-speeds; others have 10-speeds as well as hybrids and mountain bikes.

Group Trips For organized rides with other cyclists, call or write before you come to New York: **Country Cycling Tours** (140 W. 83rd St., 10024, tel. 212/874–5151) and **Staten Island Bicycling Association** (1/5 Stuyvesant St., tel. 718/273–0805). The **Floyd Bennett Field Bike Tour** (tel. 718/338–3799) is a run around the historic Brooklyn runway that launched Amelia Earhart.

Billiards

It used to be that pool halls were dusty, grimy, sticky places—and there are still a few of those around. But they've been joined by a group of oh-so-chic spots with deluxe decor, high prices, and even classical music or jazz in the background. The halls listed below are usually open late into the night, but it's best to call ahead for closing hours.

Amsterdam Billiard Club, (344 Amsterdam Ave., between 76th and 77th Sts., tel. 212/496–8180).
Billiard Club (220 W. 19th St., tel. 212/206–7665).
Chelsea Billiards (54 W. 21st St., tel. 212/989–0096).
SoHo Billiards (298 Mulberry St. at Houston St., tel. 212/925–3753).
West Side Billiards Center (601 W. 50th St., tel. 212/246–1060).

Bird-Watching

Manhattan's green parks and woodlands provide habitat for thousands of birds, everything from summer tanagers and fork-tailed flycatchers to Kentucky warblers and common nighthawks. Since the city is on the Atlantic flyway, a major migratory route, you can see birds that nest as far north as the High Arctic. May is the best season, since the songbirds are in their freshest colors—and so many are singing at once that you can hardly distinguish their songs. To find out what's been seen where, call the Rare Bird Alert (tel. 212/979–3070). For information on best bird-watching spots in various parks, call the **Urban Park Rangers,** a uniformed division of the Parks Department: Manhattan (tel. 212/427–4040); the Bronx (tel. 718/548–7070); Brooklyn (tel. 718/287–3400); Queens (tel. 718/ 699–4204); and Staten Island (tel. 718/667–6042).

Good bets include 1,146-acre **Van Cortlandt Park** in the Bronx, with its freshwater marshes and upland woods. In Brooklyn there are 526-acre **Prospect Park** and **Green-Wood Cemetery** (call superintendent at 718/768–7300 for permission to enter grounds). The Ramble in Manhattan's **Central Park** is another prime spot. In Queens, try **Jamaica Bay Wildlife Refuge,** 9,155 acres of salt marshes, fresh and brackish ponds, and open water (stop by visitor center, Crossbay Blvd., Broad Channel, Queens, tel. 718/474–0613, to get permit). In Staten Island, head for the fairly undeveloped 317-acre **Wolfe's Pond Park,** where the pond and the nearby shore can be dense with geese and ducks during the annual migrations.

Guided Walks   The **New York City Audubon Society** (71 W. 23rd, tel. 212/691–7483) has occasional bird-watching outings; call 1–4 PM for information. Also check with the **Urban Park Rangers** at the numbers listed above.

Boating

The boating available on New York City's ponds and lakes conjures up 19th-century images of a parasol-twirling lady being rowed by her swain. But there's a huge demand for it, and on weekends you'd better go early or be prepared to wait.

In **Central Park,** the boats are rowboats (plus one Venetian gondola for nighttime glides in the moonlight) and the rowing terrain is the 18-acre Central Park Lake. Rent your boat at **Loeb Boathouse** (tel. 212/517–4723), near 74th Street, from spring through fall.

Boccie

This pinless Italian version of bowling thrives in New York, with 100 city courts in the five boroughs. The easiest to get to from midtown are at 96th Street and 1st Avenue; at East River Drive and 42nd Street; and at the Thompson Street Playground (at Houston St.) in Greenwich Village. There's also a boccie court at **Il Vagabondo,** (351 E. 62nd St., tel. 212/832–9221), a vintage Italian restaurant east of Bloomingdale's.

Bowling

Standard American-style bowling refuses to flourish in Manhattan, so your options are more limited. The **Leisure Time Bowling Recreation Center** (625 8th Ave. at 42nd St., tel. 212/268–6909) offers 30 lanes on the second floor of the Port Authority Bus Terminal. **Bowlmor** (110 University Pl., tel. 212/255–8188) is a funky 44-lane operation frequented by a colorful Village crowd.

Boxing

The recent trendiness of the sport is reflected in its availability to the casual participant. **Crosby Street Studio** (56 Crosby St., entrance at 512 Broadway, between Spring and Broome Sts., tel. 212/941–8313) is the first boxing gym run by a woman, offering classes led by professional fighters for beginners and intermediates, sparring sessions and one-on-one training for the enthusiast, plus Thai and kickboxing. Brooklyn's venerable **Gleason's** (75 Front St., tel. 718/797–2872), home of 106 world champs, including Jake LaMotta and Muhammad Ali, also welcomes visitors.

Chess and Checkers

Central Park's Chess & Checkers House is picturesquely situated atop a massive stone outcrop. Ten tables are available for indoor play on weekends, 11:30–4:30, and 24 outdoor tables are available during all daylight hours. Pick up playing pieces at the **Dairy** (midpark at 64th St., tel. 212/794–6565) 11–4 daily; there is no charge, but a deposit is required.

Downtown in Greenwich Village, the **Village Chess Shop** (230 Thompson St., tel. 212/475–9580) is always an active spot. Uptown, the **Manhattan Chess Club** (353 W. 46th St., tel. 212/333–5888) sponsors tournaments and exhibitions; instruction is available on both beginning and intermediate levels.

Dance and Aerobics

Naturally enough, New York gives birth to many a new fitness trend, and an aerobics class here may turn out to be executed on rollerblades or to the accompaniment of live gospel singing. Some top studios to check out are: **Crosby Street** (56 Crosby St., entrance at 512 Broadway, tel. 212/941–8313), **Crunch** (140 Charles St., tel. 212/633–6863; 54 E. 13th St., tel. 212/475–2018; and 162 W. 83rd St., tel. 212/875–1902), **Equinox** (344 Amsterdam Ave., tel. 212/721–4200, and 897 Broadway, between 19th and 20th Sts., tel. 212/780–9300), **Molly Fox** (27 W. 20th St., tel. 212/807–7266), and **Printing House** (421 Hudson St., tel. 212/243–7600). None requires membership for classes.

Golf

Many New Yorkers are avid golfers, and on weekends they jam the handful of verdant, well-kept city courses.

Bethpage State Park (tel. 516/249–8917), in the Long Island town of Bethpage, about one hour and 20 minutes from Manhattan, is home to five golf courses, including its 7,065-yard par-71 Black, generally ranked among the nation's top 25 public courses. Reservations for tee times are not accepted; on weekends and Monday, the line starts forming at midnight for the Black course's tee-time tickets to go on sale at 4 AM. It's not so congested on other days, or on the other four courses on the property.

Of the 13 city courses, the 6,585-yard Split Rock in **Pelham Bay Park,** the Bronx, is considered the most challenging (tel. 718/885–1258). Slightly easier is its sister course, the 6,405-yard Pelham, which has fewer trees to contend with. **Van Cortlandt Park** has the nation's first municipal golf course, established in 1895—the hilly 6,052-yard Van Cortlandt (tel. 718/543–4595). Queens has a 5,431-yard course at **Forest Park** in Woodhaven (Park La. S and Forest Pkwy., tel. 718/ 296–0999); Staten Island has the 5,891-yard **Silver Lake** (915 Victory Blvd., one block south of Forest Ave., tel. 718/447–5686).

Driving Range In midtown Manhattan you can practice your swing in netted cages, with bull's-eye backdrops, at the **Richard Metz Golf Studio** (425 Madison Ave. at 49th St., 3rd Floor, tel. 212/759–6940). **Midtown Golf Club** (7 W. 45th St., tel. 212/869–3636) offers netted cages, golf simulators, and putting greens.

Miniature Golf Putting courses are at **Gotham Miniature Golf** (at Wollman Rink, Central Park near 64th St., tel. 212/517–4800), where, from late April through early October, putters maneuver outdoors around scale models of city landmarks.

Horseback Riding

A trot on the bridle path around Central Park's Reservoir, renovated in 1987, provides a pleasant look at New York. The carefully run **Claremont Riding Academy** (175 W. 89th St., tel. 212/724–5100) is the city's oldest riding academy and the only riding stable left in Manhattan. Private lessons, including dressage, are available at beginner through advanced levels, for $35 per half hour. Experienced riders can rent horses, at $33 per hour, for a walk, trot, or canter (but not a gallop) in nearby Central Park; call ahead to reserve.

Hotel Health Clubs

Although space is tight in Manhattan hotels, most of them offer some kind of fitness facility, even if it's just an arrangement enabling guests to use a nearby health club (*see* Chapter 10). These hotels have some of the better on-premises workout centers for their guests:

Doral Fitness Center (90 Park Ave., tel. 212/370–9692), available to guests of the **Doral Park Avenue, Doral Court,** and **Doral Tuscany.** This serious health club offers a number of workout programs, including one-on-one training, aerobic equipment, and Nautilus and Eagle equipment. **The Four Seasons** (57 E. 57th St., tel. 212/758– 5700) has a spacious and high-tech facility, including an aerobics room with video, free weights, stairmaster, and Nautilus. **Holiday Inn Crowne Plaza** (1605 Broadway at 49th St., tel. 212/977–4000) has a facility operated by the New York Sports Club. Features include a lap pool, fitness and cardiovascular equipment, and an aerobics studio. **The Peninsula** (700 5th Ave., tel. 212/247–2200) reserves floors 21–23 for its health club, with a pool on the 22nd floor, plus exercise machines and a poolside dining terrace. **Sheraton Manhattan** (790 7th Ave. at 51st St., tel. 212/581–3300) has a health club with a large pool, aerobic and aquatic exercise equipment, swimming lessons, and a sun deck. **Vanderbilt YMCA** (224 E. 47th St., tel. 212/755–2410) offers guests access to the Y's athletic facilities—pools, gym, running track, weight room, machines, and exercise classes.

Ice Skating

Each of the city's rinks has its own character, but all have scheduled skating sessions, with the surfaces tended between times. Lockers, skate rentals, music, and snack bars complete the picture. Major rinks include the one in **Rockefeller Center** (50th St. at 5th Ave., lower plaza, tel. 212/757–5730), postage-stamp size and utterly romantic, especially when the enormous Christmas tree towers above it; **Sky Rink** (450 W. 33rd St., 16th Floor, tel. 212/239–8385), the city's biggest indoor skating spot and its only year-round rink; and the beautifully situated **Wollman Memorial Rink** (6th Ave. at 59th St., tel. 212/517–4800). Be prepared for crowds on weekends.

In-Line Skating

In-line skating is very popular in New York. **Peck & Goodie** (917 8th Ave. at 54th St., tel. 212/246–6123; 1414 2nd Ave. at 73rd St., tel. 212/249–3178) sells and rents skates and also gives in-line skating lessons in Central Park's Wollman Rink and in Brooklyn's Prospect Park. Downtown, the specialists at **Alex Sport** (295 Greenwich St., tel. 212/964–1944) can furnish you with skates and all the gear and accessories you'll ever need; rentals are also available.

Those who think skates should be used for disco dancing can be found, whirling and twirling and wearing headphones, weekends in Central Park between the Mall and Bethesda Fountain. **Wollman Rink** (6th Ave. at 59th St., tel. 212/517–4800) converts to a roller rink during warm months, and rentals are available. You can also rent at **Blades West** (105 W. 72nd St., tel. 212/787–3911), **Blades East** (160 E. 86th St., tel. 212/996–1644), and **Manhattan Sports** (740 7th Ave. at 49th St., tel. 212/664–1360).

Jogging and Racewalking

Jogging In New York, dog-walkers jog, librarians jog, rock stars jog, and parents jog (sometimes pushing their toddlers ahead of them in speedy Baby Jogger strollers). Publicity notwithstanding, crime is not a problem as long as you jog when and where everybody else does.

In Manhattan, **Central Park** is the busiest spot, specifically along the 1.58-mile track circling the **Reservoir.** A runners' lane has been designated along the park roads, which are closed to traffic weekdays 10–3 and 7–10, and from 7 PM Friday to 6 AM Monday. A good 1.72-mile route starts at Tavern on the Green along the West Drive, heads south around the bottom of the park to the East Drive, and circles back west on the 72nd Street park road to your starting point. **Riverside Park,** along the Hudson River bank in Manhattan, is glorious at sunset. You can cover 4½ miles by running from 72nd to 116th streets and back. On Manhattan streets, figure 20 north–south blocks per mile.

Other favorite Manhattan circuits are around **Gramercy Park** (⅙ mile), **Washington Square Park** (½ mile), and the **Battery Park City Esplanade** (about 2 miles). In Brooklyn, try the **Brooklyn Heights Esplanade,** facing the Manhattan skyline, or the roads in **Prospect Park.**

Races and Group Runs A full, year-round schedule is organized by the **New York Road Runners Club** (9 E. 89th St., tel. 212/860–4455), including group runs at 6:30 PM and 7:15 PM on weekdays, starting at the club headquarters, and at 10 AM Saturday at 90th Street and 5th Avenue in Central Park. One of the most popular events is the 5-mile Runner's World Midnight Run, held on New Year's Eve with many of the runners wearing inventive costumes.

Racewalking Elbows pumping vigorously at their sides, racewalkers can move as fast as some joggers, the great difference being that their heels are planted firmly with every stride. A number of competitive racewalking events are held regularly in Central Park and around the metropolitan area; you can also join in Wednesday-evening and Sunday-morning group racewalks in Central Park. For information, contact the **Park Walker's Club** (320 E. 33rd St., tel. 212/628–1317).

Rock Climbing

Yes, you can scale mountains in Manhattan. Okay, it's a wall, at **Manhattan Plaza** (450 W. 43rd St., tel 212/594–0554), with rental of shoes, carabiners, harness, and everything you need. People also climb **Central Park**'s rocky outcrops (tel. 212/397–3166).

Swimming

With the wave of city budget cuts, many municipal pools have been closed; among the few that remain is the **Carmine Street Pool** (7th Ave. S and Clarkson St., tel. 212/242–5228). The **U.N. Plaza** (1 United Nations Plaza, tel. 212/702–5016) and **Parker Meridien** (119 W. 56th St., tel. 212/245–5000) hotels have lovely rooftop swimming pools that can be used by nonguests for a $30-a-day fee. The **YWCA** has a sparkling 75-foot lap pool available at $6 per half hour to members of all YWCAs (610 Lexington Ave. at 53rd St., tel. 212/755–4500).

Tennis

The New York City Parks Department maintains scores of tennis courts. Some of the most scenic are the 26 clay courts and four hard courts in **Central Park** (mid-park near 94th St., tel. 212/280–0205), set in a thicket of trees with the skyline beyond. Modestly priced, same-day, single-play admissions are available at the Tennis House adjoining the courts.

You can also play where John McEnroe and Ivan Lendl do: at the **U.S.T.A. National Tennis Center** (tel. 718/592–8000) in Flushing Meadows–Corona Park, Queens, site of the U.S. Open tournament. The center has 29 outdoor and nine indoor courts, all Deco Turf II. Reservations are accepted up to an hour in advance, though a call two days in advance is suggested. A $150 million expansion of the center added 15 new courts open to the public and three new stadiums.

Local clubs that will book courts to nonmembers include:

Crosstown Tennis (14 W. 31st St., tel. 212/947–5780), with four indoor hard courts that are air-conditioned in summer.

HRC Tennis (Piers 13 and 14, East River at Wall St., tel. 212/422–9300), with eight Har-Tru courts under two bubbles, which are air-conditioned in summer. HRC Tennis is also affiliated with **Village Tennis Courts** (10 University Pl., tel. 212/989–2300), with two courts that are air-conditioned in summer.

Manhattan Plaza Racquet Club (450 W. 43rd St., tel. 212/594–0554), on whose five courts Virginia Slims and U.S. Open players have been known to practice—not to mention a soap opera star or two, since many actors live in special housing near the club.

Beaches

Fine weather brings sun-worshiping New Yorkers out in force. Early in the season, the nearest park or even a rooftop is just fine for catching rays, but later on everyone heads for New York City beaches. Before you go, call to check on swimming conditions.

City Beaches

The tame waves of **Coney Island** (tel. 718/946–1353) are the closest many New Yorkers get to a surf all year. The last stop in Brooklyn on the B, D, F, and N lines, the beach here, which has the boardwalk and the amusement park skyline of the "Cyclone" and the "Wonder Wheel" as its backdrop, is busy every day that the sun shines. (*See* Exploring the Other Boroughs). For more surf and slightly fewer boom boxes, venture out on the A or C trains to the beaches at 9th Street, 23rd Street, or 80–118th streets in the **Rockaways** (tel. 718/318–4000).

Great Kills Park on Staten Island is part of the extensive Gateway National Recreation Area (tel. 718/338–3687) and offers one of the quietest sandy stretches within the city limits. Also on Staten Island is the more populous and more surfy **Wolfe's Pond Park** (tel. 718/984–8266). Bus 103 from the Staten Island Ferry Terminal takes you to both beaches.

Long Island

New Yorkers' favorite strand may be **Jones Beach** (tel. 516/785–1600), one of the great man-made beaches of the world, built during the era of the famous parks commissioner Robert Moses. Up the shore is another good beach at **Robert Moses State Park** on Fire Island (tel. 516/669–0449). The Long Island Railroad (tel. 718/217–5477) runs regular transportation in the summer from Penn Station to Jones Beach, Robert Moses State Park, and Long Beach.

8 Shopping

By Karen Cure

Updated by Dick Kagan

Shopping in New York is theater, architecture, and people-watching all rolled into one. Big stores and small ones, one-of-a-kinds and chains together present an overwhelming array of "Things." There are fabulous department stores, with something for everyone, and tiny specialists: You can find a store full of balloons (**Toy Balloon,** 204 E. 38th St., tel. 212/682–3803), and others offering paper products (**Kate's Paperie,** 561 Broadway, tel. 212/941–9816), personal and business security equipment (**Counter Spy Shop,** 630 3rd Ave., tel. 212/557–3040; by appointment only), and skeletons and fossils (**Maxilla & Mandible,** 451 Columbus Ave. at 80th St., tel. 212/724–6173).

Another big Manhattan shopping lure is the bargain. Major intersections are instant markets as street peddlers hawk fake Gucci and Cartier watches at $15–$25 each. (These may just possibly last a year or two.) There are thrift shops and resale shops where, it's whispered, Jackie O sends her castoffs and Catherine Deneuve snaps up antique lace. At off-price and discount stores, mark-offs are, as locals say, "to die for," and the sales are even better. Designers' showroom sales allow you to buy cheap at the source; auctions promise good prices as well.

Shopping Hours

Stores are generally open Monday–Saturday from 10 AM to 5 or 6 PM, but neighborhood peculiarities do exist. In midtown and lower Manhattan, shops are often closed all weekend. Most stores on the Lower East Side and in the diamond district on 47th Street close on Friday afternoon and all day Saturday for the Jewish Sabbath while keeping normal hours on Sunday. Sunday hours, also common on the West Side and in the Village and SoHo, are the exception on the Upper East Side.

Sales

Sales take place late June and July (for summer merchandise) and late December and January (for winter wares); these sales are announced in the papers. Sales of special merit may end up in *New York* magazine's "Sales and Bargains" column. These often include sales in manufacturers' showrooms that are otherwise never promoted to the public. If your visit is planned for April or October, when most take place, you might phone your favorite designer and ask whether one is in the offing. Find out before you go whether the seller requires cash or accepts credit cards and checks (whether local or out-of-state).

Shopping Neighborhoods

New York shops are collected in neighborhoods rather than in malls, so there's nothing more pleasant than shop-crawling when the weather is fine. Locations, if not included here, can be found in store listings below.

South Street Seaport

The Seaport's shops are located along the cobbled, pedestrians-only extension to Fulton Street; in the Fulton Market building, the original home of the city's fish market; and on the three levels of Pier 17. You'll find some of the best of the country's upscale retailers: **Ann Taylor** and **Laura Ashley** for women's clothing, **Brookstone** for fancy gadgets and hardware, **Caswell-Massey** for fragrances, and **Sharper Image** for high-tech gimmickry. The big catalogue house **J. Crew** chose the Seaport as the location for its first retail outlet. There are also few-of-a-kind shops, notably the **Strand** bookstore, where second-hand volumes overflow into sidewalk bins; **Mariposa** for butterflies; and **Hats in the Belfry** for inexpensive hats. Business is brisk, especially on fine summer days and on weekends.

Manhattan Shopping Highlights

A & S Plaza, **13**

Annex Antiques Fair and Flea Market, **14**

Barneys New York, **2, 15**

Bergdorf Goodman, **4**

Bloomingdale's, **3**

Century 21, **17**

Henri Bendel, **5**

Lord & Taylor, **11**

Lower East Side (Orchard Street), **16**

Macy's, **12**

Manhattan Art and Antiques Center, **8**

Rockefeller Center, **9**

Saks Fifth Avenue, **10**

South Street Seaport, **18**

Tiffany & Co., **6**

Trump Tower, **7**

Zabar's, **1**

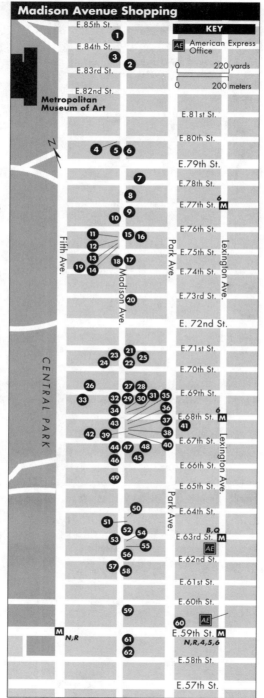

Madison Avenue Shopping

57th Street / 5th Avenue Shopping

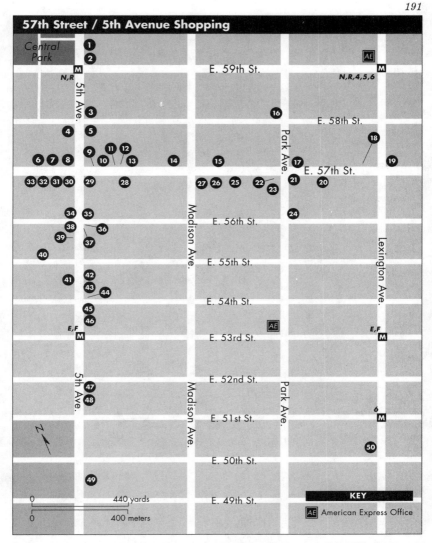

A La Vieille Russie, **2**
Alfred Dunhill of London, **22**
André Emmerich Gallery, **15**
Ann Taylor, **10**
Asprey, **35**
Bergdorf Goodman, **4, 5**
Blum Helman, **31**
Buccellati, **25**
Bulgari, **30**
Burberry's, **12**
Cartier, **47**
Chanel, **11**

Charivari 57, **32**
Ciro, **41**
David Webb, **21**
Dempsey & Carroll, **20**
F.A.O. Schwarz, **3**
Façonnable, **44**
Fortunoff, **46**
Galeries Lafayette, **28**
Gazebo, **18**
Geoffrey Beene, **1**
Godiva, **42, 50**
H. Stern, **48**
Hammacher Schlemmer, **19**
Harry Winston, **38**

Henri Bendel, **39**
Hermès, **13**
Hoya Crystal Gallery, **23**
Israel Sack, **13**
J.N. Bartfield, **33**
James Robinson, **16**
Kenneth Jay Lane, **45**
Laura Ashley, **14**
Louis Feraud, **34**
Manolo Blahnik, **40**
Matsuda, **17**
Pace Gallery, **27**
Rizzoli, **7**

Saks Fifth Avenue, **49**
Salvatore Ferragamo, **36**
Steuben, **37**
Susan Bennis Warren Edwards, **6**
T. Anthony, **24**
Takashimaya, **43**
Tiffany & Co., **29**
Van Cleef & Arpels, **8**
Victoria's Secret, **26**
Warner Bros. Studio Store, **9**

Acker Merrall &
Condit, **29**

Adriana's
Bazaar, **19**

Ann Taylor, **34**

Aris Mixon &
Company, **17**

Avventura, **11**

The Ballet
Shop, **36**

Betsey
Johnson, **30**

Charivari, **3, 9,
14, 32**

Citarella, **23**

Ecco, **22**

Endicott
Booksellers, **5**

Frank Stella
Ltd., **6**

Greenstones, **7**

Gryphon Record
Shop, **25**

Handblock, **4**

HMV, **26**

I.S. 44
Market, **20**

Laura
Ashley, **15**

Maxilla and
Mandible, **10**

Murder Ink, **1**

Only Hearts, **16**

Penny Whistle
Toys, **8**

Peter Fox, **18**

Petrossian, **37**

Pottery Barn, **24**

Putumayo, **21**

Sensuous
Bean, **33**

Shakespeare &
Company, **12**

Star Magic, **27**

Tip Top, **28**

To Boot, **31**

Tower
Records, **35**

West Side
Kids, **2**

Zabar's, **13**

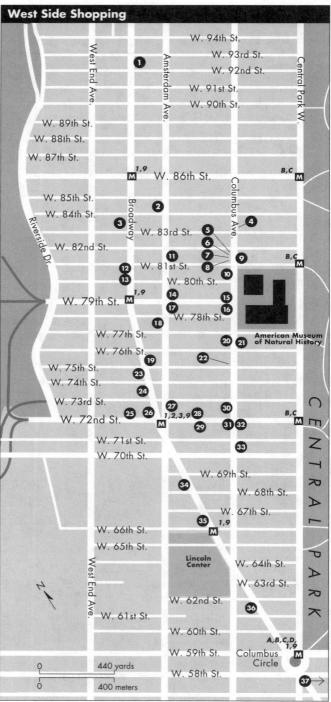

West Side Shopping

Ad Hoc
Softwares, **17**

Agnes B., **9**

A/X: Armani
Exchange, **6**

Back Pages
Antiques, **4**

Bébé
Thompson, **14**

Betsey
Johnson, **2**

Broadway
Panhandler, **25**

Canal Jean, **26**

Comme des
Garçons, **19**

Dean &
DeLuca, **7**

Ecco, **12**

Enchanted
Forest, **27**

Harriet Love, **10**

Irish Books, **5**

Joovay, **16**

Kate's Paperie, **8**

Leo Castelli, **15**

Mary Boone, **18**

Multiple
Impressions, **24**

O.K. Harris, **28**

Paula Cooper, **1**

Penny Whistle
Toys, **23**

Peter Fox, **13**

Putumayo, **22**

Think Big!, **29**

Tootsie
Plohound, **11**

Untitled, **3**

Wolfman-Gold &
Good
Company, **21**

Yohji
Yamamoto, **30**

Zona, **20**

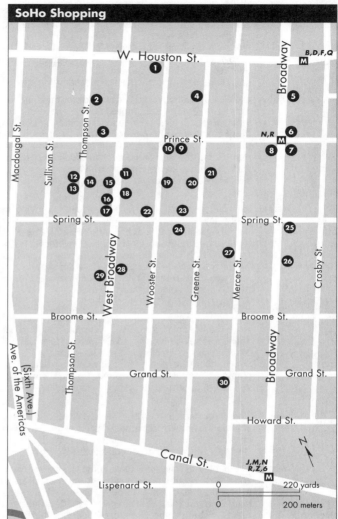

SoHo Shopping

World
Financial
Center Although the nearby World Trade Center bills its concourse as the city's busiest shopping center, the World Financial Center in Battery Park City is a shopping destination to reckon with, thanks to stores such as **Barneys New York** for clothing, **Godiva Chocolatier** for chocolates, **Mark Cross** for leather goods, **Ann Taylor,** and **Caswell-Massey. Rizzoli** has books and magazines, stocked on handsome wooden shelves, and **Downtown Sound** strives to be the ultimate compact-disc store. Most are open on Sundays.

Lower East
Side Once home to millions of Jewish immigrants from Russia and Eastern Europe, this area is New Yorkers' bargain beat. The center of it all is narrow, unprepossessing Orchard Street, which is crammed with tiny, no-nonsense clothing and shoe stores ranging from kitschy to elegant. Don't expect to schmooze with salespeople, espe-

cially on Sunday, the busiest day of the week. Start at Houston Street, walk down one side as far as Canal Street, then walk back up. Essential stops include **Fine & Klein** for handbags; **Forman's** for women's clothing; and **Lace-Up Shoes**. Grand Street (off Orchard Street, south of Delancey Street) is chockablock with linens, towels, and other items for the home; the Bowery (between Grand Street and Delancey Street), with lamps and light fixtures.

SoHo   On West Broadway, SoHo's main drag, and on Broadway and Wooster, Greene, Mercer, Prince, Spring, Broome, and Grand streets, major art galleries keep company with chic clothing stores such as **Yohji Yamamoto** and **Agnès B.** Well-known stops include decorative-items specialist **Wolfman-Gold & Good Company** and Southwest- and Italian-themed **Zona;** gourmet food emporium **Dean & DeLuca;** and the remarkable **Enchanted Forest** toy store. Many stores in SoHo close on Mondays.

Lower 5th Avenue   Fifth Avenue south of 20th Street along with the streets fanning east and west are home to some of New York's hippest shops and a lively downtown crowd. Many of the locals sport clothes from the neighborhood—a mix of **Emporio Armani, Paul Smith,** and **Matsuda** (for Japanese clothing), sometimes finished off with big black shades from **Mikli.** Book lovers head for the enormous outposts of **Barnes & Noble** and its **Sale Annex** on the southeast and southwest corners of 18th Street. **Barneys, Williams-Sonoma,** and **Pottery Barn** are within walking distance on nearby 7th Avenue.

Herald Square   Reasonable prices prevail at this intersection of 34th Street and Avenue of the Americas (6th Avenue). Giant **Macy's** has traditionally been the linchpin. Opposite is Manhattan's first **Toys "Я" Us.** Next door on 6th Avenue, the **A&S Plaza** atrium mall is anchored by the Manhattan outlet of the Brooklyn-based A&S department store, which makes for wonderful browsing, as do **Lechter's,** for home furnishings, and **Mouse N' Around,** for cartoon-emblazoned merchandise. The concentration of shops in a small area makes it a good bet in nasty weather.

Midtown Near Grand Central   The biggest men's clothiers are here on and just off the stretch of Madison Avenue nicknamed Trad Avenue: **J. Press, Brooks Brothers, Paul Stuart, F. R. Tripler,** and **Wallachs.** Most also handle women's clothing in dress-for-success styles.

5th Avenue   The boulevard that was once home to some of the biggest names in New York retailing is not what it once was, that role having been usurped by Madison Avenue north of 57th Street. But 5th Avenue from Central Park South to Rockefeller Center still shines with **F.A.O. Schwarz** and **Bergdorf Goodman** (both the main store and **Bergdorf Goodman Men** are at 58th St.), **Tiffany** and **Bulgari** jewelers (at 57th St.), **Ferragamo** and other various luxury stores in **Trump Tower** (all at 56th St.), **Steuben** crystal (also at 56th St.), **Henri Bendel,** across the street, **Takashimaya** (at 54th St.), **Cartier** jewelers (at 52nd St.), and so on down to **Saks Fifth Avenue** (at 50th St.). **Rockefeller Center** itself provides a plethora of shops. To the south (at 47th St.) is the shiny 575 atrium mall, named for its 5th Avenue address, and the venerable **Lord & Taylor** department store (at 39th St.).

57th Street   The thoroughfare of Carnegie Hall, the Russian Tea Room, and the Hard Rock Café supports stores that sell everything from remaindered books to $50,000 diamond-and-platinum bracelets. Begin at the **Compleat Strategist** game store (between 8th and 9th Aves.) and head eastward, via the **Pottery Barn, Coliseum Books,** and **Jerry Brown** and **Paron** fabric stores. As you approach 5th Avenue, you're in the creamiest New York retail territory, with **Bergdorf Goodman's** flagship store. East of 5th you'll find **Galeries Lafayette New York,** a branch of the famous French department store, the glittery, glassy new **Warner Bros. Studio Store** (1 E. 57th St. at 5th Ave., tel. 212/754–0300), with its state-of-the-art interactive elements, animation art, and vast array of children's merchandise, as well as such exclusive stores as **Chanel, Burberrys, Escada, Hermès,** and **Alfred Dunhill of London** for men's clothing and cigars (at the corner of Park Ave.). Above and alongside these stores are top art galleries such as **André Emmerich** and **Pace.**

Columbus Avenue — Between 66th and 86th streets, this former tenement district is now home to some of the city's glitziest stores. Shops are mostly modern in design, upscale but not top-of-the-line. Clothing runs the gamut from preppy for men and women (**Frank Stella Ltd.**) to high funk (**Betsey Johnson**) and high style (**Charivari**).

Upper East Side — On Madison and Lexington avenues, roughly between 57th and 79th streets, New York branches of world-renowned designer emporiums are joined by spirited retailers who fill their stores with the unique and stylish. Domestic and imported items for the home, fine antiques, and wonderful clothing predominate—and the prices aren't always sky high.

Blitz Tours

Get your subway tokens ready, and save enough cash for cab fare to lug all your packages home from these shopping itineraries. They're arranged by special interest; addresses, if not included here, can be found in the store listings below.

Antiques — Spend two hours at the **Manhattan Art & Antiques Center** (1050 2nd Ave. at 55th St.), then swing over to 57th Street for an even posher array of European, American, and Asian treasures. Stroll westward across 57th Street, stopping at **Lillian Nassau** of Tiffany lamp and art nouveau furniture fame and **Israel Sack,** nearby on 5th Avenue, with American antique furniture. Then head up Madison to **America Hurrah** (at 65th St.), **Didier Aaron** (on 67th St.), **Thomas K. Woodard** (near 69th St.), **Leigh Keno** (on 74th St.), **Stair & Company** (near 74th St.), **DeLorenzo** and **Leo Kaplan** (near 75th St.), **David A. Schorsch** (on 76th St.), **Florian Papp** (at 76th St.), and **Barry Friedman** (at 83rd St.).

Bargains — Start early at **Century 21** or **Syms** in lower Manhattan. Take a cab to Hester and Orchard streets and shop along Orchard to Houston Street. (Prowl along Grand Street if you're more interested in goods for your home than in clothing.) Leave at 2:30 and take a cab to **S&W** in Chelsea; then take the subway uptown to **Loehmann's** (open until 9 PM) in the Bronx. But remember: On Saturdays, most shops are closed on the Lower East Side.

Cook's Tour — Browse in **Zabar's** (2245 Broadway at W. 80th St., tel. 212/787–2000) for a couple of hours beginning at 8 AM; then go across town to **Kitchen Arts & Letters** bookstore (1435 Lexington Ave., between 93rd and 94th Sts., tel. 212/876–5550) and proceed down to **Bridge Kitchenware** (214 E. 52nd St., tel. 212/688–4220). Head downtown to hit **Balducci's** in the Village, **Dean & DeLuca** and **Broadway Panhandler** (520 Broadway, tel. 212/966–3434) in SoHo, and, if there's time before 6, **Kam-Man** (200 Canal St., tel. 212/571–0330) in Chinatown. If not, head up to **Macy's Cellar.** If you live in a landlocked area, make your last stop in New York **Citarella** (2135 Broadway at 75th St., tel. 212/874–0383), and have some great fish packed in ice to go.

Luxury Spend 90 minutes at **Saks Fifth Avenue,** then stroll up 5th Avenue. Leave **Trump Tower** by 2:30. Visit **Tiffany** and **Bergdorf Goodman** before closing time. On Thursday, windowshop your way across 57th Street and north on Lexington Avenue to **Bloomingdale's,** which closes at 9 PM. On other nights, clothes fanatics can take a cab to one of the two main **Barneys New York** stores for a finale.

Home Start at **Barneys New York** (on 7th and Madison Aves.), which opens
Furnishings at 10, and visit its Chelsea Passage. Then take a cab to SoHo and stroll around, making sure not to miss **Wolfman-Gold & Good Company** and **Zona.** When things there close—at 6 or 7—take the No. 6 subway to **Bloomingdale's,** if it's Thursday, or the Q, N, or R train to **Macy's,** open late Mondays, Thursdays, and Fridays.

Department Stores

Most of these stores keep regular hours on weekdays and are open until 8 at least one night a week. Many have personal shoppers who can walk you through the store at no charge.

A&S (33rd St. and 6th Ave., tel. 212/594–8500). What was the old Gimbel's, a block south of Macy's, lives again as home to A&S Plaza, whose nine floors are anchored by Abraham & Straus, working hard to become as well established here as in the outer boroughs. The sales are some of the best in town.

Barneys New York (106 7th Ave. at 17th St., tel. 212/929–9000; Madison Ave. at 61st St., tel. 212/929–9000; World Financial Center, tel. 212/945–1600). Founded as a menswear discounter some 60 years ago, Barneys is still the place to see what's hot. The still-extensive selection of menswear ranges from made-to-measure and European and American couture to mass-market natural-shouldered suits; the women's department is a showcase of current women's fashion. The ladies' accessories are some of the chicest around, and the Chelsea Passage can be counted on for distinctive housewares.

Bergdorf Goodman (754 5th Ave., between 57th and 58th Sts., tel. 212/753–7300). Good taste reigns in an elegant and understated setting. The Home Department is room after exquisite room of wonderful linens, tabletop items, and gifts. The expanded men's store, across the street, occupies the former home of the giant F.A.O. Schwarz toy store (now at 767 5th Ave.).

Bloomingdale's (1000 3rd Ave. at 59th St., tel. 212/355–5900). Only a handful of department stores occupy an entire city block; Macy's is one, and this New York institution is another. The main floor is a stupefying maze of mirrors and black walls; elsewhere the racks are overfull, salespeople overworked, and the departments constantly on the move. Still, selections are dazzling at all but the lowest price points, and the markdowns on top-of-the-line designer goods can be extremely rewarding. Exotic special promotions regularly fill the store.

Galleries Lafayette New York (4–10 E. 57th St., tel. 212/355–0022). This branch of the French fashion store, opening onto Trump Tower, carries mostly French labels in an upscale assortment of better and designer apparel. Styles here tend more toward youthful than classic. Up-to-the-minute fashion accessories can have surprisingly reasonable price tags.

Henri Bendel (712 5th Ave., between 55th and 56th Sts., tel. 212/247–1100). Now firmly established under its beautiful new roof (having moved from W. 57th Street), Bendel's continues to delight with its stylish displays and sophisticated boutiques. The second-floor café is a delight.

Lord & Taylor (424 5th Ave., between 38th and 39th Sts., tel. 212/391–3344). This store can be relied upon for the wearable, the fashionable, and the classic in clothes and accessories for women. It's refined, well stocked, and never overwhelming.

Macy's (Herald Sq., Broadway at 34th St., tel. 212/695–4400). No less than a miracle on 34th Street, Macy's main store is the largest retail store in America. Over the past two decades, it has grown chic enough to rival Bloomingdale's in the style department, but its main floor is reassuringly traditional. The latest trends are represented in almost every area the store covers. Estate Jewelry offers fine antique pieces. And for cooking gear and housewares, the Cellar nearly outdoes Zabar's.

Saks Fifth Avenue (611 5th Ave., between 49th and 50th Sts., tel. 212/753–4000). This wonderful store still embodies the spirit of service and style with which it opened in 1926. Saks believes in good manners, the ceremonies of life, and dressing for the part; the selection for men, women, and children—doubled by recent expansion—affirms this quality.

Takashimaya New York (693 5th Ave., between 54th and 55th Sts., tel. 212/350–0100). This pristine branch of Japan's largest department store carries stylish clothes for women and men and fine household items, all of which reflect a combination of Eastern and Western designs. The garden atrium and two-floor art gallery contribute to the elegant ambience.

Specialty Shops

Antiques Antiquing is fine sport in Manhattan. Goods run the gamut from rarefied museum-quality to wacky and eminently affordable. Premier shopping areas are on Madison Avenue north of 57th Street, 57th Street east of 5th Avenue, and 60th Street between 2nd and 3rd avenues, where more than 20 shops, dealing in everything from 18th-century French furniture to Art Deco lighting fixtures, cluster on one block. Around 11th and 12th streets, between University Place and Broadway, a tantalizing array of settees, tables, bedsteads, and rocking chairs overflows onto the sidewalks in front of wholesalers with "To The Trade" signs on their doors; however, a card from your hometown architect or decorator may get you inside. Most dealers are open on Saturdays.

Many small dealers cluster in two antiques "malls":

Manhattan Art & Antiques Center (1050 2nd Ave., between 55th and 56th Sts., tel. 212/355–4400). More than 100 dealers stocking everything from paisley and Judaica to satsuma, scientifica, and samovars jumble the three floors here. The level of quality is not, as a rule, up to that of Madison Avenue, but then neither are the prices.

Metropolitan Arts and Antiques Pavilion (110 W. 19th St., between 6th Ave. and 7th Ave., tel. 212/463–0200). Good for costume jewelry, off-beat bric-a-brac, and '50s kitsch, this antiques mall holds regularly scheduled auctions and specialty shows featuring rare books, photography, tribal art, Victoriana, and other lots.

American and English **America Hurrah** (766 Madison Ave., between 65th and 66th Sts., 3rd Floor, tel. 212/535–1930). Superb American patchwork quilts and other Americana can be found here.

David A. Schorsch (30 E. 76th St., No. 11A, tel. 212/439–6100). New York's Shaker specialist sees clients by appointment only.

Florian Papp (962 Madison Ave., between 75th and 76th Sts., tel. 212/288–6770). This store has an unassailed reputation among knowledgeable collectors.

Hyde Park Antiques (836 Broadway, between 12th and 13th Sts., tel. 212/477–0033). This store features English decorative arts from the 18th and 19th centuries.

Israel Sack (730 5th Ave., between 56th and 57th Sts., tel. 212/399–6562). This is widely considered one of the very best places in the country for 18th-century American furniture.

Kentshire Galleries (37 E. 12th St., tel. 212/673–6644). There are eight floors of elegant furniture displayed in room settings, with an emphasis on formal English pieces from the 18th and 19th centuries, particularly the Georgian and Regency periods. Kentshire also operates an antiques department at Bergdorf Goodman that features small collectibles such as tea caddies, ink wells, and biscuit boxes.

Leigh Keno American Furniture (19 E. 74th St., 1st Floor, tel. 212/734–2381). Before he was 30, Leigh Keno set a new auction record in the American antiques field by paying $2.75 million for a hairy-paw-foot Philadelphia wing chair. He has a good eye and an interesting inventory.

Steve Miller American Folk Art (17 E. 96th St., tel. 212/348–5219). This gallery is run by one of the country's premier folk art dealers, the author of *The Art of the Weathervane*.

Thomas K. Woodard (799 Madison Ave., between 67th and 68th Sts., 2nd Floor, tel. 212/794–9404). Americana and antique quilts are among the specialties of this prestigious dealer.

Eclectic **Newel Art Galleries** (425 E. 53rd St., tel. 212/758–1970). Located near the East Side's interior design district, this gallery, the city's biggest antiques store, has a huge collection that roams from the Renaissance to the 20th century.

European **Artisan Antiques** (81 University Pl. at 11th St., tel. 212/751–5214). Art Deco chandeliers come in merry profusion, along with lamps, sconces, and other lighting fixtures from France.

Barry Friedman (1117 Madison Ave., between 83rd and 84th Sts., tel. 212/794–8950). Wiener Werkstätte, Bauhaus, De Stijl, Russian Constructivist, and other European avant-gardists star.

Brass Antique Shop (32 Allen St., tel. 212/925–6660). Candlesticks, chandeliers, andirons, teapots, and other objects in brass, sterling, and copper fill the shelves and teeter on the tables in this old Lower East Side shop.

DeLorenzo (958 Madison Ave., between 75th and 76th Sts., tel. 212/249–7575). Come here to explore the sinuous curves, strongly articulated shapes, and highly polished surfaces of French Art Deco furniture and accessories at their best.

Didier Aaron (32 E. 67th St., tel. 212/988–5248). This highly esteemed gallery specializes in superb 18th- and 19th-century French furniture and paintings.

Leo Kaplan Ltd. (967 Madison Ave., between 75th and 76th Sts., tel. 212/249–6766). The impeccable items here include Art Nouveau glass and pottery, porcelain from 18th-century England, stunning antique and modern paperweights, and Russian artworks, including creations by Fabergé.

Malmaison Antiques (253 E. 74th St., tel. 212/288–7569). This gallery has the country's largest selection of Empire furniture and decorative arts.

Pierre Deux Antiques (369 Bleecker St., tel. 212/243–7740). The company that brought French provincial to a provincial America still offers an excellent selection.

Stair & Company (942 Madison Ave., between 74th and 75th Sts., tel. 212/517–4400). Period rooms stylishly show off fine 18th- and 19th-century English mahogany pieces.

Fun Stuff **Back Pages Antiques** (125 Greene St., tel. 212/460–5998). To acquire an antique jukebox or slot machine, just drop in.

Darrow's Fun Antiques (1101 1st Ave., between 60th and 61st Sts., tel. 212/838–0730). The first of the city's nostalgia shops, the store is full of whimsy.

John T. Johnston's Jukebox Classics (6742 5th Ave., near 68th St., Brooklyn, tel. 718/833–8455). You'll find oodles of vintage jukeboxes, pinball machines, gumball machines, and other arcade goodies, all expertly restored.

Apothecary **Aveda Aromatherapy Esthetique** (509 Madison Ave. between 52nd
and Fragrance and 53rd Sts., tel. 212/832–2416). Concoct your own perfumes from
Shops the impressive selection of essential oils.

The Body Shop (773 Lexington Ave. at 61st St., tel. 212/755–7851; A&S Plaza, 6th Ave. at 33rd St., tel. 212/268–7424; 485 Madison Ave. at 52nd St., tel. 212/832–0812; the World Trade Center, tel. 212/488–7595; and other Manhattan locations). Stop here for clean, green goodies for skin and hair.

Caswell-Massey (518 Lexington Ave. at 48th St., tel. 212/755–2254). The original store displays its fragrant toiletries in polished old cases; branches are in the World Financial Center and South Street Seaport.

Essential Products Company (90 Water St., tel. 212/344–4288). This company, established in 1895, sells knockoffs of famous fragrances at a fraction of the original price tags.

Floris (703 Madison Ave., between 62nd and 63rd Sts., tel. 212/935–9100). Floral English toiletries beloved of such beauties as Cher, Sophia Loren, and Catherine Deneuve fill this re-creation of the cozy London original.

Jean Laporte Perfumes (870 Madison Ave., between 70th and 71st Sts., tel. 212/517–8665.) Exquisite French scents and antique perfume bottles make a splendid array.

Kiehl Pharmacy (109 3rd Ave., near 13th St., tel. 212/475–3400). A favored haunt of top models and hairstylists, it's been a purveyor of quality skin and hair products since 1851.

Art Galleries America's art capital, New York has numerous wealthy collectors, so many galleries are minimuseums that welcome browsing (*see also* Auctions, *below*).

Aberbach Fine Art (980 Madison Ave., between 76th and 77th Sts., tel. 212/988–1100). Exhibits here include paintings and sculpture by various modern and contemporary artists.

André Emmerich Gallery (41 E. 57th St., tel. 212/752–0124). Located in the Art Deco Fuller Building, this gallery displays major works by major modern artists.

Art in General (79 Walker St., tel. 212/219–0473). Come here for works in a variety of mediums by emerging contemporary artists.

Blum Helman (20 W. 57th St., tel. 212/245–2888). Contemporary art by Brian Hunt, Robert Moskowitz, Joe Andoe, and Ellsworth Kelly, among others, is displayed here.

A Clean, Well-Lighted Place (363 Bleecker St., tel. 212/255–3656). Prints by well-known artists, including Sean Scully, Susan Rothenberg, Robert Motherwell, and David Hockney, are displayed here.

Colnaghi (21 E. 67th St., tel. 212/772–2266). This is the New York outpost of one of London's preeminent fine art galleries, offering European and English paintings and objets d'art.

Gagosian (980 Madison Ave., between 76th and 77th Sts., tel. 212/744–2313). Works on display are by such artists as Richard Serra, Willem De Kooning, Jasper Johns, Frank Stella, Warhol, David Salle, and Philip Taaffe.

Hirschl & Adler (21 E. 70th St., tel. 212/535–8810). A respected dealer of American painting and sculpture, this gallery also offers American decorative arts. Among the celebrated artists whose works are featured: Thomas Cole, Childe Hassam, Ralston Crawford, John Storrs, and William Merritt Chase.

Isselbacher (41 E. 78th St., tel. 212/472–1766). This gallery offers prints by late-19th- and 20th-century masters such as Henri Toulouse-Lautrec, Henri Matisse, Marc Chagall, Joan Miró, Pablo Picasso, and Edvard Munch.

Leo Castelli (420 W. Broadway, between Prince and Spring Sts., tel. 212/431–5160). He's the man who discovered Pop. Look for works by Jasper Johns, Roy Lichtenstein, Ed Ruscha, and Ed Rosenquist.

Margo Feiden Galleries (699 Madison Ave., between 62nd and 63rd Sts., tel. 212/677–5330). The specialty here are drawings and prints by theatrical caricaturist Al Hirschfeld, who has been delighting readers of the *New York Times* for more than 60 years.

Mary Boone (417 Broadway, between Prince and Spring Sts., tel. 212/431–1818.) A hot '80s gallery, it's still intriguing today, with such artists as Eric Fischl and Richard Tuttle.

Multiple Impressions (128 Spring St., tel. 212/925–1313). Twentieth-century American, European, and South American paintings and prints are offered here at reasonable prices.

O. K. Harris (383 W. Broadway, tel. 212/431–3600). The oldest gallery in SoHo, opened in 1969, O. K. Harris showcases paintings, sculpture, and photography by contemporary artists.

Pace Gallery (32 E. 57th St., tel. 212/421–3292). This gallery features such well-known modern and contemporary artists as Picasso, Alexander Calder, and Julian Schnabel.

Paula Cooper (149 and 155 Wooster St., tel. 212/674–0766). Exhibits include contemporary paintings and sculpture.

SoHo Photo (15 White St., tel. 212/226–8571). In the heart of TriBeCa, this gallery exhibits various photographers' work.

Books With so many of the country's publishing houses, magazines, and writers based here, there is an abundance of bookshops, small and large. Of course, all the big national chains are here—Barnes & Noble, B. Dalton, Brentano's, Doubleday, Waldenbooks—with branches all over town.

Biography Bookshop (400 Bleecker St., tel. 212/807–8655). Diaries, letters, and other biographical and autobiographical material fill this tidy, well-organized store.

Books & Company (939 Madison Ave., between 74th and 75th Sts., tel. 212/737–1450). A comfy sofa invites lingering here.

Coliseum Books (1771 Broadway at 57th St., tel. 212/757–8381). This supermarket of a bookstore has a huge, quirky selection of remainders, best-sellers, and scholarly works.

Endicott Booksellers (450 Columbus Ave., between 81st and 82nd Sts., tel. 212/787–6300). This intelligent, wood-paneled bookstore features evening readings once or twice a week.

Gotham Book Mart (41 W. 47th St., tel. 212/719–4448). The late Frances Steloff opened this store years ago with just $200 in her pocket, half of it on loan. But she helped launch *Ulysses*, D. H. Lawrence, and Henry Miller and is now legendary among bibliophiles, as is her bookstore, an oasis for those who love to read, with nearly a quarter of a million books.

Irish Books (580 Broadway at Prince St., 11th Floor, tel. 212/274–1923). Here you'll find the country's widest selection of books about Ireland, both current and out-of-print titles.

Kinokuniya Bookstore (10 W. 49th St., tel. 212/765–1461). Come here for everything you ever wanted to read about Japan—in English and Japanese.

Librairie de France/Libraria Hispanica (610 5th Ave., in Rockefeller Ctr., tel. 212/581–8810; 115 5th Ave. at 19th St., tel. 212/673–7400). These huge collections of foreign-language books and periodicals, some in quite exotic tongues, are among the country's largest. Both sites have books in French and Spanish.

Madison Avenue Bookshop (833 Madison Ave., between 69th and 70th Sts., tel. 212/535–6130). Serious contemporary fiction and biographies are sold here in pleasant surroundings.

Revolution Books (13 E. 16th St., tel. 212/691–3345). Come here for left-wing and Third World literature.

Rizzoli (31 W. 57th St., tel. 212/759–2424; 454 W. Broadway, tel. 212/674–1616; World Financial Center, tel. 212/385–1400). Uptown, an elegant marble entrance, oak paneling, chandeliers, and classical music accompany books on art, architecture, dance, design, foreign language, and travel; the downtown stores come without the fin-de-siècle frills.

Shakespeare & Company (2259 Broadway at 81st St., tel. 212/580–7800; 716 Broadway, near Astor Pl., tel. 212/529–1330). The stock here represents what's happening in publishing today in just about every field. Late hours are a plus.

Tower Books (383 Lafayette St., tel. 212/228–5100). Owned by the record conglomerate, this megastore discounts thousands of titles; the magazine section alone is worth the visit.

Children's Books **Bank Street College Bookstore** (2875 Broadway at 112th St., tel. 212/678–1654). Operated by the famed teachers college, here's a mini-emporium of politically correct children's books, games, and videos.

Books of Wonder (464 Hudson St., tel. 212/645–8006; 132 7th Ave. at 18th St., tel. 212/989–3270). This store offers an excellent stock of children's books for all reading levels. Oziana is a specialty, and the 18th Street branch offers antique books as well as new publications.

Maps **Hagstrom Map and Travel Center** (57 W. 43rd St., tel. 212/398–1222). This may be the ultimate map store.

Rand McNally Map & Travel (150 E. 52nd St., tel. 212/758–7488). The excellent selection covers the world.

Music **Joseph Patelson Music House** (160 W. 56th St., tel. 212/582–5840). A huge collection of scores has long made this the heart of the music lover's New York.

Music Exchange (151 W. 46th St., tel. 212/354–5858). Sheet music of popular songs can be found here.

Mystery and Suspense Whodunits are the specialty at: **Foul Play** (13 8th Ave., near 12th St., tel. 212/675–5115; 1465 2nd Ave., between 76th and 77th Sts., tel. 212/517–3222); **Murder Ink** (2486 Broadway, between 92nd and 93rd Sts., tel. 212/362–8905); and **Mysterious Bookshop** (129 W. 56th St., tel. 212/765–0900).

Rare and Used Books **Argosy Bookstore** (116 E. 59th St., tel. 212/753–4455). This sedate nook keeps a scholarly stock of books and autographs.

Bauman Rare Books (The Waldorf-Astoria, Park Ave. at 50th St., tel. 212/759–8300). This very successful Philadelphia firm now offers New Yorkers the most impossible-to-get titles.

J. N. Bartfield (30 W. 57th St., 3rd Floor, tel. 212/245–8890). This legend in the field offers old and antiquarian books distinguished by binding, author, edition, or content.

Pageant Book and Print Shop (109 E. 9th St., tel. 212/674–5296). Michael Caine browsed in this relic of old New York in Woody Allen's *Hannah and Her Sisters.*

Strand (828 Broadway at 12th St., tel. 212/473–1452). Eight miles of shelves house more than two million books at this biggest of Manhattan's used-book stores.

Ximenes Rare Books (19 E. 69th St., tel. 212/744–0226). This store spends much of its time searching for hard-to-find titles.

Travel Books **Complete Traveller Bookstore** (199 Madison Ave. at 35th St., tel. 212/685–9007). Old and new titles are sold here.

Traveller's Bookstore (22 W. 52nd St., tel. 212/664–0995). The stock includes essays and novels, as well as maps and guides.

Cameras and **Bi-Rite** (15 E. 30th St., tel. 212/685–2130). Once your turn comes, **Electronics** this tiny discounter's Hasidic salesmen offer good service, great prices. Take model numbers; there's no showroom.

47th Street Photo (67 W. 47th St., 115 W. 45th St.; tel. 212/921–1287). Prices can be better elsewhere, but these stores manned by Hasidic Jews are a heavyweight among electronics discounters. Note Friday afternoon and Saturday closings.

Harvey Electronics (2 W. 45th St., tel. 212/575–5000; 28 W. 8th St., tel. 212/982–7191). A well-informed staff offers top-of-the-line audio equipment.

Sony (550 Madison Ave., between 55th and 56th Sts., tel. 212/833–8830). Everything electronic made by Sony is available at a pair of sleek new stores that frame the lobby of the handsome Philip Johnson–designed Sony headquarters.

Willoughby's (110 W. 32nd St., tel. 212/564–1600). Calling itself the world's largest camera store, Willoughby's rates high among amateurs and pros for selection and service.

CDs, Tapes, The city's best record stores match its music scene: diversified, eso-**and Records** teric, and very in-the-know. They also provide browsers with a window to New York's hipper subcultures.

Bleecker Bob's Golden Oldies (118 W. 3rd St., tel. 212/475–9677). The staff sells punk, new wave, progressive rock, reggae, and R&B until the wee hours.

Footlight Records (113 E. 12th St., tel. 212/533–1572). Stop here to browse through New York's largest selection of old and new musicals and movie soundtracks, as well as a good choice of jazz and popular recordings.

Gryphon Record Shop (251 W. 72nd St., 2nd Floor, tel. 212/874–1588). *New York* magazine called this the city's best rare-record store, citing its 40,000 out-of-print and rare LPs.

HMV (2081 Broadway at 72nd St., tel. 212/721–5900; 1280 Lexington Ave. at 86th St., tel. 212/348–0800). These state-of-the-art record superstores stock 800,000 discs, tapes, and videos.

House of Oldies (35 Carmine St., tel. 212/243–0500). The specialty here is records made between 1950 and the present—45s and 78s, as well as LPs; there are more than a million titles.

Jazz Record Center (236 W. 26th St., 8th Floor, tel. 212/675–4480). Here is the city's only jazz-record specialist.

J&R Music World (23 Park Row, tel. 212/732–8600). This store offers a huge selection with good prices on major releases. Jazz recordings are sold at 25 Park Row, classical at No. 33.

Midnight Records (263 W. 23rd St., tel. 212/675–2768). This rare-rock specialist stocks obscure artists from the '50s on.

Tower Records (692 Broadway at 4th St., tel. 212/505–1500; 1961 Broadway at 66th St., tel. 212/799–2500; 1535 3rd Ave. at 87th St., tel. 212/369–2500). The selection of CDs and tapes can get overwhelming here. The scene is pure New York: At the Village branch, you'll see many customers in head-to-toe black; the Upper West Side outlet has good selection but more traditional clientele.

Children's Clothing **Bébé Thompson** (98 Thompson St., tel. 212/925–1122). Downtown style is evident here: plenty of black-and-white and jungle prints among the embroidered treasures. Look for sales.
Cerutti (807 Madison Ave., between 67th and 68th Sts., tel. 212/737–7540). This is where Nanny takes her Little Princess, and Yoko Ono shopped for Sean Lennon when he was a tyke.
Citykids (130 7th Ave., between 17th and 18th Sts., tel. 212/620–0906). This busy store carries colorful, fun clothing and accessories. Don't miss the hand-painted T-shirts and sweatshirts with New York themes.
Greenstones (442 Columbus Ave., between 81st and 82nd Sts., tel. 212/580–4322; 1124 Madison Ave., between 86th and 87th Sts., tel. 212/427–1665). Catering to junior yuppies, this store offers some handsome clothes, particularly sweaters.
Little Eric (1331 3rd Ave. at 76th St., tel. 212/288–8987; 1118 Madison Ave. at 83rd St., tel. 212/717–1513). Moms who love Eric can introduce their daughters to this happy footwear shop that's styled in an adult mode.
Oilily (870 Madison Ave., between 70th and 71st Sts., tel. 212/628–0100). A newcomer to these shores, this shop specializes in brightly colored play and school clothes that are designed in Holland.
Space Kiddets (46 E. 21st St., tel. 212/420–9878). Casual trendsetting clothes for kids are carried here.
Wicker Garden's Children (1327 Madison Ave., near 93rd St., tel. 212/410–7001). Top-of-the-line pretties for boys, girls, and babies are sold here.

Resale Shops **Once Upon A Time** (171 E. 92nd St., tel. 212/831–7619) and **Second Act Children's Wear** (1046 Madison Ave. at 80th St., tel. 212/988–2440) offer gently worn children's wear, sizes 0–14.

Crystal Three peerless sources are **Baccarat** (625 Madison Ave., between 58th and 59th Sts., tel. 212/826–4100); **Hoya Crystal Gallery** (450 Park Ave., between 56th and 57th Sts., tel. 212/223–6335); and **Steuben** (715 5th Ave. at 56th St., tel. 212/752–1441).

Food For food lovers, New York's gourmet specialty shops are a truly moveable feast: Much of the food can travel home with you.

Caviar **Macy's** and **Zabar's** (*see below*) feature good deals on caviars, especially when they're battling each other during their periodic "caviar wars." **Caviarteria** (502 Park Ave. at 59th St., tel. 212/759–7410) and **Petrossian** (182 W. 58th St., tel. 212/245–2217) are specialists.

Chocolate and Candy **Elk Candy Company** (240 E. 86th St., tel. 212/650–1177). This is a marzipan fantasy and a chocoholic's sweet dream.
Godiva Chocolatier (793 Madison Ave. at 67th St., tel. 212/249–9444; 701 5th Ave., between 54th and 55th Sts., tel. 212/593–2845; 560 Lexington Ave. at 50th St., tel. 212/980–9810; 33 Maiden La., tel. 212/514–6240). This famous maker features cleverly molded chocolates—and embossed gold boxes. Godiva has other locations on Columbus Avenue and Park Avenue, as well as in 30 Rockefeller Center and the World Financial Center.
La Maison du Chocolat (25 E. 73rd St., tel. 212/744–7117). This is the New York branch of the famous Parisian chocolatier, whose bon-

bons have been described in *Vogue* as "the most refined and subtle in the world."

Li-Lac Chocolates (120 Christopher St., tel. 212/242–7374). This charming nook feeds the Village's sweet tooth with homemade selections in the French tradition.

Neuchatel Chocolates (2 W. 59th St., in the Plaza Hotel, tel. 212/751–7742; 55 E. 52nd St., in Park Avenue Plaza between Park and Madison, tel. 212/759–1388). Velvety chocolates come in five dozen varieties here—all made in New York to approximate the Swiss chocolates.

Teuscher Chocolates (620 5th Ave., in Rockefeller Ctr., tel. 212/246–4416; 25 E. 61st St., tel. 212/751–8482). Fabulous chocolates made in Switzerland are flown in weekly for sale in these jewel-box shops, newly decorated each season.

Coffee **Empire Coffee and Tea Company** (592 9th Ave., between 42nd and 43rd Sts., tel. 212/586–1717). The selection here numbers almost 90 different beans.

McNulty's Tea & Coffee Company (109 Christopher St., tel. 212/242–5351). Antique wood paneling says "Old New York"—indeed, this is the city's oldest coffee and tea emporium. The barrels of beans say "Timor," "Java," and "New Guinea."

Oren's Daily Roast (434 3rd Ave. at 31st St., tel. 212/779–1241, and other locations). Choose from a huge selection of exotic—and prosaic—coffees, teas, and mugs.

Porto Rico Importing Company (201 Bleecker St., tel. 212/477–5421; 40½ St. Marks Pl., tel. 212/533–1982). This dark, old-fashioned, and highly aromatic store, a local coffee source since 1907, now has an East Village branch.

Sensuous Bean (66 W. 70th St., tel. 212/724–7725). Mocha meets such flavors as banana, peach, and orange.

Gourmet **Balducci's** (424 6th Ave. at 9th St., tel. 212/673–2600). In this former
Markets mom-and-pop food shop, now one of the city's finest food stores, mounds of baby carrots keep company with frilly lettuce, feathery dill, and superlative meats, fish, cheeses, chocolates, baked goods, pastas, vinegars, oils, and Italian specialties.

Dean & DeLuca (560 Broadway at Prince St., tel. 212/431–1691). This huge SoHo trendsetter, splendidly bright white, has an encyclopedic selection, from the heady array at the cheese counter to the shelves of crackers and the display cases of prepared foods.

Kam-Man (200 Canal St., tel. 212/571–0330). The city's premier Chinese market, Kam-Man is filled with exotic foods, the staccato sound of Chinese, and mysterious smells.

Zabar's (2245 Broadway at 80th St., tel. 212/787–2000). Enjoy the atmosphere of one of New York's favorite food markets. Dried herbs and spices, chocolates, and assorted bottled foods are downstairs, along with a fragrant jumble of fresh breads and the cheese, meat, and smoked-fish counters. Upstairs is one of New York's largest selections of kitchenware.

Spices **Adriana's Bazaar** (2152 Broadway at 75th St., tel. 212/877–5757). The fact that this store offers more than 25 chilis should tell you something about its vast spice inventory.

Pete's Spice & Everthing Nice (174 1st Ave. near 11th St., tel. 212/254–8773). Everything from anise to zathar can be found in this hot spot.

Wine **Acker Merrall & Condit** (160 W. 72nd St., tel. 212/787–1700). Known for its selection of red burgundies, this store has knowledgeable, helpful personnel.

Garnet Wines & Liquors (929 Lexington Ave., between 68th and

American Express offers Travelers Cheques built for two.

Cheques *for Two*℠ from American Express are the Travelers Cheques that allow either of you to use them because both of you have signed them. And only one of you needs to be present to purchase them.

Cheques *for Two* are accepted anywhere regular American Express Travelers Cheques are, which is just about everywhere. So stop by your bank, AAA* or any American Express Travel Service Office and ask for Cheques *for Two*.

© 1994 American Express Travel Related Services Company, Inc. *Available at participating clubs.

Pack light.
Take the one number you need for any kind of call, anywhere you travel.

Checking in with your family back home? Calling for a tow truck? When you're on the road, the phone you use might not accept your calling card. Or you might get overcharged by an unknown telephone company. Here's the solution: dial 1 800 CALL ATT.ˢᵐ You'll get flawless AT&T service, competitive calling card prices, and the lowest prices for collect calls from any phone, anywhere. Travel light. Just bring along this one simple number: 1 800 CALL ATT.

©1994 AT&T

69th Sts., tel. 212/772–3211). Its fine selection includes champagne at prices that one wine writer called "almost charitable."

Morrell & Company (535 Madison Ave., near 54th St., tel. 212/688–9370). Peter Morrell is a well-regarded and very colorful figure in the wine business; his store reflects his expertise.

Sherry-Lehmann (679 Madison Ave., between 61st and 62nd Sts., tel. 212/838–7500). It's a New York institution.

Sokolin (178 Madison Ave., between 33rd and 34th Sts., tel. 212/532–5893). Knowledgeable oenophiles have been shopping here for 50 years.

Fun and Games These are stores by adults, for adults, but with such humor and whimsy that kids will like them, too.

Compleat Strategist (11 E. 33rd St., tel. 212/685–3880; 320 W. 57th St., tel. 212/582–1272). All kinds of strategy games are supplied for the serious enthusiast.

Darts Unlimited (30 E. 20th St., tel. 212/533–8684). Exquisitely crafted English darts and boards are sold here.

Flosso Hornmann (45 W. 34th St., tel. 212/279–6079). This modest magic shop offers museum-class memorabilia, including a hand-painted crate used by Harry Houdini.

Game Show (474 6th Ave., between 11th and 12th Sts., tel. 212/633–6328; 1240 Lexington Ave., between 83rd and 84th Sts., tel. 212/472–8011). The mix here includes board games, box games, and card games.

Little Rickie (49½ 1st Ave. at 3rd St., tel. 212/505–6467). This fun spot is packed with wacky novelties and vintage treasures that baby-boomers remember from childhood.

Louis Tannen Inc. (6 W. 32nd St., 4th Floor, tel. 212/239–8383). You'll find sword chests, dove-a-matics, magic wands, and crystal balls, not to mention the all-important top hats with rabbits, at this six-decades-old magicians' supply house.

Marion & Company (147 W. 26th St., tel. 212/727–8900). Playing cards come in all shapes and sizes here.

Only Hearts (386 Columbus Ave., between 78th and 79th Sts., tel. 212/724–5608). Romance is the theme. Heart-shaped waffle irons, anyone?

Star Magic (745 Broadway, between 8th St. and Astor Pl., tel. 212/228–7770; 275 Amsterdam Ave. at 73rd St., tel. 212/769–2020; 500 Lexington Ave., between 47th and 48th Sts., tel. 212/888–1921; 1256 Lexington Ave., between 84th and 85th Sts., tel. 212/988–0300). Astronomy meets New Age in a clutter of crystals, star charts, and other celestial playthings.

Think Big! (390 W. Broadway, between Broome and Spring Sts., tel. 212/925–7300). Huge Pop Art–like replicas of various ordinary objects stock this amusing store.

Uncle Futz (408 Amsterdam Ave. at 79th St., tel. 212/799–6723; 1054 Lexington Ave. at 75th St., tel. 212/535–4686). These delicious toy shops are crammed with supercool puzzles, board games, and souped-up yo-yos.

Gizmos and Whatchamacallits **Hammacher Schlemmer** (147 E. 57th St., tel. 212/421–9000). The store that offered America its first pop-up toaster, the automatic steam iron, telephone answering machine, and microwave oven still ferrets out the outrageous, the unusual, and the best-of-kind.

Sharper Image (Pier 17, South St. Seaport, tel. 212/693–0477; 4 W. 57th St., tel. 212/265–2550; 900 Madison Ave., between 72nd and 73rd Sts., tel. 212/794–4974). This retail outlet of the catalogue company stocks gifts for the pampered executive who has everything.

Home Decor and Gifts

Aris Mixon & Company (381 Amsterdam Ave., between 78th and 79th Sts., tel. 212/724–6904). The intrigue here is in the mix of newly manufactured, handmade, and antique.

Avventura (463 Amsterdam Ave., at 82nd St., tel. 212/769–2510). Glory in Italian design in all its streamlined beauty here. Tabletop items and accessories are all stunning.

Bed, Bath & Beyond (620 6th Ave., between 19th and 20th Sts., tel. 212/255–3550). This huge Chelsea emporium has 11 sections of household items at reasonable prices.

Be Seated (66 Greenwich Ave., near 11th St., tel. 212/924–8444). Manhattan's source for African and Asian basketwork is redolent of rattan and raffia.

Charlotte Moss & Company (1027 Lexington Ave., between 73rd and 74th Sts., tel. 212/772–3320). Within what looks like a vine-wrapped, chintz-cozy English country house, you'll find English country-house-style treasures.

D. F. Sanders (952 Madison Ave. at 75th St., tel. 212/879–6161). The sleek, postmodern items on display at this design center are destined to be classics.

Gazebo (127 E. 57th St., tel. 212/832–7077). Quilts and wicker overflow this bastion of American style.

Jenny B. Goode (1194 Lexington Ave., between 80th and 81st Sts., tel. 212/794–2492). Charming china serving pieces and bibelots star.

Lexington Gardens (1011 Lexington Ave., between 72nd and 73rd Sts., tel. 212/861–4390). A favorite source for some of New York's top decorators, this delightful shop offers new and antique ornaments for both city terraces and country gardens, as well as distinctive arrangements of dried flowers.

Let There Be Neon (38 White St., between Broadway and Church St., tel. 212/226–4883). Browse among the terrific collection of new and antique neon signs, clocks, and tabletop accessories. (Open Sat. by appointment only.)

Mabel's (849 Madison Ave., between 70th and 71st Sts., tel. 212/734–3263). Enchanting animal lovers is the business of this Noah's Ark of knickknacks in animal shapes.

Mimi Russell Cloths (156 E. 64th St., tel. 212/838–1140). Done up like an Edwardian townhouse, this tasteful shop offers an exclusive line of fabrics that are at once contemporary and romantic. Also available are stools and slipper chairs covered in these same fabrics.

Miya Shoji (109 W. 17th St., tel. 212/243–6774). It offers a superb selection of beautifully crafted Japanese folding screens.

The Pillowry (132 E. 61st St., tel. 212/308–1630). The selection of decorative, one-of-a-kind pillows is vast. (Open weekday afternoons only; otherwise by appointment.)

Pottery Barn (117 E. 59th St., tel. 212/753–5424; 2109 Broadway, between 73rd and 74th Sts., tel. 212/595–5573; 250 W. 57th St., tel. 212/315–1855; 231 10th Ave., between 23rd and 24th Sts., tel. 212/206–8118; and five other locations). The emphasis here is on setting the table with reasonably priced, contemporary-style appointments. Overstocks are discounted at 10th Avenue.

Wolfman-Gold & Good Company (116 Greene St., tel. 212/431–1888). Half antique and half contemporary in spirit, this chic SoHo shop, a major New York trendsetter, is all white, with touches of blond wood and wicker. Tableware is the focus.

Zona (97 Greene St., tel. 212/925–6750). SoHo's airy, high-ceilinged bastion of the Southwestern look offers Solieri bells, earthtoned textiles, and terra-cottas, all artfully displayed.

Linens Luxurious linens enchant at **D. Porthault** (18 E. 69th St., tel. 212/688–1660), **E. Braun** (717 Madison Ave., between 63rd and 64th

Sts., tel. 212/838–0650), **Frette** (799 Madison Ave., between 67th and 68th Sts., tel. 212/988–5221), and **Pratesi** (829 Madison Ave. at 69th St., tel. 212/288–2315). Chic prevails at lower prices at **Ad Hoc Softwares** (410 W. Broadway at Spring St., tel. 212/925–2652) and **Descamps** (723 Madison Ave., between 63rd and 64th Sts., tel. 212/355–2522). Antique linens, including whimsically ruffled pillow shams, are at **Jana Starr/Jean Hoffman Antiques** (236 E. 80th St., tel. 212/861–8256). For bargains, check out the Lower East Side's dry-goods merchants (most on Grand St.) and **Century 21** (22 Cortlandt St., between Broadway and Church St., tel. 212/227–9092; 472 86th St., Bay Ridge, Brooklyn, tel. 718/748–3266).

Jewelry, Watches, and Silver

Most of the world's premier jewelers have retail outlets in New York, and the nation's jewelry wholesale center is on 47th Street.

A La Vieille Russie (781 5th Ave., between 59th and 60th Sts., tel. 212/752–1727). Stop here to behold bibelots by Fabergé and others, enameled or encrusted with jewels.

Asprey (725 5th Ave. at 56th St., tel. 212/688–1811). The only branch of the distinguished London jeweler, which holds three royal warrants, this store is just the place to go when seeking crystal, silver, leather goods or, perhaps, a brooch fit for a queen. The store is closed on Saturday during the summer.

Buccellati (46 E. 57th St., tel. 212/308–5533). The exquisite, Florentine-finish Italian jewelry here makes a statement; as does the silver.

Bulgari (730 5th Ave. at 57th St., tel. 212/315–9000; 2 E. 61st St., in the Pierre Hotel, tel. 212/486–0326). The expertly crafted jewelry here has an understated, tailored look.

Camilla Dietz Bergeron (116 E. 68th St., tel. 212/794–9100). Antique cufflinks here date back to the Roaring '20s. (Open by appointment only.)

Cartier (2 E. 52nd St., tel. 212/446–3400). Simple but superb pieces are displayed in the former mansion of the late yachtsman and society king Morton F. Plant.

David Webb (445 Park Ave. at 57th St., tel. 212/421–3030) features gem-studded pieces, often enameled and in animal forms.

Fortunoff (681 5th Ave., between 53rd and 54th Sts., tel. 212/758–6660). Good prices on gold and silver jewelry, flatware, and hollowware draw crowds to this large store.

Harry Winston (718 5th Ave. at 56th St., tel. 212/245–2000). The moneyed clientele here appreciates this store's oversize stones and impeccable quality.

H. Stern (645 5th Ave., between 50th and 51st Sts., tel. 212/688–0300). Gemstones in contemporary settings are the specialty of this Brazilian firm.

James Robinson (480 Park Ave. at 58th St., tel. 212/752–6166). This family-owned business features wonderful new and antique silver, fine estate jewelry, and table accessories.

Jean Silversmiths (16 W. 45th St., tel. 212/575–0723). Where to replace the butter knife missing from your great-aunt's set? Try this dusty, crowded shop.

Tiffany & Co. (727 5th Ave. at 57th St., tel. 212/755–8000). A shiny robin's-egg-blue box from this venerable New York jeweler announces the contents as something very special. Along with the $80,000 platinum-and-diamond bracelets, there is a great deal that's affordable on a whim.

Van Cleef & Arpels (744 5th Ave. at 57th St., tel. 212/644–9500). The jewelry here is sheer perfection.

Costume Jewelry Fabulously faux wares can be found at **Ciro** (694 5th Ave., between 54th and 55th Sts., tel. 212/247–0927, and other locations) and **Kenneth Jay Lane** (677 5th Ave., between 53rd and 54th Sts., tel. 212/750–2858). Jewelry inspired by Etruscan, Renaissance, and Baroque designs is the specialty of **Jaded** (24 W. 57th St., between 5th and 6th Aves., tel. 212/956–5757; 1048 Madison Ave., near 80th St., tel. 212/288–6631).

Luggage and Leather Goods **Altman Luggage** (135 Orchard St., between Delancey and Rivington Sts., tel. 212/254–7275). Come here for reasonably priced leather items.

Bottega Veneta (635 Madison Ave., between 59th and 60th Sts., tel. 212/371–5511). The superb Italian goods here are for people who know real quality.

Crouch & Fitzgerald (400 Madison Ave. at 48th St., tel. 212/755–5888). Since 1839, this store has offered a terrific selection in hard- and soft-sided luggage, plus handbags.

Fine & Klein (119 Orchard St., tel. 212/674–6720). Fabulous handbags are discounted here.

Lederer Leather Goods (613 Madison Ave. at 58th St., tel. 212/355–5515). The excellent selection here includes exotic skins.

North Beach Leather (772 Madison Ave. at 66th St., tel. 212/772–0707). High-fashion leather wear comes in many colors here.

T. Anthony (445 Park Ave. at 56th St., tel. 212/750–9797). This store's hard- and soft-sided luggage of coated fabric with leather trim has brass fasteners that look like precision machines.

Menswear **Alfred Dunhill of London** (450 Park Ave. at 57th St., tel. 212/753–9292). Corporate brass comes here for finely tailored clothing, both ready-made and custom-order, and smoking accessories; the walk-in humidor stores top-quality tobacco and cigars.

Brooks Brothers (346 Madison Ave. at 44th St., tel. 212/682–8800). An American-menswear institution, with conservative styles and fine tailoring.

Façonnable (689 5th Ave. at 54th St., tel. 212/319–0111). Designed in France, the well-made traditional clothing and sportswear has an international appeal.

Frank Stella Ltd. (440 Columbus Ave. at 81st St., tel. 212/877–5566; 1388 6th Ave., between 56th and 57th Sts., tel. 212/757–2295). Classic clothing with subtle variations is offered here.

J. Press (16 E. 44th St., tel. 212/687–7642). This store emphasizes the oxford-cloth shirt, natural-shoulder suit, madras-patch Bermuda shorts, and amusing club tie.

Paul Smith (108 5th Ave. at 16th St., tel. 212/627–9770). Dark mahogany Victorian cases display downtown styles.

Paul Stuart (Madison Ave. at 45th St., tel. 212/682–0320). The fabric selection is interesting, the tailoring superb, and the look traditional but not stodgy.

Saint Laurie, Ltd. (897 Broadway, between 19th and 20th Sts., tel. 212/473–0100). This family-owned business sells suits manufactured on the premises in styles ranging from the boxy to the Italianate in lovely fabrics.

Discounts New York men looking for bargains rely on **BFO** (149 5th Ave. at 21st St., tel. 212/254–0059); **Eisenberg and Eisenberg** (85 5th Ave. at 16th St., tel. 212/627–1290); **Moe Ginsburg** (162 5th Ave. at 21st St., tel. 212/242–3482); **Rothman's** (200 Park Ave. S at 17th St., tel. 212/777–7400); and **Syms** (42 Trinity Pl., tel. 212/797–1199; cash or store credit card only).

Men's Hats **Worth & Worth** (331 Madison Ave. at 43rd St., tel. 212/867–6058). Come here for elegant handmade headwear—everything from driving caps to fedoras.

Men's Shoes **Billy Martin's** (812 Madison Ave. at 68th St., tel. 212/861–3100). Quality hand-tooled and custom-made boots are carried here.

Church's English Shoes (428 Madison Ave. at 49th St., tel. 212/755–4313). This store has been selling beautifully made English shoes since 1873.

Shoe Express (1420 2nd Ave. at 74th St., tel. 212/734–3967). The stylish selection includes rugged classics, western-style boots, and name-brand dress shoes.

Tip Top (155 W. 72nd St., tel. 212/787–4960). You'll find comfortable walking shoes and sandals here.

To Boot (256 Columbus Ave., between 71st and 72nd Sts., tel. 212/724–8249). Here you'll find stylish shoes and boots for a more fashionable business look.

Tootsie Plohound (413 W. Broadway, between Prince and Spring Sts., tel. 212/925–8931). This shop is tops in "downtown" shoes: fun, funky, and cool. It carries women's styles, too.

Needlecraft *Fabric* Seamstresses prize the selection and prices at shops in the upper 30s and on 40th Street, between Broadway and 8th Avenue, such as **K&M** (250 W. 39th St., tel. 212/354–9360). Luxurious imports fill **Jerry Brown** (37 W. 57th St., tel. 212/753–3626), **Paron Fabrics** (60 W. 57th St., tel. 212/247–6451), **Paron Fabrics West** (239 W. 39th St., tel. 212/768–3266), which discounts remnants, and **Weller** (24 W. 57th St., tel. 212/247–3790). Good buys can be had at the fabric shops on Orchard Street between Delancey and Houston streets.

Trimming Dingy 38th Street between 5th and 6th avenues is a treasure chest. Jewels include **Hyman Hendler & Sons** (67 W. 38th St., tel. 212/840–8393), the ribbon king, since 1900; and **Tinsel Trading** (47 W. 38th St., tel. 212/730–1030), for new and antique trims and tassels. Nearby **M & J Trimming** (1008 6th Ave. near 37th St., tel. 212/391–9072) stocks more than 100 styles of tassels and tiebacks. Uptown, buttons overflow the charming **Tender Buttons** (143 E. 62nd St., tel. 212/758–7004).

Yarns **Erica Wilson** (717 Madison Ave., between 63rd and 64th Sts., 2nd Floor, tel. 212/832–7290). The eponymous British-born needlepoint authority is a top resource.

Pamela Duval (833 Lexington Ave., between 63rd and 64th Sts., tel. 212/751–2126). Look for the needlepoint canvases with funny quotations.

Wallis Mayers Needlework (30 E. 68th St., tel. 212/861–5318). Have fun choosing among oodles of yarns and offbeat hand-painted canvases here.

Yarn Center (1011 6th Ave., between 37th and 38th Sts., 2nd Floor, tel. 212/719–5648). There's a huge selection of yarns here to suit many purposes.

Paper, Greeting Cards, Stationery **Dempsey & Carroll** (110 E. 57th St., tel. 212/486–7526). Supplying New York's high society for a century, this firm is always correct but seldom straitlaced.

Kate's Paperie (561 Broadway, near Prince St., tel. 212/941–9816; 8 W. 13th St., tel. 212/633–0570). This wonderful spot features fabulous wrapping papers, some handmade; bound blank books; and more.

Untitled (159 Prince St., tel. 212/982–2088). The stock here includes thousands of tasteful greeting cards and postcards.

Performing Arts Memorabilia

The Ballet Shop (1887 Broadway, between 62nd and 63rd Sts., tel. 212/581–7990). This balletomane's delight near Lincoln Center showcases dance ephemera and artifacts.

Drama Book Shop (723 7th Ave., between 48th and 49th Sts., tel. 212/944–0595). The comprehensive stock here includes scripts, scores, and libretti.

Motion Picture Arts Gallery (133 E. 58th St., 10th Floor, tel. 212/223–1009). Vintage posters enchant collectors here.

Movie Star News (134 W. 18th St., tel. 212/620–8160). The film memorabilia emphasizes Hollywood glamour.

One Shubert Alley (Shubert Alley, between 44th and 45th Sts. west of Broadway, tel. 212/944–4133). Souvenirs from past and present Broadway hits reign at this Theater District shop.

Paper Collectibles (126 E. 12th St., basement, tel. 212/473–2404). The variety ranges from movie posters and stills to back-date magazines and vintage toys.

Richard Stoddard (18 E. 16th St., Room 305, tel. 212/645–9576). This veteran dealer offers out-of-print books, back issues of magazines, old programs, and other printed matter.

Triton Gallery (323 W. 45th St., between 8th and 9th Aves., tel. 212/765–2472). Theatrical posters large and small can be found here for hits and flops.

Posters

Chisholm Prats Gallery (145 8th Ave., between 17th and 18th Sts., tel. 212/741–1703). European posters from the 1920s and '30s as well as European film posters fill the quarters of this Chelsea dealer near the Joyce Theatre.

Poster America (138 W. 18th St., tel. 212/206–0499). Original advertising posters dating from 1915 to 1965 and vintage photographs are displayed in this renovated carriage house, the country's oldest store of its type.

Souvenirs of New York City

Ordinary Big Apple souvenirs can be found in and around major tourist attractions. More unusual items can be found at:

Accent New York (489 5th Ave., between 41st and 42nd Sts., tel. 212/599–3661). This store features every possible variation of the New York souvenir T-shirt, mug, key chain, and so on.

Citybooks (61 Chambers St., tel. 212/669–8245). Come here for calendars, maps, books, seals, subway-token tietacks, traffic signs ("Don't Even Think of Parking Here"), Sanitation Department T-shirts, and teddy bears. The store is closed on weekends.

New York Bound Bookshop (50 Rockefeller Plaza, tel. 212/245–8503). Old or rare New York books and prints are the specialty in this delightfully knowledgeable store.

Think New York (875 7th Ave., between 55th and 56th Sts., tel. 212/957–8511). Here you'll find New York City landmarks featured on mugs, aprons, and many other objects, some surprising and unusual.

Transit Museum Gift Shop (Grand Central Terminal, main concourse, near Vanderbilt Ave. entrance, tel. 212/682–7572). Coffee mugs, T-shirts, and other items emblazoned with the transit system logos are the stock in trade here, along with banks in the form of city buses, motormen's hats, and jewelry made out of old subway tokens.

Toys

Many toy companies are headquartered here, and the windows of the Toy Center at 23rd Street and 5th Avenue display the latest thing, especially during February's Toy Week, when all the out-of-town buyers come to place orders for the Christmas season (*see also* Fun and Games, *above*).

Big City Kite Co. (1201 Lexington Ave. at 81st St., tel. 212/472–2623). Kites of all sizes and shapes are found here.

Enchanted Forest (85 Mercer St., tel. 212/925–6677). Fancy reigns in this shop's stock of unique handmades.

F.A.O. Schwarz (767 5th Ave. at 58th St., tel. 212/644–9400). You will be hooked on this sprawling two-level children's store from the minute you walk through the door and one of the costumed staff members—a donkey, a clown, a cave woman, or a mad scientist—extends a welcome. Beyond a wonderful mechanical clock with many dials and dingbats are all the stuffed animals in the world, dolls large and small, things to build with (including blocks by the pound), computer games, toy cars (including a multi-thousand-dollar Ferrari), and more.

Penny Whistle Toys (132 Spring St., tel. 212/925–2088; 448 Columbus Ave., between 81st and 82nd Sts., tel. 212/873–9090; 1283 Madison Ave., between 91st and 92nd Sts., tel. 212/369–3868). Meredith Brokaw, wife of TV anchorman Tom Brokaw, has developed an intriguing selection of quality toys here.

West Side Kids (498 Amsterdam Ave. at 84th St., tel. 212/496–7282). The shrewd selection here mixes educational toys with a grab bag of fun little playthings.

Dolls and Miniatures **Dollhouse Antics** (1343 Madison Ave. at 94th St., tel. 212/876–2288). This is a miniaturist's paradise, with infinitesimal accessories such as a small *New York Times*.

Iris Brown's Victorian Doll and Miniature Shop (253 E. 57 St., tel. 212/593–2882.) A sweet, knowledgeable owner presides over the antique dolls, dollhouses, and miniatures.

Trains and Models Railroad aficionados will be dazzled by the vast selections at: **America's Hobby Center** (146 W. 22nd St., tel. 212/675–8922); **Red Caboose** (16 W. 45th St., 4th Floor, tel. 212/575–0155); and **Train Shop** (23 W. 45th St., basement level, tel. 212/730–0409).

Umbrellas and Canes **Stanley Novak** (115 W. 30th St., Room 400, tel. 212/947–8466). The cane's the thing, and there are hundreds here.

Uncle Sam Umbrella (161 W. 57th St., tel. 212/247–7163). The city's top umbrella dealer offers both basics and oddball stuff.

Women's Clothing The department stores' collections are always good: **Saks** for its designers; **Macy's** for its breadth; **Bloomingdale's** for its extremes; **Barneys, Galleries Lafayette,** and **Henri Bendel** for their trendy chic; and **Lord & Taylor** for its classicism. **Bergdorf Goodman** offers a range from updated classics to up-to-the-minute, all of the highest quality. The following add another dimension.

Classicists **Ann Taylor** (2017 Broadway, near 69th St., tel. 212/873–7344; 25 Fulton St., tel. 212/608–5600; 805 3rd Ave. at 50th St., tel. 212/308–5333; 3 E. 57th St., tel. 212/832–2010; and other locations). These stores provide what the elegant young woman with a sense of style needs for work and play.

Burberry's (9 E. 57th St., tel. 212/371–5010). The look is classic and conservative—and nobody does a better trench coat.

Designer Showcases **Betsey Johnson** (130 Thompson St., tel. 212/420–0169; 251 E. 60th St., tel. 212/319–7699; 248 Columbus Ave., between 71st and 72nd Sts., tel. 212/362–3364; 1060 Madison Ave., between 80th and 81st Sts., tel. 212/734–1257). The look here is still hip and quirky.

Chanel (5 E. 57th St., tel. 212/355–5050). The classic designs here never go out of style; neither do those wonderful Chanel perfumes.

Comme des Garçons (116 Wooster St., tel. 212/219–0660). This SoHo shop showcases a Japanese designer.

Emanuel Ungaro (803 Madison Ave., between 67th and 68th Sts., tel. 212/249–4090). The style here is body-conscious, but it's never flashy.

Emporio Armani (110 5th Ave., between 16th and 17th Sts., tel. 212/727–3240). The Italian designer's casual line is featured.

Geoffrey Beene (783 5th Ave., between 58th and 59th Sts., tel. 212/935–0470). A splendid-looking boutique houses exquisite day and evening wear by America's master designer.

Gianni Versace (817 Madison Ave., between 68th and 69th Sts., tel. 212/744–6868). An Italian maestro of color and form continues to dazzle with his daring.

Giorgio Armani (815 Madison Ave., between 67th and 68th Sts., tel. 212/988–9191). In this lofty blond-and-beige space with grand, arched windows and doors, Armani's high-end line looks oh-so-chic.

Givenchy (954 Madison Ave. at 75th St., tel. 212/772–1040). This designer is famous for timeless elegance.

Hermès (11 E. 57th St., tel. 212/751–3181). Patterned silk scarves and the so-called "Kelly" handbags are hallmarks.

Louis Feraud (3 W. 56th St., tel. 212/956–7010). An artist as well as a couturier, his deft hand is seen in the superb cut and colorations of well-tailored clothes at the only free-standing boutique bearing his name in North America.

Matsuda (156 5th Ave., between 20th and 21st Sts., tel. 212/645–5151; 465 Park Ave. at 57th St., tel. 212/935–6969). Kudos go out for wonderful cuts and fine muted hues.

Missoni (836 Madison Ave. at 69th St., tel. 212/517–9339). Wonderfully textured knits, suits, and sportswear stand out.

Nicole Miller (780 Madison Ave., between 66th and 67th Sts., tel. 212/288–9779). Sexy and colorful, these clothes for a woman by a woman are spirited and sassy.

Norma Kamali O.M.O. (11 W. 56th St., tel. 212/957–9797). The look here ranges from sweatshirts to evening gowns.

Polo/Ralph Lauren (867 Madison Ave. at 72nd St., tel. 212/606–2100). Lauren's flagship store is one of New York's most distinctive shopping experiences, in a grand, carefully renovated turn-of-the-century town house. The new **Polo Sport** is directly across the street.

Sonia Rykiel (792 Madison Ave. at 67th St., tel. 212/744–0880). Signature knits for day and evening pack the racks.

Valentino (823 Madison Ave., between 68th and 69th Sts., tel. 212/744–0200). The mix here is at once audacious and beautifully cut, with the best of France and Italy on its racks.

Vera Wang (991 Madison Ave. at 77th St., tel. 212/628–3400). Sumptuous, made-to-order bridal and evening wear is shown here by appointment only. Their periodic prêt-à porter sales offer designer dresses for a (relative) song.

Yohji Yamamoto (103 Grand St., tel. 212/966–9066). Severe, beautifully cut fashions come from fashion's Zen master.

Yves St. Laurent Rive Gauche 859 Madison Ave., between 70th and 71st Sts., tel. 212/517–7400). The looks range from chic to classic for day and evening.

Discount **Aaron's** (627 5th Ave. at 17th St., Park Slope, Brooklyn, tel. 718/768–5400). If your taste runs to expensive labels, you'll appreciate the significant savings. You'll have your own salesperson assigned to you, and there's free parking in the store's lot. Even if you don't have a car, it's worth calling for subway directions.

Bolton's (225 E. 57th St., tel. 212/755–2527; other locations). The styles won't stop traffic, but you can count on finding basics at moderate prices.

Century 21 (22 Cortlandt St., between Broadway and Church St., tel. 212/227–9092; 472 86th St., Bay Ridge, Brooklyn, tel. 718/748–3266). Spiffy quarters make bargain-hunting a pleasure, and there are fabulous buys on very high fashion. Note that there are no try-ons, but items may be returned within 12 working days after purchase.

Daffy's (111 5th Ave. at 18th St., tel. 212/529–4477; 335 Madison Ave. at 44th St., tel. 212/557–4422). Cheap stuff is priced cheaper, and pricey stuff is marked way down. Only for the most patient, indefatigable shopper.

Forman's (82 Orchard St., tel. 212/228–2500). This is an unexpectedly attractive longtime mainstay of the Lower East Side.

Loehmann's (236th St. and Broadway, the Bronx, tel. 718/543–6420). The flagship store of this premier off-price outlet is an institution among shopaholics. Other New York stores are located in Queens and Brooklyn.

S&W (165 W. 26th St., tel. 212/924–6656). Prices here are good to great on coats, suits, shoes, handbags, and accessories.

Ethnic Looks **Handblock** (860 Lexington Ave., between 64th and 65th Sts., tel. 212/570–1816; 487 Columbus Ave., between 83rd and 84th Sts., tel. 212/799–4342). In addition to the frocks in Provençal, African, and Indian prints, the stores carry table and bed linens in similar fabrics. The color combinations here are luscious.

Putumayo (857 Lexington Ave., between 64th and 65th Sts., tel. 212/734–3111; 341 Columbus Ave., between 76th and 77th Sts., tel. 212/595–3441; 147 Spring St., tel. 212/966–4458). There's cool cotton clothing here, much of it crinkly and easy to pack.

Hip Styles **A/X: Armani Exchange** (568 Broadway near Prince St., tel. 212/431–6000). Here's Giorgio Armani's answer to the Gap—with a sleek European touch and a higher price tag.

Canal Jean (504 Broadway, between Spring and Broome Sts., tel. 212/226–1130). Casual funk draws hip shoppers.

The Limited (691 Madison Ave. at 62nd St., tel. 212/838–8787). Considering the address, prices are moderate for well-styled though not outrageous clothing, much of it casual.

Limited Express (7 W. 34th St., tel. 212/629–6838; and other locations). Mass-market chic includes great leggings, sweaters, and microscopic dresses—all with a Gallic accent.

Reminiscence (74 5th Ave., between 13th and 14th Sts., tel. 212/243–2292). The theme is strictly '50s and '60s, in vintage and new clothing.

Trash and Vaudeville (4 St. Marks Pl., tel. 212/982–3590). Black, white, and electric colors are the focus here.

Women's Workout Gear (121 7th Ave., between 17th and 18th Sts., tel. 212/627–1117). Come here for exercise wear in all colors.

Lingerie Exquisite little things in silk and lace, both naughty and nice, are found at **Joovay** (436 W. Broadway, tel. 212/431–6386); **Montenapoleone** (789 Madison Ave. at 67th St., tel. 212/535–2660); and **Victoria's Secret** (34 E. 57th St., tel. 212/758–5592).

Romantics **Laura Ashley** (21 E. 57th St., tel. 212/752–7300; 398 Columbus Ave. at 79th St., tel. 212/496–5110). Old-fashioned English frocks abound here. There's a small branch at the South Street Seaport.

Trendsetters **Agnès B.** (116 Prince St., tel. 212/925–4649). This Euro-style boutique has maintained its SoHo popularity for several years.

Charivari (2315 Broadway, between 83rd and 84th Sts., tel. 212/873–1424). Since Selma Weiser founded this store on the Upper West Side, she has made a name for herself internationally for her eagle eye on the up-and-coming and avant-garde. The branches, too, take a high-style approach: **Charivari Sport** (201 W. 79th St., tel. 212/799–8650); **Charivari Workshop** (441 Columbus Ave. at 81st St., tel. 212/496–8700); **Charivari 72** (58 W. 72nd St., tel. 212/787–7272); **Charivari 57** (18 W. 57th St., tel. 212/333–4040); and **Charivari on Madison** (1001 Madison Ave. at 77th St., tel. 212/650–0078).

Patricia Field (10 E. 8th St., tel. 212/254–1699). This store collects the essence of the downtown look.

Vintage **Harriet Love** (126 Prince St., tel. 212/966–2280). This is the doyenne of the city's vintage clothing scene.

Screaming Mimi's (382 Lafayette St., between 4th and Great Jones Sts., tel. 212/677–6464). Vintage clothes and the avant-garde go together here.

Women's **Manolo Blahnik** (15 E. 55th St., tel. 212/582–3007). It's possibly the
Shoes hautest—and costliest—footwear in town, by England's top shoe
Designer Shoes designer.

Maud Frizon (19 E. 69th St., tel. 212/249–5368). These extravagant styles come in outrageous shapes and sizzling colors.

Peter Fox (105 Thompson St., tel. 212/431–7426 and 212/431–6359; 378 Amsterdam Ave. at 78th St., tel. 212/874–6399). Looks here are outside the fashion mainstream—really fun.

Robert Clergerie (41 E. 60 St., tel. 212/207–8600). Exquisite, high-style French footwear includes the chicest platform sandals imaginable.

Salvatore Ferragamo (725 5th Ave. at 56th St., tel. 212/759–3822). No stylistic gimmicks here, just beautiful shoemaking.

Susan Bennis Warren Edwards (22 W. 57th St., tel. 212/755–4197). Here you'll find alligator, silk, satin, suede, canvas, and buttery-soft leather exquisitely worked.

Tanino Crisci (795 Madison Ave., between 67th and 68th Sts., tel. 212/535–1014). Well-made shoes in classic styles and subtle variations of basic colors are the highlight here. All are made in Italy.

Discount and Discounters dot Reade Street between Church and West Broadway,
Lower-Price including **Anbar** (60 Reade St., tel. 212/227–0253). Several Orchard
Shoes Street stores discount uptown shoe styles; try **Lace-Up Shoes** (110 Orchard St., tel. 212/475–8040) for moderate discounts on very high-style shoes.

Moderately The shoes at these stores tend toward the classic, in a good range of
Priced Shoes colors and styles: **Ecco** (324 Columbus Ave., between 75th and 76th Sts., tel. 212/799–5229; 94 7th Ave., between 15th and 16th Sts., tel. 212/675–5180; 111 Thompson St., tel. 212/925–8010); **Galo** (825 Lexington Ave. at 63rd St., tel. 212/832–3922; 504 Madison Ave. at 52nd St., tel. 212/832–7150; 692 Madison Ave., between 62nd and 63rd Sts., tel. 212/688–6276); **Joan & David** (816 Madison Ave. at 68th St., tel. 212/772–3970; 104 5th Ave. at 16th St., tel. 212/627–1780); **Maraolo** (782 Lexington Ave., between 60th and 61st Sts., tel. 212/832–8182); **Ritz** (14 W. 8th St., between 5th and 6th Aves., tel. 212/228–5377; 505 Park Ave. at 59th St., tel. 212/838–2556); **Shoe Express** (1420 2nd Ave. at 74th St., tel. 212/734–3967); and **Vamps** (1421 2nd Ave. at 74th St., tel. 212/744–0227).

Secondhand Shops

Resale Shops To find top-of-the-line designs at secondhand prices, try: **Encore** (1132 Madison Ave., between 84th and 85th Sts., upstairs, tel. 212/879–2850); **Exchange Unlimited** (563 2nd Ave. at 31st St., tel. 212/889–3229); **Michael's Resale** (1041 Madison Ave., between 79th and 80th Sts., tel. 212/737–7273); and **Renate's** (235 E. 81st St., tel. 212/472–1698).

Thrift Shops Affluent New Yorkers donate castoffs to thrift shops run for charity. And, oh, such castoffs! Often they're supplemented by closeouts from major stores. Hours are limited, so call ahead.

Arthritis Foundation Thrift Shop (121 E. 77th St., tel. 212/772–8816).

Council Thrift Shop (767 9th Ave., between 51st and 52nd Sts., tel. 212/757–6132).

Everybody's Thrift Shop (261 Park Ave. S, between 20th and 21st Sts., tel. 212/355–9263).

Irvington Institute for Medical Research Thrift Shop (1534 2nd Ave. at 80th St., tel. 212/879–4555).

Memorial Sloan-Kettering Cancer Center Thrift Shop (1440 3rd Ave., between 81st and 82nd Sts., tel. 212/535–1250).

New York Hospital Auxiliary Thrift Shop (439 E. 71st St., tel. 212/535–0965).

Spence-Chapin Thrift Shop (1430 3rd Ave., between 81st and 82nd Sts., tel. 212/737–8448).

Auctions

New York's lively auction scene means regular sales from internationally known houses. Sales are advertised in the *New York Times*, particularly in Friday's "Weekend" and Sunday's "Arts & Leisure" sections. If you note a sale of interest, attend the exhibition to inspect the wares, peruse the catalogue, discuss possible payment methods, and find out whether you'll need a paddle for bidding.

Christie's (502 Park Ave. at 59th St., tel. 212/546–1000, 212/371–5438 for recorded schedules). This London firm, more than 200 years old, has had an American presence for more than a decade. The annex is **Christie's East** (219 E. 67th St., tel. 212/606–0400).

Sotheby's (1334 York Ave. at 72nd St., tel. 212/606–7000, 212/606–7245 for recorded schedules). This is Christie's chief rival, also originally from London. Check out the **Arcade** auctions, where interesting and well-priced also-rans go on the block.

William Doyle Galleries (175 E. 87th St., tel. 212/427–2730, 212/427–4885 for recorded schedules). The charismatic and amazingly energetic William Doyle has turned his instinct for accumulation into a major force on the New York auction scene.

Smaller houses include **Gotham Galleries** (80 4th Ave., between 10th and 11th Sts., tel. 212/677–3303); **Guernsey's** (108 E. 73rd St., tel. 212/794–2280); **Lubin Galleries** (30 W. 26th St., tel. 212/924–3777); **Swann Galleries** (104 E. 25th St., 6th Floor, tel. 212/254–4710); and **Tepper Galleries** (110 E. 25th St., tel. 212/677–5300).

Flea Markets

The season runs from March or April through November or December at most of these markets in school playgrounds and parking lots.

Annex Antiques Fair and Flea Market (6th Ave., between 25th and 26th Sts., tel. 212/243–5343), Saturday and Sunday.

The Garage (112 W. 25th St., between 6th and 7th Aves., tel. 212/463–0200). The newest flea market in town, this one is indoors, in a 23,000-square-foot, two-story former parking garage.

I.S. 44 Market (Columbus Ave., between 76th and 77th Sts., tel. 212/721–0900 evenings), Sunday.

P.S. 41 (Greenwich Ave. at Charles St.), Saturday.

P.S. 183 Market (67th St., between York and 1st Aves.), Saturday.

9 Dining

by J. Walman

Syndicated travel, food, and wine journalist J. Walman dispenses culinary advice to the 2 million listeners of WEVD-AM, writes regularly for Chocolatier, and is president of Punch In International Syndicate, an electronic publishing company specializing in travel, restaurants, entertainment, and wine.

There are better French restaurants in France and better Italian restaurants in Italy. While Paris boasts its Taillevent, London its Le Gavroche, and Brussels the Villa Lorraine, New York is conspicuously lacking a genuinely distinguished *grand luxe* restaurant, one that is glamorous and incredibly elegant, where food, wine, and service fulfill the promise of the decor. While seafood restaurants are improving, there are still precious few outstanding ones, given that the city is a port. And despite the prevalence of small Indian restaurants, their menus and spicing are painfully similar. Alas, the Spanish kitchen has never taken flight in Manhattan. As for Brazilian fare, an authentic *feijoada*, the stew of black beans with smoked meats, is better described on menus than executed in the kitchen. The city has lost all but one Czech restaurant and a handful of Hungarians.

Still, that international appendage to the United States known as the Big Apple supports more good restaurants, and more kinds of them, than any other city in the world; food is one of the city's joys. Its restaurant mix also has an idiosyncratic charm. Hotel dining rooms—which have resources to provide the professional service staff, fine china, comprehensive wine cellar, and top-flight kitchen required for serious dining—are increasingly common, with a life and often an entrance of their own. New York bistros and trattorias are as excellent as they are inexpensive and abundant. Star chefs such as Larry Forgione, Daniel Boulud, David Burke, and Gray Kunz have given the city a coterie of innovative kitchens, whose graduates have assured that even neighborhood eateries serve more than usually interesting fare.

New York's best eating is not limited to so-called tablecloth restaurants. For about the same price as a Big Whatever, you can experiment in dozens of Greek coffee shops where you can invariably find fresh salads and appetizing plates at modest prices. A strip of 1st Avenue north of 5th or 6th streets is full of small Polish restaurants where, for a song, you can consume a satisfying bowl of soup or dish of dumplings.

Such small ethnic eating spots are legend in New York, their mix constantly changing with shifting immigration patterns; countries like Afghanistan, Thailand, Turkey, and Jamaica are currently adding culinary breadth to the dining scene. There are more Chinese options than ever, and you must no longer endure rude service and dingy surroundings: Brightening today's Chinatown are noisy, gaudy eating emporiums in the Hong Kong style. Szechuan may be out but Cantonese home cooking is in, with its fresh ingredients and simple cooking. The Chinese tea lunch known as dim sum (meaning "odds and ends of food or snacks")—consisting of various dumplings, small cooked dishes, rice, noodles, puffs, balls, claws, you name it—is holding strong; point at what you want as trolleys bearing these delicacies wheel past your table. The next wave? Caribbean cuisine is hip. Even Spanish cuisine may eventually gain a foothold.

Bottom line? Take a chance. Not every venture will be a success. But the whole experience will be rewarding. That's a promise.

Planning Your Culinary Itinerary

In most great restaurant towns, there is generally one best restaurant; New York generously offers a variety of candidates. Times being what they are, top restaurants have short lives, chefs play musical kitchens, and today's star is often tomorrow's laggard. As in France, it's prudent to seek out restaurants on their way up, and approach celebrities with caution. Temper your visits to famous restaurants with informed selections from among lesser-knowns. Can a famous restaurant produce a really spectacular dinner? Probably. Will an unknown diner receive a great meal on the first visit to a fashionable restaurant? Probably not. Even in these recessionary times the snob snub is not dead. What about Siberia? You, too, will quickly learn the meaning of the Yiddish word chutzpah (as in "the nerve of the man") when you are led to the unappealing upstairs annex of a major restaurant after reserving a month in advance.

Our Selections We firmly believe that everybody should be treated like a somebody, and our recommendations consider the reception as well as the food, decor, service, and wines. When there are several restaurants of a genre, we choose the most interesting. Some famous restaurants, elsewhere held in high regard, have not captured our accolades; others are omitted because they treat guests shabbily or are poor value. This is the '90s, so you will also find a strong selection of inexpensive, moderately priced, and ethnic restaurants. To familiarize you with the kitchen's style, we also mention dishes we have sampled. Although menu changes may eliminate some of them, you should be able to find similar fare. Stars (★) highlight restaurants that offer outstanding experiences.

Wine New York won't disappoint on this score. Generally, the most expensive wines have the smallest markup, the middle of the price spectrum offers the best values, and the least expensive offerings are poor values if not what's known in the trade as mouthwash. Half bottles are hard to find. Increasingly common instead is wine by the glass; younger restaurants as well as a number of old-timers offer serious vintages at sensible prices. If the wine list is large, have an aperitif and take your time in ordering. Remember: You're the buyer. Note that many restaurants allow you to bring your own bottle, charging a service fee ranging from $5 to about $25.

Tipping Rules are simple. Never tip the maître d' unless you're out to impress your companion. In most restaurants, tip the waiter at least 15% to 20%. (To figure the amount quickly, just double the tax noted on the check—it's 8¼% of your bill—and round up or slightly down.)

In stylish establishments, give 5% to the captain, even if he did most of the work, and 15% to the waiter. To a busboy, a couple of dollars is appreciated but hardly expected. Give wine stewards about $5 per bottle, more if you order important wines that require decanting or other special services. Give the captain or sommelier his or her tip, palmed in your hand, with a friendly shake and a smile. Tip $1 per coat checked.

Prices New York gets a bum rap. Of course, you can order caviar and champagne or Bordeaux of great years; you will pay accordingly. But you will also do that in Nashville, Chicago, and Los Angeles. Our point is that each price stratum has its own equilibrium. Translation: $20 is only inexpensive if you get $20 of value, and $100 may be a bargain.

Category	Cost*
$$$$	over $60
$$$	$40–$59
$$	$20–$39
$	under $20

per person, excluding drinks, service, and sales tax (8¼%)

Restaurants marked with two prices ($–$$, for example) include both more modest restaurants where choosing the most expensive dishes can push your check into the next category as well as pricier restaurants where you can lower your tab by opting for the less expensive fare or choosing a prix fixe meal such as $19.95 lunches or dinners found in many New York restaurants. Brunches are also price-wise, although the menu that you go to the restaurant to enjoy may have been replaced by one that highlights egg dishes. If it matters, call before you make your plans. Most prix fixe menus don't include coffee and drinks.

Especially if you're watching your budget, always ask the price of specials, which have become a way for restaurants to charge higher-than-normal prices. Rather than being sensibly attached to the menu European-style, specials are often recited by the waiter without mention of cost. Ask.

Finally, always go over your bill. Mistakes do occur (and not always in the favor of the house).

Dress New York is relatively formal. "Casual" usually refers to the casual-trendy clothing you might see in *Vogue* or *GQ* rather than to the attire worn to country clubs or for hikes in the woods. Use common sense. Dress up for grand restaurants, casually for casual spots. Midtown is more conservative than residential neighborhoods, SoHo and TriBeCa trendier than the Upper East and Upper West Sides. Shorts are appropriate only in summer and in the most casual spots. When in doubt, call ahead.

Reservations Make a reservation. If you change your mind, cancel—it's only courteous. Tables can be hard to come by between 7 and 9; if a restaurant tells you that they can seat you only before 6 or after 10, you may decide that they don't need you. Or you may be persuaded that eating early or late is okay. Eating after a play or concert is quite common in New York, and there's no shortage of options then.

Smoking If you smoke, say so when reserving; local laws mandate smoker segregation. Also speak up if you prefer to sit in a certain area or if you want a certain table.

If you can't negotiate an acceptable arrangement, remember that there are always a plethora of palatable pinch hitters. As a New Yorker might say: "What do you feel like tonight? Chinese, Italian, pizza, pasta, French, Spanish, Greek, Japanese, Afghan, Korean, Thai, or Burmese...?"

Lower Manhattan

$$$
American-
Contemporary
★

Hudson River Club. Spacious and clubby, with river views and soft piano music, it improves with age. Always creative, chef Waldy Malouf celebrates Hudson River Valley produce with a talent that speaks for itself in his striped bass with fennel and roasted garlic, rabbit pot pie, and apple-smoked salmon napoleon with caviar. Desserts like the signature tower of chocolate—brownie, mousse, and meringue—are edible sculptures. The regional American wine list is superb; apart from the sometimes distant reception, the service is pleasant, if on occasion slow. *4 World Financial Center, tel. 212/786–1500. Reservations required. Jacket and tie required. AE, D, DC, MC, V. No lunch Sat.*

Le Pactole. The Hudson, which turns gold at night, makes a breathtaking backdrop to this refined restaurant, which boasts spacious seating, burnished cherry wood chairs, dramatic lighting, and live piano music. That executive chef Alain Quirin has energized the

Downtown Manhattan Dining

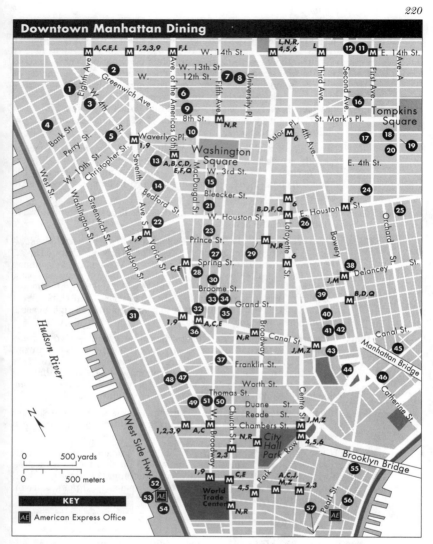

Arturo's, **21**

Au Mandarin, **53**

Ballato's, **26**

Boca Chica, **24**

Bondini, **9**

Barolo, **30**

Bouley, **49**

Bridge Café, **55**

Brother's Bar-B-Q, **22**

Café, **28**

Capsouto Frères, **31**

Chanterelle, **47**

C111, **10**

Da Nico, **39**

Diva, **34**

Duane Park Cafe, **51**

Dusit Thai, **14**

El Teddy's, **37**

Fannie's Oyster Bar, **4**

Felix, **33**

Fraunces Tavern, **57**

French Roast, **6**

Gianni's, **56**

Golden Unicorn, **46**

Gotham Bar & Grill, **8**

Grand Ticino, **15**

Home, **13**

Hudson River Club, **52**

Jean Claude, **23**

Kin Khao, **27**

La Metarie, **5**

L'Auberge Du Midi, **3**

Le Pactole, **54**

Lucky Strike, **35**

Ludlow Street Cafe, **25**

Manhattan Brewing Company, **32**

Manila Garden, **12**

Markham, **7**

Mi Cocina, **1**

Montrachet, **37**

New Viet Huong, **43**

98 Mott Street, **41**

Nosmo King, **36**

Odeon, **50**

Oriental Pearl, **42**

Pisces, **19**

Roettelle A. G., **18**

Sammy's Roumanian Steak House, **38**

Second Avenue Deli, **16**

S.P.Q.R., **40**

Takahachi, **20**

Tea and Sympathy, **2**

Teresa's, **17**

TriBeCa Grill, **48**

Triple Eight Palace, **45**

20 Mott, **44**

Zoë, **29**

Uptown Manhattan Dining

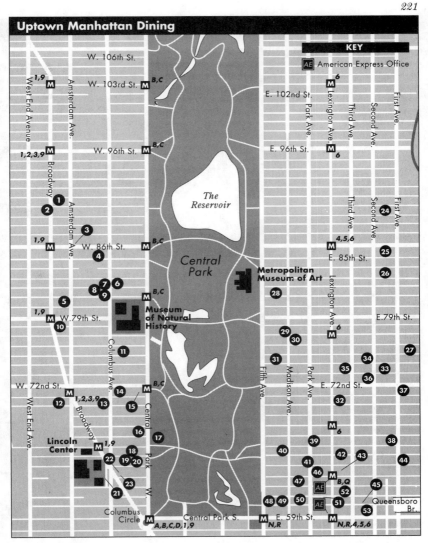

KEY

AE American Express Office

Amsterdam's, **5**
Arizona 206, **53**
Aureole, **50**
Baraonda, **34**
Boonthai, **36**
Café Crocodile, **33**
Café des Artistes, **16**
Café Luxembourg, **12**
Café Pierre, **48**
Carmine's, **1**
Coco Pazzo, **31**
Daniel, **30**
Dish, **8**
Dock's, **2**

Ferrier, **40**
Fiorello's Roman
Café, **23**
Fishin Eddie, **14**
Fujiyama Mama, **6**
High Life, **37**
Iridium, **21**
Jack's Firehouse, **4**
Jo Jo, **43**
Josephina, **22**
La Palette, **35**
L' Ardoise, **38**
L'Auberge, **44**
Le Cirque, **41**
Le Pistou, **51**

Mad. 61, **49**
Main Street, **9**
Mark's, **29**
Matthew's, **52**
Memphis, **11**
Parioli
Romanissimo, **28**
Park Avenue Café, **46**
Picholine, **20**
Poiret, **7**
Popover Café, **3**
Post House, **47**
Red Tulip, **27**
Sala Thai, **24**
Serendipity 3, **45**

Sette Mezzo, **32**
Seventh Regiment
Mess and Bar, **39**
Sfuzzi, **19**
Shun Lee West, **18**
Sidewalker's, **15**
Sign of the Dove, **42**
Tavern on
the Green, **17**
The Pie, **25**
Triangolo, **26**
Two Two Two, **10**
Ying, **13**

Midtown Manhattan Dining

kitchen is evident in the salad of warm duck confit and fresh foie gras, the sparkling shellfish, the roasted monkfish fillet on white cabbage, and the tuna steak grilled with ginger and served with cucumber coulis. For dessert, try the honey parfait with caramelized pistachios. *2 World Financial Center, tel. 212/945–9444. Reservations required. Jacket and tie advised. AE, DC, MC, V. Closed Sat., Sun. dinner.*

Chinese **Au Mandarin.** This extraordinary World Financial Center restaurant is one of the best bets in Manhattan for haute Chinese fare. It's also the restaurant of choice for Chinese banquets. The dining experience combines a refined atmosphere, careful service, and exquisite food. You might start with vegetarian dumplings and Shanghai buns, then move on to shark's fin soup, Shanghai prawns, or General Tao's scallops; Peking duck, tangerine beef, and delicate rice noodles with julienne vegetables are other possible courses. Wines are serious and work well with the food here. *200–250 Vesey St., tel. 212/385–0313. Reservations advised. Jacket and tie advised. AE, DC, MC, V.*

$$ **Fraunces Tavern.** Opened in 1762 by Samuel Fraunces, George
American Washington's steward, this landmark with a clubby bar is a good spot for cocktails (they're rather good) and for basic eggs-bacon-and-oatmeal breakfasts. Any other time, stick to steaks and grills. A museum is upstairs. *54 Pearl St. at Broad, tel. 212/269–0144. Reservations advised. Jacket advised. AE, DC, MC, V. Closed weekends.*

Seafood **Gianni's.** This is the most serious and attractive restaurant near South Street Seaport, an area not noted for gastronomic excellence. Ten pastas, varied antipasto, and garlic bread with Gorgonzola give Italian overtones to the eclectic American menu; although there's meat and poultry, the best choice is seafood. Try the pepper-seared tuna steak with citrus vinaigrette and shaved fennel or the roasted lobster with onion-mashed potatoes and chive butter; among the agreeable desserts is cheesecake with cranberry. There's a good selection of wines, especially from California. *15 Fulton St., tel. 212/608–7300. Reservations advised. Dress: casual. AE, DC, MC, V.*

$ **Bridge Café.** If you yearn for solid food with a touch of class, head for
American- this antique spot sequestered on a tiny lane near the Seaport. From
Contemporary the subtle soup of monkfish, scallops, and butternut squash to the hearty braised lamb shank with red lentils and pearl onions, the food is honest and realistically priced. Orange-pecan pie and peanut butter cheesecake are knockouts. The wine list is all-American, heavy on whites and regionals. Rumor has it that the ghost of Gallis Megs roams the rooms upstairs; this feisty lady of the evening wore suspenders and bit off the ears of those who refused to pay up. *279 Water St. at Dover, tel. 212/227–3344. Dress: casual. AE, DC, MC, V. Closed Sat. lunch.*

SoHo and TriBeCa

$$$$ **Bouley.** In this striking TriBeCa room with vaulted ceilings, wild-
American- flower bouquets, and impressionistic paintings, your tab is one of
Contemporary the city's highest. Wines are outrageously expensive. Waits between courses can be painful. Moreover, there can be an attitude problem. Yet it's fiendishly difficult to pull off an 8 PM reservation, because chef David Bouley is a star. Dinner might commence with a teaser of peppered skate or calamari with 100-year-old balsamic vinegar, then move on to foie gras roasted in salt with figs, tomatoes, and Armagnac; organic pigeon and foie gras in savoy cabbage; or lobster

with pineapple, sage, and julienned asparagus. For dessert? Sorbets in fig sauce, chocolate gratin with ice cream, or plum and apple clafouti. The $85 tasting dinner and $32 prix fixe lunch are good values. *165 Duane St., between Greenwich and Hudson, tel. 212/608–3852. Jacket and tie required. AE, DC, MC, V. Closed Sat. lunch, Sun.*

★ **Chanterelle.** Soft peach walls, luxuriously spaced tables, and flawless service set the stage for David Waltuck's masterpieces, all original, carefully prepared, and beautifully presented, such as the signature seafood sausage, a delicate asparagus flan, an understated halibut with fava beans, seared tuna with seaweed and wasabi, and crispy bass with sage. Don't miss such exceptional desserts as chocolate mille-feuille and fruit soup with coconut sorbet. The cheese selection is remarkable. Trust your sommelier to find value in the outstanding wine list; trust Karen Waltuck to supervise with grace and enthusiasm. Dinner is prix fixe. In TriBeCa. *2 Harrison St. near Hudson, tel. 212/966–6960. Reservations required. Dress: casual but smart. AE, MC, DC, V. Closed Sun.–Mon.*

$$$
French

Montrachet. Chef Deborah Ponzek's cuisine at this TriBeCa leader, owned by TriBeCa Grill's Drew Nieporent, is at once unpretentious and distinguished by great finesse, as in the outstanding pasta in lobster-truffle cream sauce with foie gras and wild mushrooms, and saddle of rabbit with Swiss chard and turnips; banana and chocolate gratin and cold chocolate truffle torte make radiant conclusions. The premises are smallish, with wine-red banquettes against refined gray walls in a discreet front room and at tables in the comfortable if less chic back room. Daniel Johnnes epitomizes the young, knowledgeable American sommelier. The wine list complements the cuisine beautifully. *239 W. Broadway, between Walker and White, tel. 212/219–2777. Reservations a must. Dress: casual. AE. Closed Sun.; no lunch Mon.–Thurs. or Sat.*

$$
American-Contemporary
★

Duane Park Café. This TriBeCa find with a Japanese chef can spoil you with its excellent service, its serious but fairly priced wines, and its eclectic international menu. Try skewers of grilled shrimp and calamari with olives and Greek-style garlic-mashed potatoes or moist salmon in a pinot noir sauce with roasted autumn vegetables, then finish with intense sorbets such as orange-spice tea, or concord grape, ginger-lime, and apple cider. The design is warm and original, with dark columns and peach walls. *157 Duane St., between W. Broadway and Hudson, tel. 212/732–5555. Reservations required. Dress: casual. AE, DC, MC, V. D. Closed Sat. lunch, Sun.*

Nosmo King. The name of this TriBeCan, a play on the phrase "no smoking," is not its only quirk. It's all deliciously eccentric. There are crystal chandeliers and watermelon margaritas, fresh-squeezed juices, and organic wines. Nothing on the fascinating menu is run-of-the-mill, and chef Allen Harding knows his stuff, seasoning fearlessly in sweet potato–black bean quesadillas; beet, goat cheese, and potato tart; and spicy duck ragout with hominy corn bread and collard greens. Not to miss: some of Manhattan's best seared tuna and roast chicken. Chocolate blackout cake is grand. *54 Varick St., south of Canal, tel. 212/966–1239. Reservations advised. Dress: casual. AE, DC, MC, V. No lunch weekends.*

TriBeCa Grill. This cavernous brick-walled restaurant, subtly lighted and anchored by the bar from the old Maxwell's Plum, displays art by the late Robert De Niro, Sr., father of the actor who opened it with various celebrity partners and now owns it with Montrachet's Drew Nieporent. The best dishes are simple: crisp fried oysters with garlic-anchovy aioli, roast chicken with whipped potatoes and wild mushrooms, rack of lamb with lentils and stuffed sweet peppers; desserts are amicable (try banana tart with milk chocolate ice cream), as is the staff. The wine list offers interesting choices, especially Californians. *375 Greenwich St. near Franklin, tel. 212/941–3900. Reservations advised. Dress: casual. AE, DC, MC, V. Closed Sat. lunch.*

Zoë. Thalia and Stephen Loffredo's colorful, high-ceilinged SoHo eatery with terra-cotta columns and floor is relatively noisy. But the open kitchen produces tasty food: calamari with Vietnamese dipping sauce, smoked salmon with wasabi potatoes and oriental crisps, roasted monkfish on home fries chunked with lobster, and braised lamb shank with gnocchi. Mexican-chocolate pecan pie and chocolate-peanut butter semifreddo are irresistible—especially at these prices. Zoë also has an outstanding wine list and a fine group of carefully tended wines by the glass. There's brunch on weekends. *90 Prince St., between Broadway and Mercer, tel. 212/966–6722. Reservations advised. Dress: casual. AE, DC, MC, V. Closed Mon.*

French **Capsouto Frères.** With its top-notch service, classical music, and
★ reasonable prices, this romantic spot in an 1891 TriBeCa landmark is a winner. Chef Charles Tutino prepares classics with a solid, contemporary touch—masterful stuffed fresh sardines meunière, heavenly mahimahi quenelles with lobster-sauterne sauce, extraordinary quail grilled with raspberry butter. Dessert soufflés around town pale against the light, delicious versions here. The carte du vin is sound and tolerably priced. Weekend brunch. *451 Washington St. near Watts, tel. 212/966–4900. Reservations required. Dress: casual. AE, DC, MC, V. No lunch Mon.*

Italian **Barolo.** Most SoHo restaurants use space in architecturally interesting ways. This large spot with a contemporary Piedmontese menu is no exception. With its appealing display of appetizers, the bar is attractive, and the huge garden, past the dining room, is remarkable with its balcony and dramatically lighted trees. Start with tuna carpaccio or fresh mozzarella salad. Then move on to the nicely grilled veal chop or the whole sea bass, baked in salt and deboned table-side. There's also a carefully chosen wine list. *398 W. Broadway, between Spring and Broome, tel. 212/226–1102. Reservations advised. Dress: casual. AE, DC, MC, V.*

Mexican **El Teddy's.** The margaritas need only a bit more lime to be perfect, and the food is mostly wonderful, revealing both authentic Mexican subtleties and contemporary creativity, from the fabulous salsa and roasted corn soup to the smoked chicken and goat cheese quesadilla and the pork, chicken, and fruit stew. The roster of inventive desserts includes summer bread pudding and chocolate tamales—odd-sounding but yummy. It's a Mexican restaurant like no other—Kafkaesque in its mirrors, tiles, glitter, and grotesque use of colors. *219 W. Broadway, between Franklin and White, tel. 212/941–7070. Reservations advised. Dress: casual. AE, DC, MC, V. No lunch weekends.*

$–$$ **Odeon.** Downtown's first trendy restaurant is still one of the best.
American- The art deco cafeteria look, pleasant service, low prices, and well-
Contemporary chosen wine list are all pluses. But let's not neglect the food: crab and corn cakes with chili sauce, excellent grilled free-range chicken with mashed potatoes and spinach, grilled salmon with soy-scallion vinaigrette, and grilled lamb and leek sandwich on country bread, which still makes our mouth water. Desserts are honest, if not up to the main event. Omelets and pizza are always available. In TriBeCa. *145 W. Broadway at Thomas St., tel. 212/233–0507. Reservations advised. Dress: casual. AE, DC, MC, V.*

French **Café.** With its high-back chairs, velvet drapes, and soft lighting,
★ there's a look of Paris to this fashionable SoHo café owned by Richard Widmaier-Picasso, the artist's grandson. Sleek model types and beautiful Europeans fill the two exquisite rooms and outside terrace. The food, largely that of southwestern France, is served with warmth, and it can be extraordinary: Grilled pigs' feet with celery-root rémoulade are light and greaseless, vegetable terrine bursts with flavor, and roast free-range chicken with mashed potatoes is perfect. So are praline-nougat ice cream with chocolate sauce and lemon tart with crème anglaise and raspberry coulis. The wine list is on target. Go for the three-course dinner or weekend brunch. *210 Spring St., off 6th Ave., tel. 212/274–0505. Reservations advised. Dress: casual. AE, DC, MC, V. No lunch weekdays.*

Felix. No, you haven't traveled 3,000 miles to Paris's Left Bank; this charming bistro is in SoHo, a taxi ride from midtown. Whether you dine inside or al fresco, the service is friendly, and the contemporary bistro fare, although seldom exciting, is always attractively presented. Try the chicken or rabbit fricassee; the *brioche perdu* with raspberry coulis and frozen apple pudding make satisfying exits. There's brunch on Sunday. *340 W. Broadway at Grand, tel. 212/431–0021. Dress: casual. AE. No lunch Mon.*

Italian **Diva.** You need operatic training to converse above the din in this hot SoHo spot. But you needn't be a diva to enjoy the chic scene, the robust cuisine, or the friendly prices. For tranquility, arrive by 7:30 and stick around as the sidewalk café fills up. Start with grilled vegetables in balsamic vinegar, follow with the huge veal chop stuffed with spinach and fontina. For dessert, don't miss the miraculous tartufo or the marvelous coconut sorbet, served in a hollowed-out shell. Portions are large enough to share, and only a tendency to serve food tepid flaws the kitchen. The wine list offers just enough choice. *341 W. Broadway near Grand, tel. 212/941–9024. Reservations advised. Dress: casual. AE, DC, MC, V.*

$ **Lucky Strike.** One of Manhattan's hottest, cheapest, and funkiest
American- small restaurants, this unadorned SoHo boîte doesn't look like
Casual much. But it serves a terrific steak and pommes frites at a bargain price, homey roast chicken, good burgers, and great bread pudding; the homemade bread is worth the trip. Champagnes are so ridiculously inexpensive that one assumes they have been marked incorrectly; other wines are well-priced. The crowd mobbing the bar is young, hip, and great-looking. Open until 4 AM and for brunch on weekends, Lucky Strike is a lucky find. *59 Grand St., between Wooster and W. Broadway, tel. 212/941–0479, 212/941–0772. No reservations. Dress: casual. AE, DC, V.*

Manhattan Brewing Company. This unusual SoHo brewery-restaurant, dominated by gigantic brewing vats, is housed in a walloping space recalling a German brew hall. Try the spicy beer sausage baked in brown ale with potato salad, the idiosyncratic ale soup served in a hollowed-out peasant loaf, or the out-of-the-ordinary macaroni and cheese in beer sauce with toasted pignolis. The burger, served on focaccia, rates kudos. Don't miss the fried ice cream, the ice cream made with stout, the chocolate cake spiked with chili, or the naughty ice-cream sandwich. *42 Thompson St., off W. Broadway at Broome, tel. 212/925–1515. Reservations only for 8 or more. Dress: casual. AE, MC, V. Closed Mon. lunch.*

Italian **Ballato's.** Garlic, red sauce, and soul. This SoHo old-timer, back af-
★ ter a decline, can dish up a first-rate veal chop along with winners such as broccoli rabe with sausage, crisp chicken sautéed with olive oil and garlic, and pasta with sardines, pine nuts, and raisins. If

you've never tasted tripe, Ballato's version, in a superb marinara sauce, will make a believer of you. Wines are well priced, and most entrées are bargains. *55 E. Houston St., between Mott and Mulberry, tel. 212/274–8881. Reservations advised. Dress: casual. AE, DC, MC. V.*

Thai **Kin Khao.** Hip downtowners have already discovered this inventive
★ Thai restaurant in SoHo. It's jam-packed—and worth the wait. The good bar, itself a scene, pours a remarkable ginger vodka, but the real payoff is the fabulous food. The masterful *gai tom kha*, traditional soup with chicken, coconut milk, mushrooms, and ginger, says it all; the kitchen here understands balance. Try the superb red snapper with sweet-and-sour chili sauce, the complex green curry with chicken, or Thai eggplant and basil. Sticky rice is heaven; for dessert, it comes with sesame seeds and fresh mango. *171 Spring St., between W. Broadway and Thompson, tel. 212/966–3939. Reservations only for 6 or more. Dress: casual but neat. AE, MC, V. No lunch.*

Chinatown, Little Italy, East Village, and Lower East Side

$$$$ **Sammy's Roumanian Steak House.** This Lower East Sider, although
Roumanian not much to look at, gives new meaning to the word party. For starters, there's the live music, occasional belly dancers, and wise-cracking co-owner Stanley Zimmerman. Then there are those Absolut bottles frozen in blocks of ice on the table. The chopped liver is the best you'll ever eat—full of onions fried to a crisp in schmaltz (chicken fat) and mixed at the table with more schmaltz. And what eggplant salad, stuffed cabbage, half-sour pickles, and roasted peppers. Typically Roumanian grilled meats follow: tenderloin, rib steak, or a mixed grill that includes lamb chops and sweetbread. Finish with rugelach and do-it-yourself egg creams (seltzer mixed with milk and chocolate syrup). *157 Chrystie at Delancey, tel. 212/673–0330. Reservations advised. Dress: casual. AE, DC, MC, V. No lunch.*

$$ **Golden Unicorn.** If you come to this Hong Kong–style restaurant
Cantonese with at least nine other diners, here's what happens: Young women
★ with walkie-talkies escort you to the elevator to the banquet rooms. A sign bearing your name hangs on one of them. Hand-printed menus are on the table and your personal waiter enters. For $35 to $40 a person, a 12-course banquet follows: roast suckling pig, scallops and seafood in a noodle nest, whole steamed fish, fried rice with raisins, lobster with ginger, and unusual desserts based on warm or chilled fruit or rice soups. If you can't muster the crowd, sit in the regular dining room and order from the regular menu. Dim sum is delightful. Our Chinese friends consider this one the best for authentic Cantonese fare. *18 E. Broadway at Catherine, tel. 212/941–0911. Reservations advised for banquets and groups of 4 or more. Dress: casual. AE.*

Italian **S.P.Q.R.** This spot with spacious tables and lots of fresh flowers is one of the few serious restaurants in Little Italy, an area more noted for fun than food. The good Genovese-inspired fare includes a marvelous pasta with pesto sauce and a lovely grilled salmon with a zesty herbal crust. Don't be put off by the expensive look: Despite the excellent service, warm reception, and amazing wine list (with 18 wines by the glass), prices are as reasonable as in mediocre spots nearby. *133 Mulberry St., between Hester and Grand, tel. 212/925–3120. Reservations advised. Dress: casual. AE, DC, MC, V.*

$–$$ **98 Mott Street.** Like many of New York's Hong Kong–style Chinese
Cantonese restaurants, this one is a virtual palace, with its red and gold accents and attentive waiters in spiffy uniforms. It offers not only low prices but also exciting food. Try the minced scallops in the shell with mushrooms, the hard-shell crab with chili peppers (first deep fried, then baked in salt), the flounder with Chinese vegetables, or the thin noodles, stir-fried with dried squid. *98 Mott St., between Canal and Hester, tel. 212/226–6603. Reservations only for 4 or more. Dress: casual. AE, MC, V.*

★ **Triple Eight Palace.** This quintessential Hong Kong–style emporium is wild and wonderful—loud, jam-packed with Chinese families (and lots of babies). It's also one of the pleasantest spots for dim sum. Try shrimp in phyllo, turnip cake, spicy squid, steamed pork buns, crab claws, and steamed and fried dumplings. In the evening, you can order excellent seafood, Cantonese specialties, and noodle dishes. To communicate, it helps to bring a Chinese friend. *78 E. Broadway, between Division and Market, tel. 212/941–8886. Reservations only for 6 or more. Dress: casual. AE, DC, MC, V.*

20 Mott. This restaurant, another excellent choice for dim sum, is neat if nondescript, and the service is a notch above average. To get food that's authentic, you must insist on it (or look around and point); when you do, you'll be served fabulous steamed dumplings filled with shrimp balls, pork, or mixed vegetables with brown vinegar; delicate sautéed snow pea leaves, available only for short periods of the year; ultra-crispy pan-fried whole flounder with julienned vegetables; and amazingly unpeculiar deep-fried eel with orange peel and spicy XO sauce (a Hong Kong specialty that's rare here). *20 Mott St., between Bowery and Pell, tel. 212/964–0380. Reservations only for 6 or more. Dress: casual. AE, MC. V.*

$ **Brother's Bar-B-Q.** Although this West Village joint's rakish decor
Barbecue may not win awards (formica tables, hanging lanterns, Christmas lights), the barbecue certainly will—it's better than much that's revered in the South (thanks to Guyanese chef Mike Persaud). Finger-licking-good North Carolina–style pulled pork, chopped beef brisket, and barbecued chicken and ribs come in he-man portions, and hush puppies and fried okra are paragons of greaseless frying. The sweet potato and pecan pies are mouthwatering; ditto for the Oreo cheescake. Service is surprisingly friendly. There's Bass ale on tap to quell the heat from the fabulous hot sauce and an all-you-can-eat $10.95 pig-out on Monday. *228 W. Houston St., between 6th Ave. and Varick, tel. 212/727–2775. No reservations. Dress: casual. AE.*

Cajun **Ludlow Street Café.** The food is beautifully prepared and excitingly spiced at this neat, unadorned Lower East Side Cajun restaurant, filled with young people having a good time. So will you. Pickled shrimp with dill and balsamic vinegar whet your appetite. The red bean soup and the fabulous gumbo prove how complex and exciting these robust dishes can be. Crab cakes are light as a feather, the tartar sauce is homemade, and the fried chicken with Cajun mustard and honey butter is rewarding—as are the friendly desserts. Weekends, there's brunch. *165 Ludlow St., between E. Houston and Stanton, tel. 212/353–0536. No reservations. Dress: casual. AE. No lunch weekdays.*

Cantonese **Oriental Pearl.** Already discovered by savvy Chinese families and transplanted Europeans, this interesting restaurant draws few Americans. Yet it's a virtual cornucopia of dining experiences. Breakfast or lunch is a dim sum feast. At dinner, you can go for the $11.95 Cantonese buffet with all the beer you can drink, or, for $19, sample a Mongolian hot pot buffet. Or, downstairs, you can order à la carte; try diced seafood and corn soup, Canadian crab Cantonese-style (with ground pork and fermented beans), deep-fried whole flounder, fried crispy stuffed bean curd, or the lovely coconut dessert. Everything is fresh, simple, and delicious. Service is friendly and helpful. *103 Mott St., between Hester and Canal, 212/219–8388. No reservations. Dress: casual. MC, V.*

Deli **Second Avenue Deli.** Here it is, the last of a dying breed. Rude service, huge sandwiches, matzo ball soup, chopped liver—they're alive and well at the Second Avenue Deli. Try it, you'll like it. *156 2nd Ave. at 10th, tel. 212/677–0606. No reservations. Dress: casual. AE.*

Japanese **Takahachi.** The best small Japanese restaurant in Manhattan, it's
★ neat and amazingly inexpensive, offering such unusual dishes as fried shiitake filled with ground salmon, chopped tuna sashimi with scallions, seared tuna with black pepper and mustard sauce, and grilled chicken stuffed with plum paste and siso leaf. There's also a good early bird special, served until 7 PM. Wine and beer only. *85 Ave. A, between 5th and 6th, tel. 212/505–6524. No reservations. Dress: casual. AE, MC, V. No lunch.*

Latin **Boca Chica.** This raffish East Villager, hot as a firecracker, has live
American music, dancing, and assertively seasoned food from several Latin
★ American nations at give-away prices. Check out the soupy Puerto Rican chicken-rice stew known as *asopao*, Cuban sandwiches, Bolivian sweet corn topped with chicken, and the nurturing rice pudding. Try a potent *caipirinha* (lime juice and Brazilian rum); or work your way through the exceptional list of beers from both Latin America and American boutique breweries. Don't trip over the boa constrictor by the bar. *13 1st Ave. near 1st St., tel. 212/473–0108. No reservations. Dress: casual. AE, DC, MC, V. No lunch Mon.–Sat.*

Pizza **Da Nico.** This Little Italy restaurant serves no pasta. Instead, young Nick Luizza and his mother, Annette, offer outstanding rotisserie grills, marinated vegetables, displayed on an attractive counter, and coal-oven pizza, thin-crusted and charred. The simplest is the best: the margherita, with just tomatoes, mozzarella, and basil. The roast chicken is delicious, the roast suckling pig soul-stirring. You eat up front by the bar or in a comfortable back room with brick walls and a skylight. *164 Mulberry St., between Grand and Broome, tel. 212/343–1212. No reservations. Dress: casual. AE, MC, V.*

Polish **Teresa's.** Prices at this luncheonette are in the giveaway category, and the food is satisfying. A few stars: *bigos*, the Polish national stew; sauerkraut layered with fresh and smoked meats and sausage; and the hearty, stick-to-the-ribs dumplings known as *pirogi*, filled with meat, fish, cheese, or mushrooms, boiled or fried and served with sour cream. Homesick Poles mix with perennially cost-conscious students here. *103 1st Ave., between 6th and 7th Sts., tel. 212/228–0604. No reservations. Dress: casual. No credit cards.*

Seafood **Pisces.** Who ever thought we'd see elegant fish preparations on Ave-
★ nue A? At this striking restaurant, where tables near the open windows seem to spill out into Alphabet City, as this neighborhood of lettered avenues is called, $15 buys an outstanding three-course dinner. Such sophisticated dishes as smoked salmon terrine with adobo sauce and grilled tuna, hidden under a tower of fried onions, are incongruous to the East Village scene, but after a delicious dessert it doesn't seem to matter. The wine list is well-chosen and sensibly priced. Brunch is served on weekends. *96 Ave. A at 6th, tel. 212/260–6660. Reservations advised. Dress: casual. AE, MC, V. No lunch weekdays.*

Swiss **Roettelle A. G.** If you hanker for hearty European cooking, you'll love this charming East Village town house, where you can sit in a hidden nook on one of the several dining rooms, in the cozy bar, or under an arbor in the garden sipping Swiss wine and eating *viande de Grisons* (Swiss air-dried beef) or raclette (mild melted cheese served with boiled potatoes and tiny pickles). Sauerbraten with spaetzle and red cabbage is delicious, and it's rare to taste apple strudel and Linzer torte this good. Prices are low anyway, but German-born owner Ingrid Roettelle also offers a bargain two-course fixed-price dinner. There is a short, inexpensive, all-European wine list. *126 E. 7th St., between 1st Ave. and Ave. A, tel. 212/674–4140. Reservations advised. Dress: casual. MC, V. Closed Sun.*

Vietnamese **New Viet Huong.** Inordinately popular in Paris, Vietnamese cuisine has never caught on in Manhattan. Yet it has the subtlety and elegance of French cooking, with flavors that intrigue but don't overwhelm. Here, try the remarkable barbecued beef wrapped in grape leaves, grilled shrimp paste on a sugarcane stick, and Vietnamese spring or fresh shrimp rolls. All come with lovely contrasting sauces. It is traditional to take romaine leaves and fill them with ingredients to create small lettuce sandwiches. With homemade ice cream and delicious coffee, dinner seldom tops $18. *77 Mulberry St., between Canal and Bayard, tel. 212/233–8988. Reservations not necessary. Dress: casual. AE, MC, V.*

Greenwich Village

$$$ **Gotham Bar & Grill.** Can success spoil this innovator? Probably not, since management keeps careful watch over the service (generally excellent) and the kitchen (always inventive; it was chef Alfred Portale who originated the vertical style of food presentation, which turns each plate into an artful edible tower). Try the sublime pasta filled with caponata and goat cheese, in an intense chicken stock heady with olive oil, or the lovely grilled chicken salad with couscous and preserved lemon. The wine list is intelligent, and the lofty, multilevel space was the prototype of the new-style New York restaurant, with its warm salmon-and-green color scheme, diffuse lighting from shirred-fabric fixtures, and large window overlooking a courtyard. *12 E. 12th St., tel. 212/620–4020. Reservations advised. Dress: casual. AE, DC, MC, V. No lunch weekends.*

American-Contemporary **★**

$$ **Home.** In this sliver of a storefront restaurant, David Page cooks with rare authority and honesty, from the superb onion rings served with homemade ketchup and the hearty smoked duck soup with peasant noodles and root vegetables to the grilled chicken sausages with rosemary-infused white bean stew and sweet potato hash. Nor will you soon forget the creamy chocolate pudding, lemon chiffon cake with lemon sugar glaze, and homemade cookies. Home also offers an interesting wine list, an excellent New York State Seyval Blanc by the glass, friendly service, and brunch on weekends. *20 Cornelia St., between Bleecker and W. 4th, tel. 212/243–9579. Reservations accepted for dinner only. Dress: casual. AE. Closed Mon.*

American-Contemporary

French **La Metairie.** This is the bistro you search for in Paris and discover only in New York. A French country charmer, with cooing doves and relaxing warmth, it serves regional classics with some interesting additions from owner Sylvain Fareri's home in the south of France (pork-stuffed calamari and soothing codfish stew). Seafood sausage stands out among the several inventive seafood preparations, and the good rack of lamb comes with a potato flan redolent of garlic.

Don't miss the drop-dead bread pudding. *189 W. 10th St. at W. 4th, tel. 212/989–0343. Reservations advised. Dress: casual. No credit cards.*

Italian **Bondini.** One of New York's best bets when you want to eat Italian is
★ this sleeper in a gorgeous town house, whose multilevel Victorian dining room is done in pastels, with lovely paintings, romantic lighting, and soft music. Modest prices belie the refined service and earnest, contemporary kitchen, which shows its stuff in the dill-perfumed codfish soup, asparagus risotto, mustard-sauced veal fillet with apples and mushrooms, and the grand poached pears, served with Kahlua-spiked cream. There's a good selection of Italian and California wines. *62 W. 9th St., between 5th and 6th, tel. 212/ 777–0670. Reservations advised. Dress: casual. AE, DC, MC, V.*

$–$$ **Markham.** This baby of noted restaurant consultant Clark Wolf is
American- deceptively understated with its creamy walls, comfortable green
Contemporary leather banquettes, and casual downstairs café. The food is simple and delicious; standouts are aged goat cheese and chicory salad with hot bacon vinaigrette, roasted red snapper on baked white beans, and a scrumptious butterscotch crème brûlée. A balanced wine list and five wines by the glass complete the picture. *59 5th Ave., between 12th and 13th, tel. 212/647–9391. Reservations advised. Dress: casual but neat. AE, MC, V. Closed Sat. lunch, Sun.*

French **Jean Claude.** This bistro from Bouley's former maître d' reflects its
★ owner's eccentric charm and joie de vivre. The young, beautiful crowd is a show in itself. However, your check buys not only lots of fun but also some of the best bourgeois cooking in town: sautéed tripe on white bean salad; homemade fettuccine with squid, sun-dried tomatoes, and basil, a masterpiece of contrasting tastes and textures; Atlantic salmon with cabbage, carrots, and red wine sauce. Wines are inexpensive, desserts and service easy. Note that the phone number is unlisted. *137 Sullivan St., between Houston and Prince, tel. 212/475–9232. No reservations. Dress: casual. No credit cards. No lunch.*

L'Auberge Du Midi. If you want the "perfect Greenwich Village restaurant," look no further than this seductive bistro. The welcome couldn't be more ingratiating, and the food is relatively inexpensive and honest, including sea scallops with leeks in champagne sauce (among several carefully prepared seafood dishes), roast rack of lamb with fresh thyme, bouillabaisse on Friday (chef Jean Roger is from Marseilles), or the couscous of Madame's native Fez, delicious under its typical garnish of caramelized onions. *310 W. 4th St., between W. 12th and Bank, tel. 212/242–4705. Reservations advised. Dress: casual. AE, MC, V. Closed Mon. Nov–Mar.; no lunch.*

Italian **Grand Ticino.** The restaurant that served its first meal in 1919 and put in a cameo appearance in the movie *Moonstruck* is romantic, charming, and generally pleasing. Start with grilled Portobello mushrooms or baked clams with oregano and garlic, then enjoy an excellent pasta ($8.95 and up) as an entrée or split as a second course Italian-style. There's also a fabulously simple grilled chicken, good calf's liver, and well-executed sweetbreads. The dessert cart will tempt you, especially the creamy tiramisù. *228 Thompson St., between W. 3rd and Bleecker, tel. 212/777-5922. Reservations advised. Dress: casual. AE, DC, MC, V. Closed Sun.*

$ **CIII.** The landmark Washington Square Hotel's slightly subterra-
American- nean dining room, dating from 1902, has scenic murals of Washing-
Contemporary ton Square Park, stylish tapestry banquettes, and changing displays of art work. To eat, what about wild mushrooms in puff pas-

try with truffle oil, crispy sesame calamari, the fabulous grilled leg of lamb, basil-mashed potatoes, or sautéed red kale? The vegetable plate is one of the best around. For dessert, we can't decide what's best: warm apple-walnut cake or the dense chocolate cake. CIII rates as a great value, with dinners at $15 and entrées from $8. *103 Waverly Pl. near Washington Sq., tel. 212/254–1200. Reservations accepted. Dress: casual. MC, V. No dinner Sun.–Mon.*

Cajun **Fannie's Oyster Bar.** With its pleasant garden, this bit of New Orleans, complete with bead curtains, is another find. Start with spicy shrimp with rémoulade sauce. Then sample the delicious gumbo with chicken, shrimp, smoked sausage, and rice, the jambalaya, the excellent red beans smoky with pork, chicken, and sausage, or a daily special like Cajun chicken salad with oranges, pecans, and blue cheese. You'll love inventive cocktails like Fannie's lemonade (with rum) and Cajun martinis (with jalapeños). *765 Washington St., between 12th and W. Bethune, tel. 212/255–5101. Reservations accepted. Dress: casual. AE, MC, V. No lunch.*

French **French Roast.** This casual, around-the-clock spot with a Left Bank ambience charges bargain prices for some very good bistro dishes rarely encountered in America, such as deep-fried whitebait and poached beef marrow finished with bread crumbs and served in broth. Or just stop for coffee and dessert. *458 6th Ave. at 11th, tel. 212/533–2233. No reservations. Dress: very casual. AE.*

Mexican **Mi Cocina.** This unassuming fonda is one of New York's best Mexican kitchens, neat as a pin with its gay tiles and rosy walls. And what food. Everything shines, from guacamole to dessert crepes, filled with nuts and dried fruits. Particularly unusual are the tender tamales of corn masa, encased in Swiss chard; shredded pork with black bean purée and warm tortillas; and homemade noodles with cream sauce. It's tough to get a good margarita in New York, but Mi Cocina really tries. Weekends, there's brunch. *57 Jane St., off Hudson, tel. 212/627–8273. Reservations accepted. Dress: casual. AE, DC, MC, V.*

Philippine **Manila Garden.** Philippine cuisine is delicious, with its mix of Asian and Spanish flavors. And it's authentic in this simple, neat spot, which serves a bargain buffet on Tuesday ($8.95 at lunch, $11.95 at dinner). Try the *escabeche* (pickled fish), or the wonderful barbecued skewered pork with peanut sauce, the crisp-fried marinated milk fish, the interesting oxtail stews in peanut gravy with eggplant and banana bud garnishes, and the national dish, chicken adobo, with onions, garlic, and vinegar, reduced to caramelized deliciousness. The flan is richer than its Spanish counterpart, and *halo halo*, ice cream topped with fruits, is delightful. *325 E. 14th St., tel. 212/777–6314. Reservations accepted. Dress: casual. AE, DC, MC, V.*

Pizza **Arturo's.** Guidebooks don't list this brick-walled Village landmark,
★ but the body-to-body crowds teetering on the wobbly wooden chairs suggest good things. The pizza is terrific, cooked in a coal-fired oven; if you want the works, order the Fiesta combo. Basic pastas as well as seafood, veal, and chicken concoctions with mozzarella and lots of tomato sauce come at giveaway prices. Wines are bargains. *106 W. Houston St., off Thompson, tel. 212/677–3820. No reservations. Dress: casual. AE, MC, V.*

Tea **Tea and Sympathy.** This minuscule restaurant offers a terrific English tea and other exports of the United Kingdom, including oh-so-British atmosphere. Photos of bulldogs and Winston Churchill adorn the walls. There is a chalkboard menu, and very proper dishes such as Scotch eggs, shepherd's pie, bangers and mash, and scones with clotted cream and jam are served. Desserts are bully, too: trifle and sweet treacle cake, to name but two. On weekends, there's a full English breakfast. *108 Greenwich Ave., between 12th and 13th, tel. 212/807–8329. No reservations. Dress: casual. No credit cards. BYOB.*

Thai **Dusit Thai.** Seasoning is forceful here but not unfriendly, and the
★ menu offers many dishes rarely served outside Asia. There are marvelous steamed dumplings with chicken, vegetables, and ground peanuts; deep-fried softshell crabs; whole fish topped with mango, onions, garlic, chile, and lime; and a complex shrimp and chicken curry with lotus seed and coconut milk. *256 Bleecker St., between 6th and 7th, tel. 212/627–9310. Reservations unnecessary. Dress: casual. AE, DC, MC, V. No lunch Sun.*

Gramercy Park, Murray Hill, Chelsea, and the Flatiron District

$$$ **An American Place.** One of the country's finest regional American
American- restaurants is really a celebration of the nation's cuisine. Executive
Contemporary chef Larry Forgione is one of the leading proponents of the new
★ American cuisine; his menu ranges from adobo-style barbecued duck cake in cornmeal pancakes to homemade peanut butter ice cream sandwiches. The meat and potatoes is the best you'll ever taste—providing you define "meat" as pan-seared medallions of venison with roasted garlic cream and "potatoes" as straw potatoes with basil and black-olive butter. There's an excellent all-American wine list. *2 Park Ave., tel. 212/684–2122. Reservations advised. Dress: casual but neat. AE, MC, V. Closed Sat. lunch, Sun.*

Union Square Café. In this spiffy café where mahogany moldings outline white walls hung with bright modern paintings, the disposition is unpretentious, the service friendly, and the atmosphere pleasant. Breads are carefully chosen and appetizers mostly well executed, while main courses range from delicious to heavenly—sandwiches such as the fresh-tuna salad with slab bacon and arugula on sturdy white bread at lunch, roast chicken with polenta and tomato-sourdough bread salad at dinner. The very good desserts include a chocolate marble brownie à la mode and warm three-apple crisp with butterscotch sauce. Although the wine list is excellent, one would appreciate more interesting wines by the glass. *21 E. 16th St., tel. 212/243–4020. Reservations required. Dress: casual but neat. AE, DC, MC, V. No lunch Sun.*

Water Club. This glass-enclosed barge in the East River is decidedly dramatic, with its long wood-paneled bar, fireplace, appetizing shellfish display, and panoramic water views. Chef Richard Moonen's food is attractively presented if sometimes underseasoned and imprecisely cooked. House-smoked salmon and foie gras terrine are dependable openers; pleasant entrées include grilled chicken with a roasted garlic crust, served with cranberry relish and five-grain risotto, and veal chops with melted onions, black olive–zinfandel sauce, and creamy beans. Seafood is not a strong point. Wines by the glass are pricey, but the wine list is a high point. Sunday brunch is delightful. *500 E. 30th St., tel. 212/683–3333. Reservations required. Dress: casual but neat. AE, DC, MC, V.*

Latin- **Patria.** This trendy trilevel Caribbean café, done in striking earth-
Contemporary tones with handsome mosaics and an open grill, is owned by Phillip
★ Suarez (of Vong and Jo Jo's). Apparently Mr. Suarez can do no wrong: Note the Honduran conch chowder; vegetarian Puerto Rican–style pastelle (roasted garlic, olive broth, and lemon-caper sauce on a bed of ground corn); shrimp in Ecuadorian peanut stew

with green tomato salsa; braised oxtail in Rioja sauce with green rice; and the signature dessert, a chocolate-filled cigar with spice-bread ice cream. The service is as excellent as the food; the wine list focuses on Spain, Argentina, and California. *250 Park Ave. S, at 20th, tel. 212/777-6211. Reservations required. Dress: casual. AE, MC, V.*

Italian **Le Madri.** In this Chelsea restaurant, one of Manhattan's top Ital-
★ ians, the original concept was to rotate Italian regional women chefs. However, current chef Gianni Scapine proves that gender is unimportant in the kitchen, with dishes that are at once robust and homey, such as grilled calamari with fava beans and radicchio, and tagliolini with shrimp, asparagus, and diced tomato. The top-flight service and engaging Tuscan-style space with vaulted ceiling and wood-burning pizza oven add appeal. *168 W. 18th St., tel. 212/727-8022. Reservations advised. Jacket advised. AE, DC, MC, V.*

Southwestern **Mesa Grill.** Chef Bobby Flay and owner Jerome Kretchmer have Manhattan foodies in the palms of their hands in this former bank, now done with vinyl banquettes, green and yellow walls, and industrial fans. You can't go wrong with the small menu. Try the shrimp with a roasted garlic corn tamale, the pumpkin soup with chili cream, or the cornmeal-coated rabbit with sweet potatoes. Desserts are irresistible: chocolate polenta soufflé cake and raspberry crackle ice cream. There's an excellent selection of beers from microbreweries as well as a banner wine list. Alas, service and margaritas are indifferent. *102 5th Ave., between 15th and 16th, tel. 212/807-7400. Reservations required. Dress: casual. AE, MC, V.*

$$ **Les Halles.** Many Manhattan bistros, although attractive, serve
French Americanized versions of French classics. In this one with butcher
★ paper on the tables and posters on the walls, the kitchen is authentic: Steak tartare is made table-side, seasoned to perfection, and stylishly presented with french fries that are outstanding if cut thicker than in France. Because chef-owner Jose de Meirelles is Portuguese, you also find Mediterranean fare: seductive gazpacho, chunky with raw vegetables; mackerel *escabeche;* robust calamari in tomato sauce, Portuguese-style. Service is friendly, and the wine list offers interesting selections from France and standouts from Portugal. *411 Park Ave. S, between 28th and 29th, tel. 212/679-4111. Reservations required. Dress: casual. AE, DC, MC, V.*

Italian **Follonico.** You'll like the vintage wainscoting, muted colors, and
★ open brick oven, but most of all you will like the food, which is authentic, inventive, and delicious: Tuscan bread salad, wood-oven-roasted lamb, baby octopus under a net of black pasta, whole red snapper baked in a rock salt crust, spaghetti with Dungeness crab, topped with a whole soft-shell crab. Blueberry granita and caramel semifreddo stand out among the desserts, and the wine list is unassuming and tolerably priced. *6 W. 24th St., tel. 212/691-6359. Reservations required. Dress: casual. AE, DC, MC, V. Closed Sat. lunch, Sun.*

Seafood **City Crab & Seafood Co.** A mammoth red crab looms over this huge cream-tiled café decked with fishing artifacts. Although oysters, clams, and shellfish are impeccably fresh, City Crab shines with assertively seasoned dishes: sautéed southern garlic crabs, fried trout with garlic mashed potatoes, and grouper in horseradish crust with smoked shrimp; the crab cakes are pristine wonders. Sticky, satisfying caramel parfaits and brownies à la mode with chocolate sauce are grand finales. The wine list, short on chardonnays and cabs, suggests food-wine pairings; markups are modest. Service is efficient. *235 Park Ave. S at 19th, tel. 212/529–3800. Reservations advised. Dress: casual. AE, DC, MC, V.*

Spanish-Contemporary **Bolo.** With its tile-edged brick oven, its vivid gold-red-cobalt color scheme, its state-of-the-art open kitchen, and its polished wood bar, blinds, and floors, the design here fuses Manhattan and Spain. The food aims at New York palates: A typically Spanish roasted marinated shrimp with toasted garlic comes with a contemporary flatbread garnish and paella mixes lobster and duck (albeit unsuccessfully). Other treats: grilled octopus and white bean salad stuffed in a caramelized onion, salt-cod-and-potato fritters, and trendy burnt orange-chocolate flan with cinnamon syrup. The house sangria is perfect, the wine list well chosen and well priced. *23 E. 22nd St., tel. 212/228–2200. Reservations advised. Dress: casual but neat. AE, MC, V. Closed Sat. lunch, Sun.*

$–$$ **Flowers.** Chef Jimmy Bradley's food is just trendy enough for the *Mediterranean* chic crowd gathered in a high-ceilinged front room with a semicircular bar, and in the intimate Tuscan-style dining room beyond. But the kitchen's offerings are always delicious: tuna tartare with sweet-hot mustard and chives, cured salmon carpaccio with Sevruga caviar, grilled salmon with oysters in port-balsamic vinegar sauce, and remarkable scallops stuffed with shiitake mushrooms. Desserts are a notch below the appetizers and entrées; best bets are the bread pudding, chunked with chocolate and prunes and doused with Armagnac-spiked crème anglaise, and the flourless chocolate cake with hazelnut mousse. *21 W. 17th St., tel. 212/691–8888. Reservations advised. Dress: casual. AE, MC, V. Closed Sat. lunch, Sun.*

$ **Gramercy Watering Hole.** If you were a "Cheers" fan, this spot with *American-* brick walls, potted palms, an animal mural, and a 50-foot bar is a *Casual* find. It's fun and attractive, and $10 to $15 pays the bill. The food is really good—and not only because of the oversize cocktails. St. Louis ribs? Terrific. Fajitas? Homemade potato chips? Guacamole and salsa? Here, they're better than in many Mexican restaurants; the quesadillas are tops. Cajun brunch with music is $8.95. *106 E. 19th St., tel. 212/674–5783. Reservations accepted. Dress: casual. AE, DC, MC, V.*

American- **T-Rex.** A protruding dinosaur head marks the entrance. Inside, mu-*Contemporary* rals recall the caves of the French town of Lascaux; a reptile tank echoes Jurassic Park motifs. Food can be delicious. Start with one of the fantasy cocktails, then move on to roasted corn-wild rice chowder and grilled aged sirloin with a tower of lightly fried onion rings, mushrooms, and leeks, or the haystack of seared salmon, garlic polenta, and roasted tomato sauce. And what desserts—warm chocolate bread-and-butter pudding and pineapple upside-down cake with warm caramel sauce. *358 W. 23rd St., tel. 212/620–4620. Reservations advised. Dress: casual. AE, DC, MC, V.*

French **La Lunchonette.** With its lipstick-red walls, exposed bricks, lace ★ curtains, and long bar, this boîte has a casual bistro charm that makes you wish it weren't in such a desolate part of town. Chef Jean-François Fraysse and his wife, Melva, offer outstanding food, including excellent cassoulet and couscous, and such hard-to-come-by dishes as veal sweetbreads vinaigrette, calves' brains in black butter with capers, and rabbit stew. There are only a few desserts; the tarte tatin is exceptional, the crème caramel everything you hope for and too seldom find. Service is friendly, the wine list short but well priced. *130 10th Ave. at 18th, tel. 212/675–0342. Reservations advised. Dress: casual. AE, DC, MC, V. No lunch Sat.–Sun.*

Italian **Caffe Bondi.** This interesting small restaurant with a garden in back
★ and a pastry shop in front offers marvelous updated versions of ancient Sicilian dishes: bread salad, for instance, and ziti Pauloti, (in a
cinnamon-spiked tomato-sardine sauce), whose recipe was jealously
kept for centuries at the eponymous monastery. Fried pumpkin
with olives, cauliflower and almond soup, fish-and-herb ravioli in
mussel-tomato sauce, and quail stuffed with mint and pomegranate
seeds: These are dishes you seldom encounter on Manhattan menus.
The wine list is short but excellent and fairly priced, and there are
extraordinary wines, dessert wines, and grappas by the glass. But
skip the pastries. *7 W. 20th St., tel. 212/691–8136. Reservations advised. Dress: casual. AE, MC, V.*

Turkish **Turkish Kitchen.** With Turkish carpets on floors and walls, this colorful, multilevel spot sets an attractive scene to sample this cuisine;
helpful service enhances the experience. Order anise-flavored *rika*
as an aperitif with *meze* (appetizers) such as *borek* (turnovers), eggplant purée, fried calamari with garlic sauce, or sautéed spinach
with dill in yogurt-garlic sauce. Among entrées, try the succulent
grilled lamb, sliced paper-thin; for dessert, the light almond pudding and stuffed apricots. *386 3rd Ave., between 27th and 28th, tel.
212/679–1810. Reservations advised. Dress: casual. AE, DC, MC,
V. No lunch.*

Midtown

$$$$ **The "21" Club.** Not all are treated equally in this four-story brown-
American- stone landmark, one of the world's most glamorous saloons—if
Contemporary you're not known, the greeting can be indifferent, even chilly. In-
★ side, though, service is seamless and pampering, and it's exhilarat-
ing to hobnob with celebrities and tycoons and sip a well-made
cocktail served by what feels like your own butler. Even the sommelier puts you at ease, the knowledgeable young William Phillips, who
tends one of the world's great cellars (with some 50,000 bottles). The
dining room, with banquettes and a ceiling hung with toys, offers
traditional American and continental classics. Executive chef Michael Lomonaco can knock out creditable renditions of the signature
"21" burger and chicken hash, but also finesses the more complex
culinary challenges of such dishes as his barely cooked scallops, encased in a crackling sesame seed crust, garnished with a single potato chip bearing fresh Sevruga caviar. Steamed halibut in lemon
grass and Thai curry, one of several calorie-wise options, is equally
contemporary. Desserts are not strong. *21 W. 52nd St., tel. 212/
582–7200. Reservations required. Jacket and tie required. AE, DC,
MC, V. Closed Sat. lunch, Sun.*

American-Retro **The Rainbow Room.** Some $25 million was spent to restore this
glamorous art deco dinner-and-dancing room on the 65th floor of the
GE Building. Tables clad in silver lamé rise in tiers around a revolving dance floor lit by an immense chandelier; aubergine walls frame
panoramic city views. The wine list is good and the bar excellent.
Guileless dishes like rack of lamb are best; alas, the kitchen is less
successful with other retro fare—the Caesar salad, lobster Thermi-
dor, tournedos Rossini, and baked Alaska are merely adequate—
than with the shorter, less complex menu offered in Rainbow and
Stars, the adjacent supper club. There's no democracy when it comes to sitting ringside. *30 Rockefeller Plaza, tel. 212/632–5000 or
212/632–5100. Reservations required. Jacket and tie required. AE.
Closed Mon. (Rainbow and Stars also Sun.). Music charge $15
weekdays, $20 weekends.*

French **La Côte Basque.** A sibling to the late, legendary Le Pavillon, this beautiful restaurant has captivating Bernard Lamotte murals of the French countryside, generous red banquettes, warm lighting, and bursts of fresh flowers. Chef-proprietor Jean-Jaques Rachou believes in large portions and complex presentations; his *salade gourmande,* of lobster, duck breast, artichoke hearts, and foie gras, is a typical creation. Entrées range from rack of lamb to earthy stews such as the signature cassoulet. The dacquoise is a nonpareil finale. The wine list yields values but takes patience (regions are sometimes confused and years and producers omitted). *5 E. 55th St., tel. 212/688–6525. Reservations required. Jacket and tie required. AE, DC, MC, V. Closed Sun.*

★ **Lutèce.** New York's most misunderstood restaurant, chef-owner André Soltner's house is no Le Cirque or Lespinasse, nor does it aspire to be. Instead, Lutèce is like a breath of fresh air on the first day of spring, refreshingly unpretentious. If you can go only once, make it for lunch at an off-peak hour and ask Soltner to select the menu. You might begin with a robust rabbit-duck torte, followed by a savory onion tart or snails in tiny pots of garlic butter, then move on to fillet of sole, encasing a delicate pike mousse with an intense Riesling-cream sauce. If *pièce de résistance* ever had meaning, it's in the fine saddle of rabbit with wild mushrooms and spaetzle. A lovely apricot cake with peach sorbet and a phenomenal tarte tatin precede excellent petit fours. Alsatian wines offer the best value. If Soltner is not on hand, remember that it is in the simple regional fare of his native Alsace that he excels. Both the snug upstairs room and the downstairs garden are lovely. *249 E. 50th St., tel. 212/752–2225. Reservations required. Jacket and tie required. AE, DC, MC, V. Closed Mon. and Sat. lunch, Sun., and Aug.*

Italian **Felidia.** Manhattanites frequent this celebrated bilevel ristorante as much for winning enthusiasm of owner Lydia Bastianich as for the food. Proselytizing the cuisine of her native Istria, on the northern Adriatic, this noted food educator and author will guide you through the written menu and specials. Trust her and you will enjoy only the freshest produce (our arugula came from her garden). Meals are served in an attractive front room with a wooden bar, in the rustic room beyond, and in a skylit balcony. The wine list, an exceptional Italian rendering, offers great bottles from great producers. Even martinis are wonderful. *243 E. 58th St., tel. 212/758–1479. Reservations required. Jacket and tie required. AE, DC, MC, V. Closed Sat. lunch, Sun.*

Japanese **Seryna.** This lovely restaurant vividly evokes Tokyo with its digni-
★ fied air, comfortable seating, and understated colors. Although the sushi is superbly fresh, the specialty is steak Ishiyaki, cooked table-side on a smoldering rock. In the six-course Wagyu dinner, you can choose between it and *shabu shabu,* another mealtime dish-cum-event: You begin with a broth to which you add meat (which you then eat), then vegetables, then noodles; and conclude by sipping the bracing soup. Cocktails are served in small carafes that come buried in crushed ice. Service is superb. Alas, you need a sturdy pocket-book—dinners run $98 to $115 a head. *11 E. 53rd St., tel. 212/980–9393. Reservations advised. Dress: casual. AE, DC, MC, V. Closed Sat. lunch, Sun.*

$$$–$$$$ **Four Seasons Grill Room.** The Grill at Night program brings this
American- power lunch bastion into the 20th century: For $27.50 to $37.50, you
Contemporary get the enthusiastic service, architect Philip Johnson's comfortable
★ leather banquettes and rosewood walls, and a dinner that's simple and modern: mussels in green chili, shrimp and pork in rice paper,

lamb and mushrooms in pastry, and mahimahi with pineapple and green peppercorns; delectable apple tart comes with cranberry sorbet. All this, plus wines under $30. One hopes that the energy revitalizing the Grill finds its way to the Pool Room, with its illuminated trees and spacious tables surrounding a marble pool. *99 E. 52nd St., tel. 212/754–9494. Reservations required. Jacket required. AE, DC, MC, V. Closed Sat. lunch, Sun.*

Chinese **Tse Yang.** There are Tse Yangs in Paris, Geneva, and Beverly Hills, but this one is the most dramatic with its dark polished wood, dim lighting, elegant tableware, and an exotic-fish tank. Sommelier Roger Dogorn provides one of the joys of dining here—experimenting with wine and food combinations. Try the crisp, delicate frogs' legs or the Peking duck, served traditionally with doilies and skin (the meat following as a separate course). *34 E. 51st St., tel. 212/688–5447. Reservations advised. Jacket and tie advised. AE, DC, MC, V.*

French **La Réserve.** This luxurious, exceedingly beautiful restaurant can be an excellent value if you go for the prix fixe lunch. Lighting is soft, the flowers lovely, the service smooth, and the wine list replete with great bottles from great châteaux in great years. Don't expect heavy sauces and flambés. Cuisine is a contemporary adaptation of classical French fare; stuffed quail in a potato nest, petite marmite of seafood, saddle of rabbit with fresh savory, and a simple apple tart are artfully presented. If only a bit more care were taken with some dishes and the chef would exhibit more courage in his seasoning, the cuisine at La Réserve could equal the totally agreeable experience. *4 W. 49th St., tel. 212/247–2993. Reservations advised. Jacket and tie required. AE, DC, MC, V. Closed Sat. lunch, Sun.*

Steak **Smith & Wollensky.** Great New York steak houses are scarce, but
★ this one is tops for its masculine setting, gargantuan portions, and outstanding wine list (strong in red Bordeaux and California cabernets). Meat is dry-aged in-house, and sirloins, porterhouses, and filet mignons arrive cooked to a turn; or try the excellent veal or lamb chops or a well-prepared grilled fish or lobster; order a side of hash browns or cottage fries and creamed spinach, but skip the perfunctory desserts. The bustling, less-pricey Wollensky's Grill next door shares the main restaurant's carnivorous bias, but has pleasant sidewalk seating in summer. *201 E. 49th St., tel. 212/753–1530 (Grill tel. 212/753–0444). Reservations advised. Dress: casual. AE, DC, MC, V. No lunch weekends in restaurant.*

$$$ **China Grill.** Although the menu recalls Wolfgang Puck's famous
American- Chinois on Main, this huge restaurant with jade-colored walls,
Contemporary cloud-like light fixtures, and an open kitchen has an identity all its own. The Asian-inspired cuisine may make you overlook the noise: lobster pancakes, sake-cured salmon rolls, duck in caramelized black vinegar, and, for dessert, coconut crème brûlée and chocolate hazelnut terrine with caramel sauce. The wine list is full of pleasures; the dessert wines are perfect as aperitifs and with vinegar-based and sweet-sour sauces. Check out the flavored sakes. *60 W. 53rd St., tel. 212/333–7788. Reservations advised. Dress: casual. AE, DC, MC, V. No lunch weekends.*

5757. Designed by I. M. Pei, the Four Seasons Hotel that houses this room is strikingly sleek, and its 22-foot coffered ceilings, inlaid maple floors, and onyx-studded bronze chandeliers set the tone for extraordinary food. Such outstanding appetizers as the potato crepes topped with smoked salmon, quail eggs, and Sevruga caviar hardly prepare you for the *pièce de résistance*, a lacquer box holding roasted vegetables on remarkable couscous. Desserts are equally strong, from sautéed bananas in poppyseed tuiles with rum raisin ice cream to the caramelized apple tarts with cinnamon ice cream and cider sauce. Wines are expensive but beautifully selected, with a good choice by the glass; note the martini menu. Service is superb. *57 W. 57th St., tel. 212/758–5757. Reservations advised. Jacket and tie advised. AE, DC, MC, V.*

★ **March.** With its travertine floor, working fireplace, and burled teak and English elm wainscoting, this singular restaurant is supremely, elegantly understated. Service is polished and inconspicuous, and the cuisine of chef Wayne Nish is at once restrained and inspired, with such dishes as the sushi-centered tuna tart and tartare, served with roast vegetables, and the impeccable Atlantic salmon with Middle Eastern spices revealing the oriental currents in the kitchen. The mixed grill of quail and squab with fall-vegetable ragout and the whimsical beggar's purses filled with lobster and truffles demonstrate a mastery of seasonal ingredients, precision cooking, and artful presentation. Warm walnut tart and grapefruit with grapefruit sorbet in gin syrup with coriander seed are delightful. The wine list is elite. *405 E. 58th St., tel. 212/838–9393. Reservations required. Jacket advised. AE, DC, MC, V. No lunch; closed Sun.*

Peacock Alley. This luxurious Waldorf-Astoria salon offers the professional service, fine china, and comprehensive wine cellar that distinguish many of today's hotel restaurants. It also has soft piano music, soothing lighting, and cushy seating at banquettes and spacious tables. Now, under executive chef John Doherty and chef de cuisine Laurent Manrique, the kitchen lives up to the rest of the dining experience, in dishes such as the baby rack of lamb, the fresh foie gras terrine with artichoke salad, dried apricots, and hazelnuts, and the fried wild bass with black pepper, citrus, and caramelized onions. There's a $70 tasting menu. *301 Park Ave., between 49th and 50th, tel. 212/872–4895. Reservations advised. Jacket and tie advised. AE, DC, MC, V. Closed Sat. lunch, Sun.*

French **Adrienne.** The elegant Peninsula Hotel restaurant has a first-rate kitchen: Witness the parfait of Amish hen with honey-roasted chestnuts and fresh plum compote, the rabbit tenderloin en croûte with Pomméry mustard sauce, the steamed cabbage roll with liver-rice, and the decadent caramel sampler—pecan crème caramel, butter-soaked apple-walnut torte, and roasted caramel nougatine. But it's the service that woos, wows, and knocks you over. Every detail is handled with care, although you are never aware of hovering waiters. Sunday brunch is elegance itself, with harp music. *700 5th Ave. at 55th, tel. 212/903–3918. Reservations advised. Jacket and tie advised. AE, DC, MC, V. No dinner Sun.–Mon. or lunch Sat.*

★ **La Caravelle.** New York's most Parisian restaurant has flattering lighting, spacious banquettes, and luxurious Jean Pagès murals. There's a fine line between elegance and pretention, and La Caravelle walks that line with authority. Under Japanese-born chef Tadashi Ono, the food is French but with Asian attitude, one that avoids nouvelle clichés. Appetizers include fillet of fluke with mint and chive oil, quail stuffed with wild mushrooms on lentils, and eel in puff pastry; distinguished entrées include smoked and grilled salmon with its roe in red wine sauce and rack of lamb baked in a clay crust. The array of desserts is stunning; don't miss the airy soufflés. The wine list provides an excellent choice of French and American vintages, while the reception at the door is warm and inviting, and the service among Manhattan's best. Consider the various prix fixe menus for value. *33 W. 56th St., 212/586–4252. Reservations required. Jacket and tie required. AE, DC, MC. V. Closed Sat. lunch, Sun.*

★ **Le Chantilly.** When executive chef David Ruggiero joined forces with owner–maître d'hôtel Camille Dulac, Le Chantilly joined the ranks of Manhattan's top French hideaways. Not only is the service smooth and the food glorious, the price is right. Well-spaced tables, wall sconces, and unobtrusive colors lend opulence. The creative Mr. Ruggiero produces everything from masterful appetizers (such as foie gras with warm kugelhof) and distinguished entrées (roasted lobster with foie gras, morels, and peas) to whimsical desserts (such as Golfer's Delight, chocolate mousse on a pistachio green). Nothing disappoints. Well, perhaps only the end of a perfect evening. *106 E. 57th St., tel. 212/751–2931. Reservations required. Jacket and tie required. AE, DC, MC, V. No Sun. lunch.*

★ **Le Périgord.** This exercise in elegance with spacious seating, soothing colors, and fresh flowers is also New York's most welcoming French restaurant. Service is friendly, and owner–maître d'hôtel Georges Briguet puts even first-timers at ease. Moreover, prices are a notch below those of most competitors, and the kitchen improves each year, thanks to chef de cuisine Antoine Bouterin. Lunch and dinner are prix fixe and might go like this: salmon, served tartare or marinated in spiced oil; tiny bay scallops sautéed with shallots; delicate grilled salmon medallions on sautéed cabbage; and a Lyonnaise dessert trolley laden with tarts, cakes, and floating island. There are also excellent soufflés, and the homemade brioche is divine. *405 E. 52nd St., tel. 212/755–6244. Reservations required. Jacket and tie required. AE, DC, MC, V. Closed Sun., Sat. lunch.*

★ **Lespinasse.** The pulchritudinous Louis XV decor of this dining room in the restored St. Regis Sheraton is an ideal setting for the refined cuisine of Gray Kunz, who honed his craft under Switzerland's celebrated Frédy Girardet. Kunz's Singapore heritage makes itself felt in Asian touches, as in the complex salad of spaghetti squash, poached chicken, foie gras, and crisp taro root. Or note the succulent braised oxtail, the Middle Eastern herb-crusted rack of lamb, or the squab with wild mushroom risotto; for dessert, go with the pear tart with chocolate ice cream and pear coulis, or the persimmon bursting with an airy flourless soufflé. Service is professional, the wine selection is improving. Although there is still no serious cheese trolley, Lespinasse is quickly evolving into Manhattan's long-awaited *grande luxe* restaurant. Excellent tasting menus are available. *2 E. 55th St., tel. 212/339–6719. Jacket required. AE, DC, MC, V. Closed Sun.*

Italian **Il Nido.** This fashionable restaurant is on many lists of Manhattan's top Italians. Hands-on restaurateur Adi Giovnanetti sees to it that you won't be disappointed. He finishes pastas, whisks zabaglione, and prepares the masterful blend of Gorgonzola and cognac to spread on toast. Simple pastas shine, and salmon carpaccio is a transparent wonder. Sautéed chicken for two requires 35 minutes—and is worth the wait. French wines are marked up substantially more than Italians (chauvinism knows no borders). Be prepared to wait for your table. *251 E. 53rd St., tel. 212/753–8450. Reservations required. Jacket and tie required. AE, DC, MC, V. Closed Sun.*

★ **San Pietro.** The stylish San Pietro highlights specialties of the Amalfi Coast. Among the remarkable pastas, you won't find clichés, but instead such eye-openers as homemade strips of buckwheat pasta with fontina and savoy cabbage, and chickpea–flour noodles with pesto. Similarly masterful are the grilled whole snapper and roast suckling pig, rolled around fresh herbs in white wine sauce. There are nice wines by the glass and wonderful homemade tarts and cheesecake. *18 E. 54th St., tel. 212/753–9015. Reservations advised. Jacket advised. AE, DC, MC, V. Closed Sun.*

Japanese **Nippon.** An innovator in bringing authentic Japanese cuisine to America, this spare, refined restaurant is the ideal place to enjoy a *kaiseki*, or traditional tasting dinner. Besides the buckwheat soba noodles, which are made on the premises twice daily, these meals include tempura, sushi, and a parade of tiny dishes, each distinctively and exquisitely presented, as well as (on pricier dinners) a bit of exotic fugu fish, known for its potential deadly effect. À la carte is available. *155 E. 52nd St., tel. 212/355–9020. Reservations advised. Jacket advised. AE, DC, MC, V. Closed Sat. lunch, Sun.*

Scandinavian **Aquavit.** Although you can dine in the delightful café upstairs for
★ half the price, the striking downstairs room in the late Nelson Rockefeller's town house, with its atrium and waterfall, *is* Aquavit. Confirming chef Johan Ahlstedt's talent and original style is such contemporary Swedish fare as his buckwheat blini with crème fraîche and caviar, roast squab with lemon-braised endive, baked turbot in citrus vinaigrette, and desserts such as apple sorbet and chocolate cake with caramelized pear. Service is discreet, and New York's largest aquavit list keeps company with the standout wine list. *13 W. 54th St., tel. 212/307–7311. Reservations required downstairs. Jacket and tie required. AE, DC, MC, V. Closed Sat. lunch, Sun.*

Seafood **Manhattan Ocean Club.** This sophisticated bilevel restaurant with comfortable seating is embellished with Picasso ceramics from the collection of owner Alan Stillman (also the proprietor of Smith & Wollensky). Shellfish by the piece, a good starter, is impeccably fresh. Lobster salad with flageolets and tarragon is delicious; tuna arrives seared and sushi-centered, with lattice potatoes and green salsa. Desserts include a good chocolate tart and a butterscotch sundae, and the wine list is good on light reds that work with seafood as well as whites. Kudos go to chef Jonathan Parker's clever illustrated menu. *57 W. 58th St., tel. 212/371–7777. Reservations advised. Jacket advised. AE, DC, MC, V. No lunch weekends.*

★ **Sea Grill.** At this restaurant under Four Seasons' former executive chef Seppi Renggli, winter's spectacular view of the Rockefeller Center ice rink and summer's lovely patio dining set the scene for such exemplary dishes as charred salmon with pepper ragout, tuna steak in zucchini and pancetta crust, and Prometheus chocolate cake, dusted with gold leaf. Prix fixe menus offer value, and wines are outstanding, with a fine selection by the glass. The American Festival Café (20 W. 50th St., tel. 212/246–6699) shares the view and the management, but not the good food and service; if you go, keep it simple. *19 W. 49th St., tel. 212/246–9201. Reservations advised. Jacket required. AE, DC, MC, V. Closed Sun.*

Steak **Manhattan Café.** In this steak house's softly lit rooms, you won't find the rush that you do in most of its competitors. Don't neglect the juicy sirloin, filet mignon, or porterhouse. But contemporary seafood dishes, such as blackened swordfish and lemon-pepper tuna, are also available, along with lyonnaise potatoes, potato pancakes, and sautéed spinach. There's a good selection of pastas and other Italian fare. Cheesecake and crème brûlée are fine. The wine list, above average for a steak house, offers decent bottles for $20 or so. There's brunch on Sunday. *1161 1st Ave., between 63rd and 64th, tel. 212/888–6556. Reservations advised. Dress: casual. AE, DC, MC, V. No lunch Sat.*

★ **Morton's.** Although famous for its steaks, New York has never seen anything like this branch of Chicago's famous steak house, in a masculine, dimly lit room that's easy on the spirit. Service is enthusiastic, the bar knows how to make a drink, and oh, those steaks and chops, that double-cut prime rib, and those 4½-pound lobsters! Potato skins, hash browns, and fresh asparagus are also terrific; for dessert, go straight to the cheesecake or the rich chocolate-velvet cake. The wine list offers hundreds of extraordinary reds and a smaller but interesting number of whites, and there is an excellent single-malt Scotch list. *551 5th Ave. at 45th, tel. 212/972–3315. Reservations advised. Jacket and tie advised. AE, DC, MC, V. No lunch weekends.*

Pen & Pencil. It's hard to beat this civilized and thoroughly pleasant restaurant with its comfortable bar area, fitted out with leather banquettes, and intimate main dining room, recalling a private club. Steaks and chops of the highest quality are grilled to perfection here, and grilled swordfish and sole stand out as well. Crisp, well-dressed salads, Italian entrées, and commendable pecan pie round out the menu. *205 E. 45th St., tel. 212/682–8660. Reservations advised. Jacket advised. AE, DC, MC, V. No lunch weekends.*

Sparks. This comfortably masculine room is one of New York's top five steak houses. The grilled meat and fish, listed on an intelligent, page-long menu, are professionally served, with crunchy steamed vegetables, and no pretentious sauces. Owner Pat Cetta is a wine buff, and his comprehensive list of ready-to-drink gems is priced fairly; the cellar ranks among the finest in the United States. *210 E. 46th St., tel. 212/687–4855. Reservations required. Jacket and tie advised. AE, DC, MC, V.*

$$–$$$
French
★

Raphael. Now we can all afford a Raphael, thanks to this Gallic charmer. We can't think of a more inviting room; the tiny garden is pleasant in summer, and a fireplace cozies things up in winter. Service is benevolent, and chef de cuisine Jean-Michel Bergougnoux's cooking is consistently excellent, from the perfectly roasted halibut with beets and the rare tuna sandwiched between shoestring potatoes to the napoleon of candied onions, chives, and corn. Among his desserts, the crusty, soft-centered chocolate cake and exotic-fruit mousse shine. Even house wines are good. *33 W. 54th St., tel. 212/582–8993. Reservations required. Jacket required. AE, DC, MC, V. Closed weekends (except for Sat. dinner Labor Day–Memorial Day).*

Italian

Gilda. From its intimate front room to its glamorous main dining space with high ceilings and a central bar, this restaurant is extraordinarily beautiful. The spectacular pastas include bow ties with prosciutto and corn, and fettuccine with cognac, cream, and wild mushrooms. Risotto arrives with strawberries, and fillet of red snapper is wrapped in crispy potatoes with shrimp purée. Desserts, service, and wines are up to the level of the delicious, innovative food. Or simply stop for caviar and champagne, served in the grotto below. *12 E. 49th St., tel. 212/832–2500. Reservations advised. Jacket and tie advised. AE, MC, V. Closed Sun.*

Mexican

Rosa Mexicano. Owner Josefina Howard is serious about her profession, and her authentic restaurant is a delight. The food is carefully executed, including guacamole, prepared table-side, and a cold seafood platter. A number of regional dishes are unavailable elsewhere. How often do you see duck enchiladas? Chicken, wrapped in parchment and steamed in beer? Or a pozole, that delectable soup-stew of hominy, pork, and chicken? Chocolate mousse cake with a hint of chili, set in coffee cream, provides a snappy conclusion. If only the margaritas were better! Our favorite place to sit is the front room, with its lively bar, open kitchen, and comfortable booths. *1063 1st Ave. at 58th, tel. 212/753–7407. Reservations advised. Dress: casual. AE, DC, MC, V. No lunch.*

Seafood
★ **The Captain's Table.** To be truly distinguished, a seafood restaurant must use scrupulously fresh fish and cook them precisely and with some inventiveness. This unpretentious spot, an eclectic room with Murano chandeliers and starched white linens, scores on all counts. In addition to straightforward grilled, sautéed, and poached offerings, there are preparations with international twists; some reflect the chefs' Thai and Mexican backgrounds (shrimp Bangkok-style or wrapped in jalapeños, for example), and others draw on owner Gino Musso's Italian heritage (grilled whole snapper or striped bass with an herbed olive oil-garlic-lemon sauce, for example). Don't miss the remarkable frogs' legs, stone crab, or Alaskan king crab. The wine list is that rarity, one with a few real bargains. *860 2nd Ave. at 46th, tel. 212/697-9538. Reservations advised. Dress: casual but neat. AE, DC, MC, V. Closed Sat. lunch, Sun.*

Oceana. Chef James Galileo's inventive composites range from a transparent tuna-scallop carpaccio with green horseradish and scallion wonton to a volcano of savoy cabbage wrapped around lobster and mashed potatoes; everything is as visually appealing as it is delicious—even desserts, which include chocolate torte with cappuccino ice cream, done by the chef's wife, Barbara Galileo. Not trendy or snobby, it's also rather pretty, with its pastel color scheme, muted lighting, and lovely paintings. Note the $38 three-course dinner. *55 E. 54th St., tel. 212/759-5941. Reservations advised. Jacket advised. AE, DC, MC, V. Closed Sat. lunch, Sun.*

Vietnamese **Le Colonial.** The dining room here is straight out of Somerset Maugham with its rattan chairs, potted palms, ceiling fans, shutters, and black-and-white period photographs. The food, although westernized, is usually well prepared; start with the superb *bahn cuon,* or steamed Vietnamese ravioli with chicken, shrimp, and mushrooms, and move on to crisp-fried whole snapper. Sorbets, ice creams, and fruit-based puddings are right on. Don't miss the Vietnamese coffee—strong black brew secreting a layer of condensed milk. Nirvana in a cup! The wine selection is fine. *149 E. 57th St., tel. 212/752-0808. Reservations advised. Jacket advised. AE, DC, MC, V.*

$$ **Ambassador Grill.** If it's Sunday, head for this model of modern ele-
American- gance in the Park Hyatt Hotel: The brunch buffet then is one of the
Contemporary finest in the city. But then, the dining experience here, under chef Mathew Mitnitsky, is always first-class (and at less-than-first-class prices). Favorite plates include sweet-pea blinis with goat-cheese vinaigrette, crabmeat quesadillas with cilantro oil, yellow- and blue-corn–crusted monkfish, and roasted duck breast with cider vinegar and honey sauce. There's also an amazing prix fixe dinner (sometimes preceded by an all-you-can-eat seafood buffet that entails only a small surcharge). *1 United Nations Plaza at 44th St., tel. 212/702-5014. Reservations advised. Jacket advised. AE, DC, MC, V.*

★ **Tatou.** Nostalgia bids us mourn the passing of the old Copa and Stork Club. But the food is worlds better in this restaurant in a former opera house, a tiered room with a stage up front and a colossal chandelier overhead; in fact, Scott Cohen's masterful cooking competes well with the offerings of top restaurants. Just try grilled boneless quail with crispy potato ribbons, the red snapper in tomato-basil-saffron broth, and the iron-skillet–roasted baby chicken with cornbread stuffing and sage. No pretentious tricks here. Wines, service, and desserts (especially the warm chocolate pudding in a cup) are beyond reproach. Entertainment is learning to be counterpoint to the food, rather than compete; a harpist often plays at lunch. *151 E. 50th St., tel. 212/753–1144. Reservations required. Jacket required. AE, DC, MC, V. Closed Sat. lunch, Sun.*

Chinese ★ **Chiam.** Although purists argue that the only worthy Chinese eateries are in Chinatown, such venues as this one make a persuasive case for the more westernized uptown experience. The setting is stylish, the wine list extraordinary for a Chinese restaurant. Seafood is good; the more interesting dishes, chicken and Chinese sausage steamed in a lotus leaf, for example, are often not on the menu, so solicit your captain's advice. *160 E. 48th St., tel. 212/371–2323. Reservations advised. Dress: casual but neat. AE, DC, MC, V.*

French-Thai ★ **Vong.** Jean-Georges Vongerichten's latest creation is a roaring success. The room is gorgeous with its palms and its rubbed-gold ceiling, the lighting is flattering, and the clientele chic. Most of the food is very good—don't miss the lobster and daikon roll with rosemary-ginger dip, the rabbit curry braised with carrots and cumin seed, or the coconut soup with chicken and galanga, an herb that gives special character to Thai cuisine. Unfortunately, some dishes are spotty, but desserts are surprisingly varied and delicious. Lychee and papaya soup and banana, kiwi, and passion fruit salad with white pepper ice cream stand out. Still, the prices are fair and the wines well chosen. *200 E. 54th St., tel. 212/486–9592. Reservations required. Dress: casual but neat. AE, DC, MC, V. No lunch weekends.*

Indian ★ **Dāwat.** One of the city's finest Indians, this classy, understated spot has flattering lighting, smooth service, and a menu full of consultant Madhur Jaffrey's subtle cuisine: shrimp in mustard seeds with curry leaves, lamb with white turnips, black-eyed peas and corn, and onion *kulcha*—an onion-stuffed bread flavored with fresh coriander. Dahi aloo poori, a mix of crispy noodles, potatoes, and chickpeas in a haunting sweet-and-sour sauce, is not to be missed. Dāwat demonstrates the charms of Indian sweets; try the pudding-like carrot halva, the *kheer* (rice pudding) with pistachios, and *kulfi*, a delicate frozen yogurt. *210 E. 58th St., tel. 212/355–7555. Reservations advised. Dress: casual. AE, DC, MC, V. No lunch Sun.*

Jewel of India. In the subcontinent's exotic cookery, each dish must exhibit its distinct flavor; spice plays against spice (curry powder need not apply). Jewel of India specializes in the fare of the north, which trades in the south's vegetarian dishes for subtle meat preparations. The marvelous herb-scented breads and knockout tandoori show off the kitchen's prowess. Go for the weekday lunch buffet ($12.95). *15 W. 44th St., tel. 212/869–5544. Reservations advised. Dress: casual but neat. AE, DC, MC, V.*

Italian-Kosher **Medici 56.** This beautiful multilevel restaurant, the best in the country for kosher fare, has an elegant design, lovely flowers, and stylish Italian food. In fact, the proliferation of yarmulkes in the dining room is the only clue to procedures in the kitchen. Try the fabulous arugula, endive, and radicchio salad, the charred salmon and cannellini beans, or the fried zucchini. The pasta is terrific, especially the rigatoni with herbed ricotta and plum tomatoes. Desserts are pretty as a picture. *25 W. 56th St., tel. 212/767–1234. Reservations advised. Dress: casual but neat. AE, DC, MC, V. Closed Sat.*

Seafood ★ **Dock's.** The large brass-trimmed bar of this striking, high-ceilinged art deco brasserie displays scrupulously fresh shellfish, which are presented on tiered platters. Cooked preparations run the gamut from traditional American to inventive-eclectic. Alaskan white king-salmon with caviar beurre blanc is inspired, and the slaw is a paragon. For dessert, try the gooey key lime pie or mud fudge pie-cake. Service is knowledgeable, and the unusual list of wine, beer, and single-malt Scotches and bourbons is a pleasure. *633 3rd Ave. at 40th, tel. 212/986–8080. Dress: casual but neat. Reservations advised. AE, DC, MC, V. No lunch Sat.*

$–$$ **The Brasserie.** This modern Manhattan version of a French
French brasserie in the Mies van der Rohe–designed Seagram Building is open around the clock and has been packing in New Yorkers for years, thanks to expert management, an authentically French joie de vivre, and solid food based on quality ingredients. Breakfast is a delight with great croissants, wonderful egg dishes, terrific pastries, and marvelous coffee. Lunch or dinner can also be good, though more olive oil, garlic, and pizzazz wouldn't hurt. Wines are well-priced and service is pleasant. *100 E. 53rd St., tel. 212/751–4840. Reservations advised. Dress: neat but casual. AE, DC, MC, V.*

$ **Ipanema.** This snug, modern restaurant is a comfortable place to
Brazilian sample Brazil's exotic cuisine. Feijoada, the national dish—black beans with smoked meats, collard greens, oranges, chili peppers, and a comforting grain named farofa—is good here if not authentic. Shrimp sautéed in the shell and codfish fritters are tasty, as is the boiled cod and vegetable platter with herb-infused olive oil. For dessert, try the custard-like *dolce de leite.* And don't miss the great sweet Brazilian rum drinks—*cachaças* (with coconut milk) and *caipirinhas* (with lime juice). *13 W. 46th St., tel. 212/730–5848. Reservations accepted. Dress: casual. AE, DC, MC, V.*

Korean **New York Kom Tang Soot Bul House.** It's the best Korean restaurant
★ on a street jammed with them, and dinner is a show. So come ready for charades (little English is spoken); wear clothes you don't mind getting smoky (from the hibachis in the center of the communal tables); and insist on the attractive second floor. Dinner starts with ten delicious sides, including kim chee, the fiery Korean pickle. Afterwards, there's soup, then the main event: You cook thin slices of beef or chicken over red-hot coals, top them with hot chilies and raw garlic, and wrap it up with lettuce. Steak dinners are just $15. *32 W. 32nd St., tel. 212/947–8482. Reservations: difficult if you don't speak Korean. Dress: casual. AE, MC, V.*

Mexican **Alamo.** This piñata-decked sleeper serves all kinds of Mexican food: real Mexican (witness the marvelous chicken in pumpkin seed sauce), Tex-Mex (the best chicken fajitas in town), Southwestern (blue quesadillas), Mexican-Italian (chili pasta), and basic Mexican-American (gringo chili, with ground meat). The fiesta platter lays out the best appetizers, and even meat-lovers love the mesquite-grilled vegetables in poblano chili butter, with jalapeño corn bread. For dessert, try the frozen chocolate-mousse pie or the whole papaya filled with ice cream. Every night is a fiesta, with 17 beers and lethal margaritas (the real thing, with Triple Sec, lime juice, and tequila). *304 E. 48th St., tel. 212/759–0590. Reservations accepted. Dress: casual. AE, DC, MC, V. Closed Sat. lunch, Sun.*

Theater District and Carnegie Hall

$$$$ **Les Célébrités.** From the moon-shaped banquettes and the plush red
French carpets to the careful lighting and paintings by celebrity artists, this intimate restaurant in the Essex House hotel is unabashedly lavish; the china is Limoges, the silver Christophle. Presentations are dramatic: For example, sea scallops with diced salmon gravlax arrives in a giant shell, which, when pried open, reveals perfectly grilled scallops in a delicate beurre blanc flecked with orange nug-

gets of the salmon, a salty contrast; the shell rests on a bed of deliciously briny sea vegetables. With similar drama, four intense sorbets are presented on a tall nest of spun sugar garnished with chocolate leaves for dessert. The six-course tasting dinner showcases the strengths of executive chef Christian Delouvrier. The wine list is extensive and expensive; best values are among California cabernets and chardonnays, but there is also a good selection of wines by the glass at affordable prices. *160 Central Park S, tel. 212/ 484–5113. Reservations essential. Jacket and tie required. AE, DC, MC, V. No lunch; closed Sun.–Mon.*

Seafood **Le Bernardin.** Even in New York, this restaurant is a star, with a superb kitchen, luxuriously spaced tables, soft lighting, high ceilings, and walls hung with gilt-framed oils of sea scenes. Le Bernardin brought a new kind of seafood to America, an elaborate and inventive cuisine based on careful undercooking of the freshest fish available. The food can still dazzle; note the black bass done ceviche-style in scallion-ginger broth or with Chinese spices, port, and wild mushrooms; the seared sea scallops, with fava beans in a diaphanous sauce of mint and peas; and sushi-center tuna with truffled herb salad. The knockout desserts include a caramel wonder under a spun sugar dome. The noise level is low, the service some of the silkiest around. The wine list is comprehensive but expensive. *155 W. 51st St., tel. 212/489–1515. Reservations required. Jacket and tie required. AE, DC, MC, V. Closed Sat. lunch, Sun.*

$$$–$$$$ **Petrossian.** With its abundance of marble, this art deco caviar bar
French and restaurant is like no other New York dining spot. Service is pol-
★ ished, and when chef Joe Pace hits the mark, the food is ethereal. A tasting dinner starts with gobs of fresh beluga on buttered toast (with no competing garnishes); then comes a huge, perfectly roasted scallop, lovely braised salmon, or tender sautéed veal; and you end with a seductive chocolate soufflé or homemade ice cream. Have vodka with the caviar or champagne throughout. If you're solo, stop at the comfortable counter bar; if you're feeling festive on Sunday, come for brunch. *182 W. 58th St., tel. 212/245–2214. Reservations advised. Jacket and tie advised. AE, DC, MC, V.*

Italian **San Domenico.** Owner Tony May has raised American consciousness
★ of the Italian cucina, and executive chef Theo Schoenegger executes dishes such as Mediterranean baby cuttlefish with vegetables, soft egg-yolk ravioli with truffle butter, and roast baby goat with authority; for dessert, try the custard with balsamic vinegar and caramel and cornmeal-chocolate soufflé. The setting is like a private villa, with terra-cotta floors, sumptuous leather chairs, and lots of warm, earthy hues. The huge wine list showcases Italy's great vintages. Your tab drops if you stick to prix fixe dinners, especially on Sunday; throw caution to the winds and you may thumb a ride home. *240 Central Park S, tel. 212/265–5959. Reservations required. Jacket and tie required; on Sun., casual but neat. AE, MC, DC, V. No lunch weekends.*

$$$ **Barbetta.** The 18th-century Venetian harpsichord in the foyer sets
Italian the mood in this venerable establishment, an island of civility in two
★ elegant, antiques-furnished town houses. The enchanting garden is verdant with century-old trees and perfumed with magnolia, wisteria, jasmine, and gardenia. Yet, although the kitchen produced northern Italian food long before most Americans knew what it was, Barbetta has not received the culinary recognition it deserves. The kitchen impresses with its simplicity and fidelity to tradition. The *carne cruda* (hand-chopped raw veal with lemon juice and olive oil) dusted with white truffles, and the fonduta, risottos, and handmade

agnolotti are superb. Or try the roasted venison or wild hare. The impeccable desserts include the *panna cotta* (milk custard), *torta di nocciole* (nut cake), and *monte bianco* (chestnut purée topped with whipped cream). In addition to the well-priced, beautifully selected short wine list, there is a long version offering more than 140 bottles dating back to 1880 (Barbetta, New York's oldest restaurant still operated by its founding family, was opened in 1906). Special prix fixe menus make Barbetta affordable. *321 W. 46th St., tel. 212/246–9171. Reservations advised. Jacket required. AE, DC, MC, V. Closed Sun., Mon. lunch.*

Remi. This stylish Italian restaurant—designed by architect Adam Tihany, who co-owns it with chef Francesco Antonucci—is a celebrity favorite, and the blue-and-white nautical decor, skylighted open atrium, and room-length mural of Venice have to compete for your attention with glimpses of stars. The contemporary Venetian cuisine is beautifully presented. A goat cheese giveaway in a lively marinara sauce with bread sticks is a perfect start. Simple grilled sardines on sour potatoes are well executed, as is goose carpaccio. Some dishes are under-seasoned, but you won't go wrong with the expertly grilled veal chop or the wonderful desserts. The wine list is exceptionally well-organized. *145 W. 53rd St., tel. 212/581–4242. Reservations advised. Dress: casual. AE, DC, MC, V. No lunch weekends.*

Russian **Russian Tea Room.** The green walls, red banquettes, and Christmas ornaments that dangle from the chandeliers create a festive mood; this place is as shiny as a gold ruble. But in addition, everybody's favorite tea room is making a stellar attempt to get into the serious-kitchen business. Predictably, blini and caviar with a selection from one of the most extensive vodka lists in town is perfect. Less predictably, traditional Russian borscht, chicken Kiev, and beef Stroganoff are less successful than such nouvelle creations as seared red snapper fillet with wild mushrooms, and grilled sea scallops and rock shrimp surrounding a gâteau made of blini, with osetra caviar and lemon vodka sauce. There's an excellent cabaret upstairs and brunch on weekends. *150 W. 57th St., tel. 212/265–0947. Reservations advised. Jackets required at dinner. AE, DC, MC, V.*

Steak **Ben Benson's.** Not only are steaks, chops, and accompaniments first-rate in this convivial spot with a rather masculine interior and a no-nonsense atmosphere; there is also a real chef in the kitchen. Witness such contemporary steak house fare as cold lobster cocktail and Maryland crab cakes; steak, chops, and the fabulous prime rib; and such excellent daily specials as Friday's crusted fish hash. Don't miss the horseradish-mashed potatoes or the excellent home fries. Cocktails are oversize, the wine list carefully chosen. *123 W. 52nd St., tel. 212/581–8888. Reservations advised. Dress: casual. AE, DC, MC, V. Closed Sat., Sun. lunch.*

Ruth Chris. Manhattan's genteel addition to this group of over 40 around the world is giving other steak houses around town a run for their money. With its impressionistic oil paintings, dark red walls, and crisp white napery on well-spaced tables, it's much more inviting than its location at the base of a nondescript office tower might suggest. Moreover, the steaks and chops, served sizzling in butter unless you specify otherwise, are tops. The menu defines degrees of doneness according to temperature and color, and the kitchen gives you just what you request. T-Bones or rib eyes, lamb chops or veal, or pork, chicken, or seafood: They do it perfectly. The shrimp cocktail, Italian salad, and lyonnaise potatoes are all terrific. Desserts? Try the fabulous bread pudding, outrageous chocolate-mousse cheesecake, or chocolate sin cake. With its remarkable wine list and excellent service, Ruth Chris sets a new standard among New York steak houses. *148 W. 51st St., tel. 212/245–9600. Reservations advised. Dress: casual but neat. AE, DC, MC, V. No lunch weekends.*

$$–$$$
Italian

Fantino. It's an elegant spot, with its crystal chandeliers, working fireplaces, and French and Italian oil paintings. The welcome of maitre d'hôtel Sandro is warm, the service polished, and the cuisine of executive chef Gennaro Villella outstanding. Largely from Umbria, Tuscany, and Liguria, it is decidedly contemporary, with a number of masterpieces: a rice tart with black truffle and Gorgonzola fondue, tagliatelle with asparagus and fresh langoustines, wild mushroom ravioli redolent of white truffle, and braised duck with vin santo, morels, and fennel. The tiramisù is perfect and the praline semifredo sheer delight. Breakfast is served daily. *112 Central Park S, in the Ritz-Carlton, tel. 212/664–7700. Reservations advised. Jacket required. AE, DC, MC, V. No lunch at press time; closed Sun.*

$$
American-Contemporary
★

Symphony Café. At this upscale brasserie near Carnegie Hall, decked with gold records and autographed photographs of songwriters, executive chef Neil Murphy's food is first-rate: Grilled tuna and quail arrive on mini-hibachis, and delicate consommé with gnocchi comes in a tiny hollowed-out pumpkin. Or try the homey wood-grilled chicken with chanterelles or delicious pan-roasted cod with lobster home fries. Pastry chef Richard Leach delights, too: Glazed pumpkin custard comes with homemade ice cream under a spun sugar dome. *950 8th Ave. at 56th, tel. 212/397–9595. Reservations accepted. Dress: casual but neat. AE, DC, MC, V.*

Cuban

Victor's Café 52. This Cuban restaurant with piano music and a Latin ambiance is more fun than a barrel of monkeys. It has improved markedly in the last few years, and whether you choose Puerto Rican or Cuban tamales, roast suckling pig, grilled seafood, or prime sirloin, you won't be disappointed. Desserts are beautifully presented, and service is friendly. Start with one of the Cuban cocktails and the place may even bring out the Latin in you. The West Side's Victor's (240 Columbus Ave., tel. 212/595–8599), under different ownership, is very different. *236 W. 52nd St., tel. 212/586–7714. Reservations accepted. Dress: casual. AE, DC, MC, V.*

French
★

Café Botanica. Inspired, decidedly French Christian Delouvrier, the Essex House executive chef, also lends his talents to this glorious café, which is as airy as the country with its high ceilings, wicker chairs, Central Park views, and striking Elke Sommer painting. The food is inventive and elegant, with a solid classical foundation. Standouts include sautéed foie gras on green lentils, porterhouse with mashed potatoes and chives, and seared salmon with celery root–sorrel coulis. Even the fresh fruit plate is lovely, each fruit in prime condition. Service is outstanding, as are the wine list and the 17 wines by the glass. Prix fixe menus can be real bargains. Or go for the outstanding Sunday brunch or extraordinary Viennese tea. *160 Central Park S, tel. 212/484–5120. Reservations advised. Dress: casual but neat (no jeans). AE, DC, MC. V.*

Italian
★

Trattoria dell'Arte. This top trattoria still displays the controversial oversize renderings of body parts. But the real draw nowadays is the delicious cuisine, American ingredients creatively prepared in the Italian style—as in the marvelous rigate with grilled vegetables and calamari, the linguini with red bean sauce and shiitake mushrooms, and the incredible whole fish with green olives and white wine. Double veal chops are mammoth, desserts fabulous. The antipasti on the bar dazzle, and the service is so good that the staff can keep your glasses filled, serve two other tables, and still have time to kibbutz. Check out the great wine list and flavored grappas. Weekends, there's brunch. *900 7th Ave., between 56th and 57th, tel. 212/ 245–9800. Reservations advised. Dress: casual. AE, DC, MC, V.*

Seafood **Christer's.** Manhattan's newest Scandinavian restaurant, from former Aquavit chef Christer Larsson, is altogether gratifying, with its warm reception, fine wine list, large portions, and moderate prices. There are five salmon specials daily; the fish may be poached in citrus broth with snow peas and asparagus; ginger-glazed and served with warm potato salad and ginger crisp; marinated with serranos, seared, and served with black beans and corn-and-tomatillo salsa; or tandoori, with chutney and lentils, in tumeric-spiked vinaigrette. There's a fantastic salmon chowder, with hints of dill and curry, a braised lamb shank, and a roasted veal chop with shoestring potatoes. One room is rustic (imagine a Norwegian log cabin); another is skylit, with fish painted on its blue floor. *145 W. 55th St., tel. 212/974-7224. Reservations advised. Dress: casual. AE, DC, MC, V. Closed Sat. lunch, Sun.*

$–$$ **Carmine's.** This cavernous family-style eatery, which started on the
Italian West Side, soon moved to Broadway. It's a good show. (*See* Upper
★ West Side.) *200 W. 44th St., tel. 212/221-3800. Reservations accepted. Dress: casual. AE.*

$ **Hard Rock Café.** This restaurant with the fins of a vintage Cadillac
American- as a marquee is best known for its loud rock music, rock star memo-
Casual rabilia, and teenyboppers. Truth is, the food is amazingly tasty. The pork barbecue, listed as a pig sandwich, is better than you often get in North Carolina. The incredible chili, with ground and chopped meats, is spiced to perfection. Or try the superlative club sandwich, crispy bacon, roast chicken, lettuce, tomato, and mayo between huge slabs of ice box bread. And the french fries, skins on, are what every french fry wants to be. Because portions are huge, everything can be split. Be sure to sample the outrageous hot fudge brownie for dessert. To avoid waits, go at opening and avoid school holidays. *221 W. 57th St., tel. 212/459-9320. No reservations. Dress: casual (earplugs may be appropriate). AE, MC, V.*

Joe Allen. With its brick walls and dark wood bar, it looks like a pub, but the food, having improved of late, warrants the smart white tablecloths: Try the inventive Cobb salad with chicken, broccoli, chickpeas, bacon, and Gorgonzola (a meal in itself); the delicious meat loaf sandwich on sourdough bread with black-eyed pea salad; or the exceptional grilled calves' liver, thinly cut and served with spinach and mashed potatoes. Chocolate pudding-cake and banana cream pie are fine, and there is a very good list of beer and inexpensive wines. You might even glimpse a celebrity or two. *326 W. 46th St., tel. 212/581-6464. Reservations advised. Dress: casual. MC, V.*

Planet Hollywood. This café owned by Bruce Willis, Demi Moore, Sylvester Stallone, Keith Barish, Robert Earl, and Arnold Schwarzenegger is fun. The walls are full of celebrity handprints outside and movie memorabilia inside; check out the gremlin. Who cares that the place rates a 10 on the decibel scale. The food is better than it has to be, but you'll be happiest if you stick with the Southwestern-style nachos, the fajitas, and the playful pizzas. Golden margaritas are good. *140 W. 57th St., tel. 212/333-7827. No reservations. Dress: casual. AE, DC, MC, V.*

Virgil's. This massive roadhouse-style restaurant in the Theater District is as funky as real Americana with its clever neon and formica decor. Start with stuffed jalapeños, buttermilk onion rings with blue-cheese dip, or the incredible buttermilk biscuits. Then go for the pig platter, piled with barbecued brisket, pork shoulder and ribs, chicken, and more. Or try the pulled lamb or the great chicken-fried steak, breaded with potato chips and corn flakes. Memphis ribs come wet or dry, and there are five terrific sauces. Most entrées can serve two and come with two excellent side dishes—mustard slaw, dirty rice, mashed potatoes and gravy, or the like. For dessert, go for peanut butter pie or devil's food cake—all winners. Wines start at $12 and there are over 60 beers. *152 W. 44th St., tel. 212/921–9494. Reservations advised. Dress: casual. AE, DC, MC, V.*

Deli **Carnegie Deli.** Although not what it was, this no-nonsense spot is still midtown's best deli, a species distinguished by crowds, noise, brusque service, and jumbo sandwiches. Try to get the counterman to hand-slice your corned beef or pastrami; the extra juiciness and superior texture warrant the extra charge. To drink? Try cream soda or celery tonic. *854 7th Ave., between 54th and 55th, tel. 212/ 757–2245. No reservations. Dress: casual. No credit cards.*

Greek **Uncle Nick's.** This hole-in-the-wall whose main decoration is its appetizing display of fresh fish is best at simple grills: Baby octopus or whole red snapper, porgy, or sea bass on the bone, with a very good Greek country salad, will delight you. The *saganakityri*, a sharp cheese baked in lemon butter and flamed, is delicious, as is yogurt drizzled with honey; skip the baklava. Retsina, the Greek white wine that's tangy with Aleppo pine resin (and resulting turpentine overtones) is not for all, but it is traditional. *402 W. 51st St., tel. 212/ 245–7992. Reservations not necessary. Dress: casual. MC, V.*

Jamaican **Island Spice.** This spotless and altogether delightful spot, with
★ green walls and plastic tablecloths, offers some of New York's best Caribbean fare. The kitchen's gastronomic reggae shows up in such dishes as the zesty jerk pork and chicken barbecue; the delicious whole red snapper, pan-fried then steamed with peppers, onions, and tomatoes; and the tender, curried goat meat, which you stuff into Indian flatbread—what a terrific sandwich. Among the honest desserts is an airy bread pudding with rum raisin sauce. You'll also appreciate the inexpensive wine, good beer, and pleasant service. Brunch is served on Sunday. *402 W. 44th, tel. 212/765–1737. Reservations advised. Dress: casual. AE, DC, MC, V.*

Middle Eastern **Kabul Cafe.** There are subtle differences among Middle Eastern foods: Afghani cuisine is robust and easy to take; Persian cooking is delicate. This spotless bilevel restaurant with Afghan rugs on the walls and waiters in native costumes offers a little of both—at bargain prices. Try the scallion-filled dumplings with yogurt and meat sauce, the crispy ground beef turnovers, or the scrumptious chicken, pickle, and potato salad to start; move on to kebabs or vegetable and meat stews, and don't miss the coriander-flavored brown rice. The wonderful sauces balance sour against hot and cold against warm. *265 W. 54th St., tel. 212/757–2037. Reservations accepted. Dress: casual. DC, MC, V.*

Upper East Side

$$$$ **Aureole.** Along with Bouley, Charles Palmer's fashionable, beauti-
American- ful restaurant is one of the town's toughest reservations. Appetizers
Contemporary are good. But entrées often seem manufactured instead of carefully prepared; desserts are masterfully presented but lack intense flavor, balance, and contrast. Wine prices are high, and the ventilation and ambience upstairs is sub-par. *4 E. 61st St., tel. 212/319–1660.*

Reservations required. Jacket and tie required. AE, DC, MC, V. Closed Sat. lunch, Sun.

French **Daniel.** Daniel Boulud's $1.9 million restaurant, elegant in a corporate way, dazzles with its celebrity clientele (Barbara Walters, Henry Kissinger) and its cuisine (at once contemporary and classic). Note the remarkable cold sweet-pea soup, delicate veal-tongue salad, intoxicating Oregon morels with chives, and roasted duck with spicy spring fruits. However, some dishes cry out for more seasoning or are over- or undercooked; skip the signature black sea bass, wrapped in a less-than-crisp potato shell. There's a special chocolate dessert menu, a lovely mille-feuille of candied chestnuts, and an unusual apple soup with apple sorbet. Daniel also has a well chosen but expensive wine list, a sidewalk café and pleasant, if casual, service. *20 E. 76th St., tel. 212/288–0033. Reservations essential. Jacket required. AE, DC, V, MC, D. Closed Sun.*

★ **Le Cirque.** The rich, the famous, and dentists from Des Moines all want to dine at this palace of international luxury; one comes here not to eat, but for the experience—although the food is of the highest quality. The cuisine has had its ups and downs, but owner Sirio Maccioni always manages to restore it to the top echelon. Current offerings by chef Sylvain Portay, including tuna tartare with a hint of curry, scallops and truffles in pastry, and lobster and rosemary risotto, are superb, as is the black bass in potato crust. Try the signature crème brûlée. The wine list is encyclopedic and tolerably priced, the service as smooth as it is friendly. *58 E. 65th St., tel. 212/794–9292. Reservations required. Jacket and tie required. AE, DC, MC, V. Closed Sun.*

Italian **Parioli Romanissimo.** This town house restaurant's elegant dining room and striking garden can produce a miraculous repast. Sample sautéed sea scallops in watercress sauce, seared lamb carpaccio in a sweet red pepper purée, saffron-porcini risotto, ravioli of goat cheese and black truffles, grilled salmon fillet with tarragon in tomato beurre blanc, and veal with broccoli purée. Floating island and passion fruit in chocolate sauce rate among desserts. Note the prime cheese trolley, with nearly a hundred top French and Italian selections. The conservative clientele is of the money-is-no-object genre. *24 E. 81st St., tel. 212/288–2391. Reservations required. Jacket and tie required. AE, DC, MC, V. No lunch; closed Sunday.*

$$$–$$$$ **Post House.** Superb grilling and first-rate ingredients are half the
Steak appeal. Good service, inventive daily specials, and the inordinately comfortable main dining room, with leather armchairs, capacious tables, and parquet floor, complete the story. A rib steak special arrives black outside, moist, rosy, and warm within. Triple lamb chops are prima, Caesar salad perfection. Frozen crème brûlée rejuvenates the dish, and the signature chocolate box, Belgian chocolate filled with white and da.k chocolat^ mousse, is t^ die for. The wine list is vast, full of wines unavailable elsewhere. *28 E. 63rd St., tel. 212/935–2888. Reservations advised. Jacket and tie advised. AE, DC, MC, V. Closed Sat. lunch, Sun.*

$$$ **Café Pierre.** This elegant room in the Pierre Hotel was always beau-
American- tiful with its ornate mirrors and cloud murals overhead. Now young
Contemporary chef Joel Somerstein has revitalized the kitchen. Prawns on creamy polenta and lobster with parsnip purée, served with potato ravioli in beurre rouge, are far from everyday. Orange-curd tart in a chocolate shell stands out, as does the service staff's youthful enthusiasm. Stay for a drink at the piano bar after dinner. *2 E. 61st St., tel. 212/940–8185. Reservations advised. Jacket and tie advised. AE, DC, MC, V.*

Mark's. This multilevel restaurant in the small, elegant Mark Hotel, sweet but not precious, presents a tranquil air with its lovely prints, gilt-framed mirrors, and the brocade pillows plumped on its banquettes. Erik Maillard prepares smoked salmon tartare with pea shoot salad and yogurt dressing; black sea bass with baby spinach, braised onions, and mashed potato gratin; and roast baby lamb with a succotash of fresh beans. Dessert stars a chocolate-pecan tart topped with caramel ice cream. Breakfast is very fine, with home-made muffins and cereals and marvelous duck hash. *25 E. 77th St., tel. 212/879–1864. Reservations advised. Jacket and tie advised. AE, DC, V.*

★ **Park Avenue Café.** American folk art, antique toys, and sheafs of dried wheat decorate this unpretentious dazzler. Presentations that would be frivolous from lesser chefs come off with flying colors in the hands of the imaginative David Burke. A delicate flan of prosciutto, peppers, and foie gras comes in an egg shell held by a porcelain rabbit. Seared salmon with ginger rests on an inverted vase. Salmon is cured like pastrami. Dessert? Inside a glass candy dish sprinkled with sugar is chocolate-milk crème brûlée and a chocolate truffle. Far from being merely conceptual, all this is also delicious. *100 E. 63rd St., tel. 212/644–1900. Reservations advised. Dress: casual. AE, DC, MC, V. Closed Sat., lunch.*

★ **Sign of the Dove.** Skylights, stunning floral arrangements, well-spaced tables, brick arches, and piano music distinguish the dining rooms here, some of the prettiest in town. From Andrew D'Amico's distinguished kitchen, don't miss the titillating Thai-spiced crab chowder, the mouthwatering Moroccan-inspired lamb bastilla, or the pan-seared tuna in green curry broth. Of the excellent desserts, we adore the espresso granita with Sambuca cream and the coconut spoon bread. The wine list, large selection by the glass, and interested service complete the experience. Prix fixe menus put the place squarely among the city's best famous-restaurant values. *1110 3rd Ave. at 65th, tel. 212/861–8080. Reservations required. Jacket and tie advised. AE, DC, MC, V. No lunch Mon.*

$$–$$$
Italian
Coco Pazzo. Here's another wildly successful Pino Luongo creation (the name means "crazy chef"), with contemporary Italian fare at its best plus strong entries from Mr. Luongo's native Tuscany, such as the soft polenta with sausage and tomato and the *cacciucca*, a fish stew. Or start with grilled octopus with cheese and polenta, then try spaghetti with garlic and oil (with unexpected notes of chili and tomato). Interesting entrées include a roasted fish of the day, pork tenderloin sautéed with shallots and rosemary, and *bistecca fiorentina*, steak anointed with herb-infused olive oil. Desserts are mouthwatering, particularly the sorbets and gelati. Service is professional. The wine list is heavy on vintages of Italy's boutique producers. *23 E. 74th St., tel. 212/794–0205. Reservations required. Dress: casual. AE, DC, MC, V.*

Mad. 61. From the aforementioned Pino Luongo comes a serious department store restaurant—this one in Barneys Uptown. Salads are inventive (warm skate and chickpeas), appetizers fabulous (grilled squid stuffed with couscous and merguez sausage in tomato-cumin broth), and seafood creditable (especially the roast cod). Other options: a melt-in-your-mouth braised lamb osso buco, grilled shell steak with onion rings, and *focaccia robiola*, a pizza filled with mild cheese and drizzled with truffle oil—as good as it sounds. There are outstanding cheese plates and even a maître-fromager (master of cheeses). Wines are well chosen, as are the nearly three dozen wines by the glass. There's also an espresso bar. *10 E. 61st St., tel. 212/ 833–2200. Reservations accepted. Dress: casual. AE, DC, MC, V.*

Sette Mezzo. It's neat and plain like other East Side Italians. But expert preparations makes even ordinary dishes extraordinary. While the menu never surprises, specials include such interesting dishes as grilled scallops on the half shell with herbs, a carefully deboned whole grilled red snapper vinaigrette, and, in season, homemade fettuccine piled with white truffles. The orange cake is sheer magic. Service is relaxed and efficient even when it's crowded. There's no liquor, and alas, the wine list is overpriced. *969 Lexington Ave., between 70th and 71st, tel. 212/472–0400. Reservations required. Dress: casual. No credit cards.*

Southwestern **Arizona 206.** Stucco walls and blanched wood create a desert look
★ here and the less expensive adjacent Arizona Café. But no Mojave truck stop serves dishes like executive chef David Walzog's lively pan-seared scallops, presented here with roasted garlic and pumpkin-seed pesto, or the tequila-cured salmon with tomatillo salsa, or the spicy grilled rabbit in cilantro oil. For dessert, try the chocolate peanut wafers with peanut-fudge-swirl ice cream. The wine list is fine, the margaritas fabulous. High prices and tight quarters are sour notes. *206 E. 60th St., tel. 212/838–0440. Dress: casual but neat. AE, DC, MC, V. No Sun. lunch.*

$$ **Matthew's.** This hot café is airy and attractive with its white shut-
American- ters, ceiling fans, jumbo potted plants, and warm colors. Young chef
Contemporary Matthew Kenny has an eclectic contemporary style. You'll find tuna tartare (more coarsely chopped here than in most new American restaurants), served with a Mediterranean green olive tapenade. There's also a terrific artichoke salad with celeriac, almond oil vinaigrette, and warm goat cheese; wood-grilled squab with delicate foie gras; and a beautifully presented charcoal-grilled lobster with spinach risotto and fresh curry leaves. *1030 3rd Ave. at 61st, tel. 212/838–4343. Reservations advised. Dress: casual. AE, DC, MC, V.*

French **Ferrier.** American chef Oliver Smith changed this great bistro with a good location and a fashionable clientele from the merely trendy to the mostly terrific. Born in Massachusetts but trained in Switzerland, he knows how to season and translates classics like cassoulet into personal masterpieces (he uses lentils instead of beans and intense reductions and herbs instead of fat). Steak tartare is zesty, and the basket of pomme frites is almost worth the price of the entire meal. Desserts are not up to the rest of the food, and wines are too expensive. *29 E. 65th St., tel. 212/772–9000. Reservations required. Dress: casual. AE, DC, MC, V.*

★ **Jo Jo.** Having satisfied, in Vong, all his inclinations to experiment with Thai flavors, chef Jean-Georges Vongerichten concentrates at this chic spot on carefully executing traditional bistro classics with contemporary touches. Most of his creations are impressive, including such dishes as sweetbreads with chestnut-truffle vinaigrette, scallops with chopped raw beets and parsley juice, pork cheeks and black bean salad, Alsatian lamb baked in a clay pot, and sautéed bass, gutsy in its salsify broth; for dessert there are lively dessert composites of fruit, ice cream, and cookies. *160 E. 64th St., tel. 212/ 223–5656. Reservations required. Dress: casual but neat. AE, MC, V. Closed Sat. lunch, Sun.*

Le Pistou. It's a poor-man's Côte Basque: The bargain prix fixe menu even offers some of the same selections as that in the pricier restaurant. But Le Pistou is second to none. The room is comfortable and charming with its platoon of folk dolls. From the quenelles, light enough to float off your plate, to the cassoulet, hearty enough to fortify you during a Manhattan winter, the kitchen perfectly executes classic recipes with a contemporary bent. The lemon soufflé is worth the surcharge; the dacquoise is imported—from La Côte Basque. *134 E. 61st St., tel. 212/838-7987. Reservations required. Dress: casual. AE, DC, MC, V. Closed Sun.*

Mediterranean **Café Crocodile.** A meal in this diminutive charmer is like eating in a private home. Andrée Abramoff cooks in the classic European style, but strong Mediterranean and Middle Eastern influences show up in the smoky baba ghannoush (eggplant purée) and hummus (chickpea purée), the homey couscous, the rosy rack of lamb with an herbal cap, and the whole red snapper, left on the bone to retain all the natural taste and texture. The intense chocolate gâteau (half cake, half terrine) is worth the calories. *354 E. 74th St., tel. 212/249-6619. Reservations required. Dress: casual but neat. AE.*

$–$$ **La Palette.** In this café with lace curtains, green banquettes, and art
French deco light fixtures, it's nice to discover such soul-satisfying food, low on pretense but high on flavor: sautéed snails in garlic butter in a roasted potato; sautéed salmon on green cabbage in red wine sauce; chicken *grand'mère* (grandmother-style), with potatoes, onions, bacon, and shallots; and, for dessert, a marvelous lemon meringue tart. The three-course prix fixe dinner is an amazing $22.50, and there are 21 decent wines by the glass. Weekends, go for brunch. *1278 3rd Ave., between 73rd and 74th, tel. 212/288-7076. Reservations advised. Dress: casual. AE, MC, V.*

Hungarian **Red Tulip.** With the gypsy violins and high-back wooden booths, the atmosphere is early Budapest (via MGM), heavy on the Gemütlichkeit. Now, thanks to vivacious co-owner–chef Mariana K. Kovacs, this restaurant founded in 1972 is better than ever. The food is light, tasty, and just a bit contemporary; try the fabulous chicken *paprikas* with egg dumplings, the crispy roast goose, the stuffed cabbage, or the wonderful sausage with onions, green peppers, and tomato sauce. Palacsinta (dessert crepes) with assorted fillings are lovely. *439 E. 75th St., tel. 212/734-4893. Reservations accepted. Dress: casual. AE, DC, MC, V. Closed Mon.–Tues.*

Italian **Baraonda.** This Roman entry onto the Italian trattoria scene is the hottest of the hot, and chic Manhattanites wait for up to 30 minutes for one of the 60 seats inside or the 20 in the sidewalk café. Why? Inside, modern art sets the scene for modern Italian cuisine at moderate prices. A salad of fried shredded artichokes and Parmesan gets things going, and a knockout pasta special—a whole split lobster, filled with spaghetti and tossed in a lobster sauce—is a must if it's available. Pastas are good buys, and although the tiramisù is above average, the Sicilian cassata is outstanding. *1439 2nd Ave. at 75th, tel. 212/288-8555. Reservations accepted. No credit cards; personal checks accepted. No lunch weekdays mid-Nov.–Apr.*

$ **High Life.** Young East Siders wait in line to sit down in this art deco
American café and then strain to hear the music or their dining companions. The draw? Soothing prices for huge portions of food that is far better than it has to be in such a hot spot. Join them—you can drink some of the best martinis in town and polish off barbecued lamb ribs, grilled vegetables carpaccio-style, catfish in beer batter with chips, steak au poivre, and blackened swordfish. Or order sushi or something from the raw bar. The wine and beer list is surprisingly acceptable. *1340 1st Ave. at 72nd, tel. 212/249-3600. No reservations. Dress: casual. AE, DC, MC, V.*
Serendipity 3. This whimsical store-cum-café has been producing excellent burgers, sandwiches, salads, and other interesting if overly

complicated plates since 1954. But most people come for the fantasy sundaes—huge, naughty, and decadent. You'll love the thick frozen hot chocolate. *225 E. 60th St., tel. 212/838–3531. Reservations accepted. Dress: casual. AE, DC, MC, V. BYOB.*

Seventh Regiment Mess and Bar. The fourth floor of the historic Seventh Regiment Armory is home to this unusual restaurant with high ceilings, wooden beams, and appropriately militaristic motifs. You won't find fancy cooking—just homey food such as chicken à la king, pork chops, roast beef, and mustardy deviled beef bones—at rock-bottom prices. *643 Park Ave. at 66th, tel. 212/744–4107. Reservations accepted. Dress: casual. AE, MC, V. Closed Sun.–Mon.*

Austrian **Kaffeehaus.** This café-cum-restaurant re-creates old Vienna with its upholstered banquettes, marble-top tables, pastry display, and racks of newspapers and magazines. There's also an inviting neighborhood feeling—not to mention terrific Viennese coffee *mit schlag* (with cream), *caffè latte* (espresso with steamed milk), unusual organic and unfiltered wheat beers, interesting Austrian wines, and food that will surprise you with its finesse. Start with dilled smoked salmon tartare on *rösti* (roast potatoes), the alpine charcuterie plate, or smoked trout with beets and horseradish cream. Then go for a classic pork Wienerschnitzel, eastern Austrian fish stew, or pan-roasted lake trout in cucumber dill sauce. Desserts look better than they taste—at least right now. *131 8th Ave., between 16th and 17th, tel. 212/229–9702. Reservations advised. Dress: casual. AE, DC, MC, V.*

French **L'Ardoise.** An unpretentious splinter of a room, with brick walls, red formica tables, votive candles, and mini chalkboards on the walls, this prepares bistro classics with gusto. Don't polish off the homemade fromage blanc; yet to come is meat terrine with Calvados, monkfish perfumed with bacon, lamb ballotine, and a *pavé de boeuf* (a slab of beef) in wild mushroom and fig sauce. *1207 1st Ave., between 66th and 67th, tel. 212/744–4752. Reservations advised. Dress: casual. No credit cards.*

Italian **Triangolo.** A bowl of pasta costs under $10 at this bustling trattoria—but you may have to stand in line for it (not as bad as it sounds if you like people-watching). The sensibly short menu offers homey, stick-to-the-ribs cooking: crepes stuffed with melted cheese and chopped prosciutto, huge portions of homemade pasta dishes like fettuccine with meat sauce and rigatoni with eggplant and mozzarella, and perfect hazelnut gelato and tiramisù. The wine list is inexpensive. *345 E. 83rd St., tel. 212/472–4488. Reservations only for 3 or more. Dress: casual. No credit cards. No lunch.*

Middle Eastern **L'Auberge.** With its flattering lighting and elegant decor,
★ L'Auberge recalls Paris more than Beirut. You'll know it's Lebanese when you dig into the delicious hummus, smoky baba ghannoush, and *kibbee* (ground lamb). Go with a group and sample the assorted *mezze* (appetizers). Most Middle Eastern entrées are letdowns, but French influences elevate Lebanon's, as evident in L'Auberge's skewered lamb meatballs, cassoulet-like white bean and lamb stew, and whole grilled sea bass with zesty red sauce. Try the prestigious Lebanese Château Musar, from the well-chosen wine list. The $6.95 all-you-can-eat weekday lunch buffet is a steal. *1191 1st Ave., between 64th and 65th, tel. 212/288–8791. Reservations accepted. Dress: casual. AE, DC, MC, V.*

Russian **The Pie.** This pint-size slice of what used to be called the Soviet Un-
★ ion, transplanted to a Yorkville storefront, specializes in Russian pies, made from crepes arranged in a casserole and bursting with

your choice of filling. Blini with herring, salmon caviar, and smoked salmon are divine appetizers. Soups are honest and satisfying. Entrées include filet mignon pie and chicken Rasputin, in a spicy tomato sauce, on noodles. Chocolate-covered pot cheese and layered meringue make delicious endings. When you order tea, a samovar arrives with cookies and jam. The owner's vivacious blond wife will guide you through the menu (and keep you in stitches). *340 E. 86th St., tel. 212/517–8717. Reservations advised. Dress: casual. AE.*

Thai **Boonthai.** In this mirrored, softly lit charmer, the owner greets you warmly, and service is unusually polished. If you're adventurous, request No. 10 (*yam sam krob*) and you're in for a treat: fish maw with yams and Thai spices. If you like it hot, try the deep-fried whole fish with chili sauce. Or order the good chicken in spicy green curry, the above-average *pad thai* (noodles with peanuts and other goodies), or, if it's available, the soft-shell crab special in garlic and black pepper sauce. To put out the fire, have a Singha, the excellent Thai beer. *1393A 2nd Ave., between 72nd and 73rd, tel. 212/249–8484. Reservations advised. Dress: casual. AE, MC, V. No lunch weekends.*

Sala Thai. Seasoning is assertive but not overwhelming in this appealing bilevel restaurant with solicitous service and a good kitchen. Try the frogs' legs, in garlic and coconut milk or with Thai basil leaves and hot peppers; the *pla lad prig*, a deep-fried whole fish topped with chilies and garlic; or *pad woon sen*, glass noodles stir-fried with shrimp, egg, bean curd, and sprouts. *1718 2nd Ave., between 89th and 90th, tel. 212/410–5557. Reservations advised. Dress: casual. AE, DC. No lunch.*

Lincoln Center

$$$ **Tavern on the Green.** The reception is perfunctory, the service inept
American- (if usually polite), and the food still hit or miss (although improved
Contemporary thanks to the direction of Marc Poidevin). Still, Warner LeRoy's lavish restaurant is a visual fantasy, and careful selection can yield a satisfying meal. Try the chilled tomato soup with avocado and paperthin, deep-fried horseradish chips, pasta with lemon sauce, or Dover sole. The wine list is a pleasure, and even three-star restaurants in France sell souvenirs. There's also jazz, dancing, and cabaret. Request the brilliant Crystal Room, for its view of the twinkle-lighted trees, or opt for al fresco dining in the engaging garden. Prix fixe menus lower the tab. *In Central Park at 67th St., tel. 212/873–3200. Reservations advised. Jacket advised. AE, DC, MC, V.*

French **Café des Artistes.** Writer-restaurant consultant George Lang's masterpiece, this most European of cafés is snug and beautiful with its polished oak woodwork and rosy Howard Chandler Christy murals of nymphs at play. The cuisine of chef Thomas Ferlesch is as refined as the setting. Four-way salmon, with tidbits of the fish that are smoked, poached, dill-marinated, and tartare, is a perfect introduction, and it would be hard to find a better *pot au feu*, a French variation on pot roast, here beautifully presented with marrow bone and traditional accompaniments. The Provençale fish stew, *bourride*, is assertive and delicious, and the desserts are appealing, especially the mocha dacquoise. Champagnes are a bargain. The Sunday brunch is especially festive. *1 W. 67th St., tel. 212/877–3500. Reservations required. Jacket and tie required at dinner. AE, DC, MC, V.*

$$–$$$
American-
Contemporary

Iridium. The decor is a knockout (chair legs in ballet positions, lots of burgundy), and the kitchen is one of the finest around Lincoln Center. Stone-oven–roasted quail with warm black beans and Thai glaze; Muscovy duck and wheatberry salad in cilantro oil; seared tuna with sweet potato, quinoa, and Indonesian plum sauce; salmon with caperberries and garlic: These taste as good as they sound (and are priced commensurate with their quality—that is, on the high side). A jazz club is downstairs and there's brunch with jazz on Sundays. The bar pours drinks in two-ounce shots, and there's a wonderful wine list. *44 W. 63rd St., tel. 212/582–2121. Reservations advised. Dress: casual. DC, MC, V.*

$$
American-
Contemporary

Josephina. Bright hand-painted murals and tables give this warm, inviting place a stylized look. Fresh juice stands in for butter in some dishes, and herb- and vegetable-infused oils in others. Fish and vegetables are fresh from the source. Try horseradish-crusted Norwegian salmon, grilled grouper over organic red lentils, or, for dessert, oat-nut apple crisp. There is an eclectic wine and beer list. *1900 Broadway, between 63rd and 64th, tel. 212/799–1000. Reservations accepted. Dress: casual. AE, MC, V. No lunch Mon.*

Café Luxembourg. A bit like SoHo on the Upper West Side, with a well-heeled clientele, this bustling, sophisticated bistro with airy arched windows, a zinc-topped bar, and racks of newspapers and magazines is just terrific. That said, we love the smoked salmon salad, the steak frites, the carefully prepared sea bass, and the soothing roast free-range chicken with mashed potatoes; a better cassoulet is hard to come by. Desserts are mostly fine, especially the delicious profiteroles. Several prix fixe menus lower the tab. There is a very good selection of wines. Be prepared for the occasional attitude problem and indifference in the service area. *200 W. 70th St., tel. 212/873–7411. Reservations advised. Dress: casual. AE, DC, MC, V. No lunch Mon.*

Chinese
★

Shun Lee West. It's a dramatically lighted study in black, accented by white dragons and monkeys. Service is good, and considering the number of people the restaurant serves, the food can be excellent. Shanghai steamed dumplings, soft-shell crabs, and giant prawns make stellar starters. Then try Peking duck, sweetbreads with hot peppers and scallions, or rack of lamb Szechuan-style. Fresh fruit makes an ideal dessert. The food in Shun Lee Palace (155 E. 55th St., tel. 212/371-8844), under the same management, is lighter and more refined, but equally good. *43 W. 65th St., tel. 212/595–8895. Reservations advised. Jacket requested. AE, DC, MC, V.*

Italian-
Contemporary

Sfuzzi. Like the Washington and Boston restaurants of which this is a clone, Sfuzzi exhibits professionalism and an appealing style that juxtaposes traditional (trompe l'oeil walls) and high-tech (video monitors, loud music). Commence with a Sfuzzi, a Bellini–frozen margarita hybrid. Then go for one of the terrific pizzas, eclectic pastas, or contemporary Italian or new American entrées—say, the firm, sweet mahimahi in a pistachio crust. Service is helpful, wines intelligently selected and affordably priced. Save room for dessert: tiramisù, or hazelnut chocolate mousse cake. There's another Sfuzzi downtown in the World Financial Center (tel. 212/385–8080). *58 W. 65th St., tel. 212/873–3700. Reservations advised. Dress: casual. AE, DC, MC, V.*

Mediterranean
★

Picholine. Dried flowers, plaid fabrics, and rough stucco create a rustic look here. Homemade breads are impressive, as are the Mediterranean spreads with just-out-of-the-oven flat bread. The delicate ricotta-Swiss chard dumplings and grilled vegetable-feta salad are special, and the *sauce Vierge*, a coriander vinaigrette, is terrific with the whole grilled bass filleted table-side. Don't miss the luscious duck risotto with wild mushrooms, pumpkin, and white truffle oil. The lamb with white bean purée and the roast baby chicken with preserved lemon are also top-notch. The best dessert is a delicate lemon napoleon. The selection of wines by the glass needs work. *35 W. 64th St., tel. 212/724–8585. Reservations advised. Dress: casual. AE, DC, MC, V. Closed Mon. lunch, Sun.*

Seafood **Fishin Eddie.** This playful spot, with a cozy, low-ceilinged bar flanked by a sofa up front and a skylighted main dining room filled with painted furniture, serves impeccably prepared seafood in styles that range from Mediterranean to new American. Favorites include a heady baccala chowder, grilled shrimp with white beans, steamed Dungeness crab, and blackened bluefish and potatoes, a special. Desserts are as good as the main event—specifically, anything in the ice cream or sorbet family. Service is casual but well meaning. *73 W. 71st St., tel. 212/874–3474. Reservations accepted. Dress: casual. AE, DC, MC, V. No lunch.*

$–$$ **Fiorello's Roman Café.** Although Trattoria dell'Arte's corporate
Italian cousin gets better with each visit, it is largely unsung. (Perhaps people still remember it as a place for deep-dish pizza or perhaps it's the prices that intimidate, which are high by West Side standards.) Those in the know enjoy fabulous thin-crust pizza, good pastas, excellent baby chicken (roasted in a clay pot with vegetables), lovely salads, and grand desserts, such as almond pound cake with gelati. There's also a sidewalk café in summer and a bargain wine list. *1900 Broadway, between 63rd and 64th, tel. 212/595–5330. Reservations advised. Dress: casual. AE, MC. V.*

$ **Ying.** Charming, energetic Tina Ying runs an attractive Cantonese-
Chinese Szechuan restaurant with inviting wicker chairs, live piano music, and excellent service. Vietnamese chicken rolls are uncommonly crisp, orange chicken is perfect, and yu-shun chicken awakens even jaded palates. Peking duck is moist and greaseless, although the accompanying doilies could be warmer. *117 W. 70th St., tel. 212/724–2031. Reservations accepted. Dress: casual. AE, MC, V.*

Upper West Side

$$ **Popover Café.** There's a certain captivating, innocent quality to the
American- honest American food in this vintage West Side tea room-cum-res-
Casual taurant full of teddy bears. Besides the superb popovers (you'll swear they're no less than the best in creation), there are terrific soups (try the vegetarian black-bean chili with the works, the excellent gazpacho, or the intense vegetarian pea soup), there are sandwiches with names like Mad Russian. The delicious Sunday brunch packs 'em in, and the dinner menu stars fried catfish, breaded in pecans and cornmeal, good lamb chops, and a half beef-half veal burger. There's also a health-watch prix fixe menu and an inexpensive wine and beer list. *551 Amsterdam Ave., between 86th and 87th, tel. 212/595–8555. Reservations advised. Dress: casual. AE, MC, V.*

American- **Memphis.** This handsome restaurant with elaborate cast-iron col-
Contemporary umns, a balcony, and a long bar that displays house-made flavored vodkas doesn't have a sign outside, yet it's going strong. Chef Richard Oswald's innovative menu brings striking Asian notes to the West Side scene, and his executions reveal a firm grasp of his craft. Try the appetizer special of mashed potatoes, spinach, mushrooms, and escargots, if it's available. Seared tuna with Jim Beam–peppercorn sauce, couscous, and oysters may sound complicated, but the flavors and textures marry well to create an uncommonly delicious

dish. For dessert, try the homey fruit crisp or seasonal fruit pies. The wine selection is interesting and agreeably priced, there are also good wine specials by the glass—and don't forget about those delightful flavored vodkas. *329 Columbus Ave., between 75th and 76th, tel. 212/496–1840. Dress: casual. AE, MC, V. No lunch.*

Two Two Two. Frank Valenza, who first made headlines in the 1970s as the owner of New York's most expensive restaurant, The Palace, returns to the local scene here with chef Frank Della Riva (late of La Côte Basque and Aureole), who looks like a kid but cooks like a pro. Shrimp and creamy polenta in a tomato–roast garlic broth is terrific; sautéed Atlantic salmon with wild mushroom ravioli and caramelized-shallot butter is lovely. The oak-paneled room, on the ground level of a brownstone, is classy for the neighborhood; the garden is a pleasure. Wines are inexpensive. *222 W. 79th St., tel. 212/799–0400. Reservations advised. Dress: casual but neat. AE, DC, MC, V. No lunch.*

Japanese **Fujiyama Mama.** White-slipcovered side chairs line up like statues in the vitrine of this creative restaurant with a high-tech design. In the startling spirit of the place, dishes have names like Poseidon Adventure and Bermuda Triangle. But the food is serious, inventive, and invariably first-rate, including marinated chicken in a blue Curaçao sauce and sparkling toro, tuna, fluke, yellow tail, sea trout and salmon sushi, sashimi, and hand rolls. Tell the waiter it's your birthday and fork over $10.50, and your tempura deep-fried ice cream comes with flickering sparklers while the DJ lays on a "Happy Birthday to You" from his collection of weird recordings of the classic. *467 Columbus Ave., between 82nd and 83rd, tel. 212/769–1144. Reservations advised. Dress: casual. AE. Dinner only.*

Seafood **Dock's.** The menu is similar to the one at the downtown version (*see* Murray Hill, *above*). But at this Dock's, the space is smaller, a slender storefront with lots of black and tan tiles, and the crowd is mainly casual neighborhood types. *2427 Broadway near 90th, tel. 212/724–5588. Dress: casual. Reservations advised. AE, DC, MC, V. No lunch Sat.*

$–$$ **Main Street.** Bring kids, friends, and an appetite—everything is
American served family style. Picture a whole roast chicken, a really good meat loaf (the whole loaf), turkey with all the trimmings. This American-as-apple-pie café in a heroic space does them all well. Since every order is large enough to split four ways, you can spend a mere $5 or $6 per entrée. And what desserts: Check out the terrific chocolate pudding and stupendous peanut butter pie. The lighting could be better, and the decibel level is unfortunate. *446 Columbus Ave., between 81st and 82nd, tel. 212/873–5025. Reservations only for 6 or more. Dress: casual. AE, DC, MC, V.*

American- **Poiret.** Walls emblazoned with red roses and green vines, green ban-
Contemporary quettes, beautiful wood floors, faux marble columns, and a chic neighborhood clientele make this area standout look more expensive than it is. By all means, split the oversize appetizers—peppered duck rillettes and potato galette with smoked salmon and onion confiture, for instance, or warm spinach salad with endive, frisée, artichokes, shallots, and a Gruyère cheese fondue. At $13.95, the garlicky herbed roast chicken with a tower of straw potatoes—the signature dish of executive chef and American culinary star Jonathan Waxman—is not to be missed. The outstanding crème brûlée makes a stellar conclusion. You'll also find pleasant wines by the glass. *474 Columbus Ave., near 82nd, tel. 212/724–6880. Reservations advised. Dress: casual but neat. AE, DC, MC, V.*

Italian **Carmine's.** Dark woodwork and old-fashioned black-and-white tiles
★ make this hotspot look like an old-timer. It isn't. Still, savvy West
Siders are only too glad to line up for its homestyle cooking, served
family style. Yet despite the mobs and the low prices, Carmine's is
good. Kick off a meal with homemade mozzarella-tomato salad or
garlicky spedini; move on to the pastas, perhaps rigatoni in a rollick-
ing broccoli, sausage, and white bean sauce. Calamari and veal
scaloppine are fine, and desserts, especially the biscuit tortoni, are
on target. Wines are inexpensive. *2450 Broadway, between 90th and
91st, tel. 212/362–2200. Reservations only for 6 or more. Dress: casual. AE. Dinner only.*

Seafood **Sidewalker's.** The Maryland-style spiced crabs here—hard-shell
crabs coated with Old Bay spice, steamed, and cracked open with
knife and mallet—are at least as good as Baltimore's. You can also
get steamed, chilled Dungeness crab and crunchy corn on the cob,
both so sweet they don't need drawn butter, as well as expertly prepared blackened grouper and chunky, spicy, addictive coleslaw.
Desserts are so-so—but who needs 'em after all that cornbread. On
Monday night, there's a $19.95 all-you-can-eat crab bash. There's an
inexpensive wine list and good beer by the pitcher or bottle. *12 W.
72nd St., tel. 212/799–6070. Reservations advised. Dress: casual.
AE, DC, MC, V. No lunch.*

$ **Amsterdam's.** Tables under the checkered cloths in this unpreten-
American- tious bistro often need a matchbook, chairs are none too com-
Casual fortable, and the noise challenges conversation. But the food is
reliable and tasty. The house antipasto for two includes a delicious
Italian crostini, firm toast spread with chicken-liver pâté. Every-
thing from the rotisserie is great, and there's a different chicken
special every day. Amsterdam's has a reasonable wine selection,
and all night on Sunday and before 7 on weeknights, children under
11 eat free (although a $3 donation to a charity is requested). *428
Amsterdam Ave., between 80th and 81st, tel. 212/874–1377.
Reservations not necessary. Dress: casual. AE, MC, V. No lunch
Mon.*

Jack's Firehouse. There's a reason this find calls itself a firehouse:
The sauce they use gives the plain chicken enough kick to get you to
Jamaica without an airplane, and the pizza topped with that chicken
is not much milder. Still, you can get other varieties, too, and the
crust is high, crisp, and delicious. You'll also find good Buffalo
wings, chili, and a tasty green salad with sun-dried tomatoes and
grilled chicken strips. Or you can try the so-called sexy fries, with
cheese dipping sauce, or go for a burger (mild, medium, or inferno).
Check out the micro-brewery beers and the brownies. Open until 4
AM. *522 Columbus Ave., between 85th and 86th, tel. 212/787–3473.
No reservations. Dress: casual. AE, MC, V.*

American- **Dish.** Here's the concept: Cook healthy food, cook it well, and serve
Contemporary large portions in huge dishes. Start with a house salad, then have
the half rotisserie chicken or the rosemary version on wild rice with
vegetables. Or try the spicy pepper steak, served with sautéed peppers and onions. The fat-free, sugar-free cobbler and white chocolate mousse–filled cannoli steal the sweets show. There's Sunday
brunch and a wine list that starts at $12. With its rough wood on
walls and floors and its angular, contemporary design, Dish is very
pleasant. *100 W. 82nd St., tel. 212/724–8700. Reservations advised.
Dress: casual. AE, DC, MC, V. No lunch.*

Worth a Special Trip

$$$$
American-
Contemporary
★

River Café. One of New York's most romantic restaurants. Sipping a perfect cocktail or a glass of wine from the extensive list and watching the sun set over Lower Manhattan, just across the East River, is one of the city's great treats. So is the food by Rick Laakkonen. Favorite dishes include fruitwood-smoked salmon on johnnycake; a remarkable poached salmon in a ginger, green onion, and lime-leaf broth; halibut fillet in rice paper with braised mushrooms and Thompson grapes; and roast loin of lamb with bordelaise sauce, curried couscous seasoned with fenugreek, and caramelized onion. Desserts are dramatic and delicious: the Brooklyn Bridge sculpted of Valrhona chocolate, hot soufflés, and tabbouleh made with fresh tropical fruit and served with cardamom tuiles. Prices are high—$58 for a three-course dinner or $78 for an elaborate six-course tasting, but service is some of the best in the business. Sunday brunch is a joy, lunch less hectic. It's a $15 cab ride from midtown. *1 Water St. at the East River, tel. 718/522–5200. Reservations advised. Jacket advised. AE, DC, MC, V.*

$–$$
American-
Contemporary
★

Henry's End. Quarters may be tight, but this plain-Jane local hangout in chic Brooklyn Heights offers some of the borough's most interesting food. During fall's wild game festival, you might sample barbecued rattlesnake or elk chops with honey-mustard glaze. Otherwise, go with raspberry duck, pumpkin ravioli, or blackened salmon or tuna. Desserts are homey; try fresh apple cobbler or black-bottom pie. Beer and wine selections are superb. To get home, we usually call the Atlantic car service (tel. 718/797–5666); it's under $20 to midtown. *44 Henry St. near Cranberry, Brooklyn, tel. 718/ 834–1776. Reservations advised. Dress: casual. AE, DC, MC, V. No lunch.*

$
Colombian

Tierras Colombianas. Come to Queens and ignore the coffee-shop decor for standout stick-to-the-ribs food at bargain prices. He-man bowls of soup arrive bursting with beef ribs, corn on the cob, vegetables, and rice, accompanied by the delicious corn cake known as *arepa*. The combination plate—a variety of meats, plantains, and cassava—is mammoth. Or try the parchment-crisp hunk of pork called *chicharron* (served rind and all). It's in a colorful neighborhood, a block from the 82nd Street stop on the No. 7 train—about 20 minutes in all from Manhattan. *82-16 Roosevelt Ave., Jackson Heights, Queens, tel. 718/426–8868. Dress: casual. No reservations. No credit cards. BYOB.*

Greek
★

Roumeli Taverna. One of the best bets in a predominantly Greek area of Queens, this spot with lighted grape vines on walls and ceiling and bouzouki music in the air is only a short cab ride from midtown or about 15 minutes from Manhattan via the N train. Hot and cold appetizers such as grilled octopus, fried cheese, and taramasalata are incredible. There are appetizing Greek salads and such delicious entrées as moussaka, grilled quail, and souvlaki; barbecued shrimp are the size of your fist. It's all fresh and special. Greek reds offer good value. *33-04 Broadway, between 33rd and 34th, Astoria, Queens, tel. 718/278–7533. Reservations accepted. Dress: casual. AE.*

Indian

Jackson Diner. Queens's Jackson Heights, full of sari salons and exotic jewelry shops, is also home to New York's best Indian food. In the Little India here, this skinny restaurant stands out from the crowd. Bette Davis's line, "What a dump," comes to mind when you see it. But who cares when $15 buys a fabulous dinner of delicate, elegant, and sensual South Indian specialties: delicious steamed lentil cakes, unusual South Indian stuffed pancakes, fragrant goat curry, marvelous breads and vegetables, and crepes filled with potatoes, peas, and nuts—all superbly spiced. In a city choked with small, predictable Indian restaurants, the Jackson Diner reigns supreme. It's in a well-trafficked neighborhood, 2 blocks from the 74th Street/Roosevelt Avenue stop on the E, F, D, R, and 7 trains—about 10 minutes in all from Manhattan. *37-03 74th St., Jackson Heights, Queens, tel. 718/672-1232. No reservations. Dress: casual. No credit cards. BYOB.*

Coffee Bars and Cafés

Cafés have been a New York institution since beat days. Yet only recently have coffee bars on the Seattle model taken off. Still, they're multiplying at an exponential rate. Plain and decaffeinated drip coffee and espresso are standard. (Note: "Regular coffee" in New York comes with milk or cream; you must add your own sugar if you want your brew sweetened.) You will also find appellations that were never uttered in Italy: *ristretto*, a highly refined espresso; *macchiato*, espresso with just a bit of foam; *caffè latte*, espresso with steamed milk; *cappuccino*, half espresso and half steamed milk, with foam; *caffè mocha*, espresso with steamed chocolate milk; *mochaccino*, cappuccino flavored with chocolate. Most come in a decaf variant or with skim, low-fat, and soy milk, half-and-half, and cream as well as plain whole milk. Many offer snacks; others are restaurants in coffee-bar drag. While prices can top $2 for an espresso, all offer a bit of civilized sipping.

Greenwich and SoHo
Black Medicine, 554 Hudson St. at Perry, tel. 212/633-1171.
Caffè Vivaldi, 32 Jones St. near Bleecker, tel. 212/929-9384.
Dean & Deluca, 75 University Pl. at 11th, tel. 212/473-1908; 121 Prince St., between Green and Wooster, tel. 212/254-8776; and 560 Broadway at Prince, tel. 212/431-1691.
Espresso Lounge, 5 St. Marks Pl. near Bowery, tel. 212/614-0830.
Flavor-Cup Coffee, 117 W. 10th St., tel. 212/675-3733.
French Roast, 458 6th Ave. at 11th, tel. 212/533-2233.
New World Coffee, 449 6th Ave., between 10th and 11th, tel. 212/343-0552; 412 W. Broadway, between Spring and Prince, tel. 212/431-1015.
Oren's Daily Roast, 31 Waverly Pl., tel. 212/420-5958.

Chelsea, Flatiron
Barnes & Noble Café, 675 6th Ave. at 21st, tel. 212/717-1227.
Caffè Bondi, 7 W. 20th St., tel. 212/691-8136.
Eureka Joe, 168 5th Ave. near 22nd, tel. 212/741-7500.
Newsbar, 2 W. 19th St., tel. 212/255-3996.
Seattle Coffee Roasters, 150 5th Ave. at 20th, tel. 212/675-9700.
T-Rex, 358 W. 23rd St., tel. 212/620-4620.

Midtown, Theater District
Au Café, 1700 Broadway at 53rd, tel. 212/757-2233.
Caffè del Corso, 19 W. 55th St., tel. 212/957-1500.
Dean & Deluca, 1 Rockefeller Plaza, tel. 212/664-1363; in the Paramount Hotel, 135 W. 46th St., tel. 212/869-6890.
New World Coffee, 400 Madison Ave. at 47th, tel. 212/838-2854.
Oh-La-La, 229 W. 45th St., tel. 212/704-8937.
Oren's Daily Roast, 434 3rd Ave., between 30th and 31st, tel. 212/779-1241.
Philip's Coffee, 155 W. 56th St., tel. 212/582-7347; 14 E. 33rd St., tel. 212/685-2620.
Simon Sips, Bryant Park, 6th Ave. at 42nd St., tel. 212/354-1668; 605 3rd Ave., lobby, between 39th and 40th, tel. 212/986-7537.
Timothy's, 1285 6th Ave. (entrance on 51st), tel. 212/956-0690; 122

E. 42nd St., tel. 212/370–1662; 553 7th Ave. at 39th, tel. 212/869–7696.

Upper East Side
Baratti & Milano, 697 Madison Ave., between 62nd and 63rd, tel. 212/888–9494.

Barneys Uptown, Madison Ave. at 61st, tel. 212/833–2200.

Café Demitasse, in Galeries Lafayette, 10 E. 57th St., tel. 212/355–2905.

Café Equense, 1291 Madison Ave., between 91st and 92nd, tel. 212/860–2300.

Caffè Grazie, 26 E. 84th St., tel. 212/717–4407.

L'Ardoise, 1207 1st Ave. near 66th, tel. 212/744–4752.

New World Coffee, 1159 3rd Ave. at 68th, tel. 212/472–1598.

Oren's Daily Roast, 1574 1st Ave., between 81st and 82nd, tel. 212/737–2690; 1144 Lexington Ave. at 79th, tel. 212/472–6830; 33 E. 58th St., tel. 212/838–3345.

Portico, 1431 2nd Ave., between 74th and 75th, tel. 212/704–1032.

Sabine's, 1223 3rd Ave. at 71st St., tel. 212/737–9445.

Seattle Bean Company, 1573 2nd Ave. near 81st St., tel. 212/794–4233.

Sylvester's, 1131 2nd Ave., between 59th and 60th, tel. 212/752–3513.

Timothy's, 1296 Madison Ave. at 92nd, tel. 212/987–3272; 1675 3rd Ave. at 94th, tel. 212/987–3094; and 1033 3rd Ave., between 61st and 62nd, tel. 212/755–6456.

Upper West Side
Barnes & Noble Café, 2289 Broadway, between 82nd and 83rd, tel. 212/362–8835.

Cooper's, 2151 Broadway, between 75th and 76th, tel. 212/496–0300; 2315 Broadway, between 83rd and 84th, tel. 212/724–0300; 159 Columbus Ave., between 67th and 68th, tel. 212/362–0100.

Edgar's, 255 W. 84th St., tel. 212/496–6126.

joe bar, 2459 Broadway at 91st, tel. 212/787–3684.

Seattle Coffee Roasters, 188 Columbus Ave., between 68th and 69th, tel. 212/877–6699.

Starbucks, 2379 Broadway at 87th, tel. 212/875–8470.

Zabar's, 2245 Broadway at 80th, tel. 212/787–2000.

10 Lodging

By Jane Hershey

Updated by Kate Sekules

If any single element of your trip to New York City is going to cost you a lot of money, it'll be your hotel bill. European cities may offer plenty of low-priced lodgings, but New York tends not to. Real estate is at a premium here, and labor costs are high, so hoteliers start out with a lot of expenses to cover. And there are enough well-heeled visitors to support competition at the premium end of the spectrum, which is where the profits are. Considering the healthy occupancy rate, market forces are not likely to drive current prices down. Fleabags and flophouses aside, there's precious little here for under $100 a night. Furthermore, the city has the country's highest tax rate on hotel rooms: an average of 21¼%, a total of 4% state sales tax, 4¼% city sales tax, 6% city occupancy tax, $2 per night on a room costing $40 or more, plus an additional 5% on rooms over $100. (At press time, there was talk of repealing this last, newest tax.) We have noted a few budget properties, but even our "Inexpensive" category includes hotels that run as high as $135 for one night's stay in a double.

Once you've accepted that you must pay the going price, though, you'll have plenty of choices. In general, Manhattan hotels don't measure up to those in other U.S. cities in terms of room size, parking, or outside landscaping. But, this being a sophisticated city, New York hotels usually compensate with fastidious service, sprucely maintained properties, and restaurants that hold their own in a city of knowledgeable diners. Where else can you sleep in Frank Lloyd Wright's former apartment, swim with a view of the Empire State Building, or eat breakfast in bed while watching sea lions at play?

Price is by no means the perfect indicator of impeccable service, pleasant surroundings, or delicious cuisine, so we've tried to indicate the shortcomings of various properties, as well as their strong points. Common sense should tell you not to anticipate the same kind of personal service from even a top-flight convention hotel, such as the New York Hilton, as you would from a smaller, sedate property like the Doral Tuscany, even though both have rooms in the same price range. Know your own taste and choose accordingly. If you like bright lights, a lively lobby, and a central location, a residential-style hotel could disappoint you, no matter how elegant it is.

Basic rules of decorum and dress are observed at the better hotels. With few exceptions, jackets (and frequently ties) are required in formal dining and bar areas after 5 or 6 PM. Bare feet or beach sandals are not allowed, and an overall sloppy appearance won't encourage good service.

Women on their own, even at upscale hotels, should be aware that they may be accosted in public areas, either by male guests trying to find companions or by hotel staff trying to chase away the hookers who transact business in hotel lobbies. Because these "working girls" often look quite respectable, any single woman may be suspect. You might want to ask the concierge to point out places where you'll feel comfortable relaxing on your own. Many female travelers find VIP floors, with their concierge-controlled lounges and complimentary beverages and snacks, a boon for avoiding such situations.

Note: Even the most exclusive hotels have security gaps. Be discreet with valuables everywhere, and stay alert in public areas.

Within each price category, our listings are organized by location. Exact prices could be misleading: Properties change their so-called "rack rates" seasonally, and most hotels offer weekend packages that include such tempting extras as complimentary meals, drinks, or tickets to events. Your travel agent may have brochures about such packages; also look for advertisements in travel magazines or the Sunday travel sections of major newspapers such as the *New York Times*, the *Washington Post*, or the *Los Angeles Times*. Note: Many hotels offer corporate rates to regular customers if they ask, and it is by no means unknown for rates—especially at the expensive end of the market—to be negotiable during periods of low occupancy.

Visitors can also take advantage of reputable discount booking services such as **Express Hotel Reservations.** This Boulder, Colorado, company offers savings of 20%–30% on superior rooms at a variety of New York hotels. There is no charge for any of the company's services (it is used frequently by major companies, such as Hallmark and the Limited). Call 800/356–1123 for further information.

Highly recommended lodgings are indicated by a star ★.

Category	Cost*
$$$$	over $260
$$$	$190–$260
$$	$135–$190
$	under $135

All prices are for a standard double room, excluding 21¼% city and state taxes.

Reservations New York is constantly full of vacationers, conventioneers, and business travelers, all requiring hotel space. Try to book your room as far in advance as possible, using a major credit card to guarantee the reservation; you might even want to work through a travel agent. Because this is a tight market, overbooking can be a problem, and "lost" reservations are not unheard of. Most properties, especially those that are part of national or worldwide chains or associations (i.e., Marriott or The Leading Hotels of the World), are cooperative and generous when a reservation is lost, but guaranteed reservations usually prevent any problems. When signing in, take a pleasant but firm attitude; if there is a mix-up, chances are the outcome will be an upgrade or a free night.

Hotels with famous restaurants appreciate it when guests who want to use those facilities book tables when they make their room reservations. All chefs mentioned were in charge at press time. Call to confirm the name under the toque. It can make *all* the difference.

Services Unless otherwise noted in the individual descriptions, all the hotels listed have the following features and services: private baths, central heating, air-conditioning, private telephones, on-premises dining, valet and room service (though not necessarily 24-hour or short-notice), TV (including cable and pay-per-view films), and a routine concierge staff. Larger hotels will generally have video or high-speed checkout capability.

New York City has finally allowed liquor minibars to be installed in rooms. Most hotels have added this much-anticipated amenity—at least in their more expensive units.

Pools are a rarity, but most properties have fitness centers; we note only those that are on the premises, but other hotels usually have arrangements for guests at nearby facilities. Some hotels also make nominal charges for guests' use of in-house fitness centers.

Those bringing a car to Manhattan should note the lack of hotel parking. Many properties in all price ranges *do* offer parking facilities, but they are often at independent garages that charge up to $20 or more per day.

$$$$

Upper East Side ★

The Carlyle. Museum Mile and the tony boutiques of Madison Avenue are on the doorstep of New York's least hysterical grand hotel, where European tradition and Manhattan swank shake hands. The mood is English manor house; larger rooms and suites, many of them decorated by the famous interior designer Mark Hampton, have terraces, pantries, and antique furnishings. Baths, though more subdued than others in town, are marble and chock-full of de rigueur amenities such as hair dryers, fine toiletries, and makeup mirrors. Most visitors have heard about the famous Café Carlyle, where performers such as Bobby Short entertain. But the hotel also contains the charming Bemelman's Bar, named after Ludwig Bemelman, illustrator of the beloved children's book character Madeline and the "twelve little girls in two straight lines"; he created the murals here as well as in the formal Carlyle Restaurant, known for French cuisine and old-fashioned courtly service. There's a jewel of a fitness center that is ultraprivate and luxurious. This is one of the few grand hotels where friendliness and old-school elegance really mix; you don't have to be a famous face to get a smile or good treatment. The concierge and housekeeping service is especially excellent. *35 E. 76th St., 10021, tel. 212/744–1600, fax 212/717–4682. 190 rooms. Facilities: restaurant, café, bar, lounge, VCRs and stereos, fax machines, kitchenettes and pantries in larger units, fitness center, meeting rooms. AE, DC, MC, V.*

★ The Mark. Find this friendliest of baby grand hotels one block north of the Carlyle and steps from Central Park. Thanks partly to Raymond Bickson, who manages the place with his stylish brand of laid-back efficiency, there's a feeling of calm pervading the Biedermeier-furnished marble lobby that follows you into the welcoming deep-green and burgundy bar, where lone women travelers can feel comfortable. The serenity continues at Mark's Restaurant (*see* Chapter 9, Dining), whose afternoon tea has become an institution. Philippe Boulot's modern French menus and special vintners dinners draw raves. Bedrooms are cozy and cosseting, with creamy walls hung with museum-quality prints, plump armchairs, a potted palm or two, double phone lines, VCRs, and Belgian bed linens. The Italian black and white marble bathrooms have oversize tubs and a generous selection of toiletries. *25 E. 77th St., 10021, tel. 212/744–4300 or 800/843–6275, fax 212/744–2749. 180 rooms. Facilities: restaurant, café, lounge, meeting rooms, VIP suites with terraces. AE, DC, MC, V.*

East 60s

The Lowell. Think how nice it would be to arrive in New York and find that a rich uncle had offered you the run of his elegant pied-à-terre—that's the feeling you'll get here. There's no lobby in the true sense, just a regal front-desk area with a few chairs and newspapers. Upstairs, on the second floor, is a picture-perfect tea and lunch room in the English country house style; adjacent is a first-rate steak restaurant, the Post House (*see* Chapter 9). The guest rooms, mostly suites, are both fashionable and homey: Furnishings are an eclectic mix of traditional pieces with surprisingly modern accents. Bathrooms have good lighting and generous Saks Fifth Avenue amenities. Some rooms have wood-burning fireplaces, a relative rarity in the city. There's even one super suite with its own fitness center. *28 E. 63rd St., 10021, tel. 212/838–1400 or 800/221–4444, fax 212/838–9194. 60 rooms. Facilities: restaurant, small meeting room, some kitchenettes. AE, DC, MC, V.*

★ **The Mayfair Baglioni.** General manager Dario Mariotti adds a cheery Italian influence to this low-key, gracious hotel. Locals know it for its traditional tea lounge and its first-rate restaurant, Le Cirque (*see* Chapter 9). Even the smallest of the guest rooms has marble baths and traditional-style, peach-tone decor with up-to-date extras such as dual-line telephones and outlets to accommodate portable computers and fax machines. Service is superefficient; guests are offered umbrellas, room humidifiers, customized pillow selection, and the ingenuity of longtime concierge Bruno Brunelli, who can usually conjure up impossible tickets or reservations. While its overall appearance isn't quite as glitzy as that of some other hotels in this price category, the Mayfair more than makes up for its slightly lived-in feel (which many guests, incidentally, prefer) with friendliness and an always-lively atmosphere. *610 Park Ave., 10021, tel. 212/288–0800 or 800/545–4000, fax 201/737–0538. 150 rooms. Facilities: restaurant, lounge, meeting rooms, unlimited local phone calls. AE, DC, MC, V.*

The Pierre. Before Canada's Four Seasons hotel group opened its eponymous flagship on 57th Street, the Pierre was its pride and joy, and it remains a high-profile presence, its distinctive, stepped stories bordering Central Park well known to New Yorkers, some of whom still reside in the hotel. Quite the opposite of the understated style of the Four Seasons, the Pierre's decor owes a lot to the Palace of Versailles, with chandeliers and handmade carpets, murals depicting putti and Corinthian columns in the Rotunda lounge (great for tea), and much muted damask and mahogany in the rooms. It manages not to be ostentatious or stuffy, though, and the staff conveys a sense of fun about working in these posh surroundings. Some $30 million was lavished on renovation a couple of years ago. Bathrooms were upgraded then as well as bedrooms, of which the Boudoir suites, overlooking the Central Park zoo and Wollman Rink, are worth the extra price. This one's a classic whose fans remain faithful. *5th Ave. at 61st St., 10021, tel. 212/838–8000 or 800/332–3442, fax 212/940–8109. 204 rooms. Facilities: restaurant, bar, tearoom, meeting rooms, manned elevators, packing service upon request, hand-laundry service. AE, DC, MC, V.*

The Plaza Athénée. The French half of Forte Hotels' (formerly Trusthouse Forte) New York offerings used to be rather snooty to noncelebrities; however, much of that has changed. What hasn't changed, thankfully, is the quiet elegance of the guest rooms and baths. Even small rooms are well thought out, if not opulent. The red and yellow penthouses are breathtaking—and their price tags aren't, considering the space and attractiveness. The staff seems more generous with its smiles these days, even if you aren't Liz Taylor. *37 E. 64th St., tel. 212/734–9100 or 800/225–5843, fax 212/772–0958. 160 rooms. Facilities: restaurant, bar, meeting rooms. AE, DC, MC, V.*

The Westbury. The English half of Forte Hotels' New York empire combines understated British formality with genuine friendliness. Sedate and comfortable, it delivers good service. Rooms and suites are decorated in either masculine "hunt-style" Ralph Lauren fabrics or in more demure Laura Ashley fashion. Some units, though elegant, are small; all baths are less than spacious when compared to baths in other hotels in this price range—some extremely so—though all are luxurious in terms of fittings and amenities. The Polo restaurant is a pleasant place to enjoy traditional cuisine with a modern touch. There is also a new, comprehensive fitness area. *69th*

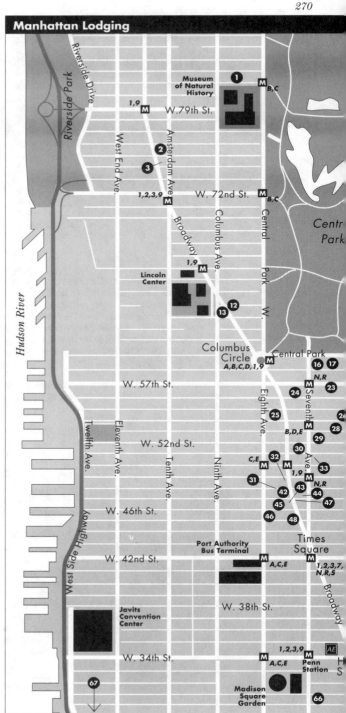

Manhattan Lodging

Sheraton
Manhattan, **30**
Sheraton New York
Hotel & Towers, **29**
Southgate Tower, **66**
Surrey Hotel, **6**
Tudor, **53**
U.N. Plaza–Park
Hyatt, **50**
Vanderbilt YMCA, **41**
Waldorf-Astoria, **39**
Warwick, **27**
Washington
Square, **64**
Wellington, **24**
West Side YMCA, **12**
Westbury, **7**

St. at Madison Ave., 10021, tel. 212/535–2000 or 800/321–1569, fax 212/535–5058. 235 rooms. Facilities: restaurant, lounge, meeting rooms, fitness center. AE, DC, MC, V.

East 50s **The Four Seasons.** If you shop at Barneys and prefer Woody Allen's Ingmar Bergman imitations to his comedies, you'll love New York's tallest, newest, most expensive hotel. I. M. Pei—he of the Louvre Pyramid, among other modernist icons—designed this limestone-clad, stepped spire amid the prime shops of 57th Street, and he made it big. The guest rooms are big (600 square feet on average), the windows in the stagelike 5757 restaurant (*see* Chapter 9) are big, the lobby is bigger than big. Leading into the aptly named Grand Foyer, it is dauntingly sky high, and its French limestone pillars, marble, onyx, and acre upon acre of blonde wood are a study in earth-toned elegance. What could possibly justify the astronomical rates? Gleaming English sycamore dressing areas with a giant mirror perhaps, and enough closets to hold a year's worth of clothing. Fridges, security entry locks, beige blackout drapes you operate by bedside button, and high-quality modern art on the flesh-colored walls are further classy touches. The superb bathrooms have deep tubs that fill and empty in a New York minute, glass-walled showers, TVs, phones, and lighting that makes your hair shine. The boring house toiletries don't measure up. Wear Armani, Gucci, or Lauren, or you'll feel out of place. And bring your own color. 57 E. 57th St., tel. 212/758–5700, fax 212/758–5711. 367 rooms. Facilities: restaurant, bar, lounge café, meeting rooms, business center, fitness center, sauna, spa; fax machines and VCRs available on request, complimentary newspaper. AE, DC, MC, V.

The Peninsula. The former Gotham Hotel on 5th Avenue has, for more than five years now, been owned and operated by the respected Peninsula Group whose Hong Kong flagship consistently gets top ratings. There's nothing wrong with this one either, with its marble Art Nouveau lobby off 54th Street, respected contemporary-American restaurant, Adrienne (*see* Chapter 9), and unobtrusive, ultra-efficient service. Most of the guest rooms are of a generous size, deep-carpeted, and soberly furnished. They're matched by sumptuous (by New York or any standards) marble baths with bidets, outsize tubs, many of them Jacuzzis, and collectible, bergamot-scented Lanvin goodies. Even the smaller rooms have graceful sculpted Art Nouveau-style headboards, desks, and armoires; some also have the same sweeping views down 5th Avenue as the more expensive suites. The rooftop health club, with state-of-the-art exercise machines, a decent-size pool, massage and facial services, and a dining area with a terrace, is a knockout. 700 5th Ave., 10019, tel. 212/247–2200 or 800/262–9467, fax 212/903–3949. 250 rooms. Facilities: restaurant, café, lounge, meeting rooms, pool, fitness center. AE, DC, MC, V.

The St. Regis. When Sheraton decided to restore this 5th Avenue Beaux-Arts landmark, planners set a new company standard for themselves, with prices to match. Is the experience transporting enough to merit such a splurge? On the plus side is chef Gray Kunz's inspired menu in the otherwise slightly stilted, very opulent restaurant, Lespinasse (*see* Chapter 9), and the delightful King Cole Bar, home to the famous Maxfield Parrish mural, and second home to visiting screen stars. Afternoon tea in the Astor Court can compete proudly with the best in town. Guest rooms are filled with Louis XV–style furnishings and expensive amenities. Marble bathrooms, with tubs, stall showers, and double sinks, are outstanding, although there are disappointments such as cheap wall-unit hair dryers and no disposable laundry bags. A fitness center is adequate.

2 E. 55th St., 10022, tel. 212/753–4500 or 800/759–7550, fax 212/787–3447. 365 rooms. Facilities: restaurant, bar, lounge, banquet room, meeting rooms, business center, fitness center, unlimited local phone calls, butler service. AE, DC, MC, V.

West 50s **The Michelangelo.** The Theater District's only true deluxe hotel, having been through several incarnations, most recently as the Parc 51 and the Grand Bay, seems to have settled happily with the Italian Starhotels company, and is better and friendlier than in the past. A very long, wide, low lobby/lounge caters to Italophiles, with plenty of multihued marble, Vivaldi in the air, and Veronese-esque oil paintings on the walls. Upstairs, the rooms are bigger than they need be, and have either French country decor or a distinctly deco feel (curvy black lacquered or pale oak closets concealing TVs, or fitted bar areas in the larger rooms; much chrome and glass). All have king-size beds, multiline phones, and fine—Italian, of course—marble bathrooms with bidets, TVs, and phones. Besides checking out a small workout room in the hotel, guests can use the nearby Equitable Health and Swim Club for a nominal charge. The staff is helpful, with a concierge who is a cut above the usual found in New York City hotels. *152 W. 51st St., 10019, tel. 212/765–1900 or 800/237–0990, fax 212/581–7618. 178 rooms. Facilities: restaurant, lobby lounge and bar, meeting rooms, fitness center; VCRs, CDs, and fax machines and other business equipment available upon request. AE, DC, MC, V.*

Central Park South/59th Street ★ **Essex House.** The owners, Japan's Nikko Hotels, have done wonders for this stately Central Park South property. The public interiors are an Art Deco masterpiece fit for Fred and Ginger. The talented Christian Delouvrier oversees the cuisine, both in the informal Café Botanica, which faces Central Park and resembles a lush prewar English greenhouse, and in the intimate Les Célébrités, which features surprisingly competent celebrity artwork from folks like Billy Dee Williams and James Dean (*see* Chapter 9). Journey's, the hotel's wood-paneled bar, has a working fireplace. The delights continue upstairs, where guest rooms and baths resemble those in a splendid English country home. Fabrics and furnishings are elegant and inviting. Baths are all marble and chrome and feature double sinks and separate stall showers. The staff is discreet, efficient, and friendly. This is the place to take advantage of weekend rates and book that dreamed-about suite on the park. *160 Central Park S (near 7th Ave.), 10019, tel. 212/247–0300, fax 212/315–1839. 593 rooms. Facilities: 3 restaurants, bar, ballroom, fitness center, meeting rooms, business center. AE, DC, MC, V.*

The Plaza. Occupying the entire southwest corner of Central Park West and 5th Avenue, with its front-yard fountain and unsurpassed location opposite Central Park and F.A.O. Schwarz, the Plaza is probably the most high-profile of all New York hotels. Donald Trump bought it (in 1988), the fictional Eloise ran riot in it (and her "portrait" adorns the Palm Court), and film upon film has featured it—from *North by Northwest* in the 1950s and *Breakfast at Tiffany's* and *Barefoot in the Park* in the 1960s, through the 1971 *Plaza Suite*, and the more recent *Sleepless in Seattle, Scent of a Woman,* and *Home Alone 2.* And does the institution live up to the hype? Reports are good. Furnishings, though still hotel-like in most units, are of high quality. The color schemes are in burgundy or teal blue; fresh, floral-patterned quilted spreads grace the large beds. Bathrooms, even those not fully redone, have fluffy new towels and toiletries. One real advantage here is the size of guest rooms—only a handful of other classic properties can offer similar spaciousness in nearly all accommodations. One thing's for sure: Even if it's your first time in New York, a quick nip at the dimly lit Oak Bar or a stroll by the fin-de-siècle Palm Court will make you feel part of what makes the city tick. *5th Ave. at 59th St., 10019, tel. 212/759–3000 or 800/228–3000, fax 212/546–5324. 807 rooms. Facilities: 2 restaurants, 2 bars, café, art gallery, disabled-accessible rooms, meeting rooms, packing service upon request, large concierge staff. AE, DC, MC, V.*

★ **The Ritz-Carlton.** This property—once hot, then lukewarm—has recently been brought under genuine Ritz-Carlton management, and overall service has been raised to the company's high standards. Guest rooms have been refurbished in the R-C manner: brocade bedspreads, marble baths, and rich wood accents. Some suites have been added, the small fitness center has been pumped up, and public areas have been given a face-lift; $20 million was lavished on the place last year, in fact, and it shows. The rooms with Central Park views are definitely preferable, but all accommodations are identical in decor and amenities. The staff is especially friendly and helpful. The elegant Fantino restaurant serves superb northern Italian fare under executive chef Gennaro Villella (*see* Chapter 9), and in the warm, clubby lounge, bartender Norman Bukofzer draws a coterie of convivial celebrities. *112 Central Park S, 10019, tel. 212/757–1900 or 800/241–3333, fax 212/757–9620. 196 rooms. Facilities: restaurant, bar, meeting rooms, concierge floor, fitness center, complimentary limousine service to Wall Street. AE, DC, MC, V.*

Downtown **The Millenium Hilton.** This sleek black monolith is the class act of downtown, outpacing both the Marriott and Vista in terms of elegance. Rooms and suites are modern, decorated in beige tones with wood accents. A unique feature is the wide "sprawl" of window shelf space, perfect for business travelers' portable computers, fax machines, and briefcases. Higher floors have delightful views of landmark buildings and both the Hudson and the East rivers. The hotel's main restaurant, Taliesin, named after architect Frank Lloyd Wright's homes, offers modern American cuisine. The more casual Millenium Grill is served by the same kitchen. Prices are reasonable for hotel fare of this caliber. The adjacent Connoisseur Bar is packed with Wall Streeters. The health club has an attractive pool with a skylight wall that looks out on St. Paul's Church. *55 Church St., 10007, tel. 212/693–2001, fax 212/571–2317. 561 rooms. Facilities: 2 restaurants, bar, meeting rooms, fitness center with pool, business center. AE, DC, M, V.*

$$$

Airport **LaGuardia Marriott Airport Hotel.** A quarter-mile from the airport and—barring traffic—within 20 minutes of Manhattan, this hotel is out of the direct line of most flights. Guests have access to a bar and free Continental breakfast on the comfortable concierge floor. *102–05 Ditmars Blvd., East Elmhurst, 11369, tel. 718/565–8900 or 800/228–9290, fax 718/899–0764. 432 rooms, 5 suites. AE, D, DC, MC, V.*

East 60s **The Regency.** Loews's upper-echelon property is a favorite for power breakfasts and fancy press events (the working rich-and-famous enjoy its discreet and surprisingly relaxed atmosphere). The stately, chandeliered lobby is reminiscent of the kind of private apartment house that comes with a personal staff to help with every need. Guest rooms and suites feature high-quality dark-wood furniture and brocade bedspreads. Bathrooms are of marble, and some have tiny TVs. The 540 Park restaurant has an inventive lower-priced menu featuring grilled meats and seafood. Service is paramount at this property, where the King—Loews Hotel's president, Jonathan Tisch—really does stand guard (and eats breakfast every day). *540 Park Ave., 10021, tel. 212/759-4100 or 800/233-2356, fax 212/826-5674. 400 rooms. Facilities: restaurant, lounge, meeting rooms, fitness center. AE, DC, MC, V.*

East 50s **The Drake.** This Swissôtel property is favored by many business travelers for its solid service and highly desirable location, just off Park Avenue at 56th Street. Since the remodeling of the public areas and updating of guest rooms and bathrooms, it has kept up with the competition. Although the closure of its once-starry restaurant, Lafayette, lowered the Drake's profile somewhat, at press time there were plans to lease the space to an independent restaurateur. The great advantage here is room size: The prewar building was originally designed as an apartment house, so the rooms have enough space for refrigerators and other homey touches, which the staff's definite tendency toward graciousness underline. Many locals enjoy Swiss specialties and hard-to-find Swiss wines at the airy Drake Bar. There's more comfort here than spit and polish, more efficiency than character, but the Drake makes a safe choice for a no-nonsense midtown base, with moderate weekend rates for the leisure traveler. *440 Park Ave., 10022, tel. 212/421-0900 or 800/637-9477, fax 212/371-4190. 600 rooms. Facilities: bar, meeting rooms, complimentary limousine service to Wall Street, luggage check-in for Swissair passengers. AE, DC, MC, V.*

The New York Palace. This glass monolith with a landmark palazzo at its feet is many visitors' vision of the ideal New York hotel: big, slightly overwrought, and always busy. Palace rooms are generous by Manhattan standards; those on the higher floors enjoy views of St. Patrick's Cathedral and the East Side from windows which, rather worryingly, open wide at the bottom. All parts of the Palace, from rooms to elevators, are punctuated with crimson plush and gilt moldings, with bedroom walls of faded duck-egg blue and a faux limed-oak finish on the reproduction furniture. In-room amenities are back-to-front: The minibar is empty, and there's no robe or in-room safe, but there *is* a shoe polishing machine, an iron, and Caswell Massey toiletries. Public rooms, many of them located in the 100-year-old Villard Houses at the hotel's base, contain valuable pieces of art and lovely architectural details, and there are a variety of bars and eating spots. The staff is friendly, if occasionally harried. *455 Madison Ave., 10022, tel. 212/888-7000 or 800/221-4982, fax 212/355-0820. 963 rooms. Facilities: restaurant, 2 lounges, 2 bars, tearoom, use of nearby fitness center (fee), meeting rooms, kitchenettes in suites. AE, DC, MC, V.*

The Waldorf-Astoria. Along with the Plaza (*see* $$$$, *above*), this Art Deco masterpiece personifies New York at its most lavish and powerful. Hilton, its owner, spent a fortune on refurbishing both public areas and guest rooms a couple of years ago, and the bloom hasn't faded yet, from the original murals and mosaics and elaborate plaster ornamentation to the fine old-wood walls and doors. In the guest rooms, some of which start at the low end of this category, there are new bedspreads, carpets, and other signs of upgrading. Bathrooms throughout are old but beautifully kept up and rather spacious. Of course, in the very private Tower section, everything becomes just that much grander. The chef is French at Peacock Alley, where Waldorf salad first made news; you'll find much more than chopped Macs in mayo nowadays (*see* Chapter 9). The Plus One fitness center stresses individual training. The hotel's richly tinted, hushed lobby serves as an interior centerpoint of city life. *301 Park Ave., 10022, tel. 212/355-3000 or 800/HILTONS, fax 212/421-8103. 1,692 rooms.*

Facilities: 3 restaurants, coffee shop, tearoom, lounge, ballroom, fitness center, meeting rooms. AE, DC, MC, V.

West 50s **Le Parker Meridien.** This dramatic, modern French hotel, whose soaring blonde-wood lobby links 56th and 57th streets, is near some of the city's finest stores and cultural spots. For fitness-minded visitors, there's an airy rooftop swimming pool and a state-of-the-art basement-level workout center—both complimentary to guests. Since all the guest rooms underwent renovation last year, you can count on fresh decor, with the bathrooms, stocked with luxurious Lanvin, up to the same standard. The hotel's service is anything but snooty. *118 W. 57th St., 10019, tel. 212/245–5000 or 800/543–4300, fax 212/307–1776. 700 rooms. Facilities: restaurant, café, bar, meeting rooms, voice mail, fitness center, pool, accompanied jogging. AE, DC, MC, V.*

The New York Hilton. In a sense, this is the city's premier hotel for professional meetings, large and small. It has a special conference center, a business center run by the *Wall Street Journal*, and loads of multilingual help. Hilton spends vast sums on keeping it trim, and it shows: There's a distinctive landscaped driveway, and a sprawling, brassy lobby, businesslike rather than beautiful to behold, but always buzzing. Considering the size of this property (more than 2,000 rooms), guest areas are surprisingly well maintained, if not always spacious or terribly fashionable. Guests who pay extra for Tower Level accommodations get slightly larger rooms and use of a lounge with a separate boardroom and complimentary drinks and snacks. Otherwise, rooms tend toward the small side, and it might be as well to request one of the 919 rooms that had either a face-lift or complete reconstructive surgery last year. The Grill 53 restaurant has standard but generally competent hotel fare. If you don't expect high levels of personal attention or unfaltering elegance, this well-run machine will usually satisfy, although housekeeping can lapse when the hotel is full. *1335 6th Ave., 10019, tel. 212/586–7000 or 800/HILTONS, fax 212/315–1374. 2,042 rooms. Facilities: restaurant, nightclub, 2 cafés, bar, meeting rooms, multilingual desk, VIP floor, fitness center, business center, American Express desk. AE, DC, MC, V.*

Midtown **Doral Court, Doral Park Avenue,** and **Doral Tuscany.** Doral has cre-
East/Murray ated a cozy enclave of three hotels in the East 30s Murray Hill dis-
Hill trict. Guests at any one property can sign for meals and drinks at all
★ three; they also have complimentary access to the Doral Saturnia Fitness Center at 90 Park Avenue. The Doral Tuscany and its adjacent neighbor, the Doral Court (which has slightly lower prices that actually put it in the "$$" category), have attractive, traditionally furnished guest rooms and suites; the Tuscany's baths and bedrooms are more formal and elegant, though both properties are well maintained. The Doral Park Avenue, refurbished by designer Sarah Lee, has rooms furnished in restful cream and beige tones. All three have good restaurants, the best and most acclaimed being the Tuscany's Time and Again, which features a changing menu of American nouvelle specialties. The Doral Court's Courtyard Café offers one of the city's nicer outdoor dining spaces. *Doral Court, 130 E. 39th St., 10016, tel. 212/685–1100 or 800/624–0607, fax 212/889–0287. 248 rooms. Facilities: café, meeting rooms, complimentary parking on all weekend packages. AE, DC, MC, V. Doral Park Avenue, 70 Park Ave. at 38th St., 10016, tel. 212/687–7050 or 800/847–4135, fax 212/808–9029. 220 rooms. Facilities: bar, café, meeting rooms, fitness center, complimentary parking on all weekend packages. AE, DC, MC, V. Doral Tuscany, 120 E. 39th St., 10016, tel. 212/686–1600 or 800/847–4078, fax 212/779–7822. 119 rooms. Facili-*

ties: restaurant, lounge, meeting rooms, complimentary parking on all weekend packages. AE, DC, MC, V.

The Tudor. A couple of years ago, a soup-to-nuts renovation by the London-based Sarova Hotel Group transformed this neighbor of the United Nations and Grand Central Terminal into a charming, medium-size property. Interior spaces are classic and unassuming, with hardwood reproduction furniture upholstered in brocades and velvets, marble floors, and handmade carpets in the public areas. A fine marble bathroom is attached to every room; the executive rooms and suites get Jacuzzis. Some of these also have a private terrace. The 20-story landmark building dates from the '20s, part of Tudor City (*see* Tour 3 in Chapter 3), with its private park and fanciful Englishness. Business travelers are particularly well looked after here, with the requisite two-line phones, fax machines, and business center, and there's a trouser press and minibar in every room. The Tudor has a handful of "Circadian" rooms—the first in the city—designed for transatlantic schmoozers to recover their equilibrium fast. *304 E. 42nd St., 10017, tel. 212/986–8800 or 800/TRY–TUDOR, fax 212/986–1758. 303 rooms. Facilities: restaurant, lounge, meeting rooms, fitness center, business center. AE, DC, MC, V.*

★ **U.N. Plaza–Park Hyatt.** It's easy to miss the entrance to this favorite among the business and diplomatic set—it's on a quiet side street near (naturally) the United Nations. The small but striking lobby gives the illusion of endless space, thanks to clever designs in dark marble and mirrors; Japanese floral arrangements add warmth and drama. What makes this place really special, though, are the guest rooms, all with breathtaking views of Manhattan's East Side, and the delightful rooftop pool. The decor is modern but not overpoweringly sterile, and the color schemes are soothing. The burgundy-hued Ambassador Grill features grilled game in season (*see* Chapter 9); prices here are still reasonable by hotel standards, though the room rates have been edging up and now sit at the top of this price category. Service throughout the hotel is first-rate. Families with young children will especially appreciate the nearby U.N. park and the hotel's safe location. *1 United Nations Plaza, 10017, tel. 212/ 355–3400 or 800/223–1234, fax 212/702–5051. 444 rooms. Facilities: restaurant, 2 lounges, meeting rooms, pool, fitness center, complimentary limousine service to Wall Street and Theater District. AE, DC, MC, V.*

Midtown West **Embassy Suites.** Another welcome addition to the Times Square
★ area, this familiar name's flagship has far more flair than anticipated. The elevated lobby is done up in modern art-deco style; color schemes and furnishings are bold and contemporary. Suites have coffeemakers, small microwave ovens, refrigerators, and even complimentary sodas and snacks. Guest rooms, though hardly elegant, are cheerful and comfortable. Certain suites have been "child-proofed" with such safety features as bumpers placed over sharp edges. All rates include full breakfast and daily cocktails in a private lounge area. There's also a regular restaurant, the Broadway Museum Café, featuring well-priced grills and salads. A complete day-care center with trained staff is just one of many wonderful features for families. The staff seems eager to please, too. Meanwhile, Embassy might improve its street-level security; the block continues to be somewhat unsavory. *1568 Broadway at 47th St., 10036, tel. 212/ 719–1600 or 800/EMBASSY, fax 212/921–5212. 460 suites. Facilities: restaurant, bar, meeting rooms, day-care center, complimentary use of nearby health club and pool. AE, DC, MC, V.*

Holiday Inn Crowne Plaza. The deluxe flagship of the famous commercial hotel chain, a towering roseate stone edifice, was built on the exact site of the original music publishing company of Irving Berlin—he wrote the music for the movie *Holiday Inn*, from which the chain took its name. Public areas with a rose and beige color scheme are softer and more opulent than those of its neighboring competitor, the Marriott Marquis. Upstairs, the decent-size rooms continue the rose color scheme, this time with a touch of teal blue. Guest rooms start at the 16th floor so that everyone gets an eyeful from the panoramic windows. Bathrooms are beyond basic, though the amenities found within could be more lavish. Another minor drawback is the serious lack of closet space, even in the suites. The multi-tiered Samplings bar and restaurant has a terrific view of Broadway. The superior health club includes a shallow lap pool, run by the efficient New York Sports company. *1605 Broadway at 49th St., 10019, tel. 212/977-4000 or 800/HOLIDAY, fax 212/333-7393. 770 rooms. Facilities: 3 restaurants, café, lounge, concierge-level fitness center, pool, ballroom, meeting rooms, business center. AE, DC, MC, V.*

The Marriott Marquis. This seven-year-old giant is one of the places New Yorkers love to hate: It's obvious, brash, bright, and definitely geared to conventions and groups. Still, anything that brings life and light to the Times Square area is welcome. As at other Marriotts, the help is ultrafriendly and informative, if not terribly polished. Rooms (though Marriott claims otherwise) are *not* the largest in town, but they're large enough; their color schemes are restful and their bathrooms perfectly adequate and modern. Some rooms have dramatic urban views. There's a revolving restaurant, the View, on the 46th floor, and a second revolving lounge on the eighth-floor lobby level. Most patrons have booked here on some sort of reduced or group rate. *1535 Broadway at 45th St., 10036, tel. 212/398-1900 or 800/843-4898, fax 212/704-8930. 1,877 rooms. Facilities: 3 restaurants, café, 3 lounges, meeting rooms, fitness center, theater, VIP floor, business center. AE, DC, MC, V.*

Renaissance. The former Ramada Renaissance was redone to suit the business community, which provides about 70% of its patrons, though for the vacationer, off-season rates start low, and theaterland is on the doorstep. Four Olympian Atlases preside over elevators leading from street level to the third-floor lobby/lounge/reception area, where service is half snotty, half super-friendly, just as decor is half hotel-chain, half deco splendor, with brass and mahogany where chrome and pine suffice elsewhere. Rooms have two-line phones, VCRs, minibars, safes, and bathrooms with deep tubs and a generous selection of toiletries. There's a tiny gym, several boardrooms, secretarial services, and a Mediterranean restaurant called Windows on Broadway, with a great eye-level view of Times Square. Somehow, though, despite the dearth of vinyl and veneer, there's something plasticky about the Renaissance, stemming from its impersonal nature—which is, after all, what some people seek. *2 Times Sq., 10036, tel. 212/765-7676, fax 212/765-1962. 305 rooms. Facilities: restaurant, 2 bars, lounge, business center, meeting rooms, fitness room. AE, D, DC, MC, V.*

The Royalton. As hip today as it was when it opened its steel-and-glass doors to the '80s, Ian Schrager and the late Steve Rubell's second Manhattan hotel (Morgan's came first) is a second home to the world's media, music, and fashion biz folk. Even someone who has never opened a copy of *Vogue* (whose editors hang out here) can't fail to be thunderstruck by the difference between this and traditional-style hotels like, say, the Algonquin across the street. French designer Philippe Starck—he of the pointy-ended toothbrush and the chrome lemon squeezer on stilts—transformed spaces of intimidating size into a paradise for poseurs, with vividly colored, geometrically challenged but comfy chairs and couches and lots of catwalk-style gliding areas. The bathrooms are amalgams of raw slate, conical brushed steel, and sculpted water (you have to see them to understand that). Rooms, suffice it to say, are just as glamorously offbeat, some of them oddly shaped and none too big, but all of them perfectly comfortable, especially with the service you get here, which caters to people who feel it's their lot in life to be waited on. The restaurant, 44, is predictably booked solid by New York's style mafia, who also habitually hold meetings, play chess, and pick at arugula in the lobby (lounge) and bar. *44 W. 44th St., 10036, tel. 212/ 869–4400 or 800/635–9013, fax 212/869–8965. 205 rooms. Facilities: restaurant with bar, lounge, meeting rooms, fitness center, game and library areas, VCRs, stereos. AE, DC, MC, V.*

Lower Manhattan **The New York Vista.** Underground damage from the World Trade Center bombing in February 1993, added a few more million to the budget of the Hilton International Vista's already-in-progress major renovation, providing an excuse to go the extra mile. And it shows. The horrid '70s smoked glass and brass are all gone, replaced by a fabulous lobby, with grand curved staircase, fountain and skylight, a comfortable burgundy and blue lounge, a second Liberty Street entrance, and a contemporary green granite and marble main entrance. Both the Greenhouse restaurant/café, and the Tallships Bar and Grill have added windows and street entrances, and extra facilities for business guests include private dining in what was the American Harvest restaurant, and an extra floor of executive rooms, with a bigger lounge. Make sure you're booked into one of the 12 newly refurbished floors, though all should be renovated by spring 1995. The Vista was the first major Lower Manhattan hotel when it opened 12 years ago. Now the West Street Marriott and the classy Millenium have joined it, but the Vista is well up to the competition, especially when you throw the Health Club, with its big pool, new equipment, and the city's biggest indoor jogging track, into the mix. Downtown also makes a great sightseeing base, by the way, and you can walk to the restaurants of TriBeCa. *3 World Trade Center, 10048, tel. 212/938–9100, fax 212/ 321–2107. 820 rooms. Facilities: 2 restaurants, 2 lounges, meeting rooms, pool, fitness center, VIP floor, free parking with weekend packages. AE, DC, MC, V.*

$$

Airport **JFK Plaza Hotel.** This contemporary-style, 12-story hotel, a 5- to 10-minute drive from the terminals at John F. Kennedy International airport, is out of the flight path of most of the airport's traffic. Guests on the concierge level get free Continental breakfasts and hors d'oeuvres; general amenities include a weight room. *135–30 140th St., 11436, tel. 718/659–6000 or 800/445–7177, fax 718/659–4755. 349 rooms, 21 suites. AE, D, DC, MC, V.*

Vista International. Opened in 1988, the Vista is five minutes from Newark airport and 20 minutes, in light traffic, from Manhattan. Triple-glazed glass doors keep airport noise to a minimum. The hotel caters to businesspeople, but guests who need to go into Manhattan should bear in mind that traffic in the New Jersey–New York tunnels can be especially slow (in both directions) at rush hours and at various other unpredictable times. *1170 Spring St., Elizabeth, NJ 07201, tel. 201/351–3900 or 800/678–4782, fax 201/355–8059. 370 rooms, 6 suites. AE, D, DC, MC, V.*

West 60s **Radisson Empire Hotel.** A change in ownership transformed this old place into a useful and reliable option. The English country–style lobby is warm and inviting; halls are decorated in soft gray with elegant lamps. Rooms and suites are a bit like small boxes, but nicely furnished; special room features include high-tech electronics, and the small but immaculate baths have heated towel racks. There is a cozy "British" lounge on the second floor that New Yorkers in the know have discovered. Although this hotel's prices have gone up, it's still one of the city's better buys in terms of quality and location, right across the street from Lincoln Center. At press time there was no room service, but no matter: The neighborhood is loaded with all-hours dining options, and the Iridium restaurant next door (*see* Chapter 9) serves fashionable but tasty fare in a surrealistic, moonscape setting. There are plans to turn over ground-floor space to an independent restaurateur. *Broadway at 63rd St., 10023, tel. 212/265–7400, 800/221–6509, or 800/223–9868, fax 212/315–0349. 368 rooms. Facilities: voice mail. AE, DC, MC, V.*

East 50s **The Fitzpatrick.** This cozy Irish "boutique" hotel is conveniently sit-
★ uated just south of Bloomingdale's and seconds away from anchor bus and subway routes. The first American venture for an established Irish company, it's a real winner in terms of value and charm. Nearly half of the 92 units are true suites that are priced well below the market average, even on weekdays. Amenities include trouser presses, telephones with voice mail, and subdued traditional furnishings. Though not especially large, bathrooms are modern and well equipped; most come with whirlpools. A small restaurant called Fitzers features Irish seafood in season and a lively bar, which has become popular with locals. The staff is exceptionally friendly and savvy, which may be why celebs such as Gregory Peck and Stephen Rea are checking in. *687 Lexington Ave., 10022, tel. 212/355–0100 or 800/367–7701, fax 212/308–5166. 92 rooms. Facilities: restaurant, bar, small meeting room, fax machines and VCRs available upon request. AE, DC, MC, V.*

Loews New York Hotel. Loews's moderate-price New York property has an impersonal style, but most of its regulars—business travelers—don't mind because the hotel generally runs quite well. Rooms, most of them refurbished, are comfortable and well designed. Deluxe units (only slightly higher in price than standard) come with goodies, such as Godiva chocolates and complimentary liquor miniatures. The Lexington Avenue Grill, with striking maroon art-deco carpeting and a wood-tone lobby, has a reliable menu of pastas, burgers, and fish entrées. During low-occupancy periods, guests can actually book rooms here for the upper end of less expensive prices; even suites come down below the $200 range. *Lexington Ave. at 51st St., 10022, tel. 212/752–7000, fax 212/758–6311. 766 rooms. Facilities: restaurant, lounge, meeting rooms, fitness center. AE, DC, MC, V.*

The San Carlos. This small, residential-style property offers basic hotel service, clean modern rooms, and a neighborly atmosphere. Larger suites come with kitchenettes, making them a good choice for families. The small wood-paneled lobby is gracious and well lit; women travelers can feel quite secure here. *150 E. 50th St., 10022, tel. 212/755–1800 or 800/722–2012. 140 rooms. Facilities: restaurant. AE, DC, MC, V.*

West 50s **Gorham Hotel.** This small but conveniently located lodging has modern guest rooms and can be recommended to the traveler who wants a location within walking distance of the best of the East and West sides of town. There are pleasant fabrics and carpeting and surprisingly luxurious bathrooms in most units. There is an Italian restaurant downstairs, though one can easily find myriad other dining options nearby. The lobby is bright, and the small staff is informed, if not always overly friendly. *136 W. 55th St., 10019, tel. 212/245–1800 or 800/735–0710, fax 212/245–1800. 120 rooms. Facilities: independent on-premises restaurant, concierge. AE, DC, MC, V.*

The Sheraton New York Hotel & Towers, Sheraton Manhattan. The Sheraton's multimillion-dollar overhaul of the two buildings for the last Democratic Convention brought vast improvements. Though rooms—even in the superior Tower section located in the Sheraton New York—are on the small side, everything is bright and cheerful. Towers guests have a private lounge and superior amenities, including private check-in and concierge. The New York's restaurant and sports-bar complex, Hudson's, is casual and attractive, as is the Manhattan's Bistro 790, which features surprisingly tasty updated American fare. Non-Tower rooms in the New York and the Manhattan are nearly identical in decor and amenities. The Manhattan has a large renovated pool and a small fitness center, which offers swimming lessons, aquatic exercise, treadmills, and a sun deck. The public spaces of both properties are welcoming, workaday, and busy, busy, busy. Sheraton New York: *811 7th Ave. at 53rd St., 10019, tel. 212/581–1000 or 800/325–3535, fax 212/262–4410. 1,800 rooms.* Sheraton Manhattan: *790 7th Ave. at 51st St., tel. 212/581–3300 or 800/325–3535, fax 212/541–9219. 650 rooms. Combined facilities: 2 restaurants, 2 bars, pool, fitness center, upgraded Tower rooms with private lounge, ballroom, extensive meeting space. AE, DC, MC, V.*

The Warwick. Catercorner from the New York Hilton and therefore well placed for theater and points west, this handsome and cozy classic belonging to a Geneva-based chain is still undergoing a major overhaul, with the third through 17th floors complete at press time, and seven more that were scheduled to be finished by summer 1994. Be sure to get one of the new, Regency-style rooms, with hardwood furniture and floral drapes, or you could get stuck in a '70s nightmare of giant bamboo- or autumn leaf-print wallpaper and lurid yellow-tiled bathrooms, with no price difference to lighten the blow. The lobby-lounge is most inviting, with a dark green bar and the huge Tudor murals of the Ciao Europa restaurant on either side of the entrance, lots of armchairs, and marble floors. *65 W. 54th St., tel. 212/247–2700, fax 212/957–8915. 425 rooms. Facilities: restaurant, bar, lounge, meeting rooms. AE, DC, MC, V.*

Midtown East/Murray Hill

Journey's End. This Canadian chain's first Manhattan property features no-nonsense, clean, attractive rooms and baths at one fixed price. Most accommodations come with queen-size beds; all have modern TVs and telephones with long cords. Guests can use a small lounge area for complimentary coffee and newspapers. There is an independently owned Italian restaurant on the premises. At night, this part of midtown is somewhat quiet and therefore subject to street crime. However, security at the hotel appears to be superior. Another plus—it's just a few blocks away from the airport bus departure area on Park Avenue near Grand Central Terminal. *3 E. 40th St., 10016, tel. 212/447–1500 or 800/668–4200. 189 rooms. Facilities: lounge, independent on-premises restaurant, business services on request. AE, DC, MC, V.*

★ **Manhattan Suites East.** Here's a group of good-value properties for the traveler who likes to combine full hotel service with independent pied-à-terre living. These nine midtown hotels have different characters and varying prices, though all have been edging up and most now top the $$ category in busy seasons. The four best are the recently redone **Beekman Tower** (3 Mitchell Pl.), near the United Nations; the **Dumont Plaza** (150 E. 34th St.); the **Surrey Hotel** (20 E. 76th St.), in the neighborhood of Madison Avenue art galleries and designer boutiques; and the **Southgate Tower** (371 7th Ave.), an attractive and secure place to sleep near Madison Square Garden and Penn Station, with the lowest rates of the bunch. Except for the modern style at the Dumont, all have traditional guest-room decor; the Surrey's rooms border on the truly elegant. Most accommodations have pantries, and larger units have dining areas with full-size tables. Other hotels in this group tend to be more residential, except for the full-service **Shelburne** (303 Lexington Ave.); many top corporations use them as interim lodgings for newly relocated executives. The Beekman, Surrey, Shelburne, and Dumont Plaza have restaurants (the art deco-style Zephyr Grill at the Beekman has an extensive spa menu), which can also be used for room service. The Dumont, Southgate, and the Shelburne have on-premises fitness centers. The older hotels in the group do have some disappointing rooms, but overall these properties are outstanding for the price, considering their convenience, location, and space. Their weekend package rates are hard to beat. *Sales office, 505 E. 75th St., 10001, tel. 212/772-2900 or 800/ME-SUITE. AE, DC, MC, V.*

★ **Morgans.** Until recently, the first hotel in nightclub mavens Ian Schrager and the late Steve Rubell's triumphant triumvirate was so discreet, it eschewed publicity of all kinds, but now it doesn't mind if you manage to find it. There's no sign outside or in the monochrome lobby to assist you, which, for many of the guests, some of them famous, is a definite turn-on. The stunning rooms, created by Andree Putman, are less wacky than at the Starck-designed Royalton (*see* $$$, *above*) and Paramount (*see* $, *below*), but if you prefer the colorized version of *It's a Wonderful Life*, you'll spend all your time looking for the tone control. Yes, from the speckled beige-gray-white walls to the cushions on the windowseat, from the built-in-closet doors to the specially commissioned Mapplethorpe photographs, everything is pretty much in shades that jump between black and white. Exquisite, tiny bathrooms have checkered tile stripes like on the old cabs, crystal glass doors on the shower, brushed steel sinks, and snob-value Kiehl's toiletries. There are vague plans afoot to add a restaurant, but for now, there's only a laid-back breakfast room with a complimentary buffet. If you care deeply about style, can't afford the Royalton, or don't want to be on show, there is no better place to stay in New York. *237 Madison Ave., 10016, tel. 212/686-0300, fax 212/779-8352. 112 rooms. Facilities: breakfast room. AE, DC, MC, V.*

Midtown West **The Algonquin.** While this landmark property's English-drawing-room atmosphere and burnished-wood lobby have been kept mercifully intact, its working parts (the plumbing, for instance) and bedrooms have been renovated. This much-beloved hotel, where the Round Table group of writers and wits once met for lunch, still shelters celebrities, particularly literary types visiting nearby publishing houses or the *New Yorker* magazine offices. Late-night performances go on as usual at the Oak Room. Bathrooms and sleeping quarters retain Victorian-style fixtures and furnishings, only now there are larger, firmer beds, modern TVs, VCRs (upon request), computerized phones, and Caswell-Massey toiletries. Tubs, tiles, and sinks are still too old-fashioned for these prices—although new management by Westin may change that. Even if you stay elsewhere, stop by the Algonquin for afternoon tea or a drink in its cozy lobby, then ask at the newsstand for a look at the album of the hotel cat's life in pictures and her fan mail. *59 W. 44th St., 10036, tel. 212/840-6800 or 800/548-0345, fax 212/944-1419. 165 rooms. Facilities: restaurant, 2 lounges, meeting rooms, complimentary parking on weekends, business center. AE, DC, MC, V.*

Downtown **Best Western Seaport Inn.** This thoroughly pleasant, restored 19th-century building is one block from the waterfront, making it convenient for South Street Seaport and lower Manhattan sightseeing, not to mention early morning forays among the ripe aromas of Fulton Street fish market. The decor is somewhere between colonial sea-captain's house and chain hotel, (with a video fire crackling in the lobby grate). The reasonably priced rooms feature dark wood, white walls, and floral nylon bedcovers. There's a fine view of Brooklyn Bridge from rooms on the fifth to seventh floors facing Front Street. Ask about weekend rates. *33 Peck Slip, 10038, tel. 212/766–6600 or 800/468–3569, fax 212/766–6615. 65 rooms. AE, DC, MC, V.*

$

East 60s **The Barbizon.** Three blocks from Bloomingdale's is this 22-story tawny brick neo-Gothic hotel, famous until the mid-70s as the Barbizon Hotel for Women, where Grace Kelly and Candice Bergen, among others, rested unmolested in the library or tea lounge. Refurbishment all but halved the room total (to 300) and doubled the size of most, but try for one of the still-small studio rooms, of which there are some 35: at under $100 a night, they're a great deal for the neighborhood. These rooms come with the same facilities as the more expensive rooms and suites (which are nothing special)—in-house movies on TV, individual air-conditioning control and phone, as well as access to the newly spruced-up lobby and Star Bar, with its cobalt blue and gold zodiac ceiling, of which the management is justly proud. *140 E. 63rd St., 10021, tel. 212/838–5700, fax 212/753–0360. 345 rooms with bath. Facilities: restaurant, bar, theater-ticket desk, meeting rooms. AE, DC, MC, V.*

East 50s **Pickwick Arms Hotel.** This convenient East Side establishment charges $80 a night for standard renovated doubles but has older singles with shared baths for as little as $40. The marble-clad lobby is small but brightly lit, and the staff is friendly. Guest rooms have been comfortably furnished in white bamboo. Guests have access to a roof garden; although there is no restaurant, the neighborhood is loaded with places to eat, and a café on the ground floor sells sandwiches, snacks, and a great cup of coffee. This is an acceptable budget alternative in a good area. *230 E. 51st St., 10022, tel. 212/355–0300 or 800/PICKWIK, fax 212/755–5729. 400 rooms. AE, MC, V.*

Upper West Side **Broadway American.** The Upper West Side has become one of New York's hottest neighborhoods. Those wishing to be in its midst should try this small but surprisingly stylish lodging. The least expensive singles have shared baths, though most rooms come with private facilities. Decor is functional modern, with high-tech touches such as TVs with cable. The dominating color scheme is soft gray. Baths are basic but no worse than others in more expensive units around town. Everything was clean at press time. The only drawback is that some of this former single-room-occupancy hotel's oddball occupants are living in old-style rooms not yet converted for transient use. *2178 Broadway, 10024, tel. 212/362–1100 or 800/446–4556, fax 212/787–9521. 200 rooms. Facilities: independent on-premises restaurant, vending machines, laundry service, AE, DC, MC, V.*

The Excelsior. This property is very much like those dependable second-class hotels you find in Paris in such abundance. A great location (right across from the American Museum of Natural History and the Hayden Planetarium), clean, pleasant rooms, a helpful staff, and low prices make this a find. Furnishings are relatively new; baths are old but in good condition. Rooms on higher floors have lovely views of Central Park. There is frequent bus and subway service nearby. *45 W. 81st St., 10024, tel. 212/362–9200 or 800/368– 4575, fax 212/721–2994. 120 rooms. Facilities: coffee shop, kitchenettes in suites. AE, DC, MC, V.*

Hotel Beacon. Here's another upper Broadway residential building that's been largely converted to a spiffy hotel that should appeal to visitors who can make their own dining and sightseeing arrangements. The decent-size rooms come with full kitchenettes—a real advantage, because some of New York's best gourmet food stores, such as Zabar's and Fairway, are in the immediate area. Furnishings are less institutional than expected, and baths are modern if not elegant. Downstairs is the well-known nightspot, the China Club, and the neighborhood offers numerous delis and ethnic restaurants. The front-desk staff seems adequate when it comes to security consciousness. *2130 Broadway, 10023, tel. 212/787–1100 or 800/572– 4969, fax 212/724–0839. 115 rooms. AE, DC, MC, V.*

West 50s **Ameritania.** This converted single-room-occupancy hotel is a pleasant choice for the theater goer or business traveler with an eye on the bottom line, especially since a lot of updating was completed only recently, ensuring that everything from the lobby to the simple rooms is modern and cheerful. Some units have superior baths and amenities. There is a full-service Italian restaurant and small fitness center on the premises. The hotel's proximity to Broadway hits and popular night spots such as the Ritz should keep the clientele on the youthful side. *1701 Broadway, 10019, tel. 212/247–5000, fax 212/ 247–3316. 250 rooms. Facilities: restaurant, lounge, fitness room. AE, DC, MC, V.*

Wellington Hotel. This large, old-fashioned property's main advantages are reasonable prices and a midtown location very near Carnegie Hall, which attract many budget-conscious Europeans. Rooms are small but clean and reasonably cheery; baths are serviceable. Standard hotel services are available upon request. The brightly lit lobby provides a reassuring welcome for late-night returns. *871 7th Ave. at 55th St., 10019, tel. 212/247–3900 or 800/652–1212, fax 212/ 768–3477. 700 rooms. Facilities: restaurant. AE, DC, MC, V.*

Midtown East **Jolly Madison Towers.** Who could resist that name? Actually, it refers not to the ambience but to the Italian chain that took this place off Best Western's hands about three years ago and proceeded with an overdue remodeling. For this safe and tony neighborhood, prices are reasonable, especially since decor, service, and facilities are unobjectionable, if unspectacular. Rooms are small but handsome in their new deep sapphire and dove gray colors, with dark wood headboards and desks; king-size beds in the superiors, queen-size elsewhere. Bathrooms are tiny and shiny, with marbelized vanities and white tiles around compact tubs. Italophiles may find the atmosphere jolly after all, with *buona seras* echoing around the coffee shop (which is just that) and the wood-beamed, tallship-theme bar. Half of the guests, after all, are Italian. *22 E. 38th St., 10016, tel. 212/685–3700, fax 212/447–0747. 225 rooms. Facilities: bar, coffee shop, health club (fee). AE, DC, MC, V.*

★ **Vanderbilt YMCA.** Of the various Manhattan Ys offering accommodations, this is the best as far as location and facilities are concerned. Although rooms hold up to four people, they are little more than dormitory-style cells—even with only one or two beds to a room, you may feel crowded. Each room does have a late-model TV, however. There are no private baths; communal showers and toilets are clean. Guests are provided with basics such as towels and soap. Besides the low price, this Y offers membership to its huge health club, which has 2 pools, gym, running track, exercise rooms, and sauna. Many of the athletic and public areas, including the pool, have been remodeled. Rooms have been recently refreshed, too. An informal cafeteria and a friendly hospitality desk encourage travelers to mix with one another. The Turtle Bay neighborhood is safe, convenient, and interesting (the United Nations is a few short blocks away). Other YMCAs in town include the 561-room **West Side Y** (5 W. 63rd St., 10023, tel. 212/787–4400), which may be hard to get into but is in the desirable Lincoln Center area; and the 1,490-room **Sloane House YMCA** (356 W. 34th St., 10001, tel. 212/760–5860), which is in a gritty and somewhat unsafe neighborhood. *224 E. 47th St., 10017, tel. 212/755–2410, fax 212/752–0210. 430 rooms. Facilities: cafeteria, meeting rooms, self-service laundry, gift shop, luggage storage, 2 pools, fitness center. No credit cards.*

Midtown West   **Chatwal Inns.** This hotel group features six properties, located mostly in the Broadway-midtown area, that provide clean, attractively designed rooms at relatively unpainful prices. All guests receive a complimentary continental breakfast and discounts to several affiliated restaurants. Some of the larger properties, such as the **Best Western** affiliate (234 W. 48th St.), have on-premises full-service restaurants as well. Rooms, though relatively small throughout all six hotels, are immaculate and have all the basic amenities travelers have come to expect, including bathroom toiletries, modern telephones, and TVs. Since many of the buildings were, until recently, rather dilapidated, don't be put off by the dingy facades of Chatwal properties like **the Quality Inn Midtown** (157 W. 47th St.) or **the Chatwal Inn** (132 W. 45th St.); their interiors are among the chain's nicest. Sant S. Chatwal, owner of Bombay Palace restaurants, is to be applauded for his restoration and pricing efforts. *Tel. 800/826–4667; in Canada: 800/621–4667. Facilities: restaurants, small meeting rooms, lounges, depending on the property. AE, DC, MC, V.*

★ **Hotel Edison.** A popular budget stop for tour groups from here and abroad, this offbeat old hotel has gotten a face-lift. A gruesome murder scene for *The Godfather* was shot in what is now Sophia's restaurant, and the pink-plaster coffee shop has become a hot place to eavesdrop on show-business gossip thanks to such celebrity regulars as Jackie Mason. Guest rooms are brighter and fresher than the dark corridors seem to hint. There's no room service, but this part of the Theater District has so many restaurants and delis that it doesn't matter much. The crowd here is perfectly wholesome, so save money on your room and spend the big bucks on theater tickets. *228 W. 47th St., 10036, tel. 212/840–5000, fax 212/596–6850. 1,000 rooms. Facilities: restaurant, coffee shop, bar. AE, DC, MC, V.*

Hotel Wentworth. This relatively small prewar hotel is on a midtown street that's usually pulsating with South American atmosphere—some of the city's best-known Brazilian restaurants are right outside. The lobby, hallways, and many of the rooms have been modernized, making this a far more welcoming property than before. The atmosphere is similar to that of many second-class European hotels. This is a popular stop for South Americans, although one frequently sees well-dressed U.S. businessmen, too. Single women might find the area a bit eerie at night. *59 W. 46th St., 10036, tel. 212/719–2300 or 800/223–1900. 250 rooms. AE, DC, MC, V.*

★ **Paramount.** What used to be the dowdy Century Paramount was completely transformed by the same team that owns the Royalton (*see* $$$, *above*), and Morgans (*see* $$, *above*), into a cut-rate version of the same, so irresistible it's nearly always full. In the Phillippe Starck lobby, a cliff of concrete and glamorous sweep of staircase lead to a mezzanine gallery of squashy seating and tiny nightclub-style table lamps for dining and spying on the glitterati below, a separate bar, and a hilarious children's playroom. Despite appearances, the staff is most welcoming, and there's a perennial scene in the other bar off the lobby, which remains packed into the wee hours. Rumors that the bedrooms are minute are true. They make up for it with wacky touches, like lights that reproduce the look of dappled sunlight, zebra-striped headboards, and conical steel sinks in the bathrooms—all bearing the Starck stamp—and VCRs as standard issue. There's a Dean & DeLuca takeout off the lobby, and the independently run Brasserie des Théâtres on the other side, plus a fitness center. For the forever young and arty, it's the best place. *235 W. 46th St., 10036, tel. 212/764–5500 or 800/225–7474, fax 212/354–5237. 610 rooms. Facilities: 2 restaurants, privately owned bar, take-out food shop, fitness center, children's playroom, business center, VCRs in rooms. AE, DC, MC, V.*

Downtown **Carlton Arms.** If the East Village is your spiritual home, and if you would like to step into a Kandinsky or Pollock or Lichtenstein and live there, then this Gramercy Park bargain is your place. It isn't arty, it's art—every wall, ceiling, and, indeed, surface is engulfed by paintings chosen over the years by the hip but friendly team of managers. They themselves immortalized on the lobby corridor wall, surrounded by the Manhattan skyline and bearing the legend: "If you think that it's better to have a party than nothing, you work here." The youthful guests do sometimes have a party, so noisy it can be. But the Carlton Arms is also clean, though this fact is overwhelmed by the roses and auto accidents in cobalt blue by F. Dominguez (room 4A), the 1987 sunset-colored nudes by Steven (room 11A), or the psychedelic religious symbolism and aquarium bedspread in room 8A. Rooms have double-glazed windows but are phoneless, TV-less, almost free of furniture, and sometimes bathless (these start at $44, with a further 10% student discount), and there are fans instead of air conditioning. But that's hardly the point. Where the Chelsea Hotel of '60s legend left off, the Carlton Arms begins. *160 E. 25th St., 10010, tel. 212/684–8337, reservations 212/769–0680. 54 rooms. MC, V.*

★ **Gramercy Park.** The terra-cotta–colored, Queen Anne–style hotel is lmost the only one in this elegant neighborhood, which boasts the city's least-populated park. The park remains thus because it's locked, but hotel guests can use it. Further advantages to staying here include more peace and quiet than is usual, and a bar straight out of a Cole Porter lyric, with pianist, hot hors d'oeuvres, and wicked martinis. A favorite of British actors and TV people, for some reason, the Gramercy is also particularly friendly, with staff who have spent their careers here. Don't expect too much from the rooms, but they are mostly way above average for this price range. *2 Lexington Ave., 10010, tel. 212/475–4320, fax 212/505–0535. 180 rooms. Facilities: bar, lounge, access to Gramercy Park. AE, D, DC, MC, V.*

Washington Square Hotel. This cozy hotel has a true European feel and style, from the wrought-iron and brass in the small but elegant lobby to the personal attention given by the staff. Rooms and baths are simple but pleasant, not that you'll spend much time in them, with so many shopping, eating, and drinking opportunities on the doorstep. Complimentary continental breakfast is included in the room rate. There's also a good and surprisingly reasonably priced restaurant, CIII (*see* Chapter 9). The manager has strong ties to the local jazz community and can provide tips if you want to catch a set at the nearby Blue Note, or one of the other famous clubs around here. *103 Waverly Pl., 10011, tel. 212/777–9515 or 800/222–0418, fax 212/*

979–8373. 160 rooms. Facilities: independent on-premises restaurant, laundry service. AE, DC, MC, V.

Bed-and-Breakfasts

Hundreds of rooms are available on a bed-and-breakfast basis in Manhattan and the other boroughs, principally Brooklyn. B&Bs almost always cost well below $100 a night; some singles are available for under $50. New York B&Bs, however, are not the quaint old mansions you find in other localities. They fall largely into two categories: (1) *hosted apartments*, a bedroom in an apartment where the host is present; (2) *unhosted apartments*, entire apartments that are temporarily vacant, scarcer and more expensive.

Along with helping you save money, B&Bs permit you to stay in "real" neighborhoods rather than in tourist enclaves. But accommodations, amenities, service, and privacy may fall short of what you get in hotels. Sometimes you really do get breakfast and sometimes you don't. And you usually can't pay by credit card.

A few reservation agencies book B&B accommodations in and near Manhattan. There is no fee for the service, but they advise you to make reservations as far in advance as possible. It's a good idea to find out something about the city before you contact them, and then to request accommodations in a neighborhood that you prefer.

Bed and Breakfast Network of New York (134 W. 32nd St., Suite 602, 10001, tel. 212/645–8134).

City Lights Bed and Breakfast, Ltd. (Box 20355, Cherokee Station, 10028, tel. 212/737–7049).

New World Bed and Breakfast (150 5th Ave., Suite 711, 10011, tel. 212/675–5600 or 800/443–3800).

Urban Ventures (306 W. 38th St., 10018, tel. 212/594–5650).

11 The Arts

By Susan
Spano Wells

Updated by
David Low

On a bad day in New York—when it's raining and a cab can't be engaged for blood or money, the subways are flooded, and the line at the cash machine seems to stretch to Poughkeepsie—many New Yorkers may feel as if they'd sell the city back to the Indians for two bits. But in the end, they put up with the urban hassles for at least one obvious reason: New York's unrivaled artistic life. Despite the immense competition and the threat of cuts in city aid to the arts, artists from all disciplines continue to come to the city to find their compatriots and to produce their work. Audiences can only benefit.

There are somewhere between 200 and 250 legitimate theaters in New York, and many more ad hoc venues—parks, churches, universities, museums, lofts, galleries, streets, and rooftops—where performances ranging from Shakespeare to sword-dancing take place. The city is, as well, a revolving door of festivals and special events: Summer jazz, one-act play marathons, international film series, and musical celebrations from the classical to the avant-garde are just a few.

In New York, the arts routinely make the headlines. Pick up a week's worth of newspapers and you'll learn of casting disputes at the Metropolitan Opera, prima ballerinas with bruised knees, big Broadway musicals whose directors are replaced hours before opening, and the constant entertaining haggles among backers, artists, and critics. It's chaos. What a town!

New York's most renowned centers for the arts are tourist attractions in themselves:

Lincoln Center (W. 62nd to 66th Sts., Columbus to Amsterdam Aves., tel. 212/875–5000) is a 14-acre complex that houses the Metropolitan Opera, the New York Philharmonic, the Juilliard School, the New York City Ballet, the American Ballet Theatre, the New York City Opera, the Film Society of Lincoln Center, the Chamber Music Society of Lincoln Center, the Lincoln Center Theater, the School of American Ballet, and the New York Public Library's Library and Museum of the Performing Arts. Tours of Lincoln Center are available (tel. 212/875–5351; *see* Tour 8 in Chapter 3).

Carnegie Hall (881 7th Ave. at 57th St., tel. 212/247–7800) is a premier hall for concerts. Music masters such as Arturo Toscanini, Leonard Bernstein, Isaac Stern, Yo-Yo Ma, Jessye Norman, Frank Sinatra, and the Beatles, along with great orchestras from around the world, have made up the Carnegie bill. Performances are held in both its main auditorium (opened in 1891 with a concert conducted by Tchaikovsky) and in Weill Recital Hall, where debuting talents often make their first New York splash. The emphasis is on classical music, but Carnegie also hosts jazz, cabaret, and folk music series.

Radio City Music Hall (1260 6th Ave. at 50th St., tel. 212/247–4777), an art-deco gem, opened in 1932 with 6,000 seats, a 60-foot-high foyer, two-ton chandeliers, and a powerful Wurlitzer organ. On this vast stage you'll find everything from rock and pop concerts to Christmas and Easter extravaganzas (featuring the perennial Rockettes kickline), and star-studded TV specials. Tours (tel. 212/632–4041) are conducted daily (*see* Tour 1 in Chapter 3).

City Center (131 W. 55th St., tel. 212/581–7907; mailing address for ticket orders: Citytix, 130 W. 56th St., 4th Floor, 10019), under its eccentric, tiled Spanish dome (built in 1923 by the Ancient and Accepted Order of the Mystic Shrine and saved from demolition in 1943 by Mayor Fiorello La Guardia) hosts dance troupes such as Alvin Ailey, Paul Taylor, and Merce Cunningham. The Manhattan Theatre Club (*see* Theater, *below*) also resides here, with its highly touted bill of innovative contemporary drama.

Madison Square Garden (W. 31st to W. 33rd St. on 7th Ave., tel. 212/ 465–6000), camped atop Penn Station, includes a recently renovated 20,000-seat arena, and the sleek 5,600-seat Paramount Theater. Sports events such as basketball, ice hockey, tennis, and boxing, plus big-draw pop music concerts by stars as diverse as Barry Manilow, Paul Simon, and Madonna, keep the Garden rocking. There's even room for the Knicks and the Rangers to call it home. Should your favorite rock band not be appearing at the Garden, check out its suburban sister halls: the **Nassau Coliseum** (Long Island, tel. 516/794–9300) and the **Meadowlands Arena** (New Jersey, tel. 201/935–3900).

Brooklyn Academy of Music (BAM; 30 Lafayette Ave., Brooklyn, tel. 718/636–4100) is America's oldest performing arts center (begun in 1859), but its reputation is decidedly contemporary thanks to daring and innovative dance, music, opera, and theater productions. The main hall is the Opera House, a white Renaissance Revival palace built in 1908; other spaces at BAM are the Majestic Theatre (a partly restored vaudeville house around the corner), the Helen Owen Carey Playhouse, and the Lepercq Space.

Other important arts centers include **Town Hall** (123 W. 43rd St., tel. 212/840–2824) for, among other things, concert versions of lost Broadway musicals; **Merkin Concert Hall** (129 W. 67th St., tel. 212/ 362–8719), which features mainly chamber music; **Symphony Space** (2537 Broadway at 95th St., tel. 212/864–5400), a cavernous converted movie theater with an eclectic offering that ranges from Irish folk music to short stories read by stars; the **Sylvia and Danny Kaye Playhouse** (Hunter College, 68th St., between Park and Lexington Aves., tel. 212/772–4448), a state-of-the-art concert hall presenting music, dance, opera, and theater performances; the **92nd Street Y** (1395 Lexington Ave., tel. 212/996–1100), known for its classical music concerts, readings by famous writers, and the Lyrics and Lyricists series; and **the Kitchen** (512 W. 19th St., tel. 212/255– 5793), a showcase for "downtown," avant-garde videos, music, performance art, and dance.

Getting Tickets

Much has been made of the ballooning cost of tickets, especially for Broadway shows—though major concerts and recitals don't come cheap in New York, either. The top Broadway ticket prices for musicals are $65; the best seats for nonmusicals usually cost $50, although they occasionally hit the $75 mark as well.

On the positive side, tickets for New York City's arts events aren't hard to come by—unless, of course, you're dead set on seeing the season's hottest, sold-out show. Generally, a theater or concert hall's box office is the best place to buy tickets, since in-house ticket sellers make it their business to know about their theaters and shows and don't mind pointing out (on a chart) where you'll be seated. It's always a good idea to purchase tickets in advance to avoid disappointment, especially if you're traveling a long distance. For advance purchase, send the theater or hall a certified check or money order, several alternate dates, and a self-addressed stamped envelope.

You can also pull out a credit card and call **Tele-Charge** (tel. 212/239– 6200), or **Ticketmaster** (tel. 212/307-4100 for Broadway and Off-

Broadway shows, 212/307–7171 for other events) to reserve tickets—newspaper ads generally will specify which you should use for any given event. A surcharge ($2–$5) will be added to the total, and your tickets will be waiting for you at the theater.

For those willing to pay top dollar to see that show or concert everyone's talking about but no one can get tickets for, try a ticket broker. Recently, brokers charged $100–$150 for tickets to *The Phantom of the Opera;* had the same seat been available at the box office, it would have sold for $65. A few brokers to try are **N.Y. Theatre Tickets** (tel. 201/392–0999 or 800/457–0999), and **Continental/Golden/Leblangs Theatre Tickets** (tel. 212/944–8910 or 800/942–9455). Also, check the lobbies of major hotels for ticket broker outlets.

You may be tempted to buy from the ticket scalpers who frequently haunt the lobbies of hit shows. But beware: They have reportedly sold tickets to *Les Misérables* for $100–$150, when seats were still available at the box office for much less.

Off- and Off-Off-Broadway theaters have their own joint box office called **Ticket Central** (416 W. 42nd St., tel. 212/279–4200). While there are no discounts here, tickets to performances in these theaters are less expensive than Broadway tickets—Ticket Central prices average $10–$35 per person—and they cover an array of events, including legitimate theater, performance art, and dance. Some Off-Broadway plays now allow you to charge tickets through **EZ-TIXZ** (tel. 212/777–7474).

Discount Tickets New York's best-known discount source is the **TKTS booth** in Duffy Square (47th St. and Broadway, tel. 212/768–1818). TKTS sells day-of-performance tickets for Broadway and some Off-Broadway plays at discounts that, depending on a show's popularity, often go as low as half price (plus a $2.50 surcharge per ticket). The names of shows available on that day are posted on boards in front of the booth. If you're interested in a Wednesday or Saturday matinee, go to the booth between 10 and 2, check out what's offered, and then wait in line. For evening performances, the booth is open 3–8; for Sunday matinee and evening performances, noon–8. One caution: TKTS accepts only cash or traveler's checks—no credit cards. The wait is generally pleasant (weather permitting), as the bright lights and babble of Broadway surround you. You're likely to meet friendly theater lovers eager to review shows they've recently seen; often you'll even meet struggling actors who can give you the inside scoop. By the time you get to the booth, you may be willing to take a gamble on a show you would otherwise never have picked, and it just might be more memorable than one of the long-running hits.

So successful has TKTS proved that auxiliary booths operate in the Wall Street area (2 World Trade Center mezzanine) and in Brooklyn Heights (near the intersection of Court and Montague Sts.). The World Trade Center Branch is open weekdays 11–5:30, Saturday 11–3:30; for matinees and Sundays, 11–closing the day before the performance. In Brooklyn, evening-performance tickets are on sale weekdays 11–5:30, Saturday 11–3:30; tickets for matinees and Sundays are sold a day ahead; Off-Broadway tickets are sold until 1. The lines at these TKTS outstations are shorter than those at Duffy Square, though occasionally the offerings are somewhat limited.

A setup similar to TKTS has arisen in the **Bryant Park Music and Dance Tickets Booth,** located on 42nd Street and 6th Avenue in Bryant Park, just west of the New York Public Library. This booth sells half-price day-of-performance tickets for several music and dance events around the city (and full-price tickets for other concerts as well). It's open Tuesday–Sunday noon–2 and 3–7. Unlike TKTS, the Bryant Park booth has a telephone information line (tel. 212/382–2323). It accepts only cash and traveler's checks.

Discounts on big-name, long-running shows (such as *Miss Saigon* and *Les Misérables*) are often available if you can lay your hands on a couple of "twofers"—discount ticket coupons found on various cash registers around town, near the lines at TKTS, at the Times Square visitor information office (at the northwest corner of 7th Ave. and 42nd St.), at the New York Visitors and Convention Bureau (at 2 Columbus Circle), and at the office of their producer, the **Hit Show Club** (630 9th Ave., 8th Floor, tel. 212/581–4211; open weekdays 9–4).

The **Joseph Papp Public Theater** (425 Lafayette St., tel. 212/598–7150) regularly sets aside some of its tickets for sale at a discount through its **Quiktix.** Join the Quiktix line anytime before 6 PM for evening performances, and before 1 PM for matinees. Tickets are sold on a first-come, first-served basis and cost $10–$15. Some other theaters, such as **Classic Stage Company** (136 E. 13th St., tel. 212/677–4210), also offer reduced rates on unsold tickets the day of the performance, often one hour before curtain time. These special discounts are usually noted in the newspaper theater listings or ads.

Some Broadway and Off-Broadway shows sell reduced-priced tickets for perormances scheduled before opening night. Look at newspaper ads for discounted previews, or consult the box office. Tickets may cost less at matinees, particularly on Wednesday.

A slew of ticket clubs exist to serve repeat theatergoers, so if you plan to be in the city for a long time, they may be worth investigating. **Advance Entertainment New York** (tel. 212/239–2570) offers its members (for $119 a year) constant updates on theater ticket procurement—sometimes at a discount and with special attention paid to getting good seats. AENY can be used on a one-time, no obligation-to-join basis for a $5 fee. Other ticket groups include **Stubs Preview Club** (tel. 212/398–8370), $50 a month, specializing in preview showings; and the **Theatre Development Fund** (1501 Broadway, tel. 212/221–0885), whose TDF vouchers are available in sets of five for $20 to students, union members, teachers, performing arts professionals, and members of volunteer groups, among others. When redeemed at the box office, the vouchers reduce the cost of a ticket for dance, theater, and musical events at Off-Off-Broadway theaters. Out-of-towners must stop by the office and present identification to qualify; residents of the metropolitan tristate area are put on the TDF mailing list to receive periodical offers.

Finding Out What's On

To find out who or what's playing where, your first stop should be the newsstand. The *New York Times* isn't a prerequisite for finding out what's going on around town, but it comes in pretty handy, especially on Friday with its "Weekend" section. On Sunday, the *Times*'s "Arts and Leisure" section features longer "think pieces" on everything from opera to TV—and a lot more ads, plus a full, detailed calendar of cultural events for the upcoming week.

If your tastes are more adventurous, try the weekly paper *The Village Voice;* its club listings are unrivaled, its "Choices" section reliable. When its club-tattler-cum-critic Michael Musto talks (in a column called "La Dolce Musto"), night prowlers and club crawlers listen. The *Voice* is published on Wednesday.

Some of the most entertaining listings can be found in the *New Yorker* magazine. "Goings On About Town" heads off each weekly issue with ruthlessly succinct reviews of theater, dance, art, music, film, and nightlife. *New York* magazine's "Cue listings" and "Hot Line" section are useful, too. *Theater Week* contains up-to-date news on theater happenings all over town. The *New York Native, Christopher Street,* and *HomoExtra* cover the gay scene.

The League of New York Theatres and Producers and *Playbill* magazine publish a biweekly *Broadway Theatre Guide,* available in hotels and at the *Playbill* magazine office (52 Vanderbilt Ave., 11th Floor, 212/557–5757). For information on the lower Manhattan cultural scene, write for a *Downtown Arts Activities Calendar* (Lower Manhattan Cultural Council, 1 World Trade Ctr., Suite 1717, New York, NY 10048, tel. 212/432–0900).

You can also get updated information by phone from NYC/ON STAGE, the Theatre Development Fund's 24-hour information service (tel. 212/768–1818).

Theater

Almost everyone who visits New York ends up spending several hours in a theater seat. The theater—not the Statue of Liberty or South Street Seaport—is the city's number-one tourist attraction, and uptown or downtown you can spot theater folk pursuing their work with customary passion and panache. Delicate little ladies tottering about in their pillbox hats are really theatrical grande dames, with fast answers to the flashers on 8th Avenue; shifty-looking guys toting battered briefcases turn out to be famous directors; and the girls and boys scuttling through stage doors are chorus members rushing to exchange their Nikes for tap shoes.

Broadway Theater District To most people, New York theater means Broadway, that region bounded by 42nd and 53rd streets, between 6th and 9th avenues, where bright, transforming lights shine upon porn theaters and jewel-box playhouses alike (*see* Theater District map). Although the area's busy sidewalks contain more than their share of hustlers and pickpockets, visitors brave them for the playhouses' plentiful delights. Extravagant plans for redevelopment of the Times Square area continue to ricochet from marquee to marquee; amid the grunge, major hotels keep springing up in this area. With every thud of the wrecker's ball, theater devotees pray for the survival of the essential character of Broadway—as Paul Goldberger put it in the *New York Times,* "the world of memory, the magical Times Square of old, the lively, glittering district of theaters, restaurants, cabarets, hotels, and neon signs that was in many ways the city's symbolic heart."

Historically speaking, the nation's entertainment capital was once composed of almost 50 theaters, which sprang up between 1899 and 1925 near the intersection of Broadway and 42nd Street. Many of those original showplaces have been gutted or turned into movie houses. The 38 legitimate theaters that remain are squeezed into side streets in such tight spaces that from the outside it's often hard to imagine that there's room inside for an audience, much less a stage.

Some of the old playhouses are as interesting for their history as for their current offerings: the **St. James** (246 W. 44th St.) is where Lauren Bacall served as an usherette in the '40s, and a sleeper of a musical called *Oklahoma!* woke up as a hit; the **Lyceum** (149 W. 45th

Theater District

St.) is New York's oldest still-functioning theater, built in 1903 with a posh apartment on top that now holds the Shubert Archive (open to scholars by appointment only); the **Shubert Theatre** (225 W. 44th St.) is where Barbra Streisand made her 1962 Broadway debut, and the long-run record-breaker, *A Chorus Line,* played for 15 years; and the **Martin Beck Theatre** (302 W. 45th St.), built in 1924 in Byzantine style, is the stage that served up premieres of Eugene O'Neill's *The Iceman Cometh,* Arthur Miller's *The Crucible,* and Tennessee Williams's *Sweet Bird of Youth.* Theater names read like a roll-call of American theater history: **Booth, Ethel Barrymore, Eugene O'Neill, Gershwin, Lunt/Fontanne, Richard Rodgers,** and **Neil Simon,** among others.

As you stroll around the theater district, you may also see: **Shubert Alley,** a shortcut between 44th and 45th streets where theater moguls used to park their limousines, today the site of a jam-packed Great White Way memorabilia store called One Shubert Alley; **Manhattan Plaza,** a largely subsidized apartment complex at 9th Avenue and 42nd Street inhabited primarily by theater people, whose rent in hard times is assessed at 30% of their income (whatever that comes to); **Theatre Row** (42nd St. between 9th and 10th Aves.), a convivial collection of small Off-Broadway theaters; and **Restaurant Row** (46th St. between 8th and 9th Aves.), which offers plenty of choices for dining before or after a show. For a deeper drink of the district, join a talk with **Backstage on Broadway Tours** (tel. 212/575–8065), hosted by a professional actor, director, stage manager, or designer (for groups only).

In determining which Broadway show to see, first consider the long-running hits: *Cats, Crazy for You, Guys and Dolls* (a revival), *Les Misérables, The Phantom of the Opera, Miss Saigon,* and others, which most magazine and newspaper listings helpfully point out. Then look beyond the marquees for both tomorrow's hits and today's resounding flops. Remember, there's something special about catching a show in previews or seeing a harshly reviewed play before it bites the dust. A lousy review can quickly close a show, even though discriminating audience members often disagree with the critics.

Beyond Broadway Ten years ago it was relatively simple to categorize the New York stage beyond Broadway. It was divided into Off-Broadway and Off-Off-Broadway, depending on a variety of factors that included theatrical contract type, location, and ticket price. Today such distinctions seem strained, as Off-Broadway prices have risen and the quality of some Off-Off-Broadway productions has improved markedly. Off- and Off-Off-Broadway is where Eric Bogosian, Ann Magnuson, John Leguizamo, and Laurie Anderson make their home and where *Driving Miss Daisy, Steel Magnolias,* and *Other People's Money* were first conceived. The recession seems to have hit Off-Broadway and Off-Off-Broadway theaters hard, forcing them to spend less on their productions and mount fewer shows a year, but attendance and ticket sales remain healthy, proving how vital this segment of the theater world is to New York culture. Recent long-running hits have included the irreverent *Nunsense, Tubes* by the surreal Blue Man Group, and *Forever Plaid,* a nostalgic tribute to 1950s popular music. Off-Broadway is also home to the romantic musical *The Fantasticks,* the longest-running play in U.S. theater history.

Name actors appear in top-flight productions at **Lincoln Center's** two theaters: the **Vivian Beaumont** and the more intimate **Mitzi E. Newhouse** (65th St. and Broadway, tel. for both 212/362–7600), which has scored some startling successes, including John Guare's *Six Degrees of Separation*, and Wendy Wasserstein's *The Sisters Rosensweig*. Downtown at the **Joseph Papp Public Theater** (425 Lafayette St., tel. 212/598–7150), renamed in 1992 to honor its late founder and long-time guiding genius, producer George C. Wolfe continues the tradition of innovative theater, mounting new and classic plays, along with film series, dance concerts, literary readings, and musical events. In the summertime, the Public's Shakespeare Festival raises its sets in Central Park's open-air Delacorte Theater (*see* Manhattan For Free in Chapter 3).

One of the major Off-Broadway enclaves is **Theatre Row,** a collection of small houses (100 seats or less)—such as the **John Houseman Theatre** (450 W. 42nd St., tel. 212/967–9077), **Douglas Fairbanks Theatre** (432 W. 42nd St., tel. 212/239–4321), and **Playwrights Horizons** (416 W. 42nd St., tel. 212/279–4200)—on the downtown side of 42nd Street between 9th and 10th avenues. A block east of Theatre Row is the **Westside Theatre** (407 W. 43rd St., tel. 212/307–4100). Another Off-Broadway neighborhood lies in Greenwich Village, around Sheridan Square. Its theaters include the **Actors Playhouse** (100 7th Ave. S., tel. 212/691–6226); **Circle Rep** (99 7th Ave. S, tel. 212/924–7100), a showcase for new playwrights; the **Cherry Lane Theatre** (38 Commerce St., tel. 212/989–2020); the **Lucille Lortel Theatre** (121 Christopher St., tel. 212/924–8782); the **Minetta Lane Theatre** (18 Minetta La., tel. 212/420–8000); the **Perry Street Theatre** (31 Perry St., tel. 212/691–2509); the **Provincetown Playhouse** (133 MacDougal St., tel. 212/477–5048); and the **Sullivan Street Playhouse** (181 Sullivan St., tel. 212/674–3838). Other estimable Off-Broadway theaters are flung across the Manhattan map: the **Astor Place Theatre** (434 Lafayette St., tel. 212/254–4370); the **Orpheum Theatre** (126 2nd Ave. at 8th St., tel. 212/477–2477); the **Variety Arts Theatre** (110 3rd Ave. at 14th St., tel. 212/239–6200); the **WPA Theatre** (519 W. 23rd St., tel. 212/206–0523), showcasing new works by American playwrights; the **Promenade Theatre** (Broadway at 76th St., tel. 212/580–1313); and the **Manhattan Theatre Club** (at City Center, 131 W. 55th St., tel. 212/581–1212).

Here are a few other Off- and Off-Off-Broadway theater groups to keep your eye on:

American Jewish Theatre (307 W. 26th St., tel. 212/633–9797) stages contemporary plays and revivals of musicals, more often than not with a Jewish theme.
The Classic Stage Company (CSC) (136 E. 13th St., tel. 212/677–4210), providing a showcase for the classics—some arcane, others European—in new translations and adaptations.
The Ensemble Studio Theatre (549 W. 52nd St., tel. 212/247–3405), with its tried-and-true roster of players, stressing new dramatic works.
Irish Arts Center (553 W. 51st St., tel. 212/757–3318), presenting classic and contemporary Irish plays.
Jean Cocteau Repertory (Bouwerie Lane Theatre, 330 Bowery, tel. 212/677–0060), founded in 1971, with international classics, intelligently performed by its resident acting troupe.
The Jewish Repertory Theatre (Playhouse 91, 316 E. 91st St., tel. 212/831–2000), begun in 1972, producing plays about Jewish life such as *Crossing Delancey*, the basis for the hit film.
The New York Theater Workshop (79 E. 4th St., tel. 212/302–6989), producing challenging new theater by American and international artists.
The Pan Asian Repertory Theatre (Playhouse 46 in St. Clement's

Church, 423 W. 46th St., tel. 212/245–2660), a center for Asian and Asian-American artists, producing new works or adapted Western plays.

Pearl Theatre Company (125 W. 22nd St., tel. 212/645–7708), with resident players focusing on a repertory of classics.

Primary Stages (354 W. 45th St., tel. 212/333–7471), devoted to new work by emerging American playwrights.

Repertorio Español (Gramercy Arts Theatre, 138 E. 27th St., tel. 212/889–2850), an Obie-award-winning Spanish arts repertory theater whose productions are in Spanish.

Second Stage (McGinn/Cazale Theatre, 2162 Broadway at W. 76th St., tel. 212/873–6103), producing new works and recent plays that may not have been given a fair shake their first time around.

The Soho Rep (46 Walker St., below Canal St. between Broadway and Church St., tel. 212/977–5955), dedicated to contemporary plays on controversial issues.

Theatre for a New Audience (St. Clement's Church, 423 W. 46th St., tel. 212/279–4200) performs both Shakespearean productions and new plays by important contemporary playwrights.

York Theatre Company (Church of the Heavenly Rest, 2 E. 90th St., and Theatre at St. Peter's Church, 54th St. at Lexington Ave., tel. 212/534–5366), presenting revivals of plays and musicals in addition to new theater works.

Avant-Garde Last, but not at all least, is New York's fabled theatrical avant-garde. The "experimental theater" movement's founders may no longer be the long-haired hippies they were when they first started doing mixed-media productions and promoting off-center playwrights (such as Sam Shepard) in the '60s, but they continue at the forefront. Take Ellen Stewart, also known, simply and elegantly, as "LaMama." Over the past two decades, her East Village organization has branched out to import European innovators and has grown physically as well. **La MaMa E.T.C.** (74A E. 4th St., tel. 212/475–7710) now encompasses a First Floor Theater, an Annex theater, and a club. Productions include everything from African fables to New Wave opera to reinterpretations of the Greek classics; past triumphs have included the original performances of *Godspell* and *Torch Song Trilogy*.

A four-theater cultural complex is home to the experimentalist **Theater for the New City** (155 1st Ave., tel. 212/254–1109), which devotes its productions to new playwrights. The complex also sponsors a free street-theater program, arts festivals, and Christmas and Halloween spectacles. Founded by the late Charles Ludlam in 1972, the **Ridiculous Theatrical Company** (1 Sheridan Sq., tel. 212/691–2271) still keeps audiences laughing with its unique performance style: a blend of classical acting—usually in drag—and high camp.

Performance Art At the vanishing point of the avant-garde is that curious mélange of artistic disciplines known as performance art. Intentionally difficult to categorize, it blends music and sound, dance, video and lights, words, and whatever else comes to the performance artist's mind, to produce events of erratic success—sometimes fascinating, sometimes deadening. Performance art is almost exclusively a downtown endeavor, though it is also showcased in the outer boroughs, especially Brooklyn, where the **Brooklyn Academy of Music** (30 Lafayette Ave., Brooklyn, tel. 718/636–4100) has built its considerable reputation on its annual Next Wave Festival, which features many performance works.

Other performance-art showcases are:

Dixon Place (258 Bowery, between Houston and Prince Sts., tel. 212/219–3088) presents an eccentric, eclectic schedule, including comedy acts, musicians, and readings.

Franklin Furnace (112 Franklin St., tel. 212/925–4671), since 1976 a supporter of off-center, emerging artists—this is where Eric Bogosian got his start. Holly Hughes and Tim Hunter have appeared here recently.

The Kitchen (512 W. 19th St., tel. 212/255–5793), perhaps *the* Manhattan center for performance art, although video, dance, and music have their moments here, too.

Performance Space 122, or **P.S. 122** (150 1st Ave., tel. 212/477–5288), called by the *Village Voice* "the petri dish of downtown culture." Occupying a former public school that was comedian George Burns's alma mater, P.S. 122 presents exhibitions and productions that come and go quickly but seldom fail in freshness. Look especially for its annual marathon in February, in which scores of dazzling downtowners take part.

Music

"Gentlemen," conductor Serge Koussevitzky once told the assembled Boston Symphony Orchestra, "maybe it's good enough for Cleveland or Cincinnati, but it's not good enough for New York." That's New York's place in the musical world, in a nutshell; quite simply, it's the top, for performers and music lovers alike.

New York possesses not only the country's oldest symphony, the New York Philharmonic, but also three renowned conservatories— The Juilliard School, The Manhattan School of Music, and Mannes College of Music—plus myriad musical performance groups. Since the turn of the century, the world's great orchestras and soloists have made Manhattan a principal stopping point. In recent years, live TV and radio broadcasts have brought the music played in New York to millions more listeners across the North American continent.

To those who visit the city for its music, New York opens like a Stradivarius case. In an average week, between 50 and 150 events— everything from zydeco to Debussy, Cole Porter, Kurt Weill, and reggae—appear in newspaper and magazine listings, and weekly concert calendars are published in all of the major newspapers. Record and music shops—such as the cavernous **Tower Records** (692 Broadway at 4th St., tel. 212/505–1500, 1535 3rd Ave. at 86th St., tel. 212/369–2500, and 1961 Broadway at 66th St., tel. 212/799– 2500), **HMV** (2081 Broadway at 72nd St., tel. 212/721–5900; 1280 Lexington Ave. at 86th St., tel. 212/348–0800), **J & R Music World** (23 Park Row, across from City Hall, tel. 212/732–8600), the reliable **Bleecker Bob's Golden Oldies** (118 W. 3rd St., tel. 212/475–9677), and the classy **Patelson's** (160 W. 56th St., tel. 212/582–5840)— serve as music information centers, too, as do the city's radio stations. WNYC (FM 93.9 and AM 820) and WQXR (FM 96.3 and AM 1560) update listeners on current musical events. The **Bryant Park Music and Dance Tickets Booth** (42nd St. just east of 6th Ave., tel. 212/382–2323) also lists music around town.

Classical Music **Lincoln Center** (W. 62nd St. and Broadway) remains the city's musical nerve center, especially when it comes to the classics. The **New York Philharmonic,** led by musical director Kurt Masur, performs at **Avery Fisher Hall** (tel. 212/875–5030) late September to early June. In addition to its magical concerts showcasing exceptional guest artists and the works of specific composers, the Philharmonic also schedules weeknight "Rush Hour" Concerts at 6:45 PM and Casual Saturdays Concerts at 2 PM; these special events, offered throughout the season, last one hour and are priced lower than the regular subscription concerts. "Rush Hour" Concerts are followed by receptions with the conductor on the Grand Promenade, and Casual Saturdays Concerts feature discussions after the performances. The Philharmonic also sponsors a series of pre-concert lectures with certain subscription events. Call 212/875–5656 for details.

In summer, the popular **Mostly Mozart** concert series presents an impressive roster of classical performers. Avery Fisher Hall, designed by Max Abramovitz, opened in 1961 as Philharmonic Hall, but underwent drastic renovation in 1976 to improve the acoustics (at a price tag of $5 million). The result is an auditorium that follows the classic European rectangular pattern. To its stage come the world's great musicians; to its boxes, the black-tie-and-diamond-tiara set.

A note for New York Philharmonic devotees: The orchestra rehearses Wednesday and Thursday mornings at 9:45. In season, and when conductors and soloists are amenable, rehearsals are open to the public for $10. Call 212/875–5656 for information.

Near Avery Fisher is Alice Tully Hall (tel. 212/875–5050), an intimate "little white box," considered as acoustically perfect as concert houses get. Here the **Chamber Music Society of Lincoln Center** tunes up, along with promising Juilliard students, chamber music ensembles such as the Guarneri Quartet and Kronos Quartet, music on period instruments, choral music, famous soloists, and concert groups. Lincoln Center's outdoor Damrosch Park, and Bruno Walter Auditorium (in the Library of the Performing Arts, tel. 212/870–1630) often offer free concerts; two summer programs, **Serious Fun** and **Classical Jazz,** have been added in recent years to the Lincoln Center bill.

While Lincoln Center is only 30 years old, another famous classical music palace—**Carnegie Hall** (W. 57th St. at 7th Ave., tel. 212/247–7800)—recently celebrated its 100th birthday. This is the place where the great pianist Paderewski was attacked by ebullient crowds (who claimed kisses and locks of his hair) after a performance in 1891; where young Leonard Bernstein, standing in for New York Philharmonic conductor Bruno Walter, made his triumphant debut in 1943; where Jack Benny and Isaac Stern fiddled together; and where the Beatles played one of their first U.S. concerts. When threats of the wrecker's ball loomed large in 1960, a consortium of Carnegie loyalists (headed by Isaac Stern) rose to save it; an eventual multimillion-dollar renovation in 1986 worked cosmetic wonders.

Other prime classical music locales are:

Aaron Davis Hall at City College (W. 133rd St. at Convent Ave., tel. 212/650–6900), uptown scene of world music events and a variety of classical concerts and dance programs.
Grace Rainey Rogers Auditorium at the Metropolitan Museum of Art (5th Ave. at 82nd St., tel. 212/570–3949), providing classical music in classic surroundings.
Merkin Concert Hall at the Abraham Goodman House (129 W. 67th St., tel. 212/362–8719), almost as prestigious as the concert halls at Lincoln Center.
Miller Theatre (Columbia University, Broadway at 116th St., 212/854–7799), featuring a varied program of classical performers, such as the New York Virtuosi Chamber Symphony.
Kaufman Concert Hall at the 92nd St. Y (1395 Lexington Ave., tel.

212/996–1100), with the New York Chamber Symphony in residence, plus star recitalists and chamber music groups.

Sylvia and Danny Kaye Playhouse (Hunter College, 68th St., between Park and Lexington Aves., tel. 212/772–4448), presenting a varied program of events, including distinguished soloists and chamber music groups, in a state-of-the-art concert hall.

Bargemusic at the Fulton Ferry Landing in Brooklyn (tel. 718/624–4061), with chamber music bubbling year-round from an old barge with a fabulous skyline view.

Brooklyn Academy of Music (30 Lafayette Ave., tel. 718/636–4100), ever experimenting with new and old musical styles, and still a showcase for the Brooklyn Philharmonic.

Outdoor Concerts Weather permitting, the city's great outdoors becomes one wide concert hall. Each August, the plaza around Lincoln Center explodes with the **Lincoln Center Out-of-Doors** series. In the summertime, both the **Metropolitan Opera** and the **New York Philharmonic** decamp to municipal parks to play free concerts, rocking the greenswards with the trills of *La Bohème* or the thunder of the *1812 Overture*. (For information call Lincoln Center, tel. 212/875–5400, or the City Parks Events Hotline, tel. 212/360–3456.) **Summerstage** (Naumburg Bandshell, Central Park at 72nd St., tel. 212/360–2756) fills a Roman-temple-like setting with free music programs, ranging from grand opera to experimental rock, generally on Sunday afternoon from June through August. The Museum of Modern Art hosts free Friday and Saturday evening concerts of 20th-century music in their sculpture garden as part of the **Summergarden** series (tel. 212/708–9480). A **Jazzmobile** (tel. 212/866–4900) trucks jazz and Latin music to parks throughout the five boroughs, and Prospect Park comes alive with the sounds of its annual **Celebrate Brooklyn Concert Series** (9th St. Bandshell, Prospect Park, Brooklyn, tel. 718/788–0055). Starlit Saturday evenings at South Street Seaport turn Pier 16 into **Summerpier** (tel. 212/SEA–PORT), featuring a range of musical styles.

Lunchtime Concerts During the work week, more and more lunchtime concerts provide musical midday breaks at public atriums all over the city. Events are generally free, and bag-lunching is encouraged. Check out the **World Financial Center's Winter Garden Atrium** (across the West Side Highway from the World Trade Center), the **IBM Atrium** (57th St. and Madison Ave.), and the **Citicorp Center Marketplace** (54th St. and Lexington Ave.). And, of course, everywhere—in parks, on street corners, and down under in the subway—aspiring musicians of all kinds hold forth, with their instrument cases thrown open for contributions. True, some are hacks, but others are bona fide professionals: moonlighting violinists, Broadway chorus members indulging their love of the barbershop quartet, or horn players prowling up from clubs to take in the fresh air.

Downtown, the venerable **St. Paul's Chapel** (Fulton St. and Broadway, tel. 212/602–0874) presents free lunchtime concerts of mostly classical music on Monday and Thursday at noon. A $2 contribution is suggested.

A midtown music break can be found at **St. Peter's Lutheran Church** (619 Lexington Ave., at the Citicorp Ctr., tel. 212/935–2200), with its Wednesday series of lunchtime jazz at 12:30 and occasional lunchtime musical events on other days of the week.

Opera

Recent decades have sharply intensified the public's appreciation for grand opera—partly because of the charismatic personalities of such great singers as Luciano Pavarotti and Jessye Norman, and partly because of the efforts of New York's magnetic **Metropolitan Opera.** A Met premiere draws the rich and famous, the critics, and the connoisseurs. At the Met's elegant Lincoln Center home, with its Marc Chagall murals and weighty Austrian-crystal chandeliers, the supercharged atmosphere gives audiences a sense that something special is going to happen, even before the curtain goes up. Luciano Pavarotti put it best: "When it comes to classical music, New York can truly be called a beacon of light—with that special quality that makes it *'unico in mondo,'* unique in the world."

The Metropolitan Opera (tel. 212/362–6000) performs its vaunted repertoire from October to mid-April, and though tickets can cost more than $100, many less expensive seats and standing room are available. The top-priced tickets are the center box seats, which are actually few in number and almost never available without a subscription. Unlike Broadway theaters, the Metropolitan Opera House has several different price levels, with some 600 seats sold at $22; bear in mind that weekday prices are slightly lower than weekend prices. Standing room tickets for the week's performance go on sale on Saturday.

The **New York City Opera,** which performs from September through November and in March and April at Lincoln Center's New York State Theater (212/870–5570) continues its tradition of offering a diverse repertoire consisting of adventurous and rarely seen works as well as beloved classic opera and operetta favorites. City Opera has widened its program to include several time-honored musicals, such as *Brigadoon, A Little Night Music, The Most Happy Fella,* and *Cinderella.* The Company persists in nurturing the talent of young American stars-to-be. (A surprising number of the world's finest singers, such as Placido Domingo, Frederica von Stade, and Beverly Sills, began their careers at City Opera.) The Company maintains its ingenious practice of "supertitling"—electronically displaying above the stage, line-by-line English translation of foreign-language operas. Recent seasons have included such old favorites as *Carmen, Madama Butterfly,* and *La Traviata.*

Opera aficionados should also keep track of the **Carnegie Hall** schedule (tel. 212/247–7800) for debuting singers and performances by the Opera Orchestra of New York, which specializes in presenting rarely performed operas in concert form, often with star soloists. Pay close attention to provocative offerings at the **Brooklyn Academy of Music** (tel. 718/636–4100), which often premieres avant-garde works difficult to see elsewhere.

Other city opera groups include:

Amato Opera Theatre (319 Bowery, tel. 212/228–8200), a showcase for rising singers.
New York Gilbert and Sullivan Players (251 W. 91st St., Apt. 4C, tel. 212/769–1000; box office, tel. 212/864–5400), performing G & S classics, usually at Symphony Space (95th and Broadway).
Opera Ebony (2109 Broadway, Suite 1418, tel. 212/874–7245), an African-American company performing major and minor works September–June at Aaron Davis Hall, City College (W. 133rd St. and Convent Ave.).

True devotees might consider a New York opera theme tour—several days of concentrated immersion, usually conducted by an expert. Check *Opera News* (70 Lincoln Center Plaza, 10023, tel. 212/769–7080), which publishes ads for tour firms.

Dance

Ballet Visiting balletomanes live out their dreams in New York, where two powerhouse companies—the New York City Ballet and the American Ballet Theatre—continue to please and astonish.

The **New York City Ballet,** a hallmark troupe for over 40 years, recently presented a highly acclaimed production of *The Sleeping Beauty,* created by the Company's Master-in-Chief, Peter Martins; his streamlined, two-act version combines the drama and beauty of the original choreography by Marius Petipa with the speed and energy for which NYCB is known. The company's vast repertory includes works by George Balanchine, Jerome Robbins, Martins, and others. NYCB performs in Lincoln Center's New York State Theater (tel. 212/870–5570). Its winter season runs from mid-November through February—with the beloved annual production of *George Balanchine's The Nutcracker* ushering in the December holiday season—while its spring season lasts from mid-April through June.

Founded by Lincoln Kirstein and Balanchine in 1948, NYCB continues to stress dance as a whole above individual ballet stars, though that hasn't stopped a number of principal dancers (such as Kyra Nichols, Darci Kistler, Damian Woetzel, and Peter Boal) from standing out. The Company has more than 100 dancers and performs and maintains an active repertoire of 20th-century works unmatched in the world.

Across the plaza at Lincoln Center, the Metropolitan Opera House (tel. 212/362–6000) is home to the **American Ballet Theatre,** renowned for its brilliant renditions of the great 19th-century classics (*Swan Lake, Giselle, The Sleeping Beauty,* and *The Nutcracker*), as well as for the unique scope of its eclectic contemporary repertoire (including works by all the 20th-century masters—Balanchine, Tudor, Robbins, de Mille, among others). Since its inception in 1940, the Company has included some of the greatest dancers of the century, such as Mikhail Baryshnikov, Natalia Makarova, Rudolf Nureyev, Gelsey Kirkland, and Cynthia Gregory. Since 1992, American Ballet Theatre has been directed by Kevin McKenzie, one of the Company's leading male dancers in the 1980s. Its New York season runs from April to June.

Part of Lincoln Center's dance vitality is accounted for by the presence of the **School of American Ballet,** the focus for the dreams of young dancers across the country. Some 2,000 of them vie for spots in SAB's summer session, and a talented handful of the 200 who make it into the summer group go on to join the school. Here the Balanchine legacy lives on, and soulful-eyed baby dancers are molded into professional performers. You can see SAB students dashing across 66th and Broadway with leotard-stuffed bags slung over their shoulders, or congregating in **The Ballet Shop** (1887 Broadway, between 62nd and 63rd Sts., tel. 212/581–7990).

When the ABT and NYCB take a break from performing, Lincoln Center acts as impresario for dozens of world-renowned companies, such as the Bolshoi and Royal Danish ballets.

The varied bill at **City Center** (131 W. 55th St., tel. 212/581–7907) often includes touring ballet companies; recently the Matsuyama Ballet from Japan performed there.

Modern Dance At City Center (131 W. 55th St., tel. 212/581–7907), the moderns hold sway. In seasons past, the **Alvin Ailey Dance Company, Twyla Tharp and Dancers,** the **Martha Graham Dance Company,** the **Paul Taylor Dance Company,** the **Dance Theater of Harlem,** and the **Merce Cunningham Dance Company** have performed here. The **Brooklyn Academy of Music** (30 Lafayette Ave., tel. 718/636–4100) features both American and foreign contemporary dance troupes as part of its **Next Wave Festival** every fall.

A growing international modern dance center is the **Joyce Theater** (175 8th Ave., tel. 212/242–0800), housed in a former Art Deco movie theater. The Joyce is the permanent home of **Feld Ballets/NY,** founded in 1974 by an upstart ABT dancer who went on to become a principal fixture on the dance scene. Other featured companies include the **Garth Fagan Dance** company, the avant-garde **ZeroMoving Company,** and the loony acrobats of **Pilobolus.** The Joyce has an eclectic program, including tap, jazz, ballroom, and ethnic dance, and it also showcases emerging choreographers. At **Symphony Space** (2537 Broadway, tel. 212/864–1414), the bill often features ethnic dance.

Here's a sampling of other, mostly experimental and avant-garde, dance forums:

Dance Theater Workshop (219 W. 19th St., tel. 212/691–6500), one of New York's most successful laboratories for new dance.
Danspace Project (at St. Mark's-in-the-Bowery Church, 10th St. and 2nd Ave., tel. 212/674–8194), with a series of avant-garde choreography that runs from September through June.
DIA Center for the Arts (155 Mercer St., tel. 212/431–9232) hosts a number of performances by interesting local dancers.
Merce Cunningham Studio (55 Bethune St., tel. 212/691–9751) sponsors performances by up-and-coming modern dance companies.
P.S. 122 (150 1st Ave., tel. 212/477–5288), where dance events border on performance art; among others, Meredith Monk occasionally cavorts here.
Repertorio Español (138 E. 27th St., tel. 212/889–2850), oft-visited by the famed Spanish stylist Pilar Rioja.

Film and Video

On any given week, New York City seems a kind of film archive featuring all the major new releases, classics renowned and arcane, unusual foreign offerings, small independent flicks, and cutting-edge experimental works. Because you don't usually need to buy tickets in advance, except on Friday and Saturday evenings, movie-going is a great spur-of-the-moment way to rest from the rigors of sightseeing. You may have to stand a while in a line that winds around the block, but even that can be entertaining—conversations overheard in such queues are generally just as good as the previews of coming attractions. Note, however, that these lines are generally for people who have already bought their tickets; be sure, as you approach the theater, to ask if there are separate lines for ticket *holders* and ticket *buyers*.

For information on first-run movie schedules and theaters, dial 212/777–FILM, the MovieFone sponsored by WQHT 97 FM and the *New York Times*.

Festivals New York's numero uno film program remains the **New York Film Festival,** conducted by the Film Society of Lincoln Center every September and October at Alice Tully and Avery Fisher halls (tel. 212/875–5050). Its program includes 25–50 exceptional movies, most of them never seen before in the United States; the festival's hits usually make their way into local movie houses over the following couple of months. This festival has presented the U.S. premieres of such memorable movies as Martin Scorsese's *Mean Streets,* François Truffaut's *Day For Night,* Akira Kurosawa's *Ran,* and Neil Jordan's *The Crying Game.* In March the Film Society joins forces with the Museum of Modern Art to produce a **New Directors/New Films** series, where the best works by up-and-coming directors get their moment to flicker. This series is held at MOMA's Roy and Niuta Titus theatres (11 W. 53rd St., tel. 212/708–9480).

Museums The **American Museum of the Moving Image** (35th Ave. at 36th St., Queens, tel. 718/784–0077) is the only U.S. museum devoted to motion pictures, video, and interactive media. Located on the site of the historic Kaufman Astoria Studios, it offers multiple galleries that are a movie buff's paradise, as are its 195-seat Riklis Theatre and 60-seat Warner Communications Screening Room. The museum presents changing exhibits and provocative film programs, including major artist-oriented retrospectives, Hollywood classics, experimental videos, and TV documentaries.

In midtown Manhattan, the **Museum of Television & Radio** (25 W. 52nd St., tel. 212/621–6800 has a gigantic collection of 60,000 radio and TV shows, including everything from *The Dick Van Dyke Show* to *Soap, Cheers,* and *Taxi.* The museum's library provides 96 consoles, where you can watch or listen to whatever you wish for up to two hours at a time. The museum presents scheduled theater screenings, gallery exhibits, and series for children.

First-Run New suburban-style multiscreen complexes have sprung up all over
Houses town, even in such hip urban neighborhoods as SoHo (Houston and Mercer Sts.), the East Village (2nd Ave. at 12th St. and 3rd Ave. at 11th St.), the Flatiron District (890 Broadway at 19th St.), and Hell's Kitchen (Worldwide Plaza, 320 W. 50th St.). While this increase in the number of screens seems to have eased lines at the box office somewhat, these cinemas often seem to show the same mainstream commercial movies, so long lines still snake around the corner at the few theaters that show more offbeat fare.

Only two New York theaters preserve the size and allure of the great old movie houses: The **Ziegfeld** (141 W. 54th St., west of 6th Ave., tel. 212/765–7600), with its awesome sound system, and **Radio City Music Hall** (1260 6th Ave., tel. 212/247–4777), with its 34-foot-high screen and 4,500-watt projector, only rarely used for movie screenings.

The Times Square area is still a movie mecca, though action flicks prevail on 42nd Street, and viewers should be warned to sit tight and hold on to their purses. Posh East Side first-run theaters line 3rd Avenue between 57th and 60th streets and continue up 2nd Avenue into the 60s. Other groups are clustered around East 34th Street, West 23rd Street, and Broadway between 60th and 63rd streets.

Midnight At a handful of Greenwich Village theaters, midnight madness con-
Movies tinues with late and late-late showings of eccentric classics such as *Blue Velvet* and *The Rocky Horror Picture Show.* The **Angelika Film Center** (W. Houston and Mercer Sts., tel. 212/995–2000) and the **Waverly Twin** (6th Ave. at W. 3rd St., tel. 212/929–8037) are good theaters to check out for these; occasional midnight programs ap-

pear also at the **Quad Cinema** (13th St., between 5th and 6th Aves., tel. 212/255–8800).

Revival Houses One of the best places to see old films in Manhattan opened in 1991: the **Walter Reade Theater** at Lincoln Center (70 Lincoln Plaza, Broadway and 65th St., tel. 212/875–5600), operated by the Film Society of Lincoln Center. This comfortable movie house presents several fascinating series that run concurrently, devoted to specific themes or a certain director's body of work; movies for kids are featured Saturday morning. The state-of-the-art auditorium is a little gem with excellent sight lines, and tickets can be purchased at the box office weeks in advance.

Revivals can also be found at:

American Museum of the Moving Image (35th Ave. at 36th St., Queens, tel. 718/784–0077), offering American film series, often in historical contexts.
Film Forum (209 W. Houston St., tel. 212/727–8110), with three screens showing often quirky series based on movie genres, directors, and other film artists.
The Museum of Modern Art (11 W. 53rd St., tel. 212/708–9480), which includes rare classic films in its many series.
Theatre 80 St. Marks (80 St. Marks Pl., tel. 212/254–7400), small and shabby but convivial, specializing in double-features from the '30s and '40s.

Foreign and Independent Films Between the interest generated by the Film Festival, the city's population of foreign executives and diplomats, a resident corps of independent filmmakers, and a large contingent of cosmopolitan *cinéastes*, there's always an audience here for foreign films and for innovative new American films and videos that buck the Hollywood currents. The following cinemas more or less specialize in such films:

Angelika 57 (225 W. 57th St., tel. 212/586–1900), showing film programs similar to its downtown sister theater (*see below*).
Angelika Film Center (W. Houston and Mercer Sts., tel. 212/995–2000), offering several screens devoted to off-beat independent and foreign films, as well as a lively café catering to a youthful crowd.
Anthology Film Archives (32 2nd Ave. at 2nd St., tel. 212/505–5181), presenting esoteric independent fare.
Carnegie Hall Cinemas (887 7th Ave., between 56th and 57th Sts., tel. 212/265–2520), where intriguing new films find long runs.
Cinema Village 12th Street (12th St., between 5th Ave. and University Pl., tel. 212/924–3363), offering innovative independent features and occasional animation festivals.
Eastside Playhouse (3rd Ave., between 55th and 56th Sts., tel. 212/755–3020), with an emphasis on first-run art films.
Film Forum (209 W. Houston St., tel. 212/727–8110) presenting some of the best new independent films and hard-to-see foreign movies.
The Joseph Papp Public Theater (425 Lafayette St., tel. 212/598–7171), a reliable forum for experimental and independent film.
Lincoln Plaza (Broadway, between 62nd and 63rd Sts., tel. 212/757–2280), six subterranean cinemas playing long-run foreign hits.
Loews Paris (58th St., between 5th and 6th Aves., tel. 212/980–5656), a showcase for much-talked-about new American and foreign entries.
Millennium (66 E. 4th St., tel. 212/673–0090), with an emphasis on the avant-garde.
68th Street Playhouse (3rd Ave. at 68th St., tel. 212/734–0302), with exclusive extended runs of critically acclaimed films.

Quad Cinema (13th St., between 5th and 6th Aves., tel. 212/255–8800), with first-run Hollywood, art, and foreign films.
Village East Cinemas (2nd Ave. at 12th St., tel. 212/529–6799), presenting cutting-edge independent features alongside mainstream Hollywood productions.

Readings and Lectures

The New York City Poetry Calendar (60 E. 4th St., Apt. 21, 10003, tel. 212/475–7110), published monthly, provides an extensive list of prose and poetry readings around the city. The calendar is available by subscription and free at several Manhattan bookstores. Check also listings for readings in *New York* magazine, the *New Yorker*, and the *Village Voice*.

A major reading and talk series held at the **Lincoln Center Library for the Performing Arts** (tel. 212/870–1630) specializes in musicians, directors, singers, and actors. In fact, the entire **New York Public Library** system (tel. 212/930–0571) is a wide-open field for reading events, as is the **Brooklyn Public Library** network (tel. 718/780–7700).

At the **Metropolitan Museum of Art** (5th Ave. at 82nd St., tel. 212/535–7710 or 570–3949), seasonal lectures regularly draw sell-out crowds. Artists such as David Hockney hold forth here, as do the world's eminent art historians.

Authors, poets, lyricists, and travelogue-spinners take the stage at the **92nd St. Y** (1395 Lexington Ave., tel. 212/996–1100), while the **West Side YMCA** (5 W. 63rd St., tel. 212/875–4124) offers readings by major novelists, poets, and humorists in a series called "The Writer's Voice." **Symphony Space** (Broadway at 95th St., tel. 212/864–5400) holds a number of readings, including the Selected Shorts series of stories read by prominent actors. **Dixon Place** (258 Bowery, between Houston and Prince Sts., tel. 212/219–3088) and **The Kitchen** (512 W. 19th St., tel. 212/255–5793) both sponsor readings regularly, some of which border on performance art.

Many Manhattan bookstores organize evening readings by authors of recently published books. Best bets are **Barnes & Noble** (1280 Lexington Ave. at 86th St., tel. 212/423–9900; 2289 Broadway at 82nd St., tel. 212/362–8835); **Books & Co.** (939 Madison Ave. near 74th St., tel. 212/737–1450), **Brentano's** (597 5th Ave. near 48th St., tel. 212/826–2450) **Endicott Booksellers** (450 Columbus Ave. near 81st St., tel. 212/787–6300), **Rizzoli Bookstore** (454 W. Broadway, between Prince and Houston Sts., tel. 212/674–1616). **Three Lives and Co.** (154 W. 10th St., tel. 212/741–2069), and **Tower Books** (383 Lafayette St. at 4th St., tel. 212/228–5100). For readings by gay and lesbian authors, try **A Different Light** (548 Hudson St., tel. 212/989–4850) and **Judith's Room** (681 Washington St., between 10th and Charles Sts., tel. 212/727–7330).

12 Nightlife

*By Susan
Spano Wells*

*Updated by
Andrew
Collins*

Okay, so you've taken the Staten Island Ferry, you've lunched at the Plaza, and you've visited the Met. But don't tuck yourself in just yet. Instead, get yourself truly attuned to the Big Apple's schedule, which runs more by New York nocturnal than by eastern standard time. Even if you're not a night owl by habit, it's worth staying up late at least once, for by night, Manhattan takes on a whole new identity.

Clubs and Entertainment

New York nightlife really started to swing in 1914, when a pair of ballroom dancers, Florence and Maurice Walton, took over management of the Parisian Room, in what is today's Theater District. At Chez Maurice, as the new club was called, the city's café society learned a sensual dance at "Tango Teas." Then came the Harlem Renaissance of the 1920s and '30s, and the New York jazz scene shifted north of 110th Street. In the 1950s night spots mushroomed in Greenwich Village and the East 50s. Along 52nd Street in those years, recalls columnist Pete Hamill, "you could walk down a single block and hear Art Tatum, Billie Holiday, and Charlie Parker. And you could go to the Latin Quarter and see girls running around with bananas on their heads. On the other hand, Babe Ruth doesn't play for the Yankees anymore, either."

Well, maybe not, but Patrick Ewing does play for the Knicks, and the old Copacabana Club has been reincarnated now as a discotheque. *Plus ça change* . . . In truth, the current nightclub scene is probably more varied and vital than it ever was, but in different ways. To begin with, it has moved downtown—along with just about everything else—to dead-looking East Village dives that come alive nightly, to classic jazz joints in the West Village, to sleekly decorated TriBeCa see-and-be-seen traps, and to preppy hangouts around Wall Street.

There are enough dedicated club-hoppers here to support night spots for almost every idiosyncratic taste. But keep in mind that *when* you go is just as important as where you go in clubland. Clubs vary their themes every night of the week. Depending on where you go, an appropriate costume for a night on the town could include anything from blue suede shoes to an Armani coat to a Balenciaga gown; anything from an orange fright wig to leather and chains to a vintage pink poodle skirt.

That doesn't mean that "anything goes," however, for exclusivity is the name of the game. At certain clubs, gimlet-eyed door staff zealously guard the barrier of velvet rope outside, selecting customers according to arbitrary standards. For a new crop of gypsy clubs, only those in the know can even find out where the group is meeting this week.

On Friday, the *New York Times*'s "Weekend" section carries a "Sounds Around Town" column that can give you a picture of what's in the air, as can the *Village Voice*, which probably has more nightclub ads than any other rag in the world. Or stop by Tower Records (Broadway and E. 4th St., tel. 212/505–1500; Broadway and W. 66th St., tel. 212/799–2500), where fliers about coming events and club passes are stacked outside. You may also get good tips from a suitably au courant hotel concierge. Just remember that what's hot and what's not changes almost weekly in this city, so visitors are at a distinct disadvantage. We've tried to give you a rounded sample of reliable hangouts—establishments that are likely to be still in business by the time you use this book—but clubs come and go as fast as spawning tsetse flies, so phone ahead to make sure your target night spot hasn't closed or turned into a polka hall. Most will charge a cover of at least $10 a head; some go as high as $20–$50 (nobody said catting around was going to be cheap!). Take cash because many places don't accept plastic.

Putting on the Ritz

You and your date are wearing Oscar de la Renta and Armani finery; your transport's a white stretch limo; and you've just come from dinner at Lutèce. Just remember to hide this guidebook in your tux pocket or your rhinestone clutch so people won't guess you're not regulars at:

The Ballroom (253 W. 28th St., tel. 212/244–3005). This very hip Chelsea spot has an extensive tapas bar and a nightclub where some of the great chanteuses—including Phoebe Légère and Helen Schneider—rhapsodize, and where Broadway's best moonlight after the shows on their nights off.

The Carlyle (35 E. 76th St., tel. 212/744–1600). The hotel's discreetly sophisticated Café Carlyle is where Bobby Short plays when he's in town; otherwise, you might find Eartha Kitt purring by a piano. Bemelmans Bar, with murals by the author of the Madeline books, regularly stars jazz pianist Barbara Carroll.

Nell's (246 W. 14th St., tel. 212/675–1567). Back in vogue, Nell Campbell (of *Rocky Horror* fame) reintroduced sophistication to nightlife with her club. The tone in the upstairs jazz salon is Victorian; downstairs is for tête-à-têtes and dancing. The boîte opens at 10 PM and closes at 3 AM (4 AM weekends).

The Oak Room (at the Algonquin Hotel, 59 W. 44th St., tel. 212/840–6800). You'll hear that the Algonquin has faded, but this room still offers yesteryear's charms. Just head straight for the long, narrow club-cum-watering hole; at the piano you'll find, perhaps, the hopelessly romantic Andrea Marcovicci or the charming Jeff Harnar.

The Rainbow Room and **Rainbow and Stars Club** (30 Rockefeller Plaza, tel. 212/632–5000). You can find two kinds of heaven high up on Rockefeller Center's 65th floor. The Rainbow Room serves dinner (*see* Chapter 9), and dancing to the strains of a live orchestra takes place on a floor right out of an Astaire-Rogers musical. At the intimate Rainbow and Stars Club, singers such as Maureen McGovern and Rosemary Clooney entertain, backlit by a view of the twinkling lights of the city.

The Russian Tea Room (150 W. 57th St., tel. 212/265–0947). This darling of the cabaret scene features seasoned performers such as Betty Buckley and Margaret Whiting as well as newcomers on Sunday evening on the second floor.

Supper Club (240 W. 47th St., tel. 212/921–1940). Note the last four digits of the telephone number. This huge, prix fixe dinner-and-dancing club specializes in cheek-to-cheek Big Band sounds, with a vocalist and quartet nightly, alternating with a full orchestra on weekends.

Boogie and Be Seen

The city's busiest dance floors are seeing all kinds of styles revived, from voguing to the Twist to bebop swings and lifts. Revelers come to socialize, to find romance, to scream business deals over the music, to show off their glad rags, or to be photographed rubbing shoulders with stars.

Club USA. (218 W. 47th St., tel. 212/869–6001) This five-story wonder, housed in a former burlesque theater, offers two floors (joined by a 100-foot Plexiglas slide) for as many as 2,000 happy dancers.

Crane Club (408 Amsterdam Ave., tel. 212/877–3097). A plush club with a good-looking crowd (if you can stand investment bankers) offers Top-40 hits and dinner every Thursday, Friday, and Saturday.

Dukie's (in the Gold Bar, 345 E. 9th St., tel. 212/505–8270). This classic East Village neighborhood bar is transformed into a dance club on Friday night. Interior design is not Dukie's trademark—unless you're inspired by the silver toilet seat over the bar.

Juke Box (304 E. 39th St., tel. 212/685–1556). Nineteen-fifties and early '60s nostalgia—and '90s music, too—is offered here. One floor is a sports lounge where you can play air hockey or watch a game on pay-cable. The mood is that of a nonstop giddy graduation prom.

Laura Belle (120 W. 43rd St., tel. 212/819–1000). Updated '40s-style glam reigns and swing music plays for most of the night (the rock sounds come later) at this split-level club.

Le Bar Bat (311 W. 57th St., tel. 212/307–7228). The third jewel of West 57th Street's tourist hubs may follow Planet Hollywood and the Hard Rock Café in popularity, but a flashy good time can be had here.

Limelight (47 W. 20th St., tel. 212/807–7850). In this transformed Chelsea church, the stained-glass windows endure amid catwalks and spiral staircases—a virtual showcase of the diversity of New York club culture.

Palladium (126 E. 14th St., tel. 212/473–7171). A native New Yorker hasn't crossed its threshold in years, but it's still a hoot with the suburban bridge-and-tunnel set.

Roseland (239 W. 52nd St., tel. 212/247–0200). This famous old ballroom-dance floor is still open Tuesday and Sunday; come and swing to the big bands.

Roxy (515 W. 18th St., tel. 212/645–5156). This place wins the award for the city's most cavernous club to date. The crowd is always beautiful and never modest.

Soul Kitchen (Monday night at the Grand, 76 E. 13th St., tel. 212/777–0600). Some say this weekly soul and hip-hop party is the raison d'être of that otherwise gloomy post-weekend curse: Monday.

Sound Factory Bar (12 W. 21st St., tel. 212/206–7770). Straight on Friday, gay on Saturday, this is the smaller but still frenetic version of its cousin on 27th Street.

Sound Factory (530 W. 27th St., tel. 212/643–0728, Saturday night only). Doors don't open until 1 AM, there's no alcohol, and usually a $15 to $20 cover, but serious dancers of all persuasions would never miss a night at the Sound Factory—and the party lasts until noon Sunday.

Tatou (151 E. 50th St., tel. 212/753–1144). This pleasing addition to the supper-club scene offers dinner, dancing, and cabaret under one stylish roof. The contemporary American food goes down particularly well.

Webster Hall (125 E. 11th St., tel. 212/353–1600). Not quite as happening as it was a year ago, Webster Hall still packs in the usual club suspects.

Jazz Notes

Jazz players always come home to Manhattan. Somehow, the city evokes their sound. Greenwich Village is still the mecca, with more than 12 jazz nightclubs, although plenty of others are strewn around town. Pick up *New York* magazine, the *Village Voice*, or any of the dozens of free weekly papers for day-by-day listings. Here are some classics:

Anarchy Café (27 3rd Ave., tel. 212/475–1270). Acid jazz, Afro-Cuban jazz, free jazz—stop in for a truly memorable slice of the above.

Arthur's Tavern (57 Grove St., tel. 212/675–6879). The place starts to cook late (say 1 or 2 AM) and eschews all fancy trappings. It offers jazz on the steamy side until 4 AM.

Birdland (2745 Broadway, tel. 212/749–2228). Although way up on the West Side (at 105th St.), this spot is still close to the Village at heart. You'll find lots of up-and-coming groups here.

The Blue Note (131 W. 3rd St., tel. 212/475–8592). This club may be the jazz capital of the world. Just an average week could bring Spyro Gyra, the Modern Jazz Quartet, and Joe Hendricks. Expect a steep music charge.

Bradley's (70 University Pl., tel. 212/228–6440). With brighter-than-usual lighting and, generally, jazz piano (and sometimes a sax), this is a spot for serious fans of jazz.

Dan Lynch's Blues Bar (221 2nd Ave., tel. 212/677–0911). This jazz surprise in the East Village bustles, with jam sessions on Saturday and Sunday afternoons.

Deanna's (130 E. 7th St., tel. 212/505–5288). You won't see many familiar names at this funky East Village club, but it's cheap, casual, and the music keeps 'em coming back for more.

Down Beat Club (70 Grove St., tel. 212/620–4000). It's been some time since a new jazz club opened downtown, but a slew of new and established acts have headlined here since its 1993 debut.

Fat Tuesday's (190 3rd Ave., tel. 212/533–7902). The Les Paul trio plays Monday in the intimate basement of this legendary spot just off Union Square.

Five Spot (4 W. 31st St., tel. 212/631–0100). This recent addition to the jazz scene features new and established musicians in a sleek restaurant setting.

The Knitting Factory (47 E. Houston St., tel. 212/219–3055). It looks seedy on the outside, but inside there's often fine avant-gardish jazz, anything from a trio to a full orchestra.

Red Blazer Too (349 W. 46th St., tel. 212/262–3112). Roaring '20s, Dixieland, and above all swing music are on tap here. It's a hot spot for after the theater.

Sweet Basil (88 7th Ave. S, tel. 212/242–1785). A little ritzy, though reliable, this night spot presents a range that runs from swing to fusion. Sunday brunch with trumpeter Doc Cheatham is truly a religious experience.

Tramps (45 W. 21st St., tel. 212/727–7788). The place has been on the scene for two decades now, with the likes of Albert Collins and NRBQ. Come here for a little Chicago blues in the big city.

The Village Gate (Bleecker and Thompson Sts., tel. 212/475–5120). This is another of the classic Village jazz joints. Music starts at 10 PM. Upstairs there's a cabaret theater.

The Village Vanguard (178 7th Ave. S, tel. 212/255–4037). This old Thelonius Monk haunt, the prototype of the old-world jazz club, lives on in a smoky cellar.

Yardbirds (35 Cooper Sq., tel. 212/288–5800). For those unable—or unwilling—to shell out a day's salary for an evening's entertainment, this new club has a low cover but high-spirited jazz and blues—as often as not with a foreign accent.

Zinno (126 W. 13th St., tel. 212/924–5182). The food (northern Italian) is actually as good as the jazz (usually duos and trios) at this mellow village club.

Rock Around the Clock

The roots of rock may lie in America's heartland, but New York has added its own spin. Crowds at the Big Apple's rocketerias are young, enthusiastic, and hungry; the noise is often deafening, but you can catch many a rising star in this lively scene. Here's where to go:

The Bitter End (147 Bleecker St., tel. 212/673–7030). This old Village standby still serves up its share of new talent, as it once did Joan Armatrading and Warren Zevon. Check before arriving; blues, country, and jazz all make appearances here.

CBGB & OMFUG (315 Bowery, tel. 212/982–4052). The full name is "Country Blue Grass Blues & Other Music For Uplifting Gourmandizers," which basically means: rock. American punk rock was born here, in this long black tunnel of a club featuring bands with inventive names: Die Monster Die, the Lunachicks, and Iron Prostate.

Continental Divide (25 3rd Ave., tel. 212/529–6924). This knockdown version of CBGB appeals to thrifty college kids on their last nickel.

The Rock 'n' Roll Café (149 Bleecker St., tel. 212/677–7630). A week's worth of band names should clue you in: the Maudlins, the Illegitimate Sons of the Blues Brothers, and of course, Kiss My Cobra.

Wetlands Preserve (161 Hudson St., tel. 212/966–5244). Billed as a "watering hole for activists," recent acts have included Mountain and Alex Chilton.

The Latin and Island Beat

Next to dependable jazz, Latin music is the sound of the moment in New York clubs. Salsa, samba, merengue—all offer an exotic counterpoint to the city's rhythms, and Big Apple musicians have found ways to integrate the Latin strain with indigenous styles. Check them out at:

The Ballroom (253 W. 28 St., tel. 212/244–3005) now includes Latin sounds at its hip nightclub.

Club Broadway (2551 Broadway, tel. 212/864–7600). This Upper West Side club is a tradition on the Latin music scene. Look for special "Salsa Nights," on which women are admitted at a discount.

S.O.B.'s (204 Varick St., tel. 212/243–4940). Since 1982, this has been the—and we mean *the*—place for reggae, Trinidadian carnival, zydeco, African, and especially Latin tunes. The initials stand for Sounds of Brazil, just in case you wondered. The decor is à la Tropicana; the favored drink, a Brazilian *caipirinha*.

Down-Home Sounds

The Bottom Line (15 W. 4th St., tel. 212/228–7880). Clubs come and go, but this granddaddy has stayed around since 1974. Its reputation is for showcasing talents on their way up, as it did for both Stevie Wonder and Bruce Springsteen. Recent visitors have included Luka Bloom and Tasmin Archer.

Eagle Tavern (355 W. 14th St., tel. 212/924–0275). Come here for Irish folk music two nights a week, bluegrass and comedy the rest.

The Lone Star Roadhouse (240 W. 52nd St., tel. 212/245–2950). Inhabiting a heady two-story space, it has a long bar for picking up long drinks. The food runs to chili and deep-fried crayfish; the music, from doo-wop to gospel.

Manny's Car Wash (1558 3rd Ave., tel. 212/369–2583). Powerhouse blues jams on Manhattan's soul-free Upper East Side? Sounds shocking, but such is the scene every night at Manny's.

O'Lunney's (12 W. 44th St., tel. 212/840–6688). Green tablecloths and the smell of stale beer accompany live music—contemporary, folk, country-western—Monday–Saturday.

Rodeo Bar (375 3rd Ave., tel. 212/683–6500). This night spot lets loose jamming fiddles and accordions.

Comic Relief

The *Village Voice* covers the comedy scene well, and it's worth checking its listings because lots of music clubs book comedians for periods between sets. Some cabarets and music spots that often bring in stand-ups are Eighty-eight's, Michael's Pub, the Duplex (*see* The Show's the Thing, *below*), and the Village Gate (*see* Jazz Notes, *above*). Several clubs, however, are exclusively devoted to comedy acts:

The Boston Comedy Club (82 W. 3rd St., tel. 212/477–1000). It's so named because the owner's from Beantown, but comedians come here from all over the country to test their stuff.

Caroline's Comedy Club (1626 Broadway, between 49th and 50th Sts., tel. 212/757–4100). This popular club features established names as well as comedians on the edge of stardom.

Catch a Rising Star (1487 1st Ave., tel. 212/397–3000). Johnny Carson got his start here, and talent scouts still show up to test the comic current. This place is neither trendy nor cutting edge, but it is reliable.

Chicago City Limits (351 E. 74th St., tel. 212/772–8707). This troupe's been doing improvisational comedy for a long time, and it seldom fails to whip its audiences into a laughing frenzy. Chicago City Limits performs in an East Side church and is very strong on audience participation.

Comedy Cellar (117 MacDougal St., tel. 212/254–3630). This spot has been running for some years now beneath the Olive Tree Café, with a bill that's a good barometer of who's hot.

The Comic Strip (1568 2nd Ave., tel. 212/861–9386). The atmosphere here is strictly corner bar. The stage is brilliantly lit but minuscule (8 by 10 feet); the bill, unpredictable but worth checking out.

Dangerfield's (1118 1st Ave., tel. 212/593–1650). Since 1969, this has been an important showcase for prime comic talent. It's owned and occasionally visited by comedian Rodney Dangerfield himself.

Freestyle Repertory Company (120 W. 28th St., tel. 212/642–8202). Here's an improvisational theater group that's a step above the others. On one night, they may ask you to step on stage and quickly tell your life story, which five actors will then adapt into scenes; on other evenings, they may make a Shakespearean tragedy the funniest show in town.

The Improvisation (433 W. 34th St., tel. 212/279–3446). The Improv, which moved to a bigger home in 1993, is to comedy what the Blue Note is to jazz. Lots of now-famous comedians got their first laughs here, among them Richard Pryor and Robin Williams.

Stand-Up N.Y. (236 W. 78th St., tel. 212/595–0850). A 175-seat Upper West Side option for comedy devotees, this club books lots of bright faces coming off recent TV gigs.

The Show's the Thing

Cabaret takes many forms in New York City, from a lone crooner at the piano to a full-fledged song-and-dance revue. Various night spots have stages; here are some of the most consistently entertaining.

Asti (13 E. 12th St., tel. 212/741–9105). Even if the hokey notion of singing waiters traditionally dampens your appetite, give this place a chance—the professionally trained staff here will knock your socks off.

Danny's Skylight Room (346 W. 46th St., tel. 212/265–8133). Danny's is housed in the Grand Sea Palace, a fixture on Restaurant Row. It offers a little bit of everything: jazz, crooners, ivory-tinklers, and monologuists.

Don't Tell Mama (343 W. 46th St., tel. 212/757–0788). At this convivial Theater District spot, composer-lyricist hopefuls show their stuff until 4 AM. Extroverts will be tempted by the open-mike policy of the piano bar in front.

The Duplex (61 Christopher St., tel. 212/255–5438). Catch a singing luminary on the rise or watch a comedienne polish up her act at this long-time Village favorite on Sheridan Square.

Eighty Eight's (228 W. 10th St., tel. 212/924–0088). Come here to hear songs by the best of Broadway's tunesmiths (among other things) and inventively assembled programs.

55 Grove Street (near Christopher St. and 7th Ave. S, tel. 212/366–5438). You may see a Judy Garland impersonator sparring with an Ann Miller impersonator, or a mother-and-daughter team that decided all anyone needs to succeed in show business is nerve—but you'll also find good entertainment, as well.

Judy's (49 W. 44th St., tel. 212/764–8930). Located in the lobby of the Hotel Iroquois, this club is known for singing pianists in the Michael Feinstein mold.

Michael's Pub (211 E. 55th St., tel. 212/758–2272). Woody Allen often moonlights on the clarinet here on Monday night. On other evenings, other fine performers such as Mel Tormé take the stage. The crowd is very monied, very uptown.

Steve McGraw's (158 W. 72nd St., tel. 212/595–7400). This West Side supper club and bar presents sophisticated comedy revues, such as *Forever Plaid*, which originated here.

West Bank Café (407 W. 42nd St., tel. 212/695–6909). In an attractive bistro-type restaurant across from Theater Row, moonlighting musical-comedy triple threats (actor-singer-dancers) show off; on occasion, new plays are read.

Bars

While the health-club craze may have hit New York hard, there's little danger that Manhattanites will abandon their bars. Drinking establishments thrive and multiply, particularly in TriBeCa, where it appears bar design has become a minor art. The city's liquor laws allow bars to stay open until 4 AM, so it's easy to add on a watering stop at the end of an evening's merriment.

Vintage Classics

The Algonquin Hotel Lounge (59 W. 44th St., tel. 212/840–6800). This is a venerable spot, not only because it was the site of the fabled literary Round Table, but also for its elegant tone. (*See also* The Oak Room in Putting on the Ritz, *above*).

Café des Artistes (1 W. 67th St., tel. 212/877–3500). This restaurant, as well known for its glorious Beaux Art murals as for its food (*see* Chapter 9), has a small, warm bar where interesting strangers tell their life stories and the house drink is pear champagne.

Elaine's (1703 2nd Ave., tel. 212/534–8103). The food's nothing special, and you will be relegated to an inferior table, but go to crane your neck and gawk. Woody Allen's favorite table is by the cappuccino machine. It's best to visit late, when the stars rise in Elaine's firmament.

The Four Seasons (99 E. 52nd St., tel. 212/754–9494). Miró tapestries greet you as you enter this power bar through the Grill Room (*see* Chapter 9). Watch for Kissingers and Trumps.

The Jockey Club (112 Central Park S, tel. 212/757–1900). Dressy and traditional, this is a slice of upper-crust New York in the lobby of the Ritz-Carlton. It's a very double-martini sort of place.

King Cole Bar (at the St. Regis Hotel, 2 E. 55th St., tel. 212/753–4500.) The famed Maxwell Parrish mural is a welcome sight at this midtown landmark, happily open again following a thorough and sensitive restoration.

The Oak Bar (at the Plaza Hotel, 5th Ave. and 59th St., tel. 212/759–3000). With its plummy, dark-wood furnishings, this old favorite continues to age well. Its great location draws sophisticates, shoppers, tourists in the know, and stars.

Pen Top Lounge (at the Peninsula Hotel, 700 5th Ave., tel. 212/247–2200). Drinks are pricey, but the Manhattan views are jaw-dropping at this spectacular, glass-lined penthouse bar.

The River Café (1 Water St., Brooklyn, tel. 718/522–5200). An eminently romantic spot, hidden at the foot of the Brooklyn Bridge, this restaurant offers smashing views of Wall Street and the East River.

Top of the Tower (3 Mitchell Pl., near 1st Ave. at 49th St., tel. 212/355–7300). There are other, higher hotel-top lounges, but this one on the 26th floor of the Beekman Tower Hotel still feels as if it's halfway to heaven. The atmosphere is elegant and subdued, with piano arpeggios in the background.

"21" Club (21 W. 52nd St., tel. 212/582–7200). Famous for its oldtime club atmosphere even before it was filmed in *All About Eve*, this isn't exactly a swinging joint, but its conservative environs evoke a sense of connections, power, and prestige. It's tough to get in unless you plan to eat here, too (*see* Chapter 9).

Drinking Spots Around Town

South of Houston Street
The Bridge Café (279 Water St., tel. 212/227–3344). This busy little restaurant flanks the Brooklyn Bridge, a hop, skip, and a jump from South Street Seaport. The bar is abridged, but between lunch and dinner you can pass a pleasant afternoon sipping a good selection of domestic wines at a table.

Broome Street Bar (363 W. Broadway at Broome St., tel. 212/925–2086). A classic hangout, this SoHo standard attracts local artsy types on weekdays, the same from other boroughs on weekends.

Ear Inn (326 Spring St., tel. 212/226–9060). There's nothing fancy here, though it inhabits an 1817 Federal house. It's the artsy crowd that makes the place, along with Saturday afternoon poetry readings—they call them "lunch for the ear."

Fanelli's (94 Prince St., tel. 212/226–9412). This is a casual SoHo neighborhood bar, where many come on Sundays with the fat *New York Times* under their arms. The food's good, too.

I Tre Merli (463 W. Broadway, tel. 212/254–8699). The sound of happy drinkers spills out of the massive doors of this wide, inviting restaurant-bar. Wine by the glass is a favorite here.

Lucky Strike (59 Grand St., tel. 212/941–0479). Very chic and international, this French bistro draws a who's who of SoHo luminaries.

Merc Bar (151 Mercer St., tel. 212/966–2727). Once upon a time there were plans to open a classy hotel in SoHo, of which this bar was to be the cornerstone. Well, still no word on the hotel, but the martinis here are wonderful.

NoHo Star (330 Lafayette St. at Bleecker St., tel. 212/925–0070). The mood is casual at this with-it bar and diner, popular with locals and even families.

Raoul's (180 Prince St., tel. 212/966–3518). The decor is 1950s chic; the clientele, upscale downtown.

The Sporting Club (99 Hudson St., tel. 212/219–0900). Lots of TV monitors here stay tuned to the evening's major sports event. Aficionados come in after punching out on Wall Street.

Spring Street Bar and Restaurant (162 Spring St., tel. 212/219–0157). At the heart of trendy SoHo, this spot possesses a sleek bar and attracts an artsy clientele.

Chelsea and the Village   For perhaps the most bizarre bar crawl Manhattan has to offer, consider a mug-hoisting stroll along the West Village's esoteric and enchanting Washington Street, which is one street east of the West Side Highway. Begin while it's light out at the dingy corner of West 13th Street with a visit to **Hogs & Heifers** (859 Washington St., tel. 212/929–0655); this seems to be Gotham's homage to the movie *Deliverance*. Next, walk south through the meat-packing district to **Braque** (775 Washington St., tel. 212/255–0709), an outdoor café frequented by the likes of Ru Paul. Across the street, you should pop into **Tortilla Flats** (767 Washington St., tel. 212/243–1053) for an icy margarita. Proceed next to the French bistro–inspired **Black Sheep** (11th and Washington Sts., tel. 212/242–1010), before stumbling on to the always hopping **Automatic Slims** (733 Washington St., tel. 212/645–8660)—from which you can finish off an A-1 evening by calling a cab.

Alcatraz (132 Ave. A, tel. 212/473–3370). The loudest, hardest, and, some say, best juke box in New York rears its ugly head at this Tompkins Square landmark.

Café Tabac (232 E. 9th St., tel. 212/674–7072). It is said Madonna sometimes appears within the hallowed walls of this pretentious salon that's all the rage these days. Practice your glare before entering.

Cedar Tavern (82 University Pl., tel. 212/243–9355). Here's a very informal, warm spot for a post-double-feature beer.

Chelsea Commons (312 10th Ave., tel. 212/675–9233). An old-fashioned pub in front and a small tree-shaded courtyard in back, this West Chelsea bar draws a disparate but friendly crowd of bookworms, sports fans, and slackers.

Chumley's (86 Bedford St., tel. 212/675–4449). There's no sign to help you find this place—they took it down during Chumley's speakeasy days—but when you reach the corner of Barrow Street, you're very close. A fireplace warms this relaxed spot where the burgers are hearty, and the kitchen stays open past 10 PM.

Cloisters Café (238 E. 9th St., tel. 212/777–9128). With one of Manhattan's largest and leafiest outdoor gardens, the Cloisters is a perfect perch for stargazing and elbow bending.

Coffee Shop (29 Union Sq. W, tel. 212/243–7969). A hip, 23-hour-a-day hangout from Tuesday through Saturday (closed 6–7 AM), the place is fueled by attitude. (Open 20 hours Sunday and Monday; closed 3–7 AM.)

Cornelia Street Café (29 Cornelia St., tel. 212/989–9319). A streetside table on this quaint West Village lane is a romantic spot to share a bottle of Merlot—or two. Inside you can dance to live jazz.

Flight 151 (151 8th Ave., tel. 212/229–1868). This popular, unpretentious neighborhood hangout serves lunch, dinner, and a bargain all-you-can-eat brunch on weekends. The polished wood bar, candlelit booths, and friendly staff create a welcoming atmosphere. Don't miss Tuesday's Flip Night—you call it, you win it!

McSorley's Old Ale House (15 E. 7th St., tel. 212/473–9148). One of New York's oldest saloons (opened in 1854), this is a must-see for first-timers to Gotham.

Peter MacManus Café (152 7th Ave., tel. 212/463–7620). It's known simply as MacManus's to the regulars, who like this bar's unpretentiousness. Among them are lots of actors, fresh from classes in the neighborhood.

Metropolis Café (31 Union Sq. W, tel. 212/675–2300). Soaring ceilings and lots of white marble distinguish this pretty yuppie drink palace—it's so pretty, in fact, that it's often used as a backdrop for movies and commercials.

Old Town Bar and Restaurant (45 E. 18th St., tel. 212/529–6732). Tawdry and proudly unpretentious, with waiters' accents as thick as slush, signs here announce "quiche not served here" and "the coffee is only four hours old." True to its name, the Old Town has been around since 1897.

Peculier Pub (145 Bleecker St., tel. 212/353–1327). Here, in the heart of the Village, you'll find 325 brands of beer, from Aass Amber to Zyweic.

Pete's Tavern (129 E. 18th St., tel. 212/473–7676). This saloon is famous as the place where O. Henry wrote "The Gift of the Magi" (at the second booth to the right as you come in). These days, it's still crowded with noisy, friendly souls.

Stella's (24 1st Ave., no phone). What used to be a *busy* bathhouse is now a haven for grungers and other deliberately scruffy bar-goers; its claim to fame is a hot tub (no longer heated) swimming with tropical fish—you can feed them for a small fee.

The White Horse Tavern (567 Hudson St., tel. 212/243–9260). Famous among the literati, this is the place where Dylan Thomas drained his last cup to the dregs. From April through October, there's outdoor café drinking.

Midtown and the Theater District

Barrymore's (267 W. 45th St., tel. 212/391–8400). This is a pleasantly downscale Theater District spot, with the requisite show posters on the wall. Listen in on the conversations at the bar and you'll hear a few tawdry, true stories of what goes on behind Broadway stage doors.

Café Un Deux Trois (123 W. 44th St., tel. 212/354–4148). This old hotel lobby, charmingly converted, is chicly peopled. The bar itself is small, but it's a hot spot before and after the theater.

Century Café (132 W. 43rd St., tel. 212/398–1988). An immense vintage neon sign lights up the bar at this trendy, friendly Theater-District bistro where you *won't* find the requisite show posters.

Halcyon Bar (at the Rihga Royal Hotel, 151 W. 54th St., tel. 212/307–5000). A big, airy hotel bar, with large and well-spaced tables, it's great for a private chat.

Hard Rock Café (221 W. 57th St., tel. 212/459–9320). Formerly embraced by the kids of stars—now, in fact, its clientele seems eternally prepubescent kids accompanied by muttering parents who find it big, crowded, and far too noisy for talk.

Joe Allen (326 W. 46th St., tel. 212/581–6464). At this old reliable on Restaurant Row celebrated in the musical version of *All About Eve*, everybody's en route to or from a show. Its walls offer a change of pace: The posters that adorn it are from Broadway musicals that quickly bombed.

The Landmark Tavern (626 11th Ave., tel. 212/757–8595). This aged redbrick pub (opened in 1868) is blessed by the glow of warming fireplaces on each of its three floors.

Planet Hollywood (140 W. 57th St., tel. 212/333–7827). It's touristy, it doesn't take reservations, and waiting lines are long. Still, the place has cachet, an undeniable star quality, and such movie memorabilia as C3PO and Dorothy's red shoes, which make up for the very compact bar.

Sardi's (234 W. 44th St., tel. 212/221–8440). "The theater is certainly not what it was," croons a cat in *Cats*—and he could be referring to this venerable spot as well. Still, if you care for the theater, don't leave New York without visiting this establishment.

Top of the Sixes (666 5th Ave., tel. 212/757–6662). This bar has an impressive nighttime view, whether you view St. Patrick's Cathedral to the east or Central Park to the north, from 39 stories up above 5th Avenue.

The Whiskey (at the Paramount Hotel, 235 W. 46th St., tel. 212/764–5500). A downstairs bar graces this chic, revamped Times Square hotel that's sleek and hip, and ideal après-theater. Also fun for evening drinks is the mezzanine lounge, pure Philippe Starck-meets-the-'40s. Wear black.

East Side **Dakota Bar & Grill** (1576 3rd Ave., tel. 212/427–8889). A mix of yuppies fresh out of college and neighborhood lifers congregate around the 52-foot bar, one of the longest in Manhattan.

Harglo's (974 2nd Ave., tel. 212/759–9820). The spicy Cajun food and bright neon sign attract white collars who just can't seem to go straight home after a long day at the office.

Jim McMullen's (1341 3rd Ave., tel. 212/861–4700). A young, quintessential Upper East Side watering hole, McMullen's has a large, busy bar decked with bouquets of fresh flowers. Here you'll find lots of Gold Cards, tennis talk, and alumni fund gatherings.

La Famille (2017 5th Ave., tel. 212/534–9909). The cuisine is southern at this longtime Harlem favorite, where you'll find a warm drinking lounge downstairs.

Mark's Bar (at Mark Hotel, 25 E. 77th St., tel. 212/879–1864). This sleek East Side bar in a sleek East Side hotel attracts monied Europeans and—what else?—sleek East Siders.

P.J. Clarke's (915 3rd Ave., tel. 212/759–1650). New York's most famous Irish bar, this establishment comes complete with the requisite mirrors and polished wood. Lots of after-workers like unwinding here, in a place that recalls the days of Tammany Hall.

The Polo Lounge (at the Westbury Hotel, 15 E. 69th St., tel. 212/439–4835). This place is, in a word, classy; it's frequented by European royalty and Knickerbocker New York.

The Water Club (500 E. 30th St., tel. 212/683–3333). Right on the East River, with a pleasing outside deck (you're not on a boat, but you'll somehow feel you are), this is a special-occasion kind of place—especially for those who've already been to all the special landlocked spots in town.

The Terrace (at the Hotel Inter-Continental, 111 E. 48th St., tel. 212/421–0836). A gilded, gargantuan birdcage greets you as you enter. To your left is a spacious lounge, called Bar 111, with a pianist reinforcing the sophisticated atmosphere.

West Side **Black Bass** (370 Columbus Ave., tel. 212/362–3559). Every night is a big, nasty fraternity party that leaves you smelling like a beer-sodden cigarette the next day; hence, its popularity.

China Club (2130 Broadway, tel. 212/877–1166). If you don't spot someone famous here within 30 minutes, you just aren't trying hard enough. Monday nights it's the place to be on the Upper West Side.

The Conservatory (at the Mayflower Hotel, 15 Central Park West, tel. 212/581–1293). Furnished, perhaps, out of a Bloomingdale's window, this is reputedly the haunt of Hollywood movie barons in town to cut deals. Beyond all that, it's a pleasant, quiet place in which to talk and drink.

Dublin House (225 W. 79th St., tel. 212/874–9528). Above the door glows a small neon harp; inside you'll find lots of very young professionals, Columbia students, and softball teams throwing back two-bit drafts.

Lucy's Retired Surfer Bar (503 Columbus Ave., tel. 212/787–3009). One of the many bars to claim to be "Home of the Jello Shot," this southern California–Mex hangout is a hit with young Upper West Siders, who pack themselves into the bar area and sometimes even manage to dance. The decor is playful gulf beach hut.

Museum Café (366 Columbus Ave., tel. 212/799–0150). Trendy, overdesigned joints on Columbus Avenue come and go, but this one across from the American Museum of Natural History endures thanks to nice streetside windows and high, airy ceilings. Split a homemade pizza as you enjoy the passing afternoon parade.

O'Neal's Lincoln Center (49 W. 64th St., tel. 212/787–4663). Mike O'Neal, the owner of the beloved but now defunct Ginger Man, has moved the bar from that establishment down the street and created a series of rooms (one with a fireplace) serving good pub food.

The Saloon (1920 Broadway, tel. 212/874–1500). The menu goes on and on; the bar is large and informal; and the waitresses and waiters cruise around on roller skates. It may be gimmicky, but the spirit of fun is infectious.

Gay Bars

For advice on the bar scene, health issues, and other assorted quandaries of the gay community, call the **Gay and Lesbian Switchboard** (tel. 212/777–1800) or stop by the **Lesbian and Gay Community Center** (208 W. 13th St., tel. 212/620–7310).

Dance Clubs **Bump!** (Club USA, 218 W. 47th St., tel. 212/258–2872). New York's fave dance club glows pink on Sundays. The stage and main floor is house and hip-hop, the fifth-floor German Expressionist–inspired Mugler Room post-disco, and the basement lounge . . . well, you remember that bar in *Star Wars?*

Lick It! and **Res-Erection** (Limelight, 47 W. 20th St., tel. 212/807–7850). On Wednesday and Friday respectively, Chelsea's church of sin turns up the heat. Music-wise it's nothing special; cruise-wise it's an action-packed adventure, replete with go-go boys.

1984 (Crowbar, 339 E. 10th St., tel. 212/420–0670). The tiny dance floor here pulses and throbs every Friday to a fabulous array of new wave syntho-garbage.

Men's Bars **The Break** (232 8th Ave., tel. 212/627–0072). The scene is usually quite young and swells according to the number and generosity of the night's drink specials.

Cleo's 9th Avenue Saloon (656 9th Ave., tel. 212/307–1503). Near the Theater District, this small, narrow neighborhood bar draws a convivial, laid-back older crowd.

Crowbar (339 E. 10th St., tel. 212/420–0670). Gay grungers and NYU students mingle happily at this East Village hot spot. Very big on Wednesday and Friday (*see* 1984, *above*).

The Eagle (142 11th Ave., tel. 212/691–8451). This leather-and-Levi bar is serious about three things: drinking, glaring, and shooting pool.

The Monster (80 Grove St., tel. 212/924–3558). Upstairs, the tone-deaf gather and sing around the piano; downstairs, the rhythm-impaired gyrate in a campy pitch-black disco. This place has been at it for twelve years, though, and continues to draw a busy mix of ages, races, and genders.

Rawhide (212 8th Ave., tel. 212/242–9332). The older Wild West crowd of this small Chelsea bar is mostly local and usually leathered-up.

The Spike (120 11th Ave., tel. 212/243–9688). The ultimate parade of black leather, chains, and Levis, the bark here is always bigger than the bite.

Splash (50 W. 17th St., tel. 212/691–0073). The staggering popularity of this three-year-old bar is due as much to its size as to anything else. Most nights go-go dancers writhe in translucent shower-cubicles.

Stonewall (53 Christopher St., tel. 212/463–0950). An odd mix of tourists chasing down gay history and down-to-earth locals, the scene is everything but trendy.

The Townhouse (236 E. 58th St., tel. 212/754–4649). On good nights it's like stepping into a Brooks Brothers catalogue—cashmere sweaters, Rolex watches, distinguished-looking gentlemen—and it's surprisingly festive.

Ty's (114 Christopher St., tel. 212/741–9641). Though fiercely loyal, this small, jeans-and-flannel neighborhood saloon never turns away friendly strangers.

The Works (428 Columbus Ave., tel. 212/799–7365). Whether it's Thursday's $1 margarita party, or just a regular Upper West Side afternoon, the crowd is usually J. Crew–style or disco hangover.

Women's Bars **Crazy Nanny's** (21 7th Ave. S, tel. 212/366–6312). The crowd is wide-ranging—from urban chic to shaved head—and tends toward the young and wild side.

Henrietta Hudson (438 Hudson St., tel. 212/243–9879). A little more upscale than Crazy Nanny's. The dance floor here is tiny but well utilized.

Julie's (204 E. 58th St., tel. 212/688–1294). Popular with the sophisticated-lady, upper-crust crowd, this brownstone basement has a piano bar.

Shescapes (various locations, tel. 212/645–6479). This roving dance party is probably the most popular of Manhattan's lesbian soirées. It's often held on Wednesday at the chic **Crane Club** (408 Amsterdam Ave., tel. 212/877–3097). Other parties are on weekends; call for the latest venue.

Index

Discover New England all over again this year

HALLIDAY'S NEW ENGLAND FOOD EXPLORER
Tours for Food Lovers

Now — a guidebook to New England for food lovers. In 12 tours through 6 states, discover the region's best markets, restaurants, farms, inns, even road-side stands in the literate, opinionated company of veteran food writer Fred Halliday. The best place to start the most delicious vacation of your life.

FODOR'S BED & BREAKFASTS AND COUNTRY INNS — NEW ENGLAND

This meticulously honest and thoroughly up-to-date guide includes critical reviews of more than 280 inns and B&Bs, plus everything you need to know about what to see and do — and where to eat — when you get there. Includes 109 illustrations and 36 pages of maps and charts.

FODOR'S NEW ENGLAND '95
A Four Season Guide with the Best of the B&Bs and Ski Resorts

All the best of New England — its top hotels, resorts, inns, and B&Bs in every category, great restaurants, cafes, and diners, wonderful shops for antiques and crafts, where to stay at 50 ski resorts, festivals and seasonal events, fishing, camping, and other outdoor sports, and 51 pages of maps.

COMPASS MAINE '95
First edition

Discover the captivating beauty and compelling history of Maine in this dramatically illustrated and evocatively written guide to the Down East state.

At bookstores, or call **1-800-533-6478**   **Fodor's**

Fodor's has your guide to New York!

FLASHMAPS NEW YORK
The Ultimate Street and Information Finder

"Best organized and most digestible locator-directory."—*New York Magazine*

The key to the city, with state-of-the-art full-color maps linked to thousands of essential addresses, telephone numbers, and facts.

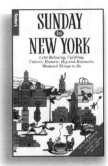

SUNDAY IN NEW YORK

"Will help even well-informed New Yorkers get to know their city better."—*New York Magazine*

Sunday brunch and much more...here's a lively insider's guide for weekend visitors, suburban day-trippers and natives on the lookout for something new.

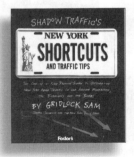

SHADOW TRAFFIC'S SHORTCUTS AND TRAFFIC TIPS
The One-of-a-Kind Driving Guide to Outsmarting New York Area Traffic in and Around Manhattan, the Boroughs and the 'Burbs

From former New York City traffic commissioner Gridlock Sam — and Shadow Traffic: New York's #1 traffic information service — an indispensable guide packed full of easy-to-use maps, detailed directions, shortcuts and escape routes.

COMPASS MANHATTAN '95
First Edition

A dazzling tour of the city's most celebrated attractions—from the Metropolitan and Wall Street to the Empire State Building — as well as the island's smaller unsung pleasures, from the pick-up soccer games just a few hundred yards from the Met to tiny neighborhood eateries.
(available November 1994)

At bookstores, or call **1-800-533-6478**

AT LAST

YOUR OWN PERSONALIZED LIST OF WHAT'S GOING ON IN THE CITIES YOU'RE VISITING.

KEYED TO THE DAYS WHEN YOU'LL BE THERE, CUSTOMIZED FOR YOUR INTERESTS, AND SENT TO YOU BEFORE YOU LEAVE HOME.

Fodor's WORLDVIEW
TRAVEL UPDATE

GET THE INSIDER'S PERSPECTIVE. . .

UP-TO-THE-MINUTE
ACCURATE
EASY TO ORDER
DELIVERED WHEN YOU NEED IT

Now there is a revolutionary way to get customized, time-sensitive travel information just before your trip.

Now you can obtain detailed information about what's going on in each city you'll be visiting <u>before</u> you leave home—up-to-the-minute, objective information about the events and activities that interest you most.

Your Itinerary:
Customized reports available for 160 destinations

Travel Updates contain the kind of time-sensitive insider information you can get only from local contacts – or from city magazines and newspapers once you arrive. But now you can have the same information before you leave for your trip.

The choice is yours: current art exhibits, theater, music festivals and special concerts, sporting events, antiques and flower shows, shopping, fitness, and more.

The information comes from hundreds of correspondents and thousands of sources worldwide. Updated continuously, it's like having your own personal concierge or friend in the city.

You specify the cities and when you'll be there. We'll do the rest — personalizing the information for you the way no guidebook can.

It's the perfect extension to your Fodor's guide and the best way to make the most of your valuable travel time.

Use Order Form on back or call 1-800-799-9609

a
tot
990
Regent
The ann
in this a
domain of
tion as Joe
worthwhile.
the perfomanc
Tickets are usua
venue. Alternate
mances are cancelle
given. For more infor
Open-Air Theatre, Inne
NW1 4NP Open Air Th
Tel: 935-5756. Ends: 9-11-9
International Air Tattoo
Held biennially, the
military air dis
demost

Personalized:
Prepared expressly
for you.

Up-to-the-minute:
Includes the most current
information available.

Your travel dates:
Covers only days
when you will be
there.

June 1

Fodor's/Worldview presents a Travel Update for:

Mr. Gavin Lynch
201 East 50th Street
New York, New York, 10022

Fodor's
WORLDVIEW

LONDON, UK

ARRIVE 23 Jun DEPART: 21 Jul

Your Interests:
Features only
those categories
that matter to you.

HIGHLIGHTS—EVENTS

Wimbledon Lawn Tennis Championships

Seats for the Wimbledon championships, especiall
those for the men's and women's finals on the
Centre Court, are the hottest tickets in Lo
summer. Each winter there is a ballo
and No. 1 Court seats for the fol'
nament. Through this ballot, te
e chance of securing a ticket.
s for top matches are included
combining hotel accommodati
s available from the tourname
ator, NAA Events Internation
7/04.

Open Air Theatre Season

ason of open-air theater produ
and lovely park, once the e
cy dandies, is as much of an
Broadway in the Park and e
e to bring your largest umbrel
often interrupted by showe
ilable for the almost 1,200-seat
s are offered when perfor-
to rain, but refunds are not
contact Sheila Benjam'
Regent's Park
Regent'

Ordering is easy.

You can order a Travel Update up to a few days
before you leave. We need 48 hours to prepare
Updates, and you have to allow for delivery time.

You can also order as much as three months before
you leave. We can send your Travel Update
immediately, or if you prefer, we can hold your
order until just before you leave so that the
information is as current as possible.

There's an order form at the end of this special
section. Choose your destinations and interests; mail
or fax the completed form to us. Or if you prefer, you
can call us toll-free. We'll send out your personalized
Update within 48 hours.

**Special concerts—
who's performing
what and where**

**One-of-a-kind,
one-time-only events**

**Special interest,
in-depth listings**

Children — Events
Angel Canal Festival
The festivities include a children's funfair, entertainers, a boat rally and displays on the water. Regent's Canal. Islington. N1. Tube: Angel. Tel: 267 9100. 11:30am-5:30pm. 7/04.
Blackheath Summer Kite Festival
Stunt kite displays with parachuting teddy bears and trade stands. Free admission. SE3. BR: Blackheath. 10am. 6/27.
Megabugs
Children will delight in this infestation of giant robotic insects, including a praying mantis 60 times life size. Mon-Sat 10am-6pm; Sun 11am-6pm. Admission 4.50 pounds. Natural History Museum, Cromwell Road. SW7. Tube: South Kensington. Tel: 938 9123. Ends 10/01.
Childminders
This establishment employs only women, providing nurses and qualified nannies to

Music — Jazz & Blues
Tito Puente's Golden Men of Latin Jazz
The father of mambo and Cuban rumba king comes to town. Royal Festival Hall. South Bank. SE1. Tube: Waterloo. Tel: 928 8800. 8pm. 7/15.
Georgie Fame and The New York Band
Riding a popular tide with his latest album, the smoky-voiced Fame and his keyboard are on a tour yet again. The Grand. Clapham Junction. SW11. BR: Clapham Junction. Tel: 738 9000. 7:30pm. 7/07.
Jacques Loussier Play Bach Trio
The French jazz classicist and colleagues. Kenwood Lakeside. Hampstead Lane. Kenwood. NW3. Tube: Golders Green, then bus 210. Tel: 413 1443. 7pm. 7/10.
Tony Bennett and Ronnie Scott
Royal Festival Hall. South Bank. SE1. Tube: Waterloo. Tel: 928 8800. 8pm. 7/11.
Santana
Royal Festival Hall. South Bank. SE1. Tube: Waterloo. Tel: 928 8800. 8pm. 7/12.
Count Basie Orchestra and Nancy Wilson Trio
Royal Festival Hall. South Bank. SE1. Tube: Waterloo. Tel: 928 8800. 8pm. 7/14.
King Pleasure and the Biscuit Boys
Royal Festival Hall. South Bank. SE1. Tube: Waterloo. Tel: 928 8800. 6:30 and 9pm. 7/16.
Al Green and the London Community Gospel Choir
Royal Festival Hall. South Bank. SE1. Tube: Waterloo. Tel: 928 8800. 8pm. 7/13.
BB King and Linda Hopkins
Mother of the blues and successor to Bessie Smith, Hopkins meets up with "Blues Boy" Royal Festival Hall. South Bank. SE

Music — Classical
Marylebone Sinfonia
Kenneth Gowen conducts music by Puce and Rossini. Queen Elizabeth Hall. So Bank. SE1. Tube: Waterloo. Tel: 928 88 7:45pm. 7/16.
London Philharmonic
Franz Welser-Moest and George Benja conduct selections by Alexander Go Messiaen, and some of Benjamin's own positions. Queen Elizabeth Hall. South B SE1. Tube: Waterloo. Tel: 928 8800. 8pm
London Pro Arte Orchestra and Forest C
Murray Stewart conducts selection Rossini, Haydn and Jonathan Willcocks. Queen Elizabeth Hall. South Bank. Tube: Waterloo. Tel: 928 8800. 7:45pm.
Kensington Symphony Orchestra
Russell Keable conducts Dvorak's D

Here's what you get . . .

Detailed information about what's going on — precisely when you'll be there.

Show openings during your visit

Handy pocket-size booklet

Reviews by local critics

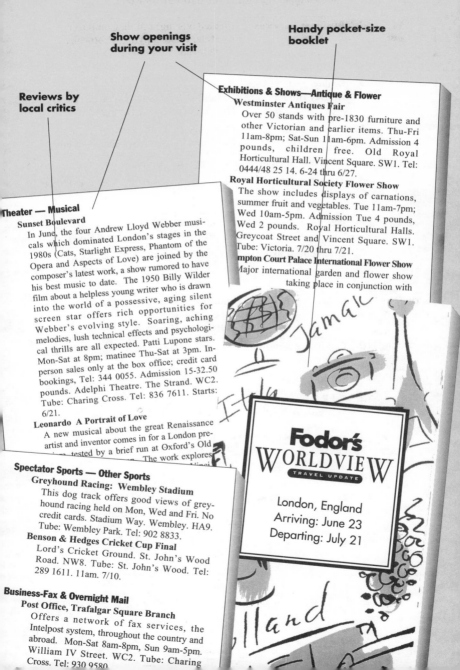

Exhibitions & Shows—Antique & Flower

Westminster Antiques Fair

Over 50 stands with pre-1830 furniture and other Victorian and earlier items. Thu-Fri 11am-8pm; Sat-Sun 11am-6pm. Admission 4 pounds, children free. Old Royal Horticultural Hall. Vincent Square. SW1. Tel: 0444/48 25 14. 6-24 thru 6/27.

Royal Horticultural Society Flower Show

The show includes displays of carnations, summer fruit and vegetables. Tue 11am-7pm; Wed 10am-5pm. Admission Tue 4 pounds, Wed 2 pounds. Royal Horticultural Halls. Greycoat Street and Vincent Square. SW1. Tube: Victoria. 7/20 thru 7/21.

Hampton Court Palace International Flower Show

Major international garden and flower show taking place in conjunction with

Theater — Musical

Sunset Boulevard

In June, the four Andrew Lloyd Webber musicals which dominated London's stages in the 1980s (Cats, Starlight Express, Phantom of the Opera and Aspects of Love) are joined by the composer's latest work, a show rumored to have his best music to date. The 1950 Billy Wilder film about a helpless young writer who is drawn into the world of a possessive, aging silent screen star offers rich opportunities for Webber's evolving style. Soaring, aching melodies, lush technical effects and psychological thrills are all expected. Patti Lupone stars. Mon-Sat at 8pm; matinee Thu-Sat at 3pm. In-person sales only at the box office; credit card bookings, Tel: 344 0055. Admission 15-32.50 pounds. Adelphi Theatre. The Strand. WC2. Tube: Charing Cross. Tel: 836 7611. Starts: 6/21.

Leonardo A Portrait of Love

A new musical about the great Renaissance artist and inventor comes in for a London pre-... tested by a brief run at Oxford's Old ... The work explores ...

Spectator Sports — Other Sports

Greyhound Racing: Wembley Stadium

This dog track offers good views of greyhound racing held on Mon, Wed and Fri. No credit cards. Stadium Way. Wembley. HA9. Tube: Wembley Park. Tel: 902 8833.

Benson & Hedges Cricket Cup Final

Lord's Cricket Ground. St. John's Wood Road. NW8. Tube: St. John's Wood. Tel: 289 1611. 11am. 7/10.

Business-Fax & Overnight Mail

Post Office, Trafalgar Square Branch

Offers a network of fax services, the Intelpost system, throughout the country and abroad. Mon-Sat 8am-8pm, Sun 9am-5pm. William IV Street. WC2. Tube: Charing Cross. Tel: 930 9580

Fodor's WORLDVIEW
TRAVEL UPDATE

London, England
Arriving: June 23
Departing: July 21

Interest Categories

For <u>your</u> personalized Travel Update, choose the categories you're most interested in from this list. Every Travel Update automatically provides you with *Event Highlights* - the best of what's happening during the dates of your trip.

1.	**Business Services**	Fax & Overnight Mail, Computer Rentals, Photocopying, Protocol, Secretarial, Messenger, Translation Services

Dining

2.	**All Day Dining**	Breakfast & Brunch, Cafes & Tea Rooms, Late-Night Dining
3.	**Local Cuisine**	In Every Price Range—from Budget Restaurants to the Special Splurge
4.	**European Cuisine**	Continental, French, Italian
5.	**Asian Cuisine**	Chinese, Far Eastern, Japanese, Other
6.	**Americas Cuisine**	American, Mexican & Latin
7.	**Nightlife**	Bars, Dance Clubs, Casinos, Comedy Clubs, Ethnic, Pubs & Beer Halls
8.	**Entertainment**	Theater—Comedy, Drama, English Language, Musicals, Dance, Ticket Agencies
9.	**Music**	Country/Western/Folk, Classical, Traditional & Ethnic, Opera, Jazz & Blues, Pop, Rock
10.	**Children's Activities**	Events, Attractions
11.	**Tours**	Local Tours, Day Trips, Overnight Excursions, Cruises
12.	**Exhibitions, Festivals & Shows**	Antiques & Flower, History & Cultural, Art Exhibitions, Fairs & Craft Shows, Music & Art Festivals
13.	**Shopping**	Districts & Malls, Markets, Regional Specialities
14.	**Fitness**	Bicycling, Health Clubs, Hiking, Jogging
15.	**Recreational Sports**	Boating/Sailing, Fishing, Golf, Ice Skating, Skiing, Snorkeling/Scuba, Swimming, Tennis & Racquet
16.	**Spectator Sports**	Auto Racing, Baseball, Basketball, Boating & Sailing, Football, Golf, Horse Racing, Ice Hockey, Rugby, Soccer, Tennis, Track & Field, Other Sports

Please note that interest category content will vary by season, destination, and length of stay.